PDR® Guide

Biological and

emical Warfare

Response™

THOMSON

™

**PHYSICIANS'
DESK REFERENCE**

PDR Guide to Biological and Chemical Warfare Response

FOREWORD BY JOHN G. BARTLETT, M.D.
Chief, Division of Infectious Diseases,
The Johns Hopkins University School of Medicine

Editor: DAVID W. SIFTON
Vice President of Design and Production: A. MICHAEL VELTHAUS
Art Director: ROBERT HARTMAN
Assistant Editor: GWYNNED L. KELLY
Production Manager: STEVE CURRLIN
Production Design Supervisor: ADELINE RICH

Physicians' Desk Reference

Executive Vice President, Directory Services: PAUL WALSH
Vice President, Clinical Communications
  and New Business Development: MUKESH MEHTA, R.PH.
New Business Development Manager: JEFFREY D. DUBIN
Vice President, Sales and Marketing: DIKRAN N. BARSAMIAN
Director of Trade Sales: BILL GAFFNEY
Director of Direct Marketing: MICHAEL BENNETT
Direct Mail Managers: JENNIFER M. FRONZAGLIA, LORRAINE M. LOENING
Promotion Manager: LINDA LEVINE

ISBN: 1-56363-426-0

Contents

Section 4: Antibiotic Prescribing Information

Foreword

There have been varying degrees of concern about the possibility of chemical or biological warfare for many years. The United States abandoned its biowarfare program in 1969, but others have continued or started such programs. Perhaps the largest was the program of the Soviet Union, which had very sophisticated science and 60,000 employees prior to its disassembly with the collapse of the Soviet Union. There is now good evidence of substantial bioweaponry in at least six countries, including Iraq. There is also substantial concern about the use of such weapons by terrorists.

Estimates of the danger have been quite divergent. On the one hand, mathematical analyses by WHO and other organizations have shown that anthrax spores, for example, delivered by aerosol in the right meteorological conditions over Washington, D.C. could produce mortality and morbidity that is comparable to a nuclear bomb. Furthermore, the technology necessary to accomplish this heinous task is relatively modest, consisting primarily of proper "milling" to produce spores in particles of one to five microns. On the other hand, despite such concerns, there were many skeptics who felt that this would never happen, or that those attempting it would be too inept to accomplish the task. For example, although the Am Shinryko, a terrorist group in Japan, delivered an aerosol of anthrax spores near Tokyo in 1993, there were no deleterious consequences because they used the veterinary strain, which is inactivated for vaccine purposes. Nevertheless the Am Shinryko subsequently gained appropriate notoriety with the sarin gas attack in the Tokyo subway system.

The potential impact of bioterrorism in the U.S. became a universally accepted issue on October 3, 2001 with the initial case of lethal inhalation anthrax in Florida. By year's end, there were 22 confirmed cases of intentional anthrax, with five deaths. Although this experience seems incredibly modest compared to prior estimates based on different delivery systems, the impact was extraordinary. There were a total of 32,000 persons with possible exposures who received antimicrobial prophylaxis; Washington, D.C. established a network of communication between emergency rooms with hourly conference calls; and New York City established a round-the-clock hotline that required substantial medical expertise in dealing with difficult issues both medically and psychologically.

The anthrax experience was relatively modest in terms of its medical toll, but it brought into sharp focus the limitations of the medical care system in dealing with mass casualties and the companion issues of triage, medical management, prophylaxis, and public hysteria. Medical care is inherently a local or regional issue, involving health care systems and medical care providers located at or near the site of attack. Although this effort needs to be orchestrated with public health officials and law enforcement agencies, due to their obvious interrelated roles, it is up to the health care professionals on the scene to deal with either small- or large-scale events with medical consequences. We will be the ones who detect the cases, manage the medical problems, and give the prophylaxis.

It is for such times of emergency that this book has been prepared. It is designed not as a text or treatise, but a ready reference for on-the-spot consultation in a suspected terror attack. It makes no attempt to provide encyclopedic information on each microbial agent or toxin. Instead, it focuses on the telltale signs that serve to identify the nature of the attack and the key elements of an effective clinical response.

Included are the essential facts you'll need to know about incubation, progression, prognosis, and recovery, together with hands-on guidelines for necessary decontamination and infection control. Also presented, in condensed form, are the highlights of supportive care. For indicated treatments, you'll find detailed information on dosing, administration, and significant precautionary measures; and for the most useful antibiotics and vaccines, the book provides you with complete prescribing information.

It is a great misfortune that a reference such as this needs to be published. But in the event it should ever become necessary, we hope it will help you mitigate and contain the attack as calmly, confidently, and effectively as possible.

John G. Bartlett, MD
Chief, Division of Infectious Diseases, Johns Hopkins University School of Medicine

How To Use This Book

Few physicians can honestly say that they're fully prepared to deal with a biological or chemical attack. The agents likely to be employed are exotic and insidious, and treatment requirements are beyond the scope of daily practice. To cope effectively under these conditions, every clinician needs a ready source of essential facts about unfamiliar biological and chemical threats—and the appropriate medical response to each.

The *PDR Guide to Biological and Chemical Warfare Response* is designed to meet this pressing new need. It begins with concise overviews of 51 toxic warfare agents — outlining their telltale signs and symptoms and summarizing the appropriate clinical counter-measures. Next comes essential information on 52 antidotes, vaccines, and other therapeutic modalities. This quick-reference data is followed by full prescribing information on 22 antibiotics indicated for various bioterror agents, plus an extended discussion of anthrax and smallpox vaccines. A brief medical safety section summarizes the precautions needed during a biological attack, and a compilation of

key government advisories rounds out the book. Here is a closer look at each section.

Section 1: Biological Agents

The entries in this section are divided into three parts: First, under "Clinical Effects" you'll find background information on the nature of each agent, a brief review of its place in biological warfare, and a description of the clinical picture at various stages of infection. Communicability, complications, and prognosis may also be discussed. Next, "Treatment" provides you with an overview of any recommended decontamination procedures, a review of indicated therapy, a summary of any other needed treatments and care, and a list of monitoring parameters. Finally, "Range of Toxicity" quantifies the virulence of the agent.

Section 2: Chemical Agents

Like the entries in Section 1, entries in this section have three parts. "Clinical Effects" provides you with background information on the agent and a description of the symptoms caused by each type of exposure. Under "Treatment" you'll find directions for decontamination, an overview of antidotes and other forms of care, and a list of clinical values to be monitored. "Range of Toxicity" provides an estimate of toxic and lethal doses.

Section 3: Treatment Modalities in an Attack

Each entry in this section begins with the treatment modality's generic name, any major brand names the compound may have, its therapeutic class, and the forms and strengths in which it's supplied. Information on the compound is organized under a series of headings that appear whenever applicable.

Under "Use" you'll find a summary of the compound's indications after a biological or chemical attack. "Adult Dosage" gives the recommended dose for each of these indications. "Pediatric Dosage" gives available dosage recommendations for children. "Administration" summarizes any special measures to take when giving the agent. "Dose Adjustments" alerts you to conditions that may require a change in dosage, such as renal impairment or liver disease. "Precautionary Information" includes contraindications, notable adverse effects, drugs and herbal products with which the compound may interact, the compound's FDA pregnancy category, and

information on its safety during breastfeeding.

Note that these highly abbreviated profiles are intended only for quick reference in an emergency. They do not cover all FDA-approved indications and dosages, and additional precautions and adverse effects may be found in approved product labeling.

Section 4: Antibiotic Prescribing Information

For further reference, this section provides you with the complete, FDA-approved package insert for many of the antibiotics most likely to be needed during a biological attack.

Section 5: Vaccine Information

In this section, you'll find extended discussions of the anthrax and smallpox vaccines covered briefly in Section 3. Included in each entry is detailed information on dosing, contraindications, precautions, adverse reactions, drug interactions, and monitoring parameters, as well as a discussion of the vaccine's mechanism of action and place in therapy. Key references are also supplied.

Section 6: Medical Safety

Here you'll find an overview of the precautions to take when confronted with a victim of biowarfare. Also included in this section are the CDC's full recommendations regarding protective clothing, plus a directory of protective clothing suppliers.

Section 7: Government Guidelines and Advisories

This final section of the book supplies you with the complete text of selected bioterror advisories from the Centers for Disease Control and the Department of Health and Human Services, focusing on the diagnosis and treatment of anthrax and the current recommendations regarding pre- and postrelease vaccination against smallpox.

How the Book Was Compiled

The concise monographs in Sections 1, 2, and 3 are adapted from a toxicological database maintained by Micromedex, Inc. The world leader in information on poisons, hazardous materials, and pharmaceutical remedies, Micromedex employs more than 100 clinicians to review the medical literature and create the information in these monographs. The content is then peer reviewed by hundreds of clinical experts at leading institutions throughout the United States.

The antibiotic information found in Section 4 is reproduced verbatim from PDR's database of FDA-approved prescribing information.

The discussions of anthrax and smallpox vaccines in Section 5 are adapted from *DrugDex® Drug Evaluations,* a database of detailed drug information created and maintained by Micromedex. The information on medical safety precautions and protective clothing suppliers found in Section 6 is also adapted from data collected by Micromedex.

All information in this book is intended for use only by healthcare professionals in conjunction with clinical data. While diligent efforts have been made to assure the accuracy of the information, it is presented without guarantees by the publisher, who disclaims all liability in connection with its use. Inclusion of a product in this book does not signify its endorsement by the publisher, nor does the absence of a product imply a criticism or rejection. The publisher is not advocating the use of any product described in this book, does not warrant or guarantee any of these products, and has not performed any independent analysis in connection with the product information contained herein.

The antibiotic prescribing information contained in Section 4 is reproduced verbatim from the manufacturer's FDA-approved package labeling as published in the 2002 edition of *Physicians' Desk Reference®.* The publisher does not assume, and expressly disclaims, any obligation to obtain and include in this material any information other than that contained in approved product labeling, nor is the publisher responsible for misuse of a product due to typographical error. Additional information on any product may be obtained from the manufacturer.

Section 1

Biological Agents

Aflatoxins

Clinical Effects

Background

Aflatoxins are naturally occurring bisfuranocoumarin compounds produced from the molds *Aspergillus flavus* and *A. parasiticus*. More than 12 of these compounds have been identified. Aflatoxins are found as contaminants on corn, peanuts, tree nuts, cotton seed, and certain meats. They have also been found in hypoallergenic milks. Exposure to aflatoxins may occur via ingestion, inhalation, or through the skin. The risk of systemic toxicity resulting from dermal exposure increases in the presence of high toxin concentrations, occlusion, and vehicles which enhance penetration.

Biological Warfare

Aflatoxins are considered potential biologic weapons.

Clinical Presentation

Protracted exposure to aflatoxins has been associated with hepatocellular carcinoma, acute hepatitis, Reye's syndrome, bile duct cell proliferation, periportal fibrosis, hemorrhage, mucous membrane jaundice, fatty liver changes, cirrhosis in malnourished children, and kwashiorkor. Inhaled aflatoxins may produce pulmonary adenomatosis.

Treatment

Decontamination

DERMAL: Remove contaminated clothing and wash exposed area thoroughly with soap and water.

INHALATION: Move patient from the toxic environment to fresh air. Monitor for respiratory distress.

ORAL: Administer activated charcoal.

Symptomatic and Supportive

No antidote is available. Symptomatic and supportive care are the mainstays of therapy.

Monitoring Parameters

Obtain liver function tests as clinically indicated.

Range Of Toxicity

There does not seem to be a direct dose-response to aflatoxin toxicity. Chronic ingestion appears to be more dangerous than acute ingestion. Aflatoxin ingestion of 2 to 6 mg/kg per day for over a month resulted in an epidemic of hepatitis in India.

Anthrax

Clinical Effects

Background

A zoonotic disease of the skin, respiratory, or GI tract due to anthrax bacillus/spore-contaminated animal products, soil, or aerosolized agents. Highly virulent.

Biological Warfare

Spores have been weaponized in an aerosolized form.

Clinical Presentation

Dependent on route, size of inoculum, patient's health, and toxicity/virulence of the Bacillus anthracis strain.

INHALATION: Initially, similar to mild upper respiratory infection, with tachycardia and respiratory distress. Progresses to pulmonary edema. Inhalational anthrax is almost always fatal. Respiratory failure can occur within 3 to 5 days after a flu-like prodrome.

CUTANEOUS: Most common form. Presents with itching (first 2 to 3 hours), followed by a papular, then vesiculated lesion.

Mild: Necrotic eschar (36 hours) that falls off without scarring.

Serious: Malignant edema, edematous tissue (2-6 days), and necrosis/blistering.

INTESTINAL: Uncommon; can occur in explosive outbreaks. Presents with abdominal distress, rapidly developing ascites, cholera-like diarrhea, fever, hypovolemia, and signs of sepsis.

OROPHARYNGEAL: Severe sore throat with neck swelling, adenopathy, dysphagia, and occasionally tracheal compression and dyspnea.

Communicability

Human to human transmission is NOT known to occur. However, lesion discharge is potentially infectious.

Complications

Septicemia, shock (may result from all routes of exposure), dehydration, meningoencephalitis, renal failure, and death.

Treatment

Respiratory Failure

Inhalational exposure requires aggressive ventilatory support.

Hypotension

Infuse isotonic fluid and dopamine or norepinephrine as needed.

Pulmonary Edema (Noncardiogenic)

Ventilation and oxygenation; monitor ABGs or pulse oximetry frequently. Early use of PEEP and mechanical ventilation may be needed.

Antibiotic Therapy

Begin treatment if anthrax is even suspected.

DRUGS OF CHOICE:
Contained Casualty Setting: Initial therapy: Ciprofloxacin, doxycycline. Optimal therapy if strain is proven susceptible: penicillin G, doxycycline.

Mass Casualty Setting or for Postexposure Prophylaxis: Ciprofloxacin. Optimal therapy if strain is proven susceptible:

Amoxicillin, doxycycline. Other agents with in vitro activity that have been suggested for use in conjunction with ciprofloxacin or doxycycline include rifampin, vancomycin, penicillin, ampicillin, chloramphenicol, imipenem, clindamycin, and clarithromycin.

TETRACYCLINE: May be considered; Adult: 1 gram IV every 24 hours.

STREPTOMYCIN: 30 mg/kg IM daily may be given in conjunction with penicillin.

CHLORAMPHENICOL: Alternate antibiotic for anthracis meningitis. Pediatric: 75 - 100 mg/kg/day IV in 4 divided doses; Adult: 4 - 6 grams/day IV in 4 divided doses.

NOTE: Inhalation anthrax has a delayed onset of disease. Antibiotics are only effective against germinating/vegetative *B. anthracis*, but are NOT effective against the nonvegetative/spore form. If an antibiotic is discontinued too soon, and there are enough nongerminated spores to overwhelm the immune system when they germinate, disease will develop.

Other

Steroids may be indicated for severe tracheal edema with inhalation anthrax AND indicated to treat severe cutaneous anthrax.

Monitoring Parameters

Obtain CBC, electrolytes, renal function tests, and cultures of blood, CSF, ascites fluid, or pleural effusions as clinically indicated. Obtain chest X-ray for suspected inhalational anthrax; generally distinctive for a widened mediastinum and pleural effusions. Skin testing appears valuable for early diagnosis of acute anthrax, but may not be widely available. Cultures of infected blisters in cutaneous anthrax can be diagnostic. ELISA and Western blot may be valuable serologic tests.

Range Of Toxicity

Inhalation of 8,000 to 50,000 anthrax spores is an infective dose.

Botulism

Clinical Effects

Background

Botulinum toxins are a group of 7 toxins produced by *Clostridium botulinum*. Spores are ubiquitous; they germinate producing bacteria that generate toxins during an aerobic incubation (large-scale fermentation can produce vast quantities of toxin for biologic warfare). Presynaptic inhibition affects both autonomic (muscarinic) and motor (nicotinic) receptors. Botulism naturally occurs in three forms: foodborne, infantile, and wound.

Biological Warfare

Primary threat as biological warfare agent is delivery by aerosol release. Lethal intoxication in experimental animals has occurred with this method; may also be delivered through contamination of food or water.

Clinical Presentation

INCUBATION: 24 to 36 hours for foodborne; 3 or more days for wound; 72 hours in 3 known cases for inhalation.

SYMPTOMS: Autonomic features are characteristic: anticholinergic effects (dry mouth, ileus, constipation, urinary retention), mydriasis (50% of cases) and nausea/vomiting secondary to functional obstruction).

Descending paralysis is the prominent neurological feature and includes ptosis, diplopia, blurred vision, enlarged and sluggish pupils, dysarthria, dysphonia, and dysphagia. Respiratory failure may occur secondary to muscle weakness. Botulism does not cross the blood-brain barrier; sensorium remains intact.

Treatment

Decontamination

GASTRIC DECONTAMINATION: May be of benefit in patients, immediately following ingestion of food or a pharmaceutical known to contain the botulism toxin.

IPECAC: Symptomatic patients should not receive ipecac.

ACTIVATED CHARCOAL: Theoretically, activated charcoal may inactivate type A botulinum toxin. Evidence is uncertain if course of illness is altered by use of activated charcoal.

Symptomatic and Supportive

Intensive supportive care is required:
- Immediately assess respiratory function.
- Intubation and mechanical ventilation may be required as neurotoxicity progresses.
- Nasogastric suction should be performed if ileus is suspected.
- Bowel and bladder care as needed.

Hydration

Immediate intravenous access is required. Administration of maintenance fluids is mandatory. Persistent symptoms may require hyperalimentation and central venous access.

Antitoxin

Trivalent antitoxin can be obtained from the Centers for Disease Control and Prevention via state and local health departments. The antitoxin should be administered as soon as possible to neutralize the circulating toxin. In a mass casualty setting, if neurological findings are present, do not delay antitoxin use for laboratory confirmation.

The dose for an individual with no known sensitivity is a single

10-mL vial IV, diluted 1:10 in 0.9% saline solution.

Treatment of botulism in patients with known sensitivity requires serial administration of diluted antitoxin/serum at 20 minute intervals, (as long as no adverse reactions occur).

Range Of Toxicity

Inhalation (Aerosol)

The lethal dose for Type A is 0.001 mcg/kg.

Oral

The oral human lethal dose is 1 pcg/kg. Due to biodegradation or inactivation in the gut, it is difficult to determine what percent of the toxin is actually absorbed.

Brucellosis

Clinical Effects

Background

Brucellosis is a multisystem, bacterial, zoonotic disease. It is caused by the genus *Brucella*, a small, gram-negative, aerobic coccobacillus that is nonmotile and lacks spores or capsules. Humans become infected via ingestion of animal products, by direct contact with infected animals, and by inhalation of infectious aerosols.

Biological Warfare

B. melitensis and *B. suis* are potential biological terrorism agents.

Clinical Presentation

INCUBATION: The incubation period ranges from 3 to 5 days to several weeks. Relapses are common.

ACUTE STAGE: The acute stage is characterized by a febrile flu-like illness with chills, sweats, headache, myalgia, arthralgia, and weakness, usually without any localizing signs. Cough, chest pain, dyspnea, fatigue, hepatomegaly, dysuria, and lymphadenopathy may also develop. Onset may be sudden or insidious.

SUBACUTE STAGE: Signs and symptoms persist for 2 to 12 months; similar to acute stage.

CHRONIC STAGE: Signs and symptoms are present for greater than 12 months. This stage is uncommon following adequate treatment of acute illness. Neuropsychiatric symptoms predominate; characterized by fever, malaise, headache, anxiety, depression. Treated persons with chronic illness usually have suppurative localization (especially of bone or joints).

Communicability

Brucellosis is highly infectious by aerosol. Person-to-person transmission is rare.

Fatalities

Rare; usually occurring in association with central nervous system disease or endocardial infection.

Recovery

Prolonged, even with antibiotic therapy.

Treatment

Decontamination

DERMAL: Sites exposed to blood, body fluids, secretions, or excretions from patients with suspected Brucellosis infections should be immediately washed with soap and water.

INHALATION: Wear protective masks and utilize strict barrier nursing techniques when working with infected patients or material.

Symptomatic and Supportive

Early antibiotic therapy is indicated in all cases. Steroids are indicated in severe cases. Supportive measures include antipyretics and analgesics for myalgia, arthralgia, and headache. No commercial vaccine exists for prophylaxis of brucellosis.

Antibiotic Therapy

Combination antibiotic therapy is indicated because of high relapse rate with single-drug therapy.

UNCOMPLICATED BRUCELLOSIS:
Adults: Doxycycline 100 mg PO BID for 6 weeks, PLUS gentamicin (preferred) 2 mg/kg loading dose, then 1.7 mg/kg IV Q8H, or 5 mg/kg IV QD, for 7 to 10 days. Either streptomycin or rifampin may be given in place of gentamicin.

Children Over 8 Years:
Doxycycline 1 to 2 mg/kg PO BID for 6 weeks, PLUS gentamicin (preferred) 2 mg/kg IV Q8H for 7 to 10 days. Either streptomycin or rifampin may be given in place of gentamicin.

Children Less Than 8 Years:
5 mg/kg TMP and 50 mg/kg SMX PO Q12H for 6 weeks, PLUS gentamicin 2 mg/kg IV Q8H for 7 to 10 days.

NEUROBRUCELLOSIS:
Adults: Gentamicin: 2 mg/kg loading dose, then 1.7 mg/kg IV Q8H, or 5 to 7 mg/kg IV QD, for 2 to 4 weeks, PLUS doxycycline 100 mg PO BID for 8 to 12 weeks, PLUS rifampin 600 to 900 mg PO QD for 8 to 12 weeks.

Children: Gentamicin: 2 mg/kg IV Q8H for 2 to 4 weeks, PLUS either doxycycline (over 8 years): 2 mg/kg PO BID for minimum of 8 weeks OR TMP/SMX (less than 8 years): 5 mg/kg TMP and 50 mg/kg SMX PO Q12H for minimum of 8 weeks PLUS rifampin 20 mg/kg (max 600 mg) PO QD for minimum of 8 weeks.

Fluids/Electrolyte Therapy

Dehydrated patients should receive dextrose and electrolyte solutions by IV infusion.

Airway Management

Airway compromise may require endotracheal intubation and mechanical ventilation.

Range Of Toxicity

The organism can be delivered as a slurry in bomblets or, theoretically, as a dry aerosol. It is highly infectious by aerosol. It survives for 6 weeks in dust and 10 weeks in soil or water. Large aerosol doses may shorten the incubation period and increase clinical attack rate.

Crimean-Congo Hemorrhagic Fever

Clinical Effects

Background

Crimean-Congo hemorrhagic fever (CCHF) is a severe viral hemorrhagic fever of the Nairovirus group. It is characterized by hepatitis, coagulopathy, major bleeding, and severe thrombocytopenia. CCHF virus is transmitted to humans principally by the bite of Hyalomma ticks.

Biological Warfare

The virus can be transmitted as an aerosol in terrorist attacks.

Clinical Presentation

INCUBATION: The incubation period is usually 2 to 9 days (range 1 to 12 days). In a biological warfare clinical presentation, incubation period may be days to months.

INITIAL SYMPTOMS: The prehemorrhagic onset is sudden and acute, with fever, headache, myalgia, joint pain, weakness, vomiting, diarrhea, and leukopenia.

PROGRESSION OF SYMPTOMS: The hemorrhagic stage begins rapidly, usually on days 3 to 5 with bradycardia (not in children), muffled heart sounds, hypotension, hepatosplenomegaly, and jaundice in some cases. Hemorrhages, ranging in size from petechiae to large hematomas, develop on mucous membranes and skin. There is bleeding of the gums, buccal mucosa, and the nose bleed; intestinal and uterine hemorrhages occur. In about 15% of patients only a hemorrhagic rash appears. Pallor and tachycardia with profuse hemorrhage may occur. About 10% of cases develop hemorrhagic pneumonia. Evidence of disseminated intravascular coagulation carries a poor prognosis. Adult Respiratory Distress Syndrome (ARDS) may develop in severe cases.

Communicability

CCHF is highly infectious, particularly from contact with acutely ill individuals.

Fatalities

Cardiovascular collapse and cardiac arrest may occur due to massive hemorrhage. Autopsy findings include numerous hemorrhages into all organs and tissues. Death can occur between 7 to 16 days after symptom onset.

Recovery

Usually convalescence begins rapidly on about day 15-20 of illness with no hemorrhagic relapse.

Treatment

Decontamination

DERMAL: Sites exposed to blood, body fluids, secretions, or excretions from patients with suspected CCHF infections should be immediately washed with soap and water.

INHALATION: Medical personnel working with known CCHF infected patients should wear protective masks and utilize strict barrier nursing techniques. Respirators should be used when caring for patients with coughing, vomiting, diarrhea, or hemorrhage.

Symptomatic and Supportive

No antidote or vaccine is available. Early, aggressive treatment is imperative. Therapy begun after late symptoms of infection are present may be ineffective. Strict barrier precautions are mandatory for all patient care.

Medication

Antibiotics are ineffective unless a secondary infection is present. Ribavirin is recommended.

TREATMENT: Administer 30 mg/kg IV as a loading dose, followed by 16 mg/kg IV Q6H for 4 days, then 8 mg/kg IV Q8H for 6 days.

PROPHYLAXIS: High risk contacts should be given ribavirin 500 mg PO Q6H for 7 days as prophylaxis.

Transfusions

Fresh frozen plasma and packed red cells should be transfused as needed for bleeding and coagulopathy.

Hypotension

Administer IV fluids; large amounts may be necessary. If unresponsive to these measures, administer dopamine or norepinephrine and titrate as needed to desired response.

Pulmonary Edema (Noncardiogenic)

Maintain ventilation and oxygenation. Monitor ABGs/pulse oximetry frequently. Early use of PEEP and mechanical ventilation may be needed.

Monitoring Parameters

CBC with differential, platelets, electrolytes, renal function tests, PT/INR, PTT, fibrinogen, fibrin degradation products, blood cultures, and liver function tests as indicated.

Range Of Toxicity

Nairovirus is highly infectious by the aerosol route. The virus may replicate sufficiently well in cell culture to permit weaponization. Mortality has been reported to be 15% to 20%, and up to 50% in some reports.

Ebola and Marburg Filoviruses

Clinical Effects

Background

Filoviruses are not known to be transmitted from human-to-human via inhalation; however, researchers have shown a potential for aerogenic infection by Ebola virus.

Biological Warfare

Use of Ebola virus as a biological warfare agent has been proposed due to its highly contagious and lethal properties. Its use in warfare requires a stable aerosolized form. It is unknown whether this is currently available.

Clinical Presentation

Clinical symptomatology appears almost identical between the two infections, which are difficult to differentiate as they are caused by morphologically identical, though immunologically distinct, viruses.

INCUBATION: The incubation period is about 1 week (range 2 to 21 days) for Ebola infections and 3 to 9 days for Marburg infections.

INITIAL SYMPTOMS: Initially, the illness resembles an influenza-like syndrome (fever, headache, myalgia, joint pain, and sore throat), commonly followed by vomiting, diarrhea, and abdominal pain. A transient, morbilliform and desquamating skin rash often appears 5 to 7 days later.

PROGRESSION OF SYMPTOMS: After the third day of illness, hemorrhagic manifestations commonly occur. They include petechiae and frank bleeding, which may arise from any part of the gastrointestinal tract and from multiple other sites.

DIC and thrombocytopenia are common, and correlate with severity of disease. High fever and delirium may be persistent. A short normothermic period can precede multiorgan failure and fatal shock.

Recovery

May take up to several weeks.

Treatment

Decontamination

DERMAL: Sites exposed to blood, body fluids, secretions, or excretions from patients with suspected filovirus infections should be immediately washed with soap and water.

INHALATION: Medical personnel working with known filovirus infected patients should wear protective masks and utilize strict barrier nursing techniques. Respirators should be used when caring for patients with coughing, vomiting, diarrhea, or hemorrhage.

Symptomatic and Supportive

Intensive supportive care is the

mainstay of therapy. No antidote or vaccine is available for filovirus infections. Strict barrier precautions are mandatory for all patient care.

Transfusions
Transfusions of fresh frozen plasma and packed red cells should be instituted in cases of severe bleeding.

Hypotension
Administer IV fluids; large amounts may be necessary. If unresponsive to these measures, administer dopamine (first choice) or norepinephrine.

Pulmonary Edema (Noncardiogenic)
Maintain ventilation and oxygenation. Monitor ABGs/pulse oximetry frequently. Early use of PEEP and mechanical ventilation may be needed.

Extracorporeal Elimination
Hemodialysis may be necessary in cases of renal failure.

Monitoring Parameters
Obtain CBC, electrolytes, renal function tests, blood cultures, CSF, ascites fluid, or pleural fluid as clinically indicated. Monitor INR or prothrombin levels.

Range Of Toxicity

Animal experiments have shown fatal inhalation doses of Ebola virus to be 400 plaque-forming units of virus.

E. Coli 0157:H7

Clinical Effects

Background
Escherichia coli, a member of the Gram-negative family of bacteria called *Enterobacteriaceae*, is a normal intestinal commensal. Pathogenic strains include:

- Enteropathogenic *E. coli* (EPEC) - a cause of childhood diarrhea
- Enteroinvasive *E. coli* (EIEC) - a cause of dysentery-like disease
- Enterotoxigenic *E. coli* (ETEC) - a cause of travelers' diarrhea
- Enteroadherent *E. coli* (EAEC) - a cause of chronic diarrhea in young children
- Verotoxin-producing *E. coli* (VTEC)
- Strains of enterohemorrhagic *E. coli* (EHEC) especially serotype 0157 (Shiga-producing *E. coli*), which cause bloody diarrhea, hemorrhagic colitis, hemolytic uremic syndrome, and thrombotic thrombocytopenic purpura.

Biological Warfare
Considered to have potential as a biologic weapon.

Clinical Presentation
INCUBATION: Average interval between exposure and symptoms is 3 days; the range is 1 to 8 days.

SYMPTOMS: Although *E. coli* 0157:H7 infection can be asymptomatic, initial symptoms may include nonbloody or bloody diarrhea, abdominal cramping, nausea, vomiting, and occasionally fever.

Complications

Complications include hemolytic-uremic syndrome (HUS) (more common in young children), thrombocytopenic purpura (more common in adults and the elderly), and death.

In children with HUS, extrarenal complications have included pancreatitis, colonic necrosis, glucose intolerance, coma, stroke, seizures, myocardial dysfunction, pericardial effusions, adult respiratory distress syndrome (ARDS), and pleural effusions.

Sequelae

Include permanent renal impairment and neurological injuries.

Treatment

Medications

ANTIBIOTICS: The role of antimicrobial therapy in patients with hemorrhagic colitis caused by EHEC is uncertain. Retrospective data suggest that treatment with trimethoprim/sulfamethoxazole is associated with an increased risk of HUS in patients with *E. coli* O157:H7 infection. Antibiotics may eliminate competing bowel flora and allow overgrowth of *E. coli* O157:H7, particularly when this serotype is resistant to the antibiotic given. Alternatively antibiotics may cause lysis of or sublethal damage to the infecting *E. coli*, with a subsequent libera-

tion of bacterial cytotoxins into the gut lumen.

ANTIDIARRHEALS: May increase the duration of hemorrhagic colitis associated with HUS. Antimotility drugs are probably contraindicated, as their administration is a risk factor for the development of HUS.

Hemolytic-Uremic Syndrome

Hemodialysis or peritoneal dialysis may be required. Children have been treated with plasmapheresis, total parenteral nutrition (TPN), administration of immune globulin, and platelets (contraindicated unless there is active bleeding; give slowly; raise platelet count to >50k), fresh frozen plasma, and packed red blood cell transfusions. The efficacy of these treatments are unknown.

Fluids/Electrolytes

Maintain a normal fluid and electrolyte balance.

Experimental Vaccine

A polyvalent *E. coli* vaccine has been tested in human volunteers and found to be safe. It is efficacious in increasing antibody levels against *E. coli*, but is not generally available.

Monitoring Parameters

In high-risk patients (young children and the elderly), monitor for development of complications with peripheral blood smears, CBC, renal function tests, and urinalysis; an enzyme-linked immunosorbent assay rapidly detects *E. coli*

O157:H7 in stool specimens. Methylene blue staining of stool or rectal mucous specimens may detect fecal white blood cells in as many as 65% of patients with *E. coli* O157:H7.

Range Of Toxicity

The infectious dose of *E. coli* O157:H7 is very low (less than 1000 organisms). One outbreak was associated with swallowing lake water containing greater than a mean of 50 enterococci per deciliter.

Glanders

Clinical Effects

Background

Glanders is caused by *Burkholderia mallei*, an aerobic, gram-negative, non-spore-forming bacillus. Disease occurs primarily in solipeds (horses, donkeys, and mules), but humans are also susceptible. The organism exists in nature only in infected susceptible hosts and is not found in water, soil, or plants. Transmission in humans has occurred through the organism's invasion of the nasal, oral, and conjunctival mucous membranes, by inhalation into the lungs, and through invasion of abraded or lacerated skin. In a laboratory setting, aerosols from cultures have been observed to be highly infectious to laboratory personnel. Person-to-person airborne transmission is unlikely, but possible. In humans, glanders may occur in 3 forms: as an acute localized infection, as a rapidly fatal septicemic illness, or as an acute pulmonary infection.

Biological Warfare

Aerosol spread by a terrorist attack could be efficient.

Clinical Presentation

INHALATION EXPOSURE: The incubation period is 10 to 14 days after an inhalation exposure. Symptoms include fever, chills, sweats, myalgia, headache, pleuritic chest pain, cervical adenopathy, splenomegaly, and generalized papular/pustular eruptions. The disease manifests as pneumonia, bronchopneumonia, or lobar pneumonia, with or without bacteremia and is almost always fatal without treatment.

DERMAL EXPOSURE: Localized infection with nodule formation and lymphadenitis.

MUCOCUTANEOUS EXPOSURE: Mucopurulent discharge from the eyes, nose, or lips, with the subsequent development of granulomatous ulcers and abscesses, often involving the extremities.

CHRONIC: A chronic form with lymphangitis, regional adenopathy, and cutaneous and intramuscular abscesses may develop.

Treatment

Decontamination

DERMAL: Intact skin should be washed with soap under running water. Cuts should be encouraged to bleed, then placed under running water. Use contact precautions while caring for patients with skin involvement.

OCULAR: Exposed eyes should be irrigated with copious amounts of room temperature water for at least 15 minutes.

INHALATION: Respiratory isolation pending exclusion of a plague diagnosis is advisable if sputum studies disclose gram-negative bacilli with bipolar "safety pin" appearance when using Wright's or methylene blue stains.

PRECAUTIONS: Standard precautions (surgical mask, face shield, and gown) should be taken to prevent potential person-to-person transmission of the disease in proven or suspected cases of glanders.

ENVIRONMENT: A 0.5% hypochlorite solution is effective to decontaminate an area.

Symptomatic and Supportive

Treatment is symptomatic; no vaccine is currently available.

Antibiotic Therapy

Antibiotics are the mainstay of therapy. Duration of therapy is 60-150 days.

Localized disease:
- Amoxicillin/clavulanate: 60 mg/kg/day in 3 divided oral doses, OR
- Tetracycline: 40 mg/kg/day in 3 divided oral doses (NOT recommended for pregnant women or children less than 8 years old), OR
- Trimethoprim/sulfa (TMP 4 mg/kg/day and sulfa 20 mg/kg/day) in 4 divided oral doses.

Extrapulmonary suppurative disease: Administer antibiotic therapy as above for a total of 6-12 months. Surgical drainage of abscesses is indicated.

Severe and/or septic disease: Ceftazidime 120 mg/kg/day in 3 divided doses, combined with TMP/sulfa (TMP 8 mg/kg/day and sulfa 40 mg/kg/day in 4 divided doses). Medication is initially given intravenously for 2 weeks, followed by oral therapy for 6 months.

Hypotension

Administer IV fluids; large amounts may be necessary. If unresponsive, administer dopamine or norepinephrine and titrate as needed.

Monitoring Parameters

Obtain CBC, liver function tests, and blood or sputum cultures in all suspected cases of glanders.

Hantavirus Pulmonary Syndrome

Clinical Effects

Background

Hantavirus Pulmonary Syndrome (HPS) in the United States is caused by at least 3 pathogenic hantaviruses, each of which has a distinct primary rodent host or reservoir. *Sin Nombre* (no-name) virus (SNV) (formerly known as *Muerto Canyon* virus) is the most common cause of HPS in North America. The principal host for SNV is the deer mouse. The exact mechanism of hantavirus transmission to humans is unknown. Potentially hazardous exposures include direct aerosolization of urine and other potentially infective rodent body fluids, secondary aerosolization of dried rodent excreta, contamination of food, and direct contact with virus-bearing rodents or their excreta or saliva.

Biological Warfare

A risk exists for use as a biologic weapon.

Clinical Presentation

INCUBATION: 2 weeks post-exposure.

PRODROMAL PHASE: Generally lasts for 3 to 6 days. Characterized by flu-like illness with fever, myalgia and often GI symptoms. Respiratory symptoms are often absent initially. Laboratory findings may include elevated LDH, AST and ALT, lactic acidosis, and the triad of thrombocytopenia, leukocytosis with left shift, and large immunoblastic lymphocytes.

CARDIOPULMONARY PHASE: Generally heralded by progressive cough and dyspnea accompanied by tachypnea, tachycardia, fever, and hypotension. Adult Respiratory Distress Syndrome (ARDS) with progressive hypoxemia (requiring intubation and mechanical ventilation) is common. Intractable hypotension and myocardial depression leading to fatal cardiac dysrhythmias may also occur.

CONVALESCENT PHASE: Improved oxygenation and hemodynamic function are observed. No long-term sequelae usually occur.

Treatment

Decontamination

OCULAR: Irrigate exposed eyes with copious amounts of 0.9% saline or water at room temperature for at least 15 minutes.

DERMAL: Remove contaminated clothing and wash exposed area thoroughly with soap and water.

INHALATION: Person-to-person or nosocomial transmission of HPS has not been documented and is unlikely to occur in health care settings. However, universal precautions and respiratory isolation of all suspected cases is advised (infection is presumed to be contracted by inhalation of infectious particles). Particle masks are required for all persons entering the room; outside venting rooms are recommended, but not required. Once patients have clinical remission, they may be transferred to private rooms where universal precautions must be maintained.

Symptomatic and Supportive

Supportive measures (intensive care monitoring, airway management, and cardiovascular support) are the basis for therapy.

Airway Management

Treat respiratory distress and hypoxemia with oxygen; intubation and mechanical ventilation may be needed.

Hypotension

Administer IV fluids; large amounts may be necessary. If unresponsive to these measures, administer dopamine or norepinephrine and titrate as needed.

Pulmonary Edema (Noncardiogenic)

Maintain ventilation and oxygenation. Monitor ABGs/pulse oximetry frequently. Early use of PEEP and mechanical ventilation may be needed.

Transfusions

RBCs are indicated to maintain oxygen delivery if hemoglobin level decreases.

Monitoring Parameters

Obtain CBC, liver function tests, ABGs, and ECG as clinically indicated. Chest x-ray is indicated for all patients with suspected HPS.

Range Of Toxicity

HPS is fatal in up to 50% of patients. Of patients with mild HPS (rare), 100% recover within 48-72 hours of admission. Patients with severe HPS, such as those requiring ventilation for up to 48 hours, may have a fatal outcome. The difference in mortality between moderate and severe cases appears to be due to early recognition and initiation of medical ICU-level care.

Junin (Argentine Hemorrhagic Fever)

Clinical Effects

Background

Junin is a viral hemorrhagic disease caused by an arenavirus. Life-threatening loss of blood volume may occur without treatment. Transmission occurs from field mice to man via probable contamination of superficial wounds by mouse urine and/or excreta. Person-to-person transmission requires close personal contact or contact with blood, secretions, or excreta and mucous membranes. No evidence exists of secondary transmission from casual contact.

Biological Warfare

Use of Junin virus as a biological warfare agent has been proposed due to its contagious and lethal properties. The virus has been shown to be stable in aerosol, and the aerosol route is a likely method of intentional dissemination during a terrorist attack.

Clinical Presentation

INCUBATION: Usually 7 to 16 days.

INITIAL SYMPTOMS: Illness begins insidiously, with early symptoms of fever, sore throat, weakness, headache, myalgia, and malaise. Nonproductive cough commonly follows. Retrosternal or epigastric pain, vomiting, diarrhea, and abdominal discomfort are also common.

PROGRESSION OF SYMPTOMS: More severe cases progress to bleeding, tremors of tongue and hands, shock, aseptic meningitis, and coma.

DURATION: Illness generally lasts 7 to 15 days.

Treatment

Decontamination

DERMAL: Sites exposed to blood, body fluids, secretions, or excretions from patients with suspected Junin fever should be immediately washed with soap and water.

INHALATION: Medical personnel working with known infected patients should wear protective masks and utilize strict barrier nursing techniques. Respirators should be used when caring for patients with coughing, vomiting, diarrhea, or hemorrhage.

Symptomatic and Supportive

Early, aggressive treatment is imperative. Aggressive management of secondary infections and hypotension is important. No antidote or vaccine is available for these infections.

Medication

Ribavirin is recommended for the treatment of Junin fever. The loading dose is 30 mg/kg of body weight IV, followed by 16 mg/kg IV Q6H for 4 days, then 8 mg/kg IV Q8H for 6 days (total treatment time 10 days).

Transfusions

Transfusions of fresh frozen plasma and packed red cells should be instituted in cases of severe bleeding or coagulopathy.

Hypotension

Administer IV fluids; large amounts may be necessary. If unresponsive, administer dopamine or norepinephrine, titrate to desired response.

Pulmonary Edema (Noncardiogenic)

Maintain ventilation and oxygenation. Monitor ABGs/pulse oximetry frequently. Early use of PEEP and mechanical ventilation may be needed.

Seizures

Administer a benzodiazepine intravenously.

Diazepam: The recommended adult dosage is 5 to 10 mg IV; repeat every 10 to 15 minutes as needed. For children, the recommended dosage is 0.2 to 0.5 mg/kg; repeat every 5 minutes as needed.

Lorazepam: The recommended adult dosage is 4 to 8 mg. For children, 0.05 to 0.1 mg/kg is recommended.

Consider phenobarbital if seizures recur after diazepam 30 mg (adults) or 10 mg (children >5 years).

Monitoring Parameters

Monitor CBC with differential, platelets, electrolytes, renal function tests, PT/INR, PTT, fibrinogen, fibrin degradation products, blood cultures, and liver function tests as indicated.

Range Of Toxicity

The mortality rate for patients hospitalized with Junin virus is 15% to 30%. Biosafety level 4 containment.

Lassa Fever

Clinical Effects

Background

Lassa fever is a severe viral hemorrhagic fever caused by an arenavirus (Lassa virus). Transmission occurs from rodent to man via probable contamination of superficial wounds by rodent urine and/or excreta. Person-to-person transmission requires close personal contact or contact with blood, secretions, or excreta and mucous membranes. There is no evidence of secondary transmission from casual contact.

Biological Warfare

Lassa virus has potential for use as a biological warfare agent due to its contagious and lethal properties. Aerosol preparations are stable at low humidity and present a likely method of intentional dissemination during a terrorist attack

Clinical Presentation

INCUBATION: Usually 10 to 14 days.

INITIAL SYMPTOMS: The illness begins insidiously, with fever, sore throat, weakness, and malaise. Pains in the joints and lower back, headache, and nonproductive cough commonly follow. Exudative pharyngitis, conjunctivitis, and elevations of hepatic enzymes may develop. Retrosternal or epigastric pain, vomiting, diarrhea, and abdominal discomfort are also common. Duration of illness is 1 to 4 weeks.

PROGRESSION OF SYMPTOMS: During the second week of illness, diffuse rales and pleural and pericardial friction rub may be detected. Facial and neck edema, conjunctival hemorrhages, mucosal bleeding, central cyanosis, encephalopathy, and shock occur in most severe cases. Some patients develop adult respiratory distress syndrome. Life-threatening blood loss is rare, about 20% of hospital-ized patients develop mucosal hemorrhage, especially gingival. Death is preceded by hypovolemic shock, tissue edema, respiratory distress syndrome, encephalopathy, and occasionally hemorrhage.

RECOVERY: In milder cases, the patient begins to recover within 8 to 10 days of disease onset. The most common complication is deafness (25%).

Treatment

Decontamination

DERMAL: Sites exposed to blood, body fluids, secretions, or excre-tions should be immediately washed with soap and water.

INHALATION: Medical personnel should wear protective masks and utilize strict barrier nursing tech-niques. Respirators should be used when caring for patients with coughing, vomiting, diarrhea or hemorrhage.

Symptomatic and Supportive

Early, aggressive treatment is war-ranted, with management of sec-ondary infections and hypotension. No antidote or vaccine is available.

Medication

Ribavirin is recommended. The loading dose is 30 mg/kg of body weight IV, followed by 16 mg/kg IV Q6H for 4 days, then 8 mg/kg IV Q8H for 6 days (total treatment time 10 days).

Transfusions

Transfusions of fresh frozen plas-ma and packed red cells should be instituted as needed for bleeding or coagulopathy.

Hypotension

Administer IV fluids; large amounts may be necessary. If unre-sponsive, administer dopamine or norepinephrine.

Pulmonary Edema (Noncardiogenic)

Maintain ventilation and oxygena-tion. Monitor ABGs/pulse oxime-try frequently. Early use of PEEP and mechanical ventilation may be needed.

Seizures

Administer a benzodiazepine intra-venously.

Diazepam: The recommended adult dosage is 5 to 10 mg IV; repeat every 10 to 15 minutes as needed. For children, the recom-mended dosage is 0.2 to 0.5 mg/kg; repeat every 5 minutes as needed.

Lorazepam: The recommended adult dosage is 4 to 8 mg. For chil-dren, 0.05 to 0.1 mg/kg is recom-mended.

Consider phenobarbital if seizures recur after diazepam 30 mg (adults) or 10 mg (children >5 years).

Monitoring Parameters

Monitor CBC with platelets and differential, electrolytes, renal function tests, PT/INR, PTT, blood cultures, and liver function tests as clinically indicated.

Range Of Toxicity

The mortality rate for hospitalized patients is 15% to 20%. Prognosis is particularly poor for women in the third trimester of pregnancy, and a high rate of fetal wastage occurs.

Paralytic Shellfish Toxins

Clinical Effects

Background

Paralytic shellfish poisoning results from the consumption of mussels, clams, oysters, and scallops that have ingested toxic dinoflagellates. Dinoflagellates are plankton that are consumed as food by a large number of marine animals.

Biological Warfare

There are several paralytic shellfish toxins, including neosaxitoxin, saxitoxin, gonyautoxin I, gonyautoxin II, gonyautoxin III, and gonyautoxin IV. These are considered to have potential for use as biological weapons.

Clinical Presentation

PRODROME: Typical clinical presentation begins with a brief gastrointestinal prodrome (nausea, vomiting) followed by sensory disturbances and progressive paralysis of skeletal muscles occurring within 30 minutes to several hours. The duration of the illness may last from several hours to days.

MILD: Paresthesias and numbness of the lips, tongue, face, and neck, spreading to the fingertips and toes. Accompanied by nausea, dizziness, and headache.

MODERATE: Difficulty with speech, weakness of arms and legs. The extremities may become numb, tingling, stiff and/or uncoordinated. Tachycardia, dyspnea, and rhabdomyolysis may also develop.

SEVERE: Muscle paralysis, hypotension, severe respiratory difficulty, and a choking sensation. Respiratory failure resulting in death may occur, usually within 12 hours of the onset of symptoms.

Prognosis

Patients who survive the first 12 hours generally have a good prognosis and recover without sequelae.

Treatment

Decontamination

Activated charcoal, gastric lavage. A patient may experience rapid onset of respiratory paralysis and loss of gag reflex; ipecac is NOT recommended.

Symptomatic and Supportive
No specific antidote is available. Treatment is symptomatic and supportive.

Fluid/Electrolytes
Replace fluid and electrolyte deficits; maintain hydration. Maintain urine output of 1 to 2 mL/kg/hr if rhabdomyolysis develops.

Hypotension
Administer IV fluids. If unresponsive, administer dopamine or norepinephrine.

Dysrhythmias
Adults should be treated with lidocaine 1 to 1.5 mg/kg by IV push, followed by 1 to 4 mg per minute as needed. The recommended pediatric dosage is 1 mg/kg IV bolus, followed by an infusion of 20 to 50 mcg/kg per minute.

Airway Management
Administer oxygen, perform endotracheal intubation and provide mechanical ventilation as clinically indicated.

Monitoring Parameters
Serum electrolytes, BUN, creatinine, calcium, magnesium, phosphorus, urine output, CPK, ECG, and pulse oximetry

Range Of Toxicity
Toxicity has been reported with intake estimated to be as low as 124 mcg. The estimated lethal dose is 500 mcg.

Plague

Clinical Effects

Background
Plague is a zoonotic disease caused by *Yersinia pestis*, a gram-negative, nonmotile and nonspore-forming bacillus that grows in anaerobic and aerobic conditions. It spreads through lymphatics to lymph nodes to the bloodstream to involve all organs. A high index of suspicion is required for diagnosis because of lack of pathognomonic features. Common syndromes include bubonic, pneumonic (most likely to be used in warfare/bioterrorism), and septicemic plague

Biological Warfare
In non-endemic areas, the possible use as a biological terrorist agent should be considered. If present, quarantine is necessary.

Clinical Presentation
The incubation period is 2-6 days (primary pneumonic plague may be 1- 2 days). Direct person-to-person transmission is seen only in the setting of pneumonic plague. Early symptoms include fever, nausea, vomiting, diarrhea, and myalgias.

BUBONIC: High fever, buboes (painful, tender, swollen lymph nodes; most commonly inguinal).

PNEUMONIC: Fulminant respiratory symptoms (tachypnea, productive cough, blood-tinged sputum, cyanosis, rales, rhonchi); rapidly fatal if untreated. Direct, person-to-person transmission is seen only in the setting of pneumonic plague.

SEPTICEMIC: Acute febrile illness, no lymphadenopathy, rapid progression to septic shock is typical.

Complications
Septic shock, ARDS (in 5% with 50% mortality), DIC, bacterial meningitis, seizures (generally an ominous sign) and skin necrosis (black plague).

Treatment

Decontamination
Universal Precautions are warranted. Isolate the infected/suspected patients for a minimum of 48 hours (continue until drainage stops). Strict isolation for pneumonic plague is recommended for at least 72 hours after the start of antibiotic therapy. Gloves and gowns are needed when in contact with infective material. Contaminated dressings and bedclothes should be burned or autoclaved. Dermal exposure to contaminated fluids should be immediately washed with soap and water.

Symptomatic and Supportive
Because of rapid disease progression (grows slowly in culture), start antibiotic therapy empirically if plague is suspected.

Pulmonary Edema (Non-Cardiogenic)
Intubation and mechanical ventilation may be necessary. Monitor ABGs/pulse oximetry. PEEP as needed.

Antibiotics Of Choice
Streptomycin, gentamicin, doxycycline, ciprofloxacin, or chloramphenicol.

Hypotension
Isotonic (0.9% saline) IV fluids, dopamine, norepinephrine.

Monitoring Parameters
Blood, sputum, bubo aspirate Gram's stain and culture, antibody titer, CBC, urinalysis. Chest x-ray: Pneumonic infiltrates or hilar adenopathy.

BACTERIOLOGY: High yield in pneumonic and septicemic plague; Y pestis appears as bipolar "safety pin" on Gram's stain; cultures may not be positive for 48 hrs.

ANTIBODY TITER: Hemagglutinating antibody titer rises in 8-14 days.

Range Of Toxicity

Mortality ranges from 50% to 60% for untreated bubonic plague and up to 100% for untreated septicemic or pneumonic plague.

Q Fever

Clinical Effects

Background
Q fever is a ubiquitous zoonosis caused by the rickettsia-like bacteria *Coxiella burnetii*, a

coccobacillus. *C. burnetii* forms spore-like structures. It resists environmental destruction and can survive for many weeks or years. The organism resides within the phagolysosome in the cytoplasm of an infected cell. Infection occurs as an acute or chronic disease.

Coxiella burnetii organisms can persist in the environment for many years in contaminated dust or aerosols, posing the potential for human infection through inhalation. Infection occurs most often by inhalation of dust or aerosols derived from infected domestic animals. Person to person spread is rare. Infection may be transmitted from animals to humans by ticks.

Biological Warfare

Because of the stability of the organism and its ability to be transmitted via inhalation, the aerosol form of this agent has the potential for use in bioterrorism.

Clinical Presentation

INCUBATION: The usual incubation period is about 20 days; the normal range is 14 to 22 days.

ACUTE STAGE: Acute Q fever is a self-limited flu-like illness, with high fevers, relative bradycardia, severe headaches, cough, nausea, vomiting, and diarrhea. Myocarditis, pericarditis, meningitis, and optic neuritis are less common. Atypical pneumonia and granulomatous hepatitis may develop 4 to 7 days after the onset of illness.

CHRONIC STAGE: Chronic Q fever may occur with or without a recognized antecedent acute episode; endocarditis appears to be the primary manifestation of chronic Q fever.

Recovery

The acute form is self-limiting (2 to 7 days) or easily treated with antibiotics. The chronic stage, which occurs in about 5% of patients, lasts longer than 6 months after disease onset.

Treatment

Decontamination

DERMAL: Remove contaminated clothing and wash exposed area thoroughly with soap and water.

INHALATION: Medical personnel should wear protective masks and utilize strict barrier nursing techniques.

Symptomatic and Supportive

Vaccines are not available. Early antibiotic therapy is recommended.

Antibiotic Therapy

ACUTE Q FEVER:

Adults: Use one of the following regimens for 2 to 3 weeks or until the patient is afebrile for one week:

- doxycycline 100 mg orally twice daily, OR
- tetracycline 500 mg PO 4 times daily, OR
- ofloxacin 200 mg PO every 12 hours, OR
- pefloxacin 400 mg IV or PO every 12 hours

Hydroxychloroquine added to antibiotic therapy has increased the effectiveness of therapy.

Children: For children over 8 years old, give tetracycline 25 mg/kg/day, in divided doses, for 2 to 3 weeks.

CHRONIC Q FEVER:

Adults: Treatment for chronic Q fever ranges from 3 years to lifetime. Regimens are:

- doxycycline 200 milligrams PO daily, OR
- ofloxacin 400 to 600 milligrams PO daily

Chloroquine or hydroxychloroquine has been added to these regimens to alkalize fluids and potentiate the eradication of organisms in phagocytes.

Corticosteroid Therapy

Granulomatous hepatitis may respond to treatment with corticosteroids. Treat with oral prednisone (0.5 mg/kg/day) if fever persists following appropriate antibiotic therapy.

Monitoring Parameters

CBC and platelet count, renal and hepatic function, and urinalysis. Diagnosis is confirmed by acute and convalescent serology. Chest x-ray is indicated for patients with pulmonary signs or symptoms. Laboratory work with *Coxiella burnetii* is designated as biosafety level-3.

Range of Toxicity

One organism is capable of causing disease. Complications may occur depending on the initial infecting dose. The length of the incubation period is inversely related to the size of the initial infecting dose.

Ricin (Toxalbumins)

Clinical Effects

Background

Ricin is a potent cytotoxin (a toxalbumin) made up of two hemagglutinins and two toxins (RCL III and RCL IV) derived from the beans of the castor plant (*ricinus communis*). Castor beans are ubiquitous and the toxin is relatively easy to extract. It can be prepared in liquid or crystalline forms or lyophilized to create a dry powder. Routes of exposure include inhalation (aerosol), ingestion (through contaminated food or water) and parenteral (injected into a victim). Ricin is NOT communicable person to person.

Biological Warfare

Ricin is less toxic than botulinum; a large quantity would be required to cover a significant area.

Clinical Presentation

INHALATION: The incubation period is 18 to 24 hours. Limited data indicate that symptoms present as acute onset of fever, chest tightness, cough, dyspnea, nausea, and arthralgias in 4 to 8 hours. The aerosol route can produce necrosis of the upper and lower respiratory system. Other effects would likely include cyanosis, respiratory inflammation, and pulmonary edema. Based on animal data, a lethal human aerosol exposure would likely result in adult respiratory distress syndrome and respiratory failure. Time to death in animal studies was dose-dependent and occurred within 36 to 72 hours.

INGESTION: Toxalbumins cause severe gastrointestinal lesions with irritation of the oropharynx, esophagus, or stomach when directly exposed. Although clinically similar to alkaline caustic burns, lesions are usually delayed 2 or more hours after exposure. Ingestion may cause abdominal pain, nausea, vomiting, and profuse bloody diarrhea. In severe cases, shock develops. Late phase complications include cytotoxic effects on the liver, central nervous system, kidney, and adrenal glands, typically 2 to 5 days after exposure. The patient may be asymptomatic during the preceding 1 to 5 days.

PARENTERAL: Parenteral exposure causes local tissue and muscle necrosis. Assassinations have been carried out by implantation of ricin-containing pellets into the body.

Treatment

Decontamination

ORAL: Vigorous decontamination is warranted, using activated charcoal and gastric lavage.

INHALATION: Ricin is non-volatile; secondary aerosols are not expected to endanger healthcare workers.

FIRST AID MEASURES: Use of a protective mask is effective in preventing aerosol exposure to medical personnel. Decontaminate exposed areas with soap and water. A hypochlorite solution (0.1% sodium hypochlorite) can inactivate ricin.

Symptomatic and Supportive

Treatment is based on the route of exposure. A vaccine is currently under development. Respiratory support includes oxygen, intubation, and mechanical ventilation as needed. Gastrointestinal support includes monitoring of fluid and electrolyte status and fluid replacement.

Pulmonary Edema (Noncardiogenic)

Maintain adequate ventilation and oxygenation; monitor ABGs and/or pulse oximetry frequently. Early use of PEEP may be necessary.

Monitoring Parameters

Collect serum and respiratory secretions for antigen detection (ELISA and ECL) testing. Obtain chest x-ray if respiratory symptoms are present (findings: bilateral infiltrates). Monitor

ABGs/pulse oximetry, CBC with differential.

Range of Toxicity

The LD50 for mice is 3 to 5 mcg/kg.

Rocky Mountain Spotted Fever

Clinical Effects

Background

Rocky Mountain Spotted Fever (RMSF) is caused by *Rickettsia rickettsii*. It is transmitted through the bite of the wood tick or dog tick.

Biological Warfare

RMSF has been cited by the military as a possible, although not likely, terrorist threat.

Clinical Presentation

INCUBATION: The incubation period is 2 to 14 days (mean 5 days) following the tick bite; in severe cases the incubation period may be 1 to 5 days. RMSF should be considered in patients with unexplained febrile illness, even if there is no history of tick bite.

INITIAL SYMPTOMS: The initial symptoms are nonspecific and include fever, headache, myalgias, malaise, nausea, and vomiting. Atypical presentations are common in adults. A flu-like prodrome (fever, chills, myalgias, headache) occurs 3 to 10 days after the tick

bite. A maculopapular rash develops 2 to 6 days after the onset of fever. It begins on the wrists and ankles, then spreads to the extremities, trunk, and face. It may become petechial; the palms and soles are involved. Some patients (5% to 15%) never develop a rash (Rocky Mountain Spotless Fever).

PROGRESSION OF SYMPTOMS: Reported clinical effects include tachycardia, hypotension, generalized edema, myocarditis, dysrhythmias, anorexia, abdominal pain and tenderness, muscular rigidity, splenomegaly, arthralgias, restlessness, irritability, altered mental status (with delirium, lethargy and coma), and dehydration.

COMPLICATIONS: Disseminated intravascular coagulation (DIC), noncardiogenic pulmonary edema, renal failure, shock, rapid death.

Treatment

Prevention

Individuals entering tick-infested areas should wear light-colored clothing with long sleeves and pants, use tick repellents, and check the entire body for ticks daily. Permethrin sprayed on clothing lasts up to 1 month. The most effective repellents contain DEET; application should be repeated every 1 to 2 hours. Tick repellents may have toxic effects and should be used cautiously in children.

TICK REMOVAL: Promptly

remove attached ticks before transmission of *R. rickettsii* can occur. Disinfect the bite site. Using blunt tweezers, grasp the tick as close to the skin surface as possible and pull upward with steady even pressure.

Symptomatic and Supportive

COOLING MEASURES: If temperature is >38.9 C, use a cooling blanket or tepid sponging.

HYDRATION: Give IV fluids (Normal Saline or Lactated Ringers) and titrate to hydration.

OXYGEN: Titrate to oxygen saturation >90%.

FRESH FROZEN PLASMA: May be needed if DIC occurs.

Antibiotic Therapy

Patients exposed to ticks who develop fever, petechial rash, and vomiting require urgent antibiotic therapy; initiate before laboratory confirmation is available.

DOXYCYCLINE: This is the drug of choice, and should be used even for children because of the potential for severe or fatal cases. Adults should receive 100 mg PO or IV BID for 7 days and for at least 48 hours after defervescence. The recommended dose for children is 1.5 mg/kg.

CHLORAMPHENICOL: An alternative choice in pregnant or allergic patients. The recommended dose for adults is 500 mg PO or IV QID for 7 days and for at least 48 hours after defervescence. For children, the dose is 75 mg/kg/day PO or IV in 4 divided doses for the same duration as adults.

Monitoring Parameters

Monitor ECG, CBC, electrolytes, ABG, renal and hepatic function.

DIAGNOSIS: Laboratory data lend only nonspecific support to the diagnosis of RMSF. The diagnosis can be confirmed by immunofluorescent antibody tests in paired sera. Only serology is specific for rickettsial infection; however, therapy should not await serologic confirmation. An immunohistochemical stain of lesion is the best rapid diagnostic test available. PCR may prove useful in early diagnosis of RMSF.

Range of Toxicity

One tick may be enough to cause an infection. The risk of infection increases if the tick is attached longer than 48 to 72 hours.

Shigella

Clinical Effects

Background

The genus *Shigella* is made up of small, nonmotile, gram-negative rods that have the same characteristics (morphologically and biochemically) as *E. coli*. *Shigella* is divided into four species: *S. boydii*, *S. dysenteriae*, *S. flexneri*, and *S. sonnei*. In general, *Shigella* outbreaks are more likely to be caused by *S. sonnei* and *S. flexneri* species in developed countries, while *S. dysenteriae* is more frequently found in developing countries. Transmission can occur from person-to-person contact and can easily occur by the fecal-oral route (more common than transmission by food or water contamination).

Biological Warfare

Shigella is considered to have the potential for use as a biologic weapon.

Clinical Presentation

INCUBATION: The incubation period is usually 24 to 48 hours.

SYMPTOMS: The presentation varies by individual, with some having only minor symptoms of watery diarrhea, fever, and abdominal pain. More severe forms result in true dysentery, which includes high fever, tenesmus, nausea, crampy abdominal pain, and profuse watery diarrhea (stools are odorless, yellow-green, commonly mucoid, and bloody) that evolves over hours to a few days. Respiratory symptoms (coughing and rhinorrhea) are common; vomiting is uncommon. Febrile seizures can occur, and are more likely in children less than 2 years old. Symptoms generally resolve in 5 to 7 days.

Treatment

Decontamination

Emetics and purgatives are not indicated. Antidiarrheals such as paregoric are also to be avoided, since the toxin is eliminated by vomiting and diarrhea.

Fluid and Electrolytes

Fluid and electrolyte replacement is indicated in moderately to severely dehydrated patients. Rehydration should take place over 30 to 45 minutes with normal saline or Lactated Ringers solution (children: 20 mL/kg; adults: 1 to 2 liters). Repeat a bolus (children: 10 mL/kg; adults: 0.5 to 1 liter) over 30 to 45 minutes if response is poor.

Antibiotic Therapy

The drug of choice is trimethoprim/sulfamethoxazole. The recommended dose for adults is 160 mg TMP and 800 mg SMX PO BID for 5 days. For children, the recommendation is 10 mg/kg/day TMP and 50 mg/kg/day SMX PO in 2 divided doses for 5 days.

Alternately, ampicillin 500 mg PO QID for 7 days can be given to individuals over 20 kg. Individuals less than 20 kg can receive 50 to 100 mg/kg/day PO in 4 to 6 divided doses for 7 days.

Tetracycline is another treatment option for adults (2.5 gm PO in a single dose).

Monitoring Parameters

CBC, serum electrolytes, and stool cultures as indicated.

Range of Toxicity

A small inoculum (10 to 200 organisms) is able to produce infection.

Smallpox

Clinical Effects

Background

Variola major is a DNA virus of genus *orthopoxvirus*. It is transmitted person-to-person, usually from airborne and droplet exposure and by contact with skin lesions or secretions. Transmission is also possible via contaminated clothing and bedding. The infection can spread widely and rapidly throughout a country. Vaccination against smallpox does NOT reliably confer lifelong immunity; even previously vaccinated persons should be considered susceptible to smallpox.

Biological Warfare

Smallpox poses a serious threat to civilian populations because of a 30% mortality rate in unvaccinated persons and the absence of specific therapy. In the United States, few persons under 27 years of age have been vaccinated.

Clinical Presentation

INCUBATION: The incubation period is 7 to 17 days (average 12 days).

SYMPTOMS: Smallpox is initially identified by its characteristic skin lesions. Patients experience an abrupt onset of fever, vomiting, malaise, headache, and backache. Two to 5 days later, a macular rash develops. The rash quickly becomes papular (the papules evolve into vesicles within 2 days, then progress to pustules). Crusting begins on day 8 or 9 of illness, with scabs separating over the next 2 to 3 weeks followed by a pigment-free skin. Scarring and pitting develops.

Transmission is only possible from the time of the first appearance of the rash until the last scab has separated. Lesions on mucous membranes shed infected epithelial cells, which are responsible for highly infectious oropharyngeal secretions during the first few days of eruptive illness. Although the virus disseminates systemically, other organs are seldom involved. Cough and bronchitis occur occasionally, but pneumonia is rare.

MALIGNANT FORM: Rapidly progressive disease develops in 5% to 10% of smallpox patients and is usually fatal within 5 to 7 days. The lesions are so densely confluent that the skin resembles crepe rubber; bleeding into the skin and intestinal tract may occur. Patients are highly infectious.

HEMORRHAGIC SMALLPOX: Characterized by a severely prostrating prodromal illness with high fever and head, back, and abdominal pain, followed by a dusky erythema, then petechiae and frank hemorrhages into the skin and mucous membranes. Pregnant women are particularly susceptible. May be mistaken for meningococcemia or severe acute leukemia.

OUTCOME: Most deaths occur during the second week of illness, most likely as a result of toxemia. Hemorrhagic and malignant forms usually cause death within a week.

Treatment

Decontamination
ORAL: Oral decontamination measures following exposure to *variola* or *vaccinia* viruses have not proven to be effective and are not recommended. Drainage material from smallpox lesions is potentially highly infectious; barrier precautions should be used.

MUCOUS MEMBRANES: Mucous membranes should be rinsed with copious amounts of water in the event of contact with infectious materials.

OCULAR: Remove contact lenses and irrigate eyes with copious amounts of 0.9% saline or water at room temperature for at least 15 minutes.

DERMAL: Intact skin should be washed with soap and running water. Cuts should be encouraged to bleed, then placed under running water. Wash the exposed area thoroughly with soap and water.

CLOTHING: Personal protective equipment should include eye protection and gloves to reduce the risk of infected material contacting mucous membranes and non-intact skin. Bag soiled clothing or dressings in clearly labeled leak-proof polyethylene bags until autoclaved or incinerated.

Symptomatic and Supportive
There is no specific treatment for smallpox. Immediate vaccination for ALL potential contacts, including healthcare workers, may prevent or lessen disease if given within 4 days of exposure. If more than 3 days have passed since exposure, give with vaccinia immune-globulin. Seventeen days of observation of contacts for fever and rash is required. Respiratory isolation is required for at least 17 days after symptoms appear.

HYPOTENSION: Infuse 10 to 20 mL/kg isotonic fluid. If symptoms persist, administer dopamine or norepinephrine.

TESTING: Requires biosafety level 4 facility. Contact state laboratory authorities or CDC for decisions regarding obtaining and processing diagnostic specimens.

Monitoring Parameters
Vital signs, including temperature.

Range of Toxicity

The virus is very stable and may persist for 24 hours or more under favorable circumstances. It travels surprisingly far in the air and infects at very low doses. About 30% of susceptible persons would become infected.

Staphylococcus

Clinical Effects

Background

The majority of cases associated with *Staphylococcus aureus* are the result of enterotoxin A; other enterotoxins include B, C, D, and E. Common carriers of *S. aureus* include humans (food handlers), their purulent secretions, nasal discharge, and normal skin. Most foods (particularly those high in protein) will support staphylococcal growth. Staphylococcal toxins can be formed within a few hours when foods are kept at room temperature.

Biological Warfare

The pyrogenic toxin *Staphylococcus aureus* enterotoxin B (SEB), which is usually associated with food poisoning after ingestion of improperly handled foodstuffs, causes a markedly different clinical syndrome when inhaled. Extreme potency and stability, along with its low incapacitating-lethality ratio, make SEB a likely candidate as an incapacitating bioterrorist agent.

Clinical Presentation

INCUBATION: The incubation period following ingestion is 1 to 6 hours. With inhalational exposure, incubation takes 3 to 12 hours.

ORAL EXPOSURE: Staphylococcal food poisoning presents as violent retching and vomiting accompanied by crampy abdominal pain and diarrhea. Patients may appear dehydrated and generally are afebrile. Headache, weakness, and dizziness may be noted. Attack rates are about 75%; the duration of illness is <24 hours (usually between 6 and 10 hours);

INHALATION EXPOSURE: Symptoms of inhaled SEB include sudden onset of fever, headache, chills, myalgia, and nonproductive cough. Dyspnea and retrosternal chest pain may develop in more severe cases. Nausea, vomiting, and diarrhea occur as a result of inadvertent swallowing of toxin. Conjunctival injection may be present. Postural hypotension may develop due to fluid losses. Most patients recover from inhalation exposure within 1 to 2 weeks. Mortality is <1%.

Treatment

Decontamination

Wear proper protective clothing to prevent contamination.

Antidote

There is no specific antidote.

Symptomatic and Supportive

INHALATION: Airway management, oxygen, mechanical ventilation.

ORAL: Emetics and purgatives are NOT indicated. Control vomiting, give fluids for dehydration, take measures to prevent the development of shock.

ANTIEMETICS: Antiemetics are not usually required if alteration of the diet is successful. However, they may be given for significant nausea and vomiting. Adult dose are:

- Promethazine 25 to 50 mg IM or IV.
- Prochlorperazine 10 mg IM or IV; or 25 mg rectally twice a day.
- Hydroxyzine 25 to 100 mg IM
- Trimethobenzamine 250 mg PO 3 to 4 times a day; or 200 mg IM or rectally 3 to 4 times a day.

ANTIDIARRHEALS: Paregoric or diphenoxylate/atropine (Lomotil) may be effective in controlling pain, tenesmus, and diarrhea. However, evidence suggests that Lomotil may prolong the symptoms and duration of some bacterial infections

Monitoring Parameters

Staphylococcal food poisoning is usually a self limited illness; often no laboratory evaluation is required. Monitor electrolytes and fluid balance in patients with significant volume loss from vomiting and diarrhea. Food cultures or assays for enterotoxins may help to identify the source of an outbreak but are not generally useful for clinical management. Cultures of stool and vomitus may also confirm the diagnosis but are generally not used to guide therapy.

Diagnosis

Laboratory findings are not helpful. The toxin is difficult to detect in the serum by the time symptoms occur. Urine samples may be tested for SEB to confirm diagnosis, but is not generally used for clinical management. Because most patients will develop a significant antibody response to the toxin, acute and convalescent serum may be used retrospectively to confirm diagnosis.

Range of Toxicity

INHALATION: The aerosol-incapacitating dose is 30 ng/person; the lethal dose is approximately 1.7 mcg/person.

ORAL: Most cases are mild in nature. Only a small amount of toxin (approximately 200 ng) is required to cause clinical illness.

Tetrodotoxin

Clinical Effects

Background

Tetrodotoxin (TTX) is a potent neurotoxin that blocks sodium ion channels responsible for nerve and muscle excitability. It is found in various marine organisms, particularly the puffer fish, and causes paralytic poisoning following ingestion. Poisonings are caused by consumption of flesh, viscera, or skin containing TTX. The highest concentration is in the viscera.

Clinical Presentation

Ingestion of marine organisms containing TTX may result in hypothermia, diaphoresis, laryngismus, hypotension, hypertension, bradycardia, nausea and vomiting, paresthesias, dizziness, weakness, cyanosis, respiratory depression, seizures, and paralysis. Symptoms usually occur within 10 to 45 minutes, but may be delayed for up to 3 hours. Death may occur within the first 6 to 24 hours post-ingestion, usually secondary to muscle weakening that leads to respiratory paralysis.

Prognosis

Good, if the patient survives the first 24 hours.

Treatment

Decontamination

Administer activated charcoal and gastric lavage. Ipecac is NOT recommended due to rapid respiratory paralysis caused by the tetrodotoxin.

Symptomatic and Supportive

There is no specific antidote or treatment for TTX toxicity. Supportive care of blood pressure and airway management are critical.

Airway Management

Administer oxygen, perform endotracheal intubation and mechanical ventilation as indicated.

Hypotension

Administer IV fluids; large amounts may be necessary. If the patient is unresponsive to these measures, administer dopamine or norepinephrine and titrate to desired response.

Hypertension

Mild/moderate asymptomatic hypertension: Pharmacologic treatment is generally not necessary.

Severe hypertension: Preferred therapy is nitroprusside by IV infusion, 0.1mcg/kg/min, titrate up to desired response. Alternatives: labetalol, nitroglycerin, phentolamine.

Bradycardia

Administer atropine: Adult dose 0.5 to 1 mg IV every 5 min.

Bradyasystolic Arrest

Adults: Atropine 1 mg IV every 5 min. Maximum total dose 0.04 mg/kg. Minimum single dose 0.5 mg.

Pediatric patients: Atropine 0.02 mg/kg IV repeat every 5 min. Minimum single dose 0.1 mg. Maximum single dose: 0.5 mg for a child, 1 mg for an adolescent. Maximum total dose: 1 mg for a child, 2 mg for an adolescent.

Seizures
IV benzodiazepines, barbiturates.

Monitoring Parameters
Vital signs and ECG as indicated. Monitor pulse oximetry and/or ABGs. Pulmonary function tests (negative inspiratory force and forced vital capacity) may help anticipate the need for ventilatory support.

Range of Toxicity

An oral dose of as little as 10 mcg/kg of TTX may be fatal. Eating as little as 1/4 ounce of TTX-poisoned fish has resulted in signs and symptoms of TTX poisoning.

Trichothecene Mycotoxins

Clinical Effects

Background
Trichothecenes are mycotoxins produced by a number of species of the fungal genus Fusarium, often found growing on various agricultural crops such as corn, wheat, and barley. Over 100 trichothecenes have been identified. The most frequent natural contaminants are deoxynivalenol, diacetoxyscripenol, HT-toxin, nivalenol, and T-2 toxin.

Biological Warfare
Human and/or animal exposure occurs via contaminated food, in chemotherapy, and in chemical warfare.

Clinical Presentation
Trichothecene toxins are multitoxins affecting many systems. Acute toxicity resembles the damage done by radiation, nitrogen mustard, or mitomycin C. Primary damage is to the gastrointestinal tract and the lymphoid and hematopoietic systems. Symptoms may occur 2 to 4 hours following exposure, regardless of route.

DERMAL: Pain, pruritus, erythema, and necrosis.

INHALATION: Cough, dyspnea, wheezing, chest pain, and hemoptysis.

INGESTION: Consumption of contaminated grain has resulted in alimentary toxic aleukia characterized by 4 stages.

First stage: Typical symptoms include hyperemia of the mucosa accompanied by weakness, fever, nausea, and vomiting. Severe cases may be marked by acute esophagitis, gastritis, and gastroenteritis. Rarely seen are seizures and circulatory failure.

Second stage: Leukopenia, granulopenia, and progressive lymphocytosis.

Third stage: Symptoms include severe hemorrhagic diathesis and severe necrotic pharyngitis and laryngitis, in some instances resulting in death due to total closure of the larynx. Severe bone marrow suppression is possible. Mortality is high secondary to hemorrhage, sepsis, and airway occlusion from swelling.

Fourth stage: Characterized by recovery, which may take several weeks to months.

Treatment

Decontamination
DERMAL: Remove contaminated clothing and wash exposed area extremely thoroughly with soap and water.

INHALATION: Move patient from the toxic environment to fresh air. Monitor for respiratory distress. If cough or difficulty in breathing develops, evaluate for hypoxia, respiratory tract irritation, bronchitis, or pneumonitis.

OCULAR: Irrigate exposed eyes with copious amounts of tepid water for at least 15 minutes.

ORAL: Administer activated charcoal.

Symptomatic and Supportive
There are no known vaccines or antidotes to trichothecene mycotoxins. Treatments are directed at supporting hemopoietic abnormalities, gastrointestinal damage, and skin damage.

Bone Marrow Suppression
Thrombocytopenia: Monitor platelets and clotting activity.

Replace with platelets or fresh plasma as necessary.

Neutropenia: Antibiotics or isolation may be necessary while the patient is in a compromised state. Consider use of filgrastim in selected patients with severe neutropenia. The usual dose is 5 mcg/kg/day subcutaneously or intravenously.

Hypotension
Administer IV fluids; large amounts may be necessary. If the patient is unresponsive, administer dopamine or norepinephrine.

Monitoring Parameters
Obtain serial CBC with differential and platelet count, electrolytes, ABGs and/or pulse oximetry, and chest x-ray as clinically indicated.

Range of Toxicity

Leukopenia may be caused by as little as 0.1 mg/kg/day for a few weeks, however the exact dose necessary to cause serious human toxicity is unknown.

Tularemia

Clinical Effects

Background
Tularemia is a highly contagious, acute febrile zoonotic disease caused by *Francisella tularensis*, a gram-negative, pleomorphic coccobacillus. It is associated with skin, glandular, respiratory, or gas-

trointestinal manifestations, depending on the route of infection and the virulence of the infecting strain. The disease is transmitted to humans by direct contact with infected animal tissues, body fluids, and pelts; by bites of infected or contaminated animals or arthropods; by ingestion of contaminated meat or water; and by inhalation of infected aerosols.

Biological Warfare

The organism can survive prolonged periods of time (including freezing and desiccation) and still cause infection. Because of the rapid onset of action, nonspecific nature of complaints, and difficulty in identifying and culturing the organism, *F. tularensis* is a potential biologic weapon. Respiratory exposure by aerosol, as in a terrorist attack, would cause typhoidal tularemia, which often has a pneumonic component. Humans are highly susceptible to *F. tularensis* infection.

Clinical Presentation

INCUBATION: 1 to 14 days (usually 3 to 5 days).

TYPHOIDAL TULAREMIA: Fever, myalgias, malaise, headache, diarrhea, vomiting, abdominal pain, meningismus, and pneumonic component with cough, dyspnea, sputum, pleural effusions, pneumonia, and hilar lymphadenopathy about 3 to 5 days after exposure.

OTHER: Forms of tularemia that can present, but are not likely in aerosol attack, include:

Ulceroglandular: Ulcerative skin lesions, painful regional adenopathy, may suppurate.

Glandular: Headache, chills, myalgias, fever, vomiting, local adenopathy.

Oculoglandular: Severe conjunctivitis, corneal granulomas or ulcers, regional adenopathy.

Oropharyngeal: Exudative tonsillitis, cervical adenopathy.

Gastrointestinal: Fever, bloody diarrhea, abdominal pain.

Meningeal: Headache, neck stiffness, delirium, CSF pleocytosis.

Complications

Without treatment, the disease may progress to respiratory failure, sepsis, shock, and death. Target organs include lungs, lymph nodes, spleen, liver, and kidneys. Tularemia has a slower progression of illness and a lower case-fatality rate than either inhalational plague or anthrax. Isolation and identification of the organism using routine laboratory procedures could take several weeks.

Recovery

In untreated cases, symptoms may persist for several weeks or months, generally with progressive debility. Early diagnosis and treatment usually results in complete recovery.

Treatment

Decontamination
DERMAL: Sites exposed to blood, body fluids, secretions, or excretions from patients with suspected tularemia infections should be washed immediately with soap and water.

INHALATION: Medical personnel working with known infected patients should wear protective masks and utilize strict barrier nursing techniques.

Symptomatic and Supportive
A vaccine is not yet commercially available, but one is currently under review by the FDA. Supportive measures include antipyretics and analgesics.

Antibiotic Therapy
Early use of antibiotic therapy is indicated in all cases.

DRUGS OF CHOICE:
For chemotherapy: Streptomycin, gentamicin, and ciprofloxacin.

For chemoprophylaxis: Doxycycline, tetracycline, and ciprofloxacin.

Airway Management
In cases of airway compromise, supportive measures including endotracheal intubation and mechanical ventilation may be necessary.

Monitoring Parameters
Chest x-ray is indicated in suspected tularemia pneumonia or patients with pulmonary signs and symptoms. Obtain CBC, renal and liver function tests, and blood cultures as indicated.

Range of Toxicity

Mortality is <2% if treated. Overall mortality is <7% if untreated or treatment is delayed; may increase to 30% in typhoidal tularemia with pneumonia. Risk of infection is related to the degree of exposure.

Typhus

Clinical Effects

Background
Typhus is caused by rickettsiae— gram-negative, nonmotile, small obligate intracellular coccobacilli that multiply in the cytoplasm of infected host cells. There are three types of typhus: epidemic typhus (*Rickettsia prowazekii*), endemic typhus (*Rickettsia typhi*), and scrub typhus (*Rickettsia tsutsugamushi*). Epidemic typhus is frequently fatal, while endemic (murine) typhus is rarely fatal. Epidemic typhus is transmitted person-to-person by the feces of body lice; endemic typhus is transmitted to humans by rat fleas; scrub typhus is transmitted to humans by chigger bites.

Biological Warfare

Typhus is a potential biologic weapon.

Clinical Presentation

EPIDEMIC TYPHUS: Incubation lasts about 7 days. One to 3 days of malaise precedes an abrupt onset of severe headache, chills, fever, and myalgia. Rash and petechiae are characteristic. More serious complications may include gangrene, cerebral thrombosis secondary to vasculitis, and death. Thrombocytopenia and elevations of LDH and AST may develop.

ENDEMIC TYPHUS: After a 6- to 14-day incubation period, symptoms appear abruptly. Fever is followed by headache, chills, and nausea. Rash may occur at various intervals after the onset of fever. Thrombocytopenia, leukopenia, elevated serum transaminase levels, hyponatremia, and hypocalcemia may develop. Recovery is usually uneventful; fatalities rare.

SCRUB TYPHUS: A skin papule develops within 2 days of the chigger bite and progresses to an eschar during the 6- to 18-day incubation period. Onset of symptoms is abrupt. They include unremitting fever, chills, and headache. Other symptoms have included myalgia, cough, and nausea. Generalized lymphadenopathy is the most common physical finding. Deafness, tinnitus, and conjunctival suffusion may also be indicative of scrub typhus. Without antibiotic therapy, many complications, including death, may occur.

Treatment

Decontamination

DERMAL: Remove contaminated clothing and wash exposed area extremely thoroughly with soap and water.

Prophylaxis

An epidemic typhus vaccine is available. There is no effective vaccine for endemic (murine) typhus or scrub typhus. Doxycycline, 200 mg PO per week, is recommended for travelers at high risk for scrub and epidemic typhus.

Antibiotic Therapy

DOXYCYCLINE:
Adult dose: 100 mg PO every 12 hours on day one, then 100 mg/day PO in 1 or 2 divided doses. Continue for 48 hours after fever ends.

Pediatric dose (>8 years old): 2 mg/kg PO every 12 hours on day one, then 2.2 mg/kg/day PO in 1 or 2 divided doses. Continue for 5 days after fever ends. Increase to 4.4 mg/kg divided BID for severe infection.

CHLORAMPHENICOL:
Adult and pediatric dose: 50 mg/kg/day IV in 4 divided doses. Continue for 5 days after fever ends.

Hyperthermia
Antipyretics, external cooling.

Hypotension
Isotonic IV fluids; large amounts may be necessary. If the patient is unresponsive, administer dopamine or norepinephrine and titrate to desired response.

Seizures
IV barbiturates, benzodiazepines.

Pulmonary Edema (Noncardiogenic)
Maintain ventilation and oxygenation. Monitor ABGs and/or pulse oximetry frequently. Early use of PEEP and mechanical ventilation may be needed.

Range Of Toxicity

Mortality for epidemic typhus is 30 to 70% if the disease is left untreated. Mortality for scrub typhus is up to 80% in untreated patients, depending on the strain.

Venezuelan Equine Encephalitis

Clinical Effects

Background
Venezuelan equine encephalitis (VEE) is caused by a member of the Togaviridae family of arthropod-borne viruses (arboviruses). The disease is normally transmitted by the bite of a mosquito. Principle viremic hosts are equines, but virus may be present in human pharyngeal excretions. Laboratory infections have occurred, probably due to inhalation of aerosols.

Biological Warfare
Contact or aerosol person-to-person spread is possible. This has not been epidemiologically significant in the past, but could become important if the virus is used as a biological weapon. VEE could be produced in either a wet or dried form and stabilized for use in biological warfare.

Clinical Presentation
INITIAL SYMPTOMS: After an incubation of 2 to 5 days, sudden onset of a flu-like illness occurs, with chills, spiking fevers, malaise, and headache. This is followed by myalgias, cough, nausea, vomiting, and sometimes diarrhea. Tachycardia, conjunctival infection, lymphadenopathy, and sometimes non-exudative pharyngitis may be seen on examination. Less common effects include photophobia, seizures, confusion, coma, tremors, and diplopia. Physical findings are non-specific. During the flu-like stage, some patients develop CNS involvement, including seizures, meningismus, paralysis, delirium, tremor, nystagmus, cranial neuropathies, coma, or severe encephalitis.

PROGRESSION OF SYMPTOMS: After 4 to 6 days, acute illness subsides. Convalescent signs and symptoms (asthenia, lethargy) may continue for up to 3 weeks. Occasionally a biphasic course is noted, with acute symptoms reappearing within a week after initial onset, following a brief remission,. Excellent short-term and long-term immunity results on recovery from infection.

Recovery

Full recovery usually takes 1 to 2 weeks.

Treatment

Decontamination

DERMAL: Sites exposed to blood, body fluids, secretions, or excretions from patients with suspected VEE should be immediately washed with soap and water.

INHALATION: Medical personnel working with known VEE infected patients should wear protective masks and utilize STRICT barrier isolation techniques. Droplet precautions indicated in all patients.

Symptomatic and Supportive

Intensive supportive care is the mainstay of therapy. No antidote or vaccine is available for VEE infection. Intensive supportive treatment of encephalitis or secondary infections is recommended.

Airway Management

Airway compromise may require endotracheal intubation and mechanical ventilation.

Seizures

IV benzodiazepines, or barbiturates.

Monitoring Parameters

Obtain CBC, electrolytes, blood cultures, and liver function tests, and monitor vital signs. Monitor pulse oximetry and/or ABGs in any patient with suspected encephalitis.

Range of Toxicity

Cases presenting with encephalitis may have a mortality rate approaching 50%. In severe cases, residual neurologic damage may also occur. The virus responsible for VEE appears to multiply well in mammals with high titers in the blood. VEE is designated as biosafety level 3 for laboratory work.

Section 2

Chemical Agents

Adamsite

Clinical Effects

Background

Also known as diphenylaminochloroarsine or DM, Adamsite is a riot control agent/vomiting agent. Produced by heating diphenylamine and arsenic trichloride, it comes in canary-yellow crystals that sublime easily. Adamsite is highly toxic by inhalation and ingestion, and is a strong irritant to tissue. Although it is an organic-arsenical agent, under normal circumstances and uses, systemic arsenic poisoning is NOT expected.

Clinical Presentation

Symptoms usually begin 3 to 4 minutes after exposure and may last up to 2 hours. They are similar to those of the other riot control agents, except that at higher concentrations adamsite is more likely to cause nausea, vomiting, and general malaise.

INHALATION EXPOSURE: Burning and irritation of the airways with bronchorrhea, coughing, chest pain and tightness, dyspnea, rhinorrhea, burning sensation of the nose, and sneezing. At higher concentrations, nausea, vomiting, and malaise.

OCULAR EXPOSURE: Burning sensation and lacrimation. Symptoms usually resolve rapidly and spontaneously, within 1 to 2 hours.

DERMAL EXPOSURE: Unlike other riot-control agents, adamsite causes little irritation to the skin.

Treatment

Decontamination

INHALATION: Administer 100% humidified supplemental oxygen. Move patient to fresh air. Treat bronchospasm with beta2 agonist and corticosteroid aerosols. Monitor for 12 to 24 hours after exposure.

DERMAL: Remove contaminated clothing and wash exposed area thoroughly with soap and water, or use a mildly alkaline solution, such as sodium bicarbonate or sodium carbonate.

OCULAR: Remove contact lenses and irrigate exposed eyes with copious amounts of 0.9% saline or water at room temperature for at least 15 minutes.

PREVENTION OF CONTAMINATION: Proper protective clothing should be worn.

Symptomatic and Supportive

INHALATION: Airway management, oxygen, intubation, and mechanical ventilation as needed. If cough or difficulty in breathing develops, evaluate for hypoxia, respiratory tract irritation, bronchitis, or pneumonitis. Carefully observe patients with inhalation exposure for the development of any systemic signs or symptoms.

Administer symptomatic treatment as necessary.

OCULAR: If irritation persists following decontamination, a thorough eye examination is recommended, with symptomatic treatment as needed.

Monitoring Parameters

No specific laboratory tests are necessary. Monitor pulse oximetry or ABGs if signs and symptoms of upper airway distress exist.

Range Of Toxicity

Adamsite is a non-persistent agent; once it falls to the ground, its efficacy diminishes.

Arsine

Clinical Effects

Background

A colorless gas with a garlic-like odor, arsine is produced when water comes into contact with molten arsenic, or when an acid comes in contact with metallic arsenic. Arsine is highly toxic at extremely low concentrations. Death may occur quickly following a massive or concentrated exposure.

Clinical Presentation

Exposure to this agent results in hemolysis.

PRE-HEMOLYSIS PHASE: Serious arsine exposure may produce symptoms in 30 to 60 minutes, but symptoms may be delayed for hours. Initially, patients may look and feel well. Red staining of the conjunctiva, a garlic odor of the breath, headache, thirst, and shivering may be observed.

HEMOLYSIS PHASE: Early symptoms include generalized weakness, headache, shivering, thirst, and abdominal pain. Weakness proceeds to muscle cramps and occasionally hypotension. Anorexia, nausea, and sometimes vomiting occur.

Plasma: First sign may be the production of free Hgb in the plasma, which may be confirmed at the bedside by spinning the hematocrit tube.

Urine: Hemoglobinuria can be confirmed at the patient's bedside by dipstick testing of urine. Hematuria can occur.

POST-HEMOLYSIS PHASE: Hemoglobinuria may be followed by renal function impairment and occasionally renal shutdown. If severe, hemolysis can result in jaundice and bronzing of the skin.

Treatment

Decontamination

ORAL: Arsine is a gas at room temperature, so ingestion is unlikely.

INHALATION: Administer 100% humidified supplemental oxygen. Move patient to fresh air. Administer inhaled beta2 agonists if bronchospasm develops.

OCULAR: Remove contact lenses and irrigate exposed eyes with copious amounts of 0.9% saline or water at room temperature for at least 15 minutes.

DERMAL: Remove contaminated clothing and wash exposed area thoroughly with soap and water.

Symptomatic and Supportive
Ensure adequate hydration; start IV fluids. Because of possible severe hemolysis, oxygenation should be checked and supplemental oxygen given if necessary.

Hypotension
In the absence of frank renal failure, large volumes of IV fluids should be administered. Administer blood as needed. Plasma expanders and blood should be administered prior to the consideration of vasopressors. Low-dose dopamine may help preserve renal blood flow. Vasopressors may be needed if hypotension is severe.

Chelation
Chelation is usually not advised because the key concern is RBC hemolysis and not the presence of arsenic metal.

Extracorporeal Elimination
Hemodialysis may preserve renal function, prevent further renal damage, and assist in decreasing arsenic levels.

Exchange Transfusion
Exchange transfusion has been suggested to remove red-cell breakdown products produced by arsine-induced hemolysis. The procedure removes arsine-hemoglobin or arsine-haptoglobin complexes (not readily removed by hemodialysis) and produces significant improvement in serious arsine poisoning even when done 10 to 12 days after exposure. However, there is little difference in the long-term outcome of patients who are given exchange transfusions compared to those given solely dialysis and repeated transfusions.

Deferoxamine
This agent has been used to treat hemolysis due to G6PD deficiency. Because the mechanism of hemolysis is different, it is not known whether the use of deferoxamine for arsine-induced hemolysis is beneficial.

Monitoring Parameters
Blood arsenic levels may be useful to confirm acute arsine toxicity (may be as high as 200 mcg/dL; normal less than 20 mcg/dL), but are not useful in acute management. Follow serial CBC, BUN, ECG, creatinine, electrolytes, and urine analysis including onsite dipstick of urine for hemoglobin pigment.

Range Of Toxicity
Industrial limits and guidelines indicate that exposures in excess of 0.05 ppm are potentially toxic and

concentrations of 3 ppm are immediately dangerous to life or health
(IDLH). The general population has
urinary arsenic levels of less than
20 mcg/L. Symptoms often occur
with levels of 70 to 100 mcg/L.

Chlorine

Clinical Effects

Background

Chlorine is a greenish-yellow gas. Its
vapors are heavy and settle in low
areas; so odor is not a good indicator
of the severity of exposure. The gas
is severely irritating on contact. It is
corrosive to the eyes, skin, nose,
throat, and mucous membranes, and
exposure can result in severe or permanent eye injury. Contact with the
escaping compressed liquid (cryogenic gas) can cause frostbite and/or
chemical burns to the eyes and skin.
However, inhalation is the main
route of exposure.

The gas typically acts as a strong
irritant, but may prove corrosive to
mucous membranes when inhaled
or ingested. Contact with moist tissue may result in tissue damage;
nascent oxygen is a potent oxidizer.
Secondary irritation occurs from
acids formed during this reaction.

Clinical Presentation

MILD EXPOSURE: Acute expo-
sures, if mild, rarely result in residual pulmonary abnormalities.

MODERATE/SEVERE EXPO-
SURE: Respiratory symptoms may
be immediate or delayed up to a
few hours. Respiratory effects
include burning chest pain, wheezing, coughing, a feeling of suffocation, pulmonary edema, and respiratory arrest. Eye, nose, and throat
irritation are possible.

Sequelae

Increased airway reactivity and
decreased residual volume have
occurred for up to 12 years following an acute exposure. Elderly or
other individuals with chronic pulmonary disease may be at greatest
risk for marked airflow obstruction
or air trapping immediately
following exposure.

Treatment

Decontamination

GENERAL FIRST AID MEA-
SURES: Immediately remove the
victim from the contaminated environment. Wash contaminated areas
with soap and water. Potential for
secondary contamination is low;
the gas is not carried on contaminated clothing. Rescuers should
wear a self-contained breathing
apparatus and protective clothing,
if needed.

OCULAR: Irrigate exposed eyes
with copious amounts of tepid
water for at least 15 minutes. If
irritation, pain, swelling, lacrimation, or photophobia persist, a
physician should evaluate the
patient. Patients who experience
only minor sensations of burning

of the mucous membranes of the nose, throat, eyes, and respiratory tract (with perhaps a slight cough) require no treatment beyond removal from the contaminated environment; symptoms are likely to resolve within one hour.

Symptomatic and Supportive

Patients experiencing more severe symptoms must be treated with oxygen and other supportive measures. No specific antidotes are available.

Burns

Corrosive burns of mucous membranes and skin should receive normal burn care and prevention of secondary infection.

Oxygen

Administer humidified oxygen if respiratory symptoms present.

Bronchospasm

Treat with beta2 agonists and corticosteroid aerosols.

Airway Management

Manage airway aggressively in patients with evidence of upper airway burns or edema.

Pulmonary Edema (Noncardiogenic)

Symptoms may be delayed. Maintain ventilation and oxygenation; monitor ABGs and/or pulse oximetry frequently. Early use of PEEP and mechanical ventilation may be needed.

Steroids

May be useful; however, conclusive efficacy data are lacking.

Monitoring Parameters

Monitor for pulmonary edema for up to 24 hours following exposure; symptoms can be delayed. Examine mucous membranes for corrosive effects.

Range Of Toxicity

Environmental persistence is low. Chloride dissipates rapidly in warm climates without leaving environmental residue. Exposure to 1 to 3 ppm causes mild irritation; 10 to 20 ppm causes severe irritation.

Chloropicrin

Clinical Effects

Background

A military choking agent. Chloropicrin is an SN2 alkylating agent with an activated halogen group. Primarily, it combines with sulfhydryl groups to inactivate enzymes. It can also interfere with oxygen transport by its reaction with SH-groups in hemoglobin. There may also be a photochemical transformation of chloropicrin into phosgene. It is both a lacrimator and lung irritant.

Clinical Presentation

CUTANEOUS: Patients present with severe skin irritation, difficulty breathing, headache, and cyanosis.

INHALATION: Most severe toxicity results from this route. Patients present with severe irritation, nausea, vomiting, difficulty breathing, headache, dizziness, cyanosis, pulmonary edema, and possibly death. With high concentrations, the lower respiratory tract can become profoundly inflamed, resulting in potentially fatal pulmonary edema. Secondary infection and bronchiolitis obliterans are potential late effects.

OCULAR: Severe irritation, tearing, and eye damage.

ORAL: Oral burns, sore throat, vomiting, esophageal/stomach burns, difficulty breathing, headache, dizziness, and cyanosis.

Treatment

Decontamination

DERMAL EXPOSURE: Remove contaminated clothing and wash exposed area extremely thoroughly with soap and water.

INHALATION: Move patient from the toxic environment to fresh air. Monitor for respiratory distress.

OCULAR EXPOSURE: Irrigate exposed eyes with copious amounts of tepid water for at least 15 minutes.

ORAL EXPOSURE: Dilute immediately with milk or water; no more than 8 ounces in adults and 4 ounces in children. Consider nasogastric suction. Ipecac is contraindicated.

Symptomatic and Supportive

Initially, administer 10% humidified oxygen for as long as needed to assure adequate oxygenation. Then adjust oxygen concentration to the comfort of the patient.

Bronchospasm

Administer beta2 adrenergic agonists. Consider use of inhaled corticosteroids and ipratropium.

Pulmonary Edema (Noncardiogenic)

Maintain ventilation and oxygenation. Monitor ABGs/pulse oximetry frequently. Early use of PEEP and mechanical ventilation may be needed.

Endoscopy

May be indicated in adults with any signs or symptoms attributable to inadvertent ingestion, and in children with stridor, vomiting, drooling, dysphagia, or refusal to swallow, significant oral burns, or abdominal pain after unintentional ingestion.

Monitoring Parameters

Monitor pulse oximetry, ABGs, and chest x-ray as clinically indicated.

CN

Clinical Effects

Background

Agent CN, also known as tear gas or mace (Military Classification: Riot Control Agent), is a clear to yellow-brown solid with an apple-blossom odor. It is dispersed as an aerosol. CN inhibits SH-containing enzymes at sensory nerve endings in the ocular mucous membranes, resulting in pain and lacrimation.

Clinical Presentation

INHALATION: High concentrations may cause upper respiratory tract irritation, pulmonary edema, skin vesicle formation, and visual impairment.

OCULAR: Ocular symptoms are a characteristic feature of exposure. They include lacrimation, burning, lid swelling, sharp pain, photophobia, and temporary blindness. They peak within minutes and resolve in 1 to 2 hours. Splash contact may cause burns and corneal opacity.

DERMAL: Splash contact may cause papulovesicular dermatitis and superficial skin burns.

ORAL: Ingestion of contaminated food and water causes nausea, vomiting, and diarrhea.

Sequelae

Likely to cause corneal damage; permanent blindness has NOT been reported. Exacerbates asthma.

Treatment

Decontamination

OCULAR: Wash eyes with copious amounts of water. Avoid rubbing eyes.

DERMAL: Remove contaminated clothing to avoid further self-exposure; place clothing in a bag to minimize escape of vapors.

PREVENTION OF CONTAMINATION: Potential for secondary contamination is high. Residual CN can be transferred from hands to the face or eyes, so wear disposable gloves. Contact lenses may protect the eyes from secondary contamination.

FIRST AID MEASURES: Move patient to fresh air; monitor for respiratory distress (airway support and 100% humidified oxygen with assisted ventilation may be needed).

Symptomatic and Supportive

Rapidly assess respiratory function; laryngospasm may require intubation/ventilation. Administer supplemental oxygen as needed. No antidote is available.

Bronchospasm

Treat with beta2 agonist and corticosteroid aerosols.

Ocular Irritation

For persistent irritation, administer ophthalmic corticosteroids or local anesthetic ointments.

Dermal Irritation

For persistent dermatitis lasting >1 hour, apply wet dressings of Burrow's solution 1:40, followed by corticosteroid creams or calamine lotion. Administer antibiotics for secondary infections as necessary.

Range Of Toxicity

CN is not environmentally persistent. Once it falls to the ground, its efficacy is diminished.

CR

Clinical Effects

Background

Agent CR, identified chemically as dibenoxazepine (Military Classification: Riot Control Agent), is a pale yellow, crystalline solid with a pepper-like odor. It is usually mixed with a pyrotechnic compound in a grenade/canister. It has limited solubility in water, is not hydrolyzed in aqueous solutions, and is sometimes disseminated from liquid dispensers containing 0.1% CR in 80 parts propylene glycol and 20 parts water. Its pathophysiological actions are thought to be similar to those of CS.

Clinical Presentation

INHALATION: CR is less toxic than CS following inhalation. Initial symptoms include a burning sensation, pain in the upper respiratory tract and lungs followed by a "feeling of suffocation," anxiety, mild epistaxis, nasal burning, and fatigue.

OCULAR: CR is an eye irritant at concentrations of 0.0025% or lower in organic solution. Initial symptoms include violent lacrimation lasting for 10–15 minutes; violent burning and conjunctivitis lasting up to 30 minutes; and lid erythema lasting up to 1 hour. Symptoms are exacerbated in hot or humid weather.

DERMAL: CR produces more dermal effects than CS. The primary symptom is burning, especially in moist areas, aggravated by contact with water. Inflammation and blistering are possible with prolonged exposure, especially in fair-skinned individuals.

ORAL: Contamination of food or water may produce gastroenteritis.

Possible Sequelae

Prognosis is generally good. Skin reactions may require several weeks to heal. Chronic reactive airway disease has not been reported, but is a possibility.

Treatment

Decontamination

OCULAR: Wash eyes with copious amounts of water. Avoid rubbing eyes.

DERMAL: Remove contaminated clothing to avoid further self-exposure; place clothing in a bag to minimize escape of vapors. Decontaminate with a 5 or 10% sodium bicarbonate solution (if immediately available), which is more effective than water. Use normal saline if a wound is present.

PREVENTION OF CONTAMINATION: Potential for secondary contamination is high. Residual CR can be transferred from hands to the face or eyes, so wear disposable gloves. Contact lenses may protect the eyes from secondary contamination.

FIRST AID MEASURES: Move patient to fresh air; monitor for respiratory distress (airway support and 100% humidified oxygen with assisted ventilation may be needed).

Symptomatic and Supportive

Rapidly assess respiratory function; laryngospasm may require intubation/ventilation. Supplemental oxygen may be required. No antidote is available.

Bronchospasm

Treat with beta2 agonist and corticosteroid aerosols.

Ocular Irritation

For persistent irritation, administer ophthalmic corticosteroids or local anesthetic ointments.

Dermal Irritation

For persistent dermatitis lasting >1 hour, apply wet dressings of Burrow's solution 1:40, followed by corticosteroid creams or calamine lotion. Administer antibiotics for secondary infections and antihistamines for pruritus.

Other

If preexisting pulmonary disease is present, observe for exacerbation. A 10% mortality was seen in adults (in enclosed areas) during the Vietnam War. Similar effects are suspected during the Gulf War.

Range Of Toxicity

CR more persistent in the environment and on clothing than CS.

CS

Clinical Effects

Background

Identified chemically as orthochloro-benzylidene malononitrile (Military Classification: Riot Control Agent), CS is a white, crystalline solid with a pepper-like odor. It is usually mixed with a pyrotechnic compound in a grenade/canister and delivered as a fog of suspended particles (a grenade can form a white cloud 6 to 9 meters in diameter). It can also be mixed with anti-agglomerant (CS1) or silicone water repellent (CS2) that remains active for weeks when dusted on soil. CS is metabolized to cyanide in peripheral tissues (clinical significance is controversial). High concentrations produce pulmonary edema.

Clinical Presentation

INHALATION EXPOSURE: Initial symptoms include a burning sensation or pain in the upper respiratory tract and lungs, followed by "feelings of suffocation," anxiety, nasal burning, mild epistaxis, and fatigue. At high concentrations, pneumonitis, pulmonary edema, heart failure, hepatotoxicity, and death are possible.

OCULAR EXPOSURE: Initial symptoms include violent lacrimation for 10 to 15 minutes, a burning sensation/conjunctivitis for up to 30 minutes, and lid erythema for up to 1 hour. Symptoms are worse in hot, humid weather. Discharge of gas at close range can cause powder infiltration of the conjunctiva, cornea, and sclera, resulting in further injury.

DERMAL EXPOSURE: Symptoms include burning, especially on moist skin, that is aggravated by contact with water. Inflammation and blistering are possible with prolonged exposure, especially in fair-skinned individuals.

ORAL EXPOSURE: Contamination of food or water may produce gastroenteritis.

Possible Sequelae

The prognosis is generally good. Dermal reactions may take up to several weeks to heal. Pneumonitis and chronic reactive airway may occur. Penetrating trauma may result from exploding CS canisters.

Treatment

Decontamination

GENERAL: Wash eyes with copious amounts of water; avoid rubbing eyes. Remove contaminated clothing to avoid further self-exposure; place clothing in a bag to minimize escape of vapors. Wash clothes in COLD water only; hot water will cause vaporization.

DERMAL: Decontaminate with a 5 or 10% sodium bicarbonate solution (if immediately available); it is more effective than water. Use normal saline if a wound is present. Avoid chloramine (found in military moist towelettes) and phenol, which contain chlorine that can react with CS to form a strong irritant.

PREVENTION OF CONTAMINATION: Potential for secondary contamination is high. The agent can be transferred from the hands to the face or eyes. Wear disposable gloves. Contact lenses may protect the eyes from secondary contamination.

FIRST AID MEASURES: Move patient to fresh air; monitor for respiratory distress (airway support and 100% humidified oxygen with assisted ventilation may be needed).

Symptomatic and Supportive

Rapidly assess respiratory function. Laryngospasm may require intubation/ventilation. Supplemental oxygen may be required. No antidote is available.

Bronchospasm

Treat with beta2 agonist and corticosteroid aerosols.

Ocular Irritation

For persistent irritation, administer ophthalmic corticosteroids or local anesthetic ointments.

Dermal Irritation

For persistent dermatitis lasting >1 hour, apply wet dressings of

Burrow's solution 1:40, followed by corticosteroid creams or calamine lotion. Administer antibiotic therapy for secondary infections and antihistamines for pruritus.

Other

If preexisting pulmonary disease is present, observe for exacerbation. 10% mortality occurred in adults (in enclosed areas) during the Vietnam War; similar effects are suspected during Gulf War.

Range Of Toxicity

CS is rapidly hydrolyzed by water, with a half-life of 15 minutes at 25 degrees centigrade. CS1 remains active for up to 5 days in favorable weather; CS2 for up to 45 days in the presence of water.

Cyanide

Clinical Effects

Clinical Presentation

INITIAL SYMPTOMS: Flushing, tachycardia, hypertension, tachypnea, headache, and dizziness.

MILD TO MODERATE SYMPTOMS: Nausea/vomiting, palpitations, confusion, agitation, anxiety, vertigo, hyperventilation, and anion gap metabolic acidosis.

SEVERE SYMPTOMS: Stupor, coma, apnea, seizures, bradycardia, hypotension, acidemia, cyanosis (late finding), dysrhythmias, and pulmonary edema.

INGESTION: Cyanide salts cause oral/esophageal burns.

Treatment

Decontamination

INHALATION: Immediately begin 100% oxygen. Move patient to fresh air. Because high concentrations of cyanide gas may cause rapid loss of consciousness, rescuers should wear a self-contained positive-pressure breathing apparatus.

INGESTION: Gastric lavage and activated charcoal have limited utility because absorption is rapid.

Antidotes

Use a cyanide antidote kit for symptomatic exposures.

AMYL NITRITE: For adults, 0.18 to 0.3 mL by inhalation; may be used when intravenous access is delayed or not possible. The ampule should be broken and inhaled for 30 seconds each minute. Use a new ampule every 3 minutes. Discontinue when intravenous sodium nitrite is administered.

SODIUM NITRITE: For adults, administer IV 10 mL of 3% solution (300 mg) over no less than 5 minutes. Children with a normal Hgb concentration can receive 0.15 to 0.33 mL/kg up to 10 mL of a 3% solution over no less than 5 minutes. Be sure to dose correctly in children because incorrect dosing can cause fatal methemo-globinemia. Monitor blood pressure frequently.

SODIUM THIOSULFATE:
Administer IV immediately following sodium nitrite. For adults, give 12.5 grams over 10 minutes. For children, use 1.65 mL/kg of 25% solution. Repeat one-half of initial doses of both agents in 30 minutes if clinical response is inadequate.

Acidosis
Sodium bicarbonate 1 to 2 mEq/kg IV if pH <7.1.

Seizures
IV benzodiazepines or barbiturates.

Hypotension
0.9% NaCl, dopamine, norepinephrine, central venous pressure monitoring.

Pulmonary Edema (Non-Cardiogenic)
Maintain adequate ventilation and oxygenation; monitor ABGs and/or pulse oximetry frequently.
Ventilation and PEEP may be necessary.

Oxygen
Combining 100% oxygen with traditional nitrite/thiosulfate therapy is more effective than thiosulfate alone.

HBO
May improve clinical outcome, especially in those patients with CNS toxicity not responding to traditional therapy.

Monitoring Parameters
Whole blood cyanide levels, ABGs, CBC, electrolytes, serum lactate, MetHb levels.

Range Of Toxicity

Air concentrations of 0.2 to 0.3 milligram/cubic meter (200 to 300 parts per million) are rapidly fatal; 50 ppm are immediately dangerous to life and health.

Cyanogen

Clinical Effects

Clinical Presentation
INITIAL SYMPTOMS: Flushing, tachycardia, hypertension, tachypnea, headache, and dizziness.

MILD TO MODERATE SYMPTOMS: Nausea/vomiting, palpitations, confusion, agitation, anxiety, vertigo, hyperventilation, and anion gap metabolic acidosis.

SEVERE SYMPTOMS: Stupor, coma, apnea, seizures, bradycardia, hypotension, acidemia, cyanosis (late finding), dysrhythmias, and pulmonary edema.

INGESTION: Cyanide salts cause oral/esophageal burns.

Treatment

Decontamination
INHALATION: Immediately begin 100% oxygen. Move patient to fresh air. Because high concentrations of cyanide gas may cause rapid loss of consciousness, res-

cuers should wear a self-contained positive-pressure breathing apparatus.

INGESTION: Gastric lavage and activated charcoal have limited utility because absorption is rapid.

Antidotes
Use a cyanide antidote kit for symptomatic exposures.

AMYL NITRITE: May be used when intravenous access is delayed or not possible. For adults, administer 0.18 to 0.3 mL by inhalation. The ampule should be broken and inhaled for 30 seconds each minute. Use a new ampule every 3 minutes. Discontinue when intravenous sodium nitrite is administered.

SODIUM NITRITE: For adults, administer IV 10 mL of 3% solution (300 mg) over no less than 5 minutes. Children with normal Hgb concentrations can receive 0.15 to 0.33 mL/kg up to 10 mL of a 3% solution over no less than 5 minutes. Be sure to dose children correctly because an incorrect dose can cause fatal methemoglobinemia. Monitor blood pressure frequently.

SODIUM THIOSULFATE: Administer IV immediately following sodium nitrite. For adults, give 12.5 grams over 10 minutes. For children, use 1.65 mL/kg of 25% solution. Repeat one-half of initial doses of both agents in 30 minutes if clinical response is inadequate.

Acidosis
Sodium bicarbonate 1 to 2 mEq/kg IV if pH <7.1.

Seizures
IV benzodiazepines or barbiturates.

Hypotension
0.9% NaCl, dopamine, norepinephrine, central venous pressure monitoring.

Pulmonary Edema (Non-Cardiogenic)
Maintain adequate ventilation and oxygenation; monitor ABGs and/or pulse oximetry frequently. Ventilation and PEEP may be necessary.

Oxygen
100% oxygen combined with traditional nitrite/thiosulfate therapy is more effective than thiosulfate alone.

HBO
May improve clinical outcome, especially in those patients with CNS toxicity not responding to traditional therapy.

Monitoring Parameters
Whole blood cyanide levels, ABGs, CBC, electrolytes, serum lactate, and MetHb levels.

Range Of Toxicity

Air concentrations of 0.2 to 0.3 milligram/cubic meter (200 to 300 parts per million) are rapidly fatal; 50 ppm are immediately dangerous to life and health.

Cyanogen Bromide

Clinical Effects

Clinical Presentation

INITIAL SYMPTOMS: Flushing, tachycardia, hypertension, tachypnea, headache, and dizziness.

MILD TO MODERATE SYMPTOMS: Nausea/vomiting, palpitations, confusion, agitation, anxiety, vertigo, hyperventilation, and anion gap metabolic acidosis.

SEVERE SYMPTOMS: Stupor, coma, apnea, seizures, bradycardia, hypotension, acidemia, cyanosis (late finding), dysrhythmias, and pulmonary edema.

INGESTION: Cyanide salts cause oral/esophageal burns.

Treatment

Decontamination

INHALATION: Immediately begin 100% oxygen. Move patient to fresh air. Because high concentrations of cyanide gas may cause rapid loss of consciousness, rescuers should wear a self-contained positive-pressure breathing apparatus.

INGESTION: Gastric lavage and activated charcoal have limited utility because absorption is rapid.

Antidotes

Use a cyanide antidote kit for symptomatic exposures.

AMYL NITRITE: May be used when intravenous access is delayed or not possible. For adults, administer 0.18 to 0.3 mL by inhalation. The ampule should be broken and inhaled for 30 seconds each minute. Use a new ampule every 3 minutes. Discontinue when intravenous sodium nitrite is administered.

SODIUM NITRITE: For adults, administer IV 10 mL of 3% solution (300 mg) over no less than 5 minutes. Children with normal Hgb concentrations can receive 0.15 to 0.33 mL/kg up to 10 mL of a 3% solution over no less than 5 minutes. Be sure to dose children correctly because an incorrect dose can cause fatal methemoglobinemia. Monitor blood pressure frequently.

SODIUM THIOSULFATE: Administer IV immediately following sodium nitrite. Adults should receive 12.5 grams over 10 minutes. Children should receive 1.65 mL/kg of 25% solution. Repeat one-half of initial doses of both agents in 30 minutes if clinical response is inadequate.

Acidosis

Sodium bicarbonate 1 to 2 mEq/kg IV if pH <7.1.

Seizures

IV benzodiazepines or barbiturates.

Hypotension

0.9% NaCl, dopamine, norepinephrine, central venous pressure monitoring.

Pulmonary Edema (Non-Cardiogenic)

Maintain adequate ventilation and oxygenation; monitor ABGs and/or pulse oximetry frequently. Ventilation and PEEP may be necessary.

Oxygen

Combining 100% oxygen with traditional nitrite/thiosulfate therapy is more effective than using thiosulfate alone.

HBO

May improve clinical outcome, especially in those patients with CNS toxicity not responding to traditional therapy.

Monitoring Parameters

Whole blood cyanide levels, ABGs, CBC, electrolytes, serum lactate, and MetHb levels.

Range Of Toxicity

Air concentrations of 0.2 to 0.3 milligram/cubic meter (200 to 300 parts per million) are rapidly fatal; 50 ppm are immediately dangerous to life and health.

Cyanogen Chloride

Clinical Effects

Clinical Presentation

INITIAL SYMPTOMS: Flushing, tachycardia, hypertension, tachypnea, headache, and dizziness.

MILD TO MODERATE SYMPTOMS: Nausea/vomiting, palpitations, confusion, agitation, anxiety, vertigo, hyperventilation, and anion gap metabolic acidosis.

SEVERE SYMPTOMS: Stupor, coma, apnea, seizures, bradycardia, hypotension, acidemia, cyanosis (late finding), dysrhythmias, and pulmonary edema.

INGESTION: Cyanide salts cause oral/esophageal burns.

Treatment

Decontamination

INHALATION: Immediately begin 100% oxygen. Move patient to fresh air. Because high concentrations of cyanide gas may cause rapid loss of consciousness, rescuers should wear a self-contained positive-pressure breathing apparatus.

INGESTION: Gastric lavage and activated charcoal have limited utility because absorption is rapid.

Antidotes

Use a cyanide antidote kit for symptomatic exposures.

AMYL NITRITE: May be used when intravenous access is delayed or not possible. For adults, administer 0.18 to 0.3 mL by inhalation. The ampule should be broken and inhaled for 30 seconds each minute. Use a new ampule every 3 minutes. Discontinue when intravenous sodium nitrite is administered.

SODIUM NITRITE: For adults, administer IV 10 mL of 3% solution (300 mg) over no less than 5 minutes. Children with a normal Hgb concentration can receive 0.15 to 0.33 mL/kg up to 10 mL of a 3% solution over no less than 5 minutes. Be sure to dose correctly in children because an incorrect dose can cause fatal methemoglobinemia. Monitor blood pressure frequently.

SODIUM THIOSULFATE: Administer IV immediately following sodium nitrite. For adults, administer 12.5 grams over 10 minutes. For children, administer 1.65 mL/kg of 25% solution. Repeat one-half of initial doses of both agents in 30 minutes if there is inadequate clinical response.

Acidosis
Sodium bicarbonate 1 to 2 mEq/kg IV if pH <7.1.

Seizures
IV benzodiazepines or barbiturates.

Hypotension
0.9% NaCl, dopamine, norepinephrine, central venous pressure monitoring.

Pulmonary Edema (Non-Cardiogenic)
Maintain adequate ventilation and oxygenation; monitor ABGs and/or pulse oximetry frequently. Ventilation and PEEP may be necessary.

Oxygen
Combining 100% oxygen with traditional nitrite/thiosulfate therapy is more effective than using thiosulfate alone.

HBO
May improve clinical outcome, especially in those patients with CNS toxicity not responding to traditional therapy.

Monitoring Parameters
Whole blood cyanide levels, ABGs, CBC, electrolytes, serum lactate, MetHb levels.

Range Of Toxicity

Air concentrations of 0.2 to 0.3 milligram/cubic meter (200 to 300 parts per million) are rapidly fatal; 50 ppm are immediately dangerous to life and health.

Cyanogen Iodide

Clinical Effects

Clinical Presentation
INITIAL SYMPTOMS: Flushing, tachycardia, hypertension, tachypnea, headache, and dizziness.

MILD TO MODERATE SYMPTOMS: Nausea/vomiting, palpitations, confusion, agitation, anxiety, vertigo, hyperventilation, and anion gap metabolic acidosis.

SEVERE SYMPTOMS: Stupor, coma, apnea, seizures, bradycardia, hypotension, acidemia, cyanosis (late finding), dysrhythmias, and pulmonary edema.

INGESTION: Cyanide salts cause oral/esophageal burns.

Treatment

Decontamination

INHALATION: Immediately begin 100% oxygen. Move to fresh air. Since high concentrations of cyanide gas may cause rapid loss of consciousness, rescuers should wear a self-contained positive-pressure breathing apparatus.

INGESTION: Gastric lavage and activated charcoal have limited utility because absorption is rapid.

Antidotes

Use a cyanide antidote kit for symptomatic exposures.

AMYL NITRITE: May be used when intravenous access is delayed or not possible. For adults, 0.18 to 0.3 mL by inhalation. The ampule should be broken and inhaled for 30 seconds each minute. Use a new ampule every 3 minutes. Discontinue when intravenous sodium nitrite is administered.

SODIUM NITRITE: For adults, administer IV 10 mL of 3% solution (300 mg) over no less than 5 minutes. Children with a normal Hgb concentration can receive 0.15 to 0.33 mL/kg up to 10 mL of a 3% solution over no less than 5 minutes. Dose correctly in children, as incorrect doses can cause fatal methemoglobinemia. Monitor blood pressure frequently.

SODIUM THIOSULFATE: Administer IV immediately following sodium nitrite. For adults, administer 12.5 grams over 10 minutes. For children, administer 1.65 mL/kg of 25% solution. Repeat one-half of initial doses of both agents in 30 minutes if there is inadequate clinical response.

Acidosis

Sodium bicarbonate 1 to 2 mEq/kg IV if pH <7.1.

Seizures

IV benzodiazepines or barbiturates.

Hypotension

0.9% NaCl, dopamine, norepinephrine, and central venous pressure monitoring.

Pulmonary Edema (Non-Cardiogenic)

Maintain adequate ventilation and oxygenation; monitor ABGs and/or pulse oximetry frequently. Ventilation and PEEP may be necessary.

Oxygen

Combining 100% oxygen with traditional nitrite/thiosulfate therapy is more effective than using thiosulfate alone.

HBO

May improve clinical outcome, especially in those patients with CNS toxicity not responding to traditional therapy.

Monitoring Parameters

Whole blood cyanide levels, ABGs, CBC, electrolytes, serum lactate, MetHb levels.

Range Of Toxicity

Air concentrations of 0.2 to 0.3 milligram/cubic meter (200 to 300 parts per million) are rapidly fatal; 50 ppm are immediately dangerous to life and health.

Diphenylchloroarsine

Clinical Effects

Background

Diphenylchloroarsine (DA) is a riot-control agent/vomiting agent. It takes the form of colorless crystals or a dark-brown liquid which slowly becomes semi-solid. It is derived when benzene and arsenic trichloride are heated in the presence of aluminum chloride. Diphenylchloroarsine is highly toxic by inhalation, and is a strong irritant to tissue. It is an organic-arsenical agent, but under normal circumstances and uses, systemic arsenic poisoning is not expected. Symptoms usually begin 3 to 4 minutes after the onset of exposure and may last up to 2 hours. Exposure symptoms are similar to other riot-control agents, with the exception that diphenylchloroarsine, a vomiting agent, at higher concentrations is expected to cause more nausea, vomiting, and general malaise.

Clinical Presentation

INHALATION EXPOSURE: Burning and irritation of the airways with bronchorrhea, coughing, chest pain and tightness, dyspnea, rhinorrhea, burning sensation of the nose, and sneezing. At higher concentrations, the agent may cause nausea, vomiting, and malaise.

OCULAR EXPOSURE: Burning sensation and lacrimation. Symptoms usually resolve rapidly and spontaneously, within 1 to 2 hours.

DERMAL EXPOSURE: Unlike other riot-control agents, diphenylchloroarsine has little irritancy to the skin.

Treatment

Decontamination

INHALATION: Administer 100% humidified supplemental oxygen. Move patient to fresh air. Monitor for 12 to 24 hours after exposure.

OCULAR: Remove contact lenses and irrigate exposed eyes with copious amounts of 0.9% saline or water at room temperature for at least 15 minutes.

DERMAL: Remove contaminated clothing and wash exposed area thoroughly with soap and water, or use a mildly alkaline solution such as sodium bicarbonate or sodium carbonate.

PREVENTION OF CONTAMINATION: Proper protective clothing should be worn.

Symptomatic and Supportive

INHALATION: Airway management, oxygen, intubation, mechanical ventilation as needed. If cough or difficulty in breathing develops, evaluate for hypoxia, respiratory tract irritation, bronchitis, or pneumonitis. Carefully observe patients with inhalation exposure for the development of any systemic signs or symptoms and administer symptomatic treatment as necessary.

OCULAR: If irritation persists following decontamination, thorough eye examination is recommended with symptomatic treatment as needed.

Bronchospasm

Treat with beta2 agonist and corticosteroid aerosols.

Monitoring Parameters

No specific laboratory tests are necessary. Monitor pulse oximetry or ABGs if the patients shows signs or symptoms of upper airway distress.

Range Of Toxicity

Diphenylchloroarsine is a non-persistent agent; once fallen to the ground, the efficacy is diminished.

Diphosgene

Clinical Effects

Background

Diphosgene (DP) is also known as trichloromethyl chloroformate, carbonochloridic acid, and trichloromethyl ester. It is a colorless liquid with an odor of newly mown hay. It is highly toxic by inhalation and ingestion, and is a strong irritant to tissue.

Diphosgene is easily decomposed by heat, alkali, water, or steam, producing phosgene. Phosgene gas is then degraded by water condensates such as rain or fog.

Clinical Presentation

INITIAL SYMPTOMS: Immediate irritant effects such as conjunctivitis, rhinitis, pharyngitis, bronchitis, lacrimation, blepharospasm, conjunctival hyperemia, and upper respiratory tract irritation may occur after exposure to concentrations of 3 to 5 ppm.

PROGRESSION OF SYMPTOMS: Severe pulmonary toxicity may develop after exposure to higher doses. Rarely, signs/symptoms of pulmonary involvement may be delayed for up to 24 hours (or as long as 72 hours in some instances). They include choking, chest tightness, severe dyspnea, pulmonary edema, cough, production of foaming bloody sputum, nausea, and anxiety. Cardiac failure has occasionally occurred as a complication of severe pulmonary edema. Release of liquefied phosgene from a pressurized cylinder produces a cryogenic gas that poses a frostbite hazard and has caused corneal opacification.

Prognosis

If the victim survives for 24 to 48 hours, prognosis is usually favorable.

Treatment

Decontamination

INHALATION: Administer 100% humidified supplemental oxygen. Move patient to fresh air. Treat bronchospasm with beta2 agonist and corticosteroid aerosols. Monitor for 12 to 24 hours after exposure.

DERMAL: Remove contaminated clothing and wash exposed area thoroughly with soap and water.

OCULAR: Remove contact lenses and irrigate exposed eyes with copious amounts of 0.9% saline or water at room temperature for at least 15 minutes.

PREVENTION OF CONTAMINA-TION: To avoid becoming secondary victims, rescuers must not enter areas with potential high airborne concentrations of this agent without self-contained breathing apparatus (SCBA). Proper protective clothing should be worn. Remove contaminated clothing.

Symptomatic and Supportive

Airway management, oxygen, intubation, and mechanical ventilation as needed.

Pulmonary Edema (Non-Cardiogenic)

Onset may be delayed up to 6 to 15 hours. Maintain ventilation and oxygenation. Monitor ABGs/pulse oximetry frequently. Early use of PEEP and mechanical ventilation may be needed. Animal studies and anecdotal experience suggest that the following therapies may be of benefit with exposures that are sufficient to place patients at risk for pulmonary edema (a dose of 50 ppm x minute or more): ibuprofen, corticosteroids, aminophylline, N-acetylcysteine and terbutaline (aerosol or SC).

Monitoring Parameters

Plasma phosgene levels are not clinically useful. Monitor ABGs, pulmonary function, and chest x-ray for patients with significant exposure. Serial chest x-rays are recommended if significant exposure is suspected; effects can be delayed. Monitor fluid balance.

Range Of Toxicity

In concentrations of 3 to 5 ppm, irritation of the eyes, throat, and upper respiratory tract are noted. The total dose (concentration in ppm multiplied by time of exposure in minutes) determines the risk of pulmonary edema. A cumulative dose of 50 ppm x min can result in delayed pulmonary edema; a dose of 150 ppm x min will probably result in pulmonary edema, and a dose of 300 ppm x min is likely to be fatal. Exposure to 25 ppm is extremely dangerous and greater than 50 ppm may be rapidly fatal.

Hydrogen Cyanide

Clinical Effects

Clinical Presentation

INITIAL SYMPTOMS: Flushing, tachycardia, hypertension, tachypnea, headache, and dizziness.

MILD/MODERATE SYMPTOMS: Nausea/vomiting, palpitations, confusion, agitation, anxiety, vertigo, hyperventilation, and anion gap metabolic acidosis.

SEVERE SYMPTOMS: Stupor, coma, apnea, seizures, bradycardia, hypotension, acidemia, cyanosis (late finding), dysrhythmias, and pulmonary edema.

INGESTION: Oral/esophageal burns occur with cyanide salts.

Treatment

Decontamination

INHALATION: Immediately begin 100% oxygen. Move to fresh air. Since high concentrations of cyanide gas may cause rapid loss of consciousness, rescuers should wear a self-contained, positive-pressure breathing apparatus.

INGESTION: Gastric lavage and activated charcoal have limited utility because absorption is rapid.

Antidotes

Use a cyanide antidote kit for symptomatic exposures.

AMYL NITRITE: For adults, 0.18 to 0.3 mL by inhalation; may be used when intravenous access is delayed or not possible. Ampule should be broken and inhaled for 30 seconds per minute. A new ampule should be used every 3 minutes. Discontinue using when intravenous sodium nitrite is administered.

SODIUM NITRITE: For adults, administer IV 10 mL of 3% solution (300 mg) over no less than 5 minutes. Children with a normal Hgb concentration can receive 0.15 to 0.33 mL/kg up to 10 mL of a 3% solution over no less than 5 minutes. Dose correctly in a child, as incorrect doses can cause fatal methemoglobinemia. Monitor blood pressure frequently.

SODIUM THIOSULFATE: Administer IV immediately following sodium nitrite. For adults, administer 12.5 grams over 10 minutes. For children, administer 1.65 mL/kg of 25% solution). Repeat one-half of initial doses of both agents in 30 minutes if there is inadequate clinical response.

Acidosis

Sodium bicarbonate 1 to 2 mEq/kg IV if pH is <7.1.

Seizures

IV benzodiazepines or barbiturates.

Hypotension

0.9% NaCl, dopamine, norepinephrine, and central venous pressure monitoring.

Pulmonary Edema (Non-Cardiogenic)
Maintain adequate ventilation and oxygenation; monitor ABGs and/or pulse oximetry frequently. Ventilation and PEEP may be necessary.

Oxygen
100% oxygen combined with traditional nitrite/thiosulfate therapy is more effective than thiosulfate alone.

HBO
May improve clinical outcome, especially in those patients with CNS toxicity not responding to traditional therapy.

Monitoring Parameters
Whole blood cyanide levels, ABGs, CBC, electrolytes, serum lactate, MetHb levels.

Range Of Toxicity

Air concentrations of 0.2 to 0.3 milligram/cubic meter (200 to 300 parts per million) are rapidly fatal; concentrations of 50 ppm are immediately dangerous to life and health.

Lewisite

Clinical Effects

Background
Lewisite is a substituted arsine. A vesicant liquid, its has potential use as a terrorist or war agent; it can be dispersed through a bursting charge of explosive. Lewisite is similar to mustard gas in that it damages the skin, eyes, and airways. However, unlike mustard gas it produces clinical effects within seconds of exposure, and may cause systemic toxicity.

Clinical Presentation
DERMAL EXPOSURE: Immediate stinging and burning; erythema within 30 minutes. Painful blister formation may occur in 2 to 3 hours. Skin burns are deeper than those produced by mustard gas. After 5 minutes of exposure, there is often a gray area of dead epithelium similar to that noted with corrosive burns. Itching and irritation are present for about 24 hours, whether or not a blister is seen.

OCULAR EXPOSURE: Immediate stinging and burning and instant blepharospasm. Edema of the conjunctiva and lids, iritis, and corneal haziness occur over a few hours. Temporary blindness due to blistering and swelling of the lids/mucous membranes is possible. Corneal scars may develop.

INHALATION EXPOSURE: The vesicant affects mucous membranes, causing intense irritation. Vocal cord paralysis, chemical pneumonitis, pulmonary edema, and respiratory failure may result.

SYSTEMIC TOXICITY: May develop after severe dermal or inhalation exposure. Effects may include diarrhea, restlessness, pulmonary edema, subnormal temperatures, hypotension, respiratory failure, increased capillary permeability, hemoconcentration, shock, and death.

Treatment

Decontamination

DERMAL: Immediately—within one minute if possible—wash skin and clothes with 5% solution of sodium hypochlorite or diluted liquid household bleach. Wash contaminated skin with soap and water afterwards. Topical application of a 5% BAL ointment or solution within 15 minutes of an exposure has been reported to be effective in diminishing the vesicant effects of Lewisite. Wash off any protective ointment prior to applying topical BAL.

INHALATION: Move patient to fresh air; administer oxygen.

OCULAR: Irrigate exposed eyes with copious amounts of 0.9% saline or water at room temperature for at least 15 minutes. A 5% BAL compounded ophthalmic ointment or solution applied within 2 minutes may prevent a significant reaction.

ORAL: Dilution, activated charcoal, gastric lavage.

Chelation

INDICATIONS: Cough with dyspnea and frothy sputum and signs of pulmonary edema; skin burn the size of the palm of the hand or larger caused by liquid Lewisite and not decontaminated within the first 15 minutes; and skin contamination by liquid Lewisite covering 5% or more of the body surface in which there is evidence of immediate skin damage or erythema within 30 minutes.

BAL (dimercaprol): 3 mg/kg (200 mg for an average person) should be given as a deep IM injection and repeated every 4 hours for 2 days, then given every 6 hours on the third day, and every 12 hours for up to 10 days. Adverse effects include hypertension, tachycardia, nausea/vomiting, headache, burning lips, feeling of chest constriction, conjunctivitis, lacrimation, rhinorrhea, sweating, muscle aches, burning/tingling of extremities, and anxiety. Adverse effects may be dose-related. They are maximal within 10 to 30 minutes and usually subside within 30 to 50 minutes.

DMSA (succimer): Initial dose is 10 mg/kg orally every 8 hours for 5 days, then every 12 hours for the next 14 days. A repeat course may be given if indicated. A minimum of 2 weeks between courses is recommended.

DMPS: The adult oral dose is 1,200 to 2,400 mg/day in equally divided doses (100 to 200 mg 12 times daily) initially, then 100 to 300 mg 1 to 3 times daily. The adult IV dose is 250 mg IV every 3 to 4 hours (1,500 to 2,000 mg total) for first 24 hours, then 250 mg IV every 4 to 6 hours; (1,000 to 1,500 mg total) on day 2; 250 mg IV every 6 to 8 hours (750 to 1,000 mg total) on day 3; 250 mg

IV every 8 to 12 hours (500 to 750 mg total) on day 4; 250 mg IV every 8 to 24 hours (250 to 750 mg total) on days 5 and 6. Inject slowly over 3 to 5 minutes. Adverse effects include chills, fever, allergic skin reactions such as itching, exanthema or maculopapular rash. Cardiovascular effects such as hypotension, nausea, dizziness, or weakness may occur with too-rapid injection of DMPS.

Burns
Wound dressings (except first-degree burns); topical antibiotics.

Hypotension
Administer IV fluids; large amounts may be necessary; dopamine or norepinephrine.

Pulmonary Edema (Non-Cardiogenic)
Maintain ventilation and oxygenation. Monitor ABGs/pulse oximetry frequently. Early use of PEEP and mechanical ventilation may be needed.

Monitoring Parameters
Obtain CBC, electrolytes, ABGs/pulse oximetry, 24-hour urinary arsenic collection, abdominal radiograph, and chest x-ray as clinically indicated.

LSD

Clinical Effects

Background
Stimulants such as LSD cause excessive nervous activity by facilitating transmission of impulses. The effect is to flood the cortex and other higher regulatory centers with too much information, making concentration difficult and causing indecisiveness and inability to act in a purposeful manner. In a chemical warfare setting, it is likely that an agent such as LSD would be dispersed by smoke-producing munitions or aerosols, using the respiratory system as the portal of entry. Use of a protective mask is essential.

Clinical Presentation
TYPICAL PHASES:

Somatic (0 to 60 minutes):
Tension, light-headedness, mydriasis, twitching, flushing, tachycardia, hypertension, hyperreflexia.

Perceptual (30 to 60 minutes):
Visual, auditory, and sensory alterations; distortions of color, distance, shape, and time; synesthesias.

Psychic (2 to 12 hours): Euphoria, mood swings, depression, feelings of depersonalization, loss of body image, derealization.

OTHER: Hyperthermia, seizures, coma, hyperglycemia, rhabdomyolysis, and renal failure are rare effects with severe intoxication.

Treatment

Decontamination
Action generally not indicated because of rapid absorption. In a warfare/terrorist setting, LSD may

be dispersed by aerosol to create confusion; protective mask is recommended.

Agitation

Sedate with benzodiazepines or haloperidol. Provide quiet environment.

Psychosis

Sedate with benzodiazepines. Long term management may require phenothiazines or haloperidol.

Hyperthermia

Control agitation with benzodiazepines and increase evaporative heat loss (remove patients clothing, dampen skin, and use fans).

Serotonin Syndrome

Control agitation (benzodiazepines). Monitor BP; give nitroprusside, dopamine, or norepinephrine as indicated. Consider cyproheptadine.

Range Of Toxicity

Toxic dose has not been established; usual recreational dose 50 to 300 mcg.

Mustard Gas

Clinical Effects

Background

Mustard gas is an organic sulfide compound. A bifunctional alkylating agent, it is a clear, yellow/amber colored, oily liquid with a faint, sweet odor of mustard/garlic. It becomes aerosolized when dispersed by spraying or by explosive blast.

Clinical Presentation

A powerful irritant and vesicant, mustard gas produces corrosion and necrosis of the skin, eyes, and respiratory tract. While the chemical reaction with biological tissue occurs rapidly, symptoms are typically delayed by several hours. Systemic poisoning occurs more easily in warm climates.

DERMAL EXPOSURE: Itching and erythema occur 2 to 3 hours after dermal exposure. Erythema spreads over the next 24 hours; yellowish blisters appear and can become ulcerated. (They heal in 4 to 6 weeks after a transitory melanoderma.) Thinner skin (neck, axillae, and groin) is more susceptible than thicker skin.

INHALATION EXPOSURE: Cough, dyspnea, and possibly pulmonary edema may occur up to 24 hours after inhalation of the gas. Ulceration of airway mucosa may occur.

OCULAR EXPOSURE: Conjunctivitis appears early, developing 4 to 6 hours after exposure. Lacrimation, dryness, pain, photophobia, corneal ulceration, and loss of vision may occur. Effects may persist for up to 10 days.

INGESTION: Nausea, vomiting, diarrhea, and abdominal pain may follow ingestion. Cough, fever, and severe bronchitis are common.

CHILDREN: Time to onset of symptoms may be shorter and severity of skin lesions may be greater as compared to adults. Ophthalmic, pulmonary, and gastrointestinal lesions are more common in children than adults.

SYSTEMIC TOXICITY: Myelosuppression may occur after significant dermal or inhalation exposure.

Treatment

Decontamination

INHALATION: Time is of the essence. Move to fresh air; administer 100% humidified oxygen. Administer inhaled beta agonists if wheezing develops. Manage airway aggressively if severe respiratory distress develops. A nebulized 2.5% solution of sodium thiosulfate may have some value in neutralization if exposure has occurred in the past 15 minutes.

DERMAL: Immediately flush skin with water for at least 20 minutes. Neutralize with a 2.5% solution of sodium thiosulfate. Avoid spreading material on unaffected skin. Avoid contact with contaminated material. The US Military previously used a Skin Decontamination Kit containing the resins Ambergard XE-555 and XE-556. If water is scarce, talcum powder, flour, and Fuller's earth can be used. Dilute (0.5%) hypochlorite (bleach) solutions can also be used.

OCULAR: Irrigate with copious amounts of tepid water for at least 15 minutes. Neutralize with a 2.5% solution of sodium thiosulfate.

PREVENTION OF CONTAMINATION: May penetrate clothing and even leather; wear protective clothing, gloves, and eye protection. Remove and isolate contaminated clothing and shoes.

Antidotes

There is no specific antidote. Experimental evidence suggests that sodium thiosulfate, N-acetylcysteine (NAC) [a potential mustard gas antagonist], and prednisone may be useful. While not proven effective by human studies, these agents have limited toxicity and should be considered.

SODIUM THIOSULFATE: Dose recommended includes 50 mL of a 25% sodium thiosulfate solution (12.5 grams total) administered IV over 10 minutes.

NAC: Proposed dosage includes an oral loading dose of 140 mg/kg, followed by 40 mg/kg every 4 hours for a total of 17 doses.

PREDNISONE: This drug has been given in doses of 60 to 125 mg/day for pulmonary toxicity.

OTHERS: Promethazine and dexamethasone have also been used.

Monitoring Parameters

The gas and its metabolite (thiodiglycol) can be detected in urine for up to a week. Monitor fluids/electrolytes, CBC with differential, platelets for 2 weeks or until nadir is passed. If respiratory symptoms develop, monitor ABGs/pulse oximetry, chest x-ray, pulmonary function tests.

Range Of Toxicity

The lowest published lethal inhalation exposure is 23 ppm for 10 minutes. The lowest published lethal dermal exposure is 60 to 64 mg/kg for 1 hour contact time. As little as 65 mcg has produced skin injury. Cellular damage begins within 1 to 2 minutes of contact; clinical effects begin within 2 to 24 hours; onset is inversely proportional to dose.

Nitrogen Mustard

Clinical Effects

Background

Nitrogen mustard is a vesicant. A mobile, oily, colorless to pale yellow liquid, it has a faint garlic or mustard odor.

Clinical Presentation

INHALATION EXPOSURE: Onset of irritation/congestion occurs in 4 to 6 hours. Burning throat pain, nasal secretions, hoarseness, aphonia, dry cough, dyspnea, moist rales, and erythema, edema, and necrosis of affected mucosa may develop. Respiratory tract irritation can progress to pulmonary edema; symptoms can be delayed up to 24 to 72 hours after exposure in some cases. Death secondary to pulmonary edema, mechanical asphyxia, or superimposed bacterial infection is possible.

Acute Stage: Upper airway obstruction; respiratory failure from pulmonary edema and hemorrhage.

Subacute Stage: Lasts hours to several days. Necrosis of the tracheobronchial mucosa, hemorrhagic tracheobronchitis, persistent pulmonary edema and hemorrhage, and infection.

Chronic Stage: Lasts weeks to months. Scarring/stenosis of the tracheobronchial tree, bronchiectasis, infections, bronchiolitis obliterans, and progressive respiratory insufficiency.

OCULAR EXPOSURE

Lacrimation/irritation occurs within 20 minutes and peaks at 8 to 10 hours. Delayed effects are possible.

DERMAL EXPOSURE: Erythema, intensive itching, vesication, and necrosis; percutaneous absorption is common with liquid or vapor contact.

SYSTEMIC TOXICITY:
Low Concentrations: anorexia, anemia, bloody diarrhea, abdominal/epigastric pain, leukopenia, and vomiting.
High concentrations: GI pain, fever, seizures followed by CNS depression, prostration, shock, cardiac dysrhythmias (AV block), and cardiac arrest.

Possible Sequelae

Visual impairment, permanent blindness, cutaneous scars, bronchial stenosis, chronic bronchitis, anorexia, and sensitivity to nitrogen mustard. The agent is mutagenic and carcinogenic in man.

Treatment

Decontamination

DERMAL: Wash with copious amounts of soap and water. A 2% sodium thiosulfate solution (mix 3 parts 10% sodium thiosulfate with 12 parts sterile water) may also be used on skin only. For first aid, remove contaminated clothing and isolate for proper disposal. Decontaminate all affected areas with copious amounts of tepid water for at least 15 minutes.

PREVENTION OF CONTAMINATION: Potential for secondary contamination is high; avoid self-contamination from contact with contaminated patients or clothing.

Symptomatic and Supportive

Treatment may include oxygen, intubation, mechanical ventilation, and burn care as indicated. There is no specific antidote.

Ocular

Instill atropine for pain from ciliary spasm.

Drug Therapy

FILGRASTIM: Consider in patients with severe granulocytopenia. Adult dosage is 5 mcg/kg/day by IV infusion or subcutaneous injection. Monitor CBC and absolute granulocyte count.

Monitoring Parameters

Monitor CBC with differential and platelets, fluid and electrolyte status. If respiratory irritation is present, monitor ABGs/pulse oximetry, chest x-ray, and pulmonary function tests.

Range Of Toxicity

Nitrogen mustard persists in the environment in cold and temperate climates. Dissolution in nonvolatile products increases its persistence and decreases the effectiveness of decontamination procedures. Increased evaporation rates in hot climates result in higher air concentrations.

Nuclear Radiation

Clinical Effects

Background

A scenario of radiation exposure during terrorism or warfare includes exposure of large masses of people via detonation of nuclear weapons, resulting in mass casualties and extensive numbers of severely burned patients. The two most radiosensitive organ systems in the body are the hematopoietic and the gastrointestinal systems.

Clinical Presentation

Acute radiation syndrome, a complex of symptoms following whole body irradiation of >1 gray (Gy), has four phases: prodrome, latent, manifest illness, and recovery.

PRODROME: Occurs in the first 48 to 72 hours and is characterized by nausea, vomiting, diarrhea, intestinal cramps, salivation, and dehydration. Fatigue, weakness, apathy, fever, and hypotension are the result of neurovascular dysfunction. At doses below about 5 Gy lasts 2 to 4 days.

LATENT: Follows the prodromal phase and lasts for approximately 1 to 2-1/2 weeks. During this period, critical cell populations (leukocytes, platelets) are decreasing as a result of bone marrow insult. The duration of this period decreases with increased doses of radiation. This is the longest phase preceding bone marrow depression, which lasts 2 to 6 weeks. The latent period lasts from a few days to a week before the onset of new gastrointestinal symptoms. Neurovascular symptoms begin after the latent phase. These times are exceedingly variable and may be modified by the presence of other disease or injury.

MANIFEST ILLNESS: Overt illness develops. Clinical symptoms are associated with the major organ system injured. A neurovascular syndrome develops after exposure to 20 to 40 Gy; onset is several hours to 3 days, with altered mental status, coma, seizures, organic brain syndrome, ataxia, tremor, and death. A gastrointestinal syndrome develops after exposure to 6 to 20 Gy; onset is hours to several days after exposure with nausea, vomiting and later bloody diarrhea and potential sepsis. Myelosuppression develops after exposure to 0.7 to 4 Gy. The neutropenic nadir occurs at 2 to 4 weeks; thrombocytopenia at 3 to 4 weeks; anemia follows. Other effects may include skin burns and associated traumatic injuries.

RECOVERY: May take weeks or months.

Treatment

Immediate concerns: (1) treatment of life-threatening injuries; (2) decontamination procedures. Manage airway and ensure adequate ventilation and hemodynamic stability.

Decontamination

Proper handling to minimize the spread of radioactive contamination is of utmost importance. Decontamination with soap and water should be repeated until dosimetry readings become normal; all waste should be saved in special receptacles. All vomitus, urine, feces, and metal clothing parts should be saved for possible neutron activation analysis and estimation of dose received. All personnel involved in handling contaminated patients should wear disposable protective clothing, including caps, masks, and shoe covers.

Burns/Radiation

Patients with thermal burns and concomitant radiation exposure exhibit a marked increase in mortality. Aggressive marrow resuscitative therapeutic procedures may improve the prognosis. The primary cause of death is infection. Treat aggressively with antibiotics and fluid resuscitation.

Marrow Depression

Administer filgrastim (G-CSF) 2.5 to 5 micrograms/kilogram/day subcutaneously until the desired effect of an ANC of 10 x 10(9)/liter is reached.

Hypotension

Administer IV fluids; large amounts may be necessary. If unresponsive, administer dopamine or norepinephrine and titrate as needed.

Seizures

Administer IV benzodiazepines or barbiturates as needed.

Monitoring Parameters

Baseline studies include a CBC with differential count, platelet count, and electrolytes. Repeat frequently.

Range Of Toxicity

Whole-body radiation doses can be divided into potentially lethal (2 to 10 Gy), sublethal (less than 2 Gy), and supralethal (greater than 10 Gy) doses. In man, the median lethal dose of radiation (LD50/60) is estimated to be 3.5 Gy.

Phosgene

Clinical Effects

Background

Military designation CG. At room temperature, phosgene is a colorless, non-combustible, highly toxic gas that is easily liquefied. At high concentrations, the gas has an odor described as suffocating, strong, pungent, and irritating. At lower concentrations, the odor has been widely characterized as being haylike, similar to newly-mown, moldy or musty hay. Chlorinated hydrocarbons (eg, carbon tetrachloride, trichloroethylene, methylene chloride) that come in contact with a flame or very hot metal decompose to phosgene gas.

Clinical Presentation

INITIAL SYMPTOMS: Immediate irritant effects such as conjunctivitis, rhinitis, pharyngitis, bronchitis, lacrimation, blepharospasm, conjunctival hyperemia, and upper respiratory tract irritation may occur after exposure to concentrations of 3 to 5 ppm.

PROGRESSION OF SYMPTOMS: Severe pulmonary toxicity may develop after exposure to higher doses. Rarely, signs and symptoms of toxicity may be delayed, for up to 24 hours (or as long as 72 hours in some instances). They include choking, chest tightness, severe dyspnea, pulmonary edema, cough, production of foaming bloody sputum, nausea, and anxiety. Cardiac failure has occasionally occurred as a complication of severe pulmonary edema. Release of liquefied phosgene from a pressurized cylinder produces a cryogenic gas that is a frostbite hazard and has caused corneal opacification.

Prognosis
If the victim survives for 24 to 48 hours; prognosis is usually favorable.

Treatment

Decontamination
INHALATION: Administer 100% humidified supplemental oxygen. Move to fresh air. Treat bronchospasm with beta2 agonist and corticosteroid aerosols. Monitor for 12 to 24 hours after exposure.

DERMAL: Remove contaminated clothing and wash exposed area thoroughly with soap and water.

OCULAR: Remove contact lenses and irrigate exposed eyes with copious amounts of 0.9% saline or water at room temperature for at least 15 minutes.

PREVENTION OF CONTAMINATION: To avoid becoming secondary victims, rescuers must not enter areas with potential high airborne concentrations of this agent without self-contained breathing apparatus (SCBA). Proper protective clothing should be worn. Remove contaminated clothing.

Symptomatic and Supportive
Airway management, O2, intubation, mechanical ventilation as needed.

Pulmonary Edema (Non-Cardiogenic)
Onset may be delayed from 6 to 15 hours. Maintain ventilation and oxygenation. Monitor ABGs and/or pulse oximetry. Early use of PEEP and mechanical ventilation may be needed. Animal studies and anecdotal experience suggest that the following therapies may be of benefit in patients with exposure sufficient to place them at risk for pulmonary edema (a dose of 50 ppm x min or more): ibuprofen, corticosteroids, aminophylline, N-acetylcysteine, and terbutaline (aerosol or SC).

Monitoring Parameters
Plasma phosgene levels are not clinically useful. Monitor ABGs, pulmonary function, and chest x-ray for patients with significant exposure. Serial chest x-rays are recommended if significant exposure suspected; effects can be delayed. Monitor fluid balance.

Range Of Toxicity

In concentrations of 3 to 5 ppm, irritation of the eyes, throat, and upper respiratory tract are noted. Total dose (concentration in ppm multiplied by time of exposure in minutes) determines the risk of pulmonary edema. A cumulative dose of 50 ppm x min can result in delayed pulmonary edema; a dose of 150 ppm x min will probably result in pulmonary edema; and a dose of 300 ppm x min is likely to be fatal. Exposure to 25 ppm is extremely dangerous and to more than 50 ppm may be rapidly fatal.

Phosgene Oxime

Clinical Effects

Background

This halogenated oxime is used as a blistering agent. It is not a true vesicant and does not cause blistering, but it does cause corrosive injury to skin and tissue with liquid or vapor contact. It is generally described as an urticant or nettle agent (or a "Nettle Rush" gas).

Clinical Presentation

Following contact, extreme pain may last for several days. Damage to the eyes, skin, and airways is similar to that from mustard gas. However, unlike mustard gas, phosgene oxime does not cause damage to the bone marrow. The crystalline solid form will produce enough vapor to cause symptoms.

INHALATION EXPOSURE: Phosgene oxime is a severe respiratory irritant in low concentrations. Pulmonary edema and death secondary to respiratory arrest are possible.

OCULAR EXPOSURE: Vapors at low concentrations cause severe eye irritation. Higher concentrations can cause incapacitating inflammation and blindness.

DERMAL EXPOSURE: High concentrations cause severe skin irritation with rapid necrotizing wounds. Immediate pain is followed by blanching with an erythematous ring in 30 seconds, a wheal in 30 minutes, and necrosis in 24 hours.

Treatment

Decontamination

INHALATION: Immediately move to fresh air. Administer oxygen and assist ventilation as required. Carefully observe for any respiratory distress.

OCULAR: Flush eyes immediately with water, 0.9% saline, or isotonic sodium bicarb for at least 1 hour or until the cul-de-sacs are free of particulate matter and returned to neutrality (confirm with pH paper). Extent of eye injury (corneal opacification and perilimbal whitening) may not be apparent for 48 to 72 hours. Patients with significant eye exposure should be monitored for respiratory effects.

DERMAL: Remove contaminated clothing and wash vigorously; do repeated soap washings. Discard contaminated clothing.

Symptomatic and Supportive

There is no antidote for phosgene oxime; treatment is symptomatic.

Bronchospasm

Treat with beta2 agonist and corticosteroid aerosols.

Ocular Injuries

If damage is minor, topical mydriatics, antibiotics, and systemic analgesics may be sufficient. Ophthalmology consult is recommended.

Dermal Injuries

Treat irritation/burns with topical therapy (includes dressings and topical antibiotic ointments).

Pulmonary Edema (Non-Cardiogenic)

Maintain ventilation and oxygenation. Monitor ABGs/pulse oximetry. Early use of PEEP and mechanical ventilation may be needed.

Monitoring Parameters

Obtain CBC, liver enzymes, kidney function tests, glucose, and serum electrolytes as indicated. Obtain baseline ABGs, pulse oximetry, pulmonary function, and chest x-ray in patients following significant exposures. Serial chest x-rays and pulse oximetry and/or ABGs are recommended following inhalation exposure.

Range Of Toxicity

Information is limited. Irritation begins at 0.2 mg/min/m(3) (12 seconds) and is unbearable at 3 mg/min/m(3) (1 minute).

Quinuclidinyl Benzilate (BZ)

Clinical Effects

Background

3-Quinuclidinyl benzilate (also known as QNB or BZ) is a chemical warfare agent with anticholinergic activity affecting both the peripheral and central nervous systems. Its pharmacologic activity is similar to other anticholinergics, but has a much longer duration of action. The agent is classified as a hallucinogenic. It is odorless and, in a terrorist attack, would be disseminated as an aerosol, using the respiratory tract as a portal of entry with a secondary route of entry through the digestive tract.

Clinical Presentation

CNS SYMPTOMS: Restlessness, apprehension, abnormal speech, confusion, agitation, tremor, ataxia, stupor, and coma have been described. Hallucinations are prominent. Motor coordination, perception, cognition, and new memory formation are altered. Seizures may occur in severe poisoning.

PERIPHERAL NERVOUS SYSTEM SYMPTOMS: Mydriasis, tachycardia, hypertension, nausea/vomiting, decreased intestinal motility, hyperthermia, dry and flushed skin, dry mucous membranes, and urinary retention.

Prognosis

Good, unless secondary effects such as rhabdomyolysis develop, Patients become more lucid after they have been removed from exposure and the agent has been metabolized. Full recovery is expected within 4 days.

Treatment

Decontamination

DERMAL: Remove contaminated clothing and jewelry; wash skin, hair, and nails vigorously with repeated soap washings. All contaminated leather should be discarded. Rescue personnel and bystanders should avoid direct contact with contaminated skin, clothing, or other objects.

INHALATION: Move from the toxic environment to fresh air. Monitor for respiratory distress (eg, hypoxia, respiratory tract irritation, bronchitis, or pneumonitis).

OCULAR: Irrigate exposed eyes with copious amounts of tepid water for at least 15 minutes.

ORAL: Administer activated charcoal and gastric lavage. Ipecac is contraindicated.

Symptomatic and Supportive

Treatment is symptomatic and supportive. Without treatment following an incapacitating dose, recovery is gradual, requiring 72 to 96 hours.

Agitation

Patients with agitation or hallucinations should be sedated with benzodiazepines.

Physostigmine

A diagnostic trial with physostigmine may be initiated. Physostigmine has been reported to be relatively ineffective if given during the first 4 to 6 hours following the onset of BZ's effects. Peak impairment following aerosol BZ exposure occurs at 6 to 10 hours. If treatment with physostigmine is not maintained once begun, recovery from BZ poisoning may be slightly prolonged. For adults, use 1 to 2 mg IV over 5 minutes; for children, use 0.02 mg/kg up to 0.5 mg IV over 5 minutes.

Dysrhythmias

Monitor. Severe dysrhythmias (hemodynamic instability) may respond to physostigmine.

Lidocaine

For adults, administer 1 to 1.5 mg/kg, followed by an infusion of 1 to 4 mg/min prn. For children, administer a loading dose of 1 mg/kg, followed by an infusion of 20 to 50 mcg/kg/min.

Seizures

Administer IV benzodiazepines, barbiturates.

Hyperthermia

External cooling, control agitation.

Rhabdomyolysis

Early aggressive fluid replacement

is the mainstay of therapy and may help prevent renal insufficiency. Diuretics such as mannitol or furosemide may be needed to maintain urine output. Urinary alkalinization is not routinely recommended.

Monitoring Parameters

Obtain electrolytes, renal function tests, CPK levels, ECG, and chest x-ray as clinically indicated.

Range Of Toxicity

The range of toxicity is variable and unpredictable. Clinical judgment is more important than attempting to determine the amount inhaled.

Sarin

Clinical Effects

Background

Sarin (Agent GB) is a military "nerve agent." A colorless liquid/vapor with almost no odor, Sarin is an extremely active anticholinesterase organophosphate compound that produces toxicity via cholinergic overdrive at muscarinic, nicotinic, and CNS cholinergic sites. At ambient temperatures, Sarin is a liquid and is rapidly absorbed through skin. Inhalation is possible at high temperatures or when the agent is aerosolized by an explosion. The vapors are denser than air. Absorption can also occur following ingestion and eye contact.

Clinical Presentation

INHALATION:
Mild exposure: Symptoms include miosis, rhinorrhea, and dyspnea.

Severe exposure: Large concentrations of vapor cause sudden loss of consciousness and seizures followed by apnea and flaccid paralysis. Severe casualties have miosis and copious secretions from the nose and mouth. Unless they are paralyzed, they have fasciculations. "SLUDGE" (salivation, lacrimation, urination, defecation, and gastric emesis) occurs. Symptoms begin within seconds to minutes.

DERMAL: A very small drop may cause sweating and twitching at the site; a slightly larger drop may cause nausea, vomiting, and diarrhea. A large drop on the skin may cause loss of consciousness, seizures, apnea, and flaccid paralysis. Effects begin within 30 minutes (large amount) to 18 hours (small amount).

Sequelae

Delayed peripheral neurotoxicity is possible. Hypoxic effects may occur in the CNS and other organs.

Fatalities

Death is due to respiratory failure, CNS depression, and excessive secretions.

Treatment

Decontamination

INHALATION: Move to fresh air. Monitor for respiratory distress;

evaluate respiratory function (eg, irritation, bronchitis, or pneumonitis).

DERMAL: Remove contaminated clothing and jewelry. Discard contaminated clothing. Wash the skin, including hair and nails, vigorously with repeated soapings. Alternatively, use dilute (0.5%) hypochlorite (household bleach) followed by a thorough water rinse. A Skin Decontaminating Kit for military/civil defense has applicator pads impregnated with Ambergard 555 ion-exchange resin and activated charcoal to be rubbed over contaminated skin and discarded. Use caution, potential for secondary contamination is high.

OCULAR: Remove contact lenses; irrigate with copious amounts of room temperature 0.9% saline or water for at least 15 minutes.

Antidotes

Specific antidotes include atropine and pralidoxime.

ATROPINE: Primarily effective for muscarinic effects; will not reverse nicotinic effects. The diagnostic dose (give if diagnosis uncertain) for adults is 1 mg IV/IM; for children, 0.25 mg (about 0.01 mg/kg) IV/IM. The therapeutic dose for adults is 2 to 5 mg slowly IV; children, 0.05 mg/kg slowly IV; repeat doses may be administered every 10 to 15 minutes as needed to achieve and maintain full atropinization.

PRALIDOXIME: Severe Sarin poisoning with nicotinic and/or CNS manifestations should be treated with pralidoxime. For adults, give 1 to 2 g IV at 0.5 g/min, or mix in 250 mL of NS and infuse over 30 min. For children, give 25 to 50 mg/kg, diluted to a 5% concentration in NS and infused over 20 to 30 min. MARK I autoinjector delivers 2 mg atropine/0.7 mL and 600 mg pralidoxime chloride/2 mL into 2 separate IM sites; not to be used in children less than 10 years old.

Bronchospasm

Use inhaled beta agonists if atropine alone is inadequate.

Seizures

Administer IV benzodiazepines, barbiturates.

Pulmonary Edema (Non-Cardiogenic)

Maintain ventilation and oxygenation. Monitor ABGs and/or pulse oximetry frequently. PEEP and mechanical ventilation may be needed. Succinylcholine should be avoided for intubation because paralysis may be prolonged.

Monitoring Parameters

Monitor ECG, respiratory function.

Range Of Toxicity

Sarin has an especially rapid onset of action. A small drop of the liquid on the skin may be sufficient to cause death. LCt50 of the vapor is 100 mg/min/m(3).

Soman

Clinical Effects

Background

Soman (Agent GD) is a military "nerve agent." A colorless liquid with a fruity or camphor odor, it is an extremely active anticholinesterase organophosphate compound that produces toxicity via cholinergic overdrive at muscarinic, nicotinic, and CNS cholinergic sites. At ambient temperatures Soman is a liquid, and is rapidly absorbed through the skin. Inhalation is possible at high temperatures or when the agent is aerosolized by an explosion. The vapors are denser than air. Absorption can also occur following ingestion and eye contact.

Clinical Presentation

INHALATION:

Mild exposure: Symptoms include miosis, rhinorrhea, and dyspnea

Severe exposure: A large concentration of vapor causes sudden loss of consciousness and seizures followed by apnea and flaccid paralysis. Severe casualties have miosis and copious secretions from nose and mouth. Unless they are paralyzed, they have fasciculations. "SLUDGE" (salivation, lacrimation, urination, defecation, and gastric emesis) occurs. Effects begin within seconds to minutes.

DERMAL: A very small drop may cause sweating and twitching at the site. A slightly larger drop may cause nausea, vomiting, and diarrhea. A large drop on the skin may cause loss of consciousness, seizures, apnea, and flaccid paralysis. Effects begin within 30 minutes (large amount) to 18 hours (small amount).

Fatalities

Death is a result of respiratory failure, CNS depression, and excessive secretions.

Treatment

Decontamination

INHALATION: Move to fresh air. Monitor for respiratory distress (eg, hypoxia, respiratory tract irritation, bronchitis, or pneumonitis).

DERMAL: Remove contaminated clothing and jewelry. Discard contaminated clothing. Wash the skin, including hair and nails, vigorously with repeated soapings. Alternatively, use dilute hypochlorite (household bleach) followed by a thorough water rinse. A Skin Decontaminating Kit for military/civil defense use contains applicator pads impregnated with Ambergard 555 ion-exchange resin and activated charcoal to be rubbed over contaminated skin and discarded. Use caution; potential for secondary contamination is high.

OCULAR: Remove contact lenses and irrigate eyes with copious amounts of 0.9% saline or water at room temperature for at least 15 minutes.

Antidotes
Specific antidotes include atropine and pralidoxime.

ATROPINE: Primarily effective for muscarinic effects; will not reverse nicotinic effects. The diagnostic dose (give if diagnosis uncertain) for adults is 1 mg IV or IM; for children, 0.25 mg (about 0.01 mg/kg) IV or IM. The therapeutic dose for adults is 2 to 5 mg slowly IV; for children, 0.05 mg/kg slowly IV. Repeat doses may be administered every 10 to 15 minutes as needed to achieve and maintain full atropinization (drying of pulmonary secretions).

PRALIDOXIME: Severe Soman poisoning with nicotinic and/or CNS manifestations may be treated with pralidoxime. For adults, give 1 to 2 g IV at 0.5 g/min or mix in 250 mL of NS and infuse over 30 min. For children, give 25 to 50 mg/kg diluted to a 5% concentration in NS and infused over 20 to 30 min. MARK I autoinjector delivers 2 mg atropine/0.7 mL and 600 mg pralidoxime chloride/2 mL into two separate intramuscular sites; not to be used in children less than 10 years old.

Bronchospasm
Use inhaled beta agonists if atropine alone is inadequate.

Seizures
Administer IV benzodiazepines, barbiturates.

Pulmonary Edema (Non-Cardiogenic)
Maintain ventilation and oxygenation. Monitor ABGs and/or pulse oximetry frequently. Early use of PEEP and mechanical ventilation may be needed. Succinylcholine should be avoided for intubation because paralysis may be prolonged.

Monitoring Parameters
Monitor ECG and respiratory function.

Range Of Toxicity

The lethal dose is as low as 0.01 mg/kg. This toxin undergoes "aging" within minutes, rendering oxime therapy less effective and making poisoning much more difficult to treat. LCt50 of the vapor is 50 mg/min/m(3).

Tabun

Clinical Effects

Background
The military "nerve agent" Tabun (Agent GA) is a combustible, colorless to brownish liquid with a fruity odor of almonds. It is an extremely active anticholinesterase organophosphate compound that produces toxicity via cholinergic overdrive at muscarinic, nicotinic, and CNS cholinergic sites. It may also undergo hydrolysis in the presence of acids or water, forming hydrogen cyanide. Inhalation is possible at high temperatures or

when the agent is aerosolized by an explosion. The liquid form is absorbed rapidly through the skin. Absorption can also occur following ingestion, inhalation, and eye contact. This agent is destroyed by contact with bleaching powder, generating cyanogen chloride.

Clinical Presentation

INHALATION:

Mild exposure: Symptoms include miosis, rhinorrhea, dyspnea.

Severe exposure: A large concentration of vapor causes sudden loss of consciousness and seizures followed by apnea and flaccid paralysis. Severe casualties have miosis and copious secretions from the nose and mouth. Unless they are paralyzed, they have fasciculations. "SLUDGE" (salivation, lacrimation, urination, defecation, and gastric emesis) occurs. Effects begin within seconds to minutes.

DERMAL: A very small drop may cause sweating and twitching at the site. A slightly larger drop may cause nausea, vomiting, and diarrhea. A large drop may cause loss of consciousness, seizures, apnea, and flaccid paralysis. Effects begin within 30 minutes (large amount) to 18 hours (small amount).

Fatalities

Death is a result of respiratory failure, CNS depression, and excessive secretions.

Treatment

Decontamination

INHALATION: Move to fresh air. Monitor for respiratory distress (eg, hypoxia, irritation, bronchitis, or pneumonitis).

DERMAL: Remove contaminated clothing and jewelry. Discard contaminated clothing. Wash the skin, including hair and nails, vigorously with repeated soapings. Alternatively, use dilute (0.5%) hypochlorite (household bleach) followed by a thorough water rinse. A Skin Decontaminating Kit for military/civil defense use contains applicator pads impregnated with Ambergard 555 ion-exchange resin and activated charcoal to be rubbed over contaminated skin and discarded. Use caution, potential for secondary contamination is high.

OCULAR: Remove contact lenses and irrigate exposed eyes with copious amounts of room temperature 0.9% saline or water for at least 15 minutes.

Antidotes

Specific antidotes include atropine and pralidoxime.

ATROPINE: Primarily effective for muscarinic effects; will not reverse nicotinic effects. The diagnostic dose (give if diagnosis uncertain) for adults is 1 mg IV or IM; for children, give 0.25 mg (about 0.01 mg/kg) IV or IM. The therapeutic dose for adults is 2 to 5 mg slowly IV; for children, give 0.05 mg/kg slowly IV. Repeat doses may be administered every 10 to 15 minutes as needed to achieve and maintain full atropinization, (signaled by drying of pulmonary secretions).

PRALIDOXIME: Severe Tabun poisoning with nicotinic and/or CNS manifestations should be treated with pralidoxime. For adults, give 1 to 2 g IV at 0.5 g/min or mix in 250 mL of NS and infuse over 30 min. For children, give 25 to 50 mg/kg, diluted to a 5% concentration in NS and infused over 20 to 30 min. MARK I autoinjector delivers 2 mg atropine/0.7 mL and 600 mg pralidoxime chloride/2 mL into 2 separate IM sites; do not use in children less than 10 years old.

Bronchospasm
Use inhaled beta agonists if atropine alone is inadequate.

Seizures
Administer IV benzodiazepines, barbiturates.

Pulmonary Edema (Non-Cardiogenic)
Maintain ventilation and oxygenation. Monitor ABGs and/or pulse oximetry frequently. Early use of PEEP and mechanical ventilation may be needed. Succinylcholine should be avoided for intubation because paralysis may be prolonged.

Monitoring Parameters
Monitor ECG and respiratory function.

Range Of Toxicity

Tabun (GA) has an especially rapid onset of action; lethal doses are effective in 1 to 10 minutes. The fatal dose is approximately 0.01 mg/kg. LCt50 of the vapor is 400 mg/min/m(3). LD50 (skin) is 1.0 gram/70 kilogram man.

VX

Clinical Effects

Background
This nonvolatile military "nerve agent" is also known as Persistent Nerve Agent. An amber colored, odorless liquid, its droplets do not evaporate quickly, facilitating systemic absorption. It may remain in the environment for weeks or longer after being dispersed. VX is an extremely active anticholinesterase organophosphate compound that produces toxicity via cholinergic overdrive at muscarinic, nicotinic, and CNS cholinergic sites. Exposure can be by inhalation; the vapors are denser than air. The agent can also be absorbed following ingestion and eye contact.

Clinical Presentation
INHALATION:
Mild Exposure: Initial effects include miosis, rhinorrhea, and dyspnea.

Severe exposure: A large concentration of vapor causes sudden loss of consciousness and seizures followed by apnea and flaccid paralysis. Severe casualties have miosis and copious secretions from the nose and mouth. Unless they are paralyzed, they have fasciculations. "SLUDGE" (salivation, lacrimation, urination, defecation, and gastric emesis) occurs. Effects begin within seconds to minutes.

DERMAL: A very small drop may cause sweating and twitching at the site. A slightly larger drop may cause nausea, vomiting, and diarrhea. A large drop on the skin may cause loss of consciousness, seizures, apnea, and flaccid paralysis. Effects begin within 30 minutes (large amount) to 18 hours (small amount).

Fatalities
Death is a result of respiratory failure, CNS depression, and excessive secretions.

Treatment

Decontamination
INHALATION: Move to fresh air. Monitor for respiratory distress. If cough or difficulty in breathing develops, evaluate for hypoxia, respiratory tract irritation, bronchitis, or pneumonitis.

DERMAL: Remove contaminated clothing and jewelry. Discard contaminated clothing. Wash the skin, including hair and nails, vigorously with repeated soapings. Alternatively, use dilute (0.5%) hypochlorite (household bleach) followed by a thorough water rinse. A Skin Decontaminating Kit for military/civil defense contains applicator pads impregnated with Ambergard 555 ion-exchange resin and activated charcoal to be rubbed over contaminated skin and discarded. Use caution; potential for secondary contamination is high.

OCULAR: Remove contact lenses; irrigate eyes with copious amounts of 0.9% saline or water at room temperature for at least 15 minutes.

Antidotes
Specific antidotes include atropine and pralidoxime.

ATROPINE: Primarily effective for muscarinic effects; will not reverse nicotinic effects. The diagnostic dose (give if diagnosis uncertain) for adults is 1 mg IV or IM; for children, 0.25 mg (about 0.01 mg/kg) IV or IM. The therapeutic dose for adults is 2 to 5 mg slowly IV; for children, 0.05 mg/kg slowly IV. Repeat doses may be administered every 10 to 15 minutes as needed to achieve and maintain full atropinization (signaled by drying of pulmonary secretions).

PRALIDOXIME: Severe VX poisoning with nicotinic and/or CNS manifestations should be treated with pralidoxime. For adults, give 1 to 2 g IV at 0.5 g/min or mix in 250 mL of NS and infuse over 30 min.

For children, give 25 to 50 mg/kg, diluted to a 5% concentration in NS and infused over 20 to 30 min. MARK I autoinjector delivers 2 mg atropine/0.7 mL and 600 mg pralidoxime chloride/2 mL into two separate IM sites. Do not use in children less than 10 years old.

Bronchospasm
Use inhaled beta agonists if atropine alone is inadequate.

Seizures
Administer IV benzodiazepines, barbiturates.

Pulmonary Edema (Non-Cardiogenic)
Maintain ventilation and oxygenation. Monitor ABGs and/or pulse oximetry frequently. Early use of PEEP and mechanical ventilation may be needed. Succinylcholine should be avoided for intubation because paralysis may be prolonged.

Monitoring Parameters
Monitor ECG and respiratory function.

Range Of Toxicity

LCt50 of the vapor is 10 mg/min/m(3). LD50 (skin) is 10 mg/70 kg man.

Section 3

Treatment Modalities in an Attack

Activated Charcoal

Brand Names:
- *Actidose-Aqua*
- *Liqui-Char*

Class: *Gastrointestinal adsorbent*

How Supplied:
- Liquid: 12.5 gm, 15 gm, 25 gm, 30 gm, 50 gm

Use

Treatment of ingestion of poisons

Adult Dosage (Usual)

25 to 100 gm. Use a minimum of 240 mL of water per 30 gm.

Pediatric Dosage (Usual)

- *1 to 12 years:* 25 to 50 gm. Use a minimum of 240 mL of water per 30 gm.
- *Up to 1 year:* 1 gm/kg

Administration

- Administer as an aqueous slurry in awake patients who are able to protect their airway.
- Charcoal is most effective when administered within 1 hour of ingestion of poison.
- For vomiting (hazardous with caustic substance/volatile hydrocarbon ingestion), give saline cathartic/sorbitol with initial dose; do NOT repeat if bowel sounds are absent.

Precautionary Information

Contraindications
- Unprotected airway
- Gastrointestinal tract not anatomically intact
- Ingestion of most hydrocarbons

Common Adverse Effects
Aspiration
Black stools
GI obstruction
Vomiting

Notes

Routine use of a cathartic with activated charcoal is not recommended.

Albuterol

Brand Names:
- *Proventil*
- *Ventolin*
- *Volmax*

Class: *Sympathomimetic bronchodilator*

How Supplied:
- 90 mcg/actuation aerosol
- 8 mg extended-release tablet
- 0.083% inhalation solution
- 4 mg repeat-action tablet
- 0.5% solution for inhalation
- 4 mg sustained-release tablet
- 2 mg/5 mL syrup
- 2 mg tablet

Use

Treatment of asthma, bronchodilation

Adult Dosage (Usual)

- Aerosol, 1 to 2 puffs Q4-6H PRN
- Nebulized, 2.5 mg TID-QID
- 2 to 4 mg PO TID-QID;
  Sustained-release tablet, 4 to
  8 mg Q12H; MAX PO 32
  mg/day

Pediatric Dosage (Usual)

- *Under 12 years old:*
  Aerosol, 1 to 2 puffs QID
  Nebulized, 0.01 to 0.05 mL/kg
  0.5% solution Q4-6H
- *2 to 6 years old:* 0.1 to
  0.2 mg/kg/dose PO TID
- *6 to 12 years old:* 2 mg PO TID-
  QID, MAX 24 mg/day

Precautionary Information

Contraindications
Hypersensitivity to albuterol

Common Adverse Effects
Hypokalemia
Nausea
Nervousness
Palpitations
Tachycardia
Tremor

Drug Interactions
Monoamine Oxidase Inhibitors

Pregnancy Category
C

Breastfeeding
Unknown

Aminophylline

Class: *Xanthine bronchodilator*
How Supplied:
- Solution for injection: 25 mg/mL

Use

Phosgene inhalation exposure:
Prophylaxis of pulmonary edema
in patients exposed to 50 ppm for a
minute or more

Adult Dosage (Usual)

Post-exposure prophylaxis:
5 mg/kg IV loading dose, followed
by 1 mg/kg Q8-12H to maintain
serum levels at 10 to 20 mcg/mL

Precautionary Information

Contraindications
Hypersensitivity to ethylenedi-
amine or theophylline

Common Adverse Effects
Nausea
Tachycardia
Tremor
Vomiting

Drug Interactions
Adenosine
Allopurinol
Aminoglutethimide
Benzodiazepines
Butalbital
Carbamazepine
Cimetidine
Ciprofloxacin
Clinafloxacin
Diltiazem

Dipyridamole
Disulfiram
Enoxacin
Ephedrine
Erythromycin
Ethinyl Estradiol
Etintidine
Fluvoxamine
Fosphenytoin
Grepafloxacin
Halothane
Idrocilamide
Imipenem Interferon
Alfa-2a ipriflavone
Isoproterenol
Josamycin
Ketamine
Lithium
Mestranol
Mexiletine
Moricizine
Nilutamide
Norethindrone
Norfloxacin
Norgestrel
Pancuronium
Paroxetine
Pefloxacin
Pentobarbital
Pentoxifylline
Phenobarbital
Phenytoin
Pipemidic Acid
Piperine
Primidone
Propafenone
Propranolol
Prulifloxacin
Rifampin
Ritonavir
Ropivacaine

Secobarbital
St. John's Wort
Sulfinpyrazone
Tacrine
Tacrolimus
Thiabendazole
Ticlopidine
Troleandomycin
Verapamil
Viloxazine
Zafirlukast
Zileuton

Pregnancy Category
C

Breastfeeding
Safe

Amoxicillin

Brand Name: *Amoxil*
Class: *Penicillin*
How Supplied:
- Capsule: 250 mg, 500 mg
- Chewable tablet: 125 mg, 200 mg, 250 mg, 400 mg
- Oral suspension: 125 mg/5 mL, 200 mg/5 mL, 250 mg/5 mL, 400 mg/5 mL
- Tablet: 500 mg, 875 mg

Use

Anthrax, postexposure prophylaxis and treatment (alternative treatment)

Adult Dosage (Usual)

- *Cutaneous anthrax (alternative), proven susceptible strain:* 500 mg PO Q8H for 60 days

- *Inhaled anthrax:* Amoxicillin should not be used as single-drug therapy for treatment of inhalational anthrax.

Pediatric Dosage (Usual)

- *Postexposure prophylaxis and treatment in mass casualty settings, proven susceptible strain:* 80 mg/kg/day PO divided into 3 doses to be taken Q8H for 60 days (MAX: 500 mg/dose)
- *Cutaneous anthrax (alternative), proven susceptible strain:* 80 mg/kg/day PO divided into 3 doses to be taken Q8H for 60 days (MAX: 500 mg/dose)
- *Inhaled anthrax:* Amoxicillin should not be used as single-drug therapy for treatment of inhalational anthrax.

Dose Adjustments

Renal impairment

Administration

- Suspension is stable for 14 days; refrigeration is preferable but not required.
- Give with or without food.

Precautionary Information

Contraindications
Hypersensitivity to penicillins

Adverse Effects
Diarrhea
Headache
Nausea/vomiting
Rash
Seizures

Drug Interactions
Ethinyl Estradiol
Mestranol
Methotrexate
Norethindrone
Norgestrel
Typhoid Vaccine

Pregnancy Category
B

Breastfeeding
Safe

Amyl Nitrite

Brand Names:
- *Amyl Nitrate Aspirols*
- *Cyanide Antidote Package*

Class: *Antianginal*

How Supplied:
- Inhalant: 0.18 mL, 0.3 mL
- Kit: 0.3 mL

Use

Cyanide Exposure

Adult Dosage (Usual)

Cyanide antidote: 0.18 to 0.3 mL by inhalation

Administration

- Ampule should be broken and inhaled by the patient for 30 seconds each minute; new ampule should be used every 3 minutes.
- Ampule may be broken in gauze and held next to the nose and

mouth of spontaneously breathing patients. The broken ampule can be placed inside the resuscitation bag or into the inner lip of the face mask for patients requiring assisted ventilation.
- Stop using when sodium nitrite is administered intravenously.

Precautionary Information

Contraindications
Hypersensitivity to organic nitrates

Common Adverse Effects
Dizziness
Headache
Hemolytic anemia
Methemoglobinemia
Tachycardia

Drug Interactions
Sildenafil

Pregnancy Category
C

Breastfeeding
Unknown

Anthrax Vaccine, Adsorbed

Brand Name: *Biothrax*
Class: Vaccine
How Supplied:
- 5 mL multidose vial

Use

Immunization of high risk individuals

Adult Dosage (Usual)

- *Primary immunization:* 0.5 mL SC every 2 weeks for 3 doses, then 0.5 mL at 6, 12, and 18 months
- *Postexposure:* 0.5 mL SC immediately postexposure, repeat at 2 and 4 weeks

Pediatric Dosage (Usual)

N/A

Administration

- Give SC; different sites should be used for each injection.
- Defer vaccine when acute respiratory or other infection is present, or if patient is receiving steroid therapy.
- Postexposure: Vaccine in conjunction with antibiotic therapy (eg, ciprofloxacin) is recommended.

Precautionary Information

Contraindications
- Severe reaction to previous dose of anthrax vaccine
- Persons who have recovered from prior clinical exposure

Common Adverse Effects
Erythema
Local irritation

Pregnancy Category
C

Breastfeeding
Unknown

Atropine

Class: *Anticholinergic*
How Supplied:
- Injection: 0.1 mg/mL,
  0.4 mg/mL, 1 mg/mL

Use

Nerve gas antidote

Adult Dosage (Usual)

- *Diagnostic dose:* 1 mg IV or IM
- *Therapeutic dose:* 2 to 5 mg
  slowly IV
- *Repeat doses:* Q10-30MIN PRN
  to achieve and maintain full
  atropinization
- *Continuous infusion:* 0.02 to
  0.08 mg/kg/hr

Pediatric Dosage (Usual)

- *Diagnostic dose:* 0.25 mg (approximately 0.01 mg/kg) IV or IM
- *Therapeutic dose:* 0.05 mg/kg
  slowly IV
- *Repeat doses:* Q10-30MIN PRN
  to achieve and maintain full
  atropinization
- *Continuous infusion:* 0.02 to
  0.08 mg/kg/hr

Dose Adjustments

Geriatric

Precautionary Information

Contraindications
- Hypersensitivity to anticholinergics
- Intestinal obstruction or atonia
- Myasthenia gravis
- Narrow-angle glaucoma
- Tachycardia secondary to thyro-
  toxicosis

Adverse Effects
Arrhythmias
Hyperthermia
Sedation
Visual impairment

Pregnancy Category
C

Breastfeeding
Controversial

Botulinum Antitoxin

Name: *Equine Botulinum Trivalent
(ABE) Antitoxin*
Class: *Botulism antitoxin*
How Supplied:
- Trivalent antitoxin can be
  obtained from the CDC via state
  and local health departments. If
  state or local health departments
  are unavailable, call the CDC at
  404-639-2206 or 404-639-2888
  (after hours) to obtain antitoxin.
- The distribution of antitoxin
  from regional depots may take
  several hours; therefore, standard detoxification techniques
  should be applied immediately.

Use

Botulism treatment

Adult Dosage (Usual)

Test dose to screen for hypersensitivity:

- *Skin test (in persons with allergies):* 0.05 mL of a 1:1000 dilution (in saline) intracutaneously. Read the reaction in 5 to 30 minutes.
- *Skin test (in persons without allergies):* 0.1 mL of a 1:100 dilution (in saline). Read the reaction in 5 to 30 minutes.
- *Positive skin test:* Wheal development (borders may be irregular) and erythema. The degree of wheal and erythema development may indicate the degree of hypersensitivity.
- *Eye test:* Except in small children, may be easier and more specific. Instill a drop of a 1:10 dilution of antitoxin/serum in physiologic saline in one eye; instill a drop of physiologic saline in the other eye as a control. Positive reaction: lacrimation and conjunctivitis appear in 10 to 30 minutes in the eye treated with the antitoxin/serum.

Treatment of botulism in patients with NO KNOWN sensitivity:

- a single 10-mL vial intravenously, diluted 1:10 in 0.9% saline solution

Treatment of botulism in patients with KNOWN sensitivity:

- The schedule of serial administration of diluted antitoxin/serum subcutaneously at 20 minute intervals (as long as there are no adverse reactions), as recommended by the manufacturer, is:

a. 0.05 mL of a 1:20 dilution
b. 0.1 mL of a 1:10 dilution
c. 0.3 mL of a 1:10 dilution
d. 0.1 mL undiluted serum
e. 0.2 mL undiluted serum
f. 0.5 mL undiluted serum

If a reaction occurs during the desensitization process, injections should be stopped for one hour. Then restart the desensitization series at the last dose which failed to cause a reaction, with 20 minute intervals between each desensitization dose.

Based on clinical judgment in the individual case, intravenous administration of the antitoxin/serum may be commenced if it is determined that desensitization has been effected. The first intravenous dose should be small and injected very slowly. Example: 0.1 mL diluted with 10 mL of sterile physiologic saline, 1 mL per minute. Larger doses may then be given similarly at 30 minute intervals.

Pediatric Dosage (Usual)

Test dose to screen for hypersensitivity: Same as adults

Treatment of botulism: Same as adults

Administration

- Administer antitoxin promptly to patients at first signs of botulism; do not delay treatment for microbiological testing.

- Administer by slow intravenous infusion.
- Diphenhydramine and epinephrine should be readily available during administration of test and treatment doses in case of adverse reaction.
- Additional doses are usually not required in foodborne botulism patients.
- Adequacy of neutralization by antitoxin can be confirmed by testing serum for toxin after treatment.
- Use of antitoxin for postexposure prophylaxis is limited; asymptomatic persons who have been exposed should remain under close observation and treated at first signs of botulism.
- One vial provides between 5,500 and 8,500 IU of each type-specific antigen.

Precautionary Information

Common Adverse Effects

Hypersensitivity reactions such as urticaria, serum sickness, or anaphylaxis

Pregnancy Category

Unknown

Breastfeeding

Unknown

Chloramphenicol

Brand Name: *Choloromycetin*
Class: *Antibiotic*
How Supplied:
- Injection: 1 gm

Use

- Anthrax (alternative treatment)
- Glanders (alternative treatment)
- Plague (alternative treatment)
- Rocky Mountain Spotted Fever (preferred treatment)
- Tularemia, contained casualty setting (alternative treatment)
- Typhus (preferred treatment)

Adult Dosage (Usual)

Anthrax

50 to 100 mg/kg/day IV or PO divided every 6 hours

Glanders

50 to 100 mg/kg/day (4 to 6 gm/day) IV divided every 6 hours plus streptomycin

Plague

- *Postexposure prophylaxis (alternative):* 25 mg/kg PO four times daily for 7 days
- *Treatment/contained or mass casualty setting (alternative):* 25 mg/kg IV or PO four times daily for 10 days

Rocky Mountain Spotted Fever

50 mg/kg/day PO divided every 6 hours, or 15 to 20 mg/kg IV loading dose, then 30 to 50 mg/kg/day IV divided every 6 hours

Tularemia
15 mg/kg IV every 6 hours for 14 to 21 days

Typhus
50 mg/kg/day IV or PO divided every 6 hours; continue 5 days after fever ends

Pediatric Dosage (Usual)

Anthrax
50 to 75 mg/kg/day IV or PO divided every 6 hours

Glanders
Same as adult dose

Plague
Same as adult dose

Rocky Mountain Spotted Fever
Same as adult dose

Tularemia
Same as adult dose

Typhus
Same as adult dose

Dose Adjustments

Renal impairment
Liver disease

Administration

Adjust dose based on serum levels.

Precautionary Information

Contraindications
Hypersensitivity to chloramphenicol products

Adverse Effects
Gray baby syndrome (children)
Irreversible aplastic anemia
Myelosuppression
Nausea/vomiting
Rash

Drug Interactions
Ceftazidime
Chlorpropamide
Cyclophosphamide
Cyclosporine
Dicumarol
Entacapone
Fosphenytoin
Glimepiride
Phenobarbital
Phenytoin
Rifampin
Tacrolimus
Tetanus Toxoid
Tolbutamide
Typhoid Vaccine
Warfarin

Pregnancy Category
C

Breastfeeding
Unsafe

Ciprofloxacin

Brand Name: *Cipro*
Class: *Fluoroquinolone antibiotic*
How Supplied:
- Powder for suspension: 250 mg/5 mL, 500 mg/5 mL
- Solution for injection: 200 mg, 400 mg
- Tablet: 250 mg, 500 mg, 750 mg

Use

- Anthrax, for postexposure prophylaxis and treatment
- Food Poisoning Agents, in adults (Shigella species, Escherichia coli, Campylobacter jejuni)
- Plague
- Tularemia
- Typhus

Adult Dosage (Usual)

Anthrax

- *Postexposure prophylaxis and treatment of anthrax, mass casualty setting (preferred initial treatment):* ciprofloxacin 500 mg PO BID for 60 days
- *Treatment of inhaled anthrax (preferred initial treatment):* ciprofloxacin 400 mg IV Q12H for 60 days Combination therapy with one or two additional antimicrobial agents is recommended for treatment of inhalational anthrax
- *Treatment of cutaneous anthrax (preferred initial treatment):* ciprofloxacin 500 mg PO Q12H for 60 days

Substitute oral antibiotics for intravenous antibiotics as soon as clinical condition improves.

Food Poisoning (Presumed Bacterial Diarrhea)

Treatment of food poisoning: 500 mg PO BID for 5 to 7 days

Pneumonic Plague

- *Postexposure prophylaxis*

(preferred treatment): 500 mg PO BID for 7 days
- *Treatment of plague; contained-casualty setting (alternative treatment):* ciprofloxacin 400 mg IV Q12H for 10 days
- *Treatment of plague; mass-casualty setting (preferred treatment):* ciprofloxacin 500 mg PO BID for 10 days

Substitute oral antibiotics for intravenous antibiotics as soon as clinical condition improves.

Typhus
Treatment of typhus: 500 mg PO BID

Tularemia

- *Postexposure prophylaxis (preferred treatment):* ciprofloxacin 500 mg PO BID for 14 days
- *Treatment of tularemia; contained-casualty setting (alternative treatment):* ciprofloxacin 400 mg IV Q12H for 10 days
- *Treatment of tularemia; mass-casualty setting (preferred treatment):* ciprofloxacin 500 mg PO BID for 14 days

Substitute oral antibiotics for intravenous antibiotics as soon as clinical condition improves.

Dosage in Pregnant Women
Same dose as non-pregnant adults.

Pediatric Dosage (Usual)

Anthrax

- *Postexposure prophylaxis and treatment of anthrax, mass casualty setting (preferred initial treatment):* ciprofloxacin 20 to 30 mg/kg/day PO divided BID for 60 days

- *Treatment of inhaled anthrax (preferred initial treatment):* ciprofloxacin 20 to 30 mg/kg/day IV divided Q12H for 60 days. Combination therapy with one or two additional antimicrobial agents is recommended for treatment of inhalational anthrax.

- *Treatment of cutaneous anthrax: (preferred initial treatment):* ciprofloxacin 20 to 30 mg/kg/day PO divided BID for 60 days

Substitute oral antibiotics for intravenous antibiotics as soon as clinical condition improves. Do not exceed 1 gram per day in children.

Pneumonic Plague

- *Postexposure prophylaxis (preferred treatment):* 20 mg/kg PO BID for 7 days

- *Treatment of plague; contained casualty setting (alternative treatment):* ciprofloxacin 15 mg/kg IV Q12H for 10 days

- *Treatment of plague; mass casualty setting (preferred treatment):* ciprofloxacin 20 mg/kg PO BID for 10 days

Substitute oral antibiotics for intravenous antibiotics as soon as clinical condition improves. Do not exceed 1 gram per day in children.

Tularemia

- *Treatment of tularemia; contained casualty setting (alternative treatment):* ciprofloxacin 15 mg/kg IV Q12H for 10 days

- *Postexposure prophylaxis (preferred treatment):* ciprofloxacin 15 mg/kg PO BID for 14 days

- *Treatment of tularemia; mass casualty setting (preferred treatment):* ciprofloxacin 15 mg/kg PO twice daily for 14 days

Substitute oral antibiotics for intravenous antibiotics as soon as clinical condition improves. Do not exceed 1 gram per day in children.

Precautionary Information

Contraindications

Hypersensitivity to ciprofloxacin or other quinolones

Common Adverse Effects

Diarrhea

Dizziness

Headache

Drug Interactions

Aluminum Carbonate, Basic

Aluminum Hydroxide

Aluminum Phosphate

Azlocillin

Calcium

Didanosine

Dihydroxyaluminum Aminoacetate

Dihydroxyaluminum Sodium Carbonate

Fennel Seed

Fosphenytoin

Glyburide

Iron

Magaldrate

Magnesium Carbonate

Magnesium Hydroxide

Magnesium Oxide

Magnesium Trisilicate

Olanzapine

Phenytoin

Probenecid

Ropinirole

Sucralfate

Teicoplanin

Theophylline

Typhoid Vaccine

Warfarin

Zinc

Pregnancy Category

C

Breastfeeding

Unsafe

Notes

For gastrointestinal and oropharyngeal anthrax, use regimens recommended for inhalational anthrax.

Additional antimicrobial agents to use with ciprofloxacin include rifampin, vancomycin, penicillin, ampicillin, chloramphenicol, imipenem, clindamycin, or clarithromycin.

Dexamethasone

Brand Name: *Decadron*

Class: *Adrenal Glucocorticoid*

How Supplied:

- Elixir: 0.5 mg/5 mL
- Solution for injection: 4 mg/mL, 24 mg/mL
- Tablet: 0.25 mg, 0.5 mg, 0.75 mg, 1.5 mg, 4 mg, 6 mg

Use

- Anthrax treatment (edema)
- Chloropicrin, oral exposure
- Phosgene oxime, oral exposure

Adult Dosage (Usual)

Anthrax Treatment (Edema)

0.75 to 0.9 mg/kg/day IV, PO, or IM divided Q6H

Chloropicrin, Oral Exposure

0.1 mg/kg/day PO

Phosgene Oxime, Oral Exposure

0.1 mg/kg/day PO

Pediatric Dosage (Usual)

Anthrax Treatment (Edema):

- 0.25 to 0.5 mg/kg Q6H IV, PO, or IM

Administration

Taper dose when discontinuing

Precautionary Information

Contraindications

- Hypersensitivity to dexamethasone
- Systemic fungal infections

Common Adverse Effects

Cushing's syndrome

GI distress

Impaired skin healing

Mild euphoria/depression

Muscle weakness

Drug Interactions

Alcuronium

Aldesleukin

Aminoglutethimide
Aspirin
Atracurium
Carbamazepine
Caspofungin
Cisatracurium
Doxacurium
Echinacea
Fosphenytoin
Gallamine
Ginseng
Hexafluorenium Bromide
Human Growth Hormone
Indinavir
Irinotecan
Licorice
Ma Huang
Metocurine
Mivacurium
Pancuronium
Phenobarbital
Phenytoin
Pipecuronium
Primidone
Rifampin
Rocuronium
Rotavirus Vaccine
Saiboku-to
Saquinavir
Thalidomide
Tubocurarine
Vaccines
Vecuronium

Pregnancy Category
C

Breastfeeding
Unsafe

Diazepam

Brand Names:
- *Diastat*
- *Valium*

Class: *Benzodiazepine*

How Supplied:
- Emulsion for injection: 5 mg/mL
- Gel: 2.5 mg, 5 mg, 10 mg, 15 mg, 20 mg
- Oral solution: 5 mg/mL
- Tablet: 2 mg, 5 mg, 10 mg

Use

- Anxiety, agitation
- Seizure control

Adult Dosage (Usual)

Anxiety, Agitation
0.1 mg/kg or 10 milligrams IV, IM, or PO

Seizure Control
5 to 10 mg IV, repeat Q5-10 MIN PRN; consider second agent if seizures persist or recur after diazepam 30 mg

Pediatric Dosage (Usual)

Anxiety, Agitation
0.25 to 0.4 mg/kg IV, IM, or PO

Seizure Control
0.2 to 0.5 mg/kg IV, repeat Q5 MIN PRN; consider second agent if seizures persist or recur after diazepam 10 mg in children over 5 years or 5 mg in children under 5 years. For children 6 to 12: 1 mg Q2-5 MIN IV up to a max of

10 mg, repeat Q2-4 HRS PRN. May be given per rectum (generally use twice the usual initial dose because of decreased absorption).

Dose Adjustments
Liver disease
Geriatrics

Administration

Administer IV over 2 to 3 minutes (maximum rate: 5 mg/min)

Precautionary Information

Contraindications
- Hypersensitivity to diazepam products
- Narrow angle glaucoma
- Patients less than 6 months of age

Adverse Effects
Ataxia
Fatigue
Hypotension
Respiratory depression
Sedation

Drug Interactions
Amitriptyline
Amprenavir
Buprenorphine
Clarithromycin
Dalfopristin
Digoxin
Disulfiram
Erythromycin
Fentanyl
Fluvoxamine
Isoniazid
Itraconazole
Josamycin
Kava
Mirtazapine
Phenytoin
Quinupristin
Rifampin
Roxithromycin
Theophylline
Troleandomycin

Pregnancy Category
D

Breastfeeding
Controversial

Dimercaprol

Brand Name: *BAL in Oil*
Class: *Heavy metal chelator*
How Supplied:
- Solution for injection: 100 mg/mL

Use

Heavy metal poisoning

Adult Dosage (Usual)

Arsenic Poisoning
3 to 5 mg/kg IM Q4-12H until symptoms resolve or another chelator is substituted

Lewisite Poisoning
3 mg/kg deep IM Q4H for 2 days, then Q6H for 1 day, then Q12H for up to 10 days.

Pediatric Dosage (Usual)

Arsenic Poisoning
Adult dose

Dose Adjustments

Renal impairment

Administration

- Inject dimercaprol deep into the muscle
- 2 mL procaine 2% may be administered at the injection site

Precautionary Information

Contraindications
- G6PD deficiency
- Alkyl mercury poisoning
- Hepatic insufficiency, except post-arsenical jaundice
- Iron, cadmium, or selenium poisoning

Adverse Effects
Constricted feeling in chest, limbs, jaw, abdomen
Elevated blood pressure and pulse
Headache
Lacrimation
Nausea/vomiting
Paresthesias
Rhinorrhea
Tremor

Pregnancy Category
C

Breastfeeding
Unknown

Dopamine Hydrochloride

Class: *Adrenergic*
How Supplied:
- Solution for injection: 40 mg/mL, 80 mg/mL, 160 mg/mL

Use

Hypotension

Adult Dosage (Usual)

5 to 20 mcg/kg/min

Pediatric Dosage (Usual)

Same as adult dose

Administration

- IV infusion only
- Extravasation may cause local tissue necrosis; central venous catheter is preferred

Precautionary Information

Contraindications
- Hypersensitivity to dopamine products
- Pheochromocytoma
- Tachyarrhythmias

Adverse Effects
Arrhythmias
Injection site necrosis
Nausea/vomiting

Drug Interactions
Entacapone
Ergonovine

Ergotamine

Fosphenytoin

Isocarboxazid

Pargyline

Phenelzine

Phenytoin

Selegiline

Tranylcypromine

Pregnancy Category

C

Breastfeeding

Unknown

Doxycycline

Brand Names:

- *Doryx*
- *Doxy 100*
- *Vibramycin*
- *Vibra-Tabs*

Class: *Tetracycline antibiotic*

How Supplied:

- Capsule: 50 mg, 100 mg
- Powder for injection: 100 mg
- Powder for oral suspension: 25 mg/5 mL
- Syrup: 50 mg/5mL
- Tablet: 100 mg

Use

- Anthrax
- Brucellosis
- Plague
- Q fever
- Rocky Mountain Spotted Fever
- Tularemia
- Typhus

Adult Dosage (Usual)

Anthrax

- *Postexposure prophylaxis and treatment of anthrax, mass casualty setting (preferred initial treatment):* doxycycline 100 mg PO BID for 60 days
- *Treatment of inhaled anthrax (preferred initial treatment):* doxycycline 100 mg IV Q12H for 60 days
- Combination therapy with one or two additional antimicrobial agents is recommended for treatment of inhalational anthrax.
- *Treatment of cutaneous anthrax (preferred initial treatment):* doxycycline 100 mg PO Q12H for 60 days
- Substitute oral antibiotics for intravenous antibiotics as soon as clinical condition improves.

Brucellosis

- *Acute brucellosis:* 100 mg PO BID for 6 weeks plus gentamicin, streptomycin, or rifampin
- *Neurobrucellosis:* 100 mg PO BID for 8 to 12 weeks plus gentamicin (or streptomycin) plus rifampin

Plague

- *Postexposure prophylaxis (preferred treatment):* 100 mg PO BID for 7 days
- *Treatment of plague; contained casualty setting (alternative treatment):* 100 mg IV Q12H or 200 mg IV every day for 10 days
- *Treatment of plague; mass casualty setting (preferred treatment):* 100 mg PO Q12H for 10 days

Q Fever

- *Acute Q Fever:* 100 mg PO BID for 2 to 3 weeks or until afebrile for 1 week
- *Chronic Q Fever:* 200 mg PO daily for 3 years to lifetime

Rocky Mountain Spotted Fever

100 mg PO BID for 10 to 21 days or 4.4 mg/kg/day IV up to 200 mg/day IV in divided doses Q12H

Tularemia

- *Postexposure prophylaxis (preferred treatment):* 100 mg PO BID for 14 days
- *Treatment of tularemia; contained casualty setting (alternative treatment):* 100 mg IV BID for 14 to 21 days
- *Treatment of tularemia; mass casualty setting (preferred treatment):* 100 mg PO BID for 14 days

Typhus

100 mg PO Q12H on day 1, then 100 mg/day PO in 1 or 2 divided doses; severe infections may require 100 mg PO Q12H for at least 10 days. Continue for 48 hours after fever ends.

Pediatric Dosage (Usual)

Anthrax

Children less than 45 kilograms:
- 2.2 mg/kg IV or PO Q12H for 60 days
- Route of administration: IV for initial treatment of inhaled anthrax; PO for postexposure prophylaxis, treatment of cutaneous anthrax, and treatment of anthrax in mass casualty setting

- Combination therapy with one or two additional antimicrobial agents is recommended for treatment of inhalational anthrax
- Substitute oral antibiotics for intravenous antibiotics as soon as clinical condition improves

Children (older than 8 years) greater than 45 kilograms: See adult dosing

Brucellosis

- *Acute brucellosis, over 8 years:* 1 to 2 mg/kg PO BID for 6 weeks
- *Neurobrucellosis, over 8 years:* 2 mg/kg PO BID for minimum of 8 weeks

Plague

Children less than 45 kilograms:
- *Post-exposure prophylaxis (preferred treatment):* 2.2 mg/kg PO Q12H for 7 days
- *Treatment of plague; contained casualty setting (alternative treatment):* 2.2 mg/kg IV Q12H for 10 days
- *Treatment of plague; mass casualty setting (preferred treatment):* 2.2 mg/kg PO Q12H for 10 days

Children greater than 45 kilograms: See adult dosing

Rocky Mountain Spotted Fever

1.5 mg/kg PO or IV Q12H for 10 to 21 days

Tularemia

Children less than 45 kilograms:
- *Post-exposure prophylaxis (preferred treatment):* 2.2 mg/kg PO Q12H for 14 days

- *Treatment of tularemia; contained casualty setting (alternative treatment):* 2.2 mg/kg IV Q12H for 14 to 21 days
- *Treatment of tularemia; mass casualty setting (preferred treatment):* 2.2 mg/kg PO Q12H for 14 days

Children greater than 45 kilogram: See adult dosing

Typhus

- Treatment of typhus, over 8 years: 2 mg/kg PO Q12H on day 1, then 2.2 mg/kg/day PO in 1 to 2 divided doses; severe infections may require 4.4 mg/kg/day PO Q12H. Continue for 5 days after fever ends.

Administration

- MAX 200 mg/min; if IV administration is not feasible.
- Continuous infusion may be more beneficial than bolus dosing.

Precautionary Information

Contraindications

- Children under 8 years of age
- Hypersensitivity to doxycycline products or tetracycline

Common Adverse Effects

Epigastric distress
Photosensitivity

Drug Interactions

Aluminum Carbonate, Basic
Aluminum Hydroxide
Aluminum Phosphate
Bismuth Subsalicylate
Calcium Carbonate
Carbamazepine
Cisatracurium
Dicumarol
Dihydroxyaluminum Aminoacetate
Dihydroxyaluminum Sodium Carbonate
Ethinyl Estradiol
Fosphenytoin
Iron
Isotretinoin
Magaldrate
Magnesium
Mestranol
Methotrexate
Phenobarbital
Phenytoin
Porfimer
Rapacuronium
Rifampin
Warfarin

Pregnancy Category

D

Breastfeeding

Unknown

Notes

For gastrointestinal and oropharyngeal anthrax, use regimens recommended for inhalational anthrax.

Additional antimicrobial agents to use with ciprofloxacin include rifampin, vancomycin, penicillin, ampicillin, chloramphenicol, imipenem, clindamycin, or clarithromycin.

Erythromycin

Brand Names:
- *E-Mycin*
- *E.E.S.*
- *Eryc*
- *Eryped*
- *Ery-Tab*
- *Erythrocin*
- *PCE*

Class: *Macrolide antibiotic*

How Supplied:
- Capsule: 250 mg
- Chewable tablet: 200 mg
- Oral suspension: 100 mg/2.5 mL, 200 mg/5 ml, 400 mg/5 mL
- Solution for injection: 500 mg/vial, 1 gm/vial
- Tablet: 250 mg, 333 mg, 400 mg, 500 mg

Use

- Anthrax
- Q Fever

Adult Dosage (Usual)

Anthrax

Treatment for anthrax (alternative treatment): 250 mg PO Q6H

Q fever

Treatment for Q fever (alternative treatment): 500 mg PO QID for 10 days

Pediatric Dosage (Usual)

Anthrax

Treatment of anthrax (alternative treatment): 40 mg/kg/day PO divided Q6H

Q Fever

Treatment of Q fever (alternative treatment): 40 mg/kg/day PO in 4 divided doses for 10 days

Dose Adjustments

Liver disease

Precautionary Information

Contraindications
- Hypersensitivity to erythromycin products
- Liver disease (estolate salt)
- Concomitant therapy with astemizole or terfenadine
- Concomitant therapy with cisapride

Adverse Effects

Cramping
Diarrhea
Hepatic dysfunction
Nausea/vomiting

Drug Interactions

Alfentanil
Alprazolam
Anisindione
Astemizole
Atorvastatin
Buspirone
Carbamazepine
Cerivastatin
Cilostazol
Cisapride
Clozapine
Colchicine
Cyclosporine
Diazepam
Dicumarol
Digoxin

Dihydroergotamine
Disopyramide
Dolasetron
Entacapone
Ergotamine
Ethinyl Estradiol
Fluvastatin
Gatifloxacin
Grepafloxacin
Halofantrine
Imatinib
Itraconazole
Levonorgestrel
Lovastatin
Mestranol
Midazolam
Moxifloxacin
Norethindrone
Norgestrel
Phenprocoumon
Pimozide
Pravastatin
Quinidine
Sertraline
Sildenafil
Simvastatin
Sirolimus
Sparfloxacin
Tacrolimus
Terfenadine
Theophylline
Triazolam
Trimetrexate
Valproic Acid
Warfarin
Zafirlukast

Pregnancy Category
B

Breastfeeding
Safe

Erythromycin Lactobionate

Class: *Macrolide antibiotic*
How Supplied:
- Solution for injection:
  500 mg/vial, 1 gm/vial

Use

Anthrax

Adult Dosage (Usual)

Treatment of anthrax (alternative treatment): 15 to 20 mg/kg/day IV divided Q6H, MAX 4 gm/day

Pediatric Dosage (Usual)

Treatment of anthrax (alternative treatment): 20 to 40 mg/kg/day IV divided Q6H (1 to 2 hour infusion)

Dose Adjustments

Liver disease

Precautionary Information

Contraindications
- Hypersensitivity to erythromycin products
- Liver disease (estolate salt)
- Concomitant therapy with astemizole or terfenadine
- Concomitant therapy with cisapride

Adverse Effects
Cramping
Diarrhea

Hepatic dysfunction
Nausea/vomiting

Drug Interactions
Alfentanil
Alprazolam
Anisindione
Astemizole
Atorvastatin
Buspirone
Carbamazepine
Cerivastatin
Cilostazol
Cisapride
Clozapine
Colchicine
Cyclosporine
Diazepam
Dicumarol
Digoxin
Dihydroergotamine
Disopyramide
Dolasetron
Entacapone
Ergotamine
Ethinyl Estradiol
Fluvastatin
Gatifloxacin
Grepafloxacin
Halofantrine
Imatinib
Itraconazole
Levonorgestrel
Lovastatin
Mestranol
Midazolam
Moxifloxacin
Norethindrone
Norgestrel
Phenprocoumon
Pimozide
Pravastatin

Quinidine
Sertraline
Sildenafil
Simvastatin
Sirolimus
Sparfloxacin
Tacrolimus
Terfenadine
Theophylline
Triazolam
Trimetrexate
Valproic Acid
Warfarin
Zafirlukast

Pregnancy Category
B

Breastfeeding
Safe

Filgrastim

Brand Name: *Neupogen*
Class: *Colony stimulating factor*
How Supplied:
- Injection: 300 mcg/mL, 600 mcg/mL

Use

Treatment of neutropenia after dermal or inhalation exposure to sulfur mustard gas

Adult Dosage (Usual)

5 mcg/kg/day SC or IV over 15 to 30 minutes; continue for 2 weeks or until the absolute neutrophil count (ANC) surpasses 10,000/mm3

Precautionary Information

Contraindications
- Concomitant chemo- or radio-therapy
- Hypersensitivity to *E.coli*-derived proteins or filgrastim

Adverse Effects
Bone pain
Flu-like symptoms
Nausea/vomiting

Pregnancy Category
C

Breastfeeding
Unknown

Notes

Do not dilute to concentrations of less than 5 mcg/mL; do not dilute with saline.

Obtain CBC with platelets before initiating therapy; monitor twice weekly during therapy.

Fluorometholone

Brand Names:
- *FML Forte Liquifilm*
- *FML Liquifilm*
- *FML S.O.P.*
- *Fluor-OP*
- *Flarex*

Class: *Ophthalmic corticosteroid*

How Supplied:
- Ointment: 0.1%
- Solution: 0.1%
- Suspension: 0.25%, 0.1%

Use

Ophthalmic burns, grade 3 or 4

Adult Dosage (Usual)

Apply 2 drops every 2 hours initially, then 4 times daily

Precautionary Information

Contraindications
- Epithelial herpes simplex keratitis
- Fungal diseases of the ocular structures
- Hypersensitivity to any of the components of the preparation
- Mycobacterial infection of the eye
- Vaccinia
- Varicella and other viral diseases of the cornea and conjunctiva

Common Adverse Effects
Cataracts
Glaucoma
Infections

Pregnancy Category
C

Breastfeeding
Unknown

Gentamicin Sulfate

Brand Name: *Garamycin*
Class: *Aminoglycoside antibiotic*
How Supplied:
- Solution for injection: 10 mg/mL, 40 mg/mL

Use

- Brucellosis (preferred treatment)
- Plague (preferred treatment)
- Tularemia (preferred treatment)

Adult Dosage (Usual)

Brucellosis

- *Treatment of brucellosis:* 2 mg/kg IV loading dose, then 1.7 mg/kg IV every 8 hours or 5 mg/kg IV once daily for 7 to 10 days PLUS doxycycline OR cotrimoxazole for 6 weeks
- *Treatment of neurobrucellosis:* 2 mg/kg IV loading dose, then 1.7 mg/kg IV every 8 hours or 5 to 7mg/kg IV once daily for 2 to 4 weeks PLUS doxycycline OR cotrimoxazole PLUS rifampin for 8 to 12 weeks

Plague

Treatment of plague; contained casualty setting: 5 mg/kg IV or IM once daily, or 2 mg/kg loading dose, then 1.7 mg/kg IV or IM every 8 hours for 10 days

Tularemia

Treatment of tularemia; contained casualty setting: 5 mg/kg IV or IM once daily for 10 days

Pediatric Dosage (Usual)

Brucellosis

- *Treatment of brucellosis:* 2 mg/kg IV Q8H for 7 to 10 days PLUS doxycycline (age over 8 years) OR cotrimoxazole for 6 weeks
- *Treatment of neurobrucellosis:* 2 mg/kg IV Q8H for 2 to 4 weeks PLUS doxycycline (age over 8 years) OR cotrimoxazole PLUS rifampin for 8 to 12 weeks

Plague

- *Treatment of plague; contained casualty setting; infants and children:* 2.5 mg/kg IV every 8 hours for 10 days
- *Treatment of plague; contained casualty setting; neonates:* 2.5 mg/kg IV every 12 hours for 10 days

Tularemia

Treatment of tularemia; contained casualty setting: 2.5 mg/kg IV or IM every 8 hours for 10 days

Dose Adjustments

Geriatrics
Renal impairment

Administration

Dilute in 50 to 200 mL NS or D5W, infuse over 30 to 120 minutes

Precautionary Information

Contraindications
Hypersensitivity to gentamicin

Common Adverse Effects
Nephrotoxicity
Ototoxicity

Drug Interactions
Bumetanide
Capreomycin
Carboplatin
Cephalosporins
Cidofovir

Cyclosporine
Ethacrynic Acid
Furosemide
Indomethacin
Magnesium
Methoxyflurane
Nondepolarizing Neuromuscular
Blockers
Piretanide
Polygeline
Succinylcholine
Tacrolimus
Typhoid Vaccine
Vancomycin

Pregnancy Category
D

Breastfeeding
Controversial

Hydrocortisone

Brand Names:
■ Cortef
■ Hydrocortone

Class: *Adrenal glucocorticoid*

How Supplied:
■ Tablet: 5 mg, 10 mg, 20 mg

Use

Brucellosis

Adult Dosage (Usual)

5 mg/km/day orally in 3 divided
doses for 3 to 4 days

Dose Adjustments

Liver disease

Precautionary Information

Contraindications
■ Hypersensitivity to hydrocortisone
■ Systemic fungal infections

Common Adverse Effects
Depression
Fluid retention
GI distress
Mild euphoria

Drug Interactions
Candesartan
Chlorthalidone
Ethacrynic Acid
Furosemide
Hydrochlorothiazide
Neostigmine
Phenobarbital
Pyridostigmine
Rifampin
Vaccines

Pregnancy Category
D

Breastfeeding
Controversial

5-Hydroxy-tryptophan (5-HTP)

Class: *Antidepressant*

How Supplied:
■ Capsules: 25 mg, 50 mg,
100 mg, 200 mg

Use

LSD-induced psychosis

Adult Dosage (Usual)

400 mg/day PO, plus carbidopa 100 mg/day

Precautionary Information

Contraindications

- Hypersensitivity to 5-HTP
- Use with caution in patients taking other antidepressants

Adverse Effects

Anorexia
Ataxia
Diarrhea
Dyspnea
Eosinophilia
Headache
Hypertension
Hyperventilation
Hypotension
Insomnia
Mania
Mental agitation
Nausea/vomiting
Palpitations
Paresthesia
Psychosis
Sedation
Stomach pain

Drug Interactions

Carbidopa
Fluoxetine
Monoamine Oxidase Inhibitors

Pregnancy

Unknown

Breastfeeding

Unknown

Levofloxacin

Brand Name: *Levaquin*
Class: *Fluoroquinolone antibiotic*
How Supplied:

- Solution for injection: 5 mg/mL, 25 mg/mL
- Tablet: 250 mg , 500 mg, 750 mg

Use

Anthrax

Adult Dosage (Usual)

Treatment of anthrax; contained or mass casualty setting or postexposure prophylaxis (alternative initial treatment): 500 mg IV or PO Q24H

Dose Adjustments

Renal impairment

Administration

- Infuse IV solution over at least 60 minutes
- Do not give tablets with antacids

Precautionary Information

Contraindications

Hypersensitivity to levofloxacin products or other quinolones

Adverse Effects

Diarrhea
Headache
Nausea/vomiting
Torsade de pointes arrhythmias

Drug Interactions

Acecainide
Ajmaline
Aluminum Carbonate, Basic
Aluminum Hydroxide
Aluminum Phosphate
Amiodarone
Antidiabetic Agents
Azimilide
Bretylium
Calcium Carbonate
Didanosine
Dihydroxyaluminum Aminoacetate
Dihydroxyaluminum Sodium
Carbonate
Disopyramide
Dofetilide
Fennel Seed
Ibutilide
Iron
Magaldrate
Magnesium Carbonate
Magnesium Hydroxide
Magnesium Oxide
Magnesium Trisilicate
Moricizine
Nonsteroidal Anti-inflammatory
    Agents
Phenothiazines
Pirmenol
Prajmaline
Procainamide
Quinidine
Recainam
Sematilide
Sotalol
Sucralfate
Tedisamil
Typhoid Vaccine
Warfarin
Zinc

Pregnancy Category

C

Breastfeeding

Unsafe

Lidocaine

Brand Name: *Xylocaine*
Class: *Amide anesthetic*
How Supplied:
- Solution for injection: 1%, 1.5%

Use

Ventricular arrhythmias

Adult Dosage (Usual)

Arrhythmia: Administer bolus load of 1 to 1.5 mg/kg IVP; begin maintenance infusion of 1 to 4 mg/min; give 0.5 mg/kg bolus 10 minutes after initial load

Pediatric Dosage (Usual)

Arrhythmia: 1 mg/kg IV bolus followed by a continuous infusion of 20 to 50 mcg/kg/min

Dose Adjustments

Liver disease

Administration

- Mix in D5W or NS to a concentration of 4 mg/mL.
- For continuous caudal or epidural anesthesia repeat max doses no sooner than every 90 minutes.

Precautionary Information

Contraindications
Hypersensitivity to lidocaine or amide-type anesthetics

Common Adverse Effects
Drowsiness
Hypotension
Seizures
Tremors

Drug Interactions
Amiodarone
Amprenavir
Arbutamine
Cimetidine
Cisatracurium
Dalfopristin
Dihydroergotamine
Dofetilide
Fosphenytoin
Hyaluronidase
Metoprolol
Nadolol
Nitrous Oxide
Penbutolol
Phenytoin
Propofol
Propranolol
Quinupristin
Rapacuronium
Succinylcholine
Tocainide

Pregnancy Category
B

Breastfeeding
Safe

Lorazepam

Brand Name: *Ativan*
Class: *Benzodiazepine*
How Supplied:
- Solution for injection: 2 mg/mL, 4 mg/mL
- Tablet: 0.5 mg, 1 mg, 2 mg

Use

- Anxiety, agitation
- Seizure control

Adult Dosage (Usual)

Anxiety, Agitation
1 to 2 mg IM

Seizure Control
2 to 8 mg IV; may repeat in 10 to 15 minutes if seizures persist

Pediatric Dosage (Usual)

Seizure Control
0.05 to 0.1 mg/kg IV (max 4 mg/dose) repeated twice at intervals of 10 to 15 minutes

Dose Adjustments

Geriatrics
Liver disease
Renal impairment

Administration

Administration rate should not exceed 2mg/min

Precautionary Information

Contraindications
- Hypersensitivity to lorazepam products
- Narrow angle glaucoma
- Physical and psychological dependence

Adverse Effects
Disorientation
Dizziness
Respiratory depression
Sedation
Weakness

Drug Interactions
Kava
Probenecid
Theophylline
Valproic Acid

Pregnancy Category
D

Breastfeeding
Controversial

Magnesium Sulfate

Class: *Electrolyte/mineral/nutrient*
How Supplied:
- IV solution: 40 mg/mL, 80 mg/mL, 125 mg/mL, 500 mg/mL

Use

Arrhythmias (torsade de pointes) following acute arsenic ingestion

Adult Dosage (Usual)

Torsade de pointes: 2 gm (16 mEq) in 50 to 100 mL D5W IV over 5 minutes, followed if needed by a second 2 gm bolus and infusion of 3 to 50 mg/min in unresponsive patients or with recurrence of dysrhythmias

Pediatric Dosage (Usual)

Torsade de pointes: 25 to 50 mg/kg diluted to 10 mg/mL IV infusion over 5 to 15 minutes

Administration

For IV administration, dilute to a concentration of 20% or less in D5W or NS. Use 20% concentration in children. Infuse slowly.

Precautionary Information

Contraindications
Heart block
Severe renal disease

Adverse Effects
Flushing
Hypotension
Muscle weakness

Drug Interactions
Allopurinol
Amikacin
Amprenavir
Aspirin
Atevirdine
Captopril
Cefdinir
Cefpodoxime
Chloroquine
Ciprofloxacin
Cisatracurium

Delavirdine
Demeclocycline
Dibekacin
Dicumarol
Digoxin
Doxycycline
Enoxacin
Felodipine
Fexofenadine
Fleroxacin
Gabapentin
Gatifloxacin
Gemifloxacin
Gentamicin
Grepafloxacin
Isradipine
Itraconazole
Kanamycin
Ketoconazole
Labetalol
Lansoprazole
Levofloxacin
Lomefloxacin
Mefenamic acid
Minocycline
Misoprostol
Moxifloxacin
Mycophenolate Mofetil
Nalidixic Acid
Netilmicin
Nicardipine
Nifedipine
Norfloxacin
Ofloxacin
Oral Phosphates
Oxytetracycline
Pefloxacin
Penicillamine
Quinidine
Rapacuronium
Rocuronium

Rufloxacin
Sodium Polystyrene Sulfonate
Sotalol
Sparfloxacin
Streptomycin
Succinylcholine
Temafloxacin
Tetracycline
Ticlopidine
Tipranavir
Tobramycin
Trovafloxacin
Vecuronium
Zalcitabine

Pregnancy Category
B

Breastfeeding
Safe

Methylpred-nisolone

Brand Name:
- *Solu-Medrol*

Class: *Adrenal glucocorticoid*

How Supplied:
- Powder for solution: 40 mg, 125 mg, 500 mg, 1 gm, 2 gm

Use

- Brucellosis
- Pulmonary edema
- Shock

Adult Dosage (Usual)

Brucellosis
10 to 40 mg IV, repeat up to 6 times per day

Pulmonary Edema
- *Prophylaxis:* 1 gm IV
- *Treatment:* 1 gm IV every 12 to 24 hours for 1 or more doses

Shock
30 mg/kg IV over 30 minutes, may repeat every 4 to 6 hours, not beyond 48 to 72 hours

Administration

May be administered by IV push over 3 to 5 minutes, or dilute in D5W or NS and infuse over 20 to 30 minutes

Precautionary Information

Contraindications
Hypersensitivity to methylpred-nisolone
Systemic fungal infections

Adverse Effects
Cushing's syndrome
GI distress
Impaired skin healing
Mild euphoria/depression

Drug Interactions
Acenocoumarol
Acuronium
Aldesleukin
Aspirin
Atracurium
Carbamazepine
Cisatracurium
Clarithromycin
Cyclosporine
Dalfopristin
Diltiazem
Doxacurium

Echinacea
Fluindione
Fosphenytoin
Gallamine
Ginseng
Hexafluorenium Bromide
Human Growth Hormone
Hydrochlorothiazide
Itraconazole
Ketoconazole
Licorice
Ma Huang
Metocurine
Mibefradil
Mivacurium
Pancuronium
Phenobarbital
Phenytoin
Pipecuronium
Primidone
Quinupristin
Rifampin
Rocuronium
Rotavirus Vaccine
Saiboku-to
Tacrolimus
Troleandomycin
Tubocurarine
Vaccines
Vecuronium

Pregnancy Category
Not rated

Breastfeeding
Controversial

Metoclopramide Hydrochloride

Brand Name: *Reglan*
Class: *Antiemetic*
How Supplied:
- Solution for injection: 5 mg/mL

Use

Trichothecene mycotoxins exposure

Adult Dosage (Usual)

1 mg/kg IV in combination with PO activated charcoal, PO magnesium sulfate, and IV dexamethasone

Dose Adjustments

Renal impairment

Administration

Maximum concentration:
5 mg/mL; maximum rate: 5 mg/min

Precautionary Information

Contraindications
- Hypersensitivity to metoclopramide products
- Pheochromocytoma
- Seizures

Adverse Effects
Drowsiness
Fatigue
Restlessness

Drug Interactions
Atovaquone
Cabergoline
Cyclosporine
Digoxin
Levodopa
Mivacurium
Sertraline
Succinylcholine
Tacrolimus
Thiopental

Pregnancy Category
B

Breastfeeding
Controversial

Norepinephrine Bitartrate

Brand Name: *Levophed*
Class: *Adrenergic*
How Supplied:
- Solution for infusion: 1 mg/mL

Use

- Acute hypotension
- Cardiac arrest (adjunctive therapy)
- Shock

Adult Dosage (Usual)

Acute Hypotension
- *Initial:* 8 to 12 mcg/min IV to establish a low normal BP (systolic, 80 to 100 mmHg)
- *Maintenance:* 2 to 4 mcg/min IV

Pediatric Dosage (Usual)

Acute Hypotension
0.05 to 0.3 mcg/kg/min; infuse at 0.1 mcg/kg/min, titrate to desired effect

Administration

- Avoid extravasation
- Dilute in D5W or NS to concentration of 4 to 16 mcg/mL

Precautionary Information

Contraindications
Blood volume deficit

Common Adverse Effects
Anxiety
Arrhythmias
HTN
Nausea/vomiting
Urinary retention

Drug Interactions
Chlorpromazine
Clorgyline
Dihydroergotamine
Entacapone
Furazolidone
Guanethidine
Isocarboxazid
Moclobemide
Phenelzine
Selegiline
Tranylcypromine
Tricyclic Antidepressants

Pregnancy Category
C

Breastfeeding
Unknown

Ofloxacin

Brand Names:
- *Floxin*
- *Floxin IV*

Class: *Fluoroquinolone antibiotic*

How Supplied:
- Solution for infusion: 4 mg/mL, 40 mg/mL
- Tablet: 200 mg, 300 mg, 400 mg

Use

- Anthrax
- Q fever

Adult Dosage (Usual)

Anthrax
Contained or mass casualty setting or postexposure prophylaxis (alternative initial therapy): 400 mg IV or PO Q12H

Q fever
200 mg PO Q12H for 2 to 3 weeks or until afebrile for 1 week

Dose Adjustments

Liver disease
Renal impairment

Administration

- Do not administer with food or antacids; offer plenty of fluids.
- Intravenous ofloxacin should be infused over a period of at least 60 minutes

Precautionary Information

Contraindications

Hypersensitivity to ofloxacin or other fluoroquinolones

Adverse Effects

Diarrhea

Dizziness

Headache

Insomnia

Nausea

Drug Interactions

Aluminum Carbonate, Basic

Aluminum Hydroxide

Aluminum Phosphate

Calcium Carbonate

Didanosine

Dihydroxyaluminum Aminoacetate

Dihydroxyaluminum Sodium Carbonate

Fennel Seed

Iron

Magaldrate

Magnesium Carbonate

Magnesium Hydroxide

Magnesium Oxide

Magnesium Trisilicate

Nonsteroidal Anti-inflammatory Agents

Sucralfate

Typhoid Vaccine

Warfarin

Zinc

Pregnancy Category

C

Breastfeeding

Unsafe

Penicillin G Potassium

Brand Name: *Pfizerpen for Injection*
Class: *Penicillin*
How Supplied:
- Powder for injection: 1 million IU

Use

Anthrax (adjunctive treatment)

Adult Dosage (Usual)

Treatment of inhalational anthrax (adjunct); proven susceptible strain:
- 4 million units IV every 4 hours for 60 days
- Penicillin should not be used as single-drug therapy

Pediatric Dosage (Usual)

Treatment of inhalational anthrax (adjunct); proven susceptible strain:
- *Less than 12 years of age:* 50,000 units/kg IV every 6 hours for 60 days
- *12 years and older:* 4 million units IV every 4 hours for 60 days
- Penicillin should not be used as single-drug therapy.

Dose Adjustments

Renal impairment

Precautionary Information

Contraindications

Hypersensitivity to penicillin

Common Adverse Effects
Diarrhea
Nausea/vomiting
Rash

Drug Interactions
Cholestyramine
Ethinyl Estradiol
Mestranol
Methotrexate
Norethindrone
Norgestrel
Typhoid Vaccine

Pregnancy Category
B

Breastfeeding
Safe

Penicillin V Potassium

Brand Names:
- *Penicillin VK*
- *Veetids*

Class: *Penicillin*

How Supplied:
- Powder for oral suspension: 125 mg/5 mL, 250 mg/5 mL
- Tablet: 250 mg, 500 mg

Use

Anthrax

Adult Dosage (Usual)

- *Treatment of inhaled anthrax (adjunct):* 200 to 500 mg PO QID
- Penicillin should not be used as single-drug therapy.

Pediatric Dosage (Usual)

- *Treatment of inhaled anthrax (adjunct):* 25 to 50 mg/kg/day PO in divided doses BID or QID
- Penicillin should not be used as single-drug therapy.

Dose Adjustments

Renal impairment

Administration

Give on an empty stomach.

Precautionary Information

Contraindications
Hypersensitivity to penicillins

Common Adverse Effects
Diarrhea
Nausea/vomiting
Rash

Drug Interactions
Ethinyl Estradiol
Guar Gum
Mestranol
Methotrexate
Norethindrone
Norgestrel
Typhoid Vaccine

Pregnancy Category
B

Breastfeeding
Safe

Permethrin

Brand Names:
- *Elimite*
- *Nix*

Class: *Scabicide*

How Supplied:
- 1% scalp application
- 1%, 5% topical cream
- 1% topical lotion

Use

Typhus

Adult Dosage (Usual)

Use sufficient volume to saturate hair/scalp

Pediatric Dosage (Usual)

- *Over 2 months:* Same as adults
- *2 months and younger:* Safety and effectiveness is unknown

Administration

- Use after the hair has been washed, rinsed with water, and towel dried.
- Drug should remain in contact with the hair for 10 minutes before being rinsed off with water.
- A single treatment is sufficient for the elimination of head lice.
- In epidemic settings, a second application is recommended 2 weeks after the first.

Precautionary Information

Contraindications
Hypersensitivity to permethrin or chrysanthemums

Adverse Effects
Burning
Erythema
Pruritus
Rash
Stinging
Swelling

Pregnancy Category
B

Breastfeeding
Unknown

Phenytoin

Brand Name: *Dilantin*

Class: *Anticonvulsant*

How Supplied:
- Capsule: 100 mg
- Chewable tablet: 50 mg
- Extended-release capsule: 30 mg, 100 mg
- Oral suspension: 125 mg/5 mL
- Solution for injection: 50 mg/mL

Use

Seizure control

Adult Dosage (Usual)

- *Loading dose:* 15 to 18 mg/kg by VERY SLOW IV PUSH. Do not exceed 0.5 mg/kg/min or 50 mg/min
- *Maintenance dose:* 100 mg PO or IV Q6-8H; maintain a serum concentration between 10 to 20 mcg/mL

Pediatric Dosage (Usual)

- *Loading dose:* 15 to 20 mg/kg or 250 mg/square meter. Do not exceed 0.5 to 1.5mg/kg/min; maximum for neonates is 1 to 3 mg/kg/min

Dose Adjustments

Geriatrics
Hepatic disease
Renal impairment

Administration

If dilution is necessary, dilute with NS to a concentration of 1 to 10 mg/mL. Avoid D5W as the IV diluent.

Precautionary Information

Contraindications

Hypersensitivity to phenytoin or hydantoin products

Adverse Effects

Ataxia
Blood dyscrasias
Cardiovascular toxicity
Lethargy
Nystagmus

Drug Interactions

Acenocoumarol
Acetaminophen
Acetazolamide
Acetyldigoxin
Acyclovir
Amiodarone
Amitriptyline
Amoxapine
Amprenavir
Anisindione
Apazone
Atorvastatin
Beclamide
Betamethasone
Bleomycin
Bromfenac
Busulfan
Capecitabine
Carbamazepine
Carboplatin
Carmustine
Caspofungin
Chloramphenicol
Chlordiazepoxide
Chlorpheniramine
Cimetidine
Ciprofloxacin
Cisatracurium
Cisplatin
Clarithromycin
Clobazam
Clofazimine
Clomipramine
Clozapine
Cortisone
Cyclosporine
Deflazacort
Delavirdine
Desipramine
Dexamethasone
Diazepam
Diazoxide
Dicumarol
Digitoxin
Diltiazem
Disopyramide
Disulfiram
Dopamine
Dothiepin

Doxepin	Nisoldipine
Doxorubicin	Norethindrone
Doxorubicin Hydrochloride	Norgestrel
Liposome	Nortriptyline
Doxycycline	Omeprazole
Ethinyl Estradiol	Oxcarbazepine
Ethosuximide	Paclitaxel
Felbamate	Pancuronium
Fluconazole	Paroxetine
Fludrocortisone	Phenprocoumon
Fluoxetine	Phensuximide
Fluvoxamine	Phenylbutazone
Folic Acid	Pipecuronium
Hydrocortisone	Piperine
Ibuprofen	Praziquantel
Imipramine	Prednisolone
Indinavir	Prednisone
Isoniazid	Progabide
Itraconazole	Protriptyline
Lamotrigine	Quetiapine
Levodopa	Quinidine
Levonorgestrel	Remacemide
Levothyroxine	Rifampin
Lidocaine	Sabeluzole
Lofepramine	Saquinavir
Mebendazole	Sertraline
Meperidine	Shankhapulshpi
Mestranol	Simvastatin
Methotrexate	Sulfadiazine
Methoxsalen	Sulfamethizole
Methsuximide	Sulfaphenazole
Methylprednisolone	Sulthiame
Metocurine	Tacrolimus
Metronidazole	Tenidap
Mexiletine	Teniposide
Miconazole	Theophylline
Midazolam	Tiagabine
Nafimidone	Ticlopidine
Nelfinavir	Ticrynafen
Nifedipine	Tirilazad
Nilutamide	Tizanidine

Tolbutamide
Topiramate
Triamcinolone
Trimethoprim
Trimipramine
Tubocurarine
Valproic acid
Vecuronium
Verapamil
Vigabatrin
Viloxazine
Vinblastine
Warfarin
Zotepine

Pregnancy Category
D

Breastfeeding
Safe

Polyethylene Glycol

Brand Names:
- *Colyte*
- *Golytely*

Class: *Gastrointestinal*

How Supplied:
- Powder for oral solution

Use

Whole bowel irrigation

Adult Dosage (Usual)

Polyethylene glycol solution PO or by NG tube 2 L/hour until rectal effluent is clear and GI x-ray shows no toxin in GI tract

Pediatric Dosage (Usual)

Arsenic poisoning: polyethylene glycol solution PO or by NG tube 20 mL/kg/hour until rectal effluent is clear and GI x-ray shows no toxin in GI tract

Precautionary Information

Contraindications
- Gastrointestinal obstruction, gastric retention or perforation
- Hypersensitivity to polyethylene glycol
- Patient weight of less than 20 kilograms
- Toxic or active colitis

Common Adverse Effects
Abdominal cramping/bloating
Nausea/vomiting

Pregnancy Category
C

Breastfeeding
Unknown

Notes

Monitor fluid/electrolyte status; prolonged irrigation may produce mild metabolic acidosis.

Pralidoxime Chloride

Brand Names:
- *Protopam Chloride*
- *Combopen Autoinjector*
- *Mark 1 Autoinjector*

Class: *Antidote*

How Supplied:

- Powder for injection: 1 gm (1 gm/20 mL)
- Autoinjector: 600 mg/2 mL and atropine 2 mg/0.7 mL

Use

Nerve agent exposure, including exposure to sarin (GB), soman (GD), tabun (GA), and VX

Adult Dosage (Usual)

- 1 to 2 gm in 250 mL NS IV over 20 to 30 minutes, or 5% solution in SWFI at 0.5 gm/min. Repeat same dose in 1 hour if muscle weakness persists
- If IV administration is not possible, 1 gm IM in 3mL diluent
- Maximum: 12 gm/24 hrs

Pediatric Dosage (Usual)

- 25 to 50 mg/kg IV in NS at 50 mg/mL-concentration over 20 to 30 minutes. Repeat in 1 to 2 hours if necessary.

Dosage Adjustments

Renal impairment

Administration

- Maximum rate: 200 mg/min
- Administer Autoinjector into IM site(s); do not use in children

Precautionary Information

Contraindications

- Hypersensitity to pralidoxime
- Organophosphates without anti-cholinesterase activity
- Phosphorus or inorganic phosphate poisoning (ineffective)

Adverse Effects

Bitter aftertaste
Blurred vision
Dizziness
Headache
Nausea/vomiting

Pregnancy Category

C

Breastfeeding

Unknown

Notes

May induce myasthenic crisis in myasthenia gravis patients.

Prednisone

Brand Name: *Deltasone*
Class: *Adrenal glucocorticoid*
How Supplied:

- Syrup: 5 mg/5mL
- Tablet: 1 mg, 2.5 mg, 5 mg, 10 mg, 20 mg, 50 mg

Use

- Anthrax (for edema)
- Brucellosis
- Herxheimer-like reaction (for prophylaxis)
- Mustard gas exposure (for pulmonary toxicity)
- Q fever-induced hepatitis

Adult Dosage (Usual)

Anthrax Treatment (Edema)
1 to 2 mg/kg/day or 5 to 60 mg/day

Brucellosis
20 mg PO BID or TID up to 5 days

Herxheimer-Like Reaction (Prophylaxis)
1 mg/kg/day PO in 3 divided doses for 3 to 4 days

Mustard Gas Exposure (Pulmonary Toxicity)
60 to 125 mg/day

Q Fever-Induced Hepatitis
0.5 mg/kg/day PO, if fever persists following antibiotic therapy, taper over 1 month

Pediatric Dosage (Usual)

Anthrax treatment (edema)
0.5 to 2 mg/kg/day

Precautionary Information

Contraindications
Hypersensitivity to prednisone
Systemic fungal infections

Adverse Effects
Adrenal insufficiency
Cushing's syndrome
GI distress
Hyperglycemia
Hypertension
Impaired skin healing
Mild euphoria/depression
Tuberculosis reactivation

Drug Interactions
Alcuronium
Aldesleukin
Alfalfa
Amobarbital
Aprobarbital
Asparaginase
Aspirin
Atracurium
Butabarbital
Butalbital
Carbamazepine
Cisatracurium
Clarithromycin
Cyclosporine
Doxacurium
Echinacea
Ethinyl Estradiol
Fluconazole
Fosphenytoin
Gallamine
Ginseng
Hexafluorenium Bromide
Human Growth Hormone
Hydrochlorothiazide
Ketoconazole
Licorice
Ma Huang
Mephobarbital
Mestranol
Metocurine
Mivacurium
Montelukast
Neostigmine
Norethindrone
Norgestrel
Pancuronium
Pentobarbital
Phenobarbital
Phenytoin
Pipecuronium
Primidone
Pyridostigmine

Rifampin
Rocuronium
Rotavirus Vaccine
Saiboku-to
Secobarbital
Succinylcholine
Tubocurarine
Vaccines
Vecuronium

Pregnancy Category
B

Breastfeeding
Safe

Notes

May increase the risk of serious or
fatal infection in individuals
exposed to viral illnesses such as
chickenpox or measles

Promethazine Hydrochloride

Brand Name: *Phenergan*
Class: *Antihistamine, phenothiazine*
How Supplied:
- Injection: 25 mg/mL, 50 mg/mL
- Syrup: 6.25 mg/5 mL, 25 mg/5mL
- Suppository: 12.5 mg, 25 mg, 50 mg
- Tablet: 12.5 mg, 25 mg, 50 mg

Use

Mustard gas exposure: Prevention
of postexposure systemic or dermal
injury

Adult Dosage (Usual)

- 12.5 mg PO before meals or on retiring, or 25 mg before retiring
- 25 mg IV/IM; may repeat in 2 hours prn

Pediatric Dosage (Usual)

2 years or older:
- 6.25 to 12.5 mg PO BID or TID
- IV dose is 50% of adult, MAX 0.5 mg/lb/dose

Dose Adjustments

Geriatric

Administration

- Maximum rate of IV administration is 25 mg/min
- Maximum concentration for IV administration is 25 mg/mL

Precautionary Information

Contraindications
- Bladder or pyeloduodenal obstruction
- Children under 2 years
- Hypersensitivity to promethazine and other phenothiazines
- MAOI therapy
- Narrow-angle glaucoma
- Peptic ulcer
- Prostatic hypertrophy
- Subcutaneous or intra-arterial injection

Adverse Effects
Dizziness
Drowsiness
Extrapyramidal reactions
Xerostomia

Drug Interactions

Benztropine
Cabergoline
Cisapride
Dehydroepiandrosterone
Dofetilide
Evening Primrose Oil
Gatifloxacin
Grepafloxacin
Halofantrine
Kava
Levofloxacin
Lithium
Meperidine
Metrizamide
Moxifloxacin
Orphenadrine
Phenobarbital
Pimozide
Porfimer
Procyclidine
Sotalol
Sparfloxacin
Tramadol
Trazodone
Trihexyphenidyl

Pregnancy Category

C

Breastfeeding

Unknown

Pyridostigmine Bromide

Brand Name: *Mestinon*
Class: *Cholinergic*
How Supplied:
- Solution for injection: 5 mg/mL
- Syrup: 60 mg/5 mL syrup
- Tablet: 60 mg tablet

Use

Pretreatment prior to soman (nerve agent) exposure

Adult Dosage (Usual)

Soman (pretreatment): 30 mg PO every 8 hours for 1 to 7 days

Administration

- Pyridostigmine should NOT be given after nerve agent exposure.
- Pyridostigmine is NOT effective as a single antidote.

Precautionary Information

Contraindications
- Hypersensitivity to pyridostigmine products
- Mechanical intestinal/urinary obstruction

Common Adverse Effects

Abdominal and muscle cramps
Diarrhea
Exacerbation of asthma/bronchitis
Fasciculations
Flatulence
Impairment of respiratory function
Incontinence
Nausea/vomiting
Pulmonary edema
Salivation
Sweating
Urinary urgency/frequency
Weakness

Drug Interactions

Hydrocortisone
Prednisolone

Prednisone
Succinylcholine

Pregnancy Category
C

Breastfeeding
Unknown

Rifampin

Brand Names:
- *Rifadin*
- *Rimactane*

Class: *Antitubercular*

How Supplied:
- Capsule: 150 mg, 300 mg
- Powder for injection: 600 mg

Use

- Brucellosis, uncomplicated
- Neurobrucellosis

Adult Dosage (Usual)

Brucellosis
Treatment of brucellosis, uncomplicated (alternative treatment): 600 to 900 mg PO QD PLUS doxycycline for 6 weeks

Neurobrucellosis
Treatment of neurobrucellosis (preferred treatment): 600 to 900 mg PO QD PLUS gentamicin PLUS doxycycline for 8 to 12 weeks

Pediatric Dosage (Usual)

Brucellosis
Treatment of brucellosis, uncomplicated; children over 8 years (alternative treatment): 20 mg/kg PO QD PLUS doxycycline for 6 weeks

Neurobrucellosis
Treatment of neurobrucellosis (preferred treatment): 20 mg/kg PO QD PLUS gentamicin PLUS doxycycline (over 8 years) OR cotrimoxazole (under 8 years)

Dose Adjustments

Liver disease

Administration

Give 1 hour before, or 2 hours after meals, with full glass of water. Capsule contents may be mixed with applesauce.

Precautionary Information

Contraindications
Hypersensitivity to rifampin

Adverse Effects
Elevated LFTs
Heartburn
Nausea/vomiting
Thrombocytopenia

Drug Interactions
Acetyldigoxin
Amiodarone
Amprenavir
Anisindione
Atovaquone
Betamethasone
Bunazosin
Buspirone
Carbamazepine
Carvedilol
Caspofungin
Chloramphenicol
Chlorpropamide

Clofibrate

Clozapine

Cortisone

Cyclosporine

Dapsone

Delavirdine

Deslanoside

Dexamethasone

Diazepam

Dicumarol

Digitoxin

Digoxin

Diltiazem

Disopyramide

Doxycycline

Enalapril

Entacapone

Ethinyl Estradiol

Ethionamide

Fluconazole

Fludrocortisone

Fosphenytoin

Glyburide

Haloperidol

Hydrocortisone

Indinavir

Isoniazid

Isradipine

Itraconazole

Ketoconazole

Leflunomide

Levonorgestrel

Levothyroxine

Lorcainide

Losartan

Medroxyprogesterone

Mestranol

Methadone

Methylprednisolone

Metildigoxin

Metoprolol

Mexiletine

Morphine

Nelfinavir

Nevirapine

Nifedipine

Nisoldipine

Norethindrone

Norgestrel

Phenprocoumon

Phenytoin

Pirmenol

Prednisolone

Prednisone

Propafenone

Propranolol

Quinidine

Repaglinide

Ritonavir

Rofecoxib

Saquinavir

Sertraline

Sirolimus

Tacrolimus

Terbinafine

Theophylline

Tocainide

Tolbutamide

Triamcinolone

Triazolam

Trimetrexate

Valproic Acid

Verapamil

Warfarin

Zaleplon

Zidovudine

Zolpidem

Pregnancy Category

C

Breastfeeding

Safe

Sargramostim

Brand Name: *Leukine*
Class: *Granulocyte-macrophage colony stimulating factor* (GM-CSF)
How Supplied:

- Lyophilized powder for injection: 250 mcg (1.4 x 10(6) IU/mL)
- Liquid for injection: 500 mcg/mL (2.8 x 10(6) IU/mL)

Use

Treatment of neutropenia secondary to dermal or inhalational exposure to sulfur mustard gas

Adult Dosage (Usual)

250 mcg/m(2)/day SC or IV over 15 to 30 minutes. Give for 2 weeks or until the absolute neutrophil count (ANC) surpasses 10,000/mm3

Administration

- Reconstitute powder with 1 mL Sterile Water for Injection.
- For IV administration, dilute with NS to at least 10 mcg/mL. If final concentration is less than 10 mcg/mL add albumin at a final concentration of 0.1% prior to the addition of Leukine.
- Infuse over 2 to 24 hours.

Precautionary Information

Contraindications

- Concomitant chemo- or radiotherapy
- Excess leukemic myeloid blasts
- Hypersensitivity to GM-CSF or yeast-derived products
- Neonates (Leukine liquid or lyophilized Leukine reconstituted with Bacteriostatic Water for Injection)

Adverse Effects

Arthralgia
Chills/Fever
Rash
Bone pain
Myalgia
First dose reaction (hypotension, tachycardia, dyspnea, nausea/vomiting)

Drug Interactions

Lithium
Vincristine

Pregnancy Category

C

Breastfeeding

Unknown

Notes

Monitor for leukocytosis.

Smallpox Vaccine

Brand Name: *Dryvax*
Class: *Vaccine*
How Supplied:

- 1 vial of Dried Smallpox Vaccine and 1 container of diluent (0.25 mL) with 100 sterile bifurcated needles

Use

- Smallpox, postexposure vaccination

Adult Dosage (Usual)

Postexposure vaccination: 1 drop of vaccine delivered percutaneously with 15 punctures of a bifurcated needle

Pediatric Dosage (Usual)

Postexposure vaccination: Same as adult. Not indicated in children less than 12 months of age unless they are at risk of contracting smallpox.

Precautionary Information

Contraindications
Postexposure, none

Common Adverse Effects
Fever
Inadvertent inoculation of vaccinia of remote body sites (face, eyelid, nose, mouth, genitalia, and rectum)
Localized skin reaction
Regional lymphadenopathy

Pregnancy Category
C

Breastfeeding
Unknown

Notes

Concomitant administration of vaccinia immune globulin with the smallpox vaccine is recommended for the following patient groups considered to have an elevated risk for smallpox vaccine-related complications:

- Persons with eczema or other exfoliative skin disorders
- Persons with leukemia, lymphoma, or generalized malignancy who are receiving therapy with alkylating agents, antimetabolites, radiation, or large doses of corticosteroids
- Persons with HIV infection
- Persons with hereditary immune deficiency disorders
- Pregnant women

Sodium Bicarbonate

Class: *Electrolyte/mineral/nutrient*
How Supplied:
- Solution for injection: 4.2%, 5%, 7.5%, 8.4%

Use

Treatment of acidosis secondary to oral, parenteral, or dermal cyanide exposure

Adult Dosage (Usual)

Severely acidotic patients (pH less than 7.1): 1 mEq/kg IV. Base further sodium bicarbonate administration on serial arterial blood gas (ABG) determinations

Precautionary Information

Contraindications
- Hypocalcemia
- Hypochloremia
- Respiratory alkalosis

Adverse Effects
Alkalosis
Flatulence
GI cramps
Vomiting

Drug Interactions
Amphetamine
Aspirin
Cefpodoxime
Chlorpropamide
Dextroamphetamine
Ephedrine
Flecainide
Itraconazole
Ketoconazole
Lithium
Mecamylamine
Pseudoephedrine

Pregnancy Category
C

Breastfeeding
Unknown

Notes

In serious cyanide poisoning cases, acidosis may be difficult to correct prior to administration of antidotes.

Sodium Nitrite

Class: *Vasodilator, Cyanide antidote*
How Supplied:
- Solution for injection: 300 mg/10 mL
- Cyanide Antidote Kit

Use

Cyanide exposure

Adult Dosage (Usual)

Cyanide antidote: 10 mL (300 mg) IV over 5 minutes. May repeat 50% of initial dose after 30 minutes if response is inadequate

Pediatric Dosage (Usual)

Cyanide antidote (child with normal hemoglobin concentration): 0.15 to 0.33 mL/kg IV over no less than 5 minutes. May repeat 50% of initial dose after 30 minutes if response is inadequate. Maximum: 10 mL

Administration

- To prevent hypotension, dilute with normal saline and infuse over 20 minutes.
- Monitor blood pressure carefully; reduce nitrite administration rate if hypotension occurs.
- Monitor methemoglobin levels; maintain below 30%.

Precautionary Information

Contraindications
Hypersensitivity to nitrates

Common Adverse Effects
Abdominal pain
Headache
Light-headedness
Methemoglobinemia
Nausea/vomiting

Drug Interactions
Acetylcholine
Alcohol
Antihistamines

Beta Blockers
CNS Depressants
Epinephrine
Meperidine
Tricyclic Antidepressants

Sodium Phosphate

Brand Name: *Fleet Phospho-Soda*
Class: *Laxatives, saline*
How Supplied:
■ 2.4 gm monobasic sodium phosphate monohydrate and 0.9 gm dibasic sodium phosphate heptahydrate per 5 mL

Use

Botulism (for gastric decontamination)

Adult Dosage (Usual)

10 to 20 mL PO diluted with 120 mL of water. Follow with 240 mL of water

Precautionary Information

Contraindications
■ Ascites
■ Bowel obstruction
■ Congenital megacolon
■ Congestive heart failure

Common Adverse Effects
Dehydration
Diarrhea
Hyperphosphatemia
Hypocalcemia
Hypokalemia
Nausea/vomiting
Stomach pain

Sodium Sulfate

Class: *Saline Laxatives*
How Supplied:
■ Granules
■ Powder

Use

Botulism (for gastric decontamination)

Adult Dosage (Usual)

250 mg/kg

Precautionary Information

Contraindications
■ Ascites
■ Bowel obstruction
■ Congenital megacolon
■ Congestive heart failure

Common Adverse Effects
Dehydration
Diarrhea
Nausea/vomiting
Stomach pain

Sodium Thiosulfate

Brand Name: *Cyanide Antidote Package*
Class: *Antidotes*
How Supplied: 12.5 gm/50 mL kit

Use

■ Cyanide exposure
■ Mustard gas exposure

Adult Dosage (Usual)

Cyanide Exposure
Treatment of cyanide poisoning:
12.5 gm IV over 10 minutes (after sodium nitrite). If necessary, repeat after 30 minutes with half doses of both agents.

Mustard Gas Exposure
- *Treatment of mustard gas exposure:* 12.5 gm IV over 10 minutes.
- *Treatment of mustard gas inhalation exposure:* 2.5% solution has been used to neutralize mustard gas via nebulization when used within 15 minutes of exposure.
- *Treatment of mustard gas ocular or dermal exposure:* 2.5% topically or for irrigation.
- *Treatment of mustard gas (oral) exposure:* 150 mL of 2% solution PO.

Pediatric Dosage (Usual)

Cyanide Exposure
Treatment of cyanide poisoning:
1.65 mL/kg of a 25% solution IV (after sodium nitrite); dose varies from 1.1 mL/kg to 1.95 mL/kg with Hgb serum concentration.

Precautionary Information

Adverse Effects
Contact dermatitis

Pregnancy Category
C

Breastfeeding
Unknown

Streptomycin Sulfate

Class: *Aminoglycoside antibiotic*
How Supplied:
- Lyophilized powder: 1 gm

Use

- Anthrax
- Brucellosis
- Plague
- Tularemia

Adult Dosage (Usual)

Anthrax
Treatment of anthrax (alternative treatment, in conjunction with penicillin): 30 mg/kg/day IM or IV

Brucellosis
- *Treatment of brucellosis, uncomplicated:* 1 gm IM daily for first 10 to 14 days PLUS doxycycline for 6 weeks
- *Treatment of neurobrucellosis:* 1 gm IM daily for 2 to 4 weeks PLUS rifampin for 8 to 12 weeks PLUS either doxycycline OR cotrimoxazole for 8 to 12 weeks

Plague
Treatment of plague; contained casualty setting (preferred treatment): 1 gm IM BID for 10 days

Tularemia
Treatment of tularemia; contained casualty setting (preferred treatment): 1 gm IM BID for 10 days

Pediatric Dosage (Usual)

Brucellosis

Treatment of brucellosis, uncomplicated (over 8 years of age): 20 to 30 mg/kg/day IM divided Q12H or QD for first 10 to 14 days PLUS doxycycline for 6 weeks

Plague

Treatment of plague; contained casualty setting (preferred treatment): 15 mg/kg IM BID; maximum: 2 gm/day

Tularemia

Treatment of tularemia; contained casualty setting (preferred treatment): 15 mg/kg IM BID; maximum: 2 gm/day

Dose Adjustments

Geriatrics
Hemodialysis
Renal impairment

Precautionary Information

Contraindications

- Hypersensitivity to streptomycin or other aminoglycosides
- Hypersensitivity to sulfites

Adverse Effects

Eosinophilia
Fever
Rash
Urticaria
Vestibular ototoxicity
  (nausea/vomiting, vertigo)

Drug Interactions

Bumetanide
Capreomycin
Carboplatin
Cephalosporins
Cidofovir
Cyclosporine
Ethacrynic Acid
Furosemide
Magnesium
Nondepolarizing Neuromuscular Blockers
Piretanide
Succinylcholine
Tacrolimus
Typhoid Vaccine

Pregnancy Category

D

Breastfeeding

Safe

Succimer (DMSA)

Brand Name: *Chemet*
Class: *Heavy metal chelator*
How Supplied:
- Capsule: 100 mg

Use

Arsenic or lewisite poisoning

Adult Dosage (Usual)

10 mg/kg every 8 hours for 5 days, then 10 mg/kg every 12 hours for 14 days

Pediatric Dosage (Usual)

10 mg/kg or 350 mg/m(2) every 8 hours for 5 days, then 10 mg/kg or 350 mg/m(2) every 12 hours for 14 days

Dose Adjustments

Renal impairment

Liver disease

Administration

- Repeat course may be given if indicated by blood levels.
- A minimum of 2 weeks between courses is recommended.
- Do not use concurrently with EDTA or BAL.
- Monitor CBC differential, platelet count, LFTs weekly.
- Capsules may be separated and sprinkled onto a small amount of soft food for children unable to swallow capsules.
- No data are available for children under 8 kilograms (18 pounds).

Precautionary Information

Contraindications

Hypersensitivity to succimer

Common Adverse Effects

Anorexia

Diarrhea

Increased liver function values

Nausea

Neutropenia

Pruritus

Rash

Pregnancy Category

C

Breastfeeding

Unknown

Note

DMSA is 2,3-dimercaptosuccinic acid.

Sulfamethoxazole/ Trimethoprim

Brand Names:
- *Bactrim*
- *Septra*

Class: *Sulfonamide*

How Supplied:
- IV solution: 80 mg-16 mg/mL
- Oral suspension: 200 mg-40 mg/5 mL
- Tablet: 400 mg-80 mg, 800 mg-160 mg

Use

- Brucellosis
- Food poisoning
- Glanders
- Plague
- Q Fever

Adult Dosage (Usual)

Brucellosis

- *Brucellosis:* 1 double-strength tablet (160 mg trimethoprim) PO BID for 6 weeks PLUS gentamicin
- *Neurobrucellosis:* 1 double-strength tablet (160 mg trimethoprim) PO BID for 8 to 12 weeks PLUS gentamicin PLUS rifampin

Food Poisoning

- *Listeria:* sulfamethoxazole/ trimethoprim has been used in

patients allergic to penicillins
- *Shigella:* 1 double-strength tablet (160 mg trimethoprim) PO BID for 5 days

Glanders
- *Localized disease:* trimethoprim, 4 mg/kg/day, and sulfamethoxazole, 20 mg/kg/day, PO in 4 divided doses
- *Localized disease with mild toxicity:* combine two of the following drugs (amoxicillin/clavulanate, sulfamethoxazole/trimethoprim, tetracycline) in an oral regimen for 30 days, followed by monotherapy with either amoxicillin/clavulanate or sulfamethoxazole/trimethoprim for 60 to 150 days
- *Severe/septic disease:* ceftazidime 120 mg/kg/day in 3 divided doses, combined with trimethoprim, 8 mg/kg/day, and sulfamethoxazole, 40 mg/kg/day, in 4 divided doses. Give initially as parenteral therapy for 2 weeks, then as oral therapy for 6 months

Plague
Pregnant women: 1 to 2 double-strength tablets (160 mg trimethoprim) PO Q12H for 7 days

Q Fever
Trimethoprim may be added to a doxycycline regimen

Pediatric Dosage (Usual)

Brucellosis
- *Brucellosis:* 5 mg/kg trimethoprim and 50 mg/kg sulfamethox

azole PO Q12H for 6 weeks, PLUS gentamicin
- *Neurobrucellosis:* 5 mg/kg trimethoprim and 50 mg/kg sulfamethoxazole PO Q12H for a minimum of 8 weeks, PLUS gentamicin, PLUS rifampin

Food Poisoning
Shigella: 10 mg/kg/day trimethoprim and 50 mg/kg/day sulfamethoxazole PO in 2 divided doses for 5 days

Plague
Trimethoprim, 8 mg/kg/day, and sulfamethoxazole, 40 mg/kg/day, PO in 2 divided doses

Dose Adjustments

Renal impairment

Administration

For IV administration, dilute each 5 mL in 125 mL D5W; infuse over 60 to 90 minutes

Precautionary Information

Contraindications
- Hypersensitivity to sulfonamides or trimethoprim
- Infants less than 2 months
- Megaloblastic anemia due to folate deficiency
- Nursing mothers
- Pregnant patients at term

Adverse Effects
Anorexia
Nausea/vomiting
Rash
Urticaria

Drug Interactions

Acenocoumarol

Acetohexamide

Anisindione

Chlorpropamide

Cyclosporine

Dicumarol

Glipizide

Glyburide

Methotrexate

Metronidazole

Para-Aminobenzoic Acid (PABA) and Derivatives

Phenprocoumon

Porfimer

Pyrimethamine

Tolazamide

Tolbutamide

Typhoid Vaccine

Warfarin

Pregnancy Category

C

Breastfeeding

Controversial

Terbutaline

Brand Name: *Brethine*
Class: *Sympathomimetic bronchodilator*
How Supplied:
- Injection: 1 mg/mL
- Tablet: 2.5 mg, 5 mg

Use

- Phosgene inhalation exposure (prophylaxis following an exposure to 50 ppm for a minute or more)
- Phosgene-induced pulmonary edema

- Bronchial asthma
- Reversible bronchospasm

Adult Dosage (Usual)

- *Prophylaxis, post-exposure to phosgene (pulmonary edema):* 0.25 mg SC
- *Pulmonary edema and asthma:* 0.25 mg SC x 1; may be repeated in 15 to 30 minutes (maximum: 0.5 mg in 4 hours) or 2.5 to 5mg PO Q6H (maximum: 15 mg/day)

Pediatric Dosage (Usual)

12 years and older: 2.5 mg PO Q6H TID (maximum: 7.5 mg/day)

Precautionary Information

Contraindications

Hypersensitivity to terbutaline products

Common Adverse Effects

Headache

Nausea

Nervousness

Palpitations

Tachycardia

Tremor

Drug Interactions

Furazolidone

Monoamine Oxidase Inhibitors

Succinylcholine

Pregnancy Category

B

Breastfeeding

Safe

Tetracycline

Brand name: *Sumycin*

Class: *Tetracycline*

How Supplied:

- Capsule: 250 mg, 500 mg
- Powder : 25 gm, 100 gm, 500 gm
- Syrup: 125 mg/5 mL
- Tablet: 250 mg, 500 mg

Use

- Anthrax
- Food poisoning (shigella)
- Glanders
- Plague
- Q Fever
- Typhus

Adult Dosage (Usual)

Anthrax

Anthrax treatment (alternative to doxycycline): 250 to 500 mg PO or IV QID (IV for inhalational, GI, or meningeal anthrax)

Food poisoning

Shigella: 2.5 gm PO, single dose

Glanders

40 mg/kg/day PO in 3 divided doses for 60 to 150 days

Q Fever

500 mg PO QID for 2 to 3 weeks or until afebrile for 1 week

Typhus

500 mg PO QID for 7 days

Pediatric Dosage (Usual)

Q Fever

Inhalation exposure (over 8 years old): 25 mg/kg/day in divided doses for 2 to 3 weeks

Dose Adjustments

Liver disease
Renal impairment

Administration

- Avoid concomitant administration of aluminum, calcium, and magnesium, which can impair absorption of tetracycline.
- Give on an empty stomach.

Precautionary Information

Contraindications

Hypersensitivity to tetracycline products

Adverse Effects

Diarrhea
Nausea/Vomiting
Photosensitivity
Pseudotumor Cerebri
Rash

Drug Interactions

Aluminum Carbonate, Basic
Aluminum Hydroxide
Aluminum Phosphate
Atovaquone
Bismuth Subsalicylate
Calcium Carbonate
Cholestyramine
Cisatracurium
Colestipol

Dicumarol

Digoxin

Dihydroxyaluminum Aminoacetate

Dihydroxyaluminum Sodium
  Carbonate

Ethinyl Estradiol

Iron

Isotretinoin

Magaldrate

Magnesium

Mestranol

Methoxyflurane

Norethindrone

Norgestrel

Phenindione

Porfimer

Quinapril

Rapacuronium

Warfarin

Zinc

Pregnancy Category

D

Breastfeeding

Safe

Section 4

Antibiotic Prescribing Information

ACHROMYCIN® V ℞
[a-krō-mī-cin]
tetracycline HCl
for ORAL USE

DESCRIPTION

ACHROMYCIN V tetracycline hydrochloride is an antibiotic isolated from *Streptomyces aureofaciens*. Chemically it is the monohydrochloride of [4S -(4α,4aα,5aα,6β,12aα,)] -4-(Dimethylamino)-1,4,4a,5,5a,6,11,12a-octahydro-3, 6, 10, 12, 12a-pentahydroxy-6-methyl-1, 11-dioxo-2-naphthacenecarboxamide.

ACHROMYCIN V oral dosage forms contain the following inactive ingredients:

Capsules: Blue 1, FD&C Yellow No. 6, Gelatin, Lactose, Magnesium Stearate, Red 28, Titanium Dioxide, Yellow 10 and other ingredients.

CLINICAL PHARMACOLOGY

The tetracyclines are primarily bacteriostatic and are thought to exert their antimicrobial effect by the inhibition of protein synthesis. Tetracyclines are active against a wide range of gram-negative and gram-positive organisms.

The drugs in the tetracycline class have closely similar antimicrobial spectra, and cross-resistance among them is common.

Microorganisms may be considered susceptible if the MIC (minimum inhibitory concentration) is not more than 4 mcg/mL and intermediate if the MIC is 4 to 12.5 mcg/mL.

Susceptibility plate testing: A tetracycline disc may be used to determine microbial susceptibility to drugs in the tetracycline class. If the Kirby-Bauer method of disc susceptibility testing is used, a 30 mcg tetracycline HCl disc should give a zone of at least 19 mm when tested against a tetracycline-susceptible bacterial strain.

Tetracyclines are readily absorbed and are bound to plasma proteins in varying degrees. They are concentrated by the liver in the bile and excreted in the urine and feces at high concentrations and in a biologically active form.

INDICATIONS

ACHROMYCIN V is indicated in infections caused by the following microorganisms.

Rickettsiae: (Rocky Mountain spotted fever, typhus fever and the typhus group, Q fever, rickettsialpox, tick fevers).

Mycoplasma pneumoniae (PPLO, Eaton agent).

Agents of psittacosis and ornithosis.

Agents of lymphogranuloma venereum and granuloma inguinale.

The spirochetal agent of relapsing fever (*Borrelia recurrentis*).

The following gram-negative microorganisms:
Haemophilus ducreyi (chancroid),
Yersinia pestis and *Francisella tularensis*, formerly

Pasteurella pestis and *Pasteurella tularensis*,
Bartonella bacilliformis,
Bacteroides species,
Vibrio comma and *Vibrio fetus*,
Brucella species (in conjunction with streptomycin).

Because many strains of the following groups of microorganisms have been shown to be resistant to tetracyclines, culture and susceptibility testing are recommended.

ACHROMYCIN is indicated for treatment of infections caused by the following gram-negative microorganisms, when bacteriologic testing indicates appropriate susceptibility to the drug:

Escherichia coli,
Enterobacter aerogenes (formerly *Aerobacter aerogenes*),
Shigella species,
Mima species and *Herellea* species,
Haemophilus influenzae (respiratory infections),
Klebsiella species (respiratory and urinary infections).

ACHROMYCIN is indicated for treatment of infections caused by the following gram-positive microorganisms, when bacteriologic testing indicates appropriate susceptibility to the drug:

Streptococcus species:

Up to 44% of strains of *Streptococcus pyogenes* and 74% of *Streptococcus faecalis* have been found to be resistant to tetracycline drugs. Therefore, tetracyclines should not be used for streptococcal disease unless the organism has been demonstrated to be sensitive.

For upper respiratory infections due to Group A beta-hemolytic streptococci, penicillin is the usual drug of choice, including prophylaxis of rheumatic fever.

Streptococcus pneumoniae,
Staphylococcus aureus, skin and soft tissue infections.

Tetracyclines are not the drug of choice in the treatment of any type of staphylococcal infection.

When penicillin is contraindicated, tetracyclines are alternative drugs in the treatment of infections due to:

Neisseria gonorrhoeae,
Treponema pallidum and *Treponema pertenue* (syphilis and yaws),
Listeria monocytogenes,
Clostridium species,
Bacillus anthracis,
Fusobacterium fusiforme (Vincent's infection),
Actinomyces species.

In acute intestinal amebiasis, the tetracyclines may be a useful adjunct to amebicides. In severe acne, the tetracyclines may be useful adjunctive therapy.

ACHROMYCIN V is indicated in the treatment of trachoma, although the infectious agent is not always eliminated, as judged by immunofluorescence.

Inclusion conjunctivitis may be treated with oral tetracyclines or with a combination of oral and topical agents.

ACHROMYCIN is indicated for the treatment of uncomplicated urethral, endocervical or rectal infections in adults caused by *Chlamydia trachomatis*.[1]

CONTRAINDICATIONS

This drug is contraindicated in persons who have shown hypersensitivity to any of the tetracyclines.

WARNINGS

THE USE OF DRUGS OF THE TETRACYCLINE CLASS DURING TOOTH DEVELOPMENT (LAST HALF OF PREGNANCY, INFANCY AND CHILDHOOD TO THE AGE OF 8 YEARS) MAY CAUSE PERMANENT DISCOLORATION OF THE TEETH (YELLOW-GRAY-BROWN). This adverse reaction is more common during long-term use of the drugs but has been observed following repeated short-term courses. Enamel hypoplasia has also been reported. TETRACYCLINE DRUGS, THEREFORE, SHOULD NOT BE USED IN THIS AGE GROUP UNLESS OTHER DRUGS ARE NOT LIKELY TO BE EFFECTIVE OR ARE CONTRAINDICATED.

If renal impairment exists, even usual oral or parenteral doses may lead to excessive systemic accumulation of the drug and possible liver toxicity. Under such conditions, lower than usual total doses are indicated and, if therapy is prolonged, serum level determinations of the drug may be advisable.

Photosensitivity manifested by an exaggerated sunburn reaction has been observed in some individuals taking tetracyclines. Patients apt to be exposed to direct sunlight or ultraviolet light should be advised that this reaction can occur with tetracycline drugs, and treatment should be discontinued at the first evidence of skin erythema.

The anti-anabolic action of the tetracyclines may cause an increase in BUN. While this is not a problem in those with normal renal function, in patients with significantly impaired function, higher serum levels of tetracycline may lead to azotemia, hyperphosphatemia, and acidosis.

Usage in Pregnancy (See above **WARNINGS** about use during tooth development.) Results of animal studies indicate that tetracyclines cross the placenta, are found in fetal tissues and can have toxic effects on the developing fetus (often related to retardation of skeletal development). Evidence of embryotoxicity has also been noted in animals treated early in pregnancy.

Usage in Newborns, Infants, and Children (See above **WARNINGS** about use during tooth development.)

All tetracyclines form a stable calcium complex in any bone forming tissue. A decrease in the fibula growth rate has been observed in prematures given oral tetracycline in doses of 25 mg/kg every six hours. This reaction was shown to be reversible when the drug was discontinued.

Tetracyclines are present in the milk of lactating women who are taking a drug in this class.

PRECAUTIONS

General

Pseudotumor cerebri (benign intracranial hypertension) in adults has been associated with the use of tetracyclines. The usual clinical manifestations are headache and blurred vision. Bulging fontanels have been associated with the use of tetracyclines in infants. While both of these conditions and related symptoms usually resolve soon after discontinuation of the tetracycline, the possibility for permanent sequelae exists.

As with other antibiotics preparations, use of this drug may result in overgrowth of nonsusceptible organisms, including fungi. If superinfection occurs, the antibiotic should be discontinued and appropriate therapy should be instituted.

In venereal diseases when coexistent syphilis is suspected, darkfield examination should be done before treatment is started and the blood serology repeated monthly for at least 4 months.

In long-term therapy, periodic laboratory evaluation of organ systems, including hematopoietic, renal and hepatic studies should be performed.

All infections due to Group A beta-hemolytic streptococci should be treated for at least ten days.

Drug Interactions

Because tetracyclines have been shown to depress plasma prothrombin activity, patients who are on anticoagulant therapy may require downward adjustment of their anticoagulant dosage.

Since bacteriostatic drugs, such as the tetracycline class of antibiotics, may interfere with the bactericidal action of penicillins, it is not advisable to administer these drugs concomitantly.

Concurrent use of tetracyclines with oral contraceptives may render oral contraceptives less effective. Breakthrough bleeding has been reported.

ADVERSE REACTIONS

Gastrointestinal: Anorexia, nausea, vomiting, diarrhea, glossitis, dysphagia, enterocolitis, pancreatitis, and inflammatory lesions (with monilial overgrowth) in the anogenital region, increases in liver enzymes, and hepatic toxicity have been reported rarely. Rare instances of esophagitis and esophageal ulcerations have been reported in patients taking the tetracycline-class antibiotics in capsule and tablet form. Most of these patients took the medication immediately before going to bed (see **DOSAGE AND ADMINISTRATION**).

Skin: Maculopapular and erythematous rashes. Exfoliative dermatitis has been reported but is uncommon. Fixed drug eruptions, including balanitis, have been rarely reported. Photosensitivity is discussed above. (See **WARNINGS.**)

Renal toxicity: Rise in BUN has been reported and is apparently dose related. (See **WARNINGS.**)

Hypersensitivity reactions: Urticaria, angioneurotic edema, anaphylaxis, anaphylactoid purpura, pericarditis and exacerbation of systemic lupus erythematosus.

Blood: Hemolytic anemia, thrombocytopenia, neutropenia and eosinophilia have been reported.

CNS: Pseudotumor cerebri (benign intracranial hypertension) in adults and bulging fontanels in infants. (See **PRECAUTIONS— General.**) Dizziness, tinnitus, and visual disturbances have been reported. Myasthenic syndrome has been reported rarely.

Other: When given over prolonged periods, tetracyclines have been reported to produce brown-black microscopic discoloration of thyroid glands. No abnormalities of thyroid function studies are known to occur.

DOSAGE AND ADMINISTRATION

Therapy should be continued for at least 24 to 48 hours after symptoms and fever have subsided.

Concomitant therapy: Antacids containing aluminum, calcium, or magnesium impair absorption and should not be given to patients taking oral tetracycline.

Foods and some dairy products also interfere with absorption. Oral forms of tetracycline should be given 1 hour before or 2 hours after meals.

In patients with renal impairment: (See **WARNINGS**). Total dosage should be decreased by reduction of recommended individual doses and/or by extending time intervals between doses.

In the treatment of streptococcal infections, a therapeutic dose of tetracycline should be administered for at least ten days.

Adults: Usual daily dose, 1–2 grams divided in two or four equal doses, depending on the severity of the infection.

For children above eight years of age: Usual daily dose, 10–20 mg (25–50 mg/kg) per pound of body weight divided in two or four equal doses.

For treatment of brucellosis, 500 mg tetracycline four times daily for 3 weeks should be accompanied by streptomycin, 1 gram intramuscularly twice daily the first week and once daily the second week.

For treatment of syphilis, a total of 30–40 grams in equally divided doses over a period of 10–15 days should be given. Close follow up, including laboratory tests, is recommended.

Gonorrhea patients sensitive to pencillin may be treated with tetracycline, administered as an initial oral dose of 1.5 grams followed by 0.5 gram every 6 hours for four days to a total dosage of 9 grams.

Uncomplicated urethral, endocervical, or rectal infection in adults caused by *Chlamydia trachomatis:* 500 mg, by mouth, 4 times a day for at least 7 days.[1]

HOW SUPPLIED

ACHROMYCIN® V tetracycline HCl oral dosage forms are available as follows:

CAPSULES

500 mg - Two-piece, hard shell, elongated, opaque capsules with a blue cap and a yellow body, printed with Lederle over A5 on one half and Lederle over 500 mg on the other in gray ink, supplied as follows:

    NDC 0005-4875-23—Bottle of 100

    NDC 0005-4875-34—Bottle of 1,000

250 mg - Two-piece, hard shell, opaque capsules with a blue cap and a yellow body, printed with Lederle over A3 on one half and Lederle over 250 mg on the other in gray ink, supplied as follows:

    NDC 0005-4880-23—Bottle of 100

    NDC 0005-4880-34—Bottle of 1,000

Store at Controlled Room Temperature 15°–30°C (59°–86°F).

Reference: 1. CDC Sexually Transmitted Diseases Treatment Guidelines 1982.

Manufactured by:

LEDERLE PHARMACEUTICAL DIVISION
American Cyanamid Company
Pearl River, NY 10965

CI 4945-1   Issued September 12, 1997

AMOXIL®   ℞
[ə-mäx' ĭl]
brand of
amoxicillin
capsules, tablets, chewable tablets,
and powder for oral suspension

DESCRIPTION

Amoxil formulations contain amoxicillin, a semisynthetic antibiotic, an analog of ampicillin, with a broad spectrum of bactericidal activity against many gram-positive and gram-negative microorganisms. Chemically it is $(2S,5R,6R)$ - 6- $[(R)$ - (-) - 2 - amino - 2 - $(p$ - hydroxyphenyl)acetamido] - 3,3 - dimethyl - 7 - oxo - 4-thia-1-azabicyclo[3.2.0]heptane-2-carboxylic acid trihydrate.

The amoxicillin molecular formula is $C_{16}H_{19}N_3O_5S\cdot3H_2O$, and the molecular weight is 419.45.

Amoxil capsules, tablets, and powder for oral suspension are intended for oral administration.

Capsules: Each *Amoxil* capsule, with royal blue opaque cap and pink opaque body, contains 250 mg or 500 mg amoxicillin as the trihydrate. The cap and body of the 250-mg capsule are imprinted with the product name AMOXIL and 250; the cap and body of the 500-mg capsule are imprinted with AMOXIL and 500. Inactive ingredients: D&C Red No. 28, FD&C Blue No. 1, FD&C Red No. 40, gelatin, magnesium stearate, and titanium dioxide.

Tablets: Each tablet contains 500 mg or 875 mg amoxicillin as the trihydrate. Each film-coated, capsule-shaped, pink tablet is debossed with AMOXIL centered over 500 or 875, respectively. The 875-mg tablet is scored on the reverse side. Inactive ingredients: colloidal silicon dioxide, crospovidone, FD&C Red No. 30 aluminum lake, hydroxypropyl methylcellulose, magnesium stearate, microcrystalline cellulose, polyethylene glycol, sodium starch glycolate, and titanium dioxide.

Chewable Tablets: Each cherry-banana-peppermint-flavored tablet contains 125 mg, 200 mg, 250 mg or 400 mg amoxicillin as the trihydrate. The 125-mg and 250-mg pink, oval tablets are imprinted with the product name AMOXIL on one side and 125 or 250 on the other side. Inactive ingredients: citric acid, corn starch, FD&C Red No. 40, flavorings, glycine, mannitol, magnesium stearate, saccharin sodium, silica gel, and sucrose. Each 125-mg chewable tablet contains 0.0019 mEq (0.044 mg) of sodium; the 250-mg chewable tablet contains 0.0037 mEq (0.085 mg) of sodium.

Each 200-mg chewable tablet contains 0.0005 mEq (0.0107 mg) of sodium; the 400-mg chewable tablet contains 0.0009 mEq (0.0215 mg) of sodium. The 200-mg and 400-mg pale pink round tablets are imprinted with the product name AMOXIL and 200 or 400 along the edge

of one side. Inactive ingredients: aspartame•, crospovidone NF, FD&C Red No. 40 aluminum lake, flavorings, magnesium stearate and mannitol.

•See **PRECAUTIONS**.

Powder for Oral Suspension: Each 5 mL of reconstituted suspension contains 125 mg, 200 mg, 250 mg or 400 mg amoxicillin as the trihydrate. Each 5 mL of the 125-mg reconstituted suspension contains 0.11 mEq (2.51 mg) of sodium; each 5 mL of the 250-mg reconstituted suspension contains 0.15 mEq (3.36 mg) of sodium. Each 5 mL of the 200-mg reconstituted suspension contains 0.15 mEq (3.39 mg) of sodium; each 5 mL of the 400-mg reconstituted suspension contains 0.19 mEq (4.33 mg) of sodium.

Pediatric Drops for Oral Suspension: Each mL of reconstituted suspension contains 50 mg amoxicillin as the trihydrate and 0.03 mEq (0.69 mg) of sodium.

Amoxicillin trihydrate for oral suspension 125 mg/5 mL (reconstituted) is a strawberry-flavored pink suspension; the 200 mg/5 mL, 250 mg/5 mL (or 50 mg/mL), and 400 mg/5 mL are bubble-gum-flavored pink suspensions. Inactive ingredients: FD&C Red No. 3, flavorings, silica gel, sodium benzoate, sodium citrate, sucrose, and xanthan gum.

CLINICAL PHARMACOLOGY

Amoxicillin is stable in the presence of gastric acid and is rapidly absorbed after oral administration. The effect of food on the absorption of amoxicillin from *Amoxil* tablets and *Amoxil* suspension has been partially investigated. The 400-mg and 875-mg formulations have been studied only when administered at the start of a light meal. However, food effect studies have not been performed with the 200-mg and 500-mg formulations. Amoxicillin diffuses readily into most body tissues and fluids, with the exception of brain and spinal fluid, except when meninges are inflamed. The half-life of amoxicillin is 61.3 minutes. Most of the amoxicillin is excreted unchanged in the urine; its excretion can be delayed by concurrent administration of probenecid. In blood serum, amoxicillin is approximately 20% protein-bound.

Orally administered doses of 250 mg and 500 mg amoxicillin capsules result in average peak blood levels 1 to 2 hours after administration in the range of 3.5 µg/mL to 5.0 µg/mL and 5.5 µg/mL to 7.5 µg/mL, respectively.

Mean amoxicillin pharmacokinetic parameters from an open, two-part, single-dose crossover bioequivalence study in 27 adults comparing 875 mg of Amoxil (amoxicillin) with 875 mg of Augmentin® (amoxicillin/clavulanate potassium) showed that the 875-mg tablet of *Amoxil* produces an $AUC_{0-\infty}$ of 35.4 ± 8.1 µg.hr./mL and a C_{max} of 13.8 ± 4.1 µg/mL. Dosing was at the start of a light meal following an overnight fast.

Amoxicillin chewable tablets, 125 mg and 250 mg, produced blood levels similar to those achieved with the corresponding doses of amoxicillin oral suspensions. Orally administered doses of amoxicillin suspension, 125 mg/5 mL and 250 mg/5 mL, result in average peak blood levels 1 to 2 hours after administration in the range of 1.5 µg/mL to 3.0 µg/mL and 3.5 µg/mL to 5.0 µg/mL, respectively.

Oral administration of single doses of 400-mg *Amoxil* chewable tablets and 400-mg/5 mL suspension to 24 adult volunteers yielded comparable pharmacokinetic data:

Dose†	$AUC_{0-\infty}$ (µg.hr./mL)	C_{max} (µg/mL)‡
amoxicillin	amoxicillin (±S.D.)	amoxicillin (±S.D.)
400 mg (5 mL of suspension)	17.1 (3.1)	5.92 (1.62)
400 mg (one chewable tablet)	17.9 (2.4)	5.18 (1.64)

† Administered at the start of a light meal.
‡ Mean values of 24 normal volunteers. Peak concentrations occurred approximately 1 hour after the dose.

Detectable serum levels are observed up to 8 hours after an orally administered dose of amoxicillin. Following a 1-gram dose and utilizing a special skin window technique to determine levels of the antibiotic, it was noted that therapeutic levels were found in the interstitial fluid. Approximately 60% of an orally administered dose of amoxicillin is excreted in the urine within 6 to 8 hours.

Microbiology
Amoxicillin is similar to ampicillin in its bactericidal action against susceptible organisms during the stage of active multiplication. It acts through the inhibition of biosynthesis of cell wall mucopeptide. Amoxicillin has been shown to be active against most strains of the following microorganisms, both *in vitro* and in clinical infections as described in the **INDICATIONS AND USAGE** section.

Aerobic gram-positive microorganisms:
Enterococcus faecalis
Staphylococcus spp.† (β-lactamase-negative strains only)
Streptococcus pneumoniae
Streptococcus spp. (α- and β-hemolytic strains only)

---

† Staphylococci which are susceptible to amoxicillin but resistant to methicillin/oxacillin should be considered as resistant to amoxicillin.

Aerobic gram-negative microorganisms:
Escherichia coli (β-lactamase-negative strains only)

Haemophilus influenzae (β-lactamase-negative strains only)
Neisseria gonorrhoeae (β-lactamase-negative strains only)
Proteus mirabilis (β-lactamase-negative strains only)

Helicobacter:
Helicobacter pylori

Susceptibility tests

Dilution techniques: Quantitative methods are used to determine antimicrobial minimum inhibitory concentrations (MICs). These MICs provide estimates of the susceptibility of bacteria to antimicrobial compounds. The MICs should be determined using a standardized procedure. Standardized procedures are based on a dilution method[1] (broth or agar) or equivalent with standardized inoculum concentrations and standardized concentrations of **ampicillin** powder. Ampicillin is sometimes used to predict susceptibility of *Streptococcus pneumoniae* to amoxicillin; however, some intermediate strains have been shown to be susceptible to amoxicillin. Therefore, *Streptococcus pneumoniae* susceptibility should be tested using amoxicillin powder. The MIC values should be interpreted according to the following criteria:

For gram-positive aerobes:
Enterococcus

MIC (µg/mL)	Interpretation
≤8	Susceptible (S)
≥16	Resistant (R)

Staphylococcus[a]

MIC (µg/mL)	Interpretation
≤ 0.25	Susceptible (S)
≥0.5	Resistant (R)

Streptococcus (except *S. pneumoniae*)

MIC (µg/mL)	Interpretation
≤0.25	Susceptible (S)
0.5 to 4	Intermediate (I)
≥8	Resistant (R)

S. pneumoniae[b]
(**Amoxicillin** powder should be used to determine susceptibility.)

MIC (µg/mL)	Interpretation
≤0.5	Susceptible (S)
1	Intermediate (I)
≥2	Resistant (R)

For gram-negative aerobes:
Enterobacteriaceae

MIC (µg/mL)	Interpretation
≤8	Susceptible (S)
16	Intermediate (I)
≥32	Resistant (R)

H. influenzae[c]

MIC (µg/mL)	Interpretation
≤1	Susceptible (S)
2	Intermediate (I)
≥4	Resistant (R)

---

a. Staphylococci which are susceptible to amoxicillin but resistant to methicillin/oxacillin should be considered as resistant to amoxicillin.

b. These interpretive standards are applicable only to broth microdilution susceptibility tests using cation-adjusted Mueller-Hinton broth with 2-5% lysed horse blood.

c. These interpretive standards are applicable only to broth microdilution test with *Haemophilus influenzae* using *Haemophilus* Test Medium (HTM).[1]

A report of "Susceptible" indicates that the pathogen is likely to be inhibited if the antimicrobial compound in the blood reaches the concentrations usually achievable. A report of "Intermediate" indicates that the result should be considered equivocal, and, if the microorganism is not fully susceptible to alternative, clinically feasible drugs, the test should be repeated. This category implies possible clinical applicability in body sites where the drug is physiologically concentrated or in situations where high dosage of drug can be used. This category also provides a buffer zone which prevents small uncontrolled technical factors from causing major discrepancies in interpretation. A report of "Resistant" indicates that the pathogen is not likely to be inhibited if the antimicrobial compound in the blood reaches the concentrations usually achievable; other therapy should be selected.

Standardized susceptibility test procedures require the use of laboratory control microorganisms to control the technical aspects of the laboratory procedures. Standard **ampicillin** powder should provide the following MIC values:

Microorganism	MIC (µg/mL)
E. coli ATCC 25922	2 to 8
E. faecalis ATCC 29212	0.5 to 2
H. influenzae ATCC 49247[d]	2 to 8
S. aureus ATCC 29213	0.25 to 1

Using **amoxicillin** to determine susceptibility:

Microorganism	MIC Range (µg/mL)
S. pneumoniae ATCC 49619[e]	0.03 to 0.12

d. This quality control range is applicable to only *H. influenzae* ATCC 49247 tested by a broth microdilution procedure using HTM.[1]

e. This quality control range is applicable to only *S. pneumoniae* ATCC 49619 tested by the broth microdilution procedure with cation-adjusted Mueller-Hinton broth with 2-5% lysed horse blood.

Diffusion techniques: Quantitative methods that require measurement of zone diameters also provide reproducible estimates of the susceptibility of bacteria to antimicrobial compounds. One such standardized procedure[2] requires the use of standardized inoculum concentrations. This procedure uses paper disks impregnated with 10 µg ampicillin to test the susceptibility of microorganisms, except *S. pneumoniae*, to amoxicillin. Interpretation involves correlation of the diameter obtained in the disk test with the MIC for **ampicillin**.

Reports from the laboratory providing results of the standard single-disk susceptibility test with a 10-µg ampicillin disk should be interpreted according to the following criteria:

For gram-positive aerobes:

Enterococcus

Zone Diameter (mm)	Interpretation
≥17	Susceptible (S)
≤16	Resistant (R)

Staphylococcus[f]

Zone Diameter (mm)	Interpretation
≥29	Susceptible (S)
≤28	Resistant (R)

β-hemolytic streptococci

Zone Diameter (mm)	Interpretation
≥26	Susceptible (S)
19 to 25	Intermediate (I)
≤18	Resistant (R)

NOTE: For streptococci (other than β-hemolytic streptococci and *S. pneumoniae*), an ampicillin MIC should be determined.

S. pneumoniae

S. pneumoniae should be tested using a 1-µg oxacillin disk. Isolates with oxacillin zone sizes of ≥20 mm are susceptible to amoxicillin. An amoxicillin MIC should be determined on isolates of *S. pneumoniae* with oxacillin zone sizes of ≤19 mm.

For gram-negative aerobes:

Enterobacteriaceae

Zone Diameter (mm)	Interpretation
≥17	Susceptible (S)
14 to 16	Intermediate (I)
≤13	Resistant (R)

H. influenzae[g]

Zone Diameter (mm)	Interpretation
≥22	Susceptible (S)
19 to 21	Intermediate (I)
≤18	Resistant (R)

f. Staphylococci which are susceptible to amoxicillin but resistant to methicillin/oxacillin should be considered as resistant to amoxicillin.

g. These interpretive standards are applicable only to disk diffusion susceptibility tests with *H. influenzae* using *Haemophilus* Test Medium (HTM).[2]

Interpretation should be as stated above for results using dilution techniques.

As with standard dilution techniques, disk diffusion susceptibility test procedures require the use of laboratory control microorganisms. The 10-µg **ampicillin** disk should provide the following zone diameters in these laboratory test quality control strains:

Microorganism	Zone diameter (mm)
E. coli ATCC 25922	16 to 22
H. influenzae ATCC 49247[h]	13 to 21
S. aureus ATCC 25923	27 to 35

Using 1-μg **oxacillin** disk:

Microorganism	Zone diameter (mm)
S. pneumoniae ATCC 49619[i]	8 to 12

h. This quality control range is applicable to only H. influenzae ATCC 49247 tested by a disk diffusion procedure using HTM.[2]

i. This quality control range is applicable to only S. pneumoniae ATCC 49619 tested by a disk diffusion procedure using Mueller-Hinton agar supplemented with 5% sheep blood and incubated in 5% CO_2.

Susceptibility testing for *Helicobacter pylori*
In vitro susceptibility testing methods and diagnostic products currently available for determining minimum inhibitory concentrations (MICs) and zone sizes have not been standardized, validated, or approved for testing *H. pylori* microorganisms.

Culture and susceptibility testing should be obtained in patients who fail triple therapy. If clarithromycin resistance is found, a non-clarithromycin-containing regimen should be used.

INDICATIONS AND USAGE

Amoxil (amoxicillin) is indicated in the treatment of infections due to susceptible (ONLY β-lactamase-negative) strains of the designated microorganisms in the conditions listed below:

Infections of the ear, nose, and throat due to *Streptococcus* spp. (α- and β-hemolytic strains only), *Streptococcus pneumoniae*, *Staphylococcus* spp., or *H. influenzae*

Infections of the genitourinary tract due to *E. coli*, *P. mirabilis*, or *E. faecalis*

Infections of the skin and skin structure due to *Streptococcus* spp. (α- and β-hemolytic strains only), *Staphylococcus* spp., or *E. coli*

Infections of the lower respiratory tract due to *Streptococcus* spp. (α- and β-hemolytic strains only), *Streptococcus pneumoniae*, *Staphylococcus* spp., or *H. influenzae*

Gonorrhea, acute uncomplicated (ano-genital and urethral infections) due to *N. gonorrhoeae* (males and females)

Therapy may be instituted prior to obtaining results from bacteriological and susceptibility studies to determine the causative organisms and their susceptibility to amoxicillin.

Indicated surgical procedures should be performed.

H. pylori eradication to reduce the risk of duodenal ulcer recurrence

Triple therapy: *Amoxil*/clarithromycin/lansoprazole

Amoxil, in combination with clarithromycin plus lansoprazole as triple therapy, is indicated for the treatment of patients with *H. pylori* infection and duodenal ulcer disease (active or one-year history of a duodenal ulcer) to eradicate *H. pylori*. Eradication of *H. pylori* has been shown to reduce the risk of duodenal ulcer recurrence. (See **CLINICAL STUDIES** and **DOSAGE AND ADMINISTRATION**.)

Dual therapy: *Amoxil*/lansoprazole

Amoxil (amoxicillin), in combination with lansoprazole delayed-release capsules as dual therapy, is indicated for the treatment of patients with *H. pylori* infection and duodenal ulcer disease (active or one-year history of a duodenal ulcer) **who are either allergic or intolerant to clarithromycin or in whom resistance to clarithromycin is known or suspected.** (See the clarithromycin package insert, **MICROBIOLOGY**.) Eradication of *H. pylori* has been shown to reduce the risk of duodenal ulcer recurrence. (See **CLINICAL STUDIES** and **DOSAGE AND ADMINISTRATION**.)

CONTRAINDICATIONS

A history of allergic reaction to any of the penicillins is a contraindication.

WARNINGS

SERIOUS AND OCCASIONALLY FATAL HYPERSENSITIVITY (ANAPHYLACTIC) REACTIONS HAVE BEEN REPORTED IN PATIENTS ON PENICILLIN THERAPY. ALTHOUGH ANAPHYLAXIS IS MORE FREQUENT FOLLOWING PARENTERAL THERAPY, IT HAS OCCURRED IN PATIENTS ON ORAL PENICILLINS. THESE REACTIONS ARE MORE LIKELY TO OCCUR IN INDIVIDUALS WITH A HISTORY OF PENICILLIN HYPERSENSITIVITY AND/OR A HISTORY OF SENSITIVITY TO MULTIPLE ALLERGENS. THERE HAVE BEEN REPORTS OF INDIVIDUALS WITH A HISTORY OF PENICILLIN HYPERSENSITIVITY WHO HAVE EXPERIENCED SEVERE REACTIONS WHEN TREATED WITH CEPHALOSPORINS. BEFORE INITIATING THERAPY WITH *AMOXIL*, CAREFUL INQUIRY SHOULD BE MADE CONCERNING PREVIOUS HYPERSENSITIVITY REACTIONS TO PENICILLINS, CEPHALOSPORINS, OR OTHER ALLERGENS. IF AN ALLERGIC REACTION OCCURS, *AMOXIL* SHOULD BE DISCONTINUED AND APPROPRIATE THERAPY INSTITUTED. SERIOUS ANAPHYLACTIC REACTIONS REQUIRE IMMEDIATE EMERGENCY TREATMENT WITH EPINEPHRINE. OXYGEN, INTRAVENOUS STEROIDS, AND AIRWAY MANAGEMENT, INCLUDING INTUBATION, SHOULD ALSO BE ADMINISTERED AS INDICATED.

Pseudomembranous colitis has been reported with nearly all antibacterial agents, including amoxicillin, and may range in severity from mild to life-threatening. Therefore, it is impor-

tant to consider this diagnosis in patients who present with diarrhea subsequent to the administration of antibacterial agents.

Treatment with antibacterial agents alters the normal flora of the colon and may permit overgrowth of clostridia. Studies indicate that a toxin produced by *Clostridium difficile* is a primary cause of "antibiotic-associated colitis."

After the diagnosis of pseudomembranous colitis has been established, appropriate therapeutic measures should be initiated. Mild cases of pseudomembranous colitis usually respond to drug discontinuation alone. In moderate to severe cases, consideration should be given to management with fluids and electrolytes, protein supplementation, and treatment with an antibacterial drug clinically effective against *Clostridium difficile* colitis.

PRECAUTIONS

General: The possibility of superinfections with mycotic or bacterial pathogens should be kept in mind during therapy. If superinfections occur, amoxicillin should be discontinued and appropriate therapy instituted.

Phenylketonurics: Each 200 mg *Amoxil* chewable tablet contains 1.82 mg phenylalanine; each 400 mg chewable tablet contains 3.64 mg phenylalanine. The *Amoxil* suspensions do not contain phenylalanine and can be used by phenylketonurics.

Laboratory Tests: As with any potent drug, periodic assessment of renal, hepatic, and hematopoietic function should be made during prolonged therapy.

All patients with gonorrhea should have a serologic test for syphilis at the time of diagnosis. Patients treated with amoxicillin should have a follow-up serologic test for syphilis after 3 months.

Drug Interactions: Probenecid decreases the renal tubular secretion of amoxicillin. Concurrent use of amoxicillin and probenecid may result in increased and prolonged blood levels of amoxicillin.

Chloramphenicol, macrolides, sulfonamides, and tetracyclines may interfere with the bactericidal effects of penicillin. This has been demonstrated *in vitro*; however, the clinical significance of this interaction is not well documented.

Drug/Laboratory Test Interactions: High urine concentrations of ampicillin may result in false-positive reactions when testing for the presence of glucose in urine using Clinitest®, Benedict's Solution or Fehling's Solution. Since this effect may also occur with amoxicillin, it is recommended that glucose tests based on enzymatic glucose oxidase reactions (such as Clinistix® or Tes-Tape®) be used.

Following administration of ampicillin to pregnant women, a transient decrease in plasma concentration of total conjugated estriol, estriol-glucuronide, conjugated estrone, and estradiol has been noted. This effect may also occur with amoxicillin.

Carcinogenesis, Mutagenesis, Impairment of Fertility: Long-term studies in animals have not been performed to evaluate carcinogenic potential. Studies to detect mutagenic potential of amoxicillin alone have not been conducted; however, the following information is available from tests on a 4:1 mixture of amoxicillin and potassium clavulanate (*Augmentin*). *Augmentin* was non-mutagenic in the Ames bacterial mutation assay, and the yeast gene conversion assay. *Augmentin* was weakly positive in the mouse lymphoma assay, but the trend toward increased mutation frequencies in this assay occurred at doses that were also associated with decreased cell survival. *Augmentin* was negative in the mouse micronucleus test, and in the dominant lethal assay in mice. Potassium clavulanate alone was tested in the Ames bacterial mutation assay and in the mouse micronucleus test, and was negative in each of these assays. In a multi-generation reproduction study in rats, no impairment of fertility or other adverse reproductive effects were seen at doses up to 500 mg/kg (approximately 3 times the human dose in mg/m^2).

Pregnancy: *Teratogenic Effects. Pregnancy Category B.* Reproduction studies have been performed in mice and rats at doses up to ten (10) times the human dose and have revealed no evidence of impaired fertility or harm to the fetus due to amoxicillin. There are, however, no adequate and well-controlled studies in pregnant women. Because animal reproduction studies are not always predictive of human response, this drug should be used during pregnancy only if clearly needed.

Labor and Delivery: Oral ampicillin-class antibiotics are poorly absorbed during labor. Studies in guinea pigs showed that intravenous administration of ampicillin slightly decreased the uterine tone and frequency of contractions but moderately increased the height and duration of contractions. However, it is not known whether use of amoxicillin in humans during labor or delivery has immediate or delayed adverse effects on the fetus, prolongs the duration of labor, or increases the likelihood that forceps delivery or other obstetrical intervention or resuscitation of the newborn will be necessary.

Nursing Mothers: Penicillins have been shown to be excreted in human milk. Amoxicillin use by nursing mothers may lead to sensitization of infants. Caution should be exercised when amoxicillin is administered to a nursing woman.

Pediatric Use: Because of incompletely developed renal function in neonates and young infants, the elimination of amoxicillin may be delayed. Dosing of Amoxil (amoxicillin) should be modified in pediatric patients 12 weeks or younger (≤3 months). (See **DOSAGE AND ADMINISTRATION**—Neonates and infants.)

ADVERSE REACTIONS

As with other penicillins, it may be expected that untoward reactions will be essentially limited to sensitivity phenomena. They are more likely to occur in individuals who have previously demonstrated hypersensitivity to penicillins and in those with a history of allergy, asthma, hay fever, or urticaria. The following adverse reactions have been reported as associated with the use of penicillins:

Gastrointestinal: nausea, vomiting, diarrhea, and hemorrhagic/pseudomembranous colitis. Onset of pseudomembranous colitis symptoms may occur during or after antibiotic treatment. (See **WARNINGS**.)

Hypersensitivity Reactions: Serum sickness like reactions, erythematous maculopapular rashes, erythema multiforme, Stevens-Johnson Syndrome, exfoliative dermatitis, toxic epidermal necrolysis, hypersensitivity vasculitis and urticaria have been reported.

NOTE: These hypersensitivity reactions may be controlled with antihistamines and, if necessary, systemic corticosteroids. Whenever such reactions occur, amoxicillin should be discontinued unless, in the opinion of the physician, the condition being treated is life-threatening and amenable only to amoxicillin therapy.

Liver: A moderate rise in AST (SGOT) and/or ALT (SGPT) has been noted, but the significance of this finding is unknown. Hepatic dysfunction including cholestatic jaundice, hepatic cholestasis and acute cytolytic hepatitis have been reported.

Hemic and Lymphatic Systems: Anemia, including hemolytic anemia, thrombocytopenia, thrombocytopenic purpura, eosinophilia, leukopenia, and agranulocytosis have been reported during therapy with penicillins. These reactions are usually reversible on discontinuation of therapy and are believed to be hypersensitivity phenomena.

Central Nervous System: Reversible hyperactivity, agitation, anxiety, insomnia, confusion, convulsions, behavioral changes, and/or dizziness have been reported rarely.

Combination therapy with clarithromycin and lansoprazole

In clinical trials using combination therapy with amoxicillin plus clarithromycin and lansoprazole, and amoxicillin plus lansoprazole, no adverse reactions peculiar to these drug combinations were observed. Adverse reactions that have occurred have been limited to those that had been previously reported with amoxicillin, clarithromycin, or lansoprazole.

Triple therapy: amoxicillin/clarithromycin/lansoprazole

The most frequently reported adverse events for patients who received triple therapy were diarrhea (7%), headache (6%), and taste perversion (5%). No treatment-emergent adverse events were observed at significantly higher rates with triple therapy than with any dual therapy regimen.

Dual therapy: amoxicillin/lansoprazole

The most frequently reported adverse events for patients who received amoxicillin t.i.d. plus lansoprazole t.i.d. dual therapy were diarrhea (8%) and headache (7%). No treatment-emergent adverse events were observed at significantly higher rates with amoxicillin t.i.d. plus lansoprazole t.i.d. dual therapy than with lansoprazole alone.

For more information on adverse reactions with clarithromycin or lansoprazole, refer to their package inserts, **ADVERSE REACTIONS**.

OVERDOSAGE

In case of overdosage, discontinue medication, treat symptomatically, and institute supportive measures as required. If the overdosage is very recent and there is no contraindication, an attempt at emesis or other means of removal of drug from the stomach may be performed. A prospective study of 51 pediatric patients at a poison-control center suggested that overdosages of less than 250 mg/kg of amoxicillin are not associated with significant clinical symptoms and do not require gastric emptying.[3]

Interstitial nephritis resulting in oliguric renal failure has been reported in a small number of patients after overdosage with amoxicillin. Renal impairment appears to be reversible with cessation of drug administration. High blood levels may occur more readily in patients with impaired renal function because of decreased renal clearance of amoxicillin. Amoxicillin may be removed from circulation by hemodialysis.

DOSAGE AND ADMINISTRATION

Amoxil capsules, chewable tablets and oral suspensions may be given without regard to meals. The 400-mg suspension, 400-mg chewable tablet and the 875-mg tablet have been studied only when administered at the start of a light meal. However, food effect studies have not been performed with the 200-mg and 500-mg formulations.

Neonates and infants aged ≤12 weeks (≤3 months)

Due to incompletely developed renal function affecting elimination of amoxicillin in this age group, the recommended upper dose of Amoxil (amoxicillin) is 30 mg/kg/day divided q12h. [See table on pages 156 and 157]

After reconstitution, the required amount of suspension should be placed directly on the child's tongue for swallowing. Alternate means of administration are to add the required amount of suspension to formula, milk, fruit juice, water, ginger ale, or cold drinks. These preparations should then be taken immediately. To be certain the child is receiving full dosage, such preparations should be consumed in entirety.

All patients with gonorrhea should be evaluated for syphilis. (See **PRECAUTIONS** — Laboratory Tests.)

Larger doses may be required for stubborn or severe infections.

General: It should be recognized that in the treatment of chronic urinary tract infections, frequent bacteriological and clinical appraisals are necessary. Smaller doses than those recommended above should not be used. Even higher doses may be needed at times. In stubborn infections, therapy may be required for several weeks. It may be necessary to continue clinical and/or bacteriological follow-up for several months after cessation of therapy. Except for gonorrhea, treatment should be continued for a minimum of 48 to 72 hours beyond the time that the patient becomes asymptomatic or evidence of bacterial eradication has been obtained. It is recommended that there be at least 10 days' treatment for any infection caused by *Streptococcus pyogenes* to prevent the occurrence of acute rheumatic fever.

H. pylori eradication to reduce the risk of duodenal ulcer recurrence

Triple therapy: Amoxil/*clarithromycin*/*lansoprazole*

The recommended adult oral dose is 1 gram *Amoxil*, 500 mg clarithromycin, and 30 mg lansoprazole, all given twice daily (q12h) for 14 days. (See **INDICATIONS AND USAGE.**)

Dual therapy: Amoxil/*lansoprazole*

The recommended adult oral dose is 1 gram Amoxil (amoxicillin) and 30 mg lansoprazole, each given three times daily (q8h) for 14 days. (See **INDICATIONS AND USAGE.**)

Please refer to clarithromycin and lansoprazole full prescribing information for **CONTRAINDICATIONS** and **WARNINGS,** and for information regarding dosing in elderly and renally impaired patients.

Dosing recommendations for adults with impaired renal function:

Patients with impaired renal function do not generally require a reduction in dose unless the impairment is severe. Severely impaired patients with a glomerular filtration rate of <30 mL/minute should not receive the 875-mg tablet. Patients with a glomerular filtration rate of 10 to 30 mL/minute should receive 500 mg or 250 mg every 12 hours, depending on the severity of the infection. Patients with a less than 10 mL/minute glomerular filtration

| **Adults and pediatric patients >3 months** | | | |
Infection	Severity‡	Usual Adult Dose	Usual Dose for Children >3 months§ ‖
Ear/nose/throat	Mild/Moderate	500 mg every 12 hours or 250 mg every 8 hours	25 mg/kg/day in divided doses every 12 hours **or** 20 mg/kg/day in divided doses every 8 hours
	Severe	875 mg every 12 hours or 500 mg every 8 hours	45 mg/kg/day in divided doses every 12 hours **or** 40 mg/kg/day in divided doses every 8 hours
Lower respiratory tract	Mild/Moderate or Severe	875 mg every 12 hours or 500 mg every 8 hours	45 mg/kg/day in divided doses every 12 hours **or** 40 mg/kg/day in divided doses every 8 hours
Skin/skin structure	Mild/Moderate	500 mg every 12 hours or 250 mg every 8 hours	25 mg/kg/day in divided doses every 12 hours **or** 20 mg/kg/day in divided doses every 8 hours
	Severe	875 mg every 12 hours or 500 mg every 8 hours	45 mg/kg/day in divided doses every 12 hours **or** 40 mg/kg/day in divided doses every 8 hours

Table continued on next page

Adults and pediatric patients >3 months *(cont.)*

Infection	Severity‡	Usual Adult Dose	Usual Dose for Children >3 months§ ‖
Genitourinary tract	Mild/Moderate	500 mg every 12 hours or 250 mg every 8 hours	25 mg/kg/day in divided doses every 12 hours **or** 20 mg/kg/day in divided doses every 8 hours
	Severe	875 mg every 12 hours or 500 mg every 8 hours	45 mg/kg/day in divided doses every 12 hours **or** 40 mg/kg/day in divided doses every 8 hours
Gonorrhea Acute, uncomplicated ano-genital and urethral infections in males and females		3 grams as single oral dose	Prepubertal children: 50 mg/kg *Amoxil*, combined with 25 mg/kg probenecid as a single dose. **NOTE: SINCE PROBENECID IS CONTRAINDICATED IN CHILDREN UNDER 2 YEARS, DO NOT USE THIS REGIMEN IN THESE CASES.**

‡ Dosing for infections caused by less susceptible organisms should follow the recommendations for severe infections.

§ The children's dosage is intended for individuals whose weight is less than 40 kg. Children weighing 40 kg or more should be dosed according to the adult recommendations.

‖ Each strength of *Amoxil* suspension is available as a chewable tablet for use by older children.

rate should receive 500 mg or 250 mg every 24 hours, depending on severity of the infection. Hemodialysis patients should receive 500 mg or 250 mg every 24 hours, depending on severity of the infection. They should receive an additional dose both during and at the end of dialysis.

There are currently no dosing recommendations for pediatric patients with impaired renal function.

Directions For Mixing Oral Suspension

Prepare suspension at time of dispensing as follows: Tap bottle until all powder flows freely. Add approximately 1/3 of the total amount of water for reconstitution (see table below) and shake vigorously to wet powder. Add remainder of the water and again shake vigorously.

Bottle Size	125 mg/ 5 mL	Amount of Water Required for Reconstitution
80 mL		62 mL
100 mL		78 mL
150 mL		116 mL

Each teaspoonful (5 mL) will contain 125 mg amoxicillin.

Bottle Size	200 mg/ 5 mL	Amount of Water Required for Reconstitution
5 mL		5 mL
50 mL		39 mL
75 mL		57 mL
100 mL		76 mL

Each teaspoonful (5 mL) will contain 200 mg amoxicillin.

Bottle Size	250 mg/ 5 mL	Amount of Water Required for Reconstitution
80 mL		59 mL
100 mL		74 mL
150 mL		111 mL

Each teaspoonful (5 mL) will contain 250 mg amoxicillin.

Bottle Size	400 mg/ 5 mL	Amount of Water Required for Reconstitution
5 mL		5 mL
50 mL		36 mL

75 mL	54 mL
100 mL	71 mL

Each teaspoonful (5 mL) will contain 400 mg amoxicillin.

Directions For Mixing Pediatric Drops

Prepare pediatric drops at time of dispensing as follows: Add the required amount of water (see table below) to the bottle and shake vigorously. Each mL of suspension will then contain amoxicillin trihydrate equivalent to 50 mg amoxicillin.

Bottle Size	Amount of Water Required for Reconstitution
15 mL	12 mL
30 mL	23 mL

NOTE: SHAKE BOTH ORAL SUSPENSION AND PEDIATRIC DROPS WELL BEFORE USING. Keep bottle tightly closed. Any unused portion of the reconstituted suspension must be discarded after 14 days. Refrigeration preferable, but not required.

HOW SUPPLIED

Amoxil (amoxicillin) Capsules. Each capsule contains 250 mg or 500 mg amoxicillin as the trihydrate.

250-mg Capsule

NDC 0029-6006-30	bottles of 100
NDC 0029-6006-32	bottles of 500

500-mg Capsule

NDC 0029-6007-30	bottles of 100
NDC 0029-6007-32	bottles of 500

Amoxil (amoxicillin) Tablets. Each tablet contains 500 mg or 875 mg amoxicillin as the trihydrate.

500-mg Tablet

NDC 0029-6046-12	bottles of 20
NDC 0029-6046-20	bottles of 100
NDC 0029-6046-25	bottles of 500

875-mg Tablet

NDC 0029-6047-12	bottles of 20
NDC 0029-6047-20	bottles of 100
NDC 0029-6047-25	bottles of 500

Amoxil (amoxicillin) Chewable Tablets. Each cherry-banana-peppermint-flavored tablet contains 125 mg, 200 mg, 250 mg or 400 mg amoxicillin as the trihydrate.

125-mg Tablet

NDC 0029-6004-39	bottles of 60

200-mg Tablet

NDC 0029-6044-12	bottles of 20
NDC 0029-6044-20	bottles of 100

250-mg Tablet

NDC 0029-6005-13	bottles of 30
NDC 0029-6005-30	bottles of 100

400-mg Tablet

NDC 0029-6045-12	bottles of 20
NDC 0029-6045-20	bottles of 100

Amoxil (amoxicillin) for Oral Suspension. Each 5 mL of reconstituted strawberry-flavored suspension contains 125 mg amoxicillin as the trihydrate. Each 5 mL of reconstituted bubble-gum-flavored suspension contains 200, 250, or 400 mg amoxicillin as the trihydrate.

125 mg/5 mL

NDC 0029-6008-21	80-mL bottle
NDC 0029-6008-23	100-mL bottle
NDC 0029-6008-22	150-mL bottle

200 mg/5 mL

NDC 0029-6048-54	50-mL bottle
NDC 0029-6048-55	75-mL bottle
NDC 0029-6048-59	100-mL bottle

250 mg/5 mL

NDC 0029-6009-21	80-mL bottle
NDC 0029-6009-23	100-mL bottle
NDC 0029-6009-22	150-mL bottle

400 mg/5 mL

NDC 0029-6049-54	50-mL bottle
NDC 0029-6049-55	75-mL bottle
NDC 0029-6049-59	100-mL bottle

NDC 0029-6048-18	**200-mg unit dose bottle**
NDC 0029-6049-18	**400-mg unit dose bottle**

Amoxil (amoxicillin) Pediatric Drops for Oral Suspension. Each mL of bubble-gum-flavored reconstituted suspension contains 50 mg amoxicillin as the trihydrate.

NDC 0029-6035-20	15-mL bottle
NDC 0029-6038-39	30-mL bottle

Store capsules, unreconstituted powder, and 125-mg and 250-mg chewable tablets at or below 20°C (68°F). The 200-mg and 400-mg chewable tablets may be stored at or below 25°C (77°F). Store 500-mg and 875-mg tablets at or below 25°C (77°F). Dispense in a tight container.

CLINICAL STUDIES

H. pylori eradication to reduce the risk of duodenal ulcer recurrence

Randomized, double-blind clinical studies performed in the U.S. in patients with *H. pylori* and duodenal ulcer disease (defined as an active ulcer or history of an ulcer within one year) evaluated the efficacy of lansoprazole in combination with amoxicillin capsules and clarithromycin tablets as triple 14-day therapy, or in combination with amoxicillin capsules as dual 14-day therapy, for the eradication of *H. pylori*. Based on the results of these studies, the safety and efficacy of two different eradication regimens were established:

Triple therapy: amoxicillin 1 gram b.i.d./clarithromycin 500 mg b.i.d./lansoprazole 30 mg b.i.d.

Dual therapy: amoxicillin 1 gram t.i.d./lansoprazole 30 mg t.i.d.

All treatments were for 14 days. *H. pylori* eradication was defined as two negative tests (culture and histology) at 4 to 6 weeks following the end of treatment.

Triple therapy was shown to be more effective than all possible dual therapy combinations. Dual therapy was shown to be more effective than both monotherapies. Eradication of *H. pylori* has been shown to reduce the risk of duodenal ulcer recurrence.

***H. pylori* Eradication Rates — Triple Therapy (amoxicillin/clarithromycin/lansoprazole) Percent of Patients Cured [95% Confidence Interval] (Number of Patients)**

Study	Triple Therapy Evaluable Analysis†	Triple Therapy Intent-to-Treat Analysis‡
Study 1	92§ [80.0–97.7] (n=48)	86§ [73.3–93.5] (n=55)
Study 2	86‖ [75.7–93.6] (n=66)	83‖ [72.0–90.8] (n=70)

† This analysis was based on evaluable patients with confirmed duodenal ulcer (active or within one year) and *H. pylori* infection at baseline defined as at least two of three positive endoscopic tests from CLOtest®, (Delta West Ltd., Bentley, Australia), histology and/or culture. Patients were included in the analysis if they completed the study. Additionally, if patients dropped out of the study due to an adverse event related to the study drug, they were included in the analysis as failures of therapy.

‡ Patients were included in the analysis if they had documented *H. pylori* infection at baseline as defined above and had a confirmed duodenal ulcer (active or within one year). All dropouts were included as failures of therapy.

§ ($p<0.05$) versus lansoprazole/amoxicillin and lansoprazole/clarithromycin dual therapy.

‖ ($p<0.05$) versus clarithromycin/amoxicillin dual therapy.

***H. pylori* Eradication Rates - Dual Therapy (amoxicillin/lansoprazole) Percent of Patients Cured [95% Confidence Interval] (Number of Patients)**

Study	Dual Therapy Evaluable Analysis¶	Dual Therapy Intent-to-Treat Analysis††
Study 1	77‡‡ [62.5–87.2] (n=51)	70‡‡ [56.8–81.2] (n=60)
Study 2	66§§ [51.9–77.5] (n=58)	61§§ [48.5–72.9] (n=67)

¶ This analysis was based on evaluable patients with confirmed duodenal ulcer (active or within one year) and *H. pylori* infection at baseline defined as at least two of three positive endoscopic tests from CLOtest®, histology and/or culture. Patients were included in the analysis if they completed the study. Additionally, if patients dropped out of the study due to an adverse event related to the study drug, they were included in the analysis as failures of therapy.

†† Patients were included in the analysis if they had documented *H. pylori* infection at baseline as defined above and had a confirmed duodenal ulcer (active or within one year). All dropouts were included as failures of therapy.

‡‡ ($p<0.05$) versus lansoprazole alone.

§§ ($p<0.05$) versus lansoprazole alone or amoxicillin alone.

REFERENCES

1. National Committee for Clinical Laboratory Standards. Methods for Dilution Antimicrobial Susceptibility Tests for Bacteria that Grow Aerobically - Fourth Edition; Approved Standard. NCCLS Document M7-A4, Vol. 17, No. 2. NCCLS, Wayne, PA, January 1997.

2. National Committee for Clinical Laboratory Standards. Performance Standards for Antimicrobial Disk Susceptibility Tests - Sixth Edition; Approved Standard. NCCLS Document M2-A6, Vol. 17, No. 1. NCCLS, Wayne, PA, January 1997.

3. Swanson-Biearman B, Dean BS, Lopez G, Krenzelok EP. The effects of penicillin and cephalosporin ingestions in children less than six years of age. *Vet Hum Toxicol* 1988;30:66-67.

GlaxoSmithKline, Research Triangle Park, NC 27709

January 2000/AM:L19

AUGMENTIN®   ℞

[*äg-ment' in*]

**amoxicillin/clavulanate potassium
Powder for Oral Suspension and
Chewable Tablets**

DESCRIPTION

Augmentin is an oral antibacterial combination consisting of the semisynthetic antibiotic amoxicillin and the β-lactamase inhibitor, clavulanate potassium (the potassium salt of clavulanic acid). Amoxicillin is an analog of ampicillin, derived from the basic penicillin nucleus, 6-aminopenicillanic acid. The amoxicillin molecular formula is $C_{16}H_{19}N_3O_5S\cdot3H_2O$ and the molecular weight is 419.46. Chemically, amoxicillin is $(2S,5R,6R)$-6-[(R) - (-)-2-Amino-2- (p -hydroxyphenyl)acetamido] - 3,3 - dimethyl - 7 -oxo-4-thia-1-azabicyclo [3.2.0] heptane-2-carboxylic acid trihydrate.

Clavulanic acid is produced by the fermentation of *Streptomyces clavuligerus*. It is a β-lactam structurally related to the penicillins and possesses the ability to inactivate a wide variety of β-lactamases by blocking the active sites of these enzymes. Clavulanic acid is particularly active against the clinically important plasmid mediated β-lactamases frequently responsible for transferred drug resistance to penicillins and cephalosporins. The clavulanate potassium molecular formula is $C_8H_8KNO_5$ and the molecular weight is 237.25. Chemically clavulanate potassium is potassium (Z)-$(2R,5R)$-3-(2-hydroxyethylidene) -7-oxo-4-oxa-1-azabicyclo [3.2.0]-heptane-2-carboxylate.

Inactive Ingredients: Powder for Oral Suspension—Colloidal silicon dioxide, flavorings (See HOW SUPPLIED), succinic acid, xanthan gum, and one or more of the following: aspartame•, hydroxypropyl methylcellulose, mannitol, silica gel, silicon dioxide and sodium saccharin. Chewable Tablets—Colloidal silicon dioxide, flavorings (See HOW SUPPLIED), magnesium stearate, mannitol and one or more of the following: aspartame•, D&C Yellow No. 10, FD&C Red No. 40, glycine, sodium saccharin and succinic acid.

• See PRECAUTIONS—Information for Patients.

Each 125 mg chewable tablet and each 5 mL reconstituted *Augmentin* 125 mg/5 mL oral suspension contains 0.16 mEq potassium.
Each 250 mg chewable tablet and each 5 mL of reconstituted *Augmentin* 250 mg/5 mL oral suspension contains 0.32 mEq potassium.
Each 200 mg chewable tablet and each 5 mL of reconstituted *Augmentin* 200 mg/5 mL oral suspension contains 0.14 mEq potassium.
Each 400 mg chewable tablet and each 5 mL of reconstituted *Augmentin* 400 mg/5 mL oral suspension contains 0.29 mEq of potassium.

CLINICAL PHARMACOLOGY

Amoxicillin and clavulanate potassium are well absorbed from the gastrointestinal tract after oral administration of *Augmentin*. Dosing in the fasted or fed state has minimal effect on the pharmacokinetics of amoxicillin. While *Augmentin* can be given without regard to meals, absorption of clavulanate potassium when taken with food is greater relative to the fasted state. In one study, the relative bioavailability of clavulanate was reduced when *Augmentin* was dosed at 30 and 150 minutes after the start of a high fat breakfast. The safety and efficacy of *Augmentin* have been established in clinical trials where *Augmentin* was taken without regard to meals.

Oral administration of single doses of 400 mg *Augmentin* chewable tablets and 400 mg/5 mL suspension to 28 adult volunteers yielded comparable pharmacokinetic data:

[See table below]

Oral administration of 5 mL of *Augmentin* 250 mg/5 mL suspension or the equivalent dose of 10 mL *Augmentin* 125 mg/5 mL suspension provides average peak serum concentrations approximately 1 hour after dosing of 6.9 µg/mL for amoxicillin and 1.6 µg/mL for clavulanic acid. The areas under the serum concentration curves obtained during the first 4 hours after dosing were 12.6 µg.hr/mL for amoxicillin and 2.9 µg.hr/mL for clavulanic acid when 5 mL of *Augmentin* 250 mg/5 mL suspension or equivalent dose of 10 mL of *Augmentin* 125 mg/5 mL suspension was administered to adult volunteers. One *Augmentin*

Dose[†]	AUC $_{0-\infty}$ (µg.hr./mL)		C$_{max}$ (µg/mL)[‡]	
(amoxicillin/clavulanate potassium)	amoxicillin ($\pm$S.D.)	clavulanate potassium ($\pm$S.D.)	amoxicillin ($\pm$S.D.)	clavulanate potassium ($\pm$S.D.)
400/57 mg (5 mL of suspension)	17.29 $\pm$2.28	2.34 $\pm$0.94	6.94 $\pm$1.24	1.10 $\pm$0.42
400/57 mg (one chewable tablet)	17.24 $\pm$2.64	2.17 $\pm$0.73	6.67 $\pm$1.37	1.03 $\pm$0.33

† Administered at the start of a light meal.
‡ Mean values of 28 normal volunteers. Peak concentrations occurred approximately 1 hour after the dose.

250 mg chewable tablet or 2 *Augmentin* 125 mg chewable tablets are equivalent to 5 mL of *Augmentin* 250 mg/5 mL suspension and provide similar serum levels of amoxicillin and clavulanic acid.

Amoxicillin serum concentrations achieved with *Augmentin* are similar to those produced by the oral administration of equivalent doses of amoxicillin alone. The half-life of amoxicillin after the oral administration of *Augmentin* is 1.3 hours and that of clavulanic acid is 1.0 hour. Time above the minimum inhibitory concentration of 1.0 µg/mL for amoxicillin has been shown to be similar after corresponding q12h and q8h dosing regimens of *Augmentin* in adults and children.

Approximately 50% to 70% of the amoxicillin and approximately 25% to 40% of the clavulanic acid are excreted unchanged in urine during the first 6 hours after administration of 10 mL of *Augmentin* 250 mg/5 mL suspension. Concurrent administration of probenecid delays amoxicillin excretion but does not delay renal excretion of clavulanic acid.

Neither component in *Augmentin* is highly protein-bound; clavulanic acid has been found to be approximately 25% bound to human serum and amoxicillin approximately 18% bound.

Amoxicillin diffuses readily into most body tissues and fluids with the exception of the brain and spinal fluid. The results of experiments involving the administration of clavulanic acid to animals suggest that this compound, like amoxicillin, is well distributed in body tissues. Two hours after oral administration of a single 35 mg/kg dose of *Augmentin* suspension to fasting children, average concentrations of 3.0 µg/mL of amoxicillin and 0.5 µg/mL of clavulanic acid were detected in middle ear effusions.

Microbiology: Amoxicillin is a semisynthetic antibiotic with a broad spectrum of bactericidal activity against many gram-positive and gram-negative microorganisms. Amoxicillin is, however, susceptible to degradation by β-lactamases and, therefore, the spectrum of activity does not include organisms which produce these enzymes. Clavulanic acid is a β-lactam, structurally related to the penicillins, which possesses the ability to inactivate a wide range of β-lactamase enzymes commonly found in microorganisms resistant to penicillins and cephalosporins. In particular, it has good activity against the clinically important plasmid mediated β-lactamases frequently responsible for transferred drug resistance.

The formulation of amoxicillin and clavulanic acid in *Augmentin* protects amoxicillin from degradation by β-lactamase enzymes and effectively extends the antibiotic spectrum of amoxicillin to include many bacteria normally resistant to amoxicillin and other β-lactam antibiotics. Thus, *Augmentin* possesses the distinctive properties of a broad-spectrum antibiotic and a β-lactamase inhibitor.

Amoxicillin/clavulanic acid has been shown to be active against most strains of the following microorganisms, both *in vitro* and in clinical infections as described in the INDICATIONS AND USAGE section.

GRAM-POSITIVE AEROBES

Staphylococcus aureus (β-lactamase and non-β-lactamase producing)[§]
[§] Staphylococci which are resistant to methicillin/oxacillin must be considered resistant to amoxicillin/clavulanic acid.

GRAM-NEGATIVE AEROBES

Enterobacter species (Although most strains of *Enterobacter* species are resistant *in vitro,* clinical efficacy has been demonstrated with *Augmentin* in urinary tract infections caused by these organisms.)

Escherichia coli (β-lactamase and non-β-lactamase producing)

Haemophilus influenzae (β-lactamase and non-β-lactamase producing)

Klebsiella species (All known strains are β-lactamase producing.)

Moraxella catarrhalis (β-lactamase and non-β-lactamase producing)

The following *in vitro* data are available, **but their clinical significance is unknown.**

Amoxicillin/clavulanic acid exhibits *in vitro* minimal inhibitory concentrations (MICs) of 0.5 µg/mL or less against most (≥90%) strains of *Streptococcus pneumoniae* [||]; MICs of 0.06 µg/mL or less against most (≥90%) strains of *Neisseria gonorrhoeae;* MICs of 4 µg/mL or less against most (≥90%) strains of staphylococci and anaerobic bacteria; and MICs of 8 µg/mL or less against most (≥90%) strains of other listed organisms. However, with the exception of organisms shown to respond to amoxicillin alone, the safety and effectiveness of amoxicillin/clavulanic acid in treating clinical infections due to these microorganisms have not been established in adequate and well-controlled clinical trials.

[||] Because amoxicillin has greater *in vitro* activity against *Streptococcus pneumoniae* than does ampicillin or penicillin, the majority of *S. pneumoniae* strains with intermediate susceptibility to ampicillin or penicillin are fully susceptible to amoxicillin.

GRAM-POSITIVE AEROBES

Enterococcus faecalis [¶]

Staphylococcus epidermidis (β-lactamase and non-β-lactamase producing)

Staphylococcus saprophyticus (β-lactamase and non-β-lactamase producing)

Streptococcus pneumoniae [¶**]

Streptococcus pyogenes [¶**]

viridans group *Streptococcus* [¶**]

GRAM-NEGATIVE AEROBES

Eikenella corrodens (β-lactamase and non-β-lactamase producing)

Neisseria gonorrhoeae [¶] (β-lactamase and non-β-lactamase producing)

Proteus mirabilis [¶] (β-lactamase and non-β-lactamase producing)

ANAEROBIC BACTERIA
Bacteroides species, including *Bacteroides fragilis* (β-lactamase and non-β-lactamase producing)
Fusobacterium species (β-lactamase and non-β-lactamase producing)
Peptostreptococcus species[**]
¶ Adequate and well-controlled clinical trials have established the effectiveness of amoxicillin alone in treating certain clinical infections due to these organisms.
** These are non-β-lactamase-producing organisms and, therefore, are susceptible to amoxicillin alone.

SUSCEPTIBILITY TESTING
Dilution Techniques: Quantitative methods are used to determine antimicrobial minimal inhibitory concentrations (MICs). These MICs provide estimates of the susceptibility of bacteria to antimicrobial compounds. The MICs should be determined using a standardized procedure. Standardized procedures are based on a dilution method[1] (broth or agar) or equivalent with standardized inoculum concentrations and standardized concentrations of amoxicillin/clavulanate potassium powder.
The recommended dilution pattern utilizes a constant amoxicillin/clavulanate potassium ratio of 2 to 1 in all tubes with varying amounts of amoxicillin. MICs are expressed in terms of the amoxicillin concentration in the presence of clavulanic acid at a constant 2 parts amoxicillin to 1 part clavulanic acid. The MIC values should be interpreted according to the following criteria:

RECOMMENDED RANGES FOR AMOXICILLIN/CLAVULANIC ACID SUSCEPTIBILITY TESTING
For gram-negative enteric aerobes:

MIC (µg/mL)	Interpretation
≤8/4	Susceptible (S)
16/8	Intermediate (I)
≥32/16	Resistant (R)

For *Staphylococcus*[††] and *Haemophilus* species:

MIC (µg/mL)	Interpretation
≤4/2	Susceptible (S)
≥8/4	Resistant (R)

†† Staphylococci which are susceptible to amoxicillin/clavulanic acid but resistant to methicillin/oxacillin must be considered as resistant.

For *Streptococcus pneumoniae:* Isolates should be tested using amoxicillin/clavulanic acid and the following criteria should be used:

MIC (µg/mL)	Interpretation
≤0.5/0.25	Susceptible (S)
1/0.5	Intermediate (I)
≥2/1	Resistant (R)

A report of "Susceptible" indicates that the pathogen is likely to be inhibited if the antimicrobial compound in the blood reaches the concentration usually achievable. A report of "Intermediate" indicates that the result should be considered equivocal, and, if the microorganism is not fully susceptible to alternative, clinically feasible drugs, the test should be repeated. This category implies possible clinical applicability in body sites where the drug is physiologically concentrated or in situations where high dosage of drug can be used. This category also provides a buffer zone that prevents small uncontrolled technical factors from causing major discrepancies in interpretation. A report of "Resistant" indicates that the pathogen is not likely to be inhibited if the antimicrobial compound in the blood reaches the concentrations usually achievable; other therapy should be selected.
Standardized susceptibility test procedures require the use of laboratory control microorganisms to control the technical aspects of the laboratory procedures. Standard amoxicillin/clavulanate potassium powder should provide the following MIC values:

Microorganism	MIC Range (µg/mL)[‡‡]
Escherichia coli ATCC 25922	2 to 8
Escherichia coli ATCC 35218	4 to 16
Enterococcus faecalis ATCC 29212	0.25 to 1.0
Haemophilus influenzae ATCC 49247	2 to 16
Staphylococcus aureus ATCC 29213	0.12 to 0.5
Streptococcus pneumoniae ATCC 49619	0.03 to 0.12

‡‡ Expressed as concentration of amoxicillin in the presence of clavulanic acid at a constant 2 parts amoxicillin to 1 part clavulanic acid.

Diffusion Techniques: Quantitative methods that require measurement of zone diameters also provide reproducible estimates of the susceptibility of bacteria to antimicrobial compounds. One such standardized procedure[2] requires the use of standardized inoculum concentrations. This procedure uses paper disks impregnated with 30 µg of amoxicillin/clavulanate potassium (20 µg amoxicillin plus 10 µg clavulanate potassium) to test the susceptibility of microorganisms to amoxicillin/clavulanic acid.
Reports from the laboratory providing results of the standard single-disk susceptibility test with a 30 µg amoxicillin/clavulanate potassium (20 µg amoxicillin plus 10 µg clavulanate potassium) disk should be interpreted according to the following criteria:

RECOMMENDED RANGES FOR AMOXICILLIN/CLAVULANIC ACID SUSCEPTIBILITY TESTING
For *Staphylococcus*[§§] species and *H. influenzae*[a]:

Zone Diameter (mm)	Interpretation
≥20	Susceptible (S)
≤19	Resistant (R)

For other organisms except *S. pneumoniae*[b] and *N. gonorrhoeae*[c]:

Zone Diameter (mm)	Interpretation
≥18	Susceptible (S)
14 to 17	Intermediate (I)
≤13	Resistant (R)

[§§] Staphylococci which are resistant to methicillin/oxacillin must be considered as resistant to amoxicillin/clavulanic acid.

[a] A broth microdilution method should be used for testing *H. influenzae*. Beta-lactamase negative, ampicillin-resistant strains must be considered resistant to amoxicillin/clavulanic acid.

[b] Susceptibility of *S. pneumoniae* should be determined using a 1 µg oxacillin disk. Isolates with oxacillin zone sizes of ≥20 mm are susceptible to amoxicillin/clavulanic acid. An amoxicillin/clavulanic acid MIC should be determined on isolates of *S. pneumoniae* with oxacillin zone sizes of ≤19 mm.

[c] A broth microdilution method should be used for testing *N. gonorrhoeae* and interpreted according to penicillin breakpoints.

Interpretation should be as stated above for results using dilution techniques. Interpretation involves correlation of the diameter obtained in the disk test with the MIC for amoxicillin/clavulanic acid.

As with standardized dilution techniques, diffusion methods require the use of laboratory control microorganisms that are used to control the technical aspects of the laboratory procedures. For the diffusion technique, the 30 µg amoxicillin/clavulanate potassium (20 µg amoxicillin plus 10 µg clavulanate potassium) disk should provide the following zone diameters in these laboratory quality control strains:

Microorganism	Zone Diameter (mm)
Escherichia coli ATCC 25922	19 to 25 mm
Escherichia coli ATCC 35218	18 to 22 mm
Staphylococcus aureus ATCC 25923	28 to 36 mm

INDICATIONS AND USAGE

Augmentin is indicated in the treatment of infections caused by susceptible strains of the designated organisms in the conditions listed below:

Lower Respiratory Tract Infections—caused by β-lactamase-producing strains of *Haemophilus influenzae* and *Moraxella (Branhamella) catarrhalis*.

Otitis Media—caused by β-lactamase-producing strains of *Haemophilus influenzae* and *Moraxella (Branhamella) catarrhalis*.

Sinusitis—caused by β-lactamase-producing strains of *Haemophilus influenzae* and *Moraxella (Branhamella) catarrhalis*.

Skin and Skin Structure Infections—caused by β-lactamase-producing strains of *Staphylococcus aureus, Escherichia coli* and *Klebsiella* spp.

Urinary Tract Infections—caused by β-lactamase-producing strains of *Escherichia coli, Klebsiella* spp. and *Enterobacter* spp.

While *Augmentin* is indicated only for the conditions listed above, infections caused by ampicillin-susceptible organisms are also amenable to *Augmentin* treatment due to its amoxicillin content. Therefore, mixed infections caused by ampicillin-susceptible organisms and β-lactamase-producing organisms susceptible to *Augmentin* should not require the addition of another antibiotic. Because amoxicillin has greater *in vitro* activity against *Streptococcus pneumoniae* than does ampicillin or penicillin, the majority of *S. pneumoniae* strains with intermediate susceptibility to ampicillin or penicillin are fully susceptible to amoxicillin and *Augmentin*. (See Microbiology subsection.)

Bacteriological studies, to determine the causative organisms and their susceptibility to *Augmentin*, should be performed together with any indicated surgical procedures.

Therapy may be instituted prior to obtaining the results from bacteriological and susceptibility studies to determine the causative organisms and their susceptibility to *Augmentin* when there is reason to believe the infection may involve any of the β-lactamase-producing organisms listed above. Once the results are known, therapy should be adjusted, if appropriate.

CONTRAINDICATIONS

Augmentin is contraindicated in patients with a history of allergic reactions to any penicillin. It is also contraindicated in patients with a previous history of *Augmentin*-associated cholestatic jaundice/hepatic dysfunction.

WARNINGS

SERIOUS AND OCCASIONALLY FATAL HYPERSENSITIVITY (ANAPHYLACTIC) REACTIONS HAVE BEEN REPORTED IN PATIENTS ON PENICILLIN THERAPY. THESE REACTIONS ARE MORE LIKELY TO OCCUR IN INDIVIDUALS WITH A HISTORY OF PENICILLIN HYPERSENSITIVITY AND/OR A HISTORY OF SENSITIVITY TO MULTIPLE ALLERGENS. THERE HAVE BEEN REPORTS OF INDIVIDUALS WITH A HISTORY OF PENICILLIN HYPERSENSITIVITY WHO HAVE EXPERIENCED SEVERE REACTIONS WHEN TREATED WITH CEPHALOSPORINS. BEFORE INITIATING THERAPY WITH *AUGMENTIN*, CAREFUL

INQUIRY SHOULD BE MADE CONCERNING PREVIOUS HYPERSENSITIVITY REACTIONS TO PENICILLINS, CEPHALOSPORINS OR OTHER ALLERGENS. IF AN ALLERGIC REACTION OCCURS, *AUGMENTIN* SHOULD BE DISCONTINUED AND THE APPROPRIATE THERAPY INSTITUTED. **SERIOUS ANAPHYLACTIC REACTIONS REQUIRE IMMEDIATE EMERGENCY TREATMENT WITH EPINEPHRINE. OXYGEN, INTRAVENOUS STEROIDS AND AIRWAY MANAGEMENT, INCLUDING INTUBATION, SHOULD ALSO BE ADMINISTERED AS INDICATED.**

Pseudomembranous colitis has been reported with nearly all antibacterial agents, including *Augmentin*, and has ranged in severity from mild to life-threatening. Therefore, it is important to consider this diagnosis in patients who present with diarrhea subsequent to the administration of antibacterial agents.

Treatment with antibacterial agents alters the normal flora of the colon and may permit overgrowth of clostridia. Studies indicate that a toxin produced by *Clostridium difficile* is one primary cause of "antibiotic associated colitis." After the diagnosis of pseudomembranous colitis has been established, appropriate therapeutic measures should be initiated. Mild cases of pseudomembranous colitis usually respond to drug discontinuation alone. In moderate to severe cases, consideration should be given to management with fluids and electrolytes, protein supplementation and treatment with an antibacterial drug clinically effective against *Clostridium difficile* colitis.

Augmentin should be used with caution in patients with evidence of hepatic dysfunction. Hepatic toxicity associated with the use of *Augmentin* is usually reversible. On rare occasions, deaths have been reported (less than 1 death reported per estimated 4 million prescriptions worldwide). These have generally been cases associated with serious underlying diseases or concomitant medications. (See CONTRAINDICATIONS and ADVERSE REACTIONS—*Liver.*)

PRECAUTIONS

General: While *Augmentin* possesses the characteristic low toxicity of the penicillin group of antibiotics, periodic assessment of organ system functions, including renal, hepatic and hematopoietic function, is advisable during prolonged therapy. A high percentage of patients with mononucleosis who receive ampicillin develop an erythematous skin rash. Thus, ampicillin class antibiotics should not be administered to patients with mononucleosis.

The possibility of superinfections with mycotic or bacterial pathogens should be kept in mind during therapy. If superinfections occur (usually involving *Pseudomonas* or *Candida*), the drug should be discontinued and/or appropriate therapy instituted.

Information for the Patient: Augmentin may be taken every 8 hours or every 12 hours, depending on the strength of the product prescribed. Each dose should be taken with a meal or snack to reduce the possibility of gastrointestinal upset. Many antibiotics can cause diarrhea. If diarrhea is severe or lasts more than 2 or 3 days, call your doctor.

Make sure your child completes the entire prescribed course of treatment, even if he/she begins to feel better after a few days. Keep suspension refrigerated. Shake well before using. When dosing a child with *Augmentin* suspension (liquid), use a dosing spoon or medicine dropper. Be sure to rinse the spoon or dropper after each use. Bottles of *Augmentin* suspension may contain more liquid than required. Follow your doctor's instructions about the amount to use and the days of treatment your child requires. Discard any unused medicine.

Phenylketonurics: Each 200 mg *Augmentin* chewable tablet contains 2.1 mg phenylalanine; each 400 mg chewable tablet contains 4.2 mg phenylalanine; each 5 mL of either the 200 mg/5 mL or 400 mg/5 mL oral suspension contains 7 mg phenylalanine. The other *Augmentin* products do not contain phenylalanine and can be used by phenylketonurics. Contact your physician or pharmacist.

Drug Interactions: Probenecid decreases the renal tubular secretion of amoxicillin. Concurrent use with *Augmentin* may result in increased and prolonged blood levels of amoxicillin. Co-administration of probenecid cannot be recommended.

The concurrent administration of allopurinol and ampicillin increases substantially the incidence of rashes in patients receiving both drugs as compared to patients receiving ampicillin alone. It is not known whether this potentiation of ampicillin rashes is due to allopurinol or the hyperuricemia present in these patients. There are no data with *Augmentin* and allopurinol administered concurrently.

In common with other broad-spectrum antibiotics, *Augmentin* may reduce the efficacy of oral contraceptives.

Drug/Laboratory Test Interactions: Oral administration of *Augmentin* will result in high urine concentrations of amoxicillin. High urine concentrations of ampicillin may result in false-positive reactions when testing for the presence of glucose in urine using Clinitest®, Benedict's Solution or Fehling's Solution. Since this effect may also occur with amoxicillin and therefore *Augmentin*, it is recommended that glucose tests based on enzymatic glucose oxidase reactions (such as Clinistix® or Tes-Tape®) be used.

Following administration of ampicillin to pregnant women a transient decrease in plasma concentration of total conjugated estriol, estriol-glucuronide, conjugated estrone and estradiol has been noted. This effect may also occur with amoxicillin and therefore *Augmentin.*

Carcinogenesis, Mutagenesis, Impairment of Fertility: Long-term studies in animals have not been performed to evaluate carcinogenic potential.

Mutagenesis: The mutagenic potential of *Augmentin* was investigated *in vitro* with an Ames test, a human lymphocyte cytogenetic assay, a yeast test and a mouse lymphoma forward mutation assay, and *in vivo* with mouse micronucleus tests and a dominant lethal test. All were negative apart from the *in vitro* mouse lymphoma assay where weak activity was found at very high, cytotoxic concentrations.

Impairment of Fertility: Augmentin at oral doses of up to 1200 mg/kg/day (5.7 times the maximum human dose, 1480 mg/m^2/day, based on body surface area) was found to have no effect on fertility and reproductive performance in rats, dosed with a 2:1 ratio formulation of amoxicillin:clavulanate.

Teratogenic effects. Pregnancy (Category B): Reproduction studies performed in pregnant rats and mice given *Augmentin* at oral dosages up to 1200 mg/kg/day, equivalent to 7200 and 4080 mg/m^2/day, respectively (4.9 and 2.8 times the maximum human oral dose based on body surface area), revealed no evidence of harm to the fetus due to *Augmentin*. There are, however, no adequate and well-controlled studies in pregnant women. Because animal reproduction studies are not always predictive of human response, this drug should be used during pregnancy only if clearly needed.

Labor and Delivery: Oral ampicillin class antibiotics are generally poorly absorbed during labor. Studies in guinea pigs have shown that intravenous administration of ampicillin decreased the uterine tone, frequency of contractions, height of contractions and duration of contractions. However, it is not known whether the use of *Augmentin* in humans during labor or delivery has immediate or delayed adverse effects on the fetus, prolongs the duration of labor, or increases the likelihood that forceps delivery or other obstetrical intervention or resuscitation of the newborn will be necessary.

Nursing Mothers: Ampicillin class antibiotics are excreted in the milk; therefore, caution should be exercised when *Augmentin* is administered to a nursing woman.

Pediatric Use: Because of incompletely developed renal function in neonates and young infants, the elimination of amoxicillin may be delayed. Dosing of *Augmentin* should be modified in pediatric patients younger than 12 weeks (3 months). (See DOSAGE AND ADMINISTRATION–Pediatric.)

ADVERSE REACTIONS

Augmentin is generally well tolerated. The majority of side effects observed in clinical trials were of a mild and transient nature and less than 3% of patients discontinued therapy because of drug-related side effects. From the original premarketing studies, where both pe-diatric and adult patients were enrolled, the most frequently reported adverse effects were diarrhea/loose stools (9%), nausea (3%), skin rashes and urticaria (3%), vomiting (1%) and vaginitis (1%). The overall incidence of side effects, and in particular diarrhea, increased with the higher recommended dose. Other less frequently reported reactions include: abdominal discomfort, flatulence and headache.

In pediatric patients (aged 2 months to 12 years), one U.S./Canadian clinical trial was conducted which compared *Augmentin* 45/6.4 mg/kg/day (divided q12h) for 10 days versus *Augmentin* 40/10 mg/kg/day (divided q8h) for 10 days in the treatment of acute otitis media. A total of 575 patients were enrolled, and only the suspension formulations were used in this trial. Overall, the adverse event profile seen was comparable to that noted above. However, there were differences in the rates of diarrhea, skin rashes/urticaria, and diaper area rashes. (See CLINICAL STUDIES.)

The following adverse reactions have been reported for ampicillin class antibiotics:

Gastrointestinal: Diarrhea, nausea, vomiting, indigestion, gastritis, stomatitis, glossitis, black "hairy" tongue, mucocutaneous candidiasis, enterocolitis, and hemorrhagic/pseudomembranous colitis. Onset of pseudomembranous colitis symptoms may occur during or after antibiotic treatment. (See WARNINGS.)

Hypersensitivity Reactions: Skin rashes, pruritus, urticaria, angioedema, serum sickness-like reactions (urticaria or skin rash accompanied by arthritis, arthralgia, myalgia and frequently fever), erythema multiforme (rarely Stevens-Johnson Syndrome) and an occasional case of exfoliative dermatitis (including toxic epidermal necrolysis) have been reported. These reactions may be controlled with antihistamines and, if necessary, systemic corticosteroids. Whenever such reactions occur, the drug should be discontinued, unless the opinion of the physician dictates otherwise. Serious and occasional fatal hypersensitivity (anaphylactic) reactions can occur with oral penicillin. (See WARNINGS.)

Liver: A moderate rise in AST (SGOT) and/or ALT (SGPT) has been noted in patients treated with ampicillin class antibiotics but the significance of these findings is unknown. Hepatic dysfunction, including increases in serum transaminases (AST and/or ALT), serum bilirubin and/or alkaline phosphatase, has been infrequently reported with *Augmentin*. It has been reported more commonly in the elderly, in males, or in patients on prolonged treatment. The histologic findings on liver biopsy have consisted of predominantly cholestatic, hepatocellular, or mixed cholestatic-hepatocellular changes. The onset of signs/symptoms of hepatic dysfunction may occur during or several weeks after therapy has been discontinued. The hepatic dysfunction, which may be severe, is usually reversible. On rare occasions, deaths have been reported (less than 1 death reported per estimated 4 million prescriptions worldwide). These have generally been cases associated with serious underlying diseases or concomitant medications.

Renal: Interstitial nephritis and hematuria have been reported rarely.

Hemic and Lymphatic Systems: Anemia, including hemolytic anemia, thrombocytopenia, thrombocytopenic purpura, eosinophilia, leukopenia and agranulocytosis have been reported during therapy with penicillins. These reactions are usually reversible on discontinuation of therapy and are believed to be hypersensitivity phenomena. A slight thrombocytosis was noted in less than 1% of the patients treated with *Augmentin*. There have been reports of increased prothrombin time in patients receiving *Augmentin* and anticoagulant therapy concomitantly.

Central Nervous System: Agitation, anxiety, behavioral changes, confusion, convulsions, dizziness, insomnia, and reversible hyperactivity have been reported rarely.

OVERDOSAGE

Most patients have been asymptomatic following overdosage or have experienced primarily gastrointestinal symptoms including stomach and abdominal pain, vomiting, and diarrhea. Rash, hyperactivity, or drowsiness have also been observed in a small number of patients. In the case of overdosage, discontinue *Augmentin*, treat symptomatically, and institute supportive measures as required. If the overdosage is very recent and there is no contraindication, an attempt at emesis or other means of removal of drug from the stomach may be performed. A prospective study of 51 pediatric patients at a poison center suggested that overdosages of less than 250 mg/kg of amoxicillin are not associated with significant clinical symptoms and do not require gastric emptying.[3]

Interstitial nephritis resulting in oliguric renal failure has been reported in a small number of patients after overdosage with amoxicillin. Renal impairment appears to be reversible with cessation of drug administration. High blood levels may occur more readily in patients with impaired renal function because of decreased renal clearance of both amoxicillin and clavulanate. Both amoxicillin and clavulanate are removed from the circulation by hemodialysis.

DOSAGE AND ADMINISTRATION

Dosage:

Pediatric Patients: Based on the amoxicillin component, *Augmentin* should be dosed as follows:

Neonates and infants aged < 12 weeks (3 months)

Due to incompletely developed renal function affecting elimination of amoxicillin in this age group, the recommended dose of *Augmentin* is 30 mg/kg/day divided q12h, based on the amoxicillin component. Clavulanate elimination is unaltered in this age group. Experience with the 200 mg/5 mL formulation in this age group is limited and, thus, use of the 125 mg/5 mL oral suspension is recommended.

Patients aged 12 weeks (3 months) and older

INFECTIONS	DOSING REGIMEN	
	q12h‖ ‖	q8h
	200 mg/5 mL or 400 mg/5 mL oral suspension¶¶	125 mg/5 mL or 250 mg/5 mL oral suspension¶¶
Otitis media[***], sinusitis, lower respiratory tract infections, and more severe infections	45 mg/kg/day q12h	40 mg/kg/day q8h
Less severe infections	25 mg/kg/day q12h	20 mg/kg/day q8h

‖ ‖ The q12h regimen is recommended as it is associated with significantly less diarrhea. (See CLINICAL STUDIES.) However, the q12h formulations (200 mg and 400 mg) contain aspartame and should not be used by phenylketonurics.

¶ Each strength of *Augmentin* suspension is available as a chewable tablet for use by older children.

*** Duration of therapy studied and recommended for acute otitis media is 10 days.

Pediatric patients weighing 40 kg and more should be dosed according to the following adult recommendations: The usual adult dose is 1 *Augmentin* 500 mg tablet every 12 hours or 1 *Augmentin* 250 mg tablet every 8 hours. For more severe infections and infections of the respiratory tract, the dose should be 1 *Augmentin* 875 mg tablet every 12 hours or 1 *Augmentin* 500 mg tablet every 8 hours. Among adults treated with 875 mg every 12 hours, significantly fewer experienced severe diarrhea or withdrawals with diarrhea vs. adults treated with 500 mg every 8 hours. For detailed adult dosage recommendations, please see complete prescribing information for *Augmentin* Tablets.

Hepatically impaired patients should be dosed with caution and hepatic function monitored at regular intervals. (See WARNINGS.)

Adults: Adults who have difficulty swallowing may be given the 125 mg/5 mL or 250 mg/5 mL suspension in place of the 500 mg tablet. The 200 mg/5 mL suspension or the 400 mg/5 mL suspension may be used in place of the 875 mg tablet. See dosage recommendations above for children weighing 40 kg or more.

The *Augmentin* 250 mg tablet and the 250 mg chewable tablet do not contain the same amount of clavulanic acid (as the potassium salt). The *Augmentin* 250 mg tablet contains 125 mg of clavulanic acid, whereas the 250 mg chewable tablet contains 62.5 mg of clavulanic acid. Therefore, the *Augmentin* 250 mg tablet and the 250 mg chewable tablet should not be substituted for each other, as they are not interchangeable.

Due to the different amoxicillin to clavulanic acid ratios in the *Augmentin* 250 mg tablet (250/125) versus the *Augmentin* 250 mg chewable tablet (250/62.5), the *Augmentin* 250 mg tablet should not be used until the child weighs at least 40 kg and more.

DIRECTIONS FOR MIXING ORAL SUSPENSION

Prepare a suspension at time of dispensing as follows: Tap bottle until all the powder flows freely. Add approximately $^2/_3$ of the total amount of water for reconstitution (see table below) and shake vigorously to suspend powder. Add remainder of the water and again shake vigorously.

***Augmentin* 125 mg/5 mL Suspension**

Bottle Size	Amount of Water Required for Reconstitution
75 mL	67 mL
100 mL	90 mL
150 mL	134 mL

Each teaspoonful (5 mL) will contain 125 mg amoxicillin and 31.25 mg of clavulanic acid as the potassium salt.

***Augmentin* 200 mg/5 mL Suspension**

Bottle Size	Amount of Water Required for Reconstitution
50 mL	47 mL
75 mL	69 mL
100 mL	91 mL

Each teaspoonful (5 mL) will contain 200 mg amoxicillin and 28.5 mg of clavulanic acid as the potassium salt.

***Augmentin* 250 mg/5 mL Suspension**

Bottle Size	Amount of Water Required for Reconstitution
75 mL	65 mL
100 mL	87 mL
150 mL	130 mL

Each teaspoonful (5 mL) will contain 250 mg amoxicillin and 62.5 mg of clavulanic acid as the potassium salt.

***Augmentin* 400 mg/5 mL Suspension**

Bottle Size	Amount of Water Required for Suspension
50 mL	44 mL
75 mL	66 mL
100 mL	87 mL

Each teaspoonful (5 mL) will contain 400 mg amoxicillin and 57.0 mg of clavulanic acid as the potassium salt.

Note: SHAKE ORAL SUSPENSION WELL BEFORE USING.

Reconstituted suspension must be stored under refrigeration and discarded after 10 days.

Administration: *Augmentin* may be taken without regard to meals; however, absorption of clavulanate potassium is enhanced when *Augmentin* is administered at the start of a meal. To minimize the potential for gastrointestinal intolerance, *Augmentin* should be taken at the start of a meal.

HOW SUPPLIED

***AUGMENTIN* 125 MG/5 ML FOR ORAL SUSPENSION:** Each 5 mL of reconstituted banana-flavored suspension contains 125 mg amoxicillin and 31.25 mg clavulanic acid as the potassium salt.

NDC 0029-6085-39 .... 75 mL bottle
NDC 0029-6085-23 .... 100 mL bottle
NDC 0029-6085-22 .... 150 mL bottle

***AUGMENTIN* 200 MG/5 ML FOR ORAL SUSPENSION:** Each 5 mL of reconstituted orange-raspberry-flavored suspension contains 200 mg amoxicillin and 28.5 mg clavulanic acid as the potassium salt.

NDC 0029-6087-29 .... 50 mL bottle
NDC 0029-6087-39 .... 75 mL bottle
NDC 0029-6087-51 .... 100 mL bottle

***AUGMENTIN* 250 MG/5 ML FOR ORAL SUSPENSION:** Each 5 mL of reconstituted orange-flavored suspension contains 250 mg amoxicillin and 62.5 mg clavulanic acid as the potassium salt.

NDC 0029-6090-39 .... 75 mL bottle
NDC 0029-6090-23 .... 100 mL bottle
NDC 0029-6090-22 .... 150 mL bottle

***AUGMENTIN* 400 MG/5 ML FOR ORAL SUSPENSION:** Each 5 mL of reconstituted orange-raspberry-flavored suspension contains 400 mg amoxicillin and 57 mg clavulanic acid as the potassium salt.

NDC 0029-6092-29 .... 50 mL bottle
NDC 0029-6092-39 .... 75 mL bottle
NDC 0029-6092-51 .... 100 mL bottle

***AUGMENTIN* 125 MG CHEWABLE TABLETS:** Each mottled yellow, round, lemon-lime-flavored tablet, debossed with BMP 189, contains 125 mg amoxicillin as the trihydrate and 31.25 mg clavulanic acid as the potassium salt.

NDC 0029-6073-47 .... carton of 30 tablets

***AUGMENTIN* 200 MG CHEWABLE TABLETS:** Each mottled pink, round, biconvex, cherry-

banana-flavored tablet contains 200 mg amoxicillin as the trihydrate and 28.5 mg clavulanic acid as the potassium salt.
NDC 0029-6071-12 .... carton of 20 tablets
AUGMENTIN 250 MG CHEWABLE TABLETS:
Each mottled yellow, round, lemon-lime-flavored tablet, debossed with BMP 190, contains 250 mg amoxicillin as the trihydrate and 62.5 mg clavulanic acid as the potassium salt.
NDC 0029-6074-47 .... carton of 30 tablets
AUGMENTIN 400 MG CHEWABLE TABLETS:
Each mottled pink, round, biconvex, cherry-banana-flavored tablet contains 400 mg amoxicillin as the trihydrate and 57.0 mg clavulanic acid as the potassium salt.
NDC 0029-6072-12 .... carton of 20 tablets
AUGMENTIN is also supplied as:
AUGMENTIN 250 MG TABLETS (250 mg amoxicillin/125 mg clavulanic acid):
NDC 0029-6075-27 .... bottles of 30
NDC 0029-6075-31 .... 100 Unit Dose tablets
AUGMENTIN 500 MG TABLETS (500 mg amoxicillin/125 mg clavulanic acid):
NDC 0029-6080-12 .... bottles of 20
NDC 0029-6080-31 .... 100 Unit Dose tablets
AUGMENTIN 875 MG TABLETS (875 mg amoxicillin/125 mg clavulanic acid):
NDC 0029-6086-12 .... bottles of 20
NDC 0029-6086-21 .... 100 Unit Dose tablets
Store tablets and dry powder at or below 25°C (77°F). Dispense in original containers. Store reconstituted suspension under refrigeration. Discard unused suspension after 10 days.

CLINICAL STUDIES

In pediatric patients (aged 2 months to 12 years), one U.S./Canadian clinical trial was conducted which compared *Augmentin* 45/6.4 mg/kg/day (divided q12h) for 10 days versus *Augmentin* 40/10 mg/kg/day (divided q8h) for 10 days in the treatment of acute otitis media. Only the suspension formulations were used in this trial. A total of 575 patients were enrolled, with an even distribution among the two treatment groups and a comparable number of patients were evaluable (i.e., ≥84%) per treatment group. Strict otitis media-specific criteria were required for eligibility and a strong correlation was found at the end of therapy and follow-up between these criteria and physician assessment of clinical response. The clinical efficacy rates at the end of therapy visit (defined as 2–4 days after the completion of therapy) and at the follow-up visit (defined as 22–28 days post-completion of therapy) were comparable for the two treatment groups, with the following cure rates obtained for the evaluable patients: At end of therapy, 87.2% (n=265) and 82.3% (n=260) for 45 mg/

kg/day q12h and 40 mg/kg/day q8h, respectively. At follow-up, 67.1% (n=249) and 68.7% (n=243) for 45 mg/kg/day q12h and 40 mg/kg/day q8h, respectively.
The incidence of diarrhea††† was significantly lower in patients in the q12h treatment group compared to patients who received the q8h regimen (14.3% and 34.3%, respectively). In addition, the number of patients with either severe diarrhea or who were withdrawn with diarrhea was significantly lower in the q12h treatment group (3.1% and 7.6% for the q12h/10 day and q8h/10 day, respectively). In the q12h treatment group, 3 patients (1.0%) were withdrawn with an allergic reaction, while 1 patient (0.3%) in the q8h group was withdrawn for this reason. The number of patients with a candidal infection of the diaper area was 3.8% and 6.2% for the q12h and q8h groups, respectively.
It is not known if the finding of a statistically significant reduction in diarrhea with the oral suspensions dosed q12h, versus suspensions dosed q8h, can be extrapolated to the chewable tablets. The presence of mannitol in the chewable tablets may contribute to a different diarrhea profile. The q12h oral suspensions are sweetened with aspartame only.

††† Diarrhea was defined as either: (a) three or more watery or four or more loose/watery stools in one day; OR (b) two watery stools per day or three loose/watery stools per day for two consecutive days.

REFERENCES

1. National Committee for Clinical Laboratory Standards. Methods for Dilution Antimicrobial Susceptibility Tests for Bacteria That Grow Aerobically — Third Edition. Approved Standard NCCLS Document M7-A3, Vol. 13, No. 25. NCCLS, Villanova, PA, Dec. 1993.
2. National Committee for Clinical Laboratory Standards. Performance Standard for Antimicrobial Disk Susceptibility Tests — Fifth Edition. Approved Standard NCCLS Document M2-A5, Vol. 13, No. 24. NCCLS, Villanova, PA, Dec. 1993.
3. Swanson-Biearman B, Dean BS, Lopez G, Krenzelok EP. The effects of penicillin and cephalosporin ingestions in children less than six years of age. *Vet Hum Toxicol* 1988; 30:66-67.
GlaxoSmithKline, Research Triangle Park, NC 27709
©2001, GlaxoSmithKline
All rights reserved.
March 1999/AG:PL6

AUGMENTIN® ℞

[äg-mint' in]
brand of
amoxicillin/clavulanate potassium
Tablets

DESCRIPTION

Augmentin is an oral antibacterial combination consisting of the semisynthetic antibiotic amoxicillin and the β-lactamase inhibitor, clavulanate potassium (the potassium salt of clavulanic acid). Amoxicillin is an analog of ampicillin, derived from the basic penicillin nucleus, 6-aminopenicillanic acid. The amoxicillin molecular formula is $C_{16}H_{19}N_3O_5S\cdot3H_2O$ and the molecular weight is 419.46. Chemically, amoxicillin is (2S,5R,6R)-6-[(R)-(-)-2-Amino-2-(p-hydroxyphenyl)acetamido] -3,3- dimethyl -7-oxo-4-thia -1- azabicyclo[3.2.0]heptane-2-carboxylic acid trihydrate.

Clavulanic acid is produced by the fermentation of Streptomyces clavuligerus. It is a β-lactam structurally related to the penicillins and possesses the ability to inactivate a wide variety of β-lactamases by blocking the active sites of these enzymes. Clavulanic acid is particularly active against the clinically important plasmid mediated β-lactamases frequently responsible for transferred drug resistance to penicillins and cephalosporins. The clavulanate potassium molecular formula is $C_8H_9KNO_5$ and the molecular weight is 237.25. Chemically clavulanate potassium is potassium (Z)-(2R, 5R)-3-(2-hydroxyethylidene)-7-oxo-4-oxa-1-azabicyclo[3.2.0]-heptane-2-carboxylate.

Inactive Ingredients: Colloidal silicon dioxide, hydroxypropyl methylcellulose, magnesium stearate, microcrystalline cellulose, polyethylene glycol, sodium starch glycolate and titanium dioxide.

Each Augmentin tablet contains 0.63 mEq potassium.

CLINICAL PHARMACOLOGY

Amoxicillin and clavulanate potassium are well absorbed from the gastrointestinal tract after oral administration of Augmentin. Dosing in the fasted or fed state has minimal ef-

fect on the pharmacokinetics of amoxicillin. While Augmentin can be given without regard to meals, absorption of clavulanate potassium when taken with food is greater relative to the fasted state. In one study, the relative bioavailability of clavulanate was reduced when Augmentin was dosed at 30 and 150 minutes after the start of a high fat breakfast. The safety and efficacy of Augmentin have been established in clinical trials where Augmentin was taken without regard to meals.

Mean* amoxicillin and clavulanate potassium pharmacokinetic parameters are shown in the table below:

[See table below]

Amoxicillin serum concentrations achieved with Augmentin are similar to those produced by the oral administration of equivalent doses of amoxicillin alone. The half-life of amoxicillin after the oral administration of Augmentin is 1.3 hours and that of clavulanic acid is 1.0 hour.

Approximately 50% to 70% of the amoxicillin and approximately 25% to 40% of the clavulanic acid are excreted unchanged in urine during the first 6 hours after administration of a single Augmentin 250 mg or 500 mg tablet. Concurrent administration of probenecid delays amoxicillin excretion but does not delay renal excretion of clavulanic acid.

Neither component in Augmentin is highly protein-bound; clavulanic acid has been found to be approximately 25% bound to human serum and amoxicillin approximately 18% bound.

Amoxicillin diffuses readily into most body tissues and fluids with the exception of the brain and spinal fluid. The results of experiments involving the administration of clavulanic acid to animals suggest that this compound, like amoxicillin, is well distributed in body tissues.

Microbiology: Amoxicillin is a semisynthetic antibiotic with a broad spectrum of bactericidal activity against many gram-positive and gram-negative microorganisms. Amoxicillin is, however, susceptible to degradation by β-lactamases and, therefore, the spectrum of activity does not include organisms which produce these enzymes. Clavulanic acid is a β-lactam, structurally related to the penicillins, which

Dose† and regimen	AUC_{0-24} (µg.hr/mL)		C_{max} (µg/mL)	
amoxicillin/ clavulanate potassium	amoxicillin (±S.D.)	clavulanate potassium (±S.D.)	amoxicillin (±S.D.)	clavulanate potassium (±S.D.)
250/125 mg q8h	26.7 ± 4.56	12.6 ± 3.25	3.3 ± 1.12	1.5 ± 0.70
500/125 mg q12h	33.4 ± 6.76	8.6 ± 1.95	6.5 ± 1.41	1.8 ± 0.61
500/125 mg q8h	53.4 ± 8.87	15.7 ± 3.86	7.2 ± 2.26	2.4 ± 0.83
875/125 mg q12h	53.5 ± 12.31	10.2 ± 3.04	11.6 ± 2.78	2.2 ± 0.99

* Mean values of 14 normal volunteers (n=15 for clavulanate potassium in the low-dose regimens). Peak concentrations occurred approximately 1.5 hours after the dose.

† Administered at the start of a light meal.

possesses the ability to inactivate a wide range of β-lactamase enzymes commonly found in microorganisms resistant to penicillins and cephalosporins. In particular, it has good activity against the clinically important plasmid mediated β-lactamases frequently responsible for transferred drug resistance.

The formulation of amoxicillin and clavulanic acid in *Augmentin* protects amoxicillin from degradation by β-lactamase enzymes and effectively extends the antibiotic spectrum of amoxicillin to include many bacteria normally resistant to amoxicillin and other β-lactam antibiotics. Thus, *Augmentin* possesses the properties of a broad-spectrum antibiotic and a β-lactamase inhibitor.

Amoxicillin/clavulanic acid has been shown to be active against most strains of the following microorganisms, both *in vitro* and in clinical infections as described in the INDICATIONS AND USAGE section.

GRAM-POSITIVE AEROBES

Staphylococcus aureus (β-lactamase and non-β-lactamase producing)[‡]

[‡] Staphylococci which are resistant to methicillin/oxacillin must be considered resistant to amoxicillin/clavulanic acid.

GRAM-NEGATIVE AEROBES

Enterobacter species (Although most strains of *Enterobacter* species are resistant *in vitro*, clinical efficacy has been demonstrated with *Augmentin* in urinary tract infections caused by these organisms.)

Escherichia coli (β-lactamase and non-β-lactamase producing)

Haemophilus influenzae (β-lactamase and non-β-lactamase producing)

Klebsiella species (All known strains are β-lactamase producing.)

Moraxella catarrhalis (β-lactamase and non-β-lactamase producing)

The following *in vitro* data are available, **but their clinical significance is unknown.**

Amoxicillin/clavulanic acid exhibits *in vitro* minimal inhibitory concentrations (MICs) of 0.5 µg/mL or less against most (≥90%) strains of *Streptococcus pneumoniae*[§]; MICs of 0.06 µg/mL or less against most (≥90%) strains of *Neisseria gonorrhoeae*; MICs of 4 µg/mL or less against most (≥90%) strains of staphylococci and anaerobic bacteria; and MICs of 8 µg/mL or less against most (≥90%) strains of other listed organisms. However, with the exception of organisms shown to respond to amoxicillin alone, the safety and effectiveness of amoxicillin/clavulanic acid in treating clinical infections due to these microorganisms have not been established in adequate and well-controlled clinical trials.

[§] Because amoxicillin has greater *in vitro* activity against *Streptococcus pneumoniae* than does ampicillin or penicillin, the majority of *S. pneumoniae* strains with intermediate susceptibility to ampicillin or penicillin are fully susceptible to amoxicillin.

GRAM-POSITIVE AEROBES

Enterococcus faecalis[||]

Staphylococcus epidermidis (β-lactamase and non-β-lactamase producing)

Staphylococcus saprophyticus (β-lactamase and non-β-lactamase producing)

Streptococcus pneumoniae[|| ¶]

Streptococcus pyogenes[|| ¶]

viridans group *Streptococcus*[|| ¶]

GRAM-NEGATIVE AEROBES

Eikenella corrodens (β-lactamase and non-β-lactamase producing)

Neisseria gonorrhoeae[||] (β-lactamase and non-β-lactamase producing)

Proteus mirabilis[||] (β-lactamase and non-β-lactamase producing)

ANAEROBIC BACTERIA

Bacteroides species, including *Bacteroides fragilis* (β-lactamase and non-β-lactamase producing)

Fusobacterium species (β-lactamase and non-β-lactamase producing)

Peptostreptococcus species[¶]

[||] Adequate and well-controlled clinical trials have established the effectiveness of amoxicillin alone in treating certain clinical infections due to these organisms.

[¶] These are non-β-lactamase-producing organisms and, therefore, are susceptible to amoxicillin alone.

SUSCEPTIBILITY TESTING

Dilution Techniques: Quantitative methods are used to determine antimicrobial minimal inhibitory concentrations (MICs). These MICs provide estimates of the susceptibility of bacteria to antimicrobial compounds. The MICs should be determined using a standardized procedure. Standardized procedures are based on a dilution method[1] (broth or agar) or equivalent with standardized inoculum concentrations and standardized concentrations of amoxicillin/clavulanate potassium powder.

The recommended dilution pattern utilizes a constant amoxicillin/clavulanate potassium ratio of 2 to 1 in all tubes with varying amounts of amoxicillin. MICs are expressed in terms of the amoxicillin concentration in the presence of clavulanic acid at a constant 2 parts amoxicillin to 1 part clavulanic acid. The MIC values should be interpreted according to the following criteria:

RECOMMENDED RANGES FOR AMOXICILLIN/CLAVULANIC ACID SUSCEPTIBILITY TESTING

For gram-negative enteric aerobes:

MIC (µg/mL)	Interpretation
≤8/4	Susceptible (S)
16/8	Intermediate (I)
≥32/16	Resistant (R)

For *Staphylococcus*** and *Haemophilus* species:

MIC (µg/mL)	Interpretation
≤4/2	Susceptible (S)
≥8/4	Resistant (R)

** Staphylococci which are susceptible to amoxicillin/clavulanic acid but resistant to methicillin/oxacillin must be considered as resistant.

For *Streptococcus pneumoniae*: Isolates should be tested using amoxicillin/clavulanic acid and the following criteria should be used:

MIC (μg/mL)	Interpretation
≤0.5/0.25	Susceptible (S)
1/0.5	Intermediate (I)
≥2/1	Resistant (R)

A report of "Susceptible" indicates that the pathogen is likely to be inhibited if the antimicrobial compound in the blood reaches the concentration usually achievable. A report of "Intermediate" indicates that the result should be considered equivocal, and, if the microorganism is not fully susceptible to alternative, clinically feasible drugs, the test should be repeated. This category implies possible clinical applicability in body sites where the drug is physiologically concentrated or in situations where high dosage of drug can be used. This category also provides a buffer zone which prevents small uncontrolled technical factors from causing major discrepancies in interpretation. A report of "Resistant" indicates that the pathogen is not likely to be inhibited if the antimicrobial compound in the blood reaches the concentrations usually achievable; other therapy should be selected.

Standardized susceptibility test procedures require the use of laboratory control microorganisms to control the technical aspects of the laboratory procedures. Standard amoxicillin/clavulanate potassium powder should provide the following MIC values:

Microorganism	MIC Range (μg/mL) ††
Escherichia coli ATCC 25922	2 to 8
Escherichia coli ATCC 35218	4 to 16
Enterococcus faecalis ATCC 29212	0.25 to 1.0
Haemophilus influenzae ATCC 49247	2 to 16
Staphylococcus aureus ATCC 29213	0.12 to 0.5
Streptococcus pneumoniae ATCC 49619	0.03 to 0.12

†† Expressed as concentration of amoxicillin in the presence of clavulanic acid at a constant 2 parts amoxicillin to 1 part clavulanic acid.

Diffusion Techniques: Quantitative methods that require measurement of zone diameters also provide reproducible estimates of the susceptibility of bacteria to antimicrobial compounds. One such standardized procedure[2] requires the use of standardized inoculum concentrations. This procedure uses paper disks impregnated with 30 μg of amoxicillin/clavulanate potassium (20 μg amoxicillin plus 10 μg clavulanate potassium) to test the susceptibility of microorganisms to amoxicillin/clavulanic acid.

Reports from the laboratory providing results of the standard single-disk susceptibility test with a 30 μg amoxicillin/clavulanate acid (20 μg amoxicillin plus 10 μg clavulanate potassium) disk should be interpreted according to the following criteria:

RECOMMENDED RANGES FOR AMOXICILLIN/CLAVULANIC ACID SUSCEPTIBILITY TESTING

For *Staphylococcus*‡‡ species and *H. influenzae*[a]:

Zone Diameter (mm)	Interpretation
≥20	Susceptible (S)
≤19	Resistant (R)

For other organisms except *S. pneumoniae*[b] and *N. gonorrhoeae*[c]:

Zone Diameter (mm)	Interpretation
≥18	Susceptible (S)
14 to 17	Intermediate (I)
≤13	Resistant (R)

‡‡ Staphylococci which are resistant to methicillin/oxacillin must be considered as resistant to amoxicillin/clavulanic acid.

a A broth microdilution method should be used for testing *H. influenzae*. Beta-lactamase negative, ampicillin-resistant strains must be considered resistant to amoxicillin/clavulanic acid.

b Susceptibility of *S. pneumoniae* should be determined using a 1 μg oxacillin disk. Isolates with oxacillin zone sizes of ≥20 mm are susceptible to amoxicillin/clavulanic acid. An amoxicillin/clavulanic acid MIC should be determined on isolates of *S. pneumoniae* with oxacillin zone sizes of ≤19 mm.

c A broth microdilution method should be used for testing *N. gonorrhoeae* and interpreted according to penicillin breakpoints.

Interpretation should be as stated above for results using dilution techniques. Interpretation involves correlation of the diameter obtained in the disk test with the MIC for amoxicillin/clavulanic acid.

As with standardized dilution techniques, diffusion methods require the use of laboratory control microorganisms that are used to control the technical aspects of the laboratory procedures. For the diffusion technique, the 30 μg amoxicillin/clavulanate potassium (20 μg amoxicillin plus 10 μg clavulanate potassium) disk should provide the following zone diameters in these laboratory quality control strains:

Microorganism	Zone Diameter (mm)
Escherichia coli ATCC 25922	19 to 25
Escherichia coli ATCC 35218	18 to 22
Staphylococcus aureus ATCC 25923	28 to 36

INDICATIONS AND USAGE

Augmentin is indicated in the treatment of infections caused by susceptible strains of the designated organisms in the conditions listed below:

Lower Respiratory Tract Infections—caused by β-lactamase-producing strains of *Haemophilus influenzae* and *Moraxella (Branhamella) catarrhalis.*

Otitis Media—caused by β-lactamase-producing strains of *Haemophilus influenzae* and *Moraxella (Branhamella) catarrhalis.*

Sinusitis—caused by β-lactamase-producing strains of *Haemophilus influenzae* and *Moraxella (Branhamella) catarrhalis.*

Skin and Skin Structure Infections—caused by β-lactamase-producing strains of *Staphylococcus aureus, Escherichia coli* and *Klebsiella* spp.

Urinary Tract Infections—caused by β-lactamase-producing strains of *Escherichia coli, Klebsiella* spp. and *Enterobacter* spp.

While *Augmentin* is indicated only for the conditions listed above, infections caused by ampicillin-susceptible organisms are also amenable to *Augmentin* treatment due to its amoxicillin content. Therefore, mixed infections caused by ampicillin-susceptible organisms and β-lactamase-producing organisms susceptible to *Augmentin* should not require the addition of another antibiotic. Because amoxicillin has greater *in vitro* activity against *Streptococcus pneumoniae* than does ampicillin or penicillin, the majority of *S. pneumoniae* strains with intermediate susceptibility to ampicillin or penicillin are fully susceptible to amoxicillin and *Augmentin.* (See Microbiology subsection.)

Bacteriological studies, to determine the causative organisms and their susceptibility to *Augmentin,* should be performed together with any indicated surgical procedures.

Therapy may be instituted prior to obtaining the results from bacteriological and susceptibility studies to determine the causative organisms and their susceptibility to *Augmentin* when there is reason to believe the infection may involve any of the β-lactamase-producing organisms listed above. Once the results are known, therapy should be adjusted, if appropriate.

CONTRAINDICATIONS

Augmentin is contraindicated in patients with a history of allergic reactions to any penicillin.

It is also contraindicated in patients with a previous history of *Augmentin*-associated cholestatic jaundice/hepatic dysfunction.

WARNINGS

SERIOUS AND OCCASIONALLY FATAL HYPERSENSITIVITY (ANAPHYLACTIC) REACTIONS HAVE BEEN REPORTED IN PATIENTS ON PENICILLIN THERAPY. THESE REACTIONS ARE MORE LIKELY TO OCCUR IN INDIVIDUALS WITH A HISTORY OF PENICILLIN HYPERSENSITIVITY AND/OR A HISTORY OF SENSITIVITY TO MULTIPLE ALLERGENS. THERE HAVE BEEN REPORTS OF INDIVIDUALS WITH A HISTORY OF PENICILLIN HYPERSENSITIVITY WHO HAVE EXPERIENCED SEVERE REACTIONS WHEN TREATED WITH CEPHALOSPORINS. BEFORE INITIATING THERAPY WITH *AUGMENTIN,* CAREFUL INQUIRY SHOULD BE MADE CONCERNING PREVIOUS HYPERSENSITIVITY REACTIONS TO PENICILLINS, CEPHALOSPORINS OR OTHER ALLERGENS. IF AN ALLERGIC REACTION OCCURS, *AUGMENTIN* SHOULD BE DISCONTINUED AND THE APPROPRIATE THERAPY INSTITUTED. **SERIOUS ANAPHYLACTIC REACTIONS REQUIRE IMMEDIATE EMERGENCY TREATMENT WITH EPINEPHRINE. OXYGEN, INTRAVENOUS STEROIDS AND AIRWAY MANAGEMENT, INCLUDING INTUBATION, SHOULD ALSO BE ADMINISTERED AS INDICATED.**

Pseudomembranous colitis has been reported with nearly all antibacterial agents, including *Augmentin,* and has ranged in severity from mild to life-threatening. Therefore, it is important to consider this diagnosis in patients who present with diarrhea subsequent to the administration of antibacterial agents.

Treatment with antibacterial agents alters the normal flora of the colon and may permit overgrowth of clostridia. Studies indicate that a toxin produced by *Clostridium difficile* is one primary cause of "antibiotic associated colitis." After the diagnosis of pseudomembranous colitis has been established, appropriate therapeutic measures should be initiated. Mild cases of pseudomembranous colitis usually respond to drug discontinuation alone. In moderate to severe cases, consideration should be given to management with fluids and electrolytes, protein supplementation and treatment with an antibacterial drug clinically effective against *Clostridium difficile* colitis.

Augmentin should be used with caution in patients with evidence of hepatic dysfunction. Hepatic toxicity associated with the use of *Augmentin* is usually reversible. On rare occasions, deaths have been reported (less than 1 death reported per estimated 4 million prescriptions worldwide). These have generally been cases associated with serious underlying diseases or concomitant medications. (See CONTRAINDICATIONS and ADVERSE REACTIONS—*Liver.*)

PRECAUTIONS

General: While *Augmentin* possesses the characteristic low toxicity of the penicillin group of antibiotics, periodic assessment of organ system functions, including renal, hepatic and hematopoietic function, is advisable during prolonged therapy.

A high percentage of patients with mononucleosis who receive ampicillin develop an erythematous skin rash. Thus, ampicillin class antibiotics should not be administered to patients with mononucleosis.

The possibility of superinfections with mycotic or bacterial pathogens should be kept in mind during therapy. If superinfections occur (usually involving *Pseudomonas* or *Candida*), the drug should be discontinued and/or appropriate therapy instituted.

Drug Interactions: Probenecid decreases the renal tubular secretion of amoxicillin. Concurrent use with *Augmentin* may result in increased and prolonged blood levels of amoxicillin. Co-administration of probenecid cannot be recommended.

The concurrent administration of allopurinol and ampicillin increases substantially the incidence of rashes in patients receiving both drugs as compared to patients receiving ampicillin alone. It is not known whether this potentiation of ampicillin rashes is due to allopurinol or the hyperuricemia present in these patients. There are no data with *Augmentin* and allopurinol administered concurrently.

In common with other broad-spectrum antibiotics, *Augmentin* may reduce the efficacy of oral contraceptives.

Drug/Laboratory Test Interactions: Oral administration of *Augmentin* will result in high urine concentrations of amoxicillin. High urine concentrations of ampicillin may result in false-positive reactions when testing for the presence of glucose in urine using Clinitest®, Benedict's Solution or Fehling's Solution. Since this effect may also occur with amoxicillin and therefore *Augmentin*, it is recommended that glucose tests based on enzymatic glucose oxidase reactions (such as Clinistix® or Tes-Tape®) be used.

Following administration of ampicillin to pregnant women a transient decrease in plasma concentration of total conjugated estriol, estriol-glucuronide, conjugated estrone and estradiol has been noted. This effect may also occur with amoxicillin and therefore *Augmentin*.

Carcinogenesis, Mutagenesis, Impairment of Fertility: Long-term studies in animals have not been performed to evaluate carcinogenic potential.

Mutagenesis: The mutagenic potential of *Augmentin* was investigated *in vitro* with an Ames test, a human lymphocyte cytogenetic assay, a yeast test and a mouse lymphoma forward mutation assay, and *in vivo* with mouse micronucleus tests and a dominant lethal test.

All were negative apart from the *in vitro* mouse lymphoma assay where weak activity was found at very high, cytotoxic concentrations.

Impairment of Fertility: *Augmentin* at oral doses of up to 1200 mg/kg/day (5.7 times the maximum human dose, 1480 mg/m^2/day, based on body surface area) was found to have no effect on fertility and reproductive performance in rats, dosed with a 2:1 ratio formulation of amoxicillin:clavulanate.

Teratogenic effects. Pregnancy (Category B): Reproduction studies performed in pregnant rats and mice given *Augmentin* at oral dosages up to 1200 mg/kg/day, equivalent to 7200 and 4080 mg/m^2/day, respectively (4.9 and 2.8 times the maximum human oral dose based on body surface area), revealed no evidence of harm to the fetus due to *Augmentin*. There are, however, no adequate and well-controlled studies in pregnant women. Because animal reproduction studies are not always predictive of human response, this drug should be used during pregnancy only if clearly needed.

Labor and Delivery: Oral ampicillin class antibiotics are generally poorly absorbed during labor. Studies in guinea pigs have shown that intravenous administration of ampicillin decreased the uterine tone, frequency of contractions, height of contractions and duration of contractions. However, it is not known whether the use of *Augmentin* in humans during labor or delivery has immediate or delayed adverse effects on the fetus, prolongs the duration of labor, or increases the likelihood of forceps delivery or other obstetrical intervention or resuscitation of the newborn will be necessary.

Nursing Mothers: Ampicillin class antibiotics are excreted in the milk; therefore, caution should be exercised when *Augmentin* is administered to a nursing woman.

ADVERSE REACTIONS

Augmentin is generally well tolerated. The majority of side effects observed in clinical trials were of a mild and transient nature and less than 3% of patients discontinued therapy because of drug-related side effects. The most frequently reported adverse effects were diarrhea/loose stools (9%), nausea (3%), skin rashes and urticaria (3%), vomiting (1%) and vaginitis (1%). The overall incidence of side effects, and in particular diarrhea, increased with the higher recommended dose. Other less frequently reported reactions include: abdominal discomfort, flatulence and headache.

The following adverse reactions have been reported for ampicillin class antibiotics:

Gastrointestinal: Diarrhea, nausea, vomiting, indigestion, gastritis, stomatitis, glossitis, black "hairy" tongue, mucocutaneous candidiasis, enterocolitis, and hemorrhagic/pseudomembranous colitis. Onset of pseudomembranous colitis symptoms may occur during or after antibiotic treatment. (See WARNINGS.)

Hypersensitivity Reactions: Skin rashes, pruritus, urticaria, angioedema, serum sickness-like reactions (urticaria or skin rash accompanied by arthritis, arthralgia, myalgia and frequently fever), erythema multiforme (rarely Stevens-Johnson Syndrome) and an occasional case of exfoliative dermatitis (including toxic epidermal necrolysis) have been reported. These reactions may be controlled with antihistamines and, if necessary, systemic corticosteroids. Whenever such reactions occur, the drug should be discontinued, unless the opinion of the physician dictates otherwise. Serious and occasional fatal hypersensitivity (anaphylactic) reactions can occur with oral penicillin. (See WARNINGS.)

Liver: A moderate rise in AST (SGOT) and/or ALT (SGPT) has been noted in patients treated with ampicillin class antibiotics but the significance of these findings is unknown. Hepatic dysfunction, including increases in serum transaminases (AST and/or ALT), serum bilirubin and/or alkaline phosphatase, has been infrequently reported with *Augmentin*. It has been reported more commonly in the elderly, in males, or in patients on prolonged treatment. The histologic findings on liver biopsy have consisted of predominantly cholestatic, hepatocellular, or mixed cholestatic-hepatocellular changes. The onset of signs/symptoms of hepatic dysfunction may occur during or several weeks after therapy has been discontinued. The hepatic dysfunction, which may be severe, is usually reversible. On rare occasions, deaths have been reported (less than 1 death reported per estimated 4 million prescriptions worldwide). These have generally been cases associated with serious underlying diseases or concomitant medications.

Renal: Interstitial nephritis and hematuria have been reported rarely.

Hemic and Lymphatic Systems: Anemia, including hemolytic anemia, thrombocytopenia, thrombocytopenic purpura, eosinophilia, leukopenia and agranulocytosis have been reported during therapy with penicillins. These reactions are usually reversible on discontinuation of therapy and are believed to be hypersensitivity phenomena. A slight thrombocytosis was noted in less than 1% of the patients treated with *Augmentin*. There have been reports of increased prothrombin time in patients receiving *Augmentin* and anticoagulant therapy concomitantly.

Central Nervous System: Agitation, anxiety, behavioral changes, confusion, convulsions, dizziness, insomnia, and reversible hyperactivity have been reported rarely.

OVERDOSAGE

Most patients have been asymptomatic following overdosage or have experienced primarily gastrointestinal symptoms including stomach and abdominal pain, vomiting, and diarrhea. Rash, hyperactivity, or drowsiness have also been observed in a small number of patients.

In the case of overdosage, discontinue *Augmentin*, treat symptomatically, and institute supportive measures as required. If the overdosage is very recent and there is no contraindication, an attempt at emesis or other means of removal of drug from the stomach may be performed. A prospective study of 51 pediatric patients at a poison center suggested that overdosages of less than 250 mg/kg of amoxicillin are not associated with significant clinical symptoms and do not require gastric emptying.[3]

Interstitial nephritis resulting in oliguric renal failure has been reported in a small number of patients after overdosage with amoxicillin. Renal impairment appears to be reversible with cessation of drug administration. High blood levels may occur more readily in patients with impaired renal function because of decreased renal clearance of both amoxicillin and clavulanate. Both amoxicillin and clavulanate are removed from the circulation by hemodialysis. (See DOSAGE AND ADMINISTRATION for recommended dosing for patients with impaired renal function.)

DOSAGE AND ADMINISTRATION

Since both the *Augmentin* 250 mg and 500 mg tablets contain the same amount of clavulanic acid (125 mg, as the potassium salt), 2 *Augmentin* 250 mg tablets are not equivalent to 1 *Augmentin* 500 mg tablet. Therefore, 2 *Augmentin* 250 mg tablets should not be substituted for 1 *Augmentin* 500 mg tablet.

Dosage:

Adults: The usual adult dose is 1 *Augmentin* 500 mg tablet every 12 hours or 1 *Augmentin* 250 mg tablet every 8 hours. For more severe infections and infections of the respiratory tract, the dose should be 1 *Augmentin* 875 mg tablet every 12 hours or 1 *Augmentin* 500 mg tablet every 8 hours.

Patients with impaired renal function do not generally require a reduction in dose unless the impairment is severe. Severely impaired patients with a glomerular filtration rate of <30 mL/minute should not receive the 875 mg tablet. Patients with a glomerular filtration rate of 10 to 30 mL/minute should receive 500 mg or 250 mg every 12 hours, depending on the severity of the infection. Patients with a less than 10 mL/minute glomerular filtration rate should receive 500 mg or 250 mg every 24 hours, depending on severity of the infection. Hemodialysis patients should receive 500 mg or 250 mg every 24 hours, depending on severity of the infection. They should receive an additional dose both during and at the end of dialysis.

Hepatically impaired patients should be dosed with caution and hepatic function monitored at regular intervals. (See WARNINGS.)

Pediatric Patients: Pediatric patients weighing 40 kg or more should be dosed according to the adult recommendations.

Due to the different amoxicillin to clavulanic acid ratios in the *Augmentin* 250 mg tablet (250/125) versus the *Augmentin* 250 mg chewable tablet (250/62.5), the *Augmentin* 250 mg tablet should not be used until the pediatric patient weighs at least 40 kg or more.

Administration: *Augmentin* may be taken without regard to meals; however, absorption of clavulanate potassium is enhanced when *Augmentin* is administered at the start of a meal. To minimize the potential for gastrointestinal intolerance, *Augmentin* should be taken at the start of a meal.

HOW SUPPLIED

AUGMENTIN 250 MG TABLETS: Each white oval filmcoated tablet, debossed with AUGMENTIN on 1 side and 250/125 on the other side, contains 250 mg amoxicillin as the trihydrate and 125 mg clavulanic acid as the potassium salt.

NDC 0029-6075-27 .... bottles of 30
NDC 0029-6075-31 . Unit Dose (10×10) 100 tablets

AUGMENTIN 500 MG TABLETS: Each white oval filmcoated tablet, debossed with AUGMENTIN on 1 side and 500/125 on the other side, contains 500 mg amoxicillin as the trihydrate and 125 mg clavulanic acid as the potassium salt.

NDC 0029-6080-12 .... bottles of 20
NDC 0029-6080-31 . Unit Dose (10×10) 100 tablets

AUGMENTIN 875 MG TABLETS: Each scored white capsule-shaped tablet, debossed with AUGMENTIN 875 on 1 side and scored on the other side, contains 875 mg amoxicillin as the trihydrate and 125 mg clavulanic acid as the potassium salt.

NDC 0029-6086-12 .... bottles of 20
NDC 0029-6086-21 . Unit Dose (10×10) 100 tablets

AUGMENTIN is also supplied as:

AUGMENTIN 125 MG/5 ML (125 mg amoxicillin/31.25 mg clavulanic acid) FOR ORAL SUSPENSION:

NDC 0029-6085-39 .... 75 mL bottle
NDC 0029-6085-23 .... 100 mL bottle
NDC 0029-6085-22 .... 150 mL bottle

AUGMENTIN 200 MG/5 ML (200 mg amoxicillin/28.5 mg clavulanic acid) FOR ORAL SUSPENSION:

NDC 0029-6087-29 .... 50 mL bottle
NDC 0029-6087-39 .... 75 mL bottle
NDC 0029-6087-51 .... 100 mL bottle

AUGMENTIN 250 MG/5 ML (250 mg amoxicillin/62.5 mg clavulanic acid) FOR ORAL SUSPENSION:

NDC 0029-6090-39 .... 75 mL bottle
NDC 0029-6090-23 .... 100 mL bottle
NDC 0029-6090-22 .... 150 mL bottle

AUGMENTIN 400 MG/5 ML (400 mg amoxicillin/57 mg clavulanic acid) FOR ORAL SUSPENSION:

NDC 0029-6092-29 .... 50 mL bottle
NDC 0029-6092-39 .... 75 mL bottle

NDC 0029-6092-51 .... 100 mL bottle

AUGMENTIN 125 MG (125 mg amoxicillin/31.25 mg clavulanic acid) CHEWABLE TABLETS:

NDC 0029-6073-47 .. carton of 30 (5×6) tablets

AUGMENTIN 200 MG (200 mg amoxicillin/28.5 mg clavulanic acid) CHEWABLE TABLETS:

NDC 0029-6071-12 .... carton of 20 tablets

AUGMENTIN 250 MG (250 mg amoxicillin/62.5 mg clavulanic acid) CHEWABLE TABLETS:

NDC 0029-6074-47 .. carton of 30 (5×6) tablets

AUGMENTIN 400 MG (400 mg amoxicillin/57.0 mg clavulanic acid) CHEWABLE TABLETS:

NDC 0029-6072-12 .... carton of 20 tablets

Store tablets and dry powder at or below 25°C (77°F). Dispense in original container.

CLINICAL STUDIES

Data from two pivotal studies in 1,191 patients treated for either lower respiratory tract infections or complicated urinary tract infections compared a regimen of 875 mg *Augmentin* tablets q12h to 500 mg *Augmentin* tablets dosed q8h (584 and 607 patients, respectively). Comparable efficacy was demonstrated between the q12h and q8h dosing regimens. There was no significant difference in the percentage of adverse events in each group. The most frequently reported adverse event was diarrhea; incidence rates were similar for the 875 mg q12h and 500 mg q8h dosing regimens (14.9% and 14.3%, respectively). However, there was a statistically significant difference ($p<0.05$) in rates of severe diarrhea or withdrawals with diarrhea between the regimens: 1.0% for 875 mg q12h dosing versus 2.5% for the 500 mg q8h dosing.

In one of these pivotal studies, 629 patients with either pyelonephritis or a complicated urinary tract infection (i.e., patients with abnormalities of the urinary tract that predispose to relapse of bacteriuria following eradication) were randomized to receive either 875 mg *Augmentin* tablets q12h or 500 mg *Augmentin* tablets q8h in the following distribution:

	875 mg q12h	500 mg q8h
Pyelonephritis	173 patients	188 patients
Complicated UTI	135 patients	133 patients
Total patients	308	321

The number of bacteriologically evaluable patients was comparable between the two dosing regimens. *Augmentin* produced comparable bacteriological success rates in patients assessed 2 to 4 days immediately following end of therapy. The bacteriologic efficacy rates were comparable at one of the follow-up visits (5 to 9 days post-therapy) and at a late post-therapy visit (in the majority of cases, this was 2 to 4 weeks post-therapy), as seen in the table below:

	875 mg q12h	500 mg q8h
2 to 4 days	81%, n=58	80%, n=54
5 to 9 days	58.5%, n=41	51.9%, n=52
2 to 4 weeks	52.5%, n=101	54.8%, n=104

As noted before, though there was no significant difference in the percentage of adverse events in each group, there was a statistically significant difference in rates of severe diarrhea or withdrawals with diarrhea between the regimens.

REFERENCES

1. National Committee for Clinical Laboratory Standards. Methods for Dilution Antimicrobial Susceptibility Tests for Bacteria that Grow Aerobically—Third Edition. Approved Standard NCCLS Document M7-A3, Vol. 13, No. 25. NCCLS, Villanova, PA, December 1993.

2. National Committee for Clinical Laboratory Standards. Performance Standards for Antimicrobial Disk Susceptibility Tests—Fifth Edition. Approved Standard NCCLS Document M2-A5, Vol. 13, No. 24. NCCLS, Villanova, PA, December 1993.

3. Swanson-Biearman B, Dean BS, Lopez G, Krenzelok EP. The effects of penicillin and cephalosporin ingestions in children less than six years of age. *Vet Hum Toxicol* 1988; 30:66-67.

GlaxoSmithKline, Research Triangle Park, NC 27709
March 1999/AG:AL6

BACTRIM™ ℞
[băc ' trĭm]
brand of trimethoprim and sulfamethoxazole
DS (double strength) TABLETS,
TABLETS and PEDIATRIC SUSPENSION

The following text is complete prescribing information based on official labeling in effect June 2001.

DESCRIPTION

Bactrim (trimethoprim and sulfamethoxazole) is a synthetic antibacterial combination product available in DS (double strength) tablets, tablets and pediatric suspension for oral administration. Each DS tablet contains 160 mg trimethoprim and 800 mg sulfamethoxazole plus magnesium stearate, pregelatinized starch and sodium starch glycolate. Each tablet contains 80 mg trimethoprim and 400 mg sulfamethoxazole plus magnesium stearate, pregelatinized starch, sodium starch glycolate, FD&C Blue No. 1 lake, FD&C Yellow No. 6 lake and D&C Yellow No. 10 lake. Each teaspoonful (5 mL) of the pediatric suspension contains 40 mg trimethoprim and 200 mg sulfamethoxazole in a vehicle containing 0.3 percent alcohol, edetate disodium, glycerin, microcrystalline cellulose, parabens (methyl and propyl), polysorbate 80, saccharin sodium, simethicone, sorbitol, sucrose, FD&C Yellow No. 6, FD&C Red No. 40, flavors and water.

Trimethoprim is 2, 4-diamino-5-(3,4,5 trimethoxybenzyl)pyrimidine; the molecular formula is C_{14} H_{18} N_4 O_3. It is a white to light yellow, odorless, bitter compound with a molecular weight of 290.3.

Sulfamethoxazole is N^1-(5-methyl-3-isoxazolyl)sulfanilamide; the molecular formula is C_{10} H_{11} N_3 O_3 S. It is almost white, odorless, tasteless compound with a molecular weight of 253.28.

CLINICAL PHARMACOLOGY

Bactrim is rapidly absorbed following oral administration. Both sulfamethoxazole and trimethoprim exist in the blood as unbound, protein-bound and metabolized forms; sulfamethoxazole also exists as the conjugated form. The metabolism of sulfamethoxazole occurs predominately by N_4-acetylation, although the glucuronide conjugate has been identified. The principal metabolites of trimethoprim are the 1- and 3-oxides and the 3'- and 4'- hydroxy derivatives. The free forms of sulfamethoxazole and trimethoprim are considered to be the therapeutically active forms. Approximately 44% of trimethoprim and 70% of sulfamethoxazole are bound to plasma proteins. The presence of 10 mg percent sulfamethoxazole in plasma decreases the protein binding of trimethoprim by an insignificant degree; trimethoprim does not influence the protein binding of sulfamethoxazole. Peak blood levels for the individual components occur 1 to 4 hours after oral administration. The mean serum half-lives of sulfamethoxazole and trimethoprim are 10 and 8 to 10 hours, respectively. However, patients with severely impaired renal function exhibit an increase in the half-lives of both components, requiring dosage regimen adjustment (see DOSAGE AND ADMINISTRATION section). Detectable amounts of trimethoprim and sulfamethoxazole are present in the blood 24 hours after drug administration. During administration of 160 mg trimethoprim and 800 mg sulfamethoxazole bid, the mean steady-state plasma concentration of trimethoprim was 1.72 µg/mL. The steady-state mean plasma levels of free and total sulfamethoxazole were 57.4 µg/mL and 68.0 µg/mL, respectively. These steady-state levels were achieved after three days of drug administration.[1]

Excretion of sulfamethoxazole and trimethoprim is primarily by the kidneys through both glomerular filtration and tubular secretion. Urine concentrations of both sulfamethoxazole and trimethoprim are considerably higher than are the concentrations in the blood. The average percentage of the dose recovered in urine from 0 to 72 hours after a single oral dose of Bactrim is 84.5% for total sulfonamide and 66.8% for free trimethoprim. Thirty percent of the total sulfonamide is excreted as free sulfamethoxazole, with the remaining as N_4-acetylated metabolite.[2] When administered together as Bactrim, neither sulfamethoxazole nor trimethoprim affects the urinary excretion pattern of the other.

Both trimethoprim and sulfamethoxazole distribute to sputum, vaginal fluid and middle ear fluid; trimethoprim also distributes to bronchial secretion, and both pass the placental barrier and are excreted in human milk.

Microbiology: Trimethoprim blocks the production of tetrahydrofolic acid from dihydrofolic acid by binding to and reversibly inhibiting the required enzyme, dihydrofolate reductase. Sulfamethoxazole inhibits bacterial synthesis of dihydrofolic acid by competing with *para*-aminobenzoic acid (PABA). Thus, trimethoprim and sulfamethoxazole block two consecutive steps in the biosynthesis of nucleic acids and proteins essential to many bacteria. In vitro studies have shown that bacterial resistance develops more slowly with both trimethoprim and sulfamethoxazole in combination than with either trimethoprim or sulfamethoxazole alone.

Trimethoprim and sulfamethoxazole have been shown to be active against most strains of the following microorganisms, both in vitro and in clinical infections as described in the INDICATIONS and USAGE section.

Aerobic gram-positive microorganisms:
Streptococcus pneumoniae

Aerobic gram-negative microorganisms:
Escherichia coli (including susceptible enterotoxigenic strains implicated in traveler's diarrhea)

Microorganism		MIC (µg/mL)
Escherichia coli	ATCC 25922	≤ 0.5/9.5
Haemophilus influenzae[c]	ATCC 49247	0.03/0.59 – 0.25/4.75
Streptococcus pneumoniae[d]	ATCC 49619	0.12/2.4 – 1/19

c. This quality control range is applicable only to *Haemophilus influenzae* ATCC 49247 tested by broth microdilution procedure using *Haemophilus* Test Medium (HTM)[4].

d. This quality control range is applicable to tests performed by the broth microdilution method only using cation-adjusted Mueller-Hinton broth with 2% to 5% lysed horse blood[4].

Klebsiella species
Enterobacter species
Haemophilus influenzae
Morganella morganii
Proteus mirabilis
Proteus vulgaris
Shigella flexneri[3]
Shigella sonnei[3]
Other Organisms:
Pneumocystis carinii

Susceptibility Testing Methods:

Dilution Techniques: Quantitative methods are used to determine antimicrobial minimum inhibitory concentrations (MICs). These MICs provide estimates of the susceptibility of bacteria to antimicrobial compounds. The MICs should be determined using a standardized procedure. Standardized procedures are based on a dilution method[4] (broth or agar) or equivalent with standardized inoculum concentrations and standardized concentrations of trimethoprim/sulfamethoxazole powder. The MIC values should be interpreted according to the following criteria:

For testing *Enterobacteriaceae*:

MIC (µg/mL)	Interpretation
≤ 2/38	Susceptible (S)
≥ 4/76	Resistant (R)

When testing either *Haemophilus influenzae*[a] or *Streptococcus pneumoniae*[b]:

MIC (µg/mL)	Interpretation[b]
≤ 0.5/9.5	Susceptible (S)
1/19–2/38	Intermediate (I)
≥ 4/76	Resistant (R)

a. These interpretative standards are applicable only to broth microdilution susceptibility tests with *Haemophilus influenzae* using *Haemophilus* Test Medium (HTM)[4].

b. These interpretative standards are applicable only to broth microdilution susceptibility tests using cation-adjusted Mueller-Hinton broth with 2% to 5% lysed horse blood[4].

A report of "Susceptible" indicates that the pathogen is likely to be inhibited if the antimicrobial compound in the blood reaches the concentrations usually achievable. A report of "Intermediate" indicates that the result should be considered equivocal, and, if the microorganism is not fully susceptible to alternative, clinically feasible drugs, the test should be repeated. This category implies possible clinical applicability in body sites where the drug is physiologically concentrated or in situations where high dosage of drug can be used. This category also provides a buffer zone which prevents small uncontrolled technical factors from causing major discrepancies in interpretation. A report of "Resistant" indicates that the pathogen is not likely to be inhibited if the antimicrobial compound in the blood reaches the concentrations usually achievable; other therapy should be selected.

Quality Control

Standardized susceptibility test procedures require the use of laboratory control microorganisms to control the technical aspects of the laboratory procedures. Standard trimethoprim/sulfamethoxazole powder should provide the following range of values:

[See table above]

Diffusion Techniques:

Quantitative methods that require measurement of zone diameters also provide reproducible estimates of the susceptibility of bacteria to antimicrobial compounds. One such standardized procedure[5] requires the use of standardized inoculum concentrations. This procedure uses paper disks impregnated with 1.25/23.75 µg of trimethoprim/sulfamethoxazole to test the susceptibility of microorganisms to trimethoprim/sulfamethoxazole.

Reports from the laboratory providing results of the standard single-disk susceptibility test with a 1.25/23.75 µg of trimethoprim/sulfamethoxazole disk should be interpreted according to the following criteria:

For testing either *Enterobacteriaceae* or *Haemophilus influenzae*[e]:

Zone Diameter (mm)	Interpretation
16	Susceptible (S)
11 – 15	Intermediate (I)
10	Resistant (R)

e. These zone diameter standards are applicable only for disk diffusion testing with *Haemophilus influenzae* and *Haemophilus* Test Medium (HTM)[5].

When testing *Streptococcus pneumoniae*[f]:

Zone Diameter (mm)	Interpretation
19	Susceptible (S)
16 – 18	Intermediate (I)
15	Resistant (R)

f. These zone diameter interpretative standards are applicable only to tests performed using Mueller-Hinton agar supplemented with 5% defibrinated sheep blood when incubated in 5% CO_2[5].

Microorganism		Zone Diameter Ranges (mm)
Escherichia coli	ATCC 25922	24 – 32
Haemophilus influenzae[g]	ATCC 49247	24 – 32
Streptococcus pneumoniae[h]	ATCC 49619	20 – 28

* Mueller-Hinton agar should be checked for excessive levels of thymidine or thymine. To determine whether Mueller-Hinton medium has sufficiently low levels of thymidine and thymine, an *Enterococcus faecalis* (ATCC 29212 or ATCC 33186) may be tested with trimethoprim/sulfamethoxazole disks. A zone of inhibition $\geq$ 20 mm that is essentially free of fine colonies indicates a sufficiently low level of thymidine and thymine.

g. This quality control range is applicable only to *Haemophilus influenzae* ATCC 49247 tested by a disk diffusion procedure using *Haemophilus* Test Medium (HTM)[5].

h. This quality control range is applicable only to tests performed by disk diffusion using Mueller-Hinton agar supplemented with 5% defibrinated sheep blood when incubated in 5% CO_2[5].

Interpretation should be as stated above for results using dilution techniques. Interpretation involves correlation of the diameter obtained in the disk test with the MIC for trimethoprim/sulfamethoxazole.

Quality Control

As with standardized dilution techniques, diffusion methods require the use of laboratory control microorganisms that are used to control the technical aspects of the laboratory procedures. For the diffusion technique, the 1.25/23.75 µg trimethoprim/sulfamethoxazole disk* should provide the following zone diameters in these laboratory test quality control strains: [See table above]

INDICATIONS AND USAGE

Urinary Tract Infections: For the treatment of urinary tract infections due to susceptible strains of the following organisms: *Escherichia coli, Klebsiella* species, *Enterobacter* species, *Morganella morganii, Proteus mirabilis* and *Proteus vulgaris.* It is recommended that initial episodes of uncomplicated urinary tract infections be treated with a single effective antibacterial agent rather than the combination.

Acute Otitis Media: For the treatment of acute otitis media in pediatric patients due to susceptible strains of *Streptococcus pneumoniae* or *Haemophilus influenzae* when in the judgment of the physician Bactrim offers some advantage over the use of other antimicrobial agents. To date, there are limited data on the safety of repeated use of Bactrim in pediatric patients under two years of age. Bactrim is not indicated for prophylactic or prolonged administration in otitis media at any age.

Acute Exacerbations of Chronic Bronchitis in Adults: For the treatment of acute exacerbations of chronic bronchitis due to susceptible strains of *Streptococcus pneumoniae* or *Haemophilus influenzae* when in the judgment of the physician Bactrim offers some advantage over the use of a single antimicrobial agent.

Shigellosis: For the treatment of enteritis caused by susceptible strains of *Shigella flexneri* and *Shigella sonnei* when antibacterial therapy is indicated.

Pneumocystis Carinii Pneumonia: For the treatment of documented *Pneumocystis carinii* pneumonia and for prophylaxis against *Pneumocystis carinii* pneumonia in individuals who are immunosuppressed and considered to be at an increased risk of developing *Pneumocystis carinii* pneumonia.

Traveler's Diarrhea in Adults: For the treatment of traveler's diarrhea due to susceptible strains of enterotoxigenic *E. coli.*

CONTRAINDICATIONS

Bactrim is contraindicated in patients with a known hypersensitivity to trimethoprim or sulfonamides and in patients with documented megaloblastic anemia due to folate deficiency. Bactrim is also contraindicated in pregnant patients and nursing mothers, because sulfonamides pass the placenta and are excreted in the milk and may cause kernicterus. Bactrim is contraindicated in pediatric patients less than 2 months of age. Bactrim is also contraindicated in patients with marked hepatic damage or with severe renal insufficiency when renal function status cannot be monitored.

WARNINGS: FATALITIES ASSOCIATED WITH THE ADMINISTRATION OF SULFONAMIDES, ALTHOUGH RARE, HAVE OCCURRED DUE TO SEVERE REACTIONS INCLUDING STEVENS-JOHNSON SYNDROME, TOXIC EPIDERMAL NECROLYSIS, FULMINANT HEPATIC NECROSIS, AGRANULOCYTOSIS, APLASTIC ANEMIA AND OTHER BLOOD DYSCRASIAS.

SULFONAMIDES, INCLUDING SULFONAMIDE-CONTAINING PRODUCTS SUCH AS TRIMETHOPRIM/SULFAMETHOXAZOLE, SHOULD BE DISCONTINUED AT THE FIRST APPEARANCE OF SKIN RASH OR ANY SIGN OF ADVERSE REACTION. In rare instances, a skin rash may be followed by a more severe reaction, such as Stevens-Johnson syndrome, toxic epidermal necrolysis, hepatic necrosis, and serious blood disorders (see PRECAUTIONS).

Clinical signs such as rash, sore throat, fever, arthralgia, pallor, purpura, or jaundice may be early indications of serious reactions.

Cough, shortness of breath, and pulmonary infiltrates are hypersensitivity reactions of the respiratory tract that have been reported in association with sulfonamide treatment.

The sulfonamides should not be used for the treatment of group A β-hemolytic streptococcal infections. In an established infection, they will not eradicate the streptococcus and, therefore, will not prevent sequelae such as rheumatic fever.

Pseudomembranous colitis has been reported with nearly all antibacterial agents, including trimethoprim/sulfamethoxazole, and may range in severity from mild to life-threatening. Therefore, it is important to consider this diagnosis in patients who present with diarrhea subsequent to the administration of antibacterial agents.

Treatment with antibacterial agents alters the normal flora of the colon and may permit overgrowth of clostridia. Studies indicate that a toxin produced by *Clostridium difficile* is one primary cause of "antibiotic-associated colitis." After the diagnosis of pseudomembranous colitis has been established, therapeutic measures should be initiated. Mild cases of pseudomembranous colitis usually respond to drug discontinuation alone. In moderate to severe cases, consideration should be given to management with fluids and electrolytes, protein supplementation, and treatment with an antibacterial drug effective against *C. difficile.*

PRECAUTIONS

General: Bactrim should be given with caution to patients with impaired renal or hepatic function, to those with possible folate deficiency (eg, the elderly, chronic alcoholics, patients receiving anticonvulsant therapy, patients with malabsorption syndrome, and patients in malnutrition states) and to those with severe allergies or bronchial asthma. In glucose-6-phosphate dehydrogenase deficient individuals, hemolysis may occur. This reaction is frequently dose-related (see CLINICAL PHARMACOLOGY and DOSAGE AND ADMINISTRATION).

Cases of hypoglycemia in non-diabetic patients treated with Bactrim are seen rarely, usually occurring after a few days of therapy. Patients with renal dysfunction, liver disease, malnutrition or those receiving high doses of Bactrim are particularly at risk.

Hematological changes indicative of folic acid deficiency may occur in elderly patients or in patients with preexisting folic acid deficiency or kidney failure. These effects are reversible by folinic acid therapy.

Trimethoprim has been noted to impair phenylalanine metabolism, but this is of no significance in phenylketonuric patients on appropriate dietary restriction.

As with all drugs containing sulfonamides, caution is advisable in patients with porphyria or thyroid dysfunction.

Use in the Elderly: There may be an increased risk of severe adverse reactions in elderly patients, particularly when complicating conditions exist, eg, impaired kidney and/or liver function, or concomitant use of other drugs. Severe skin reactions, generalized bone marrow suppression (see WARNINGS and AD-

VERSE REACTIONS sections) or a specific decrease in platelets (with or without purpura) are the most frequently reported severe adverse reactions in elderly patients. In those concurrently receiving certain diuretics, primarily thiazides, an increased incidence of thrombocytopenia with purpura has been reported. Appropriate dosage adjustments should be made for patients with impaired kidney function and duration of use should be as short as possible to minimize risks of undesired reactions (see DOSAGE AND ADMINISTRATION section). The trimethoprim component of Bactrim may cause hyperkalemia when administered to patients with underlying disorders of potassium metabolism, with renal insufficiency, or when given concomitantly with drugs known to induce hyperkalemia. Close monitoring of serum potassium is warranted in these patients. Discontinuation of Bactrim treatment is recommended to help lower potassium serum levels.

Use in the Treatment of and Prophylaxis for Pneumocystis Carinii Pneumonia in Patients with Acquired Immunodeficiency Syndrome (AIDS): AIDS patients may not tolerate or respond to Bactrim in the same manner as non-AIDS patients. The incidence of side effects, particularly rash, fever, leukopenia and elevated aminotransferase (transaminase) values, with Bactrim therapy in AIDS patients who are being treated for *Pneumocystis carinii* pneumonia has been reported to be greatly increased compared with the incidence normally associated with the use of Bactrim in non-AIDS patients. The incidence of hyperkalemia appears to be increased in AIDS patients receiving Bactrim. Adverse effects are generally less severe in patients receiving Bactrim for prophylaxis. A history of mild intolerance to Bactrim in AIDS patients does not appear to predict intolerance of subsequent secondary prophylaxis.[6] However, if a patient develops skin rash or any sign of adverse reaction, therapy with Bactrim should be reevaluated (see WARNINGS).

High dosage of trimethoprim, as used in patients with *Pneumocystis carinii* pneumonia, induces a progressive but reversible increase of serum potassium concentrations in a substantial number of patients. Even treatment with recommended doses may cause hyperkalemia when trimethoprim is administered to patients with underlying disorders of potassium metabolism, with renal insufficiency, or if drugs known to induce hyperkalemia are given concomitantly. Close monitoring of serum potassium is warranted in these patients.

During treatment, adequate fluid intake and urinary output should be ensured to prevent crystalluria. Patients who are "slow acetylators" may be more prone to idiosyncratic reactions to sulfonamides.

Information for Patients: Patients should be instructed to maintain an adequate fluid intake in order to prevent crystalluria and stone formation.

Laboratory Tests: Complete blood counts should be done frequently in patients receiving Bactrim; if a significant reduction in the count of any formed blood element is noted, Bactrim should be discontinued. Urinalyses with careful microscopic examination and renal function tests should be performed during therapy, particularly for those patients with impaired renal function.

Drug Interactions: In elderly patients concurrently receiving certain diuretics, primarily thiazides, an increased incidence of thrombocytopenia with purpura has been reported. It has been reported that Bactrim may prolong the prothrombin time in patients who are receiving the anticoagulant warfarin. This interaction should be kept in mind when Bactrim is given to patients already on anticoagulant therapy, and the coagulation time should be reassessed.

Bactrim may inhibit the hepatic metabolism of phenytoin. Bactrim, given at a common clinical dosage, increased the phenytoin half-life by 39% and decreased the phenytoin metabolic clearance rate by 27%. When administering these drugs concurrently, one should be alert for possible excessive phenytoin effect.

Sulfonamides can also displace methotrexate from plasma protein binding sites and can compete with the renal transport of methotrexate, thus increasing free methotrexate concentrations.

There have been reports of marked but reversible nephrotoxicity with coadministration of Bactrim and cyclosporine in renal transplant recipients.

Increased digoxin blood levels can occur with concomitant Bactrim therapy, especially in elderly patients. Serum digoxin levels should be monitored.

Increased sulfamethoxazole blood levels may occur in patients who are also receiving indomethacin.

Occasional reports suggest that patients receiving pyrimethamine as malaria prophylaxis in doses exceeding 25 mg weekly may develop megaloblastic anemia if Bactrim is prescribed.

The efficacy of tricyclic antidepressants can decrease when coadministered with Bactrim. Like other sulfonamide-containing drugs, Bactrim potentiates the effect of oral hypoglycemics.

In the literature, a single case of toxic delirium has been reported after concomitant intake of trimethoprim/sulfamethoxazole and amantadine.

Drug/Laboratory Test Interactions: Bactrim, specifically the trimethoprim component, can interfere with a serum methotrexate assay as determined by the competitive binding protein technique (CBPA) when a bacterial dihydrofolate reductase is used as the binding protein. No interference occurs, however, if methotrex-

ate is measured by a radioimmunoassay (RIA). The presence of trimethoprim and sulfamethoxazole may also interfere with the Jaffé alkaline picrate reaction assay for creatinine, resulting in overestimations of about 10% in the range of normal values.

Carcinogenesis, Mutagenesis, Impairment of Fertility:

Carcinogenesis: Long-term studies in animals to evaluate carcinogenic potential have not been conducted with Bactrim.

Mutagenesis: Bacterial mutagenic studies have not been performed with sulfamethoxazole and trimethoprim in combination. Trimethoprim was demonstrated to be nonmutagenic in the Ames assay. No chromosomal damage was observed in human leukocytes cultured in vitro with sulfamethoxazole and trimethoprim alone or in combination; the concentrations used exceeded blood levels of these compounds following therapy with Bactrim. Observations of leukocytes obtained from patients treated with Bactrim revealed no chromosomal abnormalities.

Impairment of Fertility: No adverse effects on fertility or general reproductive performance were observed in rats given oral dosages as high as 70 mg/kg/day trimethoprim plus 350 mg/kg/day sulfamethoxazole. These doses are 10.9-fold higher than the recommended human dose for trimethoprim and sulfamethoxazole.

Pregnancy: Teratogenic Effects: Pregnancy Category C. In rats, oral doses of 533 mg/kg sulfamethoxazole (16.7-fold higher than the recommended human dose) or 200 mg/kg trimethoprim (31.3-fold higher than the recommended human dose) produced teratologic effects manifested mainly as cleft palates.

The highest dose which did not cause cleft palates in rats was 512 mg/kg sulfamethoxazole (16-fold higher than the recommended human dose) or 192 mg/kg trimethoprim (30-fold higher than the recommended human dose) when administered separately. In two studies in rats, no teratology was observed when 512 mg/kg of sulfamethoxazole (16-fold higher than the recommended human dose) was used in combination with 128 mg/kg of trimethoprim (20-fold higher than the recommended human dose). In one study, however, cleft palates were observed in one litter out of 9 when 355 mg/kg of sulfamethoxazole (11.1-fold higher than the recommended human dose) was used in combination with 88 mg/kg of trimethoprim (13.8-fold higher than the recommended human dose).

In some rabbit studies, an overall increase in fetal loss (dead and resorbed and malformed conceptuses) was associated with doses of trimethoprim 6 times the human therapeutic dose.

While there are no large, well-controlled studies on the use of trimethoprim and sulfamethoxazole in pregnant women, Brumfitt and Pursell,[7] in a retrospective study, reported the outcome of 186 pregnancies during which the mother received either placebo or trimethoprim and sulfamethoxazole. The incidence of congenital abnormalities was 4.5% (3 of 66) in those who received placebo and 3.3% (4 of 120) in those receiving trimethoprim and sulfamethoxazole. There were no abnormalities in the 10 children whose mothers received the drug during the first trimester. In a separate survey, Brumfitt and Pursell also found no congenital abnormalities in 35 children whose mothers had received oral trimethoprim and sulfamethoxazole at the time of conception or shortly thereafter.

Because trimethoprim and sulfamethoxazole may interfere with folic acid metabolism, Bactrim should be used during pregnancy only if the potential benefit justifies the potential risk to the fetus.

Nonteratogenic Effects: See CONTRAINDICATIONS section.

Nursing Mothers: See CONTRAINDICATIONS section.

Pediatric Use: Bactrim is not recommended for pediatric patients younger than 2 months of age (see INDICATIONS and CONTRAINDICATIONS sections).

ADVERSE REACTIONS: The most common adverse effects are gastrointestinal disturbances (nausea, vomiting, anorexia) and allergic skin reactions (such as rash and urticaria). **FATALITIES ASSOCIATED WITH THE ADMINISTRATION OF SULFONAMIDES, ALTHOUGH RARE, HAVE OCCURRED DUE TO SEVERE REACTIONS, INCLUDING STEVENS-JOHNSON SYNDROME, TOXIC EPIDERMAL NECROLYSIS, FULMINANT HEPATIC NECROSIS, AGRANULOCYTOSIS, APLASTIC ANEMIA AND OTHER BLOOD DYSCRASIAS (SEE WARNINGS SECTION).**

Hematologic: Agranulocytosis, aplastic anemia, thrombocytopenia, leukopenia, neutropenia, hemolytic anemia, megaloblastic anemia, hypoprothrombinemia, methemoglobinemia, eosinophilia, pancytopenia, purpura.

Allergic Reactions: Stevens-Johnson syndrome, toxic epidermal necrolysis, anaphylaxis, allergic myocarditis, erythema multiforme, exfoliative dermatitis, angioedema, drug fever, chills, Henoch-Schoenlein purpura, serum sickness-like syndrome, generalized allergic reactions, generalized skin eruptions, photosensitivity, conjunctival and scleral injection, pruritus, urticaria and rash. In addition, periarteritis nodosa and systemic lupus erythematosus have been reported.

Gastrointestinal: Hepatitis (including cholestatic jaundice and hepatic necrosis), elevation of serum transaminase and bilirubin, pseudomembranous enterocolitis, pancreatitis, stomatitis, glossitis, nausea, emesis, abdominal pain, diarrhea, anorexia.

Genitourinary: Renal failure, interstitial nephritis, BUN and serum creatinine elevation, toxic nephrosis with oliguria and anuria, crys-

talluria and nephrotoxicity in association with cyclosporine.

Metabolic and Nutritional: Hyperkalemia (see PRECAUTIONS: *Use in the Elderly* and *Use in the Treatment of and Prophylaxis for Pneumocystis Carinii Pneumonia in Patients with Acquired Immunodeficiency Syndrome [AIDS]).*

Neurologic: Aseptic meningitis, convulsions, peripheral neuritis, ataxia, vertigo, tinnitus, headache.

Psychiatric: Hallucinations, depression, apathy, nervousness.

Endocrine: The sulfonamides bear certain chemical similarities to some goitrogens, diuretics (acetazolamide and the thiazides) and oral hypoglycemic agents. Cross-sensitivity may exist with these agents. Diuresis and hypoglycemia have occurred rarely in patients receiving sulfonamides.

Musculoskeletal: Arthralgia and myalgia. Isolated cases of rhabdomyolysis have been reported with Bactrim, mainly in AIDS patients.

Respiratory: Cough, shortness of breath, and pulmonary infiltrates (see WARNINGS).

Miscellaneous: Weakness, fatigue, insomnia.

OVERDOSAGE

Acute: The amount of a single dose of Bactrim that is either associated with symptoms of overdosage or is likely to be life-threatening has not been reported. Signs and symptoms of overdosage reported with sulfonamides include anorexia, colic, nausea, vomiting, dizziness, headache, drowsiness and unconsciousness. Pyrexia, hematuria and crystalluria may be noted. Blood dyscrasias and jaundice are potential late manifestations of overdosage.

Signs of acute overdosage with trimethoprim include nausea, vomiting, dizziness, headache, mental depression, confusion and bone marrow depression.

General principles of treatment include the institution of gastric lavage or emesis, forcing oral fluids, and the administration of intravenous fluids if urine output is low and renal function is normal. Acidification of the urine will increase renal elimination of trimethoprim. The patient should be monitored with blood counts and appropriate blood chemistries, including electrolytes. If a significant blood dyscrasia or jaundice occurs, specific therapy should be instituted for these complications. Peritoneal dialysis is not effective and hemodialysis is only moderately effective in eliminating trimethoprim and sulfamethoxazole.

Chronic: Use of Bactrim at high doses and/or for extended periods of time may cause bone marrow depression manifested as thrombocytopenia, leukopenia and/or megaloblastic anemia. If signs of bone marrow depression occur, the patient should be given leucovorin 5 to 15 mg daily until normal hematopoiesis is restored.

Weight		Dose–every 12 hours	
lb	kg	Teaspoonfuls	Tablets
22	10	1 (5 mL)	—
44	20	2 (10 mL)	1
66	30	3 (15 mL)	1$\frac{1}{2}$
88	40	4 (20 mL)	2 or 1 DS tablet

Weight		Dose–every 6 hours	
lb	kg	Teaspoonfuls	Tablets
18	8	1 (5 mL)	—
35	16	2 (10 mL)	1
53	24	3 (15 mL)	1$\frac{1}{2}$
70	32	4 (20 mL)	2 or 1 DS tablet
88	40	5 (25 mL)	2$\frac{1}{2}$
106	48	6 (30 mL)	3 or 1$\frac{1}{2}$DS tablets
141	64	8 (40 mL)	4 or 2 DS tablets
176	80	10 (50 mL)	5 or 2$\frac{1}{2}$ DS Tablets

DOSAGE AND ADMINISTRATION

Not recommended for use in pediatric patients less than 2 months of age.
Urinary Tract Infections and Shigellosis in Adults and Pediatric Patients, and Acute Otitis Media in Pediatric Patients:
Adults: The usual adult dosage in the treatment of urinary tract infections is 1 Bactrim DS (double strength) tablet, 2 Bactrim tablets or 4 teaspoonfuls (20 mL) of Bactrim Pediatric Suspension every 12 hours for 10 to 14 days. An identical daily dosage is used for 5 days in the treatment of shigellosis.
Pediatric Patients: The recommended dose for pediatric patients with urinary tract infections or acute otitis media is 8 mg/kg trimethoprim and 40 mg/kg sulfamethoxazole per 24 hours, given in two divided doses every 12 hours for 10 days. An identical daily dosage is used for 5 days in the treatment of shigellosis. The following table is a guideline for the attainment of this dosage:
Pediatric Patients 2 months of age or older:
[See first table above]
For Patients with Impaired Renal Function:
When renal function is impaired, a reduced dosage should be employed using the following table:

Creatinine Clearance (mL/min)	Recommended Dosage Regimen
Above 30	Usual standard regimen
15–30	$\frac{1}{2}$ the usual regimen
Below 1[5]	Use not recommended

Acute Exacerbations of Chronic Bronchitis in Adults:
The usual adult dosage in the treatment of acute exacerbations of chronic bronchitis is 1 Bactrim DS (double strength) tablet, 2 Bactrim tablets or 4 teaspoonfuls (20 mL) of Bactrim Pediatric Suspension every 12 hours for 14 days.
Pneumocystis Carinii Pneumonia:
Treatment: Adults and Pediatric Patients:
The recommended dosage for treatment of patients with documented *Pneumocystis carinii* pneumonia is 15 to 20 mg/kg trimethoprim and 75 to 100 mg/kg sulfamethoxazole per 24 hours given in equally divided doses every 6 hours for 14 to 21 days. The following table is a guideline for the upper limit of this dosage.
[See second table above]
For the lower limit dose (15 mg/kg trimethoprim and 75 mg/kg sulfamethoxazole per 24 hours) administer 75% of the dose in the above table.
Prophylaxis:
Adults:
The recommended dosage for prophylaxis in adults is 1 Bactrim DS (double strength) tablet daily.[9]
Pediatric Patients:
For pediatric patients, the recommended dose is 150 mg/m^2/day trimethoprim with 750 mg/m^2/day sulfamethoxazole given orally in equally divided doses twice a day, on 3 consecutive days per week. The total daily dose should not exceed 320 mg trimethoprim and 1600 mg sulfamethoxazole.[10] The following table is a guideline for the attainment of this dosage in pediatric patients:
[See table at top of next page]
Traveler's Diarrhea in Adults:
For the treatment of traveler's diarrhea, the usual adult dosage is 1 Bactrim DS (double strength) tablet; 2 Bactrim tablets or 4 teaspoonfuls (20 mL) of Pediatric Suspension every 12 hours for 5 days.

HOW SUPPLIED

DS (double strength) Tablets (white, notched, capsule shaped), containing 160 mg trimetho-

Body Surface Area	Dose–every 12 hours	
(m²)	Teaspoonfuls	Tablets
0.26	¹/₂ (2.5 mL)	—
0.53	1 (5 mL)	¹/₂
1.06	2 (10 mL)	1

prim and 800 mg sulfamethoxazole—bottles of 100 (NDC 0004-0117-01), 250 (NDC 0004-0117-04) and 500 (NDC 0004-0117-14). Imprint on tablets: (front) BACTRIM-DS; (back) ROCHE.

Tablets (light green, scored, capsule shaped), containing 80 mg trimethoprim and 400 mg sulfamethoxazole—bottles of 100 (NDC 0004-0050-01). Imprint on tablets: (front) BACTRIM; (back) ROCHE.

Pediatric Suspension (pink, cherry flavored), containing 40 mg trimethoprim and 200 mg sulfamethoxazole per teaspoonful (5 mL)—bottles of 16 oz (1 pint) (NDC 0004-1033-28). TABLETS SHOULD BE STORED AT 15° to 30°C (59° to 86°F) IN A DRY PLACE AND PROTECTED FROM LIGHT.

SUSPENSION SHOULD BE STORED AT 15° to 30°C (59° to 86°F) AND PROTECTED FROM LIGHT.

REFERENCES

1. Kremers P, Duvivier J, Heusghem C. Pharmacokinetic Studies of Co-Trimoxazole in Man after Single and Repeated Doses. *J Clin Pharmacol.* Feb-Mar 1974; 14:112–117.
2. Kaplan SA, et al. Pharmacokinetic Profile of Trimethoprim-Sulfamethoxazole in Man. *J Infect Dis.* Nov 1973; 128 (Suppl): S547–S555.
3. Rudoy RC, Nelson JD, Haltalin KC. *Antimicrobial Agents Chemother.* May 1974;5:439–443.
4. National Committee for Clinical Laboratory Standards. *Methods for Dilution Antimicrobial Susceptibility Tests for Bacteria that Grow Aerobically;* Approved Standard—Fourth Edition. NCCLS Document M7-A4, Vol.17, No. 2, NCCLS, Wayne, PA, January, 1997.
5. National Committee for Clinical Laboratory Standards. *Performance Standards for Antimicrobial Disk Susceptibility Tests.* Approved Standard—Sixth Edition. NCCLS Document M2–A6, Vol. 17, No. 1, NCCLS, Wayne, PA, January, 1997.
6. Hardy DW, et al. A controlled trial of trimethoprim-sulfamethoxazole or aerosolized pentamidine for secondary prophylaxis of *Pneumocystis carinii* pneumonia in patients with the acquired immunodeficiency syndrome. *N Engl J Med.* 1992; 327: 1842–1848.
7. Brumfitt W, Pursell R. Trimethoprim/Sulfamethoxazole in the Treatment of Bacteriuria in Women. *J Infect Dis.* Nov 1973; 128 (Suppl):S657–S663.
8. Masur H. Prevention and treatment of *Pneumocystis* pneumonia. *N Engl J Med.* 1992; 327: 1853–1880.
9. Recommendations for prophylaxis against *Pneumocystis carinii* pneumonia for adults and adolescents infected with human immunodefficiency virus. *MMWR.* 1992; 41(RR-4):1–11.
10. CDC Guidelines for prophylaxis against *Pneumocystis carinii* pneumonia for children infected with human immunodeficiency virus. *MMWR.* 1991; 40(RR-2):1–13.

Revised: July 2000

CIPRO® I.V.   ℞
(ciprofloxacin)
For Intravenous Infusion

DESCRIPTION

CIPRO® I.V. (ciprofloxacin) is a synthetic broad-spectrum antimicrobial agent for intravenous (I.V.) administration. Ciprofloxacin, a fluoroquinolone, is 1-cyclopropyl-6-fluoro-1, 4-dihydro-4-oxo-7-(1-piperazinyl) -3- quinolinecarboxylic acid. Its empirical formula is $C_{17}H_{18}FN_3O_3$ and its chemical structure is:

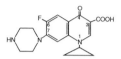

Ciprofloxacin is a faint to light yellow crystalline powder with a molecular weight of 331.4. It is soluble in dilute (0.1N) hydrochloric acid and is practically insoluble in water and ethanol. Ciprofloxacin differs from other quinolones in that it has a fluorine atom at the 6-position, a piperazine moiety at the 7-position, and a cyclopropyl ring at the 1-position. CIPRO® I.V. solutions are available as sterile 1.0% aqueous concentrates, which are intended for dilution prior to administration, and as 0.2% ready-for-use infusion solutions in 5% Dextrose Injection. All formulas contain lactic acid as a solubilizing agent and hydrochloric acid for pH adjustment. The pH range for the 1.0% aqueous concentrates in vials is 3.3 to 3.9. The pH range for the 0.2% ready-for-use infusion solutions is 3.5 to 4.6.

The plastic container is fabricated from a specially formulated polyvinyl chloride. Solutions in contact with the plastic container can leach out certain of its chemical components in very small amounts within the expiration period, e.g., di(2-ethylhexyl) phthalate (DEHP), up to 5 parts per million. The suitability of the plastic has been confirmed in tests in animals according to USP biological tests for plastic containers as well as by tissue culture toxicity studies.

CLINICAL PHARMACOLOGY

Following 60-minute intravenous infusions of 200 mg and 400 mg ciprofloxacin to normal volunteers, the mean maximum serum concentrations achieved were 2.1 and 4.6 µg/mL, respectively; the concentrations at 12 hours were 0.1 and 0.2 µg/mL, respectively.
[See table below]

The pharmacokinetics of ciprofloxacin are linear over the dose range of 200 to 400 mg administered intravenously. The serum elimination half-life is approximately 5–6 hours and the total clearance is around 35 L/hr. Comparison of the pharmacokinetic parameters following the 1st and 5th I.V. dose on a q 12 h regimen indicates no evidence of drug accumulation.

The absolute bioavailability of oral ciprofloxacin is within a range of 70–80% with no substantial loss by first pass metabolism. An intravenous infusion of 400 mg ciprofloxacin given over 60 minutes every 12 hours has been shown to produce an area under the serum concentration time curve (AUC) equivalent to that produced by a 500-mg oral dose given every 12 hours. An intravenous infusion of 400 mg ciprofloxacin given over 60 minutes every 8 hours has been shown to produce an AUC at steady-state equivalent to that produced by a 750-mg oral dose given every 12 hours. A 400-mg I.V. dose results in a C_{max} similar to that observed with a 750-mg oral dose. An infusion of 200 mg ciprofloxacin given every 12 hours produces an AUC equivalent to that produced by a 250-mg oral dose given every 12 hours.
[See table at bottom of next page]

After intravenous administration, approximately 50% to 70% of the dose is excreted in the urine as unchanged drug. Following a 200-mg I.V. dose, concentrations in the urine usually exceed 200 µg/mL 0–2 hours after dosing and are generally greater than 15 µg/mL 8–12 hours after dosing. Following a 400-mg I.V. dose, urine concentrations generally exceed 400 µg/mL 0–2 hours after dosing and are usually greater than 30 µg/mL 8–12 hours after dosing. The renal clearance is approximately 22 L/hr. The urinary excretion of ciprofloxacin is virtually complete by 24 hours after dosing.

The serum concentrations of ciprofloxacin and metronidazole were not altered when these two drugs were given concomitantly.

Co-administration of probenecid with ciprofloxacin results in about a 50% reduction in the ciprofloxacin renal clearance and a 50% increase in its concentration in the systemic circulation. Although bile concentrations of ciprofloxacin are severalfold higher than serum concentrations after intravenous dosing, only a small amount of the administered dose (<1%) is recovered from the bile as unchanged drug. Approximately 15% of an I.V. dose is recovered from the feces within 5 days after dosing.

Steady-state Ciprofloxacin Serum Concentrations (µg/mL)
After 60-minute I.V. Infusions q 12 h.

| Dose | Time after starting the infusion | | | | | |
	30 min	1 hr	3 hr	6 hr	8 hr	12 hr
200 mg	1.7	2.1	0.6	0.3	0.2	0.1
400 mg	3.7	4.6	1.3	0.7	0.5	0.2

After I.V. administration, three metabolites of ciprofloxacin have been identified in human urine which together account for approximately 10% of the intravenous dose.

Pharmacokinetic studies of the oral (single dose) and intravenous (single and multiple dose) forms of ciprofloxacin indicate that plasma concentrations of ciprofloxacin are higher in elderly subjects (>65 years) as compared to young adults. Although the C_{max} is increased 16–40%, the increase in mean AUC is approximately 30%, and can be at least partially attributed to decreased renal clearance in the elderly. Elimination half-life is only slightly ($\sim$20%) prolonged in the elderly. These differences are not considered clinically significant. (See **PRECAUTIONS: Geriatric Use.**)

In patients with reduced renal function, the half-life of ciprofloxacin is slightly prolonged and dosage adjustments may be required. (See **DOSAGE AND ADMINISTRATION.**)

In preliminary studies in patients with stable chronic liver cirrhosis, no significant changes in ciprofloxacin pharmacokinetics have been observed. However, the kinetics of ciprofloxacin in patients with acute hepatic insufficiency have not been fully elucidated.

Following infusion of 400 mg I.V. ciprofloxacin every eight hours in combination with 50 mg/kg I.V. piperacillin sodium every 4 hours, mean serum ciprofloxacin concentrations were 3.02 µg/mL ½ hour and 1.18 µg/mL between 6–8 hours after the end of infusion.

The binding of ciprofloxacin to serum proteins is 20 to 40%.

After intravenous administration, ciprofloxacin is present in saliva, nasal and bronchial secretions, sputum, skin blister fluid, lymph, peritoneal fluid, bile, and prostatic secretions. It has also been detected in the lung, skin, fat, muscle, cartilage, and bone. Although the drug diffuses into cerebrospinal (CSF), CSF concentrations are generally less than 10% of peak serum concentrations. Levels of the drug in the aqueous and vitreous chambers of the eye are lower than in serum.

Microbiology: Ciprofloxacin has *in vitro* activity against a wide range of gram-negative and gram-positive microorganisms. The bactericidal action of ciprofloxacin results from interference with the enzyme DNA gyrase which is needed for the synthesis of bacterial DNA.

Ciprofloxacin has been shown to be active against most strains of the following microorganisms, both *in vitro* and in clinical infections as described in the **INDICATIONS AND USAGE** section of the package insert for CIPRO® I.V. (ciprofloxacin for intravenous infusion).

Aerobic gram-positive microorganisms
Enterococcus faecalis
   (Many strains are only moderately susceptible.)
Staphylococcus aureus
   (methicillin susceptible)
Staphylococcus epidermidis
Staphylococcus saprophyticus
Streptococcus pneumoniae
Streptococcus pyogenes

Aerobic gram-negative microorganisms
Citrobacter diversus
Citrobacter freundii
Enterobacter cloacae
Escherichia coli
Haemophilus influenzae
Haemophilus parainfluenzae
Klebsiella pneumoniae
Moraxella catarrhalis
Morganella morganii
Proteus mirabilis
Proteus vulgaris
Providencia rettgeri
Providencia stuartii
Pseudomonas aeruginosa
Serratia marcescens

Ciprofloxacin has been shown to be active against most strains of the following microorganisms, both *in vitro* and in clinical infections as described in the **INDICATIONS AND USAGE** section of the package insert for CIPRO® (ciprofloxacin hydrochloride) Tablets.

Aerobic gram-positive microorganisms
Enterococcus faecalis
   (Many strains are only moderately susceptible.)
Staphylococcus aureus
   (methicillin susceptible)
Staphylococcus epidermidis
Staphylococcus saprophyticus
Streptococcus pneumoniae
Streptococcus pyogenes

Aerobic gram-negative microorganisms
Campylobacter jejuni
Citrobacter diversus
Citrobacter freundii
Enterobacter cloacae

Steady-state Pharmacokinetic Parameter Following Multiple Oral and I.V. Doses				
Parameters	500 mg q 12 h, P.O.	400 mg q 12 h, I.V.	750 mg q 12 h, P.O.	400 mg q 8 h, I.V.
AUC (µg•hr/mL)	13.7[a]	12.7[a]	31.6[b]	32.9[c]
C_{max} (µg/mL)	2.97	4.56	3.59	4.07

[a]AUC_{0-12h}
[b]AUC 24h=$AUC_{0-12h} \times 2$
[c]AUC 24h=$AUC_{0-8h} \times 3$

Escherichia coli
Haemophilus influenzae
Haemophilus parainfluenzae
Klebsiella pneumoniae
Moraxella catarrhalis
Morganella morganii
Neisseria gonorrhoeae
Proteus mirabilis
Proteus vulgaris
Providencia rettgeri
Providencia stuartii
Pseudomonas aeruginosa
Salmonella typhi
Serratia marcescens
Shigella boydii
Shigella dysenteriae
Shigella flexneri
Shigella sonnei

Ciprofloxacin has been shown to be active against *Bacillus anthracis* both *in vitro* and by use of serum levels as a surrogate marker (see **INDICATIONS AND USAGE** and **INHALATIONAL ANTHRAX—ADDITIONAL INFORMATION**).

The following *in vitro* data are available, **but their clinical significance is unknown**.

Ciprofloxacin exhibits *in vitro* minimum inhibitory concentrations (MICs) of 1 µg/mL or less against most (≥90%) strains of the following microorganisms; however, the safety and effectiveness of ciprofloxacin in treating clinical infections due to these microorganisms have not been established in adequate and well-controlled clinical trials.

Aerobic gram-positive microorganisms
Staphylococcus haemolyticus
Staphylococcus hominis

Aerobic gram-negative microorganisms
Acinetobacter lwoffi
Aeromonas hydrophila
Edwardsiella tarda
Enterobacter aerogenes
Klebsiella oxytoca
Legionella pneumophila
Pasteurella multocida
Salmonella enteritidis
Vibrio cholerae
Vibrio parahaemolyticus
Vibrio vulnificus
Yersinia enterocolitica

Most strains of *Burkholderia cepacia* and some strains of *Stenotrophomonas maltophilia* are resistant to ciprofloxacin as are most anaerobic bacteria, including *Bacteroides fragilis* and *Clostridium difficile*.

Ciprofloxacin is slightly less active when tested at acidic pH. The inoculum size has little effect when tested *in vitro*. The minimum bactericidal concentration (MBC) generally does not exceed the minimum inhibitory concentration (MIC) by more than a factor of 2. Resistance to ciprofloxacin *in vitro* usually develops slowly (multiple-step mutation).

Ciprofloxacin does not cross-react with other antimicrobial agents such as beta-lactams or aminoglycosides; therefore, organisms resistant to these drugs may be susceptible to ciprofloxacin.

In vitro studies have shown that additive activity often results when ciprofloxacin is combined with other antimicrobial agents such as beta-lactams, aminoglycosides, clindamycin, or metronidazole. Synergy has been reported particularly with the combination of ciprofloxacin and beta-lactam; antagonism is observed only rarely.

Susceptibility Tests

Dilution Techniques: Quantitative methods are used to determine antimicrobial minimum inhibitory concentrations (MICs). These MICs provide estimates of the susceptibility of bacteria to antimicrobial compounds. The MICs should be determined using a standardized procedure. Standardized procedures are based on a dilution method[1] (broth or agar) or equivalent with standardized inoculum concentrations and standardized concentrations of ciprofloxacin powder. The MIC values should be interpreted according to the following criteria:

For testing aerobic microorganisms other than *Haemophilus influenzae, Haemophilus parainfluenzae*, and *Neisseria gonorrhoeae*[a]:

MIC (µg/mL)	Interpretation
≤ 1	Susceptible (S)
2	Intermediate (I)
≥ 4	Resistant (R)

[a] These interpretive standards are applicable only to broth microdilution susceptibility tests with streptococci using cation-adjusted Mueller-Hinton broth with 2–5% lysed horse blood.

For testing *Haemophilus influenzae* and *Haemophilus parainfluenzae*[b]:

MIC (µg/mL)	Interpretation
≤ 1	Susceptible (S)

[b] This interpretive standard is applicable only to broth microdilution susceptibility tests with *Haemophilus influenzae* and *Haemophilus parainfluenzae* using *Haemophilus* Test Medium[1].

The current absence of data on resistant strains precludes defining any results other than "Susceptible". Strains yielding MIC results suggestive of a "nonsusceptible" category should be submitted to a reference laboratory for further testing.

For testing *Neisseria gonorrhoeae*[c]:

MIC (µg/mL)	Interpretation
≤0.06	Susceptible (S)

[c] This interpretive standard is applicable only to agar dilution test with GC agar base and 1% defined growth supplement.

Organism		MIC (µg/mL)
E. faecalis	ATCC 29212	0.25–2.0
E. coli	ATCC 25922	0.004–0.015
H. influenzae[a]	ATCC 49247	0.004–0.03
N. gonorrhoeae[b]	ATCC 49226	0.001–0.008
P. aeruginosa	ATCC 27853	0.25–1.0
S. aureus	ATCC 29213	0.12–0.5

[a] This quality control range is applicable to only *H. influenzae* ATCC 49247 tested by a broth microdilution procedure using *Haemophilus* Test Medium (HTM)[1].

[b] This quality control range is applicable to only *N. gonorrhoeae* ATCC 49226 tested by an agar dilution procedure using GC agar base and 1% defined growth supplement.

The current absence of data on resistant strains precludes defining any results other than "Susceptible". Strains yielding MIC results suggestive of a "nonsusceptible" category should be submitted to a reference laboratory for further testing.

A report of "Susceptible" indicates that the pathogen is likely to be inhibited if the antimicrobial compound in the blood reaches the concentrations usually achievable. A report of "Intermediate" indicates that the result should be considered equivocal, and, if the microorganism is not fully susceptible to alternative, clinically feasible drugs, the test should be repeated. This category implies possible clinical applicability in body sites where the drug is physiologically concentrated or in situations where high dosage of drug can be used. This category also provides a buffer zone which prevents small uncontrolled technical factors from causing major discrepancies in interpretation. A report of "Resistant" indicates that the pathogen is not likely to be inhibited if the antimicrobial compound in the blood reaches the concentrations usually achievable; other therapy should be selected.

Standardized susceptibility test procedures require the use of laboratory control microorganisms to control the technical aspects of the laboratory procedures. Standard ciprofloxacin powder should provide the following MIC values:

[See table above]

Diffusion Techniques: Quantitative methods that require measurement of zone diameters also provide reproducible estimates of the susceptibility of bacteria to antimicrobial compounds. One such standardized procedure[2] requires the use of standardized inoculum concentrations. This procedure uses paper disks impregnated with 5-µg ciprofloxacin to test the susceptibility of microorganisms to ciprofloxacin.

Reports from the laboratory providing results of the standard single-disk susceptibility test with a 5-µg ciprofloxacin disk should be interpreted according to the following criteria:

For testing aerobic microorganisms other than *Haemophilus influenzae*, *Haemophilus parainfluenzae*, and *Neisseria gonorrhoeae*[a]:

Zone Diameter (mm)	Interpretation
≥ 21	Susceptible (S)
16–20	Intermediate (I)
≤ 15	Resistant (R)

[a] These zone diameter standards are applicable only to tests performed for streptococci using Mueller-Hinton agar supplemented with 5% sheep blood incubated in 5% CO_2.

For testing *Haemophilus influenzae* and *Haemophilus parainfluenzae*[b]:

Zone Diameter (mm)	Interpretation
≥ 21	Susceptible (S)

[b] This zone diameter standard is applicable only to tests with *Haemophilus influenzae* and *Haemophilus parainfluenzae* using *Haemophilus* Test Medium (HTM)[2].

The current absence of data on resistant strains precludes defining any results other than "Susceptible". Strains yielding zone diameter results suggestive of a "nonsusceptible" category should be submitted to a reference laboratory for further testing.

For testing *Neisseria gonorrhoeae*[c]:

Zone Diameter (mm)	Interpretation
≥ 36	Susceptible (S)

[c] This zone diameter standard is applicable only to disk diffusion tests with GC agar base and 1% defined growth supplement.

The current absence of data on resistant strains precludes defining any results other than "Susceptible". Strains yielding zone diameter results suggestive of a "nonsusceptible" category should be submitted to a reference laboratory for further testing.

Interpretation should be as stated above for results using dilution techniques. Interpretation involves correlation of the diameter obtained in the disk test with the MIC for ciprofloxacin.

As with standardized dilution techniques, diffusion methods require the use of laboratory control microorganisms that are used to control the technical aspects of the laboratory procedures. For the diffusion technique, the 5-µg

Organism		Zone Diameter (mm)
E. coli	ATCC 25922	30–40
H. influenzae[a]	ATCC 49247	34–42
N. gonorrhoeae[b]	ATCC 49226	48–58
P. aeruginosa	ATCC 27853	25–33
S. aureus	ATCC 25923	22–30

[a] These quality control limits are applicable to only *H. influenzae* ATCC 49247 testing using *Haemophilus* Test Medium (HTM)[2].
[b] These quality control limits are applicable only to tests conducted with *N. gonorrhoeae* ATCC 49226 performed by disk diffusion using GC agar base and 1% defined growth supplement.

ciprofloxacin disk should provide the following zone diameters in these laboratory test quality control strains:
[See table above]

INDICATIONS AND USAGE

CIPRO® I.V. is indicated for the treatment of infections caused by susceptible strains of the designated microorganisms in the conditions listed below when the intravenous administration offers a route of administration advantageous to the patient. Please see **DOSAGE AND ADMINISTRATION** for specific recommendations.

Urinary Tract Infections caused by *Escherichia coli* (including cases with secondary bacteremia), *Klebsiella pneumoniae* subspecies *pneumoniae*, *Enterobacter cloacae*, *Serratia marcescens*, *Proteus mirabilis*, *Providencia rettgeri*, *Morganella morganii*, *Citrobacter diversus*, *Citrobacter freundii*, *Pseudomonas aeruginosa*, *Staphylococcus epidermidis*, *Staphylococcus saprophyticus*, or *Enterococcus faecalis*.

Lower Respiratory Infections caused by *Escherichia coli*, *Klebsiella pneumoniae* subspecies *pneumoniae*, *Enterobacter cloacae*, *Proteus mirabilis*, *Pseudomonas aeruginosa*, *Haemophilus influenzae*, *Haemophilus parainfluenzae*, or *Streptococcus pneumoniae*.

NOTE: Although effective in clinical trials, ciprofloxacin is not a drug of first choice in the treatment of presumed or confirmed pneumonia secondary to *Streptococcus pneumoniae*.

Nosocomial Pneumonia caused by *Haemophilus influenzae* or *Klebsiella pneumoniae*.

Skin and Skin Structure Infections caused by *Escherichia coli*, *Klebsiella pneumoniae* subspecies *pneumoniae*, *Enterobacter cloacae*, *Proteus mirabilis*, *Proteus vulgaris*, *Providencia stuartii*, *Morganella morganii*, *Citrobacter freundii*, *Pseudomonas aeruginosa*, *Staphylococcus aureus* (methicillin susceptible), *Staphylococcus epidermidis*, or *Streptococcus pyogenes*.

Bone and Joint Infections caused by *Enterobacter cloacae*, *Serratia marcescens*, or *Pseudomonas aeruginosa*.

Complicated Intra-Abdominal Infections (used in conjunction with metronidazole) caused by *Escherichia coli*, *Pseudomonas aeruginosa*, *Proteus mirabilis*, *Klebsiella pneumonia*, or *Bacteroides fragilis*. (See **DOSAGE AND ADMINISTRATION**.)

Acute Sinusitis caused by *Haemophilus influenzae*, *Streptococcus pneumoniae*, or *Moraxella catarrhalis*.

Chronic Bacterial Prostatitis caused by *Escherichia coli* or *Proteus mirabilis*.

Empirical Therapy for Febrile Neutropenic Patients in combination with piperacillin sodium. (See **DOSAGE AND ADMINISTRATION** and **CLINICAL STUDIES**.)

Inhalational anthrax (post-exposure): To reduce the incidence or progression of disease following exposure to aerosolized *Bacillus anthracis*.

Ciprofloxacin serum concentrations achieved in humans serve as a surrogate endpoint reasonably likely to predict clinical benefit and provide the basis for this indication.[4] (See also, **INHALATIONAL ANTHRAX—ADDITIONAL INFORMATION**).

If anaerobic organisms are suspected of contributing to the infection, appropriate therapy should be administered.

Appropriate culture and susceptibility tests should be performed before treatment in order to isolate and identify organisms causing infection and to determine their susceptibility to ciprofloxacin. Therapy with CIPRO® I.V. may be initiated before results of these tests are known; once results become available, appropriate therapy should be continued.

As with other drugs, some strains of *Pseudomonas aeruginosa* may develop resistance fairly rapidly during treatment with ciprofloxacin. Culture and susceptibility testing performed periodically during therapy will provide information not only on the therapeutic effect of the antimicrobial agent but also on the possible emergence of bacterial resistance.

CLINICAL STUDIES
EMPIRICAL THERAPY IN FEBRILE NEUTROPENIC PATIENTS

The safety and efficacy of ciprofloxacin, 400 mg I.V. q 8 h, in combination with piperacillin sodium 50 mg/kg I.V. q 4 h, for the empirical therapy of febrile neutropenic patients were studied in one large pivotal multicenter, randomized trial and were compared to those of tobramycin, 2 mg/kg I.V. q 8 h, in combination with piperacillin sodium, 50 mg/kg I.V. q 4 h. The demographics of the evaluable patients were as follows:
[See first table at bottom of next page]
Clinical response rates observed in this study were as follows:
[See second table at bottom of next page]

CONTRAINDICATIONS

CIPRO® I.V. (ciprofloxacin) is contraindicated in persons with a history of hypersensitivity to ciprofloxacin or any member of the quinolone class of antimicrobial agents.

WARNINGS

THE SAFETY AND EFFECTIVENESS OF CIPROFLOXACIN IN PEDIATRIC PATIENTS AND ADOLESCENTS (LESS THAN 18 YEARS OF AGE),—EXCEPT FOR USE IN INHALATIONAL ANTHRAX (POST-EXPOSURE), PREGNANT WOMEN, AND LACTATING WOMEN HAVE NOT BEEN ESTABLISHED. (See PRECAUTIONS: Pediatric Use, Pregnancy, and Nursing Mothers subsections.) Ciprofloxacin causes lameness in immature dogs. Histopathological examination of the weight-bearing joints of these dogs revealed permanent lesions of the cartilage. Related quinolone-class drugs also produce erosions of cartilage of weight-bearing joints and other signs of arthropathy in immature animals of various species. (See **ANIMAL PHARMACOLOGY.**)

Convulsions, increased intracranial pressure, and toxic psychosis have been reported in patients receiving quinolones, including ciprofloxacin. Ciprofloxacin may also cause central nervous system (CNS) events including: dizziness, confusion, tremors, hallucinations, depression, and rarely, suicidal thoughts or acts. These reactions may occur following the first dose. If these reactions occur in patients receiving ciprofloxacin, the drug should be discontinued and appropriate measures instituted. As with all quinolones, ciprofloxacin should be used with caution in patients with known or suspected CNS disorders that may predispose to seizures or lower the seizure threshold (e.g. severe cerebral arteriosclerosis, epilepsy), or in the presence of other risk factors that may predispose to seizures or lower the seizure threshold (e.g. certain drug therapy, renal dysfunction). (See **PRECAUTIONS: General: Information for Patients, Drug Interactions** and **ADVERSE REACTIONS.**)

SERIOUS AND FATAL REACTIONS HAVE BEEN REPORTED IN PATIENTS RECEIVING CONCURRENT ADMINISTRATION OF INTRAVENOUS CIPROFLOXACIN AND THEOPHYLLINE. These reactions have included cardiac arrest, seizure, status epilepticus, and respiratory failure. Although similar serious adverse events have been reported in patients receiving theophylline alone, the possibility that these reactions may be potentiated by ciprofloxacin cannot be eliminated. If concomitant use cannot be avoided, serum levels of theophylline should be monitored and dosage adjustments made as appropriate.

Serious and occasionally fatal hypersensitivity (anaphylactic) reactions, some following the first dose, have been reported in patients re-

Total	Ciprofloxacin/Piperacillin N = 233		Tobramycin/Piperacillin N = 237	
Median Age (years)	47.0	(range 19–84)	50.0	(range 18–81)
Male	114	(48.9%)	117	(49.4%)
Female	119	(51.1%)	120	(50.6%)
Leukemia/Bone Marrow Transplant	165	(70.8%)	158	(66.7%)
Solid Tumor/Lymphoma	68	(29.2%)	79	(33.3%)
Medial Duration of Neutropenia (days)	15.0	(range 1–61)	14.0	(range 1–89)

Outcomes	Ciprofloxacin/Piperacillin N = 233 Success (%)		Tobramycin/Piperacillin N = 237 Success (%)	
Clinical Resolution of Initial Febrile Episode with No Modifications of Empirical Regimen*	63	(27.0%)	52	(21.9%)
Clinical Resolution of Initial Febrile Episode Including Patients with Modifications of Empirical Regimen	187	(80.3%)	185	(78.1%)
Overall Survival	224	(96.1%)	223	(94.1%)

* To be evaluated as a clinical resolution, patients had to have: (1) resolution of fever; (2) microbiological eradication of infection (if an infection was microbiologically documented); (3) resolution of signs/symptoms of infection; and (4) no modification of empirical antibiotic regimen.

ceiving quinolone therapy. Some reactions were accompanied by cardiovascular collapse, loss of consciousness, tingling, pharyngeal or facial edema, dyspnea, urticaria, and itching. Only a few patients had a history of hypersensitivity reactions. Serious anaphylactic reactions require immediate emergency treatment with epinephrine and other resuscitation measures, including oxygen, intravenous fluids, intravenous antihistamines, corticosteroids, pressor amines, and airway management, as clinically indicated.

Severe hypersensitivity reactions characterized by rash, fever, eosinophilia, jaundice, and hepatic necrosis with fatal outcome have also been reported extremely rarely in patients receiving ciprofloxacin along with other drugs. The possibility that these reactions were related to ciprofloxacin cannot be excluded. Ciprofloxacin should be discontinued at the first appearance of a skin rash or any other sign of hypersensitivity.

Pseudomembranous colitis has been reported with nearly all antibacterial agents, including ciprofloxacin, and may range in severity from mild to life-threatening. Therefore, it is important to consider this diagnosis in patients who present with diarrhea subsequent to the administration of antibacterial agents.

Treatment with antibacterial agents alters the normal flora of the colon and may permit overgrowth of clostridia. Studies indicate that a toxin produced by *Clostridium difficile* is one primary cause of "antibiotic-associated colitis". After the diagnosis of pseudomembranous colitis has been established, therapeutic measures should be initiated. Mild cases of pseudomembranous colitis usually respond to drug discontinuation alone. In moderate to severe cases, consideration should be given to management with fluids and electrolytes, protein supplementation and treatment with an antibacterial drug clinically effective against *C. difficile* colitis.

Achilles and other tendon ruptures that required surgical repair or resulted in prolonged disability have been reported with ciprofloxacin and other quinolones. Ciprofloxacin should be discontinued if the patient experiences pain, inflammation, or rupture of a tendon.

PRECAUTIONS
General: INTRAVENOUS CIPROFLOXACIN SHOULD BE ADMINISTERED BY SLOW INFUSION OVER A PERIOD OF 60 MINUTES. Local I.V. site reactions have been reported with the intravenous administration of ciprofloxacin. These reactions are more frequent if infusion time is 30 minutes or less or if small veins of the hand are used. (See **ADVERSE REACTIONS**.)

Quinolones, including ciprofloxacin, may also cause central nervous system (CNS) events, including nervousness, agitation, insomnia, anxiety, nightmares or paranoia. (See **WARNINGS**, **Information for Patients**, and **Drug Interactions**.)

Crystals of ciprofloxacin have been observed rarely in the urine of human subjects but more frequently in the urine of laboratory animals, which is usually alkaline. (See **ANIMAL PHARMACOLOGY**.) Crystalluria related to ciprofloxacin has been reported only rarely in humans because human urine is usually acidic. Alkalinity of the urine should be avoided in patients receiving ciprofloxacin. Patients should be well hydrated to prevent the formation of highly concentrated urine.

Alteration of the dosage regimen is necessary for patients with impairment of renal function. (See **DOSAGE AND ADMINISTRATION**.)

Moderate to severe phototoxicity manifested as an exaggerated sunburn reaction has been observed in some patients who were exposed to direct sunlight while receiving some members of the quinolone class of drugs. Excessive sunlight should be avoided.

As with any potent drug, periodic assessment of organ system functions, including renal, hepatic, and hematopoietic, is advisable during prolonged therapy.

Information For Patients: Patients should be advised that ciprofloxacin may be associated with hypersensitivity reactions, even following a single dose, and to discontinue the drug at the first sign of a skin rash or other allergic reaction.

Ciprofloxacin may cause dizziness and lightheadedness; therefore, patients should know how they react to this drug before they operate an automobile or machinery or engage in activities requiring mental alertness or coordination.

Patients should be advised that ciprofloxacin may increase the effects of theophylline and caffeine. There is a possibility of caffeine accumulation when products containing caffeine are consumed while taking ciprofloxacin.

Patients should be advised to discontinue treatment; rest and refrain from exercise; and inform their physician if they experience pain, inflammation, or rupture of a tendon.

Patients should be advised that convulsions have been reported in patients taking quinolones, including ciprofloxacin, and to notify their physician before taking the drug if there is a history of this condition.

Drug Interactions: As with some other quinolones, concurrent administration of ciprofloxacin with theophylline may lead to elevated serum concentrations of theophylline and prolongation of its elimination half-life. This may result in increased risk of theophylline-related adverse reactions. (See **WARNINGS**.) If concomitant use cannot be avoided, serum levels of theophylline should be monitored and dosage adjustments made as appropriate.

Some quinolones, including ciprofloxacin, have also been shown to interfere with the metabolism of caffeine. This may lead to reduced clearance of caffeine and prolongation of its serum half-life.

Some quinolones, including ciprofloxacin, have been associated with transient elevations in serum creatinine in patients receiving cyclosporine concomitantly.

Altered serum levels of phenytoin (increased and decreased) have been reported in patients receiving concomitant ciprofloxacin.

The concomitant administration of ciprofloxacin with the sulfonylurea glyburide has, in some patients, resulted in severe hypoglycemia. Fatalities have been reported.

Quinolones have been reported to enhance the effects of the oral anticoagulant warfarin or its derivatives. When these products are administered concomitantly, prothrombin time or other suitable coagulation tests should be closely monitored.

Probenecid interferes with renal tubular secretion of ciprofloxacin and produces an increase in the level of ciprofloxacin in the serum. This should be considered if patients are receiving both drugs concomitantly.

As with other broad-spectrum antimicrobial agents, prolonged use of ciprofloxacin may result in overgrowth of nonsusceptible organisms. Repeated evaluation of the patient's condition and microbial susceptibility testing are essential. If superinfection occurs during therapy, appropriate measures should be taken.

Carcinogenesis, Mutagenesis, Impairment of Fertility: Eight *in vitro* mutagenicity tests have been conducted with ciprofloxacin. Test results are listed below:

Salmonella/Microsome Test (Negative)

E. coli DNA Repair Assay (Negative)

Mouse Lymphoma Cell Forward Mutation Assay (Positive)

Chinese Hamster V_{79} Cell HGPRT Test (Negative)

Syrian Hamster Embryo Cell Transformation Assay (Negative)

Saccharomyces cerevisiae Point Mutation Assay (Negative)

Saccharomyces cerevisiae Mitotic Crossover and Gene Conversion Assay (Negative)

Rat Hepatocyte DNA Repair Assay (Positive)

Thus, two of the eight tests were positive, but results of the following three *in vivo* test systems gave negative results:

Rat Hepatocyte DNA Repair Assay

Micronucleus Test (Mice)

Dominant Lethal Test (Mice)

Long-term carcinogenicity studies in mice and rats have been completed. After daily oral doses of 750 mg/kg (mice) and 250 mg/kg (rats) were administered for up to 2 years, there was no evidence that ciprofloxacin had any carcinogenic or tumorigenic effects in these species. Results from photo co-carcinogenicity testing indicate that ciprofloxacin dose not reduce the time to appearance of UV-induced skin tumors as compared to vehicle control. Hairless (Skh-1) mice were exposed to UVA light for 3.5 hours five times every two weeks for up to 78 weeks while concurrently being administered ciprofloxacin. The time to development of the first skin tumors was 50 weeks in mice treated concomitantly with UVA and ciprofloxacin (mouse dose approximately equal to maximum recommended human dose based upon mg/m²), as opposed to 34 weeks when animals were treated with both UVA and vehicle. The times to development of skin tumors ranged from 16–32 weeks in mice treated concomitantly with UVA and other quinolones.[3]

In this model, mice treated with ciprofloxacin alone did not develop skin or systemic tumors. There are no data from similar models using pigmented mice and/or fully haired mice. The clinical significance of these findings to humans in unknown.

Fertility studies performed in rats at oral doses of ciprofloxacin up to 100 mg/kg (0.8 times the highest recommended human dose of 1200 mg based upon body surface area) revealed no evidence of impairment.

Pregnancy: Teratogenic Effects. Pregnancy Category C: Reproduction studies have been performed in rats and mice using oral doses of up to 100 mg/kg (0.8 and 0.4 times the maximum daily human dose based upon body surface area, respectively) and I.V. doses of up to 30 mg/kg (0.24 and 0.12 times the maximum daily human dose based upon body surface area, respectively) and have revealed no evidence of harm to the fetus due to ciprofloxacin. In rabbits, ciprofloxacin (30 and 100 mg/kg orally) produced gastrointestinal disturbances resulting in maternal weight loss and an increased incidence of abortion, but no teratogenicity was observed at either dose. After intravenous administration of doses up to 20 mg/kg, no maternal toxicity was produced in the rabbit, and no embryotoxicity or teratogenicity was observed. There are, however, no adequate and well-controlled studies in pregnant women. Ciprofloxacin should be used during pregnancy only if the potential benefit justifies the potential risk to the fetus. (See **WARNINGS.**)

Nursing Mothers: Ciprofloxacin is excreted in human milk. Because of the potential for serious adverse reactions in infants nursing from mothers taking ciprofloxacin, a decision should be made whether to discontinue nursing or to discontinue the drug, taking into account the importance of the drug to the mother.

Pediatric Use: Safety and effectiveness in pediatric patients and adolescents less than 18 years of age have not been established, except for use in inhalational anthrax (post-exposure). Ciprofloxacin causes arthropathy in juvenile animals. (See **WARNINGS.**)

For the indication of inhalational anthrax (post-exposure), the risk-benefit assessment indicates that administration of ciprofloxacin to pediatric patients is appropriate. For information regarding pediatric dosing in inhalational anthrax (post-exposure), see **DOSAGE AND ADMINISTRATION** and **INHALATIONAL ANTHRAX—ADDITIONAL INFORMATION.**

Short-term safety data from a single trial in pediatric cystic fibrosis patients are available. In a randomized, double-blind clinical trial for the treatment of acute pulmonary exacerbations in cystic fibrosis patients (ages 5–17 years), 67 patients received ciprofloxacin I.V. 10 mg/kg/dose q 8 h for one week followed by ciprofloxacin tablets 20 mg/kg/dose q 12 h to complete 10–21 days treatment and 62 patients received the combination of ceftazidime I.V. 50 mg/kg/dose q 8 h and tobramycin I.V. 3 mg/kg/dose q 8 h for a total of 10–21 days. Patients less than 5 years of age were not studied. Safety monitoring in the study included periodic range of motion examinations and gait assessments by treatment-blinded examiners. Patients were followed for an average of 23 days after completing treatment (range 0–93 days). This study was not designed to determine long term effects and the safety of repeated exposure to ciprofloxacin.

In the study, injection site reactions were more common in the ciprofloxacin group (24%) than in the comparison group (8%). Other adverse events were similar in nature and frequency between treatment arms. Musculoskeletal adverse events were reported in 22% of the patients in the ciprofloxacin group and 21% in the comparison group. Decreased range of motion was reported in 12% of the subjects in the ciprofloxacin group and 16% in the comparison group. Arthralgia was reported in 10% of the patients in the ciprofloxacin group and 11% in the comparison group. One of sixty-seven patients developed arthritis of the knee nine days after a ten day course of treatment with ciprofloxacin. Clinical symptoms resolved, but an MRI showed knee effusion without other abnormalities eight months after treatment. However, the relationship of this event to the patient's course of ciprofloxacin cannot be definitively determined, particularly since patients with cystic fibrosis may develop arthralgias/arthritis as part of their underlying disease process.

Geriatric Use: In a retrospective analysis of 23 multiple-dose controlled clinical trials of ciprofloxacin encompassing over 3500 ciprofloxacin treated patients, 25% of patients were greater than or equal to 65 years of age and 10% were greater than or equal to 75 years of age. No overall differences in safety or effectiveness were observed between these subjects and younger subjects, and other reported clinical experience has not identified differences in responses between the elderly and younger patients, but greater sensitivity of some older individuals on any drug therapy cannot be ruled out. Ciprofloxacin is known to be substantially excreted by the kidney, and the risk of adverse reactions may be greater in patients with impaired renal function. No alteration of dosage is necessary for patients greater than 65 years of age with normal renal function. However, since some older individuals experience reduced renal function by virtue of their ad-

vanced age, care should be taken in dose selection for elderly patients, and renal function monitoring may be useful in these patients. (See **CLINICAL PHARMACOLOGY** and **DOSAGE AND ADMINISTRATION**.)

ADVERSE REACTIONS

The most frequently reported events, without regard to drug relationship, among patients treated with intravenous ciprofloxacin were nausea, diarrhea, central nervous system disturbance, local I.V. site reactions, abnormalities of liver associated enzymes (hepatic enzymes), and eosinophilia. Headache, restlessness, and rash were also noted in greater than 1% of patients treated with the most common doses of ciprofloxacin.

Local I.V. site reactions have been reported with the intravenous administration of ciprofloxacin. These reactions are more frequent if the infusion time is 30 minutes or less. These may appear as local skin reactions which resolve rapidly upon completion of the infusion. Subsequent intravenous administration is not contraindicated unless the reactions recur or worsen.

Additional events, without regard to drug relationship or route of administration, that occurred in 1% or less of ciprofloxacin patients are listed below:

CARDIOVASCULAR: cardiovascular collapse, cardiopulmonary arrest, myocardial infarction, arrhythmia, tachycardia, palpitation, cerebral thrombosis, syncope, cardiac murmur, hypertension, hypotension, angina pectoris

CENTRAL NERVOUS SYSTEM: convulsive seizures, paranoia, toxic psychosis, depression, dysphasia, phobia, depersonalization, manic reaction, unresponsiveness, ataxia, confusion, hallucinations, dizziness, lightheadedness, paresthesia, anxiety, tremor, insomnia, nightmares, weakness, drowsiness, irritability, malaise, lethargy

GASTROINTESTINAL: ileus, jaundice, gastrointestinal bleeding, *C. difficile* associated diarrhea, pseudomembranous colitis, pancreatitis, hepatic necrosis, intestinal perforation, dyspepsia, epigastric or abdominal pain, vomiting, constipation, oral ulceration, oral candidiasis, mouth dryness, anorexia, dysphagia, flatulence

I.V. INFUSION SITE: thrombophlebitis, burning, pain, pruritus, paresthesia, erythema, swelling

MUSCULOSKELETAL: arthralgia, jaw, arm or back pain, joint stiffness, neck and chest pain, achiness, flare up of gout

RENAL/UROGENITAL: renal failure, interstitial nephritis, hemorrhagic cystitis, renal calculi, frequent urination, acidosis, urethral bleeding, polyuria, urinary retention, gynecomastia, candiduria, vaginitis. Crystalluria, cylindruria, hematuria, and albuminuria have also been reported.

RESPIRATORY: respiratory arrest, pulmonary embolism, dyspnea, pulmonary edema, respiratory distress, pleural effusion, hemoptysis, epistaxis, hiccough
SKIN/HYPERSENSITIVITY: anaphylactic reactions, erythema multiforme/Stevens-Johnson syndrome, exfoliative dermatitis, toxic epidermal necrolysis, vasculitis, angioedema, edema of the lips, face, neck, conjunctivae, hands or lower extremities, purpura, fever, chills, flushing, pruritus, urticaria, cutaneous candidiasis, vesicles, increased perspiration, hyperpigmentation, erythema nodosum, photosensitivity (See **WARNINGS**.)
SPECIAL SENSES: decreased visual acuity, blurred vision, disturbed vision (flashing lights, change in color perception, overbrightness of lights, diplopia), eye pain, anosmia, hearing loss, tinnitus, nystagmus, a bad taste

Also reported were agranulocytosis, prolongation of prothrombin time, and possible exacerbation of myasthenia gravis.

Many of these events were described as only mild or moderate in severity, abated soon after the drug was discontinued, and required no treatment.

In several instances, nausea, vomiting, tremor, irritability, or palpitation were judged by investigators to be related to elevated serum levels of theophylline possibly as a result of drug interaction with ciprofloxacin.

In randomized, double-blind controlled clinical trials comparing ciprofloxacin (I.V. and I.V. P.O sequential) with intravenous beta-lactam control antibiotics, the CNS adverse event profile of ciprofloxacin was comparable to that of the control drugs.

Post-Marketing Adverse Events: Additional adverse events, regardless of relationship to drug, reported from worldwide marketing experience with quinolones, including ciprofloxacin, are:
BODY AS A WHOLE: change in serum phenytoin
CARDIOVASCULAR: postural hypotension, vasculitis
CENTRAL NERVOUS SYSTEM: agitation, delirium, myoclonus, toxic psychosis
HEMIC/LYMPHATIC: hemolytic anemia, methemoglobinemia
METABOLIC/NUTRITIONAL: elevation of serum triglycerides, cholesterol, blood glucose, serum potassium
MUSCULOSKELTAL: myalgia, tendinitis/tendon rupture
RENAL/UROGENITAL: vaginal candidiasis
(See **PRECAUTIONS**.)

Adverse Laboratory Changes: The most frequently reported changes in laboratory parameters with intravenous ciprofloxacin therapy, without regard to drug relationship are listed below:

Hepatic— elevations of AST (SGOT), ALT (SGPT), alkaline phos-phatase, LDH, and serum bilirubin;
Hematologic— elevated eosinophil and platelet counts, decresed platelet counts, hemoglobin and/or hematocrit;
Renal— elevations of serum creatinine, BUN, and uric acid;
Other— elevations of serum creatinine, phosphokinase, serum theophylline (in patients receiving theophylline concomitantly), blood glucose, and triglycerides.

Other changes occurring infrequently were: decreased leukocyte count, elevated atypical lymphocyte count, immature WBCs, elevated serum calcium, elevation of serum gamma-glutamyl transpeptidase (γ GT), decreased BUN, decreased uric acid, decreased total serum protein, decreased serum albumin, decreased serum potassium, elevated serum potassium, elevated serum cholesterol.

Other changes occurring rarely during administration of ciprofloxacin were: elevation of serum amylase, decrease of blood glucose, pancytopenia, leukocytosis, elevated sedimentation rate, change in serum phenytoin, decreased prothrombin time, hemolytic anemia, and bleeding diathesis.

OVERDOSAGE

In the event of acute overdosage, the patient should be carefully observed and given supportive treatment. Adequate hydration must be maintained. Only a small amount of ciprofloxacin (<10%) is removed from the body after hemodialysis or peritoneal dialysis.

In mice, rats, rabbits and dogs, significant toxicity including tonic/clonic convulsions was observed at intravenous doses of ciprofloxacin between 125 and 300 mg/kg.

DOSAGE AND ADMINISTRATION

The recommended adult dosage for urinary tract infections of mild to moderate severity is 200 mg I.V. every 12 hours. For severe or complicated urinary tract infections, the recommended dosage is 400 mg I.V. every 12 hours.

The recommended adult dosage for lower respiratory tract infections, skin and skin structure infections, and bone and joint infections of mild to moderate severity is 400 mg I.V. every 12 hours.

For severe/complicated infections of the lower respiratory tract, skin and skin structure, and bone and joint, the recommended adult dosage is 400 mg I.V. every 8 hours.

The recommended adult dosage for mild, moderate, and severe nosocomial pneumonia is 400 mg I.V. every 8 hours.

Complicated Intra-Abdominal Infections: Sequential therapy [parenteral to oral—400 mg CIPRO® I.V. q 12 h (plus I.V. metronidazole) → 500 mg CIPRO® I.V. Tablets q 12 h (plus

DOSAGE GUIDELINES
Intravenous

Infection†	Type or Severity	Unit Dose	Frequency	Daily Dose
Urinary tract	Mild/Moderate Severe/ Complicated	200 mg 400 mg	q 12 h q 12 h	400 mg 800 mg
Lower Respiratory Tract	Mild/Moderate Severe/ Complicated	400 mg 400 mg	q 12 h q 8 h	800 mg 1200 mg
Nosocomial Pneumonia	Mild/Moderate/ Severe	400 mg	q 8 h	1200 mg
Skin and Skin Structure	Mild/Moderate Severe/ Complicated	400 mg 400 mg	q 12 h q 8 h	800 mg 1200 mg
Bone and Joint	Mild/Moderate Severe/ Complicated	400 mg 400 mg	q 12 h q 8 h	800 mg 1200 mg
Intra-Abdominal*	Complicated	400 mg	q 12 h	800 mg
Acute Sinusitis	Mild/Moderate	400 mg	q 12 h	800 mg
Chronic Bacterial Prostatitis	Mild/Moderate	400 mg	q 12 h	800 mg
Empirical Therapy in Febrile Neutropenic Patients	Severe Ciprofloxacin + Piperacillin	400 mg 50 mg/kg	q 8 h q 4 h	1200 mg Not to exceed 24 g/day
Inhalational anthrax (post-exposure)**	Adult	400 mg	q 12 h	800 mg
	Pediatric	10 mg/kg per dose, not to exceed 400 mg per dose	q 12 h	Not to exceed 800 mg

* used in conjunction with metronidazole. (See product labeling for prescribing information.)
† DUE TO THE DESIGNATED PATHOGENS (See **INDICATIONS AND USAGE.**)
Drug administration should begin as soon as possible after suspected or confirmed exposure. This indication is based on a surrogate endpoint, ciprofloxacin serum concentrations achieved in humans. For a discussion of ciprofloxacin serum concentrations in various human populations, see **INHALATIONAL ANTHRAX—ADDITIONAL INFORMATION. Total duration of ciprofloxacin administration (IV or oral) for inhalational anthrax (post-exposure) is 60 days.

oral metronidazole)] can be instituted at the discretion of the physician. Metronidazole should be given according to product labeling to provide appropriate anaerobic coverage.

The recommended dosage for mild to moderate Acute Sinusitis and Chronic Bacterial Prostatitis is 400 mg I.V. every 12 hours.

The recommended adult dosage for empirical therapy of febrile neutropenic patients is 400 mg I.V. every 8 hours in combination with piperacillin sodium 50 mg/kg I.V. q 4 hours, not to exceed 24 g/day (300 mg/kg/day), for 7–14 days.

The determination of dosage for any particular patient must take into consideration the severity and nature of the infection, the susceptibility of the causative microorganism, the integrity of the patient's host-defense mechanisms and the status of renal and hepatic function.

RECOMMENDED STARTING AND MAINTENANCE DOSES
FOR PATIENTS WITH IMPAIRED RENAL FUNCTION

Creatinine Clearance (mL/min)	Dosage
> 30	See usual dosage.
5 – 29	200 – 400 mg q 18–24 hr

Men: Creatinine clearance (mL/min) = $\dfrac{\text{Weight (kg)} \times (140 - \text{age})}{72 \times \text{serum creatinine (mg/dL)}}$

Women: 0.85 × the value calculated for men.

[See table at top of previous page]

CIPRO® I.V. should be administered by intravenous infusion over a period of 60 minutes. Parenteral drug products should be inspected visually for particulate matter and discoloration prior to administration.

Ciprofloxacin hydrochloride (CIPRO® Tablets) for oral administration are available. Parenteral therapy may be changed to oral CIPRO® Tablets when the condition warrants, at the discretion of the physician. For complete dosage and administration information, see CIPRO® Tablets package insert.

Impaired Renal Function: The following table provides dosage guidelines for use in patients with renal impairment; however, monitoring of serum drug levels provides the most reliable basis for dosage adjustment.

[See first table above]

When only the serum creatinine concentration is known, the following formula may be used to estimate creatinine clearance:

[See second table above]

The serum creatinine should represent a steady state of renal function.

For patients with changing renal function or for patients with renal impairment and hepatic insufficiency, measurement of serum concentrations of ciprofloxacin will provide additional guidance for adjusting dosage.

INTRAVENOUS ADMINISTRATION

CIPRO® I.V. should be administered by intravenous infusion over a period of 60 minutes. Slow infusion of a dilute solution into a large vein will minimize patient discomfort and reduce the risk of venous irritation.

Vials (Injection Concentrate): THIS PREPARATION MUST BE DILUTED BEFORE USE. The intravenous dose should be prepared by aseptically withdrawing the concentrate from the vial of CIPRO® I.V. This should be diluted with a suitable intravenous solution to a final concentration of 1–2 mg/mL. (See **COMPATIBILITY AND STABILITY.**) The resulting solution should be infused over a period of 60 minutes by direct infusion or through a Y-type intravenous infusion set which may already be in place.

If this method or the "piggyback" method of administration is used, it is advisable to discontinue temporarily the administration of any other solutions during the infusion of CIPRO® I.V.

Flexible Containers: CIPRO® I.V. is also available as a 0.2% premixed solution in 5% dextrose in flexible containers of 100 mL or 200 mL. The solutions in flexible containers may be infused as described above.

COMPATIBILITY AND STABILITY

Ciprofloxacin injection 1% (10 mg/mL), when diluted with the following intravenous solutions to concentrations of 0.5 to 2.0 mg/mL, is stable for up to 14 days at refrigerated or room temperature storage.

0.9% Sodium Chloride Injection, USP

5% Dextrose Injection, USP

Sterile Water for Injection

10% Dextrose for Injection

5% Dextrose and 0.225% Sodium Chloride for Injection

5% Dextrose and 0.45% Sodium Chloride for Injection

Lactated Ringer's for Injection

If CIPRO® I.V. is to be given concomitantly with another drug, each drug should be given separately in accordance with the recommended dosage and route of administration for each drug.

HOW SUPPLIED

CIPRO® I.V. (ciprofloxacin) is available as a clear, colorless to slightly yellowish solution. CIPRO® I.V. is available in 200 mg and 400 mg strengths. The concentrate is supplied in vials while the premixed solution is supplied in flexible containers as follows:

VIAL:	SIZE	STRENGTH	NDC NUMBER
	20 mL	200 mg, 1%	0026-8562-20
	40 mL	400 mg, 1%	0026-8564-64

FLEXIBLE CONTAINER: manufactured for Bayer Corporation by Abbott Laboratories, North Chicago, IL 60064.

[See first table at top of next page]

FLEXIBLE CONTAINER: manufactured for Bayer Corporation by Baxter Healthcare Corporation, Deerfield, IL 60015.

[See second table at top of next page]

STORAGE

Vial:	Store between 5–30°C (41–86°F).
Flexible Container:	Store between 5–25°C (41–77°F).

Protect from light, avoid excessive heat, protect from freezing.

CIPRO® I.V. (ciprofloxacin) is also available in a 120 mL Pharmacy Bulk Package.

SIZE	STRENGTH	NDC NUMBER
100 mL 5% dextrose	200 mg, 0.2%	0026-8552-36
200 mL 5% dextrose	400 mg, 0.2%	0026-8554-63

SIZE	STRENGTH	NDC NUMBER
100 mL 5% dextrose	200 mg, 0.2%	0026-8527-36
200 mL 5% dextrose	400 mg, 0.2%	0026-8527-63

Ciprofloxacin is also available as CIPRO® (ciprofloxacin HCl) Tablets 100, 250, 500, and 750 mg and CIPRO® (ciprofloxacin) 5% and 10% Oral Suspension.

ANIMAL PHARMACOLOGY

Ciprofloxacin and other quinolones have been shown to cause arthropathy in immature animals of most species tested. (See WARNINGS.) Damage of weight-bearing joints was observed in juvenile dogs and rats. In young beagles, 100 mg/kg ciprofloxacin given daily for 4 weeks caused degenerative articular changes of the knee joint. At 30 mg/kg, the effect on the joint was minimal. In a subsequent study in beagles, removal of weight-bearing from the joint reduced the lesions but did not totally prevent them.

Crystalluria, sometimes associated with secondary nephropathy, occurs in laboratory animals dosed with ciprofloxacin. This is primarily related to the reduced solubility of ciprofloxacin under alkaline conditions, which predominate in the urine of test animals; in man, crystalluria is rare since human urine is typically acidic. In rhesus monkeys, crystalluria without nephropathy has been noted after intravenous doses as low as 5 mg/kg. After 6 months of intravenous dosing at 10 mg/kg/day, no nephropathological changes were noted; however, nephropathy was observed after dosing at 20 mg/kg/day for the same duration.

In dogs, ciprofloxacin administered at 3 and 10 mg/kg by rapid intravenous injection (15 sec.) produces pronounced hypotensive effects. These effects are considered to be related to histamine release because they are partially antagonized by pyrilamine, an antihistamine. In rhesus monkeys, rapid intravenous injection also produces hypotension, but the effect in this species is inconsistent and less pronounced.

In mice, concomitant administration of nonsteroidal anti-inflammatory drugs, such as phenylbutazone and indomethacin, with quinolones has been reported to enhance the CNS stimulatory effect of quinolones.

Ocular toxicity, seen with some related drugs, has not been observed in ciprofloxacin-treated animals.

INHALATIONAL ANTHRAX—ADDITIONAL INFORMATION

The mean serum concentrations of ciprofloxacin associated with a statistically significant improvement in survival in the rhesus monkey model of inhalational anthrax are reached or exceeded in adult and pediatric patients receiving oral and intravenous regimens. (See DOSAGE AND ADMINISTRATION.) Ciprofloxacin pharmacokinetics have been evaluated in various human populations. The mean peak serum concentration achieved at steady-state in human adults receiving 500 mg orally every 12 hours is 2.97 µg/mL, and 4.56 µg/mL following 400 mg intravenously every 12 hours. The mean trough serum concentration at steady-state for both of these regimens is 0.2 µg/mL. In a study of 10 pediatric patients between 6 and 16 years of age, the mean peak plasma concentration achieved is 8.3 µg/mL and trough concentrations range from 0.09 to 0.26 µg/mL, following two 30-minute intravenous infusions of 10 mg/kg administered 12 hours apart. After the second intravenous infusion patients switched to 15 mg/kg orally every 12 hours achieve a mean peak concentration of 3.6 µg/mL after the initial oral dose. Long-term safety data, including effects on cartilage, following the administration of ciprofloxacin to pediatric patients are limited. (For additional information, see PRECAUTIONS, Pediatric Use.) Ciprofloxacin serum concentrations achieved in humans serve as a surrogate endpoint reasonably likely to predict clinical benefit and provide the basis for this indication.[4]

A placebo-controlled animal study in rhesus monkeys exposed to an inhaled mean dose of 11 LD_{50} (∼5.5 × 10^5) spores (range 5–30 LD_{50}) of B. anthracis was conducted. The minimal inhibitory concentration (MIC) of ciprofloxacin for the anthrax strain used in this study was 0.08 µg/mL. In the animals studied, mean serum concentrations of ciprofloxacin achieved at expected T_{max} (1 hour post-dose) following oral dosing to steady-state ranged from 0.98 to 1.69 µg/mL. Mean steady-state trough concentrations at 12 hours post-dose ranged from 0.12 to 0.19 µg/mL.[5] Mortality due to anthrax for animals that received a 30-day regimen of oral ciprofloxacin beginning 24 hours post-exposure was significantly lower (1/9), compared to the placebo group (9/10) [p=0.001]. The one ciprofloxacin-treated animal that died of anthrax did so following the 30-day administration period.[6]

REFERENCES

1. National Committee for Clinical Laboratory Standards, Methods for Dilution Antimicro-

bial Susceptibility Tests for Bacteria That Grow Aerobically—Fifth Edition. Approved Standard NCCLS Document M7–A5, Vol. 20, No.2, NCCLS, Wayne, PA, January, 2000. **2.** National Committee for Clinical Laboratory Standards, Performance Standards for Antimicrobial Disk Susceptibility Tests—Seventh Edition. Approved Standard NCCLS Document M2–A7, Vol. 20, No. 1, NCCLS, Wayne, PA, January, 2000. **3.** Report presented at the FDA's Anti-Infective Drug and Dermatological Drug Product's Advisory Committee meeting, March 31, 1993, Silver Spring, MD. Report available from FDA, CDER, Advisors and Consultants Staff, HFD-21, 1901 Chapman Avenue, Room 200, Rockville, MD 20852, USA. **4.** 21 CFR 314.510 (Subpart H—Accelerated Approval of New Drugs for Life-Threatening Illnesses). **5.** Kelly DJ, et al. Serum concentrations of penicillin, doxycycline, and ciprofloxacin during prolonged therapy in rhesus monkeys. J Infect Dis 1992; 166: 1184–7. **6.** Friedlander AM, et. al. Postexposure prophylaxis against experimental inhalational anthrax. J Infect Dis 1993; 167: 1239–42.

Manufactured for:
Bayer Corporation
Pharmaceutical Division
400 Morgan Lane
West Haven, CT 06516 USA
Rx Only
PZ500175 11/00 BAY q 3939 5202-4-A-U.S.-8
©2000 Bayer Corporation 10014
58-6307   Printed in U.S.A.

CIPRO® I.V.   ℞
(ciprofloxacin)
For Intravenous Infusion

**PHARMACY BULK PACKAGE—NOT FOR
DIRECT INFUSION**

DESCRIPTION

The pharmacy bulk package is a single-entry container of a sterile preparation for parenteral use that contains many single doses. It contains ciprofloxacin as a 1% aqueous solution concentrate. The contents are intended for use in a pharmacy admixture program and are restricted to the preparation of admixtures for intravenous infusion.

CIPRO® I.V. (ciprofloxacin) is a synthetic broad-spectrum antimicrobial agent for intravenous (I.V.) administration. Ciprofloxacin, a fluoroquinolone, is 1-cyclopropyl-6-fluoro-1, 4-dihydro-4-oxo-7 - (1-piperazinyl) - 3-quinolinecarboxylic acid. Its empirical formula is $C_{17}H_{18}FN_3O_3$ and its chemical structure is:

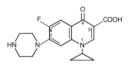

Ciprofloxacin is a faint to light yellow crystalline powder with a molecular weight of 331.4. It is soluble in dilute (0.1N) hydrochloric acid and is practically insoluble in water and ethanol. Ciprofloxacin differs from other quinolones in that it has a fluorine atom at the 6-position, a piperazine moiety at the 7-position, and a cyclopropyl ring at the 1-position. CIPRO® I.V. solutions are available as sterile 1.0% aqueous concentrate, which is intended for dilution prior to administration. Ciprofloxacin solution contains lactic acid as a solubilizing agent and hydrochloric acid for pH adjustment. The pH range for the 1.0% aqueous concentrate is 3.3 to 3.9.

CLINICAL PHARMACOLOGY

Following 60-minute intravenous infusions of 200 mg and 400 mg ciprofloxacin to normal volunteers, the mean maximum serum concentrations achieved were 2.1 and 4.6 µg/mL, respectively; the concentrations at 12 hours were 0.1 and 0.2 µg/mL, respectively.

[See table below]
The pharmacokinetics of ciprofloxacin are linear over the dose range of 200 to 400 mg administered intravenously. The serum elimination half-life is approximately 5–6 hours and the total clearance is around 35 L/hr. Comparison of the pharmacokinetic parameters following the 1st and 5th I.V. dose on a q 12 h regimen indicates no evidence of drug accumulation.

The absolute bioavailability of oral ciprofloxacin is within a range of 70–80% with no substantial loss by first pass metabolism. An intravenous infusion of 400 mg ciprofloxacin given over 60 minutes every 12 hours has been shown to produce an area under the serum concentration time curve (AUC) equivalent to that produced by a 500-mg oral dose given every 12 hours. An intravenous infusion of 400 mg ciprofloxacin given over 60 minutes every 8 hours has been shown to produce an AUC at steady-state equivalent to that produced by a 750-mg oral dose given every 12 hours. A 400-mg I.V. dose results in a C_{max} similar to that observed with a 750-mg oral dose. An infusion of 200 mg ciprofloxacin given every 12 hours produces an AUC equivalent to that produced by a 250-mg oral dose given every 12 hours.

[See table at bottom of next page]
After intravenous administration, approximately 50% to 70% of the dose is excreted in the urine as unchanged drug. Following a 200-mg I.V. dose, concentrations in the urine usually exceed 200 µg/mL 0–2 hours after dosing and are generally greater than 15 µg/mL 8–12 hours after dosing. Following a 400-mg I.V. dose, urine concentrations generally exceed 400 µg/mL 0–2 hours after dosing and are usually greater than 30 µg/mL 8–12 hours after dosing. The renal clearance is approximately 22 L/hr. The urinary excretion of ciprofloxacin is virtually complete by 24 hours after dosing.

The serum concentrations of ciprofloxacin and metronidazole were not altered when these two drugs were given concomitantly.

Co-administration of probenecid with ciprofloxacin results in about a 50% reduction in the ciprofloxacin renal clearance and a 50% increase in its concentration in the systemic circulation. Although bile concentrations of ciprofloxacin are severalfold higher than serum concentrations after intravenous dosing, only a small amount of the administered dose (<1%) is recovered from the bile as unchanged drug. Approximately 15% of an I.V. dose is recovered from the feces within 5 days after dosing.

Steady-state Ciprofloxacin Serum Concentrations (µg/mL) After 60-minute I.V. Infusions q 12 h.						
	Time after starting the infusion					
Dose	**30 min**	**1 hr**	**3 hr**	**6 hr**	**8 hr**	**12 hr**
200 mg	1.7	2.1	0.6	0.3	0.2	0.1
400 mg	3.7	4.6	1.3	0.7	0.5	0.2

After I.V. administration, three metabolites of ciprofloxacin have been identified in human urine which together account for approximately 10% of the intravenous dose.

Pharmacokinetic studies of the oral (single dose) and intravenous (single and multiple dose) forms of ciprofloxacin indicate that plasma concentrations of ciprofloxacin are higher in elderly subjects (>65 years) as compared to young adults. Although the C_{max} is increased 16–40%, the increase in mean AUC is approximately 30%, and can be at least partially attributed to decreased renal clearance in the elderly. Elimination half-life is only slightly ($\sim$20%) prolonged in the elderly. These differences are not considered clinically significant. (See **PRECAUTIONS: Geriatric Use.**)

In patients with reduced renal function, the half-life of ciprofloxacin is slightly prolonged and dosage adjustments may be required. (See **DOSAGE AND ADMINISTRATION.**)

In preliminary studies in patients with stable chronic liver cirrhosis, no significant changes in ciprofloxacin pharmacokinetics have been observed. However, the kinetics of ciprofloxacin in patients with acute hepatic insufficiency have not been fully elucidated.

Following infusion of 400 mg I.V. ciprofloxacin every eight hours in combination with 50 mg/kg I.V. piperacillin sodium every 4 hours, mean serum ciprofloxacin concentrations were 3.02 μg/mL $^1/_2$ hour and 1.18 μg/mL between 6–8 hours after the end of infusion. The binding of ciprofloxacin to serum proteins is 20 to 40%.

After intravenous administration, ciprofloxacin is present in saliva, nasal and bronchial secretions, sputum, skin blister fluid, lymph, peritoneal fluid, bile, and prostatic secretions. It has also been detected in the lung, skin, fat, muscle, cartilage, and bone. Although the drug diffuses into cerebrospinal fluid (CSF), CSF concentrations are generally less than 10% of peak serum concentrations. Levels of the drug in the aqueous and vitreous chambers of the eye are lower than in serum.

Microbiology: Ciprofloxacin has *in vitro* activity against a wide range of gram-negative and gram-positive microorganisms. The bactericidal action of ciprofloxacin results from interference with the enzyme DNA gyrase which is needed for the synthesis of bacterial DNA.

Ciprofloxacin has been shown to be active against most strains of the following microorganisms, both *in vitro* and in clinical infections as described in the **INDICATIONS AND USAGE** section of the package insert for CIPRO® I.V. (ciprofloxacin for intravenous infusion).

Aerobic gram-positive microorganisms
Enterococcus faecalis
(Many strains are only moderately susceptible.)
Staphylococcus aureus
(methicillin susceptible)
Staphylococcus epidermidis
Staphylococcus saprophyticus
Streptococcus pneumoniae
Streptococcus pyogenes

Aerobic gram-negative microorganisms
Citrobacter diversus
Citrobacter freundii
Enterobacter cloacae
Escherichia coli
Haemophilus influenzae
Haemophilus parainfluenzae
Klebsiella pneumoniae
Moraxella catarrhalis
Morganella morganii
Proteus mirabilis
Proteus vulgaris
Providencia rettgeri
Providencia stuartii
Pseudomonas aeruginosa
Serratia marcescens

Ciprofloxacin has been shown to be active against most strains of the following microorganisms, both *in vitro* and in clinical infections as described in the **INDICATIONS AND USAGE** section of the package insert for CIPRO® (ciprofloxacin hydrochloride) Tablets.

Aerobic gram-positive microorganisms
Enterococcus faecalis
(Many strains are only moderately susceptible.)
Staphylococcus aureus
(methicillin susceptible)
Staphylococcus epidermidis
Staphylococcus saprophyticus
Streptococcus pneumoniae
Streptococcus pyogenes

Aerobic gram-negative microorganisms
Campylobacter jejuni
Citrobacter diversus
Citrobacter freundii
Enterobacter cloacae

Steady-state Pharmacokinetic Parameter Following Multiple Oral and I.V. Doses

Parameters	500 mg q 12 h, P.O.	400 mg q 12 h, I.V.	750 mg q 12 h, P.O.	400 mg q 8 h, I.V.
AUC (μg•hr/mL)	13.7[a]	12.7[a]	31.6[b]	32.9[c]
C_{max} (μg/mL)	2.97	4.56	3.59	4.07

[a] AUC_{0-12h}
[b] AUC 24h=$AUC_{0-12h} \times 2$
[c] AUC 24h=$AUC_{0-8h} \times 3$

Escherichia coli
Haemophilus influenzae
Haemophilus parainfluenzae
Klebsiella pneumoniae
Moraxella catarrhalis
Morganella morganii
Neisseria gonorrhoeae
Proteus mirabilis
Proteus vulgaris
Providencia rettgeri
Providencia stuartii
Pseudomonas aeruginosa
Salmonella typhi
Serratia marcescens
Shigella boydii
Shigella dysenteriae
Shigella flexneri
Shigella sonnei

Ciprofloxacin has been shown to be active against *Bacillus anthracis* both *in vitro* and by use of serum levels as a surrogate marker (see **INDICATIONS AND USAGE** and **INHALATIONAL ANTHRAX—ADDITIONAL INFORMATION**).

The following *in vitro* data are available, **but their clinical significance is unknown.**

Ciprofloxacin exhibits *in vitro* minimum inhibitory concentrations (MICs) of 1 µg/mL or less against most (≥90%) strains of the following microorganisms; however, the safety and effectiveness of ciprofloxacin in treating clinical infections due to these microorganisms have not been established in adequate and well-controlled trials.

Aerobic gram-positive microorganisms
Staphylococcus haemolyticus
Staphylococcus hominis
Aerobic gram-negative microorganisms
Acinetobacter lwoffi
Aeromonas hydrophila
Edwardsiella tarda
Enterobacter aerogenes
Klebsiella oxytoca
Legionella pneumophila
Pasteurella multocida
Salmonella enteritidis
Vibrio cholerae
Vibrio parahaemolyticus
Vibrio vulnificus
Yersinia enterocolitica

Most strains of *Burkholderia cepacia* and some strains of *Stenotrophomonas maltophilia* are resistant to ciprofloxacin as are most anaerobic bacteria, including *Bacteroides fragilis* and *Clostridium difficile.*

Ciprofloxacin is slightly less active when tested at acidic pH. The inoculum size has little effect when tested *in vitro.* The minimum bactericidal concentration (MBC) generally does not exceed the minimum inhibitory concentration (MIC) by more than a factor of 2. Resistance to ciprofloxacin *in vitro* usually develops slowly (multiple-step mutation).

Ciprofloxacin does not cross-react with other antimicrobial agents such as beta-lactams or

aminoglycosides; therefore, organisms resistant to these drugs may be susceptible to ciprofloxacin.

In vitro studies have shown that additive activity often results when ciprofloxacin is combined with other antimicrobial agents such as beta-lactams, aminoglycosides, clindamycin, or metronidazole. Synergy has been reported particularly with the combination of ciprofloxacin and a beta-lactam; antagonism is observed only rarely.

Susceptibility Tests

Dilution Techniques: Quantitative methods are used to determine antimicrobial minimum inhibitory concentrations (MICs). These MICs provide estimates of the susceptibility of bacteria to antimicrobial compounds. The MICs should be determined using a standardized procedure. Standardized procedures are based on a dilution method[1] (broth and agar) or equivalent with standardized inoculum concentrations and standardized concentrations of ciprofloxacin powder. The MIC values should be interpreted according to the following criteria:

For testing aerobic microorganisms other than *Haemophilus influenzae, Haemophilus parainfluenzae,* and *Neisseria gonorrhoeae*[a]:

MIC (µg/mL)	Interpretation
≤ 1	Susceptible (S)
2	Intermediate (I)
≥ 4	Resistant (R)

[a] These interpretive standards are applicable only to broth microdilution susceptibility tests with streptococci using cation-adjusted Mueller-Hinton broth with 2–5% lysed horse blood.

For testing *Haemophilus influenzae,* and *Haemophilus parainfluenzae*[b]:

MIC (µg/mL)	Interpretation
≤ 1	Susceptible (S)

[b] This interpretive standard is applicable only to broth microdilution susceptibility tests with *Haemophilus influenzae* and *Haemophilus parainfluenzae* using *Haemophilus* Test Medium[1].

The current absence of data on resistant strains precludes defining any results other than "Susceptible". Strains yielding MIC results suggestive of a "nonsusceptible" category should be submitted to a reference laboratory for further testing.

For testing *Neisseria gonorrhoeae*[c]:

MIC (µg/mL)	Interpretation
≤ 0.06	Susceptible (S)

[c] This interpretive standard is applicable only to agar dilution test with GC agar base and 1% defined growth supplement.

The current absence of data on resistant strains precludes defining any results other than "Susceptible". Strains yielding MIC results suggestive of a "nonsusceptible" category should be submitted to a reference laboratory for further testing.

A report of "Susceptible" indicates that the pathogen is likely to be inhibited if the antimicrobial compound in the blood reaches the concentrations usually achievable. A report of "Intermediate" indicates that the result should be considered equivocal, and, if the microorganism is not fully susceptible to alternative, clinically feasible drugs, the test should be repeated. This category implies possible clinical applicability in body sites where the drug is physiologically concentrated or in situations where high dosage of drug can be used. This category also provides a buffer zone which prevents small uncontrolled technical factors from causing major discrepancies in interpretation. A report of "Resistant" indicates that the pathogen is not likely to be inhibited if the antimicrobial compound in the blood reaches the concentrations usually achievable; other therapy should be selected.

Standardized susceptibility test procedures require the use of laboratory control microorganisms to control the technical aspects of the laboratory procedures. Standard ciprofloxacin powder should provide the following MIC values:

Organism		MIC (μg/mL)
E. faecalis	ATCC 29212	0.25 – 2.0
E. coli	ATCC 25922	0.004 – 0.015
H. influenzae[a]	ATCC 49247	0.004 – 0.03
N. gonorrhoeae[b]	ATCC 49226	0.001 – 0.008
P. aeruginosa	ATCC 27853	0.25 – 1.0
S. aureus	ATCC 29213	0.12 – 0.5

[a] This quality control range is applicable to only H. influenzae ATCC 49247 tested by a broth microdilution procedure using Haemophilus Test Medium (HTM)[1].
[b] This quality control range is applicable to only N. gonorrhoeae ATCC 49226 tested by an agar dilution procedure using GC agar base and 1% defined growth supplement.

Diffusion Techniques: Quantitative methods that require measurement of zone diameters also provide reproducible estimates of the susceptibility of bacteria to antimicrobial compounds. One such standardized procedure[2] requires the use of standardized inoculum concentrations. This procedure uses paper disks impregnated with 5-μg ciprofloxacin to test the susceptibility of microorganisms to ciprofloxacin.

Reports from the laboratory providing results of the standard single-disk susceptibility test with a 5-μg ciprofloxacin disk should be interpreted according to the following criteria:

For testing aerobic microorganisms other than *Haemophilus influenzae*, *Haemophilus parainfluenzae*, and *Neisseria gonorrhoeae*[a]:

Zone Diameter (mm)	Interpretation
≥ 21	Susceptible (S)
16 – 20	Intermediate (I)
≤ 15	Resistant (R)

[a] These zone diameter standards are applicable only to tests performed for streptococci using Mueller-Hinton agar supplemented with 5% sheep blood incubated in 5% CO_2.

For testing *Haemophilus influenzae* and *Haemophilus parainfluenzae*[b]:

Zone Diameter (mm)	Interpretation
≥ 21	Susceptible (S)

[b] This zone diameter standard is applicable only to tests with Haemophilus influenzae and Haemophilus parainfluenzae using Haemophilus Test Medium (HTM)[2].

The current absence of data on resistant strains precludes defining any results other than "Susceptible". Strains yielding zone diameter results suggestive of a "nonsusceptible" category should be submitted to a reference laboratory for further testing.

For testing *Neisseria gonorrhoeae*[c]:

Zone Diameter (mm)	Interpretation
≥ 36	Susceptible (S)

[c] This zone diameter standard is applicable only to disk diffusion tests with GC agar base and 1% defined growth supplement.

The current absence of data on resistant strains precludes defining any results other than "Susceptible". Strains yielding zone diameter results suggestive of a "nonsusceptible" category should be submitted to a reference laboratory for further testing.

Interpretation should be as stated above for results using dilution techniques. Interpretation involves correlation of the diameter obtained in the disk test with the MIC for ciprofloxacin.

As with standardized dilution techniques, diffusion methods require the use of laboratory control microorganisms that are used to control the technical aspects of the laboratory procedures. For the diffusion technique, the 5-μg ciprofloxacin disk should provide the following zone diameters in these laboratory test quality control strains:

Organism		Zone Diameter (mm)
E. coli	ATCC 25922	30–40
H. influenzae[a]	ATCC 49247	34–42

N. gonorrhoeae[b]	ATCC 49226	48–58
P. aeruginosa	ATCC 27853	25–33
S. aureus	ATCC 25923	22–30

[a] These quality control limits are applicable to only *H. influenzae* ATCC 49247 testing using *Haemophilus* Test Medium (HTM)[2].

[b] These quality control limits are applicable only to tests conducted with *N. gonorrhoeae* ATCC 49226 performed by disk diffusion using GC agar base and 1% defined growth supplement.

INDICATIONS AND USAGE

CIPRO® I.V. is indicated for the treatment of infections caused by susceptible strains of the designated microorganisms in the conditions listed below when the intravenous administration offers a route of administration advantageous to the patient. Please see **DOSAGE AND ADMINISTRATION** for specific recommendations.

Urinary Tract Infections caused by *Escherichia coli* (including cases with secondary bacteremia), *Klebsiella pneumoniae* subspecies *pneumoniae, Enterobacter cloacae, Serratia marcescens, Proteus mirabilis, Providencia rettgeri, Morganella morganii, Citrobacter diversus, Citrobacter freundii, Pseudomonas aeruginosa, Staphylococcus epidermidis, Staphylococcus saprophyticus,* or *Enterococcus faecalis.*

Lower Respiratory Infections caused by *Escherichia coli, Klebsiella pneumoniae* subspecies *pneumoniae, Enterobacter cloacae, Proteus mirabilis, Pseudomonas aeruginosa, Haemophilus influenzae, Haemophilus parainfluenzae,* or *Streptococcus pneumoniae.*

NOTE: Although effective in clinical trials, ciprofloxacin is not a drug of first choice in the treatment of presumed or confirmed pneumonia secondary to *Streptococcus pneumoniae.*

Nosocomial Pneumonia caused by *Haemophilus influenzae* or *Klebsiella pneumoniae.*

Skin and Skin Structure Infections caused by *Escherichia coli, Klebsiella pneumoniae* subspecies *pneumoniae, Enterobacter cloacae, Proteus mirabilis, Proteus vulgaris, Providencia stuartii, Morganella morganii, Citrobacter freundii, Pseudomonas aeruginosa, Staphylococcus aureus* (methicillin susceptible), *Staphylococcus epidermidis,* or *Streptococcus pyogenes.*

Bone and Joint Infections caused by *Enterobacter cloacae, Serratia marcescens,* or *Pseudomonas aeruginosa.*

Complicated Intra-Abdominal Infections (used in conjunction with metronidazole) caused by *Escherichia coli, Pseudomonas aeruginosa, Proteus mirabilis, Klebsiella pneumoniae,* or *Bacteroides fragilis.* (See **DOSAGE AND ADMINISTRATION**.)

Acute Sinusitis caused by *Haemophilus influenzae, Streptococcus pneumoniae,* or *Moraxella catarrhalis.*

Chronic Bacterial Prostatitis caused by *Escherichia coli* or *Proteus mirabilis.*

Empirical Therapy for Febrile Neutropenic Patients in combination with piperacillin sodium. (See **DOSAGE AND ADMINISTRATION** and **CLINICAL STUDIES**.)

Inhalational anthrax (post-exposure): To reduce the incidence or progression of disease following exposure to aerosolized *Bacillus anthracis.*

Ciprofloxacin serum concentrations achieved in humans serve as a surrogate endpoint reasonably likely to predict clinical benefit and provide the basis for this indication.[4] (See also, **INHALATIONAL ANTHRAX—ADDITIONAL INFORMATION**).

If anaerobic organisms are suspected of contributing to the infection, appropriate therapy should be administered.

Appropriate culture and susceptibility tests should be performed before treatment in order to isolate and identify organisms causing infection and to determine their susceptibility to ciprofloxacin. Therapy with CIPRO® I.V. may be initiated before results of these tests are known; once results become available, appropriate therapy should be continued.

As with other drugs, some strains of *Pseudomonas aeruginosa* may develop resistance fairly rapidly during treatment with ciprofloxacin. Culture and susceptibility testing performed periodically during therapy will provide information not only on the therapeutic effect of the antimicrobial agent but also on the possible emergence of bacterial resistance.

CLINICAL STUDIES

EMPIRICAL THERAPY IN FEBRILE NEUTROPENIC PATIENTS

The safety and efficacy of ciprofloxacin, 400 mg I.V. q 8 h, in combination with piperacillin sodium, 50 mg/kg I.V. q 4 h, for the empirical therapy of febrile neutropenic patients were studied in one large pivotal multicenter, randomized trial and were compared to those of tobramycin, 2 mg/kg I.V. q 8 h, in combination with piperacillin sodium, 50 mg/kg I.V. q 4 h. The demographics of the evaluable patients were as follows:

[See first table at bottom of next page]

Clinical response rates observed in this study were as follows:

[See second table at bottom of next page]

CONTRAINDICATIONS

CIPRO® I.V. (ciprofloxacin) is contraindicated in persons with a history of hypersensitivity to ciprofloxacin or any member of the quinolone class of antimicrobial agents.

WARNINGS

THE SAFETY AND EFFECTIVENESS OF CIPROFLOXACIN IN PEDIATRIC PATIENTS AND ADOLESCENTS (LESS THAN 18 YEARS

OF AGE),—EXCEPT FOR USE IN INHALA-
TIONAL ANTHRAX (POST-EXPOSURE), PREG-
NANT WOMEN, AND LACTATING WOMEN
HAVE NOT BEEN ESTABLISHED. (See PRE-
CAUTIONS: Pediatric Use, Pregnancy, and
Nursing Mothers subsections.) Ciprofloxacin
causes lameness in immature dogs. Histopathological examination of the weight-bearing
joints of these dogs revealed permanent lesions of the cartilage. Related quinolone-class
drugs also produce erosions of cartilage of
weight-bearing joints and other signs of arthropathy in immature animals of various species. (See ANIMAL PHARMACOLOGY.)

Convulsions, increased intracranial pressure,
and toxic psychosis have been reported in patients receiving quinolones, including ciprofloxacin. Ciprofloxacin may also cause central
nervous system (CNS) events including: dizziness, confusion, tremors, hallucinations, depression, and, rarely, suicidal thoughts or acts.
These reactions may occur following the first
dose. If these reactions occur in patients receiving ciprofloxacin, the drug should be discontinued and appropriate measures instituted. As with all quinolones, ciprofloxacin
should be used with caution in patients with
known or suspected CNS disorders that may
predispose to seizures or lower the seizure
threshold (e.g. severe cerebral arteriosclerosis,
epilepsy), or in the presence of other risk factors that may predispose to seizures or lower
the seizure threshold (e.g. certain drug ther-

apy, renal dysfunction). (See PRECAU-
TIONS: General, Information for Patients,
Drug Interactions and ADVERSE REAC-
TIONS.)

SERIOUS AND FATAL REACTIONS HAVE
BEEN REPORTED IN PATIENTS RECEIVING
CONCURRENT ADMINISTRATION OF INTRA-
VENOUS CIPROFLOXACIN AND THEOPHYL-
LINE. These reactions have included cardiac
arrest, seizure, status epilepticus, and respiratory failure. Although similar serious adverse
events have been reported in patients receiving theophylline alone, the possibility that
these reactions may be potentiated by ciprofloxacin cannot be eliminated. If concomitant
use cannot be avoided, serum levels of theophylline should be monitored and dosage adjustments made as appropriate.

Serious and occasionally fatal hypersensitivity
(anaphylactic) reactions, some following the
first dose, have been reported in patients receiving quinolone therapy. Some reactions
were accompanied by cardiovascular collapse,
loss of consciousness, tingling, pharyngeal or
facial edema, dyspnea, urticaria, and itching.
Only a few patients had a history of hypersensitivity reactions. Serious anaphylactic reactions require immediate emergency treatment
with epinephrine and other resuscitation
measures, including oxygen, intravenous fluids, intravenous antihistamines, corticosteroids, pressor amines, and airway management, as clinically indicated.

Total	Ciprofloxacin/Piperacillin N = 233	Tobramycin/Piperacillin N = 237
Median Age (years)	47.0 (range 19–84)	50.0 (range 18–81)
Male	114 (48.9%)	117 (49.4%)
Female	119 (51.1%)	120 (50.6%)
Leukemia/Bone Marrow Transplant	165 (70.8%)	158 (66.7%)
Solid Tumor/Lymphoma	68 (29.2%)	79 (33.3%)
Median Duration of Neutropenia (days)	15.0 (range 1–61)	14.0 (range 1–89)

Outcomes	Ciprofloxacin/Piperacillin N = 233 Success (%)	Tobramycin/Piperacillin N = 237 Success (%)
Clinical Resolution of Initial Febrile Episode with No Modifications of Empirical Regimen*	63 (27.0%)	52 (21.9%)
Clinical Resolution of Initial Febrile Episode Including Patients with Modifications of Empirical Regimen	187 (80.3%)	185 (78.1%)
Overall Survival	224 (96.1%)	223 (94.1%)

* To be evaluated as a clinical resolution, patients had to have: (1) resolution of fever; (2) microbiological eradication of infection (if an infection was microbiologically documented); (3) resolution of signs/symptoms of infection; and (4) no modification of empirical antibiotic regimen.

Severe hypersensitivity reactions characterized by rash, fever, eosinophilia, jaundice, and hepatic necrosis with fatal outcome have also been reported extremely rarely in patients receiving ciprofloxacin along with other drugs. The possibility that these reactions were related to ciprofloxacin cannot be excluded. Ciprofloxacin should be discontinued at the first appearance of a skin rash or any other sign of hypersensitivity.

Pseudomembranous colitis has been reported with nearly all antibacterial agents, including ciprofloxacin, and may range in severity from mild to life-threatening. Therefore, it is important to consider this diagnosis in patients who present with diarrhea subsequent to the administration of antibacterial agents. Treatment with antibacterial agents alters the normal flora of the colon and may permit overgrowth of clostridia. Studies indicate that a toxin produced by *Clostridium difficile* is one primary cause of "antibiotic-associated colitis". After the diagnosis of pseudomembranous colitis has been established, therapeutic measures should be initiated. Mild cases of pseudomembranous colitis usually respond to drug discontinuation alone. In moderate to severe cases, consideration should be given to management with fluids and electrolytes, protein supplementation and treatment with an antibacterial drug clinically effective against *C. difficile* colitis.

Achilles and other tendon ruptures that required surgical repair or resulted in prolonged disability have been reported with ciprofloxacin and other quinolones. Ciprofloxacin should be discontinued if the patient experiences pain, inflammation, or rupture of a tendon.

PRECAUTIONS

General: INTRAVENOUS CIPROFLOXACIN SHOULD BE ADMINISTERED BY SLOW INFUSION OVER A PERIOD OF 60 MINUTES. Local I.V. site reactions have been reported with the intravenous administration of ciprofloxacin. These reactions are more frequent if infusion time is 30 minutes or less or if small veins of the hand are used. (See **ADVERSE REACTIONS**.)

Quinolones, including ciprofloxacin, may also cause central nervous system (CNS) events, including nervousness, agitation, insomnia, anxiety, nightmares or paranoia. (See **WARNINGS, Information for Patients,** and **Drug Interactions**.)

Crystals of ciprofloxacin have been observed rarely in the urine of human subjects but more frequently in the urine of laboratory animals, which is usually alkaline. (See **ANIMAL PHARMACOLOGY**.) Crystalluria related to ciprofloxacin has been reported only rarely in humans because human urine is usually acidic. Alkalinity of the urine should be avoided in patients receiving ciprofloxacin. Patients should be well hydrated to prevent the formation of highly concentrated urine.

Alteration of the dosage regimen is necessary for patients with impairment of renal function. (See **DOSAGE AND ADMINISTRATION**.)

Moderate to severe phototoxicity manifested as an exaggerated sunburn reaction has been observed in some patients who were exposed to direct sunlight while receiving some members of the quinolone class of drugs. Excessive sunlight should be avoided.

As with any potent drug, periodic assessment of organ system functions, including renal, hepatic, and hematopoietic, is advisable during prolonged therapy.

Information For Patients: Patients should be advised that ciprofloxacin may be associated with hypersensitivity reactions, even following a single dose, and to discontinue the drug at the first sign of a skin rash or other allergic reaction.

Ciprofloxacin may cause dizziness and light-headedness; therefore, patients should know how they react to this drug before they operate an automobile or machinery or engage in activities requiring mental alertness or coordination.

Patients should be advised that ciprofloxacin may increase the effects of theophylline and caffeine. There is a possibility of caffeine accumulation when products containing caffeine are consumed while taking ciprofloxacin.

Patients should be advised to discontinue treatment; rest and refrain from exercise; and inform their physician if they experience pain, inflammation, or rupture of a tendon.

Patients should be advised that convulsions have been reported in patients taking quinolones, including ciprofloxacin, and to notify their physician before taking the drug if there is a history of this condition.

Drug Interactions: As with some other quinolones, concurrent administration of ciprofloxacin with theophylline may lead to elevated serum concentrations of theophylline and prolongation of its elimination half-life. This may result in increased risk of theophylline-related adverse reactions. (See **WARNINGS**.) If concomitant use cannot be avoided, serum levels of theophylline should be monitored and dosage adjustments made as appropriate.

Some quinolones, including ciprofloxacin, have also been shown to interfere with the metabolism of caffeine. This may lead to reduced clearance of caffeine and prolongation of its serum half-life.

Some quinolones, including ciprofloxacin, have been associated with transient elevations in serum creatinine in patients receiving cyclosporine concomitantly.

Altered serum levels of phenytoin (increased and decreased) have been reported in patients receiving concomitant ciprofloxacin.

The concomitant administration of ciprofloxacin with the sulfonylurea glyburide has, in some patients, resulted in severe hypoglycemia. Fatalities have been reported.

Quinolones have been reported to enhance the effects of the oral anticoagulant warfarin or its derivatives. When these products are administered concomitantly, prothrombin time or other suitable coagulation tests should be closely monitored.

Probenecid interferes with renal tubular secretion of ciprofloxacin and produces an increase in the level of ciprofloxacin in the serum. This should be considered if patients are receiving both drugs concomitantly.

As with other broad-spectrum antimicrobial agents, prolonged use of ciprofloxacin may result in overgrowth of nonsusceptible organisms. Repeated evaluation of the patient's condition and microbial susceptibility testing are essential. If superinfection occurs during therapy, appropriate measures should be taken.

Carcinogenesis, Mutagenesis, Impairment of Fertility: Eight *in vitro* mutagenicity tests have been conducted with ciprofloxacin. Test results are listed below:

Salmonella/Microsome Test (Negative)
E. coli DNA Repair Assay (Negative)
Mouse Lymphoma Cell Forward Mutation Assay (Positive)
Chinese Hamster V_{79} Cell HGPRT Test (Negative)
Syrian Hamster Embryo Cell Transformation Assay (Negative)
Saccharomyces cerevisiae Point Mutation Assay (Negative)
Saccharomyces cerevisiae Mitotic Crossover and Gene Conversion Assay (Negative)
Rat Hepatocyte DNA Repair Assay (Positive)

Thus, two of the eight tests were positive, but results of the following three *in vivo* test systems gave negative results:

Rat Hepatocyte DNA Repair Assay
Micronucleus Test (Mice)
Dominant Lethal Test (Mice)

Long-term carcinogenicity studies in mice and rats have been completed. After daily oral doses of 750 mg/kg (mice) and 250 mg/kg (rats) were administered for up to 2 years, there was no evidence that ciprofloxacin had any carcinogenic or tumorigenic effects in these species. Results from photo co-carcinogenicity testing indicate that ciprofloxacin does not reduce the time to appearance of UV-induced skin tumors as compared to vehicle control. Hairless (Skh-1) mice were exposed to UVA light for 3.5 hours five times every two weeks for up to 78 weeks while concurrently being administered ciprofloxacin. The time to development of the first skin tumors was 50 weeks in mice treated concomitantly with UVA and ciprofloxacin (mouse dose approximately equal to maximum recommended human dose based upon mg/m²), as opposed to 34 weeks when animals were treated with both UVA and vehicle. The times to development of skin tumors ranged from 16–32 weeks in mice treated concomitantly with UVA and other quinolones.[3] In this model, mice treated with ciprofloxacin alone did not develop skin or systemic tumors.

There are no data from similar models using pigmented mice and/or fully haired mice. The clinical significance of these findings to humans is unknown.

Fertility studies performed in rats at oral doses of ciprofloxacin up to 100 mg/kg (0.8 times the highest recommended human dose of 1200 mg based upon body surface area) revealed no evidence of impairment.

Pregnancy: Teratogenic Effects. Pregnancy Category C: Reproduction studies have been performed in rats and mice using oral doses of up to 100 mg/kg (0.8 and 0.4 times the maximum daily human dose based upon body surface area, respectively) and I.V. doses of up to 30 mg/kg (0.24 and 0.12 times the maximum daily human dose based upon body surface area, respectively) and have revealed no evidence of harm to the fetus due to ciprofloxacin. In rabbits, ciprofloxacin (30 and 100 mg/kg orally) produced gastrointestinal disturbances resulting in maternal weight loss and an increased incidence of abortion, but no teratogenicity was observed at either dose. After intravenous administration of doses up to 20 mg/kg, no maternal toxicity was produced in the rabbit, and no embryotoxicity or teratogenicity was observed. There are, however, no adequate and well-controlled studies in pregnant women. Ciprofloxacin should be used during pregnancy only if the potential benefit justifies the potential risk to the fetus. (See **WARNINGS.**)

Nursing Mothers: Ciprofloxacin is excreted in human milk. Because of the potential for serious adverse reactions in infants nursing from mothers taking ciprofloxacin, a decision should be made whether to discontinue nursing or to discontinue the drug, taking into account the importance of the drug to the mother.

Pediatric Use: Safety and effectiveness in pediatric patients and adolescents less than 18 years of age have not been established, except for use in inhalational anthrax (post-exposure). Ciprofloxacin causes arthropathy in juvenile animals. (See **WARNINGS.**)

For the indication of inhalational anthrax (post-exposure), the risk-benefit assessment indicates that administration of ciprofloxacin to pediatric patients is appropriate. For information regarding pediatric dosing in inhalational anthrax (post-exposure), see **DOSAGE AND ADMINISTRATION** and **INHALATIONAL ANTHRAX—ADDITIONAL INFORMATION.**

Short-term safety data from a single trial in pediatric cystic fibrosis patients are available. In a randomized, double-blind clinical trial for the treatment of acute pulmonary exacerbations in cystic fibrosis patients (ages 5–17 years), 67 patients received ciprofloxacin I.V. 10 mg/kg/dose q 8 h for one week followed by ciprofloxacin tablets 20 mg/kg/dose q 12 h to complete 10–21 days treatment and 62 patients received the combination of ceftazidime

I.V. 50 mg/kg/dose q 8 h and tobramycin I.V. 3 mg/kg/dose q 8 h for a total of 10–21 days. Patients less than 5 years of age were not studied. Safety monitoring in the study included periodic range of motion examinations and gait assessments by treatment-blinded examiners. Patients were followed for an average of 23 days after completing treatment (range 0–93 days). This study was not designed to determine long term effects and the safety of repeated exposure to ciprofloxacin.

In the study, injection site reactions were more common in the ciprofloxacin group (24%) than in the comparison group (8%). Other adverse events were similar in nature and frequency between treatment arms. Musculoskeletal adverse events were reported in 22% of the patients in the ciprofloxacin group and 21% in the comparison group. Decreased range of motion was reported in 12% of the subjects in the ciprofloxacin group and 16% in the comparison group. Arthralgia was reported in 10% of the patients in the ciprofloxacin group and 11% in the comparison group. One of sixty-seven patients developed arthritis of the knee nine days after a ten day course of treatment with ciprofloxacin. Clinical symptoms resolved, but an MRI showed knee effusion without other abnormalities eight months after treatment. However, the relationship of this event to the patient's course of ciprofloxacin can not be definitively determined, particularly since patients with cystic fibrosis may develop arthralgias/arthritis as part of their underlying disease process.

Geriatric Use: In a retrospective analysis of 23 multiple-dose controlled clinical trials of ciprofloxacin encompassing over 3500 ciprofloxacin treated patients, 25% of patients were greater than or equal to 65 years of age and 10% were greater than or equal to 75 years of age. No overall differences in safety or effectiveness were observed between these subjects and younger subjects, and other reported clinical experience has not identified differences in responses between the elderly and younger patients, but greater sensitivity of some older individuals on any drug therapy cannot be ruled out. Ciprofloxacin is known to be substantially excreted by the kidney, and the risk of adverse reactions may be greater in patients with impaired renal function. No alteration of dosage is necessary for patients greater than 65 years of age with normal renal function. However, since some older individuals experience reduced renal function by virtue of their advanced age, care should be taken in dose selection for elderly patients, and renal function monitoring may be useful in these patients. (See **CLINICAL PHARMACOLOGY** and **DOSAGE AND ADMINISTRATION**.)

ADVERSE REACTIONS

The most frequently reported events, without regard to drug relationship, among patients treated with intravenous ciprofloxacin were nausea, diarrhea, central nervous system disturbance, local I.V. site reactions, abnormalities of liver associated enzymes (hepatic enzymes), and eosinophilia. Headache, restlessness, and rash were also noted in greater than 1% of patients treated with the most common doses of ciprofloxacin.

Local I.V. site reactions have been reported with the intravenous administration of ciprofloxacin. These reactions are more frequent if the infusion time is 30 minutes or less. These may appear as local skin reactions which resolve rapidly upon completion of the infusion. Subsequent intravenous administration is not contraindicated unless the reactions recur or worsen.

Additional events, without regard to drug relationship or route of administration, that occurred in 1% or less of ciprofloxacin patients are listed below:

CARDIOVASCULAR: cardiovascular collapse, cardiopulmonary arrest, myocardial infarction, arrhythmia, tachycardia, palpitation, cerebral thrombosis, syncope, cardiac murmur, hypertension, hypotension, angina pectoris

CENTRAL NERVOUS SYSTEM: convulsive seizures, paranoia, toxic psychosis, depression, dysphasia, phobia, depersonalization, manic reaction, unresponsiveness, ataxia, confusion, hallucinations, dizziness, lightheadedness, paresthesia, anxiety, tremor, insomnia, nightmares, weakness, drowsiness, irritability, malaise, lethargy

GASTROINTESTINAL: ileus, jaundice, gastrointestinal bleeding, *C. difficile* associated diarrhea, pseudomembranous colitis, pancreatitis, hepatic necrosis, intestinal perforation, dyspepsia, epigastric or abdominal pain, vomiting, constipation, oral ulceration, oral candidiasis, mouth dryness, anorexia, dysphagia, flatulence

I.V. INFUSION SITE: thrombophlebitis, burning, pain, pruritus, paresthesia, erythema, swelling

MUSCULOSKELETAL: arthralgia, jaw, arm or back pain, joint stiffness, neck and chest pain, achiness, flare up of gout

RENAL/UROGENITAL: renal failure, interstitial nephritis, hemorrhagic cystitis, renal calculi, frequent urination, acidosis, urethral bleeding, polyuria, urinary retention, gynecomastia, candiduria, vaginitis. Crystalluria, cylindruria, hematuria, and albuminuria have also been reported.

RESPIRATORY: respiratory arrest, pulmonary embolism, dyspnea, pulmonary edema, respiratory distress, pleural effusion, hemoptysis, epistaxis, hiccough

SKIN/HYPERSENSITIVITY: anaphylactic reactions, erythema multiforme/Stevens-Johnson syndrome, exfoliative dermatitis, toxic epidermal necrolysis, vasculitis, angioedema, edema of the lips, face, neck, conjunctivae, hands or lower extremities, purpura, fever, chills, flushing, pruritus, urticaria, cuta-

Hepatic	—	elevations of AST (SGOT), ALT (SGPT), alkaline phosphatase, LDH, and serum bilirubin;
Hematologic	—	elevated eosinophil and platelet counts, decreased platelet counts, hemoglobin and/or hematocrit;
Renal	—	elevations of serum creatinine, BUN, and uric acid;
Other	—	elevations of serum creatinine, phosphokinase, serum theophylline (in patients receiving theophylline concomitantly), blood glucose, and triglycerides.

neous candidiasis, vesicles, increased perspiration, hyperpigmentation, erythema nodosum, photosensitivity (See **WARNINGS**.)

SPECIAL SENSES: decreased visual acuity, blurred vision, disturbed vision (flashing lights, change in color perception, overbrightness of lights, diplopia), eye pain, anosmia, hearing loss, tinnitus, nystagmus, a bad taste Also reported were agranulocytosis, prolongation of prothrombin time, and possible exacerbation of myasthenia gravis.

Many of these events were described as only mild or moderate in severity, abated soon after the drug was discontinued, and required no treatment.

In several instances, nausea, vomiting, tremor, irritability, or palpitation were judged by investigators to be related to elevated serum levels of theophylline possibly as a result of drug interaction with ciprofloxacin.

In randomized, double-blind controlled clinical trials comparing ciprofloxacin (I.V. and I.V. P.O. sequential) with intravenous beta-lactam control antibiotics, the CNS adverse event profile of ciprofloxacin was comparable to that of the control drugs.

Post-Marketing Adverse Events: Additional adverse events, regardless of relationship to drug, reported from worldwide marketing experience with quinolones, including ciprofloxacin, are:

BODY AS A WHOLE: change in serum phenytoin

CARDIOVASCULAR: postural hypotension, vasculitis

CENTRAL NERVOUS SYSTEM: agitation, delirium, myoclonus, toxic psychosis

HEMIC/LYMPHATIC: hemolytic anemia, methemoglobinemia

METABOLIC/NUTRITIONAL: elevation of serum triglycerides, cholesterol, blood glucose, serum potassium

MUSCULOSKELETAL: myalgia, tendinitis/tendon rupture

RENAL/UROGENITAL: vaginal candidiasis (See **PRECAUTIONS**.)

Adverse Laboratory Changes: The most frequently reported changes in laboratory parameters with intravenous ciprofloxacin therapy, without regard to drug relationship are listed below:

[See table above]

Other changes occurring infrequently were: decreased leukocyte count, elevated atypical lymphocyte count, immature WBCs, elevated serum calcium, elevation of serum gamma-glutamyl transpeptidase (γ GT), decreased

BUN, decreased uric acid, decreased total serum protein, decreased serum albumin, decreased serum potassium, elevated serum potassium, elevated serum cholesterol.

Other changes occurring rarely during administration of ciprofloxacin were: elevation of serum amylase, decrease of blood glucose, pancytopenia, leukocytosis, elevated sedimentation rate, change in serum phenytoin, decreased prothrombin time, hemolytic anemia, and bleeding diathesis.

OVERDOSAGE

In the event of acute overdosage, the patient should be carefully observed and given supportive treatment. Adequate hydration must be maintained. Only a small amount of ciprofloxacin (<10%) is removed from the body after hemodialysis or peritoneal dialysis.

In mice, rats, rabbits and dogs, significant toxicity including tonic/clonic convulsions was observed at intravenous doses of ciprofloxacin between 125 and 300 mg/kg.

DOSAGE AND ADMINISTRATION

The recommended adult dosage for urinary tract infections of mild to moderate severity is 200 mg I.V. every 12 hours. For severe or complicated urinary tract infections, the recommended dosage is 400 mg I.V. every 12 hours.

The recommended adult dosage for lower respiratory tract infections, skin and skin structure infections, and bone and joint infections of mild to moderate severity is 400 mg I.V. every 12 hours.

For severe/complicated infections of the lower respiratory tract, skin and skin structure, and bone and joint, the recommended adult dosage is 400 mg I.V. every 8 hours.

The recommended adult dosage for mild, moderate, and severe nosocomial pneumonia is 400 mg I.V. every 8 hours.

Complicated Intra-Abdominal Infections: Sequential therapy [parenteral to oral - 400 mg CIPRO® I.V. q 12 h (plus I.V. metronidazole) → 500 mg CIPRO® Tablets q 12 h (plus oral metronidazole)] can be instituted at the discretion of the physician. Metronidazole should be given according to product labeling to provide appropriate anaerobic coverage.

The recommended dosage for mild to moderate Acute Sinusitis and Chronic Bacterial Prostatitis is 400 mg I.V. every 12 hours.

The recommended adult dosage for empirical therapy of febrile neutropenic patients is 400 mg I.V. every 8 hours in combination with

DOSAGE GUIDELINES
Intravenous

Infection†	Type or Severity	Unit Dose	Frequency	Daily Dose
Urinary tract	Mild/Moderate	200 mg	q 12 h	400 mg
	Severe/Complicated	400 mg	q 12 h	800 mg
Lower Respiratory Tract	Mild/Moderate	400 mg	q 12 h	800 mg
	Severe/Complicated	400 mg	q 8 h	1200 mg
Nosocomial Pneumonia	Mild/Moderate/Severe	400 mg	q 8 h	1200 mg
Skin and Skin Structure	Mild/Moderate	400 mg	q 12 h	800 mg
	Severe/Complicated	400 mg	q 8 h	1200 mg
Bone and Joint	Mild/Moderate	400 mg	q 12 h	800 mg
	Severe/Complicated	400 mg	q 8 h	1200 mg
Intra-Abdominal*	Complicated	400 mg	q 12 h	800 mg
Acute Sinusitis	Mild/Moderate	400 mg	q 12 h	800 mg
Chronic Bacterial Prostatitis	Mild/Moderate	400 mg	q 12 h	800 mg
Empirical Therapy in Febrile Neutropenic Patients	Severe Ciprofloxacin + Piperacillin	400 mg 50 mg/kg	q 8 h q 4 h	1200 mg Not to exceed 24 g/day
Inhalational anthrax (post-exposure)**	Adult	400 mg	q 12 h	800 mg
	Pediatric	10 mg/kg per dose, not to exceed 400 mg per dose	q 12 h	Not to exceed 800 mg

*   used in conjunction with metronidazole. (See product labeling for prescribing information.)
†   DUE TO THE DESIGNATED PATHOGENS (See **INDICATIONS AND USAGE**.)
** Drug administration should begin as soon as possible after suspected or confirmed exposure. This indication is based on a surrogate endpoint, ciprofloxacin serum concentrations achieved in humans. For a discussion of ciprofloxacin serum concentrations in various human populations, see **INHALATIONAL ANTHRAX—ADDITIONAL INFORMATION**. Total duration of ciprofloxacin administration (IV or oral) for inhalational anthrax (post-exposure) is 60 days.

piperacillin sodium 50 mg/kg I.V. q 4 hours, not to exceed 24 g/day (300 mg/kg/day), for 7–14 days.

The determination of dosage for any particular patient must take into consideration the severity and nature of the infection, the susceptibility of the causative microorganism, the integrity of the patient's host-defense mechanisms and the status of renal and hepatic function.

[See table above]

After dilution CIPRO® I.V. should be administered by intravenous infusion over a period of 60 minutes.

Parenteral drug products should be inspected visually for particulate matter and discoloration prior to administration.

Ciprofloxacin hydrochloride (CIPRO® Tablets) for oral administration are available. Parenteral therapy may be changed to oral CIPRO® Tablets when the condition warrants, at the discretion of the physician. For complete dosage and administration information, see CIPRO® Tablets package insert.

Impaired Renal Function: The following table provides dosage guidelines for use in patients with renal impairment; however, monitoring of serum drug levels provides the most reliable basis for dosage adjustment.

$$\text{Men: Creatinine clearance (mL/min)} = \frac{\text{Weight (kg)} \times (140 - \text{age})}{72 \times \text{serum creatinine (mg/dL)}}$$

Women: $0.85 \times$ the value calculated for men.

RECOMMENDED STARTING AND MAINTENANCE DOSES FOR PATIENTS WITH IMPAIRED RENAL FUNCTION

Creatinine Clearance (mL/min)	Dosage
> 30	See usual dosage.
5–29	200 - 400 mg q 18–24 hr

When only the serum creatinine concentration is known, the following formula may be used to estimate creatinine clearance:
[See table above]
The serum creatinine should represent a steady state of renal function.
For patients with changing renal function or for patients with renal impairment and hepatic insufficiency, measurement of serum concentrations of ciprofloxacin will provide additional guidance for adjusting dosage.

INTRAVENOUS ADMINISTRATION

After dilution, CIPRO® I.V. should be administered by intravenous infusion over a period of 60 minutes. Slow infusion of a dilute solution into a large vein will minimize patient discomfort and reduce the risk of venous irritation.

PHARMACY BULK PACKAGE: The pharmacy bulk package is a single-entry container of a sterile preparation for parenteral use that contains many single doses. It contains ciprofloxacin as a 1% aqueous solution concentrate. The contents are intended for use in a pharmacy admixture program and are restricted to the preparation of admixture for intravenous infusion. **THE CLOSURE SHALL BE PENETRATED ONLY ONE TIME** with a suitable sterile transfer set or dispensing device which allows measured dispensing of the contents.
The pharmacy bulk package is to be used only in a suitable work area such as laminar flow hood or an equivalent clean air or compounding area. **THIS PREPARATION MUST BE DILUTED BEFORE USE.** The intravenous dose should be prepared by aseptically withdrawing the CIPRO® I.V. concentrate from the pharmacy bulk package and diluting the appropriate volume with a suitable intravenous solution to a final concentration of 0.5–2 mg/mL. (See **COMPATIBILITY AND STABILITY**.) The resulting solution should be infused over a period of 60 minutes by direct infusion or through a Y-type intravenous set which may already be in place. If this method or the "piggyback" method of administration is used, it is advisable to discontinue the administration of any other intravenous solutions during the infusion of CIPRO® I.V.

COMPATIBILITY AND STABILITY

Ciprofloxacin injection 1% (10 mg/mL), when diluted with the following intravenous solutions to concentrations of 0.5 to 2.0 mg/mL, is stable for up to 14 days at refrigerated or room temperature storage.

0.9% Sodium Chloride Injection, USP
5% Dextrose Injection, USP
Sterile Water for Injection
10% Dextrose for Injection
5% Dextrose and 0.225% Sodium Chloride for Injection
5% Dextrose and 0.45% Sodium Chloride for Injection
Lactated Ringer's for Injection

If CIPRO® I.V. is to be given concomitantly with another drug, each drug should be given separately in accordance with the recommended dosage and route of administration for each drug.

HOW SUPPLIED

CIPRO® I.V. (ciprofloxacin) is available as a clear, colorless to slightly yellowish solution supplied in the pharmacy bulk package as follows:
[See table at top of next page]
Ciprofloxacin is also available as CIPRO® (ciprofloxacin HCl) Tablets 100, 250, 500, and 750 mg and CIPRO® (ciprofloxacin) 5% and 10% Oral Suspension.

STORAGE

Store between 5–30°C (41–86°F).
Protect from light, avoid excessive heat, protect from freezing.

ANIMAL PHARMACOLOGY

Ciprofloxacin and other quinolones have been shown to cause arthropathy in immature animals of most species tested. (See **WARNINGS.**) Damage of weight-bearing joints was observed in juvenile dogs and rats. In young beagles, 100 mg/kg ciprofloxacin given daily for 4 weeks caused degenerative articular changes of the knee joint. At 30 mg/kg, the effect on the joint was minimal. In a subsequent study in beagles, removal of weight-bearing from the joint reduced the lesions but did not totally prevent them.
Crystalluria, sometimes associated with secondary nephropathy, occurs in laboratory animals dosed with ciprofloxacin. This is primarily related to the reduced solubility of ciprofloxacin under alkaline conditions, which predominate in the urine of test animals; in man, crystalluria is rare since human urine is typically acidic. In rhesus monkeys, crystalluria without nephropathy has been noted after intravenous doses as low as 5 mg/kg. After 6 months of intravenous dosing at 10 mg/kg/day, no nephropathological changes were noted; however, nephropathy was observed after dosing at 20 mg/kg/day for the same duration.

CONTAINER	SIZE	STRENGTH	NDC NUMBER
Pharmacy Bulk Package:	120 mL	1200-mg, 1%	0026-8566-65

CIPRO® I.V. (ciprofloxacin) is also available as follows:

VIAL:	SIZE	STRENGTH	NDC NUMBER
	20 mL	200 mg, 1%	0026-8562-20
	40 mL	400 mg, 1%	0026-8564-64

FLEXIBLE CONTAINER: manufactured for Bayer Corporation by Abbott Laboratories, North Chicago, IL 60064.

SIZE	STRENGTH	NDC NUMBER
100 mL 5% dextrose	200 mg, 0.2%	0026-8552-36
200 mL 5% dextrose	400 mg, 0.2%	0026-8554-63

FLEXIBLE CONTAINER: manufactured for Bayer Corporation by Baxter Healthcare Corporation, Deerfield, IL 60015.

SIZE	STRENGTH	NDC NUMBER
100 mL 5% dextrose	200 mg, 0.2%	0026-8527-36
200 mL 5% dextrose	400 mg, 0.2%	0026-8527-63

In dogs, ciprofloxacin administered at 3 and 10 mg/kg by rapid intravenous injection (15 sec.) produces pronounced hypotensive effects. These effects are considered to be related to histamine release because they are partially antagonized by pyrilamine, an antihistamine. In rhesus monkeys, rapid intravenous injection also produces hypotension, but the effect in this species is inconsistent and less pronounced.

In mice, concomitant administration of non-steroidal anti-inflammatory drugs, such as phenylbutazone and indomethacin, with quinolones has been reported to enhance the CNS stimulatory effect of quinolones.

Ocular toxicity, seen with some related drugs, has not been observed in ciprofloxacin-treated animals.

INHALATIONAL ANTHRAX—ADDITIONAL INFORMATION

The mean serum concentrations of ciprofloxacin associated with a statistically significant improvement in survival in the rhesus monkey model of inhalational anthrax are reached or exceeded in adult and pediatric patients receiving oral and intravenous regimens. (See **DOSAGE AND ADMINISTRATION**.) Ciprofloxacin pharmacokinetics have been evaluated in various human populations. The mean peak serum concentration achieved at steady-state in human adults receiving 500 mg orally every 12 hours is 2.97 µg/mL, and 4.56 µg/mL following 400 mg intravenously every 12 hours. The mean trough serum concentration at steady-state for both of these regimens is 0.2 µg/mL. In a study of 10 pediatric patients between 6 and 16 years of age, the mean peak plasma concentration achieved is 8.3 µg/mL and trough concentrations range from 0.09 to 0.26 µg/mL, following two 30-minute intravenous infusions of 10 mg/kg administered 12 hours apart. After the second intravenous infusion patients switched to 15 mg/kg orally every 12 hours achieve a mean peak concentration of 3.6 µg/mL after the initial oral dose. Long-term safety data, including effects on cartilage, following the administration of ciprofloxacin to pediatric patients are limited. (For additional information, see **PRECAUTIONS, Pediatric Use**.) Ciprofloxacin serum concentrations achieved in humans serve as a surrogate endpoint reasonably likely to predict clinical benefit and provide the basis for this indication.[4]

A placebo-controlled animal study in rhesus monkeys exposed to an inhaled mean dose of 11 LD_{50} ($\sim$5.5 × 10^5) spores (range 5–30 LD_{50}) of *B. anthracis* was conducted. The minimal inhibitory concentration (MIC) of ciprofloxacin for the anthrax strain used in this study was 0.08 µg/mL. In the animals studied, mean serum concentrations of ciprofloxacin achieved at expected T_{max} (1 hour post-dose) following oral dosing to steady-state ranged from 0.98 to 1.69 µg/mL. Mean steady-state trough concentrations at 12 hours post-dose ranged from 0.12 to 0.19 µg/mL.[5] Mortality due to anthrax for animals that received a 30-day regimen of oral ciprofloxacin beginning 24 hours post-exposure was significantly lower (1/9), compared to the placebo group (9/10) [p=0.001]. The one ciprofloxacin-treated animal that died of anthrax did so following the 30-day drug administration period.[6]

REFERENCES

1. National Committee for Clinical Laboratory Standards, Methods for Dilution Antimicrobial Susceptibility Tests for Bacteria That Grow Aerobically-Fifth Edition. Approved Standard NCCLS Document M7-A5, Vol. 20, No. 2, NCCLS, Wayne, PA, January, 2000. **2.** National Committee for Clinical Laboratory Standards, Performance Standards for Antimicrobial Disk Susceptibility Tests-Seventh

Edition. Approved Standard NCCLS Document M2-A7, Vol. 20, No. 1, NCCLS, Wayne, PA, January, 2000. **3.** Report presented at the FDA's Anti-Infective Drug and Dermatological Drug Product's Advisory Committee meeting, March 31, 1993, Silver Spring, MD. Report available from FDA, CDER, Advisors and Consultants Staff, HFD-21, 1901 Chapman Avenue, Room 200, Rockville, MD 20852, USA. **4.** 21 CFR 314.510 (Subpart H – Accelerated Approval of New Drugs for Life-Threatening Illnesses). **5.** Kelly DJ, et al. Serum concentrations of penicillin, doxycycline, and ciprofloxacin during prolonged therapy in rhesus monkeys. J Infect Dis 1992; 166: 1184–7. **6.** Friedlander AM, et al. Postexposure prophylaxis against experimental inhalational anthrax. J Infect Dis 1993; 167: 1239–42.

Manufactured for:
Bayer Corporation
Pharmaceutical Division
400 Morgan Lane
West Haven, CT 06516 USA
℞ **Only**
PZ500176   11/00   BAY q 3939
5202-4-A-U.S.-7
©2000 Bayer Corporation   10046
Printed in U.S.A.

CIPRO® ℞
(ciprofloxacin hydrochloride)
TABLETS

CIPRO® ℞
(ciprofloxacin)
5% and 10% ORAL SUSPENSION

DESCRIPTION

CIPRO® (ciprofloxacin hydrochloride) Tablets and CIPRO® (ciprofloxacin) Oral Suspension are synthetic broad spectrum antimicrobial agents for oral administration. Ciprofloxacin hydrochloride, USP, a fluoroquinolone, is the monohydrochloride monohydrate salt of 1-cyclopropyl-6-fluoro-1, 4-dihydro-4-oxo-7-(1-piperazinyl)-3-quinolinecarboxylic acid. It is a faintly yellowish to light yellow crystalline substance with a molecular weight of 385.8. Its empirical formula is $C_{17}H_{18}FN_3O_3 \bullet HCl \bullet H_2O$ and its chemical structure is as follows:

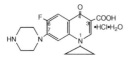

Ciprofloxacin is 1-cyclopropyl-6-fluoro-1, 4-dihydro-4-oxo-7-(1-piperazinyl)-3-quinolinecarboxylic acid. Its empirical formula is $C_{17}H_{18}FN_3O_3$ and its molecular weight is 331.4. It is a faintly yellowish to light yellow crystalline substance and its chemical structure is as follows:

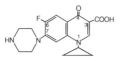

Ciprofloxacin differs from other quinolones in that it has a fluorine atom at the 6-position, a piperazine moiety at the 7-position, and a cyclopropyl ring at the 1-position.

CIPRO® film-coated tablets are available in 100-mg, 250-mg, 500-mg and 750-mg (ciprofloxacin equivalent) strengths. The inactive ingredients are starch, microcrystalline cellulose, silicon dioxide, crospovidone, magnesium stearate, hydroxypropyl methylcellulose, titanium dioxide, polyethylene glycol and water.

Ciprofloxacin Oral Suspension is available in 5% (5 g ciprofloxacin in 100 mL) and 10% (10 g ciprofloxacin in 100 mL) strengths. Ciprofloxacin Oral Suspension is a white to slightly yellowish suspension with strawberry flavor which may contain yellow-orange droplets. It is composed of ciprofloxacin microcapsules and diluent which are mixed prior to dispensing (See instructions for USE/HANDLING). The components of the suspension have the following compositions:

Microcapsules—ciprofloxacin, polyvinylpyrrolidone, methacrylic acid copolymer, hydroxypropyl methylcellulose, magnesium stearate, and Polysorbate 20.
Diluent—medium-chain triglycerides, sucrose, lecithin, water, and strawberry flavor.

CLINICAL PHARMACOLOGY

Ciprofloxacin given as an oral tablet is rapidly and well absorbed from the gastrointestinal tract after oral administration. The absolute bioavailability is approximately 70% with no substantial loss by first pass metabolism. Ciprofloxacin maximum serum concentrations and area under the curve are shown in the chart for the 250-mg to 1000-mg dose range.

Dose (mg)	Maximum Serum Concentration (µg/mL)	Area Under Curve (AUC) (µg · hr/mL)
250	1.2	4.8
500	2.4	11.6
750	4.3	20.2
1000	5.4	30.8

Maximum serum concentrations are attained 1 to 2 hours after oral dosing. Mean concentrations 12 hours after dosing with 250, 500, or 750-mg are 0.1, 0.2, and 0.4 µg/mL, respectively. The serum elimination half-life in subjects with normal renal function is approximately 4 hours. Serum concentrations increase proportionately with doses up to 1000-mg.

A 500-mg oral dose given every 12 hours has been shown to produce an area under the serum concentration time curve (AUC) equivalent to that produced by an intravenous infusion of 400 mg ciprofloxacin given over 60 minutes every 12 hours. A 750-mg oral dose given every 12 hours has been shown to produce an AUC at steady-state equivalent to that produced by an intravenous infusion of 400 mg over 60 minutes every 8 hours. A 750-mg oral dose results in a C_{max} similar to that observed with a 400-mg I.V. dose. A 250-mg oral dose given every 12 hours produces an AUC equivalent to that produced by an infusion of 200 mg ciprofloxacin given every 12 hours. [See table at bottom of next page]

The serum elimination half-life in subjects with normal renal function is approximately 4 hours. Approximately 40 to 50% of an orally administered dose is excreted in the urine as unchanged drug. After a 250-mg oral dose, urine concentrations of ciprofloxacin usually exceed 200 µg/mL during the first two hours and are approximately 30 µg/mL at 8 to 12 hours after dosing. The urinary excretion of ciprofloxacin is virtually complete within 24 hours after dosing. The renal clearance of ciprofloxacin, which is approximately 300 mL/minute, exceeds the normal glomerular filtration rate of 120 mL/minute. Thus, active tubular secretion would seem to play a significant role in its elimination. Co-administration of probenecid with ciprofloxacin results in about a 50% reduction in the ciprofloxacin renal clearance and a 50% increase in its concentration in the systemic circulation. Although bile concentrations of ciprofloxacin are several fold higher than serum concentrations after oral dosing, only a small amount of the dose administered is recovered from the bile as unchanged drug. An additional 1 to 2% of the dose is recovered from the bile in the form of metabolites. Approximately 20 to 35% of an oral dose is recovered from the feces within 5 days after dosing. This may arise from either biliary clearance or transintestinal elimination. Four metabolites have been identified in human urine which together account for approximately 15% of an oral dose. The metabolites have antimicrobial activity, but are less active than unchanged ciprofloxacin.

With oral administration, a 500-mg dose, given as 10 mL of the 5% CIPRO® Suspension (containing 250-mg ciprofloxacin/5mL) is bioequivalent to the 500-mg tablet. A 10 mL volume of the 5% CIPRO® Suspension (containing 250-mg ciprofloxacin/5mL) is bioequivalent to a 5 mL volume of the 10% CIPRO® Suspension (containing 500-mg ciprofloxacin/5mL).

When CIPRO® Tablet is given concomitantly with food, there is a delay in the absorption of the drug, resulting in peak concentrations that occur closer to 2 hours after dosing rather than 1 hour whereas there is no delay observed when CIPRO® Suspension is given with food. The overall absorption of CIPRO® Tablet or CIPRO® Suspension, however, is not substantially affected. The pharmacokinetics of ciprofloxacin given as the suspension are also not affected by food. Concurrent administration of antacids containing magnesium hydroxide or aluminum hydroxide may reduce the bioavailability of ciprofloxacin by as much as 90%. (See **PRECAUTIONS**.)

The serum concentrations of ciprofloxacin and metronidazole were not altered when these two drugs were given concomitantly.

Concomitant administration of ciprofloxacin with theophylline decreases the clearance of theophylline resulting in elevated serum theophylline levels and increased risk of a patient developing CNS or other adverse reactions. Ciprofloxacin also decreases caffeine clearance and inhibits the formation of paraxanthine after caffeine administration. (See **PRECAUTIONS**.)

Pharmacokinetic studies of the oral (single dose) and intravenous (single and multiple dose) forms of ciprofloxacin indicate that plasma concentrations of ciprofloxacin are higher in elderly subjects (>65 years) as compared to young adults. Although the C_{max} is increased 16–40%, the increase in mean AUC is approximately 30%, and can be at least partially attributed to decreased renal clearance in the elderly. Elimination half-life is only slightly ($\sim$20%) prolonged in the elderly. These differences are not considered clinically significant. (See **PRECAUTIONS: Geriatric Use**.)

In patients with reduced renal function, the half-life of ciprofloxacin is slightly prolonged. Dosage adjustments may be required. (See **DOSAGE AND ADMINISTRATION**.)

In preliminary studies in patients with stable chronic liver cirrhosis, no significant changes in ciprofloxacin pharmacokinetics have been observed. The kinetics of ciprofloxacin in patients with acute hepatic insufficiency, however, have not been fully elucidated.

The binding of ciprofloxacin to serum proteins is 20 to 40% which is not likely to be high enough to cause significant protein binding interactions with other drugs.

After oral administration, ciprofloxacin is widely distributed throughout the body. Tissue concentrations often exceed serum concentrations in both men and women, particularly in genital tissue including the prostate. Ciprofloxacin is present in active form in the saliva, nasal and bronchial secretions, mucosa of the sinuses, sputum, skin blister fluid, lymph, peritoneal fluid, bile, and prostatic secretions. Ciprofloxacin has also been detected in lung, skin, fat, muscle, cartilage, and bone. The drug diffuses into the cerebrospinal fluid (CSF); however, CSF concentrations are generally less than 10% of peak serum concentrations. Low levels of the drug have been detected in the aqueous and vitreous humors of the eye.

Microbiology: Ciprofloxacin has *in vitro* activity against a wide range of gram-negative and gram-positive organisms. The bactericidal action of ciprofloxacin results from interference with the enzyme DNA gyrase which is needed for the synthesis of bacterial DNA. Ciprofloxacin does not cross-react with other antimicrobial agents such as beta-lactams or aminoglycosides; therefore, organisms resistant to these drugs may be susceptible to

		Steady-state Pharmacokinetic Parameter Following Multiple Oral and I.V. Doses		
Parameters	500 mg q 12 h, P.O.	400 mg q 12 h, I.V.	750 mg q 12 h, P.O.	400 mg q 8 h, I.V.
AUC (µg•hr/mL)	13.7[a]	12.7[a]	31.6[b]	32.9[c]
C_{max} (µg/mL)	2.97	4.56	3.59	4.07

[a]AUC_{0-12h}
[b]AUC 24h=$AUC_{0-12h} \times 2$
[c]AUC 24h=$AUC_{0-8h} \times 3$

ciprofloxacin. *In vitro* studies have shown that additive activity often results when ciprofloxacin is combined with other antimicrobial agents such as beta-lactams, aminoglycosides, clindamycin, or metronidazole. Synergy has been reported particularly with the combination of ciprofloxacin and a beta-lactam; antagonism is observed only rarely.

Ciprofloxacin has been shown to be active against most strains of the following microorganisms, both *in vitro* and in clinical infections as described in the **INDICATIONS AND USAGE** section of the package insert for CIPRO® (ciprofloxacin hydrochloride) Tablets and CIPRO® (ciprofloxacin) 5% and 10% Oral Suspension.

Aerobic gram-positive microorganisms
Enterococcus faecalis
   (Many strains are only moderately susceptible.)
Staphylococcus aureus (methicillin susceptible)
Staphylococcus epidermidis
Staphylococcus saprophyticus
Streptococcus pneumoniae
Streptococcus pyogenes

Aerobic gram-negative microorganisms
Campylobacter jejuni
Citrobacter diversus
Citrobacter freundii
Enterobacter cloacae
Escherichia coli
Haemophilus influenzae
Haemophilus parainfluenzae
Klebsiella pneumoniae
Moraxella catarrhalis
Morganella morganii
Neisseria gonorrhoeae
Proteus mirabilis
Proteus vulgaris
Providencia rettgeri
Providencia stuartii
Pseudomonas aeruginosa
Salmonella typhi
Serratia marcescens
Shigella boydii
Shigella dysenteriae
Shigella flexneri
Shigella sonnei

Ciprofloxacin has been shown to be active against most strains of the following microorganisms, both *in vitro* and in clinical infections as described in the **INDICATIONS AND USAGE** section of the package insert for CIPRO® I.V. (ciprofloxacin for intravenous infusion).

Aerobic gram-positive microorganisms
Enterococcus faecalis
   (Many strains are only moderately susceptible.)
Staphylococcus aureus (methicillin susceptible)
Staphylococcus epidermidis
Staphylococcus saprophyticus
Streptococcus pneumoniae
Streptococcus pyogenes

Aerobic gram-negative microorganisms
Citrobacter diversus
Citrobacter freundii
Enterobacter cloacae
Escherichia coli
Haemophilus influenzae
Haemophilus parainfluenzae
Klebsiella pneumoniae
Morganella morganii
Proteus mirabilis
Proteus vulgaris
Providencia rettgeri
Providencia stuartii
Pseudomonas aeruginosa
Serratia marcescens

Ciprofloxacin has been shown to be active against *Bacillus anthracis* both *in vitro* and by use of serum levels as a surrogate marker (see **INDICATIONS AND USAGE** and **INHALATIONAL ANTHRAX—ADDITIONAL INFORMATION**).

The following *in vitro* data are available, **but their clinical significance is unknown.**

Ciprofloxacin exhibits *in vitro* minimum inhibitory concentrations (MICs) of 1 µg/mL or less against most (≥90%) strains of the following microorganisms; however, the safety and effectiveness of ciprofloxacin in treating clinical infections due to these microorganisms have not been established in adequate and well-controlled clinical trials.

Aerobic gram-positive microorganisms
Staphylococcus haemolyticus
Staphylococcus hominis

Aerobic gram-negative microorganisms
Acinetobacter lwoffi
Aeromonas hydrophila
Edwardsiella tarda
Enterobacter aerogenes
Klebsiella oxytoca
Legionella pneumophila
Pasteurella multocida
Salmonella enteritidis
Vibrio cholerae
Vibrio parahaemolyticus
Vibrio vulnificus
Yersinia enterocolitica

Most strains of *Burkholderia cepacia* and some strains of *Stenotrophomonas maltophilia* are resistant to ciprofloxacin as are most anaerobic bacteria, including *Bacteroides fragilis* and *Clostridium difficile.*

Ciprofloxacin is slightly less active when tested at acidic pH. The inoculum size has little effect when tested *in vitro*. The minimal bactericidal concentration (MBC) generally does not exceed the minimal inhibitory concentration (MIC) by more than a factor of 2. Resistance to ciprofloxacin *in vitro* develops slowly (multiple-step mutation).

Susceptibility Tests
Dilution Techniques: Quantitative methods are used to determine antimicrobial minimum inhibitory concentrations (MICs). These MICs provide estimates of the susceptibility of bacteria to antimicrobial compounds. The MICs should be determined using a standardized

procedure. Standardized procedures are based on a dilution method[1] (broth or agar) or equivalent with standardized inoculum concentrations and standardized concentrations of ciprofloxacin powder. The MIC values should be interpreted according to the following criteria:

For testing aerobic microorganisms other than *Haemophilus influenzae*, *Haemophilus parainfluenzae*, and *Neisseria gonorrhoeae*[a]:

MIC (µg/mL)	Interpretation
≤1	Susceptible (S)
2	Intermediate (I)
≥4	Resistant (R)

[a] These interpretive standards are applicable only to broth microdilution susceptibility tests with streptococci using cation-adjusted Mueller-Hinton broth with 2-5% lysed horse blood.

For testing *Haemophilus influenzae* and *Haemophilus parainfluenzae*[b]:

MIC (µg/mL)	Interpretation
≤1	Susceptible (S)

[b] This interpretive standard is applicable only to broth microdilution susceptibility tests with *Haemophilus influenzae* and *Haemophilus parainfluenzae* using *Haemophilus* Test Medium[1].

The current absence of data on resistant strains precludes defining any results other than "Susceptible." Strains yielding MIC results suggestive of a "nonsusceptible" category should be submitted to a reference laboratory for further testing.

For testing *Neisseria gonorrhoeae*[c]:

MIC (µg/mL)	Interpretation
≤0.06	Susceptible (S)

[c] This interpretive standard is applicable only to agar dilution test with GC agar base and 1% defined growth supplement.

The current absence of data on resistant strains precludes defining any results other than "Susceptible." Strains yielding MIC results suggestive of a "nonsusceptible" category should be submitted to a reference laboratory for further testing.

A report of "Susceptible" indicates that the pathogen is likely to be inhibited if the antimicrobial compound in the blood reaches the concentrations usually achievable. A report of "Intermediate" indicates that the result should be considered equivocal, and, if the microorganism is not fully susceptible to alternative, clinically feasible drugs, the test should be repeated. This category implies possible clinical applicability in body sites where the drug is physiologically concentrated or in situations where high dosage of drug can be used. This category also provides a buffer zone which prevents small uncontrolled technical factors from causing major discrepancies in interpretation. A report of "Resistant" indicates that the pathogen is not likely to be inhibited if the antimicrobial compound in the blood reaches the concentrations usually achievable; other therapy should be selected. Standardized susceptibility test procedures require the use of laboratory control microorganisms to control the technical aspects of the laboratory procedures. Standard ciprofloxacin powder should provide the following MIC values:

Organism		MIC (µg/mL)
E. faecalis	ATCC 29212	0.25 – 2.0
E. coli	ATCC 25922	0.004 – 0.015
H. influenzae[a]	ATCC 49247	0.004 – 0.03
N. gonorrhoeae[b]	ATCC 49226	0.001 – 0.008
P. aeruginosa	ATCC 27853	0.25 – 1.0
S. aureus	ATCC 29213	0.12 – 0.5

[a] This quality control range is applicable to only *H. influenzae* ATCC 49247 tested by a broth microdilution procedure using *Haemophilus* Test Medium (HTM)[1].

[b] This quality control range is applicable to only *N. gonorrhoeae* ATCC 49226 tested by an agar dilution procedure using GC agar base and 1% defined growth supplement.

Diffusion Techniques: Quantitative methods that require measurement of zone diameters also provide reproducible estimates of the susceptibility of bacteria to antimicrobial compounds. One such standardized procedure[2] requires the use of standardized inoculum concentrations. This procedure uses paper disks impregnated with 5-µg ciprofloxacin to test the susceptibility of microorganisms to ciprofloxacin.

Reports from the laboratory providing results of the standard single-disk susceptibility test with a 5-µg ciprofloxacin disk should be interpreted according to the following criteria:

For testing aerobic microorganisms other than *Haemophilus influenzae*, *Haemophilus parainfluenzae*, and *Neisseria gonorrhoeae*[a]:

Zone Diameter (mm)	Interpretation
≥21	Susceptible (S)
16–20	Intermediate (I)
≤15	Resistant (R)

[a] These zone diameter standards are applicable only to tests performed for streptococci using Mueller-Hinton agar supplemented with 5% sheep blood incubated in 5% CO_2.

For testing *Haemophilus influenzae* and *Haemophilus parainfluenzae*[b]:

Zone Diameter (mm)	Interpretation
≥21	Susceptible (S)

[b] This zone diameter standard is applicable only to tests with *Haemophilus influenzae* and *Haemophilus parainfluenzae* using *Haemophilus* Test Medium (HTM)[2].

The current absence of data on resistant strains precludes defining any results other than "Susceptible". Strains yielding zone diameter results suggestive of a "nonsusceptible" category should be submitted to a reference laboratory for further testing.

For testing *Neisseria gonorrhoeae*[c]:

Zone Diameter (mm)	Interpretation
≥36	Susceptible (S)

[c] This zone diameter standard is applicable only to disk diffusion tests with GC agar base and 1% defined growth supplement.

The current absence of data on resistant strains precludes defining any results other than "Susceptible". Strains yielding zone diameter results suggestive of a "nonsusceptible" category should be submitted to a reference laboratory for further testing.

Interpretation should be as stated above for results using dilution techniques. Interpretation involves correlation of the diameter obtained in the disk test with the MIC for ciprofloxacin.

As with standardized dilution techniques, diffusion methods require the use of laboratory control microorganisms that are used to control the technical aspects of the laboratory procedures. For the diffusion technique, the 5-μg ciprofloxacin disk should provide the following zone diameters in these laboratory test quality control strains:

Organism		Zone Diameter (mm)
E. coli	ATCC 25922	30 – 40
H. influenzae[a]	ATCC 49247	34 – 42
N. gonorrhoeae[b]	ATCC 49226	48 – 58
P. aeruginosa	ATCC 27853	25 – 33
S. aureus	ATCC 25923	22 – 30

[a] These quality control limits are applicable to only *H. influenzae* ATCC 49247 testing using *Haemophilus* Test Medium (HTM)[2].

[b] These quality control limits are applicable only to tests conducted with *N. gonorrhoeae* ATCC 49226 performed by disk diffusion using GC agar base and 1% defined growth supplement.

INDICATIONS AND USAGE

CIPRO® is indicated for the treatment of infections caused by susceptible strains of the designated microorganisms in the conditions listed below. Please see **DOSAGE AND ADMINISTRATION** for specific recommendations.

Acute Sinusitis caused by *Haemophilus influenzae*, *Streptococcus pneumoniae*, or *Moraxella catarrhalis*.

Lower Respiratory Tract Infections caused by *Escherichia coli*, *Klebsiella pneumoniae*, *Enterobacter cloacae*, *Proteus mirabilis*, *Pseudomonas aeruginosa*, *Haemophilus influenzae*, *Haemophilus parainfluenzae*, or *Streptococcus pneumoniae*. Also, *Moraxella catarrhalis* for the treatment of acute exacerbations of chronic bronchitis.

NOTE: Although effective in clinical trials, ciprofloxacin is not a drug of first choice in the treatment of presumed or confirmed penumonia secondary to *Streptococcos pneumoniae*.

Urinary Tract Infections caused by *Escherichia coli*, *Klebsiella pneumoniae*, *Enterobacter cloacae*, *Serratia marcescens*, *Proteus mirabilis*, *Providencia rettgeri*, *Morganella morganii*, *Citrobacter diversus*, *Citrobacter freundii*, *Pseudomonas aeruginosa*, *Staphylococcus epidermidis*, *Staphylococcus saprophyticus*, or *Enterococcus faecalis*.

Acute Uncomplicatd Cystitis in females caused by *Escherichia coli* or *Staphylococcus saprophyticus*. (See **DOSAGE AND ADMINISTRATION**.)

Chronic Bacterial Prostatitis caused by *Escherichia coli* or *Proteus mirabilis*.

Complicated Intra-Abdominal Infections (used in combination with metronidazole) caused by *Escherichia coli*, *Pseudomonas aeruginosa*, *Proteus mirabilis*, *Klebsiella pneumoniae*, or *Bacteroides fragilis*. (See **DOSAGE AND ADMINISTRATION**.)

Skin and Skin Structure Infections caused by *Escherichia coli*, *Klebsiella pneumoniae*, *Enterobacter cloacae*, *Proteus mirabilis*, *Proteus vulgaris*, *Providencia stuartii*, *Morganella morganii*, *Citrobacter freundii*, *Pseudomonas aeruginosa*, *Staphylococcus aureus* (methicillin susceptible), *Staphylococcus epidermidis*, or *Streptococcus pyogenes*.

Bone and Joint Infections caused by *Enterobacter cloacae*, *Serratia marcescens*, or *Pseudomonas aeruginosa*.

Infectious Diarrhea caused by *Escherichia coli* (enterotoxigenic strains), *Campylobacter jejuni*, *Shigella boydii**, *Shigella dysenteriae*, *Shigella flexneri* or *Shigella sonnei** when antibacterial therapy is indicated.

Typhoid Fever (Enteric Fever) caused by *Salmonella typhi*.

NOTE: The efficacy of ciprofloxacin in the eradication of the chronic typhoid carrier state has not been demonstrated.

Uncomplicated cervical and urethral gonorrhea due to *Neisseria gonorrhoeae*.

Inhalational anthrax (post-exposure): To reduce the incidence or progression of disease following exposure to aerosolized *Bacillus anthracis*.

Ciprofloxacin serum conentrations achieved in humans serve as a surrogate endpoint reasonably likely to predict clinical benefit and provide the basis for this indication.[4] (See also **INHALATIONAL ANTHRAX—ADDITIONAL INFORMATION**).

---

*Although treatment of infections due to this organism in this organ system demonstrated a clinically significant outcome, efficacy was studied in fewer than 10 patients.

If anaerobic organisms are suspected of contributing to the infection, appropriate therapy should be administered.

Appropriate culture and susceptibility tests should be performed before treatment in order to isolate and identify organisms causing infection and to determine their susceptibility to ciprofloxacin. Therapy with CIPRO® may be initiated before results of these tests are known; once results become available appropriate therapy should be continued. As with other drugs, some strains of *Pseudomonas aeruginosa* may develop resistance fairly rapidly during treatment with ciprofloxacin. Culture and susceptibility testing performed periodically during therapy will provide information not only on the therapeutic effect of the antimicrobial agent but also on the possible emergence of bacterial resistance.

CONTRAINDICATIONS

CIPRO® (ciprofloxacin hydrochloride) is contraindicated in persons with a history of hypersensitivity to ciprofloxacin or any member of the quinolone class of antimicrobial agents.

WARNINGS

THE SAFETY AND EFFECTIVENESS OF CIPROFLOXACIN IN PEDIATRIC PATIENTS AND ADOLESCENTS (LESS THAN 18 YEARS OF AGE),—EXCEPT FOR USE IN INHALATIONAL ANTHRAX (POST-EXPOSURE), PREGNANT WOMEN, AND LACTATING WOMEN HAVE NOT BEEN ESTABLISHED. (See **PRECAUTIONS: Pediatric Use, Pregnancy,** and **Nursing Mothers** subsections.) The oral administration of ciprofloxacin caused lameness in immature dogs. Histopathological examination of the weight-bearing joints of these dogs revealed permanent lesions of the cartilage. Related quinolone-class drugs also produce erosions of cartilage of weight-bearing joints and other signs of arthropathy in immature animals of various species. (See **ANIMAL PHARMACOLOGY.**)

Convulsions, increased intracranial pressure, and toxic psychosis have been reported in patients receiving quinolones, including ciprofloxacin. Ciprofloxacin may also cause central nervous system (CNS) events including: dizziness, confusion, tremors, hallucinations, depression, and, rarely, suicidal thoughts or acts. These reactions may occur following the first dose. If these reactions occur in patients receiving ciprofloxacin, the drug should be discontinued and appropriate measures instituted. As with all quinolones, ciprofloxacin should be used with caution in patients with known or suspected CNS disorders that may predispose to seizures or lower the seizure threshold (e.g. severe cerebral arteriosclerosis, epilepsy), or in the presence of other risk factors that may predispose to seizures or lower the seizure threshold (e.g. certain drug therapy, renal dysfunction). (See **PRECAUTIONS: General, Information for Patients, Drug Interactions** and **ADVERSE REACTIONS.**)

SERIOUS AND FATAL REACTIONS HAVE BEEN REPORTED IN PATIENTS RECEIVING CONCURRENT ADMINISTRATION OF CIPROFLOXACIN AND THEOPHYLLINE. These reactions have included cardiac arrest, seizure, status epilepticus, and respiratory failure. Although similar serious adverse effects have been reported in patients receiving theophylline alone, the possibility that these reactions may be potentiated by ciprofloxacin cannot be eliminated. If concomitant use cannot be avoided, serum levels of theophylline should be monitored and dosage adjustments made as appropriate.

Serious and occasionally fatal hypersensitivity (anaphylactic) reactions, some following the first dose, have been reported in patients receiving quinolone therapy. Some reactions were accompanied by cardiovascular collapse, loss of consciousness, tingling, pharyngeal or facial edema, dyspnea, urticaria, and itching. Only a few patients had a history of hypersensitivity reactions. Serious anaphylactic reactions require immediate emergency treatment with epinephrine. Oxygen, intravenous steroids, and airway management, including intubation, should be administered as indicated. Severe hypersensitivity reactions characterized by rash, fever, eosinophilia, jaundice, and hepatic necrosis with fatal outcome have also been rarely reported in patients receiving ciprofloxacin along with other drugs. The possibility that these reactions were related to ciprofloxacin cannot be excluded. Ciprofloxacin should be discontinued at the first appearance of a skin rash or any other sign of hypersensitivity.

Pseudomembranous colitis has been reported with nearly all antibacterial agents, including ciprofloxacin, and may range in severity from mild to life-threatening. Therefore, it is important to consider this diagnosis in patients who present with diarrhea subsequent to the administration of antibacterial agents.

Treatment with antibacterial agents alters the normal flora of the colon and may permit overgrowth of clostridia. Studies indicate that a toxin produced by *Clostridium difficile* is one primary cause of "antibiotic-associated colitis."

After the diagnosis of pseudomembranous colitis has been established, therapeutic measures should be initiated. Mild cases of pseudomembranous colitis usually respond to drug discontinuation alone. In moderate to severe cases, consideration should be given to management with fluids and electrolytes, protein supplementation, and treatment with an antibacterial drug clinically effective against *C. difficile* colitis.

Achilles and other tendon ruptures that required surgical repair or resulted in prolonged disability have been reported with ciprofloxacin and other quinolones. Ciprofloxacin should be discontinued if the patient experiences pain, inflammation, or rupture of a tendon.

Ciprofloxacin has not been shown to be effective in the treatment of syphilis. Antimicrobial agents used in high dose for short periods of time to treat gonorrhea may mask or delay the symptoms of incubating syphilis. All patients with gonorrhea should have a serologic test for syphilis at the time of diagnosis. Patients treated with ciprofloxacin should have a follow-up serologic test for syphilis after three months.

PRECAUTIONS

General: Crystals of ciprofloxacin have been observed rarely in the urine of human subjects but more frequently in the urine of laboratory animals, which is usually alkaline. (See **ANIMAL PHARMACOLOGY**.) Crystalluria related to ciprofloxacin has been reported only rarely in humans because human urine is usually acidic. Alkalinity of the urine should be avoided in patients receiving ciprofloxacin. Patients should be well hydrated to prevent the formation of highly concentrated urine.

Quinolones, including ciprofloxacin, may also cause central nervous system (CNS) events, including: nervousness, agitation, insomnia, anxiety, nightmares or paranoia. (See **WARNINGS, Information for Patients**, and **Drug Interactions**.)

Alteration of the dosage regimen is necessary for patients with impairment of renal function. (See **DOSAGE AND ADMINISTRATION**.)

Moderate to severe phototoxicity manifested as an exaggerated sunburn reaction has been observed in patients who are exposed to direct sunlight while receiving some members of the quinolone class of drugs. Excessive sunlight should be avoided. Therapy should be discontinued if phototoxicity occurs.

As with any potent drug, periodic assessment of organ system functions, including renal, hepatic, and hematopoietic function, is advisable during prolonged therapy.

Information for Patients:

Patients should be advised:

• that ciprofloxacin may be taken with or without meals and to drink fluids liberally. As with other quinolones, concurrent administration of ciprofloxacin with magnesium/

aluminum antacids, or sucralfate, Videx® (didanosine) chewable/buffered tablets or pediatric powder, or with other products containing calcium, iron or zinc should be avoided. These products may be taken two hours after or six hours before ciprofloxacin. Ciprofloxacin should not be taken concurrently with milk or yogurt alone, since absorption of ciprofloxacin may be significantly reduced. Dietary calcium as part of a meal, however, does not significantly affect ciprofloxacin absorption.

• that ciprofloxacin may be associated with hypersensitivity reactions, even following a single dose, and to discontinue the drug at the first sign of a skin rash or other allergic reaction.

• to avoid excessive sunlight or artificial ultraviolet light while receiving ciprofloxacin and to discontinue therapy if phototoxicity occurs.

• to discontinue treatment; rest and refrain from exercise; and inform their physician if they experience pain, inflammation, or rupture of a tendon.

• that ciprofloxacin may cause dizziness and lightheadedness; therefore, patients should know how they react to this drug before they operate an automobile or machinery or engage in activities requiring mental alertness or coordination.

• that ciprofloxacin may increase the effects of theophylline and caffeine. There is a possibility of caffeine accumulation when products containing caffeine are consumed while taking quinolones.

• that convulsions have been reported in patients taking quinolones, including ciprofloxacin, and to notify their physician before taking the drug if there is a history of this condition.

Drug Interactions: As with some other quinolones, concurrent administration of ciprofloxacin with theophylline may lead to elevated serum concentrations of theophylline and prolongation of its elimination half-life. This may result in increased risk of theophylline-related adverse reactions. (See **WARNINGS**.) If concomitant use cannot be avoided, serum levels of theophylline should be monitored and dosage adjustments made as appropriate.

Some quinolones, including ciprofloxacin, have also been shown to interfere with the metabolism of caffeine. This may lead to reduced clearance of caffeine and a prolongation of its serum half-life.

Concurrent administration of a quinolone, including ciprofloxacin, with multivalent cation-containing products such as magnesium/aluminum antacids, sucralfate, Videx® (didanosine) chewable/buffered tablets or pediatric powder, or products containing calcium, iron, or zinc may substantially decrease its absorption, resulting in serum and urine levels considerably lower than desired. (See

DOSAGE AND ADMINISTRATION for current administration of these agents with ciprofloxacin.)

Histamine H₂-receptor antagonists appear to have no significant effect on the bioavailability of ciprofloxacin.

Altered serum levels of phenytoin (increased and decreased) have been reported in patients receiving concomitant ciprofloxacin.

The concomitant administration of ciprofloxacin with the sulfonylurea glyburide has, on rare occasions, resulted in severe hypoglycemia.

Some quinolones, including ciprofloxacin, have been associated with transient elevations in serum creatinine in patients receiving cyclosporine concomitantly.

Quinolones have been reported to enhance the effects of the oral anticoagulant warfarin or its derivatives. When these products are administered concomitantly, prothrombin time or other suitable coagulation tests should be closely monitored.

Probenecid interferes with renal tubular secretion of ciprofloxacin and produces an increase in the level of ciprofloxacin in the serum. This should be considered if patients are receiving both drugs concomitantly.

As with other broad spectrum antimicrobial agents, prolonged use of ciprofloxacin may result in overgrowth of nonsusceptible organisms. Repeated evaluation of the patient's condition and microbial susceptibility testing is essential. If superinfection occurs during therapy, appropriate measures should be taken.

Carcinogenesis, Mutagenesis, Impairment of Fertility: Eight *in vitro* mutagenicity tests have been conducted with ciprofloxacin, and the test results are listed below:

　Salmonella/Microsome Test (Negative)

　E. coli DNA Repair Assay (Negative)

　Mouse Lymphoma Cell Forward Mutation Assay (Positive)

　Chinese Hamster V₇₉ Cell HGPRT Test (Negative)

　Syrian Hamster Embryo Cell Transformation Assay (Negative)

　Saccharomyces cerevisiae Point Mutation Assay (Negative)

　Saccharomyces cerevisiae Mitotic Crossover and Gene Conversion Assay (Negative)

　Rat Hepatocyte DNA Repair Assay (Positive)

Thus, 2 of the 8 tests were positive, but results of the following 3 *in vivo* test systems gave negative results:

Rat Hepatocyte DNA Repair Assay

Micronucleus Test (Mice)

Dominant Lethal Test (Mice)

Long-term carcinogenicity studies in mice and rats have been completed. After daily oral doses of 750 mg/kg (mice) and 250 mg/kg (rats) were administered for up to 2 years, there was no evidence that ciprofloxacin had any carcinogenic or tumorigenic effects in these species.

Results from photo co-carcinogenicity testing indicate that ciprofloxacin does not reduce the time to appearance of UV-induced skin tumors as compared to vehicle control. Hairless (Skh-1) mice were exposed to UVA light for 3.5 hours five times every two weeks for up to 78 weeks while concurrently being administered ciprofloxacin. The time to development of the first skin tumors was 50 weeks in mice treated concomitantly with UVA and ciprofloxacin (mouse dose approximately equal to maximum recommended human dose based upon mg/m²), as opposed to 34 weeks when animals were treated with both UVA and vehicle. The times to development of skin tumors ranged from 16–32 weeks in mice treated concomitantly with UVA and other quinolones.[3]

In this model, mice treated with ciprofloxacin alone did not develop skin or systemic tumors. There are no data from similar models using pigmented mice and/or fully haired mice. The clinical significance of these findings to humans is unknown.

Fertility studies performed in rats at oral doses of ciprofloxacin up to 100 mg/kg (0.8 times the highest recommended human dose of 1200 mg based upon body surface area) revealed no evidence of impairment.

Pregnancy: Teratogenic Effects. Pregnancy Category C: Reproduction studies have been performed in rats and mice using oral doses up to 100 mg/kg (0.6 and 0.3 times the maximum daily human dose based upon body surface area, respectively) and have revealed no evidence of harm to the fetus due to ciprofloxacin. In rabbits, ciprofloxacin (30 and 100 mg/kg orally) produced gastrointestinal disturbances resulting in maternal weight loss and an increased incidence of abortion, but no teratogenicity was observed at either dose. After intravenous administration of doses up to 20 mg/kg, no maternal toxicity was produced in the rabbit, and no embryotoxicity or teratogenicity was observed. There are, however, no adequate and well-controlled studies in pregnant women. Ciprofloxacin should be used during pregnancy only if the potential benefit justifies the potential risk to the fetus. (See **WARNINGS**.)

Nursing Mothers: Ciprofloxacin is excreted in human milk. Because of the potential for serious adverse reactions in infants nursing from mothers taking ciprofloxacin, a decision should be made whether to discontinue nursing or to discontinue the drug, taking into account the importance of the drug to the mother.

Pediatric Use: Safety and effectiveness in pediatric patients and adolescents less than 18 years of age have not been established, except for use in inhalational anthrax (post-exposure). Ciprofloxacin causes arthropathy in juvenile animals. (See **WARNINGS**.)

For the indication of inhalational anthrax (post-exposure), the risk-benefit assessment indicates that administration of ciprofloxacin to pediatric patients is appropriate. For information regarding pediatric dosing in inhalational anthrax (post-exposure), see **DOSAGE AND ADMINISTRATION** and **INHALATIONAL ANTHRAX—ADDITIONAL INFORMATION.**

Short-term safety data from a single trial in pediatric cystic fibrosis patients are available. In a randomized, double-blind clinical trial for the treatment of acute pulmonary exacerbations in cystic fibrosis patients (ages 5–17 years), 67 patients received ciprofloxacin I.V. 10 mg/kg/dose q 8 h for one week followed by ciprofloxacin tablets 20 mg/kg/dose q 12 h to complete 10–21 days treatment and 62 patients received the combination of ceftazidime I.V. 50 mg/kg/dose q 8 h and tobramycin I.V. 3 mg/kg/dose q 8 h for a total of 10–21 days. Patients less than 5 years of age were not studied. Safety monitoring in the study included periodic range of motion examinations and gait assessments by treatment-blinded examiners. Patients were followed for an average of 23 days after completing treatment (range 0–93 days). This study was not designed to determine long term effects and the safety of repeated exposure to ciprofloxacin.

In the study, injection site reactions were more common in the ciprofloxacin group (24%) than in the comparison group (8%). Other adverse events were similar in nature and frequency between treatment arms. Musculoskeletal adverse events were reported in 22% of the patients in the ciprofloxacin group and 21% in the comparison group. Decreased range of motion was reported in 12% of the subjects in the ciprofloxacin group and 16% in the comparison group. Arthralgia was reported in 10% of the patients in the ciprofloxacin group and 11% in the comparison group. One of sixty-seven patients developed arthritis of the knee nine days after a ten day course of treatment with ciprofloxacin. Clinical symptoms resolved, but an MRI showed knee effusion without other abnormalities eight months after treatment. However, the relationship of this event to the patient's course of ciprofloxacin can not be definitively determined, particularly since patients with cystic fibrosis may develop arthralgias/arthritis as part of their underlying disease process.

Geriatric Use: In a retrospective analysis of 23 multiple-dose controlled clinical trials of ciprofloxacin encompassing over 3500 ciprofloxacin treated patients, 25% of patients were greater than or equal to 65 years of age and 10% were greater than or equal to 75 years of age. No overall differences in safety or effectiveness were observed between these subjects and younger subjects, and other reported clinical experience has not identified differences in responses between the elderly and younger patients, but greater sensitivity of some older individuals on any drug therapy cannot be ruled out. Ciprofloxacin is known to be substantially excreted by the kidney, and the risk of adverse reactions may be greater in patients with impaired renal function. No alteration of dosage is necessary for patients greater than 65 years of age with normal renal function. However, since some older individuals experience reduced renal function by virtue of their advanced age, care should be taken in dose selection for elderly patients, and renal function monitoring may be useful in these patients. (See **CLINICAL PHARMACOLOGY** and **DOSAGE AND ADMINISTRATION**.)

ADVERSE REACTIONS

During clinical investigation with the tablet, 2,799 patients received 2,868 courses of the drug. Adverse events that were considered likely to be drug related occurred in 7.3% of patients treated, possibly related in 9.2% (total of 16.5% thought to be possibly or probably related to drug therapy), and remotely related in 3.0%. Ciprofloxacin was discontinued because of an adverse event in 3.5% of patients treated, primarily involving the gastrointestinal system (1.5%), skin (0.6%), and central nervous system (0.4%).

The most frequently reported events, drug related or not, were nausea (5.2%), diarrhea (2.3%), vomiting (2.0%), abdominal pain/discomfort (1.7%), headache (1.2%), restlessness (1.1%), and rash (1.1%).

Additional events that occurred in less than 1% of ciprofloxacin patients are listed below.

CARDIOVASCULAR: palpitation, atrial flutter, ventricular ectopy, syncope, hypertension, angina pectoris, myocardial infarction cardiopulmonary arrest, cerebral thrombosis

CENTRAL NERVOUS SYSTEM: dizziness, lightheadedness, insomnia, nightmares, hallucinations, manic reaction, irritability, tremor, ataxia, convulsive seizures, lethargy, drowsiness, weakness, malaise, anorexia, phobia, depersonalization, depression, paresthesia (See above.) (See **PRECAUTIONS**.)

GASTROINTESTINAL: painful oral mucosa, oral candidiasis, dysphagia, intestinal perforation, gastrointestinal bleeding (See above.) Cholestatic jaundice has been reported.

MUSCULOSKELETAL: arthralgia or back pain, joint stiffness, achiness, neck or chest pain, flare up of gout

RENAL/UROGENITAL: interstitial nephritis, nephritis, renal failure, polyuria, urinary retention, urethral bleeding, vaginitis, acidosis

RESPIRATORY: dyspnea, epistaxis, laryngeal or pulmonary edema, hiccough, hemoptysis, bronchospasm, pulmonary embolism

SKIN/HYPERSENSITIVITY: pruritus, urticaria, photosensitivity, flushing, fever, chills, angioedema, edema of the face, neck, lips, conjunctivae or hands, cutaneous candidiasis, hyperpigmentation, erythema nodosum (See above.)

Hepatic	—	Elevations of ALT (SGPT) (1.9%), AST (SGOT) (1.7%), alkaline phosphatase (0.8%), LDH (0.4%), serum bilirubin (0.3%).
Hematologic	—	Eosinophilia (0.6%), leukopenia (0.4%), decreased blood platelets (0.1%), elevated blood platelets (0.1%), pancytopenia (0.1%).
Renal	—	Elevations of serum creatinine (1.1%), BUN (0.9%), CRYSTALLURIA, CYLINDRURIA, AND HEMATURIA HAVE BEEN REPORTED.

Allergic reactions ranging from urticaria to anaphylactic reactions have been reported. (See **WARNINGS**.)

SPECIAL SENSES: blurred vision, disturbed vision (change in color perception, overbrightness of lights), decreased visual acuity, diplopia, eye pain, tinnitus, hearing loss, bad taste

Most of the adverse events reported were described as only mild or moderate in severity, abated soon after the drug was discontinued, and required no treatment.

In several instances nausea, vomiting, tremor, irritability, or palpitation were judged by investigators to be related to elevated serum levels of theophylline possibly as a result of drug interaction with ciprofloxacin.

In domestic clinical trials involving 214 patients receiving a single 250-mg oral dose, approximately 5% of patients reported adverse experiences without reference to drug relationship. The most common adverse experiences were vaginitis (2%), headache (1%), and vaginal pruritus (1%). Additional reactions, occurring in 0.3%–1% of patients, were abdominal discomfort, lymphadenopathy, foot pain, dizziness, and breast pain. Less than 20% of these patients had laboratory values obtained, and these results were generally consistent with the pattern noted for multi-dose therapy. In randomized, double-blind controlled clinical trials comparing ciprofloxacin tablets (500 mg BID) to cefuroxime axetil (250 mg–500 mg BID) and to clarithromycin (500 mg BID) in patients with respiratory tract infections, ciprofloxacin demonstrated a CNS adverse event profile comparable to the control drugs.

Post-Marketing Adverse Events: Additional adverse events, regardless of relationship to drug, reported from worldwide marketing experience with quinolones, including ciprofloxacin, are:

BODY AS A WHOLE: change in serum phenytoin

CARDIOVASCULAR: postural hypotension, vasculitis

CENTRAL NERVOUS SYSTEM: agitation, confusion, delirium, dysphasia, myoclonus, nystagmus, toxic psychosis

GASTROINTESTINAL: constipation, dyspepsia, flatulence, hepatic necrosis, jaundice, pancreatitis, pseudomembranous colitis (The onset of pseudomembranous colitis symptoms may occur during or after antimicrobial treatment.)

HEMIC/LYMPHATIC: agranulocytosis, hemolytic anemia, methemoglobinemia, prolongation of prothrombin time

METABOLIC/NUTRITIONAL: elevation of serum triglycerides, cholesterol, blood glucose, serum potassium

MUSCULOSKELETAL: myalgia, possible exacerbation of myasthenia gravis, tendinitis/tendon rupture

RENAL/UROGENITAL: albuminuria, candiduria, renal calculi, vaginal candidiasis

SKIN/HYPERSENSITIVITY: anaphylactic reactions, erythema multiforme/Stevens-Johnson syndrome, exfoliative dermatitis, toxic epidermal necrolysis

SPECIAL SENSES: anosmia, taste loss (See **PRECAUTIONS**.)

Adverse Laboratory Changes: Changes in laboratory parameters listed as adverse events without regard to drug relationship are listed below:

[See table above]

Other changes occurring in less than 0.1% of courses were: elevation of serum gamma-glutamyl transferase, elevation of serum amylase, reduction in blood glucose, elevated uric acid, decrease in hemoglobin, anemia, bleeding diathesis, increase in blood monocytes, leukocytosis.

OVERDOSAGE

In the event of acute overdosage, the stomach should be emptied by inducing vomiting or by gastric lavage. The patient should be carefully observed and given supportive treatment. Adequate hydration must be maintained. Only a small amount of ciprofloxacin (<10%) is removed from the body after hemodialysis or peritoneal dialysis.

In mice, rats, rabbits and dogs, significant toxicity including tonic/clonic convulsions was observed at intravenous doses of ciprofloxacin between 125 and 300 mg/kg.

Single doses of ciprofloxacin were relatively non-toxic via the oral route of administration in mice, rats, and dogs. No deaths occurred within a 14-day post treatment observation period at the highest oral doses tested; up to 5000 mg/kg in either rodent species, or up to 2500 mg/kg in the dog. Clinical signs observed included hypoactivity and cyanosis in both rodent species and severe vomiting in dogs. In rabbits, significant mortality was seen at doses of ciprofloxacin > 2500 mg/kg. Mortality was delayed in these animals, occurring 10–14 days after dosing.

DOSAGE AND ADMINISTRATION

The recommended adult dosage for acute sinusitis is 500-mg every 12 hours.

Lower respiratory tract infections may be treated with 500-mg every 12 hours. For more severe or complicated infections, a dosage of 750-mg may be given every 12 hours.

Severe/complicated urinary tract infections or urinary tract infections caused by organisms not highly susceptible to ciprofloxacin may be treated with 500-mg every 12 hours. For other mild/moderate urinary infections, the usual adult dosage is 250-mg every 12 hours.

In acute uncomplicated cystitis in females, the usual dosage is 100-mg or 250-mg every 12 hours. For acute uncomplicated cystitis in females, 3 days of treatment is recommended while 7 to 14 days is suggested for other mild/moderate, severe or complicated urinary tract infections.

The recommended adult dosage for chronic bacterial prostatitis is 500-mg every 12 hours.

The recommended adult dosage for oral sequential therapy of complicated intra-abdominal infections is 500-mg every 12 hours. (To provide appropriate anaerobic activity, metronidazole should be given according to product labeling.) (See CIPRO® I.V. package insert.)

Skin and skin structure infections and bone and joint infections may be treated with 500-mg every 12 hours. For more severe or complicated infections, a dosage of 750-mg may be given every 12 hours.

The recommended adult dosage for infectious diarrhea or typhoid fever is 500-mg every 12 hours. For the treatment of uncomplicated urethral and cervical gonococcal infections, a single 250-mg dose is recommended.

See Instructions To The Pharmacist for Use/ Handling of CIPRO® Oral Suspension.

[See first table at top of next page]

One teaspoonful (5 mL) of 5% ciprofloxacin oral suspension = 250-mg of ciprofloxacin. One teaspoonful (5 mL) of 10% ciprofloxacin oral suspension = 500-mg of ciprofloxacin. See Instructions for USE/HANDLING.

Dosage	Volume (mL) of Oral Suspension	
	5%	10%
250-mg	5 mL	2.5 mL
500-mg	10 mL	5 mL
750-mg	15 mL	7.5 mL

CIPRO (ciprofloxacin) 5% and 10% Oral Suspension should not be administered through feeding tubes due to its physical characteristics.

Complicated Intra-Abdominal Infections: Sequential therapy [parenteral to oral—400-mg CIPRO® I.V. q 12 h (plus I.V. metronidazole) → 500-mg CIPRO® Tablets q 12 h (plus oral metronidazole)] can be instituted at the discretion of the physician.

The determination of dosage for any particular patient must take into consideration the severity and nature of the infection, the susceptibility of the causative organism, the integrity of the patient's host-defense mechanisms, and the status of renal function and hepatic function.

The duration of treatment depends upon the severity of infection. Generally ciprofloxacin should be continued for at least 2 days after the signs and symptoms of infection have disappeared. The usual duration is 7 to 14 days; however, for severe and complicated infections more prolonged therapy may be required. Bone and joint infections may require treatment for 4 to 6 weeks longer. Chronic Bacterial Prostatitis should be treated for 28 days. Infectious diarrhea may be treated for 5–7 days. Typhoid fever should be treated for 10 days.

Ciprofloxacin should be administered at least 2 hours before or 6 hours after magnesium/ aluminum antacids, or sucralfate, Videx® (didanosine) chewable/buffered tablets or pediatric powder for oral solution, or other products containing calcium, iron or zinc.

Impaired Renal Function: Ciprofloxacin is eliminated primarily by renal excretion; however, the drug is also metabolized and partially cleared through the biliary system of the liver and through the intestine. These alternate pathways of drug elimination appear to compensate for the reduced renal excretion in patients with renal impairment. Nonetheless, some modification of dosage is recommended, particularly for patients with severe renal dysfunction. The following table provides dosage guidelines for use in patients with renal impairment; however, monitoring of serum drug levels provides the most reliable basis for dosage adjustment:

RECOMMENDED STARTING AND MAINTENANCE DOSES FOR PATIENTS WITH IMPAIRED RENAL FUNCTION

Creatinine Clearance (mL/min)	Dose
>50	See Usual Dosage.
30–50	250–500 mg q 12 h
5–29	250–500 mg q 18 h
Patients on hemodialysis or Peritoneal dialysis	250–500 mg q 24 h (after dialysis)

When only the serum creatinine concentration is known, the following formula may be used to estimate creatinine clearance.

[See second table on next page]

The serum creatinine should represent a steady state of renal function.

In patients with severe infections and severe renal impairment, a unit dose of 750-mg may

DOSAGE GUIDELINES

Infection	Type or Severity	Unit Dose	Frequency	Usual Durations†
Acute Sinusitis	Mild/Moderate	500-mg	q 12 h	10 Days
Lower Respiratory Tract	Mild/Moderate Severe/Complicated	500-mg 750-mg	q 12 h q 12 h	7 to 14 Days 7 to 14 Days
Urinary Tract	Acute Uncomplicated Mild/Moderate Severe/Complicated	100-mg or 250-mg 250-mg 500-mg	q 12 h q 12 h q 12 h	3 Days 7 to 14 Days 7 to 14 Days
Chronic Bacterial Prostatitis	Mild/Moderate	500-mg	q 12 h	28 Days
Intra-Abdominal*	Complicated	500-mg	q 12 h	7 to 14 Days
Skin and Skin Structure	Mild/Moderate Severe/Complicated	500-mg 750-mg	q 12 h q 12 h	7 to 14 Days 7 to 14 Days
Bone and Joint	Mild/Moderate Severe/Complicated	500-mg 750-mg	q 12 h q 12 h	≥4 to 6 weeks ≥4 to 6 weeks
Infectious Diarrhea	Mild/Moderate/Severe	500-mg	q 12 h	5 to 7 Days
Typhoid Fever	Mild/Moderate	500-mg	q 12 h	10 Days
Urethral and Cervical Gonococcal Infections	Uncomplicated	250-mg	single dose	single dose
Inhalational anthrax (post-exposure)**	Adult	500-mg	q 12 h	60 Days
	Pediatric	15 mg/kg per dose, not to exceed 500-mg per dose	q 12 h	60 Days

*   used in conjunction with metronidazole
†   Generally ciprofloxacin should be continued for at least 2 days after the signs and symptoms of infection have disappeared, except for inhalational anthrax (post-exposure).
**   Drug administration should begin as soon as possible after suspected or confirmed exposure. This indication is based on a surrogate endpoint, ciprofloxacin serum concentrations achieved in humans, reasonably likely to predict clinical benefit.[4] For a discussion of ciprofloxacin serum concentrations in various human populations, see **INHALATIONAL AN-THRAX—ADDITIONAL INFORMATION.**

Men: Creatinine clearance (mL/min) = $\dfrac{\text{Weight (kg)} \times (140 - \text{age})}{72 \times \text{serum creatinine (mg/dL)}}$

Women: 0.85 × the value calculated for men.

---

be administered at the intervals noted above; however, patients should be carefully monitored and the serum ciprofloxacin concentration should be measured periodically. Peak concentrations (1–2 hours after dosing) should generally range from 2 to 4 µg/mL.
For patients with changing renal function or for patients with renal impairment and he-

patic insufficiency, measurement of serum concentrations of ciprofloxacin will provide additional guidance for adjusting dosage.

HOW SUPPLIED

CIPRO® (ciprofloxacin hydrochloride) Tablets are available as round, slightly yellowish film-

	Strength	NDC Code	Tablet Identification	
Bottles of 50:	750-mg	NDC 0026-8514-50	CIPRO	750
Bottles of 100:	250-mg	NDC 0026-8512-51	CIPRO	250
	500-mg	NDC 0026-8513-51	CIPRO	500
Unit Dose				
Package of 100:	250-mg	NDC 0026-8512-48	CIPRO	250
	500-mg	NDC 0026-8513-48	CIPRO	500
	750-mg	NDC 0026-8514-48	CIPRO	750
Cystitis:				
Package of 6:	100-mg	NDC 0026-8511-06	CIPRO	100

Total volume after reconstitution	Ciprofloxacin contents after reconstitution	Ciprofloxacin contents per bottle	NDC Code
100 mL	250 mg/5 mL	5,000 mg	0026-8551-36
100 mL	500 mg/5 mL	10,000 mg	0026-8553-36

coded tablets containing 100-mg or 250-mg ciprofloxacin. The 100-mg tablet is coded with the word "CIPRO" on one side and "100" on the reverse side. The 250-mg tablet is coded with the word "CIPRO" on one side and "250" on the reverse side. CIPRO® is also available as capsule shaped, slightly yellowish film-coated tablets containing 500-mg or 750-mg ciprofloxacin. The 500-mg tablet is coded with the word "CIPRO" on one side and "500" on the reverse side. The 750-mg tablet is coded with the word "CIPRO" on one side and "750" on the reverse side. CIPRO® 250-mg, 500-mg, and 750-mg are available in bottles of 50, 100, and Unit Dose packages of 100. The 100-mg strength, is available only as CIPRO® Cystitis pack containing 6 tablets for use only in female patients with acute uncomplicated cystitis.
[See first table above]
Store below 30°C (86°F).
CIPRO® Oral Suspension is supplied in 5% (5g ciprofloxacin in 100 mL) and 10% (10g ciprofloxacin in 100 mL) strengths. The drug product is composed of two components (microcapsules and diluent) which are mixed prior to dispensing. See Instructions To The Pharmacist For Use/ Handling.
[See second table above]
Microcapsules and diluent should be stored below 25°C (77°F) and protected from freezing.
Reconstituted product may be stored below 30°C (86°F). Protect from freezing. A teaspoon is provided for the patient.

ANIMAL PHARMACOLOGY

Ciprofloxacin and other quinolones have been shown to cause arthropathy in immature animals of most species tested. (See **WARNINGS**.) Damage of weight bearing joints was observed in juvenile dogs and rats. In young beagles, 100 mg/kg ciprofloxacin, given daily for 4 weeks, caused degenerative articular changes of the knee joint. At 30 mg/kg, the effect on the joint was minimal. In a subsequent study in beagles, removal of weight bearing from the joint reduced the lesions but did not totally prevent them.

Crystalluria, sometimes associated with secondary nephropathy, occurs in laboratory animals dosed with ciprofloxacin. This is primarily related to the reduced solubility of ciprofloxacin under alkaline conditions, which predominate in the urine of test animals; in man, crystalluria is rare since human urine is typically acidic. In rhesus monkeys, crystalluria without nephropathy has been noted after single oral doses as low as 5 mg/kg. After 6 months of intravenous dosing at 10 mg/kg/day, no nephropathological changes were noted; however, nephropathy was observed after dosing at 20 mg/kg/day for the same duration.
In dogs, ciprofloxacin at 3 and 10 mg/kg by rapid IV injection (15 sec.) produces pronounced hypotensive effects. These effects are considered to be related to histamine release, since they are partially antagonized by pyrilamine, an antihistamine. In rhesus monkeys, rapid IV injection also produces hypotension but the effect in this species is inconsistent and less pronounced.
In mice, concomitant administration of nonsteroidal anti-inflammatory drugs such as phenylbutazone and indomethacin with quinolones has been reported to enhance the CNS stimulatory effect of quinolones.
Ocular toxicity seen with some related drugs has not been observed in ciprofloxacin-treated animals.

CLINICAL STUDIES
Acute Sinusitis Studies
Ciprofloxacin tablets (500-mg BID) were evaluated for the treatment of acute sinusitis in two randomized, double-blind, controlled clinical trials conducted in the United States. Study 1 compared ciprofloxacin with cefuroxime axetil (250-mg BID) and enrolled 501 patients (400 of which were valid for the primary efficacy analysis). Study 2 compared ciprofloxacin with clarithromycin (500-mg BID) and enrolled 560 patients (418 of whom were valid for the primary efficacy analysis). The primary test of cure endpoint was a follow-up visit performed approximately 30 days after the completion of treatment with study medication. Clinical response data from these studies are summarized below:

Drug Regimen	Clinical Response Resolution at 30 Day Follow-up n (%)
STUDY 1	
CIPRO 500-mg BID × 10 days	152/197 (77)
Cefuroxime Axetil 250-mg BID × 10 days	145/203 (71)
STUDY 2	
CIPRO 500-mg BID × 10 days	168/212 (79)
Clarithromycin 500-mg BID × 14 days	169/206 (82)

In ciprofloxacin-treated patients enrolled in controlled and uncontrolled acute sinusitis studies, all of which included antral puncture, bacteriological eradication/presumed eradication was documented at the 30 day follow-up visit in 44 of 50 (88%) *H. influenzae*, 17 of 21 (80.9%) *M. catarrhalis*, and 42 of 51 (82.3%) *S. pneumoniae*. Patients infected with *S. pneumoniae* strains whose baseline susceptibilities were intermediate or resistant to ciprofloxacin had a lower success rate than patients infected with susceptible strains.

Uncomplicated Cystitis Studies

Efficacy: Two U.S. double-blind, controlled clinical studies of acute uncomplicated cystitis in women compared ciprofloxacin 100-mg BID for 3 days to ciprofloxacin 250-mg BID for 7 days or control drug. In these two studies, using strict evaluability criteria and microbiologic and clinical response criteria at the 5–9 day post-therapy follow-up, the following clinical resolution and bacterial eradication rates were obtained:

[See table below]

INHALATIONAL ANTHRAX – ADDITIONAL INFORMATION

The mean serum concentrations of ciprofloxacin associated with a statistically significant improvement in survival in the rhesus monkey model of inhalational anthrax are reached or exceeded in adult and pediatric patients receiving oral and intravenous regimens. (See **DOSAGE AND ADMINISTRATION**.) Ciprofloxacin pharmacokinetics have been evaluated in various human populations. The mean peak serum concentration achieved at steady-state in human adults receiving 500 mg orally every 12 hours is 2.97 µg/mL, and 4.56 µg/mL following 400 mg intravenously every 12 hours. The mean trough serum concentration at steady-state for both of these regimens is 0.2 µg/mL. In a study of 10 pediatric patients between 6 and 16 years of age, the mean peak plasma concentration achieved is 8.3 µg/mL and trough concentrations range from 0.09 to 0.26 µg/mL, following two 30-minute intravenous infusions of 10 mg/kg administered 12 hours apart. After the second intravenous infusion patients switched to 15 mg/kg orally every 12 hours achieve a mean peak concentration of 3.6 µg/mL, after the initial oral dose. Long-term safety data, including effects on cartilage, following the administration of ciprofloxacin to pediatric patients are limited. (For additional information, see **PRECAUTIONS: Pediatric Use**.) Ciprofloxacin serum concentrations achieved in humans serve as a surrogate endpoint reasonably likely to predict clinical benefit and provide the basis for this indication.[4]

A placebo-controlled animal study in rhesus monkeys exposed to an inhaled mean dose of 11 LD_{50} ($\sim$5.5 × 10^5) spores (range 5–30 LD_{50}) of *B. anthracis* was conducted. The minimal inhibitory concentration (MIC) of ciprofloxacin for the anthrax strain used in this study was 0.08 µg/mL. In the animals studied, mean serum concentrations of ciprofloxacin achieved at expected T_{max} (1 hour post-dose) following oral dosing to steady-state ranged from 0.98 to 1.69 µg/mL. Mean steady-state trough concentrations at 12 hours post-dose ranged from 0.12 to 0.19 µg/mL.[5] Mortality due to anthrax for animals that received a 30-day regimen of oral ciprofloxacin beginning 24 hours post-exposure was significantly lower (1/9), compared to the placebo group (9/10) [p=0.001]. The one ciprofloxacin-treated animal that died of anthrax did so following the 30-day drug administration period.[6]

Drug Regimen	Clinical Response Resolution n (%)	Bacteriological Response By Organism (Eradication Rate)	
		E. coli n (%)	*S. saprophyticus* n (%)
STUDY 1			
CIPRO 100-mg BID × 3 days	82/94 (87)	64/70 (91)	8/8 (100)
CIPRO 250-mg BID × 7 days	81/86 (94)	67/69 (97)	4/4 (100)
STUDY 2			
CIPRO 100-mg BID × 3 days	134/141 (95)	117/123 (95)	8/8 (100)
Control (3 days)	128/133 (96)	103/105 (98)	10/10 (100)

Instructions To The Pharmacist For Use/Handling Of CIPRO® Oral Suspension:
Preparation of the suspension:

1. The small bottle contains the microcapsules, the large bottle contains the diluent.

2. Open both bottles. Child-proof cap: Press down according to instructions on the cap while turning to the left.

3. Pour the microcapsules completely into the large bottle of diluent. **Do not add water to the suspension.**

4. Remove the top layer of the diluent bottle label (to reveal the CIPRO® Oral Suspension label).

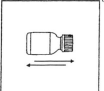

5. Close the large bottle completely according to the directions on the cap and shake vigorously for about 15 seconds. The suspension is ready for use.

Instructions To The Patient For Taking CIPRO® Oral Suspension:
Shake vigorously each time before use for approximately 15 seconds.
Swallow the prescribed amount of suspension. Do not chew the microcapsules. Reclose the bottle completely after use according to the instructions on the cap. Shake vigorously each time before use for approximately 15 seconds. The product can be used for 14 days when stored in a refrigerator or at room temperature (below 86°F). After treatment has been completed, any remaining suspension should not be reused.

REFERENCES
1. National Committee for Clinical Laboratory Standards, Methods for Dilution Antimicrobial Susceptibility Tests for Bacteria That Grow Aerobically-Fifth Edition. Approved Standard NCCLS Document M7-A5, Vol. 20, No. 2, NCCLS, Wayne, PA, January, 2000. **2.** National Committee for Clinical Laboratory Standards, Performance Standards for Antimicrobial Disk Susceptibility Tests-Seventh Edition. Approved Standard NCCLS Document M2-A7, Vol. 20, No. 1, NCCLS, Wayne, PA, January, 2000. **3.** Report presented at the FDA's Anti-Infective Drug and Dermatological Drug Product's Advisory Committee meeting, March 31, 1993, Silver Spring, MD. Report available from FDA, CDER, Advisors and Consultants Staff, HFD-21, 1901 Chapman Avenue, Room 200, Rockville, MD 20852, USA. **4.** 21 CFR 314.510 (Subpart H—Accelerated Approval of New Drugs for Life-Threatening Illnesses) **5.** Kelly DJ, et al. Serum concentrations of penicillin, doxycycline, and ciprofloxacin during prolonged therapy in rhesus monkeys. J Infect Dis 1992; 166: 1184–7. **6.** Friedlander AM, et al. Postexposure prophylaxis against experimental inhalational anthrax. J Infect Dis 1993; 167: 1239–42.

Bayer Corporation
Pharmaceutical Division
400 Morgan Lane
West Haven, CT 06516 USA
℞ Only
PZ500174 10/00 Bay o 9867 5202-2-A-U.S.-11
© 2000 Bayer Corporation   10007
CIPRO® (ciprofloxacin) 5% and 10% ORAL SUSPENSION Made in Italy
Printed in U.S.A.

DECLOMYCIN®　　　　　　　　℞
[děk-lō-mī-sĭn]
Demeclocycline Hydrochloride
For Oral Use

DESCRIPTION

DECLOMYCIN demeclocycline hydrochloride
is an antibiotic isolated from a mutant strain
of *Streptomyces aureofaciens.* Chemically it is
7-Chloro-4-(dimethylamino)-1,4, 4a,5,5a,6,11,
12a-octahydro-3,6,10,12, 12a-pentahydroxy-
1,11-dioxo-2-naphthacenecarboxamide monohydrochloride.
DECLOMYCIN contains the following inactive ingredients:
Tablets: Alginic Acid, Corn Starch, Ethylcellulose, Hydroxypropyl Methylcellulose, Magnesium Stearate, Red 7, Sorbitol, Titanium Dioxide, Yellow 10 and other ingredients. May also
contain Sodium Lauryl Sulfate.

CLINICAL PHARMACOLOGY

The tetracyclines are primarily bacteriostatic
and are thought to exert their antimicrobial
effect by the inhibition of protein synthesis.
Tetracyclines are active against a wide range
of gram-negative and gram-positive organisms.
The drugs in the tetracycline class have
closely similar antimicrobial spectra, and
cross-resistance among them is common. Microorganisms may be considered susceptible if
the MIC (minimum inhibitory concentration)
is not more than 4 mcg/mL and intermediate if
the MIC is 4 to 12.5 mcg/mL.
Susceptibility plate testing: A tetracycline disc
may be used to determine microbial susceptibility to drugs in the tetracycline class. If the
Kirby-Bauer method of disc susceptibility testing is used, a 30 mcg tetracycline disc should
give a zone of at least 19 mm when tested
against a tetracycline-susceptible bacterial
strain.
Tetracyclines are readily absorbed and are
bound to plasma proteins in varying degrees.
They are concentrated by the liver in the bile
and excreted in the urine and feces at high
concentrations and in a biologically active
form.

INDICATIONS AND USAGE

DECLOMYCIN demeclocycline hydrochloride
is indicated in infections caused by the following microorganisms:
Rickettsiae: (Rocky Mountain spotted fever,
typhus fever and the typhus group, Q fever,
rickettsialpox, tick fevers).
Mycoplasma pneumoniae (PPLO, Eaton
agent).
Agents of psittacosis and ornithosis.
Agents of lymphogranuloma venereum and
granuloma inguinale.
The spirochetal agent of relapsing fever (*Borrelia recurrentis*).
The following gram-negative microorganisms:
Haemophilus ducreyi (chancroid),

Yersinia pestis and *Francisella tularensis*, formerly *Pasteurella pestis* and *Pasteurella tularensis,*
Bartonella bacilliformis,
Bacteroides species,
Vibrio comma and *Vibrio fetus,*
Brucella species (in conjunction with streptomycin).
Because many strains of the following groups
of microorganisms have been shown to be resistant to tetracyclines, culture and susceptibility testing are recommended.
Demeclocycline is indicated for treatment of
infections caused by the following gram-negative microorganisms, when bacteriologic testing indicates appropriate susceptibility to the
drug:
Escherichia coli,
Enterobacter aerogenes (formerly *Aerobacter
aerogenes*),
Shigella species,
Mima species and *Herellea* species,
Haemophilus influenzae (respiratory
infections),
Klebsiella species (respiratory and urinary
infections).
DECLOMYCIN is indicated for treatment of
infections caused by the following gram-positive microorganisms when bacteriologic testing indicates appropriate susceptibility to the
drug:
Streptococcus species:
Up to 44% of strains of *Streptococcus pyogenes*
and 74% of *Streptococcus faecalis* have been
found to be resistant to tetracycline drugs.
Therefore, tetracyclines should not be used for
streptococcal disease unless the organism has
been demonstrated to be sensitive.
For upper respiratory infections due to Group
A beta-hemolytic streptococci, penicillin is the
usual drug of choice, including prophylaxis of
rheumatic fever.
Streptococcus pneumoniae,
Staphylococcus aureus, skin and soft tissue
infections.
Tetracyclines are not the drugs of choice in
the treatment of any type of staphylococcal
infection.
When penicillin is contraindicated, tetracy-
clines are alternative drugs in the treatment
of infections due to:
Neisseria gonorrhoeae,
Treponema pallidum and *Treponema pertenue*
(syphilis and yaws),
Listeria monocytogenes,
Clostridium species,
Bacillus anthracis,
Fusobacterium fusiforme (Vincent's infection),
Actinomyces species.
In acute intestinal amebiasis, the tetracy-
clines may be a useful adjunct to amebicides.
DECLOMYCIN demeclocycline hydrochloride
is indicated in the treatment of trachoma, al-
though the infectious agent is not always elim-
inated, as judged by immunofluorescence.

Inclusion conjunctivitis may be treated with oral tetracyclines or with a combination of oral and topical agents.

CONTRAINDICATIONS

This drug is contraindicated in persons who have shown hypersensitivity to any of the tetracyclines or any of the components of the product formulation.

WARNINGS

DEMECLOCYCLINE HYDROCHLORIDE, LIKE OTHER TETRACYCLINE-CLASS ANTIBIOTICS, CAN CAUSE FETAL HARM WHEN ADMINISTERED TO A PREGNANT WOMAN. IF ANY TETRACYCLINE IS USED DURING PREGNANCY, OR IF THE PATIENT BECOMES PREGNANT WHILE TAKING THESE DRUGS, THE PATIENT SHOULD BE APPRISED OF THE POTENTIAL HAZARD TO THE FETUS.

THE USE OF DRUGS OF THE TETRACYCLINE CLASS DURING TOOTH DEVELOPMENT (LAST HALF OF PREGNANCY, INFANCY AND CHILDHOOD TO THE AGE OF 8 YEARS) MAY CAUSE PERMANENT DISCOLORATION OF THE TEETH (YELLOW-GRAY-BROWN).

This adverse reaction is more common during long-term use of the drugs but has been observed following repeated short-term courses. Enamel hypoplasia has also been reported. TETRACYCLINE DRUGS, THEREFORE, SHOULD NOT BE USED DURING TOOTH DEVELOPMENT UNLESS OTHER DRUGS ARE NOT LIKELY TO BE EFFECTIVE OR ARE CONTRAINDICATED.

All tetracyclines form a stable calcium complex in any bone-forming tissue. A decrease in fibula growth rate has been observed in premature human infants given oral tetracycline in doses of 25 mg/kg every six hours. This reaction was shown to be reversible when the drug was discontinued.

Results of animal studies indicate that tetracyclines cross the placenta, are found in fetal tissues, and can have toxic effects on the developing fetus (often related to retardation of skeletal development). Evidence of embryotoxicity has also been noted in animals treated early in pregnancy.

The anti-anabolic action of the tetracyclines may cause an increase in BUN. While this is not a problem in those with normal renal function, in patients with significantly impaired function, higher serum levels of tetracycline may lead to azotemia, hyperphosphatemia, and acidosis.

If renal impairment exists, even usual oral or parenteral doses may lead to excessive systemic accumulation of the drug and possible liver toxicity. Under such conditions, lower than usual total doses are indicated and, if therapy is prolonged, serum level determinations of the drug may be advisable.

Photosensitivity manifested by an exaggerated sunburn reaction has been observed in some individuals taking tetracyclines. Phototoxic reactions can occur in individuals taking demeclocycline, and are characterized by severe burns of exposed surfaces resulting from direct exposure of patients to sunlight during therapy with moderate or large doses of demeclocycline. Patients apt to be exposed to direct sunlight or ultraviolet light should be advised that this reaction can occur, and treatment should be discontinued at the first evidence of erythema of the skin.

Administration of DECLOMYCIN has resulted in appearance of the diabetes insipidus syndrome (polyuria, polydipsia and weakness) in some patients on long-term therapy. The syndrome has been shown to be nephrogenic, dose-dependent and reversible on discontinuance of therapy.

Patients who are experiencing central nervous system symptoms associated with demeclocycline therapy should be cautioned about driving vehicles or using hazardous machinery while on demeclocycline therapy.

PRECAUTIONS
General

Pseudotumor cerebri (benign intracranial hypertension) in adults has been associated with the use of tetracyclines. The usual clinical manifestations are headache and blurred vision. Bulging fontanels have been associated with the use of tetracyclines in infants. While both of these conditions and related symptoms usually resolve soon after discontinuation of the tetracycline, the possibility for permanent sequelae exists.

As with other antibiotic preparations, use of this drug may result in overgrowth of nonsusceptible organisms, including fungi. If superinfection occurs, the antibiotic should be discontinued and appropriate therapy should be instituted.

Incision and drainage or other surgical procedures should be performed in conjunction with antibiotic therapy, when indicated.

All infections due to Group A beta-hemolytic streptococci should be treated for at least ten days.

Interpretation of Bacteriologic Studies: Following a course of therapy, persistence for several days in both urine and blood of bacteriosuppressive levels of demeclocycline may interfere with culture studies. These levels should not be considered therapeutic.

Information for Patients

Photosensitivity manifested by an exaggerated sunburn reaction has been observed in some individuals taking tetracyclines. Patients apt to be exposed to direct sunlight of ultraviolet light should be advised that this reaction can occur with tetracycline drugs, and treatment should be discontinued at the first evidence of skin erythema.

Concurrent use of tetracyclines with oral contraceptives may render oral contraceptives less effective (See **Drug Interactions**.)

Patients should be informed that demeclocycline hydrochloride tablets should be taken at least 1 hour before meals or 2 hours after meals (See **DOSAGE AND ADMINISTRATION.**)

Unused supplies of tetracycline antibiotics should be discarded by the expiration date.

Patients who experience central nervous system symptoms while on demeclocycline therapy should be cautioned about driving vehicles or using hazardous machinery while receiving demeclocycline therapy.

Laboratory Tests

In venereal diseases when coexistent syphilis is suspected, darkfield examination should be done before treatment is started and the blood serology repeated monthly for at least 4 months.

In long-term therapy, periodic laboratory evaluation of organ systems, including hematopoietic, renal and hepatic studies should be performed.

All patients with gonorrhea should have a serologic test for syphilis at the time of diagnosis. Patients treated with demeclocycline hydrochloride should have a follow-up serologic test for syphilis after 3 months.

Drug Interactions

Because the tetracyclines have been shown to depress plasma prothrombin activity, patients who are on anticoagulant therapy may require downward adjustment of their anticoagulant dosage.

Since bacteriostatic drugs may interfere with the bactericidal action of penicillins, it is advisable to avoid giving tetracycline-class drugs in conjunction with penicillin.

Concurrent use of tetracyclines with oral contraceptives may render oral contraceptives less effective.

The concurrent use of tetracyclines and methoxyflurane has been reported to result in fatal renal toxicity.

Absorption of tetracyclines is impaired by antacids containing aluminum, calcium or magnesium, and by iron-containing preparations.

Carcinogenesis, Mutagenesis, Impairment of Fertility

Long-term studies in animals to evaluate carcinogenic potential of demeclocycline hydrochloride have not been conducted. However, there has been evidence of oncogenic activity in rats in studies with the related antibiotics oxytetracycline (adrenal and pituitary tumors) and minocycline (thyroid tumors).

Although mutagenicity studies of demeclocycline hydrochloride have not been conducted, positive results in *in vitro* mammalian cell assays (i.e., mouse lymphoma and Chinese hamster lung cells) have been reported for related antibiotics (tetracycline hydrochloride and oxytetracycline). (See **WARNINGS.)**

Demeclocycline hydrochloride had no effect on fertility when administered in the diet to male and female rats at a daily intake of 45 times the human dose.

Pregnancy

Teratogenic effects. Pregnancy Category D. (See **WARNINGS.**) Results of animal studies indicate that tetracyclines cross the placenta, are found in fetal tissues, and can have toxic effects on the developing fetus (often related to retardation of skeletal development). Evidence of embryotoxicity has been noted in animals treated early in pregnancy.

Nonteratogenic effects. (See **WARNINGS.**)

Nursing Mothers

Tetracyclines are excreted in human milk. Because of the potential for serious adverse reactions in nursing infants from the tetracyclines, a decision should be made whether to discontinue nursing or discontinue the drug, taking into account the importance of the drug to the mother. (See **WARNINGS.**)

Pediatric Use

Not for use in patients younger than eight years of age. (See **WARNINGS, PRECAUTIONS (General** subsection) and **DOSAGE AND ADMINISTRATION.**

ADVERSE REACTIONS

The following reactions have been reported in patients receiving tetracyclines:

Gastrointestinal: Anorexia, nausea, vomiting, diarrhea, glossitis, dysphagia, enterocolitis, pancreatitis, and inflammatory lesions (with monilial overgrowth) in the anogenital region, increases in liver enzymes, and hepatic toxicity has been reported rarely.

Rarely, hepatitis and liver failure have been reported. These reactions have been caused by both the oral and parenteral administration of tetracyclines.

Instances of esophageal ulcerations have been reported in patients receiving oral tetracyclines. Most of the patients were reported to have taken the medication immediately before lying down. (See **DOSAGE AND ADMINISTRATION.**)

Skin: Maculopapular and erythematous rashes, erythema multiforme. Exfoliative dermatitis has been reported but is uncommon. Fixed drug eruptions and Stevens-Johnson syndrome have been reported rarely. Lesions occurring on the glans penis have caused balanitis. Pigmentation of the skin and mucous membranes has also been reported. Photosensitivity is discussed. (See **WARNINGS.**)

Renal toxicity: Acute renal failure. Rise in BUN has been reported and is apparently dose related. Nephrogenic diabetes insipidus. (See **WARNINGS.**)

Hypersensitivity reactions: Urticaria, angioneurotic edema, polyarthralgia, anaphylaxis, anaphylactoid purpura, pericarditis, exacerbation of systemic lupus erythematosus, lupus-like syndrome, pulmonary infiltrates with eosinophilia.

Hematologic: Hemolytic anemia, thrombocytopenia, neutropenia and eosinophilia have been reported.

CNS: Pseudotumor cerebri (benign intracranial hypertension) in adults and bulging fontanels in infants (see **PRECAUTIONS—General**). Dizziness, headache, tinnitus, and visual disturbances have been reported. Myasthenic syndrome has been reported rarely.

Other: When given over prolonged periods, tetracyclines have been reported to produce brown-black microscopic discoloration of thyroid glands. No abnormalities of thyroid function studies are known to occur. Very rare cases of abnormal thyroid function have been reported.

Tooth discoloration has occurred in pediatric patients less than 8 years of age (see **WARNINGS**), and also has been reported rarely in adults.

OVERDOSAGE

In case of overdosage, discontinue medication, treat symptomatically and institute supportive measures.

Tetracyclines are not removed in significant quantities by hemodialysis or peritoneal dialysis.

DOSAGE AND ADMINISTRATION

Therapy should be continued for at least 24 to 48 hours after symptoms and fever have subsided.

Concomitant therapy: Absorption of tetracycline is impaired by antacids containing aluminum, calcium, or magnesium, and by iron-containing preparations. Foods and some dairy products also interfere with absorption. Oral forms of tetracycline should be given at least 1 hour before or 2 hours after meals.

In patients with renal impairment: (See **WARNINGS**.) Tetracyclines should be used cautiously in patients with impaired renal function. Total dosage should be decreased by reduction of recommended individual doses and/or by extending time intervals between doses.

In patients with liver impairment: Tetracyclines should be used cautiously in patients with impaired liver function. Total dosage should be decreased by reduction of recommended individual doses and/or by extending time intervals between doses.

In the treatment of streptococcal infections, a therapeutic dose of demeclocycline should be administered for at least ten days.

Administration of adequate amounts of fluid with the oral formulations of tetracyclines is recommended to wash down the drugs and reduce the risk of esophageal irritation and ulceration. (See **ADVERSE REACTIONS**.)

Adults: Usual daily dose—Four divided doses of 150 mg each or two divided doses of 300 mg each.

For children above eight years of age: Usual daily dose, 3–6 mg per pound body weight per day, depending upon the severity of the disease, divided into two to four doses.

Gonorrhea patients sensitive to penicillin may be treated with demeclocycline administered as an initial oral dose of 600 mg followed by 300 mg every 12 hours for four days to a total of 3 grams.

HOW SUPPLIED

DECLOMYCIN® demeclocycline hydrochloride Tablets, 150 mg are round, convex, red, film coated tablets, engraved with LL on one side and D11 on the other, are supplied as follows:

NDC 0005-9218-23—Bottle of 100

DECLOMYCIN® demeclocycline hydrochloride Tablets, 300 mg are round, convex, red, film coated tablets, engraved with LL on one side and D12 on the other, are supplied as follows:

NDC 0005-9270-29—Bottle of 48

Store at controlled room temperature 20°–25°C (68–77°F).

Manufactured by:
LEDERLE PHARMACEUTICAL DIVISION
American Cyanamid Company
Pearl River, NY 10965
CI 5189-4 Revised June 13, 2001

E.E.S.® ℞
[ē-ē-s]
(ERYTHROMYCIN ETHYLSUCCINATE)
Rx only

DESCRIPTION

Erythromycin is produced by a strain of *Saccharopolyspora erythraea* (formerly *Streptomyces erythraeus*) and belongs to the macrolide group of antibiotics. It is basic and readily forms salts with acids. The base, the stearate salt, and the esters are poorly soluble in water. Erythromycin ethylsuccinate is an ester of erythromycin suitable for oral administration. Erythromycin ethylsuccinate is known chemically as erythromycin 2′-(ethylsuccinate). The molecular formula is $C_{43}H_{75}NO_{16}$ and the molecular weight is 862.06. The structural formula is:
[See chemical structure below]
E.E.S. Granules are intended for reconstitution with water. Each 5-mL teaspoonful of reconstituted cherry-flavored suspension contains erythromycin ethylsuccinate equivalent to 200 mg of erythromycin.
The pleasant tasting, fruit-flavored liquids are supplied ready for oral administration.
E.E.S. 200 Liquid: Each 5-mL teaspoonful of fruit-flavored suspension contains erythromycin ethylsuccinate equivalent to 200 mg of erythromycin.
E.E.S. 400 Liquid: Each 5-mL teaspoonful of orange-flavored suspension contains erythromycin ethylsuccinate equivalent to 400 mg of erythromycin.
Granules and ready-made suspensions are intended primarily for pediatric use but can also be used in adults.
E.E.S. 400® Filmtab® Tablets: Each tablet contains erythromycin ethylsuccinate equivalent to 400 mg of erythromycin.
The Filmtab® tablets are intended primarily for adults or older children.

Inactive Ingredients:

E.E.S. 200 Liquid: FD&C Red No. 40, methylparaben, polysorbate 60, propylparaben, sodium citrate, sucrose, water, xanthan gum and natural and artificial flavors.
E.E.S. 400 Liquid: D&C Yellow No. 10, FD&C Yellow No. 6, methylparaben, polysorbate 60, propylparaben, sodium citrate, sucrose, water, xanthan gum and natural and artificial flavors.
E.E.S. Granules: Citric acid, FD&C Red No. 3, magnesium aluminum silicate, sodium carboxymethylcellulose, sodium citrate, sucrose and artificial flavor.
E.E.S. 400 Filmtab Tablets: Cellulosic polymers, confectioner's sugar (contains corn starch), corn starch, D&C Red No. 30, D&C Yellow No. 10, FD&C Red No. 40, magnesium stearate, polacrilin potassium, polyethylene glycol, propylene glycol, sodium citrate, sorbic acid, and titanium dioxide.

CLINICAL PHARMACOLOGY

Orally administered erythromycin ethylsuccinate suspensions and Filmtab tablets are readily and reliably absorbed. Comparable serum levels of erythromycin are achieved in the fasting and nonfasting states.
Erythromycin diffuses readily into most body fluids. Only low concentrations are normally achieved in the spinal fluid, but passage of the drug across the blood-brain barrier increases in meningitis. In the presence of normal hepatic function, erythromycin is concentrated in the liver and excreted in the bile; the effect of hepatic dysfunction on excretion of erythromycin by the liver into the bile is not known. Less than 5 percent of the orally administered dose of erythromycin is excreted in active form in the urine.
Erythromycin crosses the placental barrier, but fetal plasma levels are low. The drug is excreted in human milk.
Microbiology:
Erythromycin acts by inhibition of protein synthesis by binding 50 *S* ribosomal subunits of susceptible organisms. It does not affect nucleic acid synthesis. Antagonism has been demonstrated *in vitro* between erythromycin and clindamycin, lincomycin, and chloramphenicol.
Many strains of *Haemophilus influenzae* are resistant to erythromycin alone but are susceptible to erythromycin and sulfonamides used concomitantly.
Staphylocci resistant to erythromycin may emerge during a course of therapy.

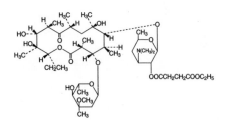

Erythromycin has been shown to be active against most strains of the following microorganisms, both *in vitro* and in clinical infections as described in the **INDICATIONS AND USAGE** section.

Gram-positive Organisms:

Corynebacterium diphtheriae

Corynebacterium minutissimum

Listeria monocytogenes

Staphylococcus aureus (resistant organisms may emerge during treatment)

Streptococcus pneumoniae

Streptococcus pyogenes

Gram-negative Organisms:

Bordetella pertussis

Legionella pneumophila

Neisseria gonorrhoeae

Other Microorganisms:

Chlamydia trachomatis

Entamoeba histolytica

Mycoplasma pneumoniae

Treponema pallidum

Ureaplasma urealyticum

The following *in vitro* data are available, **but their clinical significance is unknown.**

Erythromycin exhibits *in vitro* minimal inhibitory concentrations (MIC's) of 0.5 µg/mL or less against most (≥90%) strains of the following microorganisms; however, the safety and effectiveness of erythromycin in treating clinical infections due to these microorganisms have not been established in adequate and well controlled clinical trials.

Gram-positive Organisms:

Viridans group streptococci

Gram-negative Organisms:

Moraxella catarrhalis

Susceptibility Tests:

Dilution Techniques:

Quantitative methods are used to determine antimicrobial minimum inhibitory concentrations (MIC's). These MIC's provide estimates of the susceptibility of bacteria to antimicrobial compounds. The MIC's should be determined using a standardized procedure. Standardized procedures are based on a dilution method[1] (broth or agar) or equivalent with standardized inoculum concentrations and standardized concentrations of erythromycin powder. The MIC values should be interpreted according to the following criteria:

MIC (µg/mL)	Interpretation
≤0.5	Susceptible (S)
1–4	Intermediate (I)
≥8	Resistant (R)

A report of "Susceptible" indicates that the pathogen is likely to be inhibited if the antimicrobial compound in the blood reaches the concentrations usually achievable. A report of "Intermediate" indicates that the result should be considered equivocal, and, if the microorganism is not fully susceptible to alternative, clinically feasible drugs, the test should be repeated. This category implies possible clinical applicability in body sites where the drug is physiologically concentrated or in situations where high dosage of drug can be used. This category also provides a buffer zone which prevents small uncontrolled technical factors from causing major discrepancies in interpretation. A report of "Resistant" indicates that the pathogen is not likely to be inhibited if the antimicrobial compound in the blood reaches the concentrations usually achievable; other therapy should be selected.

Standardized susceptibility test procedures require the use of laboratory control microorganisms to control the technical aspects of the laboratory procedures. Standard erythromycin powder should provide the following MIC values:

Microorganism	MIC (µg/mL)
S. aureus ATCC 25923	0.12–0.5
E. faecalis ATCC 29212	1–4

Diffusion Techniques:

Quantitative methods that require measurement of zone diameters also provide reproducible estimates of the susceptibility of bacteria to antimicrobial compounds. One such standardized procedure[2] requires the use of standardized inoculum concentrations. This procedure uses paper disks impregnated with 15-µg erythromycin to test the susceptibility of microorganisms to erythromycin.

Reports from the laboratory providing results of the standard single-disk susceptibility test with a 15-µg erythromycin disk should be interpreted according to the following criteria:

Zone Diameter (mm)	Interpretation
≥23	Susceptible (S)
14–22	Intermediate (I)
≤13	Resistant (R)

Interpretation should be as stated above for results using dilution techniques. Interpretation involves correlation of the diameter obtained in the disk test with the MIC for erythromycin.

As with standardized dilution techniques, diffusion methods require the use of laboratory control microorganisms that are used to control the technical aspects of the laboratory procedures. For the diffusion technique, the 15-µg erythromycin disk should provide the following zone diameters in these laboratory test quality control strains:

Microorganism	Zone Diameter (mm)
S. aureus ATCC 25923	22–30

INDICATIONS AND USAGE

E.E.S. is indicated in the treatment of infections caused by susceptible strains of the designated organisms in the diseases listed below:

Upper respiratory tract infections of mild to moderate degree caused by *Streptococcus pyogenes, Streptococcus pneumoniae,* or *Haemophilus influenzae* (when used concomitantly with adequate doses of sulfonamides, since many strains of *H. influenzae* are not susceptible to the erythromycin concentrations ordinarily achieved). (See appropriate sulfonamide labeling for prescribing information.)

Lower-respiratory tract infections of mild to moderate severity caused by *Streptococcus pneumoniae* or *Streptococcus pyogenes.*

Listeriosis caused by *Listeria monocytogenes.*

Pertussis (whooping cough) caused by *Bordetella pertussis.* Erythromycin is effective in eliminating the organism from the nasopharynx of infected individuals rendering them noninfectious. Some clinical studies suggest that erythromycin may be helpful in the prophylaxis of pertussis in exposed susceptible individuals.

Respiratory tract infections due to *Mycoplasma pneumoniae.*

Skin and skin structure infections of mild to moderate severity caused by *Streptococcus pyogenes* or *Staphylococcus aureus* (resistant staphylococci may emerge during treatment).

Diphtheria: Infections due to *Corynebacterium diphtheriae,* as an adjunct to antitoxin, to prevent establishment of carriers and to eradicate the organism in carriers.

Erythrasma: In the treatment of infections due to *Corynebacterium minutissimum.*

Intestinal amebiasis caused by *Entamoeba histolytica* (oral erythromycins only). Extraenteric amebiasis requires treatment with other agents.

Acute pelvic inflammatory disease caused by *Neisseria gonorrhoeae:* As an alternative drug in treatment of acute pelvic inflammatory disease caused by *N. gonorrhoeae* in female patients with a history of sensitivity to penicillin. Patients should have a serologic test for syphilis before receiving erythromycin as treatment of gonorrhea and a follow-up serologic test for syphilis after 3 months.

Syphilis caused by *Treponema pallidum:* Erythromycin is an alternate choice of treatment for primary syphilis in patients allergic to the penicillins. In treatment of primary syphilis, spinal fluid examinations should be done before treatment and as part of follow-up after therapy.

Erythromycins are indicated for the treatment of the following infections caused by *Chlamydia trachomatis:* conjunctivitis of the newborn, pneumonia of infancy, and urogenital infections during pregnancy. When tetracyclines are contraindicated or not tolerated, erythromycin is indicated for the treatment of uncomplicated urethral, endocervical, or rectal infections in adults due to *Chlamydia trachomatis.* When tetracyclines are contraindicated or not tolerated, erythromycin is indicated for the treatment of nongonococcal urethritis caused by *Ureaplasma urealyticum.*

Legionnaires' Disease caused by *Legionella pneumophila.* Although no controlled clinical efficacy studies have been conducted, *in vitro* and limited preliminary clinical data suggest that erythromycin may be effective in treating Legionnaires' Disease.

Prophylaxis:

Prevention of Initial Attacks of Rheumatic Fever: Penicillin is considered by the American Heart Association to be the drug of choice in the prevention of initial attacks of rheumatic fever (treatment of *Streptococcus pyogenes* infections of the upper respiratory tract, e.g., tonsillitis or pharyngitis). Erythromycin is indicated for the treatment of penicillin-allergic patients.[3] The therapeutic dose should be administered for 10 days.

Prevention of Recurrent Attacks of Rheumatic Fever: Penicillin or sulfonamides are considered by the American Heart Association to be the drugs of choice in the prevention of recurrent attacks of rheumatic fever. In patients who are allergic to penicillin and sulfonamides, oral erythromycin is recommended by the American Heart Association in the long-term prophylaxis of streptococcal pharyngitis (for the prevention of recurrent attacks of rheumatic fever).[3]

CONTRAINDICATIONS

Erythromycin is contraindicated in patients with known hypersensitivity to this antibiotic.

Erythromycin is contraindicated in patients taking terfenadine, astemizole, or cisapride. (See **PRECAUTIONS** - *Drug Interactions.*)

WARNINGS

There have been reports of hepatic dysfunction, including increased liver enzymes, and hepatocellular and/or cholestatic hepatitis, with or without jaundice, occurring in patients receiving oral erythromycin products.

There have been reports suggesting that erythromycin does not reach the fetus in adequate concentration to prevent congenital syphilis. Infants born to women treated during pregnancy with oral erythromycin for early syphilis should be treated with an appropriate penicillin regimen.

Pseudomembranous colitis has been reported with nearly all antibacterial agents, including erythromycin, and may range in severity from mild to life threatening. Therefore, it is important to consider this diagnosis in patients who present with diarrhea subsequent to the administration of antibacterial agents.

Treatment with antibacterial agents alters the normal flora of the colon and may permit overgrowth of clostridia. Studies indicate that a toxin produced by *Clostridium difficile* is a primary cause of "antibiotic-associated colitis". After the diagnosis of pseudomembranous colitis has been established, therapeutic measures should be initiated. Mild cases of pseudomembranous colitis usually respond to discontinuation of the drug alone. In moderate to severe cases, consideration should be given to management with fluids and electrolytes, protein supplementation, and treatment with an antibacterial drug clinically effective against *Clostridium difficile* colitis.

Rhabdomyolysis with or without renal impairment has been reported in seriously ill patients receiving erythromycin concomitantly with lovastatin. Therefore, patients receiving concomitant lovastatin and erythromycin should be carefully monitored for creatine kinase (CK) and serum transaminase levels. (See package insert for lovastatin.)

PRECAUTIONS

General: Since erythromycin is principally excreted by the liver, caution should be exercised when erythromycin is administered to patients with impaired hepatic function. (See **CLINICAL PHARMACOLOGY** and **WARNINGS** sections.)

There have been reports that erythromycin may aggravate the weakness of patients with myasthenia gravis.

Prolonged or repeated use of erythromycin may result in an overgrowth of nonsusceptible bacteria or fungi. If superinfection occurs, erythromycin should be discontinued and appropriate therapy instituted.

When indicated, incision and drainage or other surgical procedures should be performed in conjunction with antibiotic therapy.

Drug Interactions: Erythromycin use in patients who are receiving high doses of theophylline may be associated with an increase in serum theophylline levels and potential theophylline toxicity. In case of theophylline toxicity and/or elevated serum theophylline levels, the dose of theophylline should be reduced while the patient is receiving concomitant erythromycin therapy.

Concomitant administration of erythromycin and digoxin has been reported to result in elevated digoxin serum levels.

There have been reports of increased anticoagulant effects when erythromycin and oral anticoagulants were used concomitantly. Increased anticoagulation effects due to interactions of erythromycin with various oral anticoagulants may be more pronounced in the elderly.

Concurrent use of erythromycin and ergotamine or dihydroergotamine has been associated in some patients with acute ergot toxicity characterized by severe peripheral vasospasm and dysesthesia.

Erythromycin has been reported to decrease the clearance of triazolam and midazolam and, thus, may increase the pharmacologic effect of these benzodiazepines.

The use of erythromycin in patients concurrently taking drugs metabolized by the cytochrome P450 system may be associated with elevations in serum levels of these other drugs. There have been reports of interactions of erythromycin with carbamazepine, cyclosporine, tacrolimus, hexobarbital, phenytoin, alfentanil, cisapride, disopyramide, lovastatin, bromocriptine, valproate, terfenadine, and astemizole. Serum concentrations of drugs metabolized by the cytochrome P450 system should be monitored closely in patients concurrently receiving erythromycin.

Erythromycin has been reported to significantly alter the metabolism of the nonsedating antihistamines terfenadine and astemizole when taken concomitantly. Rare cases of serious cardiovascular adverse events, including electrocardiographic QT/QT$_c$ interval prolongation, cardiac arrest, torsades de pointes, and other ventricular arrhythmias have been observed. (See **CONTRAINDICATIONS**.) In addition, deaths have been reported rarely with concomitant administration of terfenadine and erythromycin.

There have been post-marketing reports of drug interactions when erythromycin is coadministered with cisapride, resulting in QT prolongation, cardiac arrhythmias, ventricular tachycardia, ventricular fibrillation, and torsades de pointes, most likely due to inhibition of hepatic metabolism of cisapride by erythromycin. Fatalities have been reported. (See **CONTRAINDICATIONS**.)

Drug/Laboratory Test Interactions: Erythromycin interferes with the fluorometric determination of urinary catecholamines.

Carcinogenesis, Mutagenesis, Impairment of Fertility: Long-term (2-year) oral studies in rats with erythromycin ethylsuccinate and erythromycin base did not provide evidence of tumorigenicity. Mutagenicity studies have not been conducted. There was no apparent effect on male or female fertility in rats fed erythromycin (base) at levels up to 0.25% of diet.

Pregnancy: Teratogenic Effects. Pregnancy Category B: There is no evidence of teratogenicity or any other adverse effect on reproduction in female rats fed erythromycin base (up to 0.25% of diet) prior to and during mating, during gestation, and through weaning of two successive litters. There are, however, no adequate and well-controlled studies in pregnant women. Because animal reproduction studies are not always predictive of human response, this drug should be used during pregnancy only if clearly needed.

Labor and Delivery: The effect of erythromycin on labor and delivery is unknown.

Nursing Mothers: Erythromycin is excreted in human milk. Caution should be exercised when erythromycin is administered to a nursing woman.

Pediatric Use: See **INDICATIONS AND USAGE** and **DOSAGE AND ADMINISTRATION** sections.

ADVERSE REACTIONS

The most frequent side effects of oral erythromycin preparations are gastrointestinal and are dose-related. They include nausea, vomiting, abdominal pain, diarrhea and anorexia. Symptoms of hepatitis, hepatic dysfunction and/or abnormal liver function test results may occur. (See **WARNINGS**.)

Onset of pseudomembranous colitis symptoms may occur during or after antibiotic treatment. (See **WARNINGS**.)

Rarely, erythromycin has been associated with the production of ventricular arrhythmias, including ventricular tachycardia and torsades de pointes, in individuals with prolonged QT intervals.

Allergic reactions ranging from urticaria to anaphylaxis have occurred. Skin reactions ranging from mild eruptions to erythema multiforme, Stevens-Johnson syndrome, and toxic epidermal necrolysis have been reported rarely.

There have been isolated reports of reversible hearing loss occurring chiefly in patients with renal insufficiency and in patients receiving high doses of erythromycin.

OVERDOSAGE

In case of overdosage, erythromycin should be discontinued. Overdosage should be handled with the prompt elimination of unabsorbed drug and all other appropriate measures should be instituted.

Erythromycin is not removed by peritoneal dialysis or hemodialysis.

DOSAGE AND ADMINISTRATION

Erythromycin ethylsuccinate suspensions and Filmtab tablets may be administered without regard to meals.

Children: Age, weight, and severity of the infection are important factors in determining the proper dosage. In mild to moderate infections the usual dosage of erythromycin ethylsuccinate for children is 30 to 50 mg/kg/day in equally divided doses every 6 hours. For more severe infections this dosage may be doubled. If twice-a-day dosage is desired, one-half of the total daily dose may be given every 12 hours. Doses may also be given three times daily by administering one-third of the total daily dose every 8 hours.

The following dosage schedule is suggested for mild to moderate infections:

Body Weight	Total Daily Dose
Under 10 lbs	30–50 mg/kg/day 15–25 mg/kg/q 12 h
10 to 15 lbs	200 mg
16 to 25 lbs	400 mg
26 to 50 lbs	800 mg
51 to 100 lbs	1200 mg
over 100 lbs	1600 mg

Adults: 400 mg erythromycin ethylsuccinate every 6 hours is the usual dose. Dosage may be increased up to 4 g per day according to the severity of the infection. If twice-a-day dosage is desired, one-half of the total daily dose may be given every 12 hours. Doses may also be given three times daily by administering one-third of the total daily dose every 8 hours.

For adult dosage calculation, use a ratio of 400 mg of erythromycin activity as the ethylsuccinate to 250 mg of erythromycin activity as the stearate, base or estolate.

In the treatment of streptococcal infections, a therapeutic dosage of erythromycin ethylsuccinate should be administered for at least 10 days. In continuous prophylaxis against recurrences of streptococcal infections in persons with a history of rheumatic heart disease, the usual dosage is 400 mg twice a day.

For treatment of urethritis due to *C. trachomatis* or *U. urealyticum*: 800 mg three times a day for 7 days.

For treatment of primary syphilis: Adults: 48 to 64 g given in divided doses over a period of 10 to 15 days.

For intestinal amebiasis: Adults: 400 mg four times daily for 10 to 14 days. Children: 30 to 50 mg/kg/day in divided doses for 10 to 14 days.

For use in pertussis: Although optimal dosage and duration have not been established, doses of erythromycin utilized in reported clinical studies were 40 to 50 mg/kg/day, given in divided doses for 5 to 14 days.

For treatment of Legionnaires' Disease: Although optimal doses have not been established, doses utilized in reported clinical data were those recommended above (1.6 to 4 g daily in divided doses.)

HOW SUPPLIED

E.E.S. 200 LIQUID (erythromycin ethylsuccinate oral suspension, USP) is supplied in 1 pint bottles (**NDC** 0074-6306-16) and in packages of six l00-mL bottles (**NDC** 0074-6306-13).

E.E.S. 400® LIQUID (erythromycin ethylsuccinate oral suspension, USP) is supplied in 1 pint bottles (**NDC** 0074-6373-16) and in packages of six l00-mL bottles (**NDC** 0074-6373-13). Both liquid products require refrigeration to preserve taste until dispensed. Refrigeration by patient is not required if used within 14 days.

E.E.S. GRANULES (erythromycin ethylsuccinate for oral suspension, USP) is supplied in l00-mL (**NDC** 0074-6369-02) and 200-mL (**NDC** 0074-6369-10) size bottles.

E.E.S. 400 Filmtab tablets (erythromycin ethylsuccinate tablets, USP) 400 mg, are supplied as pink tablets imprinted with the Abbott logo, ⌐⌐ , and two letter Abbo-Code designation, EE, in bottles of 100 (**NDC** 0074-5729-13), 500

(**NDC** 0074-5729-53) and 1000 (**NDC** 0074-5729-19) and in ABBO-PAC unit dose strip packages of 100 (**NDC** 0074-5729-11).

Recommended storage: Store tablets below 86°F (30°C).

Store granules, prior to mixing, below 86°F (30°C). After mixing, refrigerate and use within 10 days.

REFERENCES

1. National Committee for Clinical Laboratory Standards, *Methods for Dilution Antimicrobial Susceptibility Tests for Bacteria that Grow Aerobically*, Third Edition. Approved Standard NCCLS Document M7-A3, Vol. 13, No. 25. NCCLS, Villanova, PA, December 1993.

2. National Committee for Clinical Laboratory Standards, *Performance Standards for Antimicrobial Disk Susceptibility Tests*, Fifth Edition. Approved Standard NCCLS Document M2-A5, Vol. 13, No. 24. NCCLS, Villanova, PA, December 1993.

3. Committee on Rheumatic Fever, Endocarditis, and Kawasaki Disease of the Council on Cardiovascular Disease in the Young, the American Heart Association: Prevention of Rheumatic Fever. *Circulation*. 78(4): 1082-1086, October 1988.

Filmtab—Film-sealed tablets, Abbott.

Ref. 03-5016-R20

Revised: February, 2000

ABBOTT LABORATORIES
NORTH CHICAGO, IL 60064, U.S.A.

ERYTHROMYCIN ℞
Base Filmtab®
ERYTHROMYCIN TABLETS, USP
℞ **only**

DESCRIPTION

Erythromycin Base Filmtab (erythromycin tablets, USP) is an antibacterial product containing erythromycin, USP, in a unique, non-enteric film coating for oral administration. Erythromycin Base Filmtab tablets are available in two strengths containing either 250 mg or 500 mg of erythromycin base.

Erythromycin is produced by a strain of *Saccharopolyspora erythraea* (formerly *Streptomyces erythraeus*) and belongs to the macrolide group of antibiotics. It is basic and readily forms salts with acids. Erythromycin is a white to off-white powder, slightly soluble in water, and soluble in alcohol, chloroform, and ether. Erythromycin is known chemically as (3R*, 4S*, 5S*, 6R*, 7R*, 9R*, 11R*, 12R*, 13S*, 14R*)-4-[(2,6-dideoxy-3-C-methyl-3-O-methyl-α-L-*ribo*-hexopyranosyl)oxy]-14-ethyl-7,12,13-trihydroxy-3,5,7,9,11,13-hexamethyl-6-[[3,4,6-trideoxy-3-(dimethylamino)-β-D-*xylo*-hexopyranosyl]oxy]oxacyclotetradecane-2,10-dione. The molecular formula is $C_{37}H_{67}NO_{13}$, and the molecular weight is 733.94. The structural formula is:

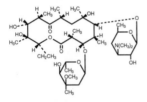

Inactive Ingredients:
Colloidal silicon dioxide, croscarmellose sodium, crospovidone, D&C Red No. 30 Aluminum Lake, hydroxypropyl cellulose, hydroxypropyl methylcellulose, hydroxypropyl methylcellulose phthalate, magnesium stearate, microcrystalline cellulose, povidone, polyethylene glycol, propylene glycol, sodium citrate, sodium hydroxide, sorbic acid, sorbitan monooleate, talc, and titanium dioxide.

CLINICAL PHARMACOLOGY

Orally administered erythromycin base and its salts are readily absorbed in the microbiologically active form. Interindividual variations in the absorption of erythromycin are, however, observed, and some patients do not achieve optimal serum levels. Erythromycin is largely bound to plasma proteins. After absorption, erythromycin diffuses readily into most body fluids. In the absence of meningeal inflammation, low concentrations are normally achieved in the spinal fluid but the passage of the drug across the blood-brain barrier increases in meningitis. Erythromycin crosses

the placental barrier, but fetal plasma levels are low. The drug is excreted in human milk. Erythromycin is not removed by peritoneal dialysis or hemodialysis.

In the presence of normal hepatic function, erythromycin is concentrated in the liver and is excreted in the bile; the effect of hepatic dysfunction on biliary excretion of erythromycin is not known. After oral administration, less than 5% of the administered dose can be recovered in the active form in the urine.

Optimal blood levels are obtained when Erythromycin Base Filmtab tablets are given in the fasting state (at least 1/2 hour and preferably 2 hours before meals). Bioavailability data are available from Abbott Laboratories, Dept. 42W.

Microbiology:
Erythromycin acts by inhibition of protein synthesis by binding 50 S ribosomal subunits of susceptible organisms. It does not affect nucleic acid synthesis. Antagonism has been demonstrated *in vitro* between erythromycin and clindamycin, lincomycin, and chloramphenicol.

Many strains of *Haemophilus influenzae* are resistant to erythromycin alone, but are susceptible to erythromycin and sulfonamides used concomitantly.

Staphylococci resistant to erythromycin may emerge during a course of erythromycin therapy. Erythromycin has been shown to be active against most strains of the following microorganisms, both *in vitro* and in clinical infections as described in the **INDICATIONS AND USAGE** section.

Gram-positive organisms:
  Corynebacterium diphtheriae
  Corynebacterium minutissimum
  Listeria monocytogenes
  Staphylococcus aureus (resistant organisms may emerge during treatment)
  Streptococcus pneumoniae
  Streptococcus pyogenes
Gram-negative organisms:
  Bordetella pertussis
  Legionella pneumophila
  Neisseria gonorrhoeae
Other microorganisms:
  Chlamydia trachomatis
  Entamoeba histolytica
  Mycoplasma pneumoniae
  Treponema pallidum
  Ureaplasma urealyticum
The following *in vitro* data are available, **but their clinical significance is unknown.**
Erythromycin exhibits *in vitro* minimal inhibitory concentrations (MIC's) of 0.5 µg/mL or less against most (≥90%) strains of the following microorganisms; however, the safety and effectiveness of erythromycin in treating clinical infections due to these microorganisms have not been established in adequate and well-controlled clinical trials.

Gram-positive organisms:
  Viridans group streptococci

Gram-negative organisms:
Moraxella catarrhalis
Susceptibility Tests:
Dilution Techniques:
Quantitative methods are used to determine antimicrobial minimum inhibitory concentrations (MIC's). These MIC's provide estimates of the susceptibility of bacteria to antimicrobial compounds. The MIC's should be determined using a standardized procedure. Standardized procedures are based on a dilution method[1] (broth or agar) or equivalent with standardized inoculum concentrations and standardized concentrations of erythromycin powder. The MIC values should be interpreted according to the following criteria:

MIC (µg/mL)	Interpretation
≤0.5	Susceptible (S)
1–4	Intermediate (I)
≥8	Resistant (R)

A report of "Susceptible" indicates that the pathogen is likely to be inhibited if the antimicrobial compound in the blood reaches the concentrations usually achievable. A report of "Intermediate" indicates that the result should be considered equivocal, and, if the microorganism is not fully susceptible to alternative, clinically feasible drugs, the test should be repeated. This category implies possible clinical applicability in body sites where the drug is physiologically concentrated or in situations where high dosage of drug can be used. This category also provides a buffer zone which prevents small uncontrolled technical factors from causing major discrepancies in interpretation. A report of "Resistant" indicates that the pathogen is not likely to be inhibited if the antimicrobial compound in the blood reaches the concentrations usually achievable; other therapy should be selected.
Standardized susceptibility test procedures require the use of laboratory control microorganisms to control the technical aspects of the laboratory procedures. Standard erythromycin powder should provide the following MIC values:

Microorganism	MIC (µg/mL)
S. aureus ATCC 29213	0.12–0.5
E. faecalis ATCC 29212	1–4

Diffusion Techniques:
Quantitative methods that require measurement of zone diameters also provide reproducible estimates of the susceptibility of bacteria to antimicrobial compounds. One such standardized procedure[2] requires the use of standardized inoculum concentrations. This procedure uses paper disks impregnated with 15-µg erythromycin to test the susceptibility of microorganisms to erythromycin.

Reports from the laboratory providing results of the standard single-disk susceptibility test with a 15-µg erythromycin disk should be interpreted according to the following criteria:

Zone Diameter (mm)	Interpretation
≥23	Susceptible (S)
14–22	Intermediate (I)
≤13	Resistant (R)

Interpretation should be as stated above for results using dilution techniques. Interpretation involves correlation of the diameter obtained in the disk test with the MIC for erythromycin.
As with standardized dilution techniques, diffusion methods require the use of laboratory control microorganisms that are used to control the technical aspects of the laboratory procedures. For the diffusion technique, the 15-µg erythromycin disk should provide the following zone diameters in these laboratory test quality control strains:

Microorganism	Zone Diameter (mm)
S. aureus ATCC 25923	22–30

INDICATIONS AND USAGE
Erythromycin Base Filmtab tablets are indicated in the treatment of infections caused by susceptible strains of the designated microorganisms in the diseases listed below:
Upper respiratory tract infections of mild to moderate degree caused by *Streptococcus pyogenes; Streptococcus pneumoniae; Haemophilus influenzae* (when used concomitantly with adequate doses of sulfonamides, since many strains of *H. influenzae* are not susceptible to the erythromycin concentrations ordinarily achieved). (See appropriate sulfonamide labeling for prescribing information.)
Lower respiratory tract infections of mild to moderate severity caused by *Streptococcus pyogenes* or *Streptococcus pneumoniae.*
Listeriosis caused by *Listeria monocytogenes.*
Respiratory tract infections due to *Mycoplasma pneumoniae.*
Skin and skin structure infections of mild to moderate severity caused by *Streptococcus pyogenes* or *Staphylococcus aureus* (resistant staphylococci may emerge during treatment).
Pertussis (whooping cough) caused by *Bordetella pertussis.* Erythromycin is effective in eliminating the organism from the nasopharynx of infected individuals, rendering them noninfectious. Some clinical studies suggest that erythromycin may be helpful in the prophylaxis of pertussis in exposed susceptible individuals.
Diphtheria: Infections due to *Corynebacterium diphtheriae,* as an adjunct to antitoxin, to prevent establishment of carriers and to eradicate the organism in carriers.

Erythrasma—In the treatment of infections due to *Corynebacterium minutissimum*.

Intestinal amebiasis caused by *Entamoeba histolytica* (oral erythromycins only). Extraenteric amebiasis requires treatment with other agents.

Acute pelvic inflammatory disease caused by *Neisseria gonorrhoeae*: Erythrocin® Lactobionate-I.V. (erythromycin lactobionate for injection, USP) followed by erythromycin base orally, as an alternative drug in treatment of acute pelvic inflammatory disease caused by *N. gonorrhoeae* in female patients with a history of sensitivity to penicillin. Patients should have a serologic test for syphilis before receiving erythromycin as treatment of gonorrhea and a follow-up serologic test for syphilis after 3 months.

Erythromycins are indicated for treatment of the following infections caused by *Chlamydia trachomatis:* conjunctivitis of the newborn, pneumonia of infancy, and urogenital infections during pregnancy. When tetracyclines are contraindicated or not tolerated, erythromycin is indicated for the treatment of uncomplicated urethral, endocervical, or rectal infections in adults due to *Chlamydia trachomatis*.[3]

When tetracyclines are contraindicated or not tolerated, erythromycin is indicated for the treatment of nongonococcal urethritis caused by *Ureaplasma urealyticum*.[3]

Primary syphilis caused by *Treponema pallidum*. Erythromycin (oral forms only) is an alternative choice of treatment for primary syphilis in patients allergic to the penicillins. In treatment of primary syphilis, spinal fluid should be examined before treatment and as part of the follow-up after therapy.

Legionnaires' Disease caused by *Legionella pneumophila*. Although no controlled clinical efficacy studies have been conducted, *in vitro* and limited preliminary clinical data suggest that erythromycin may be effective in treating Legionnaires' Disease.

Prophylaxis

Prevention of Initial Attacks of Rheumatic Fever—Penicillin is considered by the American Heart Association to be the drug of choice in the prevention of initial attacks of rheumatic fever (treatment of *Streptococcus pyogenes* infections of the upper respiratory tract e.g., tonsillitis, or pharyngitis).[3] Erythromycin is indicated for the treatment of penicillin-allergic patients. The therapeutic dose should be administered for ten days.

Prevention of Recurrent Attacks of Rheumatic Fever—Penicillin or sulfonamides are considered by the American Heart Association to be the drugs of choice in the prevention of recurrent attacks of rheumatic fever. In patients who are allergic to penicillin and sulfonamides, oral erythromycin is recommended by the American Heart Association in the longterm prophylaxis of streptococcal pharyngitis (for the prevention of recurrent attacks of rheumatic fever).[3]

CONTRAINDICATIONS

Erythromycin is contraindicated in patients with known hypersensitivity to this antibiotic. Erythromycin is contraindicated in patients taking terfenadine, astemizole, or cisapride. (See **PRECAUTIONS**—*Drug Interactions*.)

WARNINGS

There have been reports of hepatic dysfunction, including increased liver enzymes, and hepatocellular and/or cholestatic hepatitis, with or without jaundice, occurring in patients receiving oral erythromycin products.

There have been reports suggesting that erythromycin does not reach the fetus in adequate concentration to prevent congenital syphilis. Infants born to women treated during pregnancy with oral erythromycin for early syphilis should be treated with an appropriate penicillin regimen.

Rhabdomyolysis with or without renal impairment has been reported in seriously ill patients receiving erythromycin concomitantly with lovastatin. Therefore, patients receiving concomitant lovastatin and erythromycin should be carefully monitored for creatine kinase (CK) and serum transaminase levels. (See package insert for lovastatin.)

Pseudomembranous colitis has been reported with nearly all antibacterial agents, including erythromycin, and may range in severity from mild to life threatening. Therefore, it is important to consider this diagnosis in patients who present with diarrhea subsequent to the administration of antibacterial agents.

Treatment with antibacterial agents alters the normal flora of the colon and may permit overgrowth of clostridia. Studies indicate that a toxin produced by *Clostridium difficile* is a primary cause of "antibiotic-associated colitis".

After the diagnosis of pseudomembranous colitis has been established, therapeutic measures should be initiated. Mild cases of pseudomembranous colitis usually respond to discontinuation of the drug alone. In moderate to severe cases, consideration should be given to management with fluids and electrolytes, protein supplementation, and treatment with an antibacterial drug clinically effective against *Clostridium difficile* colitis.

PRECAUTIONS

General: Since erythromycin is principally excreted by the liver, caution should be exercised when erythromycin is administered to patients with impaired hepatic function. (See **CLINICAL PHARMACOLOGY** and **WARNINGS**.)

There have been reports that erythromycin may aggravate the weakness of patients with myasthenia gravis.

Prolonged or repeated use of erythromycin may result in an overgrowth of nonsusceptible bacteria or fungi. If superinfection occurs, erythromycin should be discontinued and appropriate therapy instituted.

When indicated, incision and drainage or other surgical procedures should be performed in conjunction with antibiotic therapy.

Drug Interactions: Erythromycin use in patients who are receiving high doses of theophylline may be associated with an increase in serum theophylline levels and potential theophylline toxicity. In case of theophylline toxicity and/or elevated serum theophylline levels, the dose of theophylline should be reduced while the patient is receiving concomitant erythromycin therapy.

Concomitant administration of erythromycin and digoxin has been reported to result in elevated digoxin serum levels.

There have been reports of increased anticoagulant effects when erythromycin and oral anticoagulants were used concomitantly. Increased anticoagulation effects due to interactions of erythromycin with oral anticoagulants may be more pronounced in the elderly.

Concurrent use of erythromycin and ergotamine or dihydroergotamine has been associated in some patients with acute ergot toxicity characterized by severe peripheral vasospasm and dysesthesia.

Erythromycin has been reported to decrease the clearance of triazolam and midazolam and, thus, may increase the pharmacologic effect of these benzodiazepines.

The use of erythromycin in patients concurrently taking drugs metabolized by the cytochrome P450 system may be associated with elevations in serum levels of these other drugs. There have been reports of interactions of erythromycin with carbamazepine, cyclosporine, tacrolimus, hexobarbital, phenytoin, alfentanil, cisapride, disopyramide, lovastatin, bromocriptine, valproate, terfenadine, and astemizole. Serum concentrations of drugs metabolized by the cytochrome P450 system should be monitored closely in patients concurrently receiving erythromycin.

Erythromycin has been reported to significantly alter the metabolism of the nonsedating antihistamines terfenadine and astemizole when taken concomitantly. Rare cases of serious cardiovascular adverse events, including electrocardiographic QT/QT$_c$ interval prolongation, cardiac arrest, torsades de pointes, and other ventricular arrhythmias, have been observed. (See **CONTRAINDICATIONS**.) In addition, deaths have been reported rarely with concomitant administration of terfenadine and erythromycin.

There have been post-marketing reports of drug interactions when erythromycin is coadministered with cisapride, resulting in cardiac arrhythmias (QT prolongation, ventricular tachycardia, ventricular fibrillation, and torsades de pointes) most likely due to the inhibition of hepatic metabolism of cisapride by erythromycin. Fatalities have been reported. (See **CONTRAINDICATIONS**).

Drug/Laboratory Test interactions: Erythromycin interferes with the fluorometric determination of urinary catecholamines.

Carcinogenesis, Mutagenesis, Impairment of Fertility: Long-term (2-year) oral studies conducted in rats with erythromycin base did not provide evidence of tumorigenicity. Mutagenicity studies have not been conducted. There was no apparent effect on male or female fertility in rats fed erythromycin (base) at levels up to 0.25 percent of diet.

Pregnancy: Teratogenic effects. Pregnancy Category B: There is no evidence of teratogenicity or any other adverse effect on reproduction in female rats fed erythromycin base (up to 0.25 percent of diet) prior to and during mating, during gestation, and through weaning of two successive litters. There are, however, no adequate and well-controlled studies in pregnant women. Because animal reproduction studies are not always predictive of human response, this drug should be used during pregnancy only if clearly needed.

Labor and Delivery: The effect of erythromycin on labor and delivery is unknown.

Nursing Mothers: Erythromycin is excreted in human milk. Caution should be exercised when erythromycin is administered to a nursing woman.

Pediatric Use: See **INDICATIONS AND USAGE** and **DOSAGE AND ADMINISTRATION**.

ADVERSE REACTIONS

The most frequent side effects of oral erythromycin preparations are gastrointestinal and are dose-related. They include nausea, vomiting, abdominal pain, diarrhea and anorexia. Symptoms of hepatitis, hepatic dysfunction and/or abnormal liver function test results may occur. (See **WARNINGS**.)

Onset of pseudomembranous colitis symptoms may occur during or after antibacterial treatment. (See **WARNINGS**.)

Rarely, erythromycin has been associated with the production of ventricular arrhythmias, including ventricular tachycardia and torsades de pointes, in individuals with prolonged QT interval.

Allergic reactions ranging from urticaria to anaphylaxis have occurred. Skin reactions ranging from mild eruptions to erythema multiforme, Stevens-Johnson syndrome, and toxic epidermal necrolysis have been reported rarely.

There have been isolated reports of reversible hearing loss occurring chiefly in patients with renal insufficiency and in patients receiving high doses of erythromycin.

OVERDOSAGE

In case of overdosage, erythromycin should be discontinued. Overdosage should be handled with the prompt elimination of unabsorbed drug and all other appropriate measures should be instituted.

Erythromycin is not removed by peritoneal dialysis or hemodialysis.

DOSAGE AND ADMINISTRATION

Optimal blood levels are obtained when Erythromycin Base Filmtab tablets are given in the fasting state (at least 1/2 hour and preferably 2 hours before meals).

Adults: The usual dosage of Erythromycin Base Filmtab is one 250 mg tablet four times daily in equally spaced doses or one 500 mg tablet every 12 hours. Dosage may be increased up to 4 g per day according to the severity of the infection. However, twice-a-day dosing is not recommended when doses larger than 1 g daily are administered.

Children: Age, weight, and severity of the infection are important factors in determining the proper dosage. The usual dosage is 30 to 50 mg/kg/day, in equally divided doses. For more severe infections this dosage may be doubled but should not exceed 4 g per day.

In the treatment of streptococcal infections of the upper respiratory tract (e.g., tonsillitis or pharyngitis), the therapeutic dosage of erythromycin should be administered for at least ten days.

The American Heart Association suggests a dosage of 250 mg of erythromycin orally, twice a day in long-term prophylaxis of streptococcal upper respiratory tract infections for the prevention of recurring attacks of rheumatic fever in patients allergic to penicillin and sulfonamides.[3]

Conjunctivitis of the newborn caused by *Chlamydia trachomatis:* Oral erythromycin suspension 50 mg/kg/day in 4 divided doses for at least 2 weeks.[3]

Pneumonia of infancy caused by *Chlamydia trachomatis:* Although the optimal duration of therapy has not been established, the recommended therapy is oral erythromycin suspension 50 mg/kg/day in 4 divided doses for at least 3 weeks.

Urogenital infections during pregnancy due to *Chlamydia trachomatis:* Although the optimal dose and duration of therapy have not been established, the suggested treatment is 500 mg of erythromycin by mouth four times a day on an empty stomach for at least 7 days. For women who cannot tolerate this regimen, a decreased dose of one erythromycin 500 mg tablet orally every 12 hours or 250 mg by mouth four times a day should be used for at least 14 days.[4]

For adults with uncomplicated urethral, endocervical, or rectal infections caused by *Chlamydia trachomatis,* when tetracycline is contraindicated or not tolerated: 500 mg of erythromycin by mouth four times a day for at least 7 days.[4]

For patients with nongonococcal urethritis caused by *Ureaplasma urealyticum* when tetracycline is contraindicated or not tolerated: 500 mg of erythromycin by mouth four times a day for at least seven days.[4]

Primary syphilis: 30 to 40 g given in divided doses over a period of 10 to 15 days.

Acute pelvic inflammatory disease caused by *N. gonorrhoeae:* 500 mg Erythrocin® Lactobionate-I.V. (erythromycin lactobionate for injection, USP) every 6 hours for 3 days, followed by 500 mg of erythromycin base orally every 12 hours for 7 days.

Intestinal amebiasis: Adults: 500 mg every 12 hours or 250 mg every 6 hours for 10 to 14 days. Children: 30 to 50 mg/kg/day in divided doses for 10 to 14 days.

Pertussis: Although optimal dosage and duration have not been established, doses of erythromycin utilized in reported clinical studies were 40 to 50 mg/kg/day, given in divided doses for 5 to 14 days.

Legionnaires' Disease: Although optimal dosage has not been established, doses utilized in reported clinical data were 1 to 4 g daily in divided doses.

HOW SUPPLIED

Erythromycin Base Filmtab tablets (erythromycin tablets, USP) are supplied as pink, unscored oval tablets in the following strengths and packages.

250 mg tablets (debossed with ⊇ and EB):
Bottles of 100 .... (**NDC** 0074-6326-13);
Bottles of 500 .... (**NDC** 0074-6326-53);
ABBO-PAC® unit dose strip packages
  of 100 tablets .... (**NDC** 0074-6326-11).
500 mg tablets (debossed with ⊇ and EA):
Bottles of 100 .... (**NDC** 0074-6227-13).
Recommended Storage: Store below 86°F (30°C). Keep tightly closed.

REFERENCES

1. National Committee for Clinical Laboratory Standards. *Methods for Dilution Antimicrobial Susceptibility Tests for Bacteria that Grow Aerobically,* Third Edition. Approved Standard NCCLS Document M7-A3, Vol. 13, No. 25 NCCLS, Villanova, PA, December 1993.
2. National Committee for Clinical Laboratory Standards, *Performance Standards for Antimicrobial Disk Susceptibility Tests,* Fifth Edition. Approved Standard NCCLS Document M2-A5, Vol. 13, No. 24 NCCLS, Villanova, PA, December 1993.
3. Committee on Rheumatic Fever, Endocarditis, and Kawasaki Disease of the Council on Cardiovascular Disease in the Young, the American Heart Association: Prevention of Rheumatic Fever. *Circulation.* 78(4):1082–1086, October 1988.
4. Data on file, Abbott Laboratories.
FILMTAB—Film-sealed tablets, Abbott.
Revised: October, 2000
Ref. 03-4968-R4

ABBOTT LABORATORIES
NORTH CHICAGO, IL 60064, U.S.A.
PRINTED IN U.S.A.

FLOXIN® I.V.   ℞
(Ofloxacin Injection)
FOR INTRAVENOUS INFUSION
[flŏx-ĭn]

DESCRIPTION

FLOXIN® (ofloxacin injection) I.V. is a synthetic, broad-spectrum antimicrobial agent for intravenous administration. Chemically, ofloxacin, a fluorinated carboxyquinolone, is the racemate, (±)-9-fluoro-2,3-dihydro-3-methyl-10-(4-methyl-1-piperazinyl)-7-oxo-7H-pyrido[1,2,3-de]-1,4-benzoxazine-6-carboxylic acid. The chemical structure is:

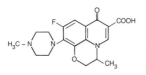

Its empirical formula is $C_{18}H_{20}FN_3O_4$, and its molecular weight is 361.4. Ofloxacin is an off-white to pale yellow crystalline powder. The relative solubility characteristics of ofloxacin at room temperature, as defined by USP nomenclature, indicate that ofloxacin is considered to be *soluble* in aqueous solutions with pH between 2 and 5. It is *sparingly* to *slightly soluble* in aqueous solutions with pH 7 (solubility falls to 4 mg/mL) and *freely soluble* in aqueous solutions with pH above 9. Ofloxacin has the potential to form stable coordination compounds with many metal ions. This *in vitro* chelation potential has the following formation order: $Fe^{+3} > Al^{+3} > Cu^{+2} > Ni^{+2} > Pb^{+2} > Zn^{+2} > Mg^{+2} > Ca^{+2} > Ba^{+2}$.

FLOXIN I.V. IN SINGLE-USE VIALS is a sterile, preservative-free aqueous solution of ofloxacin with pH ranging from 3.5 to 5.5. FLOXIN I.V. IN PRE-MIXED BOTTLES and IN PRE-MIXED FLEXIBLE CONTAINERS are sterile, preservative-free aqueous solutions of ofloxacin with pH ranging from 3.8 to 5.8. The color of FLOXIN I.V. may range from light yellow to amber. This does not adversely affect product potency. FLOXIN I.V. IN SINGLE-USE VIALS contains ofloxacin in Water for Injection. FLOXIN I.V. IN PRE-MIXED BOTTLES and IN PRE-MIXED FLEXIBLE CONTAINERS are dilute, non-pyrogenic, nearly isotonic pre-mixed solutions that con-

tain ofloxacin in 5% Dextrose (D_5W). Hydrochloric acid and sodium hydroxide may have been added to adjust the pH.

The flexible container is fabricated from a specially formulated non-plasticized, thermoplastic copolyester (CR3). The amount of water that can permeate from the container into the overwrap is insufficient to affect the solution significantly. Solutions in contact with the flexible container can leach out certain of the container's chemical components in very small amounts within the expiration period. The suitability of the container material has been confirmed by tests in animals according to USP biological tests for plastic containers.

CLINICAL PHARMACOLOGY

Following a single 60-minute intravenous infusion of 200 mg or 400 mg of ofloxacin to normal volunteers, the mean maximum plasma concentrations attained were 2.7 and 4.0 µg/mL, respectively; the concentrations at 12 hours (h) after dosing were 0.3 and 0.7 µg/mL, respectively.

Steady-state concentrations were attained after four doses, and the area under the curve (AUC) was approximately 40% higher than the AUC after a single dose. The mean peak and trough plasma steady-state levels attained following intravenous administration of 200 mg of ofloxacin q 12 h for seven days were 2.9 and 0.5 µg/mL, respectively. Following intravenous doses of 400 mg of ofloxacin q 12 h, the mean peak and trough plasma steady-state levels ranged, in two different studies, from 5.5 to 7.2 µg/mL and 1.2 to 1.9 µg/mL, respectively.

Following 7 days of intravenous administration, the elimination half-life of ofloxacin was 6 h (range 5 to 10 h). The total clearance and the volume of distribution were approximately 15 L/h and 120 L, respectively.

Elimination of ofloxacin is primarily by renal excretion. Approximately 65% of a dose is excreted renally within 48 h. Studies indicate that <5% of an administered dose is recovered in the urine as the desmethyl or N-oxide metabolites. Four to eight percent of an ofloxacin dose is excreted in the feces. This indicates a small degree of biliary excretion of ofloxacin. *In vitro*, approximately 32% of the drug in plasma is protein bound.

The single dose and steady-state plasma profiles of ofloxacin injection were comparable in extent of exposure (AUC) to those of ofloxacin

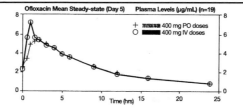

Ofloxacin Mean Steady-state (Day 5)   Plasma Levels (µg/mL) (n=19)

+ ▨▨▨▨▨ 400 mg PO doses
O ▬▬▬ 400 mg IV doses

Time (hrs)

Gram-positive aerobes

Staphylococcus epidermidis (excluding methicillin-resistant strains)	Staphylococcus haemolyticus Staphylococcus saprophyticus

Gram-negative aerobes

Acinetobacter calcoaceticus	Enterobacter cloacae	Proteus vulgaris
Aeromonas caviae	Haemophilus ducreyi	Providencia rettgeri
Aeromonas hydrophila	Klebsiella oxytoca	Providencia stuartii
Bordetella parapertussis	Moraxella catarrhalis	Serratia marcescens
Bordetella pertussis	Morganella morganii	Vibrio parahaemolyticus
Citrobacter freundii		

Anaerobes

Clostridium perfringens	Gardnerella vaginalis

Other organisms

Chlamydia pneumoniae	Mycobacterium tuberculosis (including multiple drug-resistant strains)	Mycoplasma hominis
Legionella pneumophila		Mycoplasma pneumoniae
		Ureaplasma urealyticum

tablets when the injectable and tablet formulations of ofloxacin were administered in equal doses (mg/mg). The mean $AUC_{(0-12)}$ attained after the intravenous administration of 400 mg over 60 min was 43.5 µg·h/mL; the mean $AUC_{(0-12)}$ attained after the oral administration of 400 mg was 41.2 µg•h/mL (two one-sided t-test, 90% confidence interval was 103–109). [See following chart.]

[See figure at bottom of previous page]

Between 0 and 6 h following the administration of a single 200 mg oral dose of ofloxacin to 12 healthy volunteers, the average urine ofloxacin concentration was approximately 220 µg/mL. Between 12 and 24 h after administration, the average urine ofloxacin level was approximately 34 µg/mL.

Following oral administration of recommended therapeutic doses, ofloxacin has been detected in blister fluid, cervix, lung tissue, ovary, prostatic fluid, prostatic tissue, skin, and sputum. The mean concentration of ofloxacin in each of these various body fluids and tissues after one or more doses was 0.8 to 1.5 times the concurrent plasma level. Inadequate data are presently available on the distribution or levels of ofloxacin in the cerebrospinal fluid or brain tissue.

Following the administration of oral doses of ofloxacin to healthy elderly volunteers (64–74 years of age) with normal renal function, the apparent half-life of ofloxacin was 7 to 8 h, as compared to approximately 6 h in younger adults.

Clearance of ofloxacin is reduced in patients with impaired renal function (creatinine clearance ≤ 50 mL/min), and dosage adjustment is necessary. (See **PRECAUTIONS: General** and **DOSAGE AND ADMINISTRATION**.)

Microbiology

Ofloxacin has in vitro activity against a broad-spectrum of gram-positive and gram-negative aerobic and anaerobic bacteria. Ofloxacin is often bactericidal at concentrations equal to or slightly greater than inhibitory concentrations. Ofloxacin is thought to exert a bactericidal effect on susceptible microorganisms by in-

hibiting DNA gyrase, an essential enzyme that is a critical catalyst in the duplication, transcription, and repair of bacterial DNA.

Ofloxacin has been shown to be active against most strains of the following microorganisms, both in vitro and in clinical infections as described in the **INDICATIONS AND USAGE** section:

Gram-positive aerobes

Staphylococcus aureus	Streptococcus pyogenes
Streptococcus pneumoniae	

Gram-negative aerobes

Citrobacter diversus	Klebsiella pneumoniae
Enterobacter aerogenes	Neisseria gonorrhoeae
Escherichia coli	Proteus mirabilis
Haemophilus influenzae	Pseudomonas aeruginosa

Other microorganisms

Chlamydia trachomatis

The following in vitro data are available, **but their clinical significance is unknown.**

Ofloxacin exhibits in vitro minimum inhibitory concentrations (MIC's) of 2 µg/mL or less against most (≥90%) strains of the following microorganisms; however, the safety and effectiveness of ofloxacin in treating clinical infections due to these microorganisms have not been established in adequate and well-controlled clinical trials:

[See table above]

Ofloxacin is not active against Treponema pallidum. (See **WARNINGS**.)

Many strains of other streptococcal species, Enterococcus species, and anaerobes are resistant to ofloxacin.

Resistance to ofloxacin due to spontaneous mutation in vitro is a rare occurrence (range: 10^{-9} to 10^{-11}). To date, emergence of resistance has been relatively uncommon in clinical practice. With the exception of *Pseudomonas aeruginosa* (10%), less than a 4% rate of resistance emergence has been reported for most other species. Although cross-resistance has been observed between ofloxacin and other fluoroquinolones, some organisms resistant to other quinolones may be susceptible to ofloxacin.

Susceptibility Tests

Dilution techniques:
Quantitative methods are used to determine antimicrobial minimal inhibitory concentrations (MIC's). These MIC's provide estimates of the susceptibility of bacteria to antimicrobial compounds. The MICs should be determined using a standardized procedure. Standardized procedures are based on a dilution method[1] (broth or agar) or equivalent with standardized inoculum concentrations and standardized concentrations of ofloxacin powder. The MIC values should be interpreted according to the following criteria:

MIC (μg/mL)	Interpretation
≤2	Susceptible (S)
4	Intermediate (I)
≥8	Resistant (R)

A report of "Susceptible" indicates that the pathogen is likely to be inhibited if the antimicrobial compound in the blood reaches the concentrations usually achievable. A report of "Intermediate" indicates that the result should be considered equivocal, and, if the microorganism is not fully susceptible to alternative, clinically feasible drugs, the test should be repeated. This category implies possible clinical applicability in body sites where the drug is physiologically concentrated or in situations where high dosage of drug can be used. This category also provides a buffer zone which prevents small uncontrolled technical factors from causing major discrepancies in interpretation. A report of "Resistant" indicates that the pathogen is not likely to be inhibited if the antimicrobial compound in the blood reaches the concentrations usually achievable; other therapy should be selected.

Standardized susceptibility test procedures require the use of laboratory control microorganisms to control the technical aspects of the laboratory procedures. Standard ofloxacin powder should provide the following MIC values:

Microorganism		MIC (μg/mL)
Escherichia coli	ATCC 25922	0.015–0.12
Staphylococcus aureus	ATCC 29213	0.12–1.0
Pseudomonas aeruginosa	ATCC 27853	1.0–8.0
Haemophilus influenzae	ATCC 49247	0.016–0.06

Neisseria gonorrhoeae	ATCC 49226	0.004–0.016

Diffusion techniques:
Quantitative methods that require measurement of zone diameters also provide reproducible estimates of the susceptibility of bacteria to antimicrobial compounds. One such standardized procedure[2] requires the use of standardized inoculum concentrations. This procedure uses paper disks impregnated with 5-μg ofloxacin to test the susceptibility of microorganisms to ofloxacin.

Reports from the laboratory providing results of the standard single-disk susceptibility test with a 5-μg ofloxacin disk should be interpreted according to the following criteria:

Zone Diameter (mm)	Interpretation
≥16	Susceptible (S)
13–15	Intermediate (I)
≤12	Resistant (R)

Interpretation should be as stated above for results using dilution techniques. Interpretation involves correlation of the diameter obtained in the disk test with the MIC for ofloxacin.

As with standardized dilution techniques, diffusion methods require the use of laboratory control microorganisms that are used to control the technical aspects of the laboratory procedures. For the diffusion technique, the 5-μg ofloxacin disk should provide the following zone diameters in these laboratory test quality control strains:

Microorganism		Zone Diameter (mm)
Escherichia coli	ATCC 25922	29–33
Pseudomonas aeruginosa	ATCC 27853	17–21
Haemophilus influenzae	ATCC 49247	31–40
Neisseria gonorrhoeae	ATCC 49226	43–51
Staphylococcus aureus	ATCC 25923	24–28

INDICATIONS AND USAGE

FLOXIN (ofloxacin injection) I.V. is indicated for the treatment of adults with mild to moderate infections (unless otherwise indicated) caused by susceptible strains of the designated microorganisms in the infections listed below – when intravenous administration offers a route of administration advantageous to the patient, (e.g., patient cannot tolerate an oral dosage form). Please see **DOSAGE AND ADMINISTRATION** for specific recommendations.

The safety and effectiveness of the intravenous formulation in treating patients with severe infections have not been established. NOTE: IN THE ABSENCE OF VOMITING OR OTHER FACTORS INTERFERING WITH THE ABSORPTION OF ORALLY ADMINISTERED DRUG, PATIENTS RECEIVE ESSENTIALLY THE SAME SYSTEMIC ANTIMICROBIAL THERAPY AFTER EQUIVALENT DOSES OF OFLOXACIN ADMINISTERED BY EITHER THE ORAL OR THE INTRAVENOUS ROUTE. THEREFORE, THE INTRAVENOUS FORMULATION DOES NOT PROVIDE A HIGHER DEGREE OF EFFICACY OR MORE POTENT ANTIMICROBIAL ACTIVITY THAN AN EQUIVALENT DOSE OF THE ORAL FORMULATION OF OFLOXACIN.

Acute bacterial exacerbation of chronic bronchitis due to *Haemophilus influenzae* or *Streptococcus pneumoniae.*

Community-acquired Pneumonia due to *Haemophilus influenzae* or *Streptococcus pneumoniae.*

Uncomplicated skin and skin structure infections due to *Staphylococcus aureus, Streptococcus pyogenes,* or *Proteus mirabilis.*

Acute, uncomplicated urethral and cervical gonorrhea due to *Neisseria gonorrhoeae.* (See *WARNINGS.*)

Nongonococcal urethritis and cervicitis due to *Chlamydia trachomatis.* (See *WARNINGS.*)

Mixed infections of the urethra and cervix due to *Chlamydia trachomatis* and *Neisseria gonorrhoeae.* (See *WARNINGS.*)

Acute pelvic inflammatory disease (including severe infection) due to *Chlamydia trachomatis* and/or *Neisseria gonorrhoeae.* (See *WARNINGS.*)

NOTE: If anaerobic microorganisms are suspected of contributing to the infection, appropriate therapy for anaerobic pathogens should be administered.

Uncomplicated cystitis due to *Citrobacter diversus, Enterobacter aerogenes, Escherichia coli, Klebsiella pneumoniae, Proteus mirabilis,* or *Pseudomonas aeruginosa.*

Complicated urinary tract infections due to *Escherichia coli, Klebsiella pneumoniae, Proteus mirabilis, Citrobacter diversus**, or *Pseudomonas aeruginosa**.

Prostatitis due to *Escherichia coli.*

*= Although treatment of infections due to this organism in this organ system demonstrated a clinically significant outcome, efficacy was studied in fewer than 10 patients.

Appropriate culture and susceptibility tests should be performed before treatment in order to isolate and identify organisms causing the infection and to determine their susceptibility to ofloxacin. Therapy with ofloxacin may be initiated before results of these tests are known; once results become available, appropriate therapy should be continued.

As with other drugs in this class, some strains of *Pseudomonas aeruginosa* may develop resis-

tance fairly rapidly during treatment with ofloxacin. Culture and susceptibility testing performed periodically during therapy will provide information not only on the therapeutic effect of the antimicrobial agent but also on the possible emergence of bacterial resistance.

CONTRAINDICATIONS

FLOXIN (ofloxacin) is contraindicated in persons with a history of hypersensitivity associated with the use of ofloxacin or any member of the quinolone group of antimicrobial agents.

WARNINGS

THE SAFETY AND EFFICACY OF OFLOXACIN IN CHILDREN, ADOLESCENTS (UNDER THE AGE OF 18 YEARS), PREGNANT WOMEN, AND LACTATING WOMEN HAVE NOT BEEN ESTABLISHED. (SEE PEDIATRIC USE, USE IN PREGNANCY, AND NURSING MOTHERS SUBSECTIONS IN THE PRECAUTIONS SECTION.)

In the immature rat, the oral administration of ofloxacin at 5 to 16 times the recommended maximum human dose based on mg/kg or 1–3 times based on mg/m^2 increased the incidence and severity of osteochondrosis. The lesions did not regress after 13 weeks of drug withdrawal. Other quinolones also produce similar erosions in the weight-bearing joints and other signs of arthropathy in immature animals of various species. (See *ANIMAL PHARMACOLOGY.*)

Convulsions, increased intracranial pressure, and toxic psychosis have been reported in patients receiving quinolones, including ofloxacin. Quinolones, including ofloxacin, may also cause central nervous system stimulation which may lead to: tremors, restlessness/agitation, nervousness/anxiety, lightheadedness, confusion, hallucinations, paranoia and depression, nightmares, insomnia, and rarely suicidal thoughts or acts. These reactions may occur following the first dose. If these reactions occur in patients receiving ofloxacin, the drug should be discontinued and appropriate measures instituted. As with all quinolones, ofloxacin should be used with caution in patients with a known or suspected CNS disorder that may predispose to seizures or lower the seizure threshold (e.g., severe cerebral arteriosclerosis, epilepsy) or in the presence of other risk factors that may predispose to seizures or lower the seizure threshold (e.g., certain drug therapy, renal dysfunction). (See *PRECAUTIONS: General, Information for Patients, Drug Interactions* and *ADVERSE REACTIONS.*)

Serious and occasionally fatal hypersensitivity (anaphylactic/anaphylactoid) reactions have been reported in patients receiving therapy with quinolones, including ofloxacin. These reactions often occur following the first dose. Some reactions were accompanied by cardiovascular collapse, hypotension/shock, seizure, loss of consciousness, tingling, angioedema (including tongue, laryngeal, throat or facial edema/swelling), airway obstruction (including bronchospasm, shortness of breath and acute respiratory distress), dyspnea, urticaria/hives, itching, and other serious skin reactions. A few patients had a history of hypersensitivity reactions. The drug should be discontinued immediately at the first appearance of a skin rash or any other sign of hypersensitivity. Serious acute hypersensitivity reactions may require treatment with epinephrine and other resuscitative measures, including oxygen, intravenous fluids, antihistamines, corticosteroids, pressor amines, and airway management, as clinically indicated. (See *PRECAUTIONS* and *ADVERSE REACTIONS*.)

Serious and sometimes fatal events, some due to hypersensitivity, and some due to uncertain etiology, have been reported in patients receiving therapy with quinolones, including ofloxacin. These events may be severe and generally occur following the administration of multiple doses. Clinical manifestations may include one or more of the following: fever, rash or severe dermatologic reactions (e.g., toxic epidermal necrolysis, Stevens-Johnson Syndrome); vasculitis; arthralgia; myalgia; serum sickness; allergic pneumonitis; interstitial nephritis; acute renal insufficiency/failure; hepatitis; jaundice; acute hepatic necrosis/failure; anemia, including hemolytic and aplastic; thrombocytopenia, including thrombotic thrombocytopenic purpura; leukopenia; agranulocytosis; pancytopenia; and/or other hematologic abnormalities. The drug should be discontinued immediately at the first appearance of a skin rash or any other sign of hypersensitivity and supportive measures instituted. (See *PRE-CAUTIONS: Information for Patients* and *ADVERSE REACTIONS*.)

Pseudomembranous colitis has been reported with nearly all antibacterial agents, including ofloxacin, and may range in severity from mild to life-threatening. Therefore, it is important to consider this diagnosis in patients who present with diarrhea subsequent to the administration of any antibacterial agent.

Treatment with antibacterial agents alters the normal flora of the colon and may permit overgrowth of clostridia. Studies indicate a toxin produced by *Clostridium difficile* is one primary cause of "antibiotic-associated colitis".

After the diagnosis of pseudomembranous colitis has been established, therapeutic measures should be initiated. Mild cases of pseudomembranous colitis usually respond to drug discontinuation alone. In moderate to severe cases, consideration should be given to management with fluids and electrolytes, protein supplementation, and treatment with an oral antibacterial drug clinically effective against *C. difficile* colitis. (See *ADVERSE REACTIONS*.)

Ruptures of the shoulder, hand, and Achilles tendons that required surgical repair or resulted in prolonged disability have been re-ported with ofloxacin and other quinolones. Ofloxacin should be discontinued if the patient experiences pain, inflammation, or rupture of a tendon. Patients should rest and refrain from exercise until the diagnosis of tendinitis or tendon rupture has been confidently excluded. Tendon rupture can occur at any time during or after therapy with ofloxacin.

Ofloxacin has not been shown to be effective in the treatment of syphilis. Antimicrobial agents used in high doses for short periods of time to treat gonorrhea may mask or delay the symptoms of incubating syphilis. All patients with gonorrhea should have a serologic test for syphilis at the time of diagnosis. Patients treated with ofloxacin for gonorrhea should have a follow-up serologic test for syphilis after three months and, if positive, treatment with an appropriate antimicrobial should be instituted.

PRECAUTIONS
General:

Because a rapid or bolus intravenous injection may result in hypotension, **OFLOXACIN INJECTION SHOULD ONLY BE ADMINISTERED BY SLOW INTRAVENOUS INFUSION OVER A PERIOD OF 60 MINUTES.** (See *DOSAGE AND ADMINISTRATION*.)

Adequate hydration of patients receiving ofloxacin should be maintained to prevent the formation of a highly concentrated urine.

Administer ofloxacin with caution in the presence of renal or hepatic insufficiency/impairment. In patients with known or suspected renal or hepatic insufficiency/impairment, careful clinical observation and appropriate laboratory studies should be performed prior to and during therapy since elimination of ofloxacin may be reduced. In patients with impaired renal function (creatinine clearance ≤ 50 mg/mL), alteration of the dosage regimen is necessary. (See *CLINICAL PHARMACOLOGY* and *DOSAGE AND ADMINISTRATION*.)

Moderate to severe phototoxicity reactions have been observed in patients exposed to direct sunlight while receiving some drugs in this class, including ofloxacin. Excessive sunlight should be avoided. Therapy should be discontinued if phototoxicity (e.g., a skin eruption) occurs.

As with other quinolones, ofloxacin should be used with caution in any patient with a known or suspected CNS disorder that may predispose to seizures or lower the seizure threshold (e.g., severe cerebral arteriosclerosis, epilepsy) or in the presence of other risk factors that may predispose to seizures or lower the seizure threshold (e.g., certain drug therapy, renal dysfunction). (See *WARNINGS* and *Drug Interactions*.)

A possible interaction between oral hypoglycemic drugs (e.g., glyburide/glibenclamide) or with insulin and fluoroquinolone antimicrobial agents have been reported resulting in a potentiation of the hypoglycemic action of these drugs. The mechanism for this interaction is not known. If a hypoglycemic reaction occurs in a patient being treated with ofloxacin, discontinue ofloxacin immediately and consult a physician. (See **Drug Interactions** and **ADVERSE REACTIONS**.)

As with any potent drug, periodic assessment of organ system functions, including renal, hepatic, and hematopoietic, is advisable during prolonged therapy. (See **WARNINGS** and **ADVERSE REACTIONS**.)

Information for Patients:

Patients should be advised:

— to drink fluids liberally if able to take fluids by the oral route;

— that ofloxacin may cause neurologic adverse effects (e.g., dizziness, lightheadedness) and that patients should know how they react to ofloxacin before they operate an automobile or machinery or engage in activities requiring mental alertness and coordination (See **WARNINGS** and **ADVERSE REACTIONS**);

— that ofloxacin may be associated with hypersensitivity reactions, even following the first dose, to discontinue the drug at the first sign of a skin rash, hives or other skin reactions, a rapid heartbeat, difficulty in swallowing or breathing, any swelling suggesting angioedema (e.g., swelling of the lips, tongue, face; tightness of the throat, hoarseness), or any other symptom of an allergic reaction (See **WARNINGS** and **ADVERSE REACTIONS**);

— to avoid excessive sunlight or artificial ultraviolet light while receiving ofloxacin and to discontinue therapy if phototoxicity (e.g., skin eruption) occurs;

— to discontinue treatment and inform their physician if they experience pain, inflammation, or rupture of a tendon, and to rest and refrain from exercise until the diagnosis of tendinitis or tendon rupture has been confidently excluded;

— that if they are diabetic and are being treated with insulin or an oral hypoglycemic agent, to discontinue ofloxacin immediately if a hypoglycemic reaction occurs and consult a physician (See **PRECAUTIONS: General** and **Drug Interactions**);

— that convulsions have been reported in patients taking quinolones, including ofloxacin, and to notify their physician before taking this drug if there is a history of this condition.

Drug Interactions:

Antacids, Sucralfate, Metal Cations, Multi-Vitamins: There are no data concerning an interaction of **intravenous** quinolones with **oral** antacids, sucralfate, multi-vitamins, or metal cations. However, no quinolone should be co-administered with any solution containing multivalent cations, e.g., magnesium, through the same intravenous line. (See **DOSAGE AND ADMINISTRATION**.)

Caffeine: Interactions between ofloxacin and caffeine have not been detected.

Cimetidine: Cimetidine has demonstrated interference with the elimination of some quinolones. This interference has resulted in significant increases in half-life and AUC of some quinolones. The potential for interaction between ofloxacin and cimetidine has not been studied.

Cyclosporine: Elevated serum levels of cyclosporine have been reported with concomitant use of cyclosporine with some other quinolones. The potential for interaction between ofloxacin and cyclosporine has not been studied.

Drugs metabolized by Cytochrome P450 enzymes: Most quinolone antimicrobial drugs inhibit cytochrome P450 enzyme activity. This may result in a prolonged half-life for some drugs that are also metabolized by this system (e.g., cyclosporine, theophylline/methylxanthines, warfarin) when co-administered with quinolones. The extent of this inhibition varies among different quinolones. (See other **Drug Interactions**.)

Non-steroidal anti-inflammatory drugs: The concomitant administration of a non-steroidal anti-inflammatory drug with a quinolone, including ofloxacin, may increase the risk of CNS stimulation and convulsive seizures. (See **WARNINGS** and **PRECAUTIONS: General**.)

Probenecid: The concomitant use of probenecid with certain other quinolones has been reported to affect renal tubular secretion. The effect of probenecid on the elimination of ofloxacin has not been studied.

Theophylline: Steady-state theophylline levels may increase when ofloxacin and theophylline are administered concurrently. As with other quinolones, concomitant administration of ofloxacin may prolong the half-life of theophylline, elevate serum theophylline levels, and increase the risk of theophylline-related adverse reactions. Theophylline levels should be closely monitored and theophylline dosage adjustments made, if appropriate, when ofloxacin is co-administered. Adverse reactions (including seizures) may occur with or without an elevation in the serum theophylline level. (See **WARNINGS** and **PRECAUTIONS: General**.)

Warfarin: Some quinolones have been reported to enhance the effects of the oral anticoagulant warfarin or its derivatives. Therefore, if a quinolone antimicrobial is administered concomitantly with warfarin or its derivatives, the prothrombin time or other suitable coagulation test should be closely monitored.

Antidiabetic agents (e.g., insulin, glyburide/glibenclamide): Since disturbances of blood glucose, including hyperglycemia and hypoglycemia, have been reported in patients treated concurrently with quinolones and an antidiabetic agent, careful monitoring of blood glucose is recommended when these agents are used concomitantly (See **PRECAUTIONS: General** and **Information for Patients**.)

Carcinogenesis, Mutagenesis, Impairment of Fertility:

Long-term studies to determine the carcinogenic potential of ofloxacin have not been conducted.

Ofloxacin was not mutagenic in the Ames bacterial test, *in vitro* and *in vivo* cytogenetic assay, sister chromatid exchange (Chinese Hamster and Human Cell Lines), unscheduled DNA Repair (UDS) using human fibroblasts, dominant lethal assays, or mouse micronucleus assay. Ofloxacin was positive in the UDS test using rat hepatocytes and Mouse Lymphoma Assay.

Pregnancy: Teratogenic Effects. Pregnancy Category C.

Ofloxacin has not been shown to have any teratogenic effects at oral doses as high as 810 mg/kg/day (11 times the recommended maximum human dose based on mg/m^2 or 50 times based on mg/kg) and 160 mg/kg/day (4 times the recommended maximum human dose based on mg/m^2 or 10 times based on mg/kg) when administered to pregnant rats and rabbits, respectively. Additional studies in rats with oral doses up to 360 mg/kg/day (5 times the recommended maximum human dose based on mg/m^2 or 23 times based on mg/kg) demonstrated no adverse effect on late fetal development, labor, delivery, lactation, neonatal viability, or growth of the newborn. Doses equivalent to 50 and 10 times the recommended maximum human dose of ofloxacin (based on mg/kg) were fetotoxic (i.e., decreased fetal body weight and increased fetal mortality) in rats and rabbits, respectively. Minor skeletal variations were reported in rats receiving doses of 810 mg/kg/day, which is more than 10 times higher than the recommended maximum human dose based on mg/m^2.

There are, however, no adequate and well-controlled studies in pregnant women. Ofloxacin should be used during pregnancy only if the potential benefit justifies the potential risk to the fetus. (See **WARNINGS**.)

Nursing Mothers:

In lactating females, a single oral 200-mg dose of ofloxacin resulted in concentrations of ofloxacin in milk that were similar to those found in plasma. Because of the potential for serious adverse reactions from ofloxacin in nursing infants, a decision should be made whether to discontinue nursing or to discontinue the drug, taking into account the importance of the drug to the mother. (See **WARNINGS** and **ADVERSE REACTIONS**.)

Pediatric Use:

Safety and effectiveness in children and adolescents below the age of 18 years have not been established. Ofloxacin causes arthropathy (arthrosis) and osteochondrosis in juvenile animals of several species. (See **WARNINGS**.)

ADVERSE REACTIONS

The following is a compilation of the data for ofloxacin based on clinical experience with both the oral and intravenous formulations. The incidence of drug-related adverse reactions in patients during Phase 2 and 3 clinical trials was 11%. Among patients receiving multiple-dose therapy, 4% discontinued ofloxacin due to adverse experiences.

In clinical trials, the following events were considered likely to be drug-related in patients receiving multiple doses of ofloxacin:

nausea 3%, insomnia 3%, headache 1%, dizziness 1%, diarrhea 1%, vomiting 1%, rash 1%, pruritus 1%, external genital pruritus in women 1%, vaginitis 1%, dysgeusia 1%.

Local injection site reactions (phlebitis, swelling, erythema) were reported in approximately 2% of patients treated with the 3.63 mg/mL final infusion concentration of intravenous ofloxacin used in the clinical safety trials. The final infusion concentration of intravenous ofloxacin in the commercially available intravenous preparations is 4.0 mg/mL. To date, individuals administered the 4.0 mg/mL concentration of the intravenous ofloxacin have demonstrated clinically acceptable rates of local injection site reactions. Due to the small difference in concentration, significant differences in local site reactions are unexpected with the 4.0 mg/mL concentration.

In clinical trials, the most frequently reported adverse events, regardless of relationship to drug, were:

nausea 10%, headache 9%, insomnia 7%, external genital pruritus in women 6%, dizziness 5%, vaginitis 5%, diarrhea 4%, vomiting 4%.

In clinical trials, the following events, regardless of relationship to drug occurred in 1 to 3% of patients:

Abdominal pain and cramps, chest pain, decreased appetite, dry mouth, dysgeusia, fatigue, flatulence, gastrointestinal distress, nervousness, pharyngitis, pruritus, fever, rash, sleep disorders, somnolence, trunk pain, vaginal discharge, visual disturbances, and constipation.

Additional events, occurring in clinical trials at a rate of less than 1%, regardless of relationship to drug, were:

Body as a whole:	asthenia, chills, malaise, extremity pain, pain, epistaxis
Cardiovascular System:	cardiac arrest, edema, hypertension, hypotension, palpitations, vasodilation
Gastrointestinal System:	dyspepsia
Genital/Reproductive System:	burning, irritation, pain and rash of the female genitalia; dysmenorrhea; menorrhagia; metrorrhagia

Musculoskeletal System:	arthralgia, myalgia
Nervous System:	seizures, anxiety, cognitive change, depression, dream abnormality, euphoria, hallucinations, paresthesia, syncope, vertigo, tremor, confusion
Nutritional/Metabolic:	thirst, weight loss
Respiratory System:	respiratory arrest, cough, rhinorrhea
Skin/Hypersensitivity:	angioedema, diaphoresis, urticaria, vasculitis
Special Senses:	decreased hearing acuity, tinnitus, photophobia
Urinary System:	dysuria, urinary frequency, urinary retention

The following laboratory abnormalities appeared in ≥ 1.0% of patients receiving multiple doses of ofloxacin. It is not known whether these abnormalities were caused by the drug or the underlying conditions being treated.

Hematopoietic:	anemia, leukopenia, leukocytosis, neutropenia, neutrophilia, increased band forms, lymphocytopenia, eosinophilia, lymphocytosis, thrombocytopenia, thrombocytosis, elevated ESR
Hepatic:	elevated: alkaline phosphatase, AST (SGOT), ALT (SGPT)
Serum chemistry:	hyperglycemia, hypoglycemia, elevated creatinine, elevated BUN
Urinary:	glucosuria, proteinuria, alkalinuria, hyposthenuria, hematuria, pyuria

Post-Marketing Adverse Events:
Additional adverse events, regardless of relationship to drug, reported from worldwide marketing experience with quinolones, including ofloxacin:
Clinical:

| Cardiovascular System: | cerebral thrombosis, pulmonary edema, tachycardia, hypotension/shock, syncope |
| Endocrine/Metabolic: | hyper- or hypoglycemia, especially in diabetic patients on insulin or oral hypoglycemic agents |

	(See *PRECAUTIONS: General* and *Drug Interactions*.)
Gastrointestinal System:	hepatic dysfunction including: hepatic necrosis, jaundice (cholestatic or hepatocellular), hepatitis; intestinal perforation; pseudomembranous colitis (the onset of pseudomembranous colitis symptoms may occur during or after antimicrobial treatment), GI hemorrhage; hiccough, painful oral mucosa, pyrosis (See *WARNINGS*.)
Genitourinary System:	vaginal candidiasis
Hematopoietic:	anemia, including hemolytic and aplastic; hemorrhage, pancytopenia, agranulocytosis, leukopenia, reversible bone marrow depression, thrombocytopenia, thrombotic thrombocytopenic purpura, petechiae, ecchymosis/bruising (See *WARNINGS*.)
Musculoskeletal:	tendinitis/rupture; weakness; rhabdomyolysis
Nervous System:	nightmares; suicidal thoughts or acts, disorientation, psychotic reactions, paranoia; phobia, agitation, restlessness, aggressiveness/hostility, manic reaction, emotional lability; peripheral neuropathy, ataxia, incoordination; possible exacerbation of: myasthenia gravis and extrapyramidal disorders; dysphasia, lightheadedness (See *WARNINGS* and *PRECAUTIONS*.)
Respiratory System:	dyspnea, bronchospasm, allergic pneumonitis, stridor (See *WARNINGS*.)

Skin/Hypersensitivity:	anaphylactic (-toid) reactions/shock; purpura, serum sickness, erythema multiforme/ Stevens-Johnson Syndrome, erythema nodosum, exfoliative dermatitis, hyperpigmentation, toxic epidermal necrolysis, conjunctivitis, photosensitivity, vesiculobullous eruption (See *WARNINGS* and *PRECAUTIONS*.)
Special Senses:	diplopia, nystagmus, blurred vision, disturbances of: taste, smell, hearing and equilibrium, usually reversible following discontinuation
Urinary System:	anuria, polyuria, renal calculi, renal failure, interstitial nephritis, hematuria (See *WARNINGS* and *PRECAUTIONS*.)
Laboratory: Hematopoietic:	prolongation of prothrombin time
Serum chemistry:	acidosis, elevation of: serum triglycerides, serum cholesterol, serum potassium, liver function tests including: GGTP, LDH, bilirubin
Urinary:	albuminuria, candiduria

In clinical trials using multiple-dose therapy, ophthalmologic abnormalities, including cataracts and multiple punctate lenticular opacities, have been noted in patients undergoing treatment with other quinolones. The relationship of the drugs to these events is not presently established.

CRYSTALLURIA and CYLINDRURIA HAVE BEEN REPORTED with other quinolones.

OVERDOSAGE

Information on overdosage with ofloxacin is limited. One incident of accidental overdosage has been reported. In this case, an adult female received 3 grams of ofloxacin intravenously over 45 minutes. A blood sample obtained 15 minutes after the completion of the infusion revealed an ofloxacin level of 39.3 μg/ mL. In 7 h, the level had fallen to 16.2 μg/mL, and by 24 h to 2.7 μg/mL. During the infusion, the patient developed drowsiness, nausea, dizziness, hot and cold flushes, subjective facial swelling and numbness, slurring of speech, and mild to moderate disorientation. All complaints except the dizziness subsided within 1 h after discontinuation of the infusion. The dizziness, most bothersome while standing, resolved in approximately 9 h. Laboratory testing reportedly revealed no clinically significant changes in routine parameters in this patient.

In the event of acute overdose, the patient should be observed and appropriate hydration maintained. Ofloxacin is not efficiently removed by hemodialysis or peritoneal dialysis.

DOSAGE AND ADMINISTRATION

FLOXIN I.V. should only be administered by **intravenous** infusion. It is not for intramuscular, intrathecal, intraperitoneal, or subcutaneous administration.

CAUTION: RAPID OR BOLUS INTRAVENOUS INFUSION MUST BE AVOIDED. Ofloxacin injection should be infused intravenously slowly over a period of not less than 60 minutes. (See *PRECAUTIONS*.)

Single-use vials require dilution prior to administration. (See *PREPARATION FOR ADMINISTRATION*.)

The usual dose of FLOXIN (ofloxacin injection) I.V. is 200 mg to 400 mg administered by slow infusion over 60 minutes every 12 h as described in the following dosing chart. These recommendations apply to patients with mild to moderate infection and normal renal function (i.e., creatinine clearance >50 mL/min). For patients with altered renal function (i.e., creatinine clearance ≤50 mL/min), see the *Patients with Impaired Renal Function* subsection.

[See table at bottom of next page]

Patients with Impaired Renal Function:
Dosage should be adjusted for patients with a creatinine clearance ≤ 50 mL/min. **After a normal initial dose,** dosage should be adjusted as follows:

Creatinine Clearance	Maintenance Dose	Frequency
20-50 mL/ min	the usual recommended unit dose	q24h
<20 mL/ min	1/2 the usual recommended unit dose	q24h

When only the serum creatinine is known, the following formula may be used to estimate creatinine clearance.

Men: Creatinine clearance (mL/min) =

$$\frac{\text{Weight (kg)} \times (140\text{-age})}{72 \times \text{serum creatinine (mg/dL)}}$$

Women: 0.85 × the value calculated for men.

The serum creatinine should represent a steady-state of renal function.

Patients with Cirrhosis:

The excretion of ofloxacin may be reduced in patients with severe liver function disorders (e.g., cirrhosis with or without ascites). A maximum dose of 400 mg of ofloxacin per day should therefore not be exceeded.

PREPARATION OF OFLOXACIN INJECTION FOR ADMINISTRATION

FLOXIN I.V. IN SINGLE-USE VIALS:

FLOXIN I.V. is supplied in single-use vials containing a concentrated ofloxacin solution with the equivalent of 400 mg of ofloxacin in Water for Injection. The 10 mL vials contain 40 mg of ofloxacin/mL. **THESE FLOXIN I.V. SINGLE-USE VIALS MUST BE FURTHER DILUTED WITH AN APPROPRIATE SOLUTION PRIOR TO INTRAVENOUS ADMINISTRATION. (See COMPATIBLE INTRAVENOUS SOLUTIONS.)** The concentration of the resulting diluted solution should be 4 mg/mL prior to administration.

This parenteral drug product should be inspected visually for discoloration and particulate matter prior to administration.

Since no preservative or bacteriostatic agent is present in this product, aseptic technique must be used in preparation of the final parenteral solution. **Since the vials are for single-use only, any unused portion should be discarded.**

Since only limited data are available on the compatibility of ofloxacin intravenous injection with other intravenous substances, **additives or other medications should not be added to FLOXIN I.V. in single-use vials or infused simultaneously through the same intravenous line.** If the same intravenous line is used for sequential infusion of several different drugs, the line should be flushed before and after infusion of FLOXIN I.V. with an infusion solution compatible with FLOXIN I.V. and with any other drug(s) administered via this common line.

Prepare the desired dosage of ofloxacin according to the following chart:

Patients with Normal Renal Function:

Infection[†]	Unit Dose	Frequency	Duration	Daily Dose
Acute Bacterial Exacerbation of Chronic Bronchitis	400 mg	q12h	10 days	800 mg
Comm. Acquired Pneumonia	400 mg	q12h	10 days	800 mg
Uncomplicated Skin and Skin Structure Infections	400 mg	q12h	10 days	800 mg
Acute, Uncomplicated Urethral and Cerivcal Gonorrhea	400 mg	single dose	1 day	400 mg
Nongonococcal Cervicitis/ Urethritis due to C. trachomatis	300 mg	q12h	7 days	600 mg
Mixed infection of the urethra and cervix due to C. trachomatis and N. gonorrhoeae	300 mg	q12h	7 days	600 mg
Acute Pelvic Inflammatory Disease	400 mg	q12h	10-14 days	800 mg
Uncomplicated Cystitis due to E. coli or K. pneumoniae	200 mg	q12h	3 days	400 mg
Uncomplicated Cystitis due to other approved pathogens	200 mg	q12h	7 days	400 mg
Complicated UTI's	200 mg	q12h	10 days	400 mg
Prostatitis due to E. coli	300 mg	q12h	6 wks[‡]	600 mg

†DUE TO THE DESIGNATED PATHOGENS (See **INDICATIONS AND USAGE**.)

‡BECAUSE THERE ARE NO SAFETY DATA PRESENTLY AVAILABLE TO SUPPORT THE USE OF THE INTRAVENOUS FORMULATION OF OFLOXACIN FOR MORE THAN 10 DAYS, THERAPY AFTER 10 DAYS SHOULD BE SWITCHED TO THE ORAL TABLET FORMULATION OR OTHER APPROPRIATE THERAPY.

Desired Dosage Strength	From 10 mL Vial, With-draw Volume	Volume of Diluent	Infusion Time
200 mg	5 mL	qs 50 mL	60 min
300 mg	7.5 mL	qs 75 mL	60 min
400 mg	10 mL	qs 100 mL	60 min

For example, to prepare a 200-mg dose using the 10 mL vial (40 mg/mL), withdraw 5 mL and dilute with a compatible intravenous solution to a total volume of 50 mL.

Compatible Intravenous Solutions:
Any of the following intravenous solutions may be used to prepare a 4 mg/mL ofloxacin solution with the approximate pH values:

Intravenous Fluids	pH of 4 mg/mL FLOXIN I.V. Solution
0.9% Sodium Chloride Injection, USP	4.69
5% Dextrose Injection, USP	4.57
5% Dextrose/0.9% NaCl Injection	4.56
5% Dextrose in Lactated Ringers Injection	4.94
5% Sodium Bicarbonate Injection	7.95
Plasma-Lyte® 56/5% Dextrose Injection	5.02
5% Dextrose, 0.45% Sodium Chloride, and 0.15% Potassium Chloride Injection	4.64
Sodium Lactate Injection (M/6)	5.64
Water for Injection	4.66

FLOXIN I.V. PRE-MIXED IN SINGLE-USE FLEXIBLE CONTAINERS:
FLOXIN I.V. is also supplied in 50 mL and 100 mL flexible containers containing a pre-mixed, ready-to-use ofloxacin solution in D_5W for single-use. **NO FURTHER DILUTION OF THIS PREPARATION IS NECESSARY. Each 50 mL pre-mixed flexible container already contains a dilute solution with the equivalent of 200 mg of ofloxacin (4 mg/mL) in 5% Dextrose (D_5W). Each 100 mL pre-mixed flexible container already contains a dilute solution with the equivalent of 400 mg of ofloxacin (4 mg/mL) in 5% Dextrose (D_5W).**

This parenteral drug product should be inspected visually for discoloration and particulate matter prior to administration.

Since no preservative or bacteriostatic agent is present in this product, aseptic technique must be used in preparation of the final parenteral solution. **Since the pre-mixed flexible containers are for single-use only, any unused portion should be discarded.**

Since only limited data are available on the compatibility of ofloxacin intravenous injection with other intravenous substances, **additives or other medications should not be added to FLOXIN I.V. in flexible containers or infused simultaneously through the same in-**travenous line. If the same intravenous line is used for sequential infusion of several different drugs, the line should be flushed before and after infusion of FLOXIN I.V. with an infusion solution compatible with FLOXIN I.V. and with any other drug(s) administered via this common line.

Instructions for the Use of FLOXIN I.V. PRE-MIXED IN FLEXIBLE CONTAINERS:
To open:
1. Tear outer wrap at the notch and remove solution container.
2. Check the container for minute leaks by squeezing the inner bag firmly. If leaks are found, or if the seal is not intact, discard the solution, as the sterility may be compromised.
3. Do not use if the solution is cloudy or a precipitate is present.
4. Use sterile equipment.
5. **WARNING: Do not use flexible containers in series connections.** Such use could result in air embolism due to residual air being drawn from the primary container before administration of the fluid from the secondary container is complete.

Preparation for administration:
1. Close flow control clamp of administration set.
2. Remove cover from port at bottom of container.
3. Insert piercing pin of administration set into port with a twisting motion until the pin is firmly seated. **NOTE: See full directions on administration set carton.**
4. Suspend container from hanger.
5. Squeeze and release drip chamber to establish proper fluid level in chamber during infusion of FLOXIN I.V. IN PRE-MIXED FLEXIBLE CONTAINERS.
6. Open flow control clamp to expel air from set. Close clamp.
7. Regulate rate of administration with flow control clamp.

Stability of FLOXIN I.V. as Supplied:
When stored under recommended conditions, FLOXIN I.V., as supplied in 10 mL vials, and 50 mL and 100 mL flexible containers, is stable through the expiration date printed on the label.

Stability of FLOXIN I.V. Following Dilution:
FLOXIN I.V., when diluted in a compatible intravenous fluid to a concentration between 0.4 mg/mL and 4 mg/mL, is stable for 72 h when stored at or below 75°F or 24°C for 14 days when stored under refrigeration at 41°F or 5°C in glass bottles or plastic intravenous containers. Solutions that are diluted in a compatible intravenous solution and frozen in glass bottles or plastic intravenous containers are stable for 6 months when stored at -4°F or -20°C. Once thawed, the solution is stable for up to 14 days, if refrigerated at 36°F to 46°F (2°C to 8°C). **THAW FROZEN SOLUTIONS AT ROOM TEMPERATURE (77°F OR 25°C) OR IN A REFRIGERATOR (46°F OR 8°C).**

DO NOT FORCE THAW BY MICROWAVE IRRA-DIATION OR WATER BATH IMMERSION. DO NOT REFREEZE AFTER INITIAL THAWING.

HOW SUPPLIED

SINGLE-USE VIALS:

FLOXIN (ofloxacin injection) I.V. is supplied in single-use vials. Each vial contains a concentrated solution with the equivalent of 400 mg of ofloxacin.

40 mg/mL, 10 mL vials (NDC 0062-1550-01) FLOXIN I.V. SINGLE-USE VIALS are manufactured for ORTHO-McNEIL PHARMACEUTICAL, INC. by Schering-Plough Products, Inc., Manati, PR 00674.

PRE-MIXED IN FLEXIBLE CONTAINERS:

FLOXIN (ofloxacin injection) I.V. PRE-MIXED IN FLEXIBLE CONTAINERS is supplied as a single-use, pre-mixed solution in 50 mL and 100 mL flexible containers. Each contains a dilute solution with the equivalent of 200 mg or 400 mg of ofloxacin, respectively, in 5% Dextrose (D_5W).

4 mg/mL (200 mg), 50 mL flexible container (NDC 0062-1553-01)

4 mg/mL (400 mg), 100 mL flexible container (NDC 0062-1552-02)

FLOXIN I.V. PRE-MIXED IN FLEXIBLE CONTAINERS is manufactured for ORTHO-McNEIL, PHARMACEUTICAL, INC. by Abbott Laboratories, North Chicago, IL 60064.

FLOXIN (ofloxacin injection) I.V. in SINGLE-USE VIALS should be stored at controlled room temperature 59°F to 86°F (15°C to 30°C) and protected from light. FLOXIN I.V. PRE-MIXED IN FLEXIBLE CONTAINERS should be stored at or below 77°F or 25°C; however, brief exposure up to 104°F or 40°C does not adversely affect the product. Avoid excessive heat and protect from freezing and light.

Also Available:

TABLETS

Ofloxacin is also available as FLOXIN TABLETS (ofloxacin tablets) 200, 300 and 400 mg.

ANIMAL PHARMACOLOGY

Ofloxacin, as well as other drugs of the quinolone class, has been shown to cause arthropathies (arthrosis) in immature dogs and rats. In addition, these drugs are associated with an increased incidence of osteochondrosis in rats as compared to the incidence observed in vehicle-treated rats. (See *WARNINGS*.) There is no evidence of arthropathies in fully mature dogs at intravenous doses up to 3 times the recommended maximum human dose (on a mg/m^2 basis or 5 times based on a mg/kg basis) for a one-week exposure period.

Long-term, high-dose systemic use of other quinolones in experimental animals has caused lenticular opacities; however, this finding was not observed in any animal studies with ofloxacin.

Reduced serum globulin and protein levels were observed in animals treated with other quinolones. In one ofloxacin study, minor decreases in serum globulin and protein levels were noted in female cynomolgus monkeys dosed orally with 40 mg/kg ofloxacin daily for one year. These changes, however, were considered to be within normal limits for monkeys.

Crystalluria and ocular toxicity were not observed in any animals treated with ofloxacin.

Rx only.

FLOXIN® is a trademark of ORTHO-McNEIL PHARMACEUTICAL, INC. U.S. Patent No. 4,382,892

REFERENCES

1. National Committee for Clinical Laboratory Standards. Methods for Dilution Antimicrobial Susceptibility Tests for Bacteria That Grow Aerobically — Third Edition. Approved Standard NCCLS Document M7-A3, Vol. 13, No. 25, NCCLS, Villanova, PA, December, 1993.

2. National Committee for Clinical Laboratory Standards. Performance Standards for Antimicrobial Disk Susceptibility Tests — Fifth Edition. Approved Standard NCCLS Document M2-A5, Vol. 13, No. 24, NCCLS, Villanova, PA, December, 1993.

ORTHO-McNEIL PHARMACEUTICAL, INC. Raritan, NJ USA 08869

© OMP 1998   Revised March 1998

635-10-267-4

FLOXIN® Tablets ℞
(ofloxacin tablets)
[flŏx- ĭn]

DESCRIPTION

FLOXIN® (ofloxacin tablets) Tablets is a synthetic broad-spectrum antimicrobial agent for oral administration. Chemically, ofloxacin, a fluorinated carboxyquinolone, is the racemate, (±)-9-fluoro-2,3-dihydro-3-methyl-10-(4-methyl-1-piperazinyl)-7-oxo-7H-pyrido[1,2,3-de]-1,4-benzoxazine-6-carboxylic acid. The chemical structure is:

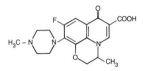

Its empirical formula is $C_{18}H_{20}FN_3O_4$, and its molecular weight is 361.4. Ofloxacin is an off-white to pale yellow crystalline powder. The molecule exists as a zwitterion at the pH conditions in the small intestine. The relative solubility characteristics of ofloxacin at room temperature, as defined by USP nomenclature, indicate that ofloxacin is considered to be *soluble* in aqueous solutions with pH between 2 and 5. It is *sparingly* to *slightly soluble* in aqueous solutions with pH 7 (solubility falls to 4 mg/mL) and *freely soluble* in aqueous solutions with pH above 9. Ofloxacin has the potential to form stable coordination compounds with many metal ions. This *in vitro* chelation potential has the following formation order: $Fe^{+3} > Al^{+3} > Cu^{+2} > Ni^{+2} > Pb^{+2} > Zn^{+2} > Mg^{+2} > Ca^{+2} > Ba^{+2}$.

FLOXIN Tablets contain the following inactive ingredients: anhydrous lactose, corn starch, hydroxypropyl cellulose, hydroxypropyl methylcellulose, magnesium stearate, polyethylene glycol, polysorbate 80, sodium starch glycolate, titanium dioxide and may also contain synthetic yellow iron oxide.

CLINICAL PHARMACOLOGY

Following oral administration, the bioavailability of ofloxacin in the tablet formulation is approximately 98%. Maximum serum concentrations are achieved one to two hours after an oral dose. Absorption of ofloxacin after single or multiple doses of 200 to 400 mg is predictable, and the amount of drug absorbed increases proportionally with the dose. Ofloxa-

cin has biphasic elimination. Following multiple oral doses at steady-state administration, the half-lives are approximately 4–5 hours and 20–25 hours. However, the longer half-life represents less than 5% of the total AUC. Accumulation at steady-state can be estimated using a half-life of 9 hours. The total clearance and volume of distribution are approximately similar after single or multiple doses. Elimination is mainly by renal excretion. The following are mean peak serum concentrations in healthy 70–80 kg male volunteers after single oral doses of 200, 300, or 400 mg of ofloxacin or after multiple oral doses of 400 mg.

[See table below]

Steady-state concentrations were attained after four oral doses, and the area under the curve (AUC) was approximately 40% higher than the AUC after single doses. Therefore, after multiple-dose administration of 200 mg and 300 mg doses, peak serum levels of 2.2 µg/mL and 3.6 µg/mL, respectively, are predicted at steady-state.

In vitro, approximately 32% of the drug in plasma is protein bound.

The single dose and steady-state plasma profiles of ofloxacin injection were comparable in extent of exposure (AUC) to those of ofloxacin tablets when the injectable and tablet formulations of ofloxacin were administered in equal doses (mg/mg) to the same group of subjects. The mean steady-state $AUC_{(0-12)}$ attained after the intravenous administration of 400 mg over 60 min was 43.5 µg•h/mL; the mean steady-state $AUC_{(0-12)}$ attained after the oral administration of 400 mg was 41.2 µg•h/mL (two one-sided t-test, 90% confidence interval was 103–109).

(See following chart.)

[See figure on next page]

Between 0 and 6 h following the administration of a single 200 mg oral dose of ofloxacin to 12 healthy volunteers, the average urine ofloxacin concentration was approximately 220 µg/mL. Between 12 and 24 hours after administration, the average urine ofloxacin level was approximately 34 µg/mL.

Following oral administration of recommended therapeutic doses, ofloxacin has been detected in blister fluid, cervix, lung tissue, ovary, prostatic fluid, prostatic tissue, skin, and sputum. The mean concentration of ofloxacin in each of these various body fluids and tissues after one or more doses was 0.8 to 1.5 times the concurrent plasma level. Inadequate data are presently available on the distribution or levels of ofloxacin in the cerebrospinal fluid or brain tissue.

Oral Dose	Serum Concentration 2 hours after admin. (µg/mL)	Area Under the Curve $(AUC_{(0-\infty)})$ (µg·h/mL)
200 mg single dose	1.5	14.1
300 mg single dose	2.4	21.2
400 mg single dose	2.9	31.4
400 mg steady-state	4.6	61.0

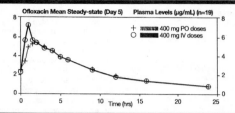

Ofloxacin Mean Steady-state (Day 5) Plasma Levels (µg/mL) (n=19)

+ 400 mg PO doses
O 400 mg IV doses

Time (hrs)

Ofloxacin has a pyridobenzoxazine ring that appears to decrease the extent of parent compound metabolism. Between 65% and 80% of an administered oral dose of ofloxacin is excreted unchanged via the kidneys within 48 hours of dosing. Studies indicate that less than 5% of an administered dose is recovered in the urine as the desmethyl or N-oxide metabolites. Four to eight percent of an ofloxacin dose is excreted in the feces. This indicates a small degree of biliary excretion of ofloxacin. The administration of FLOXIN with food does not affect the C_{max} and AUC_∞ of the drug, but T_{max} is prolonged.

Clearance of ofloxacin is reduced in patients with impaired renal function (creatinine clearance rate ≤ 50 mL/min), and dosage adjustment is necessary. (See **PRECAUTIONS: General** and **DOSAGE AND ADMINISTRATION.**)

Following oral administration to healthy elderly subjects (65–81 years of age), maximum plasma concentrations are usually achieved one to two hours after single and multiple twice-daily doses, indicating that the rate of oral absorption is unaffected by age or gender. Mean peak plasma concentrations in elderly subjects were 9–21% higher than those observed in younger subjects. Gender differences in the pharmacokinetic properties of elderly subjects have been observed. Peak plasma concentrations were 114% and 54% higher in elderly females compared to elderly males following single and multiple twice-daily doses. [This interpretation was based on study results collected from two separate studies.] Plasma concentrations increase dose-dependently with the increase in doses after single oral dose and at steady state. No differences were observed in the volume of distribution values between elderly and younger subjects. As in younger subjects, elimination is mainly by renal excretion as unchanged drug in elderly subjects, although less drug is recovered from renal excretion in elderly subjects. Consistent with younger subjects, less than 5% of an administered dose was recovered in the urine as the desmethyl and N-oxide metabolites in the elderly. A longer plasma half-life of approximately 6.4 to 7.4 hours was observed in elderly subjects, compared with 4 to 5 hours for young subjects. Slower elimination of ofloxacin is observed in elderly subjects as compared with younger subjects which may be attributable to the reduced renal function and

renal clearance observed in the elderly subjects. Because ofloxacin is known to be substantially excreted by the kidney, and elderly patients are more likely to have decreased renal function, dosage adjustment is necessary for elderly patients with impaired renal function as recommended for all patients. (See **PRECAUTIONS: General** and **DOSAGE AND ADMINISTRATION.**)

Microbiology

Ofloxacin is a quinolone antimicrobial agent. The mechanism of action of ofloxacin and other fluoroquinolone antimicrobials involves inhibition of bacterial topoisomerase IV and DNA gyrase (both of which are type II topoisomerases), enzymes required for DNA replication, transcription, repair and recombination.

Ofloxacin has in vitro activity against a wide range of gram-negative and gram-positive microorganisms. Ofloxacin is often bactericidal at concentrations equal to or slightly greater than inhibitory concentrations.

Fluoroquinolones, including ofloxacin, differ in chemical structure and mode of action from aminoglycosides, macrolides and β-lactam antibiotics, including penicillins. Fluoroquinolones may, therefore, be active against bacteria resistant to these antimicrobials.

Resistance to ofloxacin due to spontaneous mutation in vitro is a rare occurrence (range: 10^{-9} to 10^{-11}). Although cross-resistance has been observed between ofloxacin and some other fluoroquinolones, some microorganisms resistant to other fluoroquinolones may be susceptible to ofloxacin.

Ofloxacin has been shown to be active against most strains of the following microorganisms both in vitro and in clinical infections as described in the **INDICATIONS AND USAGE** section:

Aerobic gram-positive microorganisms

Staphylococcus aureus (methicillin-susceptible strains)
Streptococcus pneumoniae (penicillin-susceptible strains)
Streptococcus pyogenes

Aerobic gram-negative microorganisms

Citrobacter (diversus) koseri
Enterobacter aerogenes
Escherichia coli
Haemophilus influenzae
Klebsiella pneumoniae
Neisseria gonorrhoeae
Proteus mirabilis

Pseudomonas aeruginosa
As with other drugs in this class, some strains of *Pseudomonas aeruginosa* may develop resistance fairly rapidly during treatment with ofloxacin.

Other microorganisms
Chlamydia trachomatis
The following *in vitro* data are available, **but their clinical significance is unknown.**
Ofloxacin exhibits *in vitro* minimum inhibitory concentrations (MIC values) of 2 µg/mL or less against most (≥ 90%) strains of the following microorganisms; however, the safety and effectiveness of ofloxacin in treating clinical infections due to these microorganisms have not been established in adequate and well-controlled trials:

Aerobic gram-positive microorganisms
Staphylococcus epidermidis (methicillin-susceptible strains)
Staphylococcus saprophyticus
Streptococcus pneumoniae (penicillin-resistant strains)

Aerobic gram-negative microorganisms
Acinetobacter calcoaceticus
Bordetella pertussis
Citrobacter freundii
Enterobacter cloacae
Haemophilus ducreyi
Klebsiella oxytoca
Moraxella catarrhalis
Morganella morganii
Proteus vulgaris
Providencia rettgeri
Providencia stuartii
Serratia marcescens

Anaerobic microorganisms
Clostridium perfringens

Other microorganisms
Chlamydia pneumoniae
Gardnerella vaginalis
Legionella pneumophila
Mycoplasma hominis
Mycoplasma pneumoniae
Ureaplasma urealyticum
Ofloxacin is not active against Treponema pallidum. (See *WARNINGS*.)
Many strains of other streptococcal species, *Enterococcus* species, and anaerobes are resistant to ofloxacin.

Susceptibility Tests
Dilution techniques: Quantitative methods are used to determine antimicrobial minimum inhibitory concentrations (MIC values). These MIC values provide estimates of the susceptibility of bacteria to antimicrobial compounds. The MIC values should be determined using a standardized procedure. Standardized procedures are based on a dilution method[1] (broth or agar) or equivalent with standardized inoculum concentrations and standardized concentrations of ofloxacin powder. The MIC values should be interpreted according to the following criteria:

For testing aerobic microorganisms other than *Haemophilus influenzae*, *Neisseria gonorrhoeae*, and *Streptococcus pneumoniae*:

MIC (µg/mL)	Interpretation
≤2	Susceptible (S)
4	Intermediate (I)
≥8	Resistant (R)

For testing *Haemophilus influenzae*:[a]

MIC (µg/mL)	Interpretation
≤2.0	Susceptible (S)

[a] This interpretive standard is applicable only to broth microdilution susceptibility tests with *Haemophilus influenzae* using *Haemophilus* Test Medium[1].

The current absence of data on resistant strains precludes defining any results other than "Susceptible." Strains yielding MIC results suggestive of a "nonsusceptible" category should be submitted to a reference laboratory for further testing.

For testing *Neisseria gonorrhoeae*:[b]

MIC (µg/mL)	Interpretation
≤0.25	Susceptible (S)
0.5–1	Intermediate (I)
≥2	Resistant (R)

[b] These interpretive standards are applicable only to agar dilution tests using GC agar base and 1% defined growth supplement incubated in 5% CO_2.

For testing *Streptococcus* species including *Streptococcus pneumoniae*:[c]

MIC (µg/mL)	Interpretation
≤2	Susceptible (S)
4	Intermediate (I)
≥8	Resistant (R)

[c] These interpretive standards are applicable only to broth microdilution susceptibility tests using cation-adjusted Mueller-Hinton broth with 2–5% lysed horse blood.

A report of "Susceptible" indicates that the pathogen is likely to be inhibited if the antimicrobial compound in the blood reaches the concentrations usually achievable. A report of "Intermediate" indicates that the result should be considered equivocal, and, if the microorganism is not fully susceptible to alternative, clinically feasible drugs, the test should be repeated. This category implies possible clinical applicability in body sites where the drug is physiologically concentrated or in situations where high dosage of drug can be used. This category also provides a buffer zone which prevents small uncontrolled technical factors from causing major discrepancies in interpre-

Microorganism		MIC (µg/mL)
Escherichia coli	ATCC 25922	0.015–0.12
Haemophilus influenzae	ATCC 49247[d]	0.016–0.06
Neisseria gonorrhoeae	ATCC 49226[e]	0.004–0.016
Pseudomonas aeruginosa	ATCC 27853	1–8
Staphylococcus aureus	ATCC 29213	0.12–1
Streptococcus pneumoniae	ATCC 49619[f]	1–4

[d] This quality control range is applicable only to *H. influenzae* ATCC 49247 tested by a microdilution procedure using *Haemophilus* Test Medium (HTM)[1].

[e] This quality control range is applicable only to *N. gonorrhoeae* ATCC 49226 tested by an agar dilution procedure using GC agar base with 1% defined growth supplement incubated in 5% CO_2.

[f] This quality control range is applicable only to *S. pneumoniae* ATCC 49619 tested by a microdilution procedure using cation-adjusted Mueller-Hinton broth with 2–5% lysed horse blood.

---

tation. A report of "Resistant" indicates that the pathogen is not likely to be inhibited if the antimicrobial compound in the blood reaches the concentrations usually achievable; other therapy should be selected.

Standardized susceptibility test procedures require the use of laboratory control microorganisms to control the technical aspects of the laboratory procedures. Standard ofloxacin powder should provide the following MIC values:

[See table above]

Diffusion techniques: Quantitative methods that require measurement of zone diameters also provide reproducible estimates of the susceptibility of bacteria to antimicrobial compounds. One such standardized procedure[2] requires the use of standardized inoculum concentrations. This procedure uses paper disks impregnated with 5-µg ofloxacin to test the susceptibility of microorganisms to ofloxacin. Reports from the laboratory providing results of the standard single-disk susceptibility test with a 5-µg ofloxacin disk should be interpreted according to the following criteria:

For testing aerobic microorganisms other than *Haemophilus influenzae*, *Neisseria gonorrhoeae*, and *Streptococcus pneumoniae*:

Zone Diameter (mm)	Interpretation
≥16	Susceptible (S)
13–16	Intermediate (I)
≤12	Resistant (R)

For testing *Haemophilus influenzae*:[g]

Zone Diameter (mm)	Interpretation
≥16	Susceptible (S)

[g] This zone diameter standard is applicable only to disk diffusion tests with *Haemophilus influenzae* using *Haemophilus* Test Medium (HTM)[2] incubated in 5% CO_2.

The current absence of data on resistant strains precludes defining any results other than "Susceptible." Strains yielding zone di-

ameter results suggestive of a "nonsusceptible" category should be submitted to a reference laboratory for further testing.

For testing *Neisseria gonorrhoea*:[h]

Zone Diameter (mm)	Interpretation
≥31	Susceptible (S)
25–30	Intermediate (I)
≤24	Resistant (R)

[h] These zone diameter standards are applicable only to disk diffusion tests using GC agar base and 1% defined growth supplement incubated in 5% CO_2.

For testing *Streptococcus* species including *Streptococcus pneumoniae*:[i]

Zone Diameter (mm)	Interpretation
≥16	Susceptible (S)
13–15	Intermediate (I)
≤12	Resistant (R)

[i] These zone diameter standards are applicable only to disk diffusion tests performed using Mueller-Hinton agar supplemented with 5% defibrinated sheep blood and incubated in 5% CO_2.

Interpretation should be as stated above for results using dilution techniques. Interpretation involves correlation of the diameter obtained in the disk test with the MIC for ofloxacin.

As with standardized dilution techniques, diffusion methods require the use of laboratory control microorganisms that are used to control the technical aspects of the laboratory procedures. For the diffusion technique, the 5-µg ofloxacin disk should provide the following zone diameters in these laboratory quality control strains:

[See table at bottom of next page]

INDICATIONS AND USAGE

FLOXIN (ofloxacin tablets) Tablets are indicated for the treatment of adults with mild to moderate infections (unless otherwise indicated) caused by susceptible strains of the designated microorganisms in the infections listed below. Please see *DOSAGE AND ADMINISTRATION* for specific recommendations.

Acute bacterial exacerbations of chronic bronchitis due to *Haemophilus influenzae* or *Streptococcus pneumoniae*.

Community-acquired Pneumonia due to *Haemophilus influenzae* or *Streptococcus pneumoniae*.

Uncomplicated skin and skin structure infections due to *Staphylococcus aureus*, *Streptococcus pyogenes*, or *Proteus mirabilis*.

Acute, uncomplicated urethral and cervical gonorrhea due to *Neisseria gonorrhoeae*. (See *WARNINGS*.)

Nongonococcal urethritis and cervicitis due to *Chlamydia trachomatis*. (See *WARNINGS*.)

Mixed infections of the urethra and cervix due to *Chlamydia trachomatis* and *Neisseria gonorrhoeae*. (See *WARNINGS*.)

Acute pelvic inflammatory disease (including severe infection) due to *Chlamydia trachomatis* and/or *Neisseria gonorrhoeae*. (See *WARNINGS*.)

NOTE: If anaerobic microorganisms are suspected of contributing to the infection, appropriate therapy for anaerobic pathogens should be administered.

Uncomplicated cystitis due to *Citrobacter diversus*, *Enterobacter aerogenes*, *Escherichia coli*, *Klebsiella pneumoniae*, *Proteus mirabilis*, or *Pseudomonas aeruginosa*.

Complicated urinary tract infections due to *Escherichia coli*, *Klebsiella pneumoniae*, *Proteus mirabilis*, *Citrobacter diversus**, or *Pseudomonas aeruginosa**.

Prostatitis due to *Escherichia coli*.

* = Although treatment of infections due to this organism in this organ system demonstrated a clinically significant outcome, efficacy was studied in fewer than 10 patients.

Appropriate culture and susceptibility tests should be performed before treatment in order to isolate and identify organisms causing the infection and to determine their susceptibility to ofloxacin. Therapy with ofloxacin may be initiated before results of these tests are known; once results become available, appropriate therapy should be continued.

As with other drugs in this class, some strains of *Pseudomonas aeruginosa* may develop resistance fairly rapidly during treatment with ofloxacin. Culture and susceptibility testing performed periodically during therapy will provide information not only on the therapeutic effect of the antimicrobial agent but also on the possible emergence of bacterial resistance.

CONTRAINDICATIONS

FLOXIN (ofloxacin) is contraindicated in persons with a history of hypersensitivity associated with the use of ofloxacin or any member of the quinolone group of antimicrobial agents.

WARNINGS

THE SAFETY AND EFFICACY OF OFLOXACIN IN PEDIATRIC PATIENTS AND ADOLESCENTS (UNDER THE AGE OF 18 YEARS), PREGNANT WOMEN, AND LACTATING WOMEN HAVE NOT BEEN ESTABLISHED. (See PRECAUTIONS: Pediatric Use, Pregnancy, and Nursing Mothers subsections.)

In the immature rat, the oral administration of ofloxacin at 5 to 16 times the recommended maximum human dose based on mg/kg or 1–3 times based on mg/m² increased the incidence and severity of osteochondrosis. The lesions did not regress after 13 weeks of drug withdrawal. Other quinolones also produce similar erosions in the weight-bearing joints and other signs of arthropathy in immature animals of various species. (See *ANIMAL PHARMACOLOGY*.)

Convulsions, increased intracranial pressure, and toxic psychosis have been reported in patients receiving quinolones, including ofloxacin. Quinolones, including ofloxacin, may also cause central nervous system stimulation which may lead to: tremors, restlessness/agitation, nervousness/anxiety, lightheadedness, confusion, hallucinations, paranoia and de-

Microorganism		Zone Diameter (mm)
Escherichia coli	ATCC 25922	29–33
Haemophilus influenzae	ATCC 49247[j]	31–40
Neisseria gonorrhoeae	ATCC 49226[k]	43–51
Pseudomonas aeruginosa	ATCC 27853	17–21
Staphylococcus aureus	ATCC 25923	24–28
Streptococcus pneumoniae	ATCC 49619[l]	16–21

[j] This quality control range is applicable only to *H. influenzae* ATCC 49247 tested by a disk diffusion procedure using *Haemophilus* Test Medium (HTM)² incubated in 5% CO_2.

[k] This quality control range is applicable only to *N. gonorrhoeae* ATCC 49226 tested by a disk diffusion procedure using GC agar base with 1% defined growth supplement incubated in 5% CO_2.

[l] This quality control range is applicable only to *S. pneumoniae* ATCC 49619 tested by a disk diffusion procedure using Mueller-Hinton agar supplemented with 5% defibrinated sheep blood and incubated in 5% CO_2.

pression, nightmares, insomnia, and rarely suicidal thoughts or acts. These reactions may occur following the first dose. If these reactions occur in patients receiving ofloxacin, the drug should be discontinued and appropriate measures instituted. Insomnia may be more common with ofloxacin than some other products in the quinolone class. As with all quinolones, ofloxacin should be used with caution in patients with a known or suspected CNS disorder that may predispose to seizures or lower the seizure threshold (e.g., severe cerebral arteriosclerosis, epilepsy) or in the presence of other risk factors that may predispose to seizures or lower the seizure threshold (e.g., certain drug therapy, renal dysfunction). (See *PRECAUTIONS: General, Information for Patients, Drug Interactions* and *ADVERSE REACTIONS*.)

Serious and occasionally fatal hypersensitivity (anaphylactic/anaphylactoid) reactions have been reported in patients receiving therapy with quinolones, including ofloxacin. These reactions often occur following the first dose. Some reactions were accompanied by cardiovascular collapse, hypotension/shock, seizure, loss of consciousness, tingling, angioedema (including tongue, laryngeal, throat or facial edema/swelling), airway obstruction (including bronchospasm, shortness of breath and acute respiratory distress), dyspnea, urticaria/hives, itching, and other serious skin reactions. A few patients had a history of hypersensitivity reactions. The drug should be discontinued immediately at the first appearance of a skin rash or any other sign of hypersensitivity. Serious acute hypersensitivity reactions may require treatment with epinephrine and other resuscitative measures, including oxygen, intravenous fluids, antihistamines, corticosteroids, pressor amines, and airway management, as clinically indicated. (See *PRECAUTIONS* and *ADVERSE REACTIONS*.)

Serious and sometimes fatal events, some due to hypersensitivity, and some due to uncertain etiology, have been reported in patients receiving therapy with quinolones, including ofloxacin. These events may be severe and generally occur following the administration of multiple doses. Clinical manifestations may include one or more of the following: fever, rash or severe dermatologic reactions (e.g., toxic epidermal necrolysis, Stevens-Johnson Syndrome); vasculitis; arthralgia; myalgia; serum sickness; allergic pneumonitis; interstitial nephritis; acute renal insufficiency/failure; hepatitis; jaundice; acute hepatic necrosis/failure; anemia, including hemolytic and aplastic; thrombocytopenia, including thrombotic thrombocytopenic purpura; leukopenia; agranulocytosis; pancytopenia; and/or other hematologic abnormalities. The drug should be discontinued immediately at the first appearance of a skin rash or any other sign of hypersensitivity and supportive measures instituted. (See *PRECAUTIONS: Information for Patients* and *ADVERSE REACTIONS*.)

Pseudomembranous colitis has been reported with nearly all antibacterial agents, including ofloxacin, and may range in severity from mild to life-threatening. Therefore, it is important to consider this diagnosis in patients who present with diarrhea subsequent to the administration of any antibacterial agents.

Treatment with antibacterial agents alters the normal flora of the colon and may permit overgrowth of clostridia. Studies indicate a toxin produced by *Clostridium difficile* is one primary cause of "antibiotic-associated colitis".

After the diagnosis of pseudomembranous colitis has been established, therapeutic measures should be initiated. Mild cases of pseudomembranous colitis usually respond to drug discontinuation alone. In moderate to severe cases, consideration should be given to management with fluids and electrolytes, protein supplementation, and treatment with an antibacterial drug clinically effective against *C. difficile* colitis. (See *ADVERSE REACTIONS*.)

Ruptures of the shoulder, hand, and Achilles tendons that required surgical repair or resulted in prolonged disability have been reported with ofloxacin and other quinolones. Ofloxacin should be discontinued if the patient experiences pain, inflammation, or rupture of a tendon. Patients should rest and refrain from exercise until the diagnosis of tendinitis or tendon rupture has been confidently excluded. Tendon rupture can occur at any time during or after therapy with ofloxacin.

Ofloxacin has not been shown to be effective in the treatment of syphilis. Antimicrobial agents used in high doses for short periods of time to treat gonorrhea may mask or delay the symptoms of incubating syphilis. All patients with gonorrhea should have a serologic test for syphilis at the time of diagnosis. Patients treated with ofloxacin for gonorrhea should have a follow-up serologic test for syphilis after three months and, if positive, treatment with an appropriate antimicrobial should be instituted.

PRECAUTIONS

General:

Adequate hydration of patients receiving ofloxacin should be maintained to prevent the formation of a highly concentrated urine.

Administer ofloxacin with caution in the presence of renal or hepatic insufficiency/impairment. In patients with known or suspected renal or hepatic insufficiency/impairment, careful clinical observation and appropriate laboratory studies should be performed prior to and during therapy since elimination of ofloxacin may be reduced. In patients with impaired renal function (creatinine clearance ≤ 50 mg/mL), alteration of the dosage regimen is necessary. (See *CLINICAL PHARMACOLOGY* and *DOSAGE AND ADMINISTRATION*.)

Moderate to severe phototoxicity reactions have been observed in patients exposed to direct sunlight while receiving some drugs in this class, including ofloxacin. Excessive sunlight should be avoided. Therapy should be discontinued if phototoxicity (e.g., a skin eruption) occurs.

As with other quinolones, ofloxacin should be used with caution in any patient with a known or suspected CNS disorder that may predispose to seizures or lower the seizure threshold (e.g., severe cerebral arteriosclerosis, epilepsy) or in the presence of other risk factors that may predispose to seizures or lower the seizure threshold (e.g., certain drug therapy, renal dysfunction). (See *WARNINGS* and *Drug Interactions*.)

A possible interaction between oral hypoglycemic drugs (e.g., glyburide/glibenclamide) or with insulin and fluoroquinolone antimicrobial agents have been reported resulting in potentiation of the hypoglycemic action of these drugs. The mechanism for this interaction is not known. If a hypoglycemic reaction occurs in a patient being treated with ofloxacin, discontinue ofloxacin immediately and consult a physician. (See *Drug Interactions* and *ADVERSE REACTIONS*.)

As with any potent drug, periodic assessment of organ system functions, including renal, hepatic, and hematopoietic, is advisable during prolonged therapy. (See *WARNINGS* and *ADVERSE REACTIONS*.)

Information for Patients:
Patients should be advised:
— to drink fluids liberally;
— that mineral supplements, vitamins with iron or minerals, calcium- , aluminum-, or magnesium-based antacids, sucralfate or Videx®, (Didanosine), chewable/buffered tablets or the pediatric powder for oral solution should not be taken within the two-hour period before or within the two-hour period after taking ofloxacin (See *Drug Interactions*);
— that ofloxacin can be taken without regard to meals;
— that ofloxacin may cause neurologic adverse effects (e.g., dizziness, lightheadedness) and that patients should know how they react to ofloxacin before they operate an automobile or machinery or engage in activities requiring mental alertness and coordination (See *WARNINGS* and *ADVERSE REACTIONS*);
— to discontinue treatment and inform their physician if they experience pain, inflammation, or rupture of a tendon, and to rest and refrain from exercise until the diagnosis of tendinitis or tendon rupture has been confidently excluded;
— that ofloxacin may be associated with hypersensitivity reactions, even following the first dose, to discontinue the drug at the first sign of a skin rash, hives or other skin reactions, a rapid heartbeat, difficulty in swallowing or breathing, any swelling suggesting angioedema (e.g., swelling of the

lips, tongue, face; tightness of the throat, hoarseness), or any other symptom of an allergic reaction (See *WARNINGS* and *ADVERSE REACTIONS*);
— to avoid excessive sunlight or artificial ultraviolet light while receiving ofloxacin and to discontinue therapy if phototoxicity (e.g., skin eruption) occurs;
— that if they are diabetic and are being treated with insulin or an oral hypoglycemic drug, to discontinue ofloxacin immediately if a hypoglycemic reaction occurs and consult a physician (See *PRECAUTIONS: General* and *Drug Interactions*);
— that convulsions have been reported in patients taking quinolones, including ofloxacin, and to notify their physician before taking this drug if there is a history of this condition.

Drug Interactions:
Antacids, Sucralfate, Metal Cations, Multivitamins: Quinolones form chelates with alkaline earth and transition metal cations. Administration of quinolones with antacids containing calcium, magnesium, or aluminum, with sucralfate, with divalent or trivalent cations such as iron, or with multivitamins containing zinc or with Videx®, (Didanosine), chewable/buffered tablets or the pediatric powder for oral solution may substantially interfere with the absorption of quinolones resulting in systemic levels considerably lower than desired. These agents should not be taken within the two-hour period before or within the two-hour period after ofloxacin administration. (See *DOSAGE AND ADMINISTRATION.*)

Caffeine: Interactions between ofloxacin and caffeine have not been detected.

Cimetidine: Cimetidine has demonstrated interference with the elimination of some quinolones. This interference has resulted in significant increases in half-life and AUC of some quinolones. The potential for interaction between ofloxacin and cimetidine has not been studied.

Cyclosporine: Elevated serum levels of cyclosporine have been reported with concomitant use of cyclosporine with some other quinolones. The potential for interaction between ofloxacin and cyclosporine has not been studied.

Drugs metabolized by Cytochrome P450 enzymes: Most quinolone antimicrobial drugs inhibit cytochrome P450 enzyme activity. This may result in a prolonged half-life for some drugs that are also metabolized by this system (e.g., cyclosporine, theophylline/methylxanthines, warfarin) when co-administered with quinolones. The extent of this inhibition varies among different quinolones. (See other *Drug Interactions*.)

Non-steroidal anti-inflammatory drugs: The concomitant administration of a non-steroidal anti-inflammatory drug with a quinolone, including ofloxacin, may increase the risk of

CNS stimulation and convulsive seizures. (See *WARNINGS* and *PRECAUTIONS: General.*)

Probenecid: The concomitant use of probenecid with certain other quinolones has been reported to affect renal tubular secretion. The effect of probenecid on the elimination of ofloxacin has not been studied.

Theophylline: Steady-state theophylline levels may increase when ofloxacin and theophylline are administered concurrently. As with other quinolones, concomitant administration of ofloxacin may prolong the half-life of theophylline, elevate serum theophylline levels, and increase the risk of theophylline-related adverse reactions. Theophylline levels should be closely monitored and theophylline dosage adjustments made, if appropriate, when ofloxacin is co-administered. Adverse reactions (including seizures) may occur with or without an elevation in the serum theophylline level. (See *WARNINGS* and *PRECAUTIONS: General.*)

Warfarin: Some quinolones have been reported to enhance the effects of the oral anticoagulant warfarin or its derivatives. Therefore, if a quinolone antimicrobial is administered concomitantly with warfarin or its derivatives, the prothrombin time or other suitable coagulation test should be closely monitored.

Antidiabetic agents (e.g., insulin, glyburide/glibenclamide): Since disturbances of blood glucose, including hyperglycemia and hypoglycemia, have been reported in patients treated concurrently with quinolones and an antidiabetic agent, careful monitoring of blood glucose is recommended when these agents are used concomitantly. (See *PRECAUTIONS: General* and *Information for Patients.*)

Carcinogenesis, Mutagenesis, Impairment of Fertility:
Long-term studies to determine the carcinogenic potential of ofloxacin have not been conducted.

Ofloxacin was not mutagenic in the Ames bacterial test, *in vitro* and *in vivo* cytogenetic assay, sister chromatid exchange (Chinese Hamster and Human Cell Lines), unscheduled DNA Repair (UDS) using human fibroblasts, dominant lethal assays, or mouse micronucleus assay. Ofloxacin was positive in the UDS test using rat hepatocytes and Mouse Lymphoma Assay.

Pregnancy: Teratogenic Effects. Pregnancy Category C.
Ofloxacin has not been shown to have any teratogenic effects at oral doses as high as 810 mg/kg/day (11 times the recommended maximum human dose based on mg/m^2 or 50 times based on mg/kg) and 160 mg/kg/day (4 times the recommended maximum human dose based on mg/m^2 or 10 times based on mg/kg) when administered to pregnant rats and rabbits, respectively. Additional studies in rats with oral doses up to 360 mg/kg/day (5 times the recommended maximum human dose based on mg/m^2 or 23 times based on mg/kg) demonstrated no adverse effect on late fetal development, labor, delivery, lactation, neonatal viability, or growth of the newborn. Doses equivalent to 50 and 10 times the recommended maximum human dose of ofloxacin (based on mg/kg) were fetotoxic (i.e., decreased fetal body weight and increased fetal mortality) in rats and rabbits, respectively. Minor skeletal variations were reported in rats receiving doses of 810 mg/kg/day, which is more than 10 times higher than the recommended maximum human dose based on mg/m^2.

There are, however, no adequate and well-controlled studies in pregnant women. Ofloxacin should be used during pregnancy only if the potential benefit justifies the potential risk to the fetus. (See *WARNINGS.*)

Nursing Mothers:
In lactating females, a single oral 200-mg dose of ofloxacin resulted in concentrations of ofloxacin in milk that were similar to those found in plasma. Because of the potential for serious adverse reactions from ofloxacin in nursing infants, a decision should be made whether to discontinue nursing or to discontinue the drug, taking into account the importance of the drug to the mother. (See *WARNINGS* and *ADVERSE REACTIONS.*)

Pediatric Use:
Safety and effectiveness in pediatric patients and adolescents below the age of 18 years have not been established. Ofloxacin causes arthropathy (arthrosis) and osteochondrosis in juvenile animals of several species. (See *WARNINGS.*)

Geriatric Use:
In phase 2/3 clinical trials with ofloxacin, 688 patients (14.2%) were ≥ 65 years of age. Of these, 436 patients (9.0%) were between the ages of 65 and 74 and 252 patients (5.2%) were 75 years or older. There was no apparent difference in the frequency or severity of adverse reactions in elderly adults compared with younger adults. The pharmacokinetic properties of ofloxacin in elderly subjects are similar to those in younger subjects. Drug absorption appears to be unaffected by age. Dosage adjustment is necessary for elderly patients with impaired renal function (creatinine clearance rate ≤ 50 mL/min) due to reduced clearance of ofloxacin. In comparative studies, the frequency and severity of most drug-related nervous system events in patients ≥ 65 years of age were comparable for ofloxacin and control drugs. The only differences identified were an increase in reports of insomnia (3.9% vs 1.5%) and headache (4.7% vs 1.8%) with ofloxacin. It is important to note that these geriatric safety data are extracted from 44 comparative studies where the adverse reaction information from 20 different controls (other antibiotics or placebo) were pooled for comparison with ofloxacin. The clinical significance of such a comparison is not clear. (See *CLINICAL PHARMACOLOGY* and *DOSAGE AND ADMINISTRATION.*)

ADVERSE REACTIONS

The following is a compilation of the data for ofloxacin based on clinical experience with both the oral and intravenous formulations. The incidence of drug-related adverse reactions in patients during Phase 2 and 3 clinical trials was 11%. Among patients receiving multiple-dose therapy, 4% discontinued ofloxacin due to adverse experiences.

In clinical trials, the following events were considered likely to be drug-related in patients receiving multiple doses of ofloxacin:

nausea 3%, insomnia 3%, headache 1%, dizziness 1%, diarrhea 1%, vomiting 1%, rash 1%, pruritus 1%, external genital pruritus in women 1%, vaginitis 1%, dysgeusia 1%.

In clinical trials, the most frequently reported adverse events, regardless of relationship to drug, were:

nausea 10%, headache 9%, insomnia 7%, external genital pruritus in women 6%, dizziness 5%, vaginitis 5%, diarrhea 4%, vomiting 4%.

In clinical trials, the following events, regardless of relationship to drug, occurred in 1 to 3% of patients:

Abdominal pain and cramps, chest pain, decreased appetite, dry mouth, dysgeusia, fatigue, flatulence, gastrointestinal distress, nervousness, pharyngitis, pruritus, fever, rash, sleep disorders, somnolence, trunk pain, vaginal discharge, visual disturbances, and constipation.

Additional events, occurring in clinical trials at a rate of less than 1%, regardless of relationship to drug, were:

Body as a whole:	asthenia, chills, malaise, extremity pain, pain, epistaxis
Cardiovascular System:	cardiac arrest, edema, hypertension, hypotension, palpitations, vasodilation
Gastrointestinal System:	dyspepsia
Genital/Reproductive System:	burning, irritation, pain and rash of the female genitalia; dysmenorrhea; menorrhagia; metrorrhagia
Musculoskeletal System:	arthralgia, myalgia
Nervous System:	seizures, anxiety, cognitive change, depression, dream abnormality, euphoria, hallucinations, paresthesia, syncope, vertigo, tremor, confusion
Nutritional/Metabolic:	thirst, weight loss
Respiratory System:	respiratory arrest, cough, rhinorrhea
Skin/Hypersensitivity:	angioedema, diaphoresis, urticaria, vasculitis
Special Senses:	decreased hearing acuity, tinnitus, photophobia
Urinary System:	dysuria, urinary frequency, urinary retention

The following laboratory abnormalities appeared in ≥ 1.0% of patients receiving multiple doses of ofloxacin. It is not known whether these abnormalities were caused by the drug or the underlying conditions being treated.

Hematopoietic:	anemia, leukopenia, leukocytosis, neutropenia, neutrophilia, increased band forms, lymphocytopenia, eosinophilia, lymphocytosis, thrombocytopenia, thrombocytosis, elevated ESR
Hepatic:	elevated: alkaline phosphatase, AST (SGOT), ALT (SGPT)
Serum chemistry:	hyperglycemia, hypoglycemia, elevated creatinine, elevated BUN
Urinary:	glucosuria, proteinuria, alkalinuria, hyposthenuria, hematuria, pyuria

Post-Marketing Adverse Events:

Additional adverse events, regardless of relationship to drug, reported from worldwide marketing experience with quinolones, including ofloxacin:

Clinical:

Cardiovascular System:	cerebral thrombosis, pulmonary edema, tachycardia, hypotension/shock, syncope
Endocrine/Metabolic:	hyper- or hypoglycemia, especially in diabetic patients on insulin or oral hypoglycemic agents (See *PRECAUTIONS: General* and *Drug Interactions.*)
Gastrointestinal System:	hepatic dysfunction including: hepatic necrosis, jaundice (cholestatic or hepatocellular), hepatitis; intestinal perforation; pseudomembranous colitis (the onset of pseu-

domembranous colitis symptoms may occur during or after antimicrobial treatment), GI hemorrhage; hiccough, painful oral mucosa, pyrosis (See **WARNINGS**.)

Genital/Reproductive
System:
vaginal candidiasis

Hematopoietic:
anemia, including hemolytic and aplastic; hemorrhage, pancytopenia, agranulocytosis, leukopenia, reversible bone marrow depression, thrombocytopenia, thrombotic thrombocytopenic purpura, petechiae, ecchymosis/bruising (See **WARNINGS**.)

Musculoskeletal:
tendinitis/rupture; weakness; rhabdomyolysis

Nervous System:
nightmares; suicidal thoughts or acts, disorientation, psychotic reactions, paranoia; phobia, agitation, restlessness, aggressiveness/hostility, manic reaction, emotional lability; peripheral neuropathy, ataxia, incoordination; possible exacerbation of: myasthenia gravis and extrapyramidal disorders; dysphasia, lightheadedness (See **WARNINGS** and **PRECAUTIONS**.)

Respiratory System:
dyspnea, bronchospasm, allergic pneumonitis, stridor (See **WARNINGS**.)

Skin/Hypersensitivity:
anaphylactic (-toid) reactions/shock; purpura, serum sickness, erythema multiforme/Stevens-Johnson Syndrome, erythema nodosum, exfoliative dermatitis, hyperpigmentation, toxic epidermal necrolysis, conjunctivitis, photosensitivity, vesiculobullous eruption (See **WARNINGS** and **PRECAUTIONS**.)

Special Senses:
diplopia, nystagmus, blurred vision, disturbances of: taste, smell, hearing and equilibrium, usually reversible following discontinuation

Urinary System:
anuria, polyuria, renal calculi, renal failure, interstitial nephritis, hematuria (See **WARNINGS** and **PRECAUTIONS**.)

Laboratory:

Hematopoietic:
prolongation of prothrombin time

Serum chemistry:
acidosis, elevation of: serum triglycerides, serum cholesterol, serum potassium, liver function tests including: GGTP, LDH, bilirubin

Urinary:
albuminuria, candiduria

In clinical trials using multiple-dose therapy, ophthalmologic abnormalities, including cataracts and multiple punctate lenticular opacities, have been noted in patients undergoing treatment with other quinolones. The relationship of the drugs to these events is not presently established.

CRYSTALLURIA and CYLINDRURIA HAVE BEEN REPORTED with other quinolones.

OVERDOSAGE

Information on overdosage with ofloxacin is limited. One incident of accidental overdosage has been reported. In this case, an adult female received 3 grams of ofloxacin intravenously over 45 minutes. A blood sample obtained 15 minutes after the completion of the infusion revealed an ofloxacin level of 39.3 µg/mL. In 7 h, the level had fallen to 16.2 µg/mL, and by 24 h to 2.7 µg/mL. During the infusion, the patient developed drowsiness, nausea, dizziness, hot and cold flushes, subjective facial swelling and numbness, slurring of speech, and mild to moderate disorientation. All complaints except the dizziness subsided within 1 h after discontinuation of the infusion. The dizziness, most bothersome while standing, resolved in approximately 9 h. Laboratory testing reportedly revealed no clinically significant changes in routine parameters in this patient.

Patients with Normal Renal Function:

Infection[†]	Unit Dose	Frequency	Duration	Daily Dose
Acute Bacterial Exacerbation of Chronic Bronchitis	400 mg	q12h	10 days	800 mg
Comm. Acquired Pneumonia	400 mg	q12h	10 days	800 mg
Uncomplicated Skin and Skin Structure Infections	400 mg	q12h	10 days	800 mg
Acute, Uncomplicated Urethral and Cervical Gonorrhea	400 mg	single dose	1 day	400 mg
Nongonococcal Cervicitis/Urethritis due to *C. trachomatis*	300 mg	q12h	7 days	600 mg
Mixed Infection of the urethra and cervix due to *C. trachomatis* and *N. gonorrhoeae*	300 mg	q12h	7 days	600 mg
Acute Pelvic Inflammatory Disease	400 mg	q12h	10–14 days	800 mg
Uncomplicated Cystitis due to *E. coli* or *K. pneumoniae*	200 mg	q12h	3 days	400 mg
Uncomplicated Cystitis due to other approved pathogens	200 mg	q12h	7 days	400 mg
Complicated UTI's	200 mg	q12h	10 days	400 mg
Prostatitis due to *E. coli*	300 mg	q12h	6 weeks	600 mg

[†] DUE TO THE DESIGNATED PATHOGENS (See *INDICATIONS AND USAGE.*)

In the event of an acute overdose, the stomach should be emptied. The patient should be observed and appropriate hydration maintained. Ofloxacin is not efficiently removed by hemodialysis or peritoneal dialysis.

DOSAGE AND ADMINISTRATION

The usual dose of FLOXIN (ofloxacin tablets) Tablets is 200 mg to 400 mg orally every 12 h as described in the following dosing chart. These recommendations apply to patients with normal renal function (i.e., creatinine clearance > 50 mL/min). For patients with altered renal function (i.e., creatinine clearance ≤ 50 mL/min), see the **Patients with Impaired Renal Function** subsection.

[See table above]

Antacids containing calcium, magnesium, or aluminum; sucralfate; divalent or trivalent cations such as iron; or multivitamins containing zinc; or Videx®, (Didanosine), chewable/buffered tablets or the pediatric powder for oral solution should not be taken within the two-hour period before or within the two-hour period after taking ofloxacin. (See *PRECAUTIONS.*)

Patients with Impaired Renal Function:

Dosage should be adjusted for patients with a creatinine clearance ≤ 50 mL/min.

After a normal initial dose, dosage should be adjusted as follows:

[See first table at top of next page]

When only the serum creatinine is known, the following formula may be used to estimate creatinine clearance.

[See second table at top of next page]

The serum creatinine should represent a steady-state of renal function.

Patients with Cirrhosis:

The excretion of ofloxacin may be reduced in patients with severe liver function disorders (e.g., cirrhosis with or without ascites). A maximum dose of 400 mg of ofloxacin per day should therefore not be exceeded.

HOW SUPPLIED

FLOXIN (ofloxacin tablets) Tablets are supplied as 200 mg light yellow, 300 mg white, and 400 mg pale gold film-coated tablets. Each tablet is distinguished by "FLOXIN" and the appropriate strength. FLOXIN Tablets are packaged in bottles and in unit-dose blister strips in the following configurations:

200 mg tablets—UROPAK unit-dose/6 tablets (NDC 0062-1540-09)

200 mg tablets—bottles of 50 (NDC 0062-1540-02)

200 mg tablets—unit-dose/100 tablets (NDC 0062-1540-05)

300 mg tablets—bottles of 50 (NDC 0062-1541-02)

300 mg tablets—unit-dose/100 tablets (NDC 0062-1541-05)

400 mg tablets—bottles of 100 (NDC 0062-1542-01)

400 mg tablets—unit-dose/100 tablets (NDC 0062-1542-05)

FLOXIN Tablets should be stored in well-closed containers. Store below 86°F (30°C).

Also Available:

Ofloxacin is also available for intravenous administration in the following configurations:

FLOXIN (ofloxacin injection) I.V. IN SINGLE-USE VIALS (10 mL) containing a concentrated solution with the equivalent of 400 mg of ofloxacin.

FLOXIN (ofloxacin injection) I.V. PRE-MIXED IN FLEXIBLE CONTAINERS (50 mL and 100 mL) containing a dilute solution with the equivalent of 200 mg or 400 mg of ofloxacin, respectively, in 5% Dextrose (D_5W).

Creatinine Clearance	Maintenance Dose	Frequency
20–50 mL/min	the usual recommended unit dose	q24h
< 20 mL/min	½ the usual recommended unit dose	q24h

Men: Creatinine clearance (mL/min) = $\dfrac{\text{Weight (kg)} \times (140 - \text{age})}{72 \times \text{serum creatinine (mg/dL)}}$

Women: 0.85 × the value calculated for men.

ANIMAL PHARMACOLOGY

Ofloxacin, as well as other drugs of the quinolone class, has been shown to cause arthropathies (arthrosis) in immature dogs and rats. In addition, these drugs are associated with an increased incidence of osteochondrosis in rats as compared to the incidence observed in vehicle-treated rats. (See **WARNINGS.**) There is no evidence of arthropathies in fully mature dogs at intravenous doses up to 3 times the recommended maximum human dose (on a mg/m^2 basis or 5 times based on mg/kg basis), for a one-week exposure period.

Long-term, high-dose systemic use of other quinolones in experimental animals has caused lenticular opacities; however, this finding was not observed in any animal studies with ofloxacin.

Reduced serum globulin and protein levels were observed in animals treated with other quinolones. In one ofloxacin study, minor decreases in serum globulin and protein levels were noted in female cynomolgus monkeys dosed orally with 40 mg/kg ofloxacin daily for one year. These changes, however, were considered to be within normal limits for monkeys.

Crystalluria and ocular toxicity were not observed in any animals treated with ofloxacin. FLOXIN® is a trademark of ORTHO-McNEIL PHARMACEUTICAL, INC.

U.S. Patent No. 4,382,892

REFERENCES

1. National Committee for Clinical Laboratory Standards. Methods for Dilution Antimicrobial Susceptibility Tests for Bacteria That Grow Aerobically—Fourth Edition. Approved Standard NCCLS Document M7-A4, Vol. 17, No. 2, NCCLS, Wayne, PA, January, 1997.

2. National Committee for Clinical Laboratory Standards. Performance Standards for Antimicrobial Disk Susceptibility Tests—Sixth Edition. Approved Standard NCCLS Document M2-A6, Vol. 17, No. 1, NCCLS, Wayne, PA, January, 1997.

ORTHO-McNEIL
PHARMACEUTICAL, INC.
Raritan, New Jersey 08869
© OMP 1998   Revised February 2000
                                    7516001

LEVAQUIN® Tablets/Injection ℞
(levofloxacin tablets/injection)

Prescribing Information

DESCRIPTION

LEVAQUIN (levofloxacin tablets/injection) Tablets/Injection are synthetic broad spectrum antibacterial agents for oral and intravenous administration. Chemically, levofloxacin, a chiral fluorinated carboxyquinolone, is the pure (-)-(S)-enantiomer of the racemic drug substance ofloxacin. The chemical name is (-)-(S)-9-fluoro-2,3-dihydro-3-methyl-10-(4-methyl-1-piperazinyl)-7-oxo-7H-pyrido[1,2,3-de]-1,4-benzoxazine-6-carboxylic acid hemihydrate. The chemical structure is:

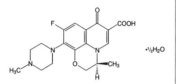

Its empirical formula is $C_{18}H_{20}FN_3O_4 \cdot \frac{1}{2} H_2O$ and its molecular weight is 370.38. Levofloxacin is a light yellowish-white to yellow-white crystal or crystalline powder. The molecule exists as a zwitterion at the pH conditions in the small intestine.

The data demonstrate that from pH 0.6 to 5.8, the solubility of levofloxacin is essentially constant (approximately 100 mg/mL). Levofloxacin is considered *soluble to freely soluble* in this pH range, as defined by USP nomenclature. Above pH 5.8, the solubility increases rapidly to its maximum at pH 6.7 (272 mg/mL) and is considered *freely soluble* in this range. Above pH 6.7, the solubility decreases and reaches a minimum value (about 50 mg/mL) at a pH of approximately 6.9.

Levofloxacin has the potential to form stable coordination compounds with many metal ions. This in vitro chelation potential has the following formation order: $Al^{+3} > Cu^{+2} > Zn^{+2} > Mg^{+2} > Ca^{+2}$.

LEVAQUIN Tablets are available as film-coated tablets and contain the following inactive ingredients:

250 mg (as expressed in the anhydrous form): hydroxypropyl methylcellulose, crospovidone, microcrystalline cellulose, magnesium stearate, polyethylene glycol, titanium dioxide, polysorbate 80 and synthetic red iron oxide.

500 mg (as expressed in the anhydrous form): hydroxypropyl methylcellulose, crospovidone, microcrystalline cellulose, magnesium stearate, polyethylene glycol, titanium dioxide, polysorbate 80 and synthetic red and yellow iron oxides.

750 mg (as expressed in the anhydrous form): hydroxypropyl methylcellulose, crospovidone, microcrystalline cellulose, magnesium stearate, polyethylene glycol, titanium dioxide, polysorbate 80.

LEVAQUIN Injection in Single-Use Vials is a sterile, preservative-free aqueous solution of levofloxacin with pH ranging from 3.8 to 5.8. LEVAQUIN Injection in Premix Flexible Containers is a sterile, preservative-free aqueous solution of levofloxacin with pH ranging from 3.8 to 5.8. The appearance of LEVAQUIN Injection may range from a clear yellow to a greenish-yellow solution. This does not adversely affect product potency.

LEVAQUIN Injection in Single-Use Vials contains levofloxacin in Water for Injection.

LEVAQUIN Injection in Premix Flexible Containers is a dilute, non-pyrogenic, nearly isotonic premixed solution that contains levofloxacin in 5% Dextrose (D_5W). Solutions of hydrochloric acid and sodium hydroxide may have been added to adjust the pH.

The flexible container is fabricated from a specially formulated non-plasticized, thermoplastic copolyester (CR3). The amount of water that can permeate from the container into the overwrap is insufficient to affect the solution significantly. Solutions in contact with the flexible container can leach out certain of the container's chemical components in very small amounts within the expiration period. The suitability of the container material has been confirmed by tests in animals according to USP biological tests for plastic containers.

CLINICAL PHARMACOLOGY

The mean $\pm SD$ pharmacokinetic parameters of levofloxacin determined under single and steady state conditions following oral (p.o.) or intravenous (i.v.) doses of levofloxacin are summarized in Table 1.

Absorption

Levofloxacin is rapidly and essentially completely absorbed after oral administration. Peak plasma concentrations are usually attained one to two hours after oral dosing. The absolute bioavailability of a 500 mg tablet and a 750 mg tablet of levofloxacin are both approximately 99%, demonstrating complete oral absorption of levofloxacin. Following a single intravenous dose of levofloxacin to healthy volunteers, the mean $\pm SD$ peak plasma concentration attained was 6.2 ± 1.0 µg/mL after a 500 mg dose given over 60 minutes and 11.5 ± 4.0 µg/mL after a 750 mg dose infused over 90 minutes.

Levofloxacin pharmacokinetics are linear and predictable after single and multiple oral/or i.v. dosing regimens. Steady-state conditions are reached within 48 hours following a 500 mg or 750 mg once-daily dose regimen. The mean $\pm SD$ peak and trough plasma concentrations attained following multiple once-daily oral dosage regimens were approximately 5.7 ± 1.4 and 0.5 ± 0.2 µg/mL after the 500 mg doses, and 8.6 ± 1.9 and 1.1 ± 0.4 µg/mL after the 750 mg doses, respectively. The mean $\pm SD$ peak and trough

Mean Levofloxacin Plasma Concentration: Time Profiles

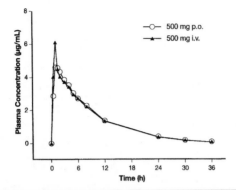

plasma concentrations attained following multiple once-daily i.v. regimens were approximately 6.4 ±0.8 and 0.6 ±0.2 µg/mL after the 500 mg doses, and 12.1 ±4.1 and 1.3 ±0.71 µg/mL after the 750 mg doses, respectively.

Oral administration of a 500-mg LEVAQUIN tablet with food slightly prolongs the time to peak concentration by approximately 1 hour and slightly decreases the peak concentration by approximately 14%. Therefore, levofloxacin tablets can be administered without regard to food.

The plasma concentration profile of levofloxacin after i.v. administration is similar and comparable in extent of exposure (AUC) to that observed for levofloxacin tablets when equal doses (mg/mg) are administered. Therefore, the oral and i.v. routes of administration can be considered interchangeable. (See following chart.)

[See figure above]

[See figure at top of next page]

Distribution

The mean volume of distribution of levofloxacin generally ranges from 74 to 112 L after single and multiple 500 mg or 750 mg doses, indicating widespread distribution into body tissues. Levofloxacin reaches its peak levels in skin tissues and in blister fluid of healthy subjects at approximately 3 hours after dosing. The skin tissue biopsy to plasma AUC ratio is approximately 2 and the blister fluid to plasma AUC ratio is approximately 1 following multiple once-daily oral administration of 750 mg and 500 mg levofloxacin, respectively, to healthy subjects. Levofloxacin also penetrates well into lung tissues. Lung tissue concentrations were generally 2- to 5- fold higher than plasma concentrations and ranged from approximately 2.4 to 11.3 µg/g over a 24-hour period after a single 500 mg oral dose.

In vitro, over a clinically relevant range (1 to 10 µg/mL) of serum/plasma levofloxacin concentrations, levofloxacin is approximately 24 to 38% bound to serum proteins across all species studied, as determined by the equilibrium dialysis method. Levofloxacin is mainly bound to serum albumin in humans. Levofloxacin binding to serum proteins is independent of the drug concentration.

Metabolism

Levofloxacin is stereochemically stable in plasma and urine and does not invert metabolically to its enantiomer, D-ofloxacin. Levofloxacin undergoes limited metabolism in humans and is primarily excreted as unchanged drug in the urine. Following oral administration, approximately 87% of an administered dose was recovered as unchanged drug in urine within 48 hours, whereas less than 4% of the dose was recovered in feces in 72 hours. Less than 5% of an administered dose was recovered in the urine as the desmethyl and N-oxide metabolites, the only metabolites identified in humans. These metabolites have little relevant pharmacological activity.

Excretion

Levofloxacin is excreted largely as unchanged drug in the urine. The mean terminal plasma elimination half-life of levofloxacin ranges from approximately 6 to 8 hours following single or multiple doses of levofloxacin given orally or intravenously. The mean apparent total body clearance and renal clearance range from approximately 144 to 226 mL/min and 96 to 142 mL/min, respectively. Renal clearance in excess of the glomerular filtration rate suggests that tubular secretion of levofloxacin occurs in addition to its glomerular filtration. Concomitant administration of either cimetidine or probenecid results in approximately 24% and 35% reduction in the levofloxacin renal clearance, respectively, indicating that secretion of levofloxacin occurs in the renal proximal tubule. No levofloxacin crystals were found in any of the urine samples freshly collected from subjects receiving levofloxacin.

Mean Levofloxacin Plasma Concentration: Time Profiles

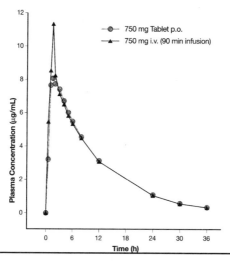

Special Populations
Geriatric: There are no significant differences in levofloxacin pharmacokinetics between young and elderly subjects when the subjects' differences in creatinine clearance are taken into consideration. Following a 500 mg oral dose of levofloxacin to healthy elderly subjects (66–80 years of age), the mean terminal plasma elimination half-life of levofloxacin was about 7.6 hours, as compared to approximately 6 hours in younger adults. The difference was attributable to the variation in renal function status of the subjects and was not believed to be clinically significant. Drug absorption appears to be unaffected by age. Levofloxacin dose adjustment based on age alone is not necessary.
Pediatric: The pharmacokinetics of levofloxacin in pediatric subjects have not been studied.
Gender: There are no significant differences in levofloxacin pharmacokinetics between male and female subjects when subjects' differences in creatinine clearance are taken into consideration. Following a 500 mg oral dose of levofloxacin to healthy male subjects, the mean terminal plasma elimination half-life of levofloxacin was about 7.5 hours, as compared to approximately 6.1 hours in female subjects. This difference was attributable to the variation in renal function status of the male and female subjects and was not believed to be clinically significant. Drug absorption appears to be unaffected by the gender of the subjects. Dose adjustment based on gender alone is not necessary.
Race: The effect of race on levofloxacin pharmacokinetics was examined through a covariate analysis performed on data from 72 subjects: 48 white and 24 nonwhite. The apparent total body clearance and apparent volume of distribution were not affected by the race of the subjects.
Renal insufficiency: Clearance of levofloxacin is substantially reduced and plasma elimination half-life is substantially prolonged in patients with impaired renal function (creatinine clearance <50 mL/min), requiring dosage adjustment in such patients to avoid accumulation. Neither hemodialysis nor continuous ambulatory peritoneal dialysis (CAPD) is effective in removal of levofloxacin from the body, indicating that supplemental doses of levofloxacin are not required following hemodialysis or CAPD. (See **PRECAUTIONS: General** and **DOSAGE AND ADMINISTRATION**.)
Hepatic insufficiency: Pharmacokinetic studies in hepatically impaired patients have not been conducted. Due to the limited extent of levofloxacin metabolism, the pharmacokinetics of levofloxacin are not expected to be affected by hepatic impairment.
Bacterial infection: The pharmacokinetics of levofloxacin in patients with serious community-acquired bacterial infections are comparable to those observed in healthy subjects.
Drug-drug interactions: The potential for pharmacokinetic drug interactions between levofloxacin and theophylline, warfarin, cyclosporine, digoxin, probenecid, cimetidine, sucralfate, and antacids has been evaluated. (See **PRECAUTIONS: Drug Interactions**.)
[See table at top of next page]

MICROBIOLOGY

Levofloxacin is the L-isomer of the racemate, ofloxacin, a quinolone antimicrobial agent. The antibacterial activity of ofloxacin resides primarily in the L-isomer. The mechanism of

Table 1. Mean ±SD Levofloxacin PK Parameters

Regimen	C_{max} (µg/mL)	T_{max} (h)	AUC (µg·h/mL)	CL/F[1] (mL/min)	Vd/F[2] (L)	$t_{1/2}$ (h)	CL_R (mL/min)
Single dose							
250 mg p.o.[3]	2.8 ± 0.4	1.6 ± 1.0	27.2 ± 3.9	156 ± 20	ND	7.3 ± 0.9	142 ± 21
500 mg p.o.[3]*	5.1 ± 0.8	1.3 ± 0.6	47.9 ± 6.8	178 ± 28	ND	6.3 ± 0.6	103 ± 30
500 mg i.v.[3]	6.2 ± 1.0	1.0 ± 0.1	48.3 ± 5.4	175 ± 20	90 ± 11	6.4 ± 0.7	112 ± 25
750 mg p.o.[5]*	9.3 ± 1.6	1.6 ± 0.8	101 ± 20	129 ± 24	83 ± 17	7.5 ± 0.9	ND
750 mg i.v.[5]	11.5 ± 4.0[4]	ND	110 ± 40	126 ± 39	75 ± 13	7.5 ± 1.6	ND
Multiple dose							
500 mg q24h p.o.[3]	5.7 ± 1.4	1.1 ± 0.4	47.5 ± 6.7	175 ± 25	102 ± 22	7.6 ± 1.6	116 ± 31
500 mg q24h i.v.[3]	6.4 ± 0.8	ND	54.6 ± 11.1	158 ± 29	91 ± 12	7.0 ± 0.8	99 ± 28
500 mg or 250 mg q24h i.v., patients with bacterial infection[6]	8.7 ± 4.0[7]	ND	72.5 ± 51.2[7]	154 ± 72	111 ± 58	ND	ND
750 mg q24h p.o.[5]	8.6 ± 1.9	1.4 ± 0.5	90.7 ± 17.6	143 ± 29	100 ± 16	8.8 ± 1.5	116 ± 28
750 mg q24h i.v.[5]	12.1 ± 4.1[4]	ND	108 ± 34	126 ± 37	80 ± 27	7.9 ± 1.9	ND
500 mg p.o. single dose, effects of gender and age:							
male[8]	5.5 ± 1.1	1.2 ± 0.4	54.4 ± 18.9	166 ± 44	89 ± 13	7.5 ± 2.1	126 ± 38
female[9]	7.0 ± 1.6	1.7 ± 0.5	67.7 ± 24.2	136 ± 44	62 ± 16	6.1 ± 0.8	106 ± 40
young[10]	5.5 ± 1.0	1.5 ± 0.6	47.5 ± 9.8	182 ± 35	83 ± 18	6.0 ± 0.9	140 ± 33
elderly[11]	7.0 ± 1.6	1.4 ± 0.5	74.7 ± 23.3	121 ± 33	67 ± 19	7.6 ± 2.0	91 ± 29
500 mg p.o. single dose, patients with renal insufficiency:							
CL_{CR} 50-80 mL/min	7.5 ± 1.8	1.5 ± 0.5	95.6 ± 11.8	88 ± 10	ND	9.1 ± 0.9	57 ± 8
CL_{CR} 20-49 mL/min	7.1 ± 3.1	2.1 ± 1.3	182.1 ± 62.6	51 ± 19	ND	27 ± 10	26 ± 13
CL_{CR} <20 mL/min	8.2 ± 2.6	1.1 ± 1.0	263.5 ± 72.5	33 ± 8	ND	35 ± 5	13 ± 3
hemodialysis	5.7 ± 1.0	2.8 ± 2.2	ND	ND	ND	76 ± 42	ND
CAPD	6.9 ± 2.3	1.4 ± 1.1	ND	ND	ND	51 ± 24	ND

[1]clearance/bioavailability
[2]volume of distribution/bioavailability
[3]healthy males 18-53 years of age
[4]60 min infusion for 250 mg and 500 mg doses, 90 min infusion for 750 mg dose
[5]healthy male and female subjects 18-54 years of age
[6]500 mg q48h for patients with moderate renal impairment (CL_{CR} 20-50 mL/min) and infections of the respiratory tract or skin
[7]dose-normalized values (to 500 mg dose), estimated by population pharmacokinetic modeling
[8]healthy males 22-75 years of age
[9]healthy females 18-80 years of age
[10]young healthy male and female subjects 18-36 years of age
[11]healthy elderly male and female subjects 66-80 years of age
*Absolute bioavailability; F = 0.99 ± 0.08 from a 500-mg tablet and F=0.99 ± 0.06 from a 750-mg tablet; ND = not determined.

action of levofloxacin and other fluoroquinolone antimicrobials involves inhibition of bacterial topoisomerase IV and DNA gyrase (both of which are type II topoisomerases), enzymes required for DNA replication, transcription, repair and recombination.

Levofloxacin has in vitro activity against a wide range of gram-negative and gram-positive microorganisms. Levofloxacin is often bactericidal at concentrations equal to or slightly greater than inhibitory concentrations.

Fluoroquinolones, including levofloxacin, differ in chemical structure and mode of action from aminoglycosides, macrolides and β-lactam antibiotics, including penicillins. Fluoroquinolones may, therefore, be active against bacteria resistant to these antimicrobials.

Resistance to levofloxacin due to spontaneous mutation in vitro is a rare occurrence (range: 10^{-9} to 10^{-10}). Although cross-resistance has been observed between levofloxacin and some other fluoroquinolones, some microorganisms resistant to other fluoroquinolones may be susceptible to levofloxacin.

Levofloxacin has been shown to be active against most strains of the following microorganisms both in vitro and in clinical infections as described in the **INDICATIONS AND USAGE** section:

Aerobic gram-positive microorganisms
Enterococcus faecalis (many strains are only moderately susceptible)
Staphylococcus aureus (methicillin-susceptible strains)
Staphylococcus saprophyticus
Streptococcus pneumoniae (including penicillin-resistant strains*)
Streptococcus pyogenes

---

*Note: penicillin-resistant *S. pneumoniae* are those strains with a penicillin MIC value of ≥2 µg/mL

Aerobic gram-negative microorganisms
Enterobacter cloacae
Escherichia coli
Haemophilus influenzae
Haemophilus parainfluenzae
Klebsiella pneumoniae
Legionella pneumophila
Moraxella catarrhalis
Proteus mirabilis
Pseudomonas aeruginosa
As with other drugs in this class, some strains of *Pseudomonas aeruginosa* may develop resistance fairly rapidly during treatment with levofloxacin.

Other microorganisms
Chlamydia pneumoniae
Mycoplasma pneumoniae
The following in vitro data are available, **but their clinical significance is unknown**.
Levofloxacin exhibits in vitro minimum inhibitory concentrations (MIC values) of 2 µg/mL or less against most (≥90%) strains of the following microorganisms; however, the safety and effectiveness of levofloxacin in treating clinical infections due to these microorganisms have not been established in adequate and well-controlled trials.

Aerobic gram-positive microorganisms
Staphylococcus epidermidis (methicillin-susceptible strains)
Streptococcus (Group C/F)
Streptococcus (Group G)
Streptococcus agalactiae
Streptococcus milleri
Viridans group streptococci

Aerobic gram-negative microorganisms
Acinetobacter baumannii
Acinetobacter lwoffii
Bordetella pertussis
Citrobacter (diversus) koseri
Citrobacter freundii
Enterobacter aerogenes
Enterobacter sakazakii
Klebsiella oxytoca
Morganella morganii
Pantoea (Enterobacter) agglomerans
Proteus vulgaris
Providencia rettgeri
Providencia stuartii
Pseudomonas fluorescens
Serratia marcescens

Anaerobic gram-positive microorganisms
Clostridium perfringens

Susceptibility Tests
Susceptibility testing for levofloxacin should be performed, as it is the optimal predictor of activity.

Dilution techniques: Quantitative methods are used to determine antimicrobial minimal inhibitory concentrations (MIC values). These MIC values provide estimates of the susceptibility of bacteria to antimicrobial compounds. The MIC values should be determined using a standardized procedure. Standardized procedures are based on a dilution method[1] (broth or agar) or equivalent with standardized inoculum concentrations and standardized concentrations of levofloxacin powder. The MIC values should be interpreted according to the following criteria:

For testing aerobic microorganisms other than *Haemophilus influenzae*, *Haemophilus parainfluenzae*, and *Streptococcus* spp. including *S. pneumoniae*:

MIC (µg/mL)	Interpretation
≤2	Susceptible (S)
4	Intermediate (I)
≥8	Resistant (R)

For testing *Haemophilus influenzae* and *Haemophilus parainfluenzae*:[a]

MIC (µg/mL)	Interpretation
≤2	Susceptible (S)

---

[a]These interpretive standards are applicable only to broth microdilution susceptibility testing with *Haemophilus influenzae* and *Haemo-*

philus parainfluenzae using Haemophilus Test Medium.[1]

The current absence of data on resistant strains precludes defining any categories other than "Susceptible". Strains yielding MIC results suggestive of a "nonsusceptible" category should be submitted to a reference laboratory for further testing.

For testing *Streptococcus* spp. including *S. pneumoniae*:[b]

MIC (µg/mL)	Interpretation
≤2	Susceptible (S)
4	Intermediate (I)
≥8	Resistant (R)

[b]These interpretive standards are applicable only to broth microdilution susceptibility tests using cation-adjusted Mueller-Hinton broth with 2–5% lysed horse blood.

A report of "Susceptible" indicates that the pathogen is likely to be inhibited if the antimicrobial compound in the blood reaches the concentrations usually achievable. A report of "Intermediate" indicates that the result should be considered equivocal, and, if the microorganism is not fully susceptible to alternative, clinically feasible drugs, the test should be repeated. This category implies possible clinical applicability in body sites where the drug is physiologically concentrated or in situations where a high dosage of drug can be used. This category also provides a buffer zone which prevents small uncontrolled technical factors from causing major discrepancies in interpretation. A report of "Resistant" indicates that the pathogen is not likely to be inhibited if the antimicrobial compound in the blood reaches the concentrations usually achievable; other therapy should be selected.

Standardized susceptibility test procedures require the use of laboratory control microorganisms to control the technical aspects of the laboratory procedures. Standard levofloxacin powder should give the following MIC values:

Microorganism		MIC (µg/mL)
Enterococcus faecalis	ATCC 29212	0.25–2
Escherichia coli	ATCC 25922	0.008–0.06
Escherichia coli	ATCC 35218	0.015–0.06
Pseudomonas aeruginosa	ATCC 27853	0.5–4
Staphylococcus aureus	ATCC 29213	0.06–0.5
Haemophilus influenzae	ATCC 49247[c]	0.008–0.03
Streptococcus pneumoniae	ATCC 49619[d]	0.5–2

[c]This quality control range is applicable to only *H. influenzae* ATCC 49247 tested by a broth microdilution procedure using Haemophilus Test Medium (HTM).[1]

[d]This quality control range is applicable to only *S. pneumoniae* ATCC 49619 tested by a broth microdilution procedure using cation-adjusted Mueller-Hinton broth with 2-5% lysed horse blood.

Diffusion techniques: Quantitative methods that require measurement of zone diameters also provide reproducible estimates of the susceptibility of bacteria to antimicrobial compounds. One such standardized procedure[2] requires the use of standardized inoculum concentrations. This procedure uses paper disks impregnated with 5-µg levofloxacin to test the susceptibility of microorganisms to levofloxacin.

Reports from the laboratory providing results of the standard single-disk susceptibility test with a 5-µg levofloxacin disk should be interpreted according to the following criteria:

For aerobic microorganisms other than *Haemophilus influenzae*, *Haemophilus parainfluenzae*, and *Streptococcus* spp. including *S. pneumoniae*:

Zone diameter (mm)	Interpretation
≥17	Susceptible (S)
14–16	Intermediate (I)
≤13	Resistant (R)

For *Haemophilus influenzae* and *Haemophilus parainfluenzae*:[e]

Zone diameter (mm)	Interpretation
≥17	Susceptible (S)

[e]These interpretive standards are applicable only to disk diffusion susceptibility testing with *Haemophilus influenzae* and *Haemophilus parainfluenzae* using Haemophilus Test Medium.[2]

The current absence of data on resistant strains preudes defining any categories other than "Susceptible". Strains yielding zone diameter results suggestive of a "nonsusceptible" category should be submitted to a reference laboratory for further testing.

For *Streptococcus* spp. including *S. pneumoniae*:[f]

Zone diameter (mm)	Interpretation
≥17	Susceptible (S)
14–16	Intermediate (I)
≤13	Resistant (R)

[f]These zone diameter standards for *Streptococcus* spp. including *S. pneumoniae* apply only to tests performed using Mueller-Hinton agar supplemented with 5% sheep blood and incubated in 5% CO_2.

Interpretation should be as stated above for results using dilution techniques. Interpretation involves correlation of the diameter obtained in the disk test with the MIC for levofloxacin.

As with standardized dilution techniques, diffusion methods require the use of laboratory control microorganisms to control the technical aspects of the laboratory procedures. For the diffusion technique, the 5-µg levofloxacin disk should provide the following zone diameters in these laboratory test quality control strains:

Microorganism		Zone Diameter (mm)
Escherichia coli	ATCC 25922	29–37
Pseudomonas aeruginosa	ATCC 27853	19–26
Staphylococcus aureus	ATCC 25923	25–30
Haemophilus influenzae	ATCC 49247[g]	32–40
Streptococcus pneumoniae	ATCC 49619[h]	20–25

[g] This quality control range is applicable to only H. influenzae ATCC 49247 tested by a disk diffusion procedure using Haemophilus Test Medium (HTM).[2]

[h] This quality control range is applicable to only S. pneumoniae ATCC 49619 tested by a disk diffusion procedure using Mueller-Hinton agar supplemented with 5% sheep blood and incubated in 5% CO_2.

INDICATIONS AND USAGE

LEVAQUIN Tablets/Injection are indicated for the treatment of adults (≥18 years of age) with mild, moderate, and severe infections caused by susceptible strains of the designated microorganisms in the conditions listed below. LEVAQUIN Injection is indicated when intravenous administration offers a route of administration advantageous to the patient (e.g., patient cannot tolerate an oral dosage form). Please see **DOSAGE AND ADMINISTRATION** for specific recommendations.

Acute maxillary sinusitis due to Streptococcus pneumoniae, Haemophilus influenzae, or Moraxella catarrhalis.

Acute bacterial exacerbation of chronic bronchitis due to Staphylococcus aureus, Streptococcus pneumoniae, Haemophilus influenzae, Haemophilus parainfluenzae, or Moraxella catarrhalis.

Community-acquired pneumonia due to Staphylococcus aureus, Streptococcus pneumoniae (including penicillin-resistant strains, MIC value for penicillin ≥2 µg/mL), Haemophilus influenzae, Haemophilus parainfluenzae, Klebsiella pneumoniae, Moraxella catarrhalis, Chlamydia pneumoniae, Legionella pneumophila, or Mycoplasma pneumoniae. (See **CLINICAL STUDIES**.)

Complicated skin and skin structure infections due to methicillin-sensitive Staphylococcus aureus, Enterococcus faecalis, Streptococcus pyogenes, or Proteus mirabilis.

Uncomplicated skin and skin structure infections (mild to moderate) including abscesses, cellulitis, furuncles, impetigo, pyoderma, wound infections, due to Staphylococcus aureus, or Streptococcus pyogenes.

Complicated urinary tract infections (mild to moderate) due to Enterococcus faecalis, Enterobacter cloacae, Escherichia coli, Klebsiella pneumoniae, Proteus mirabilis, or Pseudomonas aeruginosa.

Acute pyelonephritis (mild to moderate) caused by Escherichia coli.

Uncomplicated urinary tract infections (mild to moderate) due to Escherichia coli, Klebsiella pneumoniae, or Staphylococcus saprophyticus.

Appropriate culture and susceptibility tests should be performed before treatment in order to isolate and identify organisms causing the infection and to determine their susceptibility to levofloxacin. Therapy with levofloxacin may be initiated before results of these tests are known; once results become available, appropriate therapy should be selected.

As with other drugs in this class, some strains of Pseudomonas aeruginosa may develop resistance fairly rapidly during treatment with levofloxacin. Culture and susceptibility testing performed periodically during therapy will provide information about the continued susceptibility of the pathogens to the antimicrobial agent and also the possible emergence of bacterial resistance.

CONTRAINDICATIONS

Levofloxacin is contraindicated in persons with a history of hypersensitivity to levofloxacin, quinolone antimicrobial agents, or any other components of this product.

WARNINGS

THE SAFETY AND EFFICACY OF LEVOFLOXACIN IN PEDIATRIC PATIENTS, ADOLESCENTS (UNDER THE AGE OF 18 YEARS), PREGNANT WOMEN, AND NURSING WOMEN HAVE NOT BEEN ESTABLISHED. (See **PRECAUTIONS: Pediatric Use, Pregnancy**, and **Nursing Mothers** subsections.)

In immature rats and dogs, the oral and intravenous administration of levofloxacin increased the incidence and severity of osteochondrosis. Other fluoroquinolones also produce similar erosions in the weight bearing joints and other signs of arthropathy in immature animals of various species. (See **ANIMAL PHARMACOLOGY**.)

Convulsions and toxic psychoses have been reported in patients receiving quinolones, including levofloxacin. Quinolones may also cause increased intracranial pressure and central nervous system stimulation which may lead to tremors, restlessness, anxiety, lightheadedness, confusion, hallucinations, paranoia, depression, nightmares, insomnia, and, rarely, suicidal thoughts or acts. These reactions may occur following the first dose. If these reactions occur in patients receiving levofloxacin, the drug should be discontinued and appropriate measures instituted. As with other quinolones, levofloxacin should be used with caution in patients with a known or suspected CNS disorder that may predispose to seizures or lower the seizure threshold (e.g., severe cerebral arterioserosis, epilepsy) or in the presence of other risk factors that may predispose to seizures or lower the seizure threshold (e.g., certain drug therapy, renal dysfunction.) (See **PRECAUTIONS: General, Information for Patients, Drug Interactions** and **ADVERSE REACTIONS.**)

Serious and occasionally fatal hypersensitivity and/or anaphylactic reactions have been reported in patients receiving therapy with quinolones, including levofloxacin. These reactions often occur following the first dose. Some reactions have been accompanied by cardiovascular collapse, hypotension/shock, seizure, loss of consciousness, tingling, angioedema (including tongue, laryngeal, throat, or facial edema/swelling), airway obstruction (including bronchospasm, shortness of breath, and acute respiratory distress), dyspnea, urticaria, itching, and other serious skin reactions. Levofloxacin should be discontinued immediately at the first appearance of a skin rash or any other sign of hypersensitivity. Serious acute hypersensitivity reactions may require treatment with epinephrine and other resuscitative measures, including oxygen, intravenous fluids, antihistamines, corticosteroids, pressor amines, and airway management, as clinically indicated. (See **PRECAUTIONS** and **ADVERSE REACTIONS.**)

Serious and sometimes fatal events, some due to hypersensitivity, and some due to uncertain etiology, have been reported rarely in patients receiving therapy with quinolones, including levofloxacin. These events may be severe and generally occur following the administration of multiple doses. Clinical manifestations may include one or more of the following: fever, rash or severe dermatologic reactions (e.g., toxic epidermal necrolysis, Stevens-Johnson Syndrome); vasculitis; arthralgia; myalgia; serum sickness; allergic pneumonitis; interstitial nephritis; acute renal insufficiency or failure; hepatitis; jaundice; acute hepatic necrosis or failure; anemia, including hemolytic and aplastic; thrombocytopenia, including thrombotic thrombocytopenic purpura; leukopenia; agranulocytosis; pancytopenia; and/or other hematologic abnormalities. The drug should be discontinued immediately at the first appearance of a skin rash or any other sign of hypersensitivity and supportive measures instituted. (See **PRECAUTIONS: Information for Patients** and **ADVERSE REACTIONS.**)

Pseudomembranous colitis has been reported with nearly all antibacterial agents, including levofloxacin, and may range in severity from mild to life-threatening. Therefore, it is important to consider this diagnosis in patients who present with diarrhea subsequent to the administration of any antibacterial agent.

Treatment with antibacterial agents alters the normal flora of the colon and may permit overgrowth of ostridia. Studies indicate that a toxin produced by *Clostridium difficile* is one primary cause of "antibiotic-associated colitis." After the diagnosis of pseudomembranous colitis has been established, therapeutic measures should be initiated. Mild cases of pseudomembranous colitis usually respond to drug discontinuation alone. In moderate to severe cases, consideration should be given to management with fluids and electrolytes, protein supplementation, and treatment with an antibacterial drug clinically effective against *C. difficile* colitis. (See **ADVERSE REACTIONS.**)

Ruptures of the shoulder, hand, or Achilles tendons that required surgical repair or resulted in prolonged disability have been reported in patients receiving quinolones, including levofloxacin. Levofloxacin should be discontinued if the patient experiences pain, inflammation, or rupture of a tendon. Patients should rest and refrain from exercise until the diagnosis of tendinitis or tendon rupture has been confidently excluded. Tendon rupture can occur during or after therapy with quinolones, including levofloxacin.

PRECAUTIONS
General

Because a rapid or bolus intravenous injection may result in hypotension, LEVOFLOXACIN INJECTION SHOULD ONLY BE ADMINISTERED BY SLOW INTRAVENOUS INFUSION OVER A PERIOD OF 60 OR 90 MINUTES DEPENDING ON THE DOSAGE. (See **DOSAGE AND ADMINISTRATION.**)

Although levofloxacin is more soluble than other quinolones, adequate hydration of patients receiving levofloxacin should be maintained to prevent the formation of a highly concentrated urine.

Administer levofloxacin with caution in the presence of renal insufficiency. Careful clinical observation and appropriate laboratory studies should be performed prior to and during therapy since elimination of levofloxacin may be reduced. In patients with impaired renal function (creatinine clearance <50 mL/min), adjustment of the dosage regimen is necessary to avoid the accumulation of levofloxacin due to decreased clearance. (See **CLINICAL PHARMACOLOGY** and **DOSAGE AND ADMINISTRATION.**)

Moderate to severe phototoxicity reactions have been observed in patients exposed to direct sunlight while receiving drugs in this class. Excessive exposure to sunlight should be avoided. However, in clinical trials with levofloxacin, phototoxicity has been observed in less than 0.1% of patients. Therapy should be discontinued if phototoxicity (e.g., a skin eruption) occurs.

As with other quinolones, levofloxacin should be used with caution in any patient with a known or suspected CNS disorder that may predispose to seizures or lower the seizure threshold (e.g., severe cerebral arterioserosis, epilepsy) or in the presence of other risk factors that may predispose to seizures or lower the seizure threshold (e.g., certain drug therapy, renal dysfunction). (See **WARNINGS** and **Drug Interactions**.)

As with other quinolones, disturbances of blood glucose, including symptomatic hyper- and hypoglycemia, have been reported, usually in diabetic patients receiving concomitant treatment with an oral hypoglycemic agent (e.g., glyburide/glibenamide) or with insulin. In these patients, careful monitoring of blood glucose is recommended. If a hypoglycemic reaction occurs in a patient being treated with levofloxacin, levofloxacin should be discontinued immediately and appropriate therapy should be initiated immediately. (See **Drug Interactions** and **ADVERSE REACTIONS**.)

Some quinolones have been associated with prolongation of the QT interval on the electrocardiogram and infrequent cases of arrhythmia. During post-marketing surveillance, extremely rare cases of torsades de pointes, have been reported in patients taking levofloxacin. These reports generally involve patients who had other concurrent medical conditions and the relationship to levofloxacin has not been established. Among drugs known to cause prolongation of the QT interval, the risk of arrhythmias may be reduced by avoiding use in the presence of hypokalemia, significant bradycardia, or concurrent treatment with class Ia or class III antiarrhythmic agents.

As with any potent antimicrobial drug, periodic assessment of organ system functions, including renal, hepatic, and hematopoietic, is advisable during therapy. (See **WARNINGS** and **ADVERSE REACTIONS**.)

Information for Patients

Patients should be advised:

- to drink fluids liberally;
- that antacids containing magnesium, or aluminum, as well as sucralfate, metal cations such as iron, and multivitamin preparations with zinc or Videx®, (Didanosine), chewable/buffered tablets or the pediatric powder for oral solution should be taken at least two hours before or two hours after oral levofloxacin administration. (See **Drug Interactions**);
- that oral levofloxacin can be taken without regard to meals;
- that levofloxacin may cause neurologic adverse effects (e.g., dizziness, lightheadedness) and that patients should know how they react to levofloxacin before they operate an automobile or machinery or engage in

other activities requiring mental alertness and coordination. (See **WARNINGS** and **ADVERSE REACTIONS**);

- to discontinue treatment and inform their physician if they experience pain, inflammation, or rupture of a tendon, and to rest and refrain from exercise until the diagnosis of tendinitis or tendon rupture has been confidently excluded;
- that levofloxacin may be associated with hypersensitivity reactions, even following the first dose, and to discontinue the drug at the first sign of a skin rash, hives or other skin reactions, a rapid heartbeat, difficulty in swallowing or breathing, any swelling suggesting angioedema (e.g., swelling of the lips, tongue, face, tightness of the throat, hoarseness), or other symptoms of an allergic reaction. (See **WARNINGS** and **ADVERSE REACTIONS**);
- to avoid excessive sunlight or artificial ultraviolet light while receiving levofloxacin and to discontinue therapy if phototoxicity (i.e., skin eruption) occurs;
- that if they are diabetic and are being treated with insulin or an oral hypoglycemic agent and a hypoglycemic reaction occurs, they should discontinue levofloxacin and consult a physician. (See **PRECAUTIONS**: **General** and **Drug Interactions**.);
- that concurrent administration of warfarin and levofloxacin has been associated with increases of the International Normalized Ratio (INR) or prothrombin time and clinical episodes of bleeding. Patients should notify their physician if they are taking warfarin.
- that convulsions have been reported in patients taking quinolones, including levofloxacin, and to notify their physician before taking this drug if there is a history of this condition.

Drug Interactions

Antacids, Sucralfate, Metal Cations, Multivitamins

LEVAQUIN Tablets: While the chelation by divalent cations is less marked than with other quinolones, concurrent administration of LEVAQUIN Tablets with antacids containing magnesium, or aluminum, as well as sucralfate, metal cations such as iron, and multivitamin preparations with zinc may interfere with the gastrointestinal absorption of levofloxacin, resulting in systemic levels considerably lower than desired. Tablets with antacids containing magnesium, aluminum, as well as sucralfate, metal cations such as iron, and multivitamin preparations with zinc or Videx®, (Didanosine), chewable/buffered tablets or the pediatric powder for oral solution may substantially interfere with the gastrointestinal absorption of levofloxacin, resulting in systemic levels considerably lower than desired. These agents should be taken at least two hours before or two hours after levofloxacin administration.

LEVAQUIN Injection: There are no data concerning an interaction with **Intravenous** quinolones with oral antacids, sucralfate, multivitamins, Videx®, (Didanosine), or metal cations. However, no quinolone should be co-administered with any solution containing multivalent cations, e.g., magnesium, through the same intravenous line. (See **DOSAGE AND ADMINISTRATION**.)

Theophylline: No significant effect of levofloxacin on the plasma concentrations, AUC, and other disposition parameters for theophylline was detected in a clinical study involving 14 healthy volunteers. Similarly, no apparent effect of theophylline on levofloxacin absorption and disposition was observed. However, concomitant administration of other quinolones with theophylline has resulted in prolonged elimination half-life, elevated serum theophylline levels, and a subsequent increase in the risk of theophylline-related adverse reactions in the patient population. Therefore, theophylline levels should be closely monitored and appropriate dosage adjustments made when levofloxacin is co-administered. Adverse reactions, including seizures, may occur with or without an elevation in serum theophylline levels. (See **WARNINGS** and **PRECAUTIONS: General**.)

Warfarin: No significant effect of levofloxacin on the peak plasma concentrations, AUC, and other disposition parameters for R- and S-warfarin was detected in a clinical study involving healthy volunteers. Similarly, no apparent effect of warfarin on levofloxacin absorption and disposition was observed. There have been reports during the post-marketing experience in patients that levofloxacin enhances the effects of warfarin. Elevations of the prothrombin time in the setting of concurrent warfarin and levofloxacin use have been associated with episodes of bleeding. Prothrombin time, International Normalized Ratio (INR), or other suitable anticoagulation tests should be closely monitored if levofloxacin is administered concomitantly with warfarin. Patients should also be monitored for evidence of bleeding.

Cyclosporine: No significant effect of levofloxacin on the peak plasma concentrations, AUC, and other disposition parameters for cyclosporine was detected in a clinical study involving healthy volunteers. However, elevated serum levels of cyclosporine have been reported in the patient population when co-administered with some other quinolones. Levofloxacin C_{max} and k_e were slightly lower while T_{max} and $t_{1/2}$ were slightly longer in the presence of cyclosporine than those observed in other studies without concomitant medication. The differences, however, are not considered to be clinically significant. Therefore, no dosage adjustment is required for levofloxacin or cyclosporine when administered concomitantly.

Digoxin: No significant effect of levofloxacin on the peak plasma concentrations, AUC, and other disposition parameters for digoxin was detected in a clinical study involving healthy volunteers. Levofloxacin absorption and disposition kinetics were similar in the presence or absence of digoxin. Therefore, no dosage adjustment for levofloxacin or digoxin is required when administered concomitantly.

Probenecid and Cimetidine: No significant effect of probenecid or cimetidine on the rate and extent of levofloxacin absorption was observed in a clinical study involving healthy volunteers. The AUC and $t_{1/2}$ of levofloxacin were 27–38% and 30% higher, respectively, while CL/F and CL_R were 21–35% lower during concomitant treatment with probenecid or cimetidine compared to levofloxacin alone. Although these differences were statistically significant, the changes were not high enough to warrant dosage adjustment for levofloxacin when probenecid or cimetidine is co-administered.

Non-steroidal anti-inflammatory drugs: The concomitant administration of a non-steroidal anti-inflammatory drug with a quinolone, including levofloxacin, may increase the risk of CNS stimulation and convulsive seizures. (See **WARNINGS** and **PRECAUTIONS: General**.)

Antidiabetic agents: Disturbances of blood glucose, including hyperglycemia and hypoglycemia, have been reported in patients treated concomitantly with quinolones and an antidiabetic agent. Therefore, careful monitoring of blood glucose is recommended when these agents are co-administered.

Carcinogenesis, Mutagenesis, Impairment of Fertility

In a lifetime bioassay in rats, levofloxacin exhibited no carcinogenic potential following daily dietary administration for 2 years; the highest dose (100 mg/kg/day) was 1.4 times the highest recommended human dose (750 mg) based upon relative body surface area.

Levofloxacin was not mutagenic in the following assays; Ames bacterial mutation assay (*S. typhimurium* and *E. coli*), CHO/HGPRT forward mutation assay, mouse micronucleus test, mouse dominant lethal test, rat unscheduled DNA synthesis assay, and the mouse sister chromatid exchange assay. It was positive in the in vitro chromosomal aberration (CHL cell line) and sister chromatid exchange (CHL/IU cell line) assays.

Levofloxacin caused no impairment of fertility or reproductive performance in rats at oral doses as high as 360 mg/kg/day, corresponding to 4.2 times the highest recommended human dose based upon relative body surface area and intravenous doses as high as 100 mg/kg/day, corresponding to 1.2 times the highest recommended human dose based upon relative body surface area.

Pregnancy: Teratogenic Effects. Pregnancy Category C.

Levofloxacin was not teratogenic in rats at oral doses as high as 810 mg/kg/day which corresponds to 9.4 times the highest recommended human dose based upon relative body surface area, or at intravenous doses as high as 160 mg/kg/day corresponding to 1.9 times the highest recommended human dose based upon relative body surface area. The oral dose of 810 mg/kg/day to rats caused decreased fetal body weight and increased fetal mortality. No teratogenicity was observed when rabbits were dosed orally as high as 50 mg/kg/day which corresponds to 1.1 times the highest recommended human dose based upon relative body surface area, or when dosed intravenously as high as 25 mg/kg/day, corresponding to 0.5 times the highest recommended human dose based upon relative body surface area.

There are, however, no adequate and well-controlled studies in pregnant women. Levofloxacin should be used during pregnancy only if the potential benefit justifies the potential risk to the fetus. (See **WARNINGS**.)

Nursing Mothers

Levofloxacin has not been measured in human milk. Based upon data from ofloxacin, it can be presumed that levofloxacin will be excreted in human milk. Because of the potential for serious adverse reactions from levofloxacin in nursing infants, a decision should be made whether to discontinue nursing or to discontinue the drug, taking into account the importance of the drug to the mother.

Pediatric Use

Safety and effectiveness in pediatric patients and adolescents below the age of 18 years have not been established. Quinolones, including levofloxacin, cause arthropathy and osteochondrosis in juvenile animals of several species. (See **WARNINGS**.)

Geriatric Use

In phase 3 clinical trials, 1,190 levofloxacin-treated patients (25%) were ≥65 years of age. Of these, 675 patients (14%) were between the ages of 65 and 74 and 515 patients (11%) were 75 years or older. No overall differences in safety or effectiveness were observed between these subjects and younger subjects, and other reported clinical experience has not identified differences in responses between the elderly and younger patients, but greater sensitivity of some older individuals cannot be ruled out. The pharmacokinetic properties of levofloxacin in younger adults and elderly adults do not differ significantly when creatinine clearance is taken into consideration. However since the drug is known to be substantially excreted by the kidney, the risk of toxic reactions to this drug may be greater in patients with impaired renal function. Because elderly patients are more likely to have decreased renal function, care should be taken in dose selection, and it may be useful to monitor renal function.

ADVERSE REACTIONS

The incidence of drug-related adverse reactions in patients during Phase 3 clinical trials conducted in North America was 6.3%. Among patients receiving levofloxacin therapy, 3.9% discontinued levofloxacin therapy due to adverse experiences. The overall incidence, type and distribution of adverse events was similar in patients receiving levofloxacin doses of 750 mg once daily compared to patients receiving doses from 250 mg once daily to 500 mg twice daily.

In clinical trials, the following events were considered likely to be drug-related in patients receiving levofloxacin: nausea 1.3%, diarrhea 1.0%, vaginitis 0.7%, insomnia 0.5%, abdominal pain 0.4%, flatulence 0.4%, pruritus 0.4%, dizziness 0.3%, dyspepsia 0.3%, rash 0.3%, genital moniliasis 0.2%, taste perversion 0.2%, vomiting 0.2%, constipation 0.1%, fungal infection 0.1%, genital pruritus 0.1%, headache 0.1%, moniliasis 0.1%, nervousness 0.1%, rash erythematous 0.1%, urticaria 0.1%.

In clinical trials, the following events occurred in >3% of patients, regardless of drug relationship: nausea 7.2%, headache 6.4%, diarrhea 5.6%, insomnia 4.6%, injection site reaction 3.5%, constipation 3.2%.

In clinical trials, the following events occurred in 1 to 3% of patients, regardless of drug relationship: dizziness 2.7%, abdominal pain 2.5%, dyspepsia 2.4%, vomiting 2.3%, vaginitis 1.8%, injection site pain 1.7%, flatulence 1.5%, pain 1.4%, pruritus 1.3%, sinusitis 1.3%, chest pain 1.2%, fatigue 1.2%, rash 1.2%, back pain 1.1%, injection site inflammation 1.1%, rhinitis 1.0%, taste perversion 1.0%.

In clinical trials, the following events, of potential medical importance, occurred at a rate of less than 1.0% regardless of drug relationship:

[See table at bottom of next page]

In clinical trials using multiple-dose therapy, ophthalmologic abnormalities, including cataracts and multiple punctate lenticular opacities, have been noted in patients undergoing treatment with other quinolones. The relationship of the drugs to these events is not presently established.

Crystalluria and cylindruria have been reported with other quinolones.

The following laboratory abnormalities appeared in 2.2% of patients receiving levofloxacin. It is not known whether these abnormalities were caused by the drug or the underlying condition being treated.

Blood Chemistry: decreased glucose

Hematology: decreased lymphocytes

Post-Marketing Adverse Reactions

Additional adverse events reported from worldwide post-marketing experience with levofloxacin include: allergic pneumonitis, anaphylactic shock, anaphylactoid reaction, dysphonia, abnormal EEG, encephalopathy, eosinophilia, erythema multiforme, hemolytic anemia, multi-system organ failure, increased International Normalized Ratio (INR)/prothrombin time, Stevens-Johnson Syndrome, tendon rupture, torsades de pointes, vasodilation.

OVERDOSAGE

Levofloxacin exhibits a low potential for acute toxicity. Mice, rats, dogs and monkeys exhibited the following clinical signs after receiving a single high dose of levofloxacin: ataxia, ptosis, decreased locomotor activity, dyspnea, prostration, tremors, and convulsions. Doses in excess of 1500 mg/kg orally and 250 mg/kg i.v. produced significant mortality in rodents. In the event of an acute overdosage, the stomach should be emptied. The patient should be observed and appropriate hydration maintained. Levofloxacin is not efficiently removed by hemodialysis or peritoneal dialysis.

DOSAGE AND ADMINISTRATION

LEVAQUIN Injection should only be administered by intravenous infusion. It is not for intramuscular, intrathecal, intraperitoneal, or subcutaneous administration.

CAUTION: RAPID OR BOLUS INTRAVENOUS INFUSION MUST BE AVOIDED. Levofloxacin Injection should be infused intravenously

Autonomic Nervous System Disorders:	postural hypotension
Body as a Whole–General Disorders:	asthenia, edema, fever, malaise, rigors, substernal chest pain, syncope
Cardiovascular Disorders, General:	cardiac failure, circulatory failure, hypertension, hypotension
Central and Peripheral Nervous System Disorders:	abnormal coordination, coma, convulsions (seizures), hyperkinesia, hypertonia, hypoaesthesia, involuntary muscle contractions, paresthesia, paralysis, speech disorder, stupor, tremor, vertigo
Gastro-Intestinal System Disorders:	dry mouth, dysphagia, gastroenteritis, G.I. hemorrhage, pancreatitis, pseudomembranous colitis, tongue edema
Hearing and Vestibular Disorders:	ear disorder (not otherwise specified), tinnitus
Heart Rate and Rhythm Disorders:	arrhythmia, atrial fibrillation, bradycardia, cardiac arrest, heart block, palpitation, supraventricular tachycardia, tachycardia, ventricular fibrillation
Liver and Biliary System Disorders:	abnormal hepatic function, cholelithiasis, hepatic coma, jaundice
Metabolic and Nutritional Disorders:	aggravated diabetes mellitus, dehydration, hyperglycemia, hyperkalemia, hypokalemia, hypoglycemia, increased LDH, weight decrease
Musculo-Skeletal System Disorders:	arthralgia, arthritis, muscle weakness, myalgia, osteomyelitis, rhabdomyolysis, synovitis, tendinitis
Myo, Endo, Pericardial and Valve Disorders:	angina pectoris, coronary thrombosis, myocardial infarction
Neoplasms:	carcinoma
Other Special Senses Disorders:	parosmia
Platelet, Bleeding and Clotting Disorders:	abnormal platelets, embolism (blood clot), epistaxis, purpura, thrombocytopenia
Psychiatric Disorders:	abnormal dreaming, aggressive reaction, agitation, anorexia, anxiety, confusion, delirium, depression, emotional lability, hallucination, impaired concentration, impotence, manic reaction, mental deficiency, nervousness, paranoia sleep disorder, somnolence, withdrawal syndrome
Red Blood Cell Disorders:	anemia
Reproductive Disorders:	ejaculation failure
Resistance Mechanism Disorders:	fungal infection, genital moniliasis
Respiratory System Disorders:	ARDS, asthma, coughing, dyspnea, haemoptysis, hypoxia, pleural effusion, respiratory insufficiency
Skin and Appendages Disorders:	erythema nodosum, genital pruritus, increased sweating, skin disorder, skin exfoliation, skin ulceration, urticaria
Urinary System Disorders:	abnormal renal function, acute renal failure, face edema, haematuria
Vascular (Extracardiac) Disorders:	cerebrovascular disorder, phlebitis
Vision Disorders:	abnormal vision, conjunctivitis, diplopia
White Cell and RES Disorders:	granulocytopenia, leukocytosis, leukopenia, lymphadenopathy, WBC abnormal (not otherwise specified)

Infection*	Unit Dose	Freq.	Duration**	Daily Dose
Acute Bacterial Exacerbation of Chronic Bronchitis	500 mg	q24h	7 days	500 mg
Comm. Acquired Pneumonia	500 mg	q24h	7–14 days	500 mg
Acute Maxillary Sinusitis	500 mg	q24h	10–14 days	500 mg
Complicated SSSI	750 mg	q24h	7–14 days	750 mg
Uncomplicated SSSI	500 mg	q24h	7–10 days	500 mg
Complicated UTI	250 mg	q24h	10 days	250 mg
Acute pyelonephritis	250 mg	q24h	10 days	250 mg
Uncomplicated UTI	250 mg	q24h	3 days	250 mg

* **DUE TO THE DESIGNATED PATHOGENS** (See **INDICATIONS AND USAGE.**)
** Sequential therapy (intravenous to oral) may be instituted at the discretion of the physician.

Renal Status	Initial Dose	Subsequent Dose
Acute Bacterial Exacerbation of Chronic Bronchitis / Comm. Acquired Pneumonia / Acute Maxillary Sinusitis / Uncomplicated SSSI		
CL_{CR} from 50 to 80 mL/min	No dosage adjustment required	
CL_{CR} from 20 to 49 mL/min	500 mg	250 mg q24h
CL_{CR} from 10 to 19 mL/min	500 mg	250 mg q48h
Hemodialysis	500 mg	250 mg q48h
CAPD	500 mg	250 mg q48h
Complicated SSSI		
CL_{CR} from 50 to 80 mL/min	No dosage adjustment required	
CL_{CR} from 20 to 49 mL/min	750 mg	750 mg q48h
CL_{CR} from 10 to 19 mL/min	750 mg	500 mg q48h
Hemodialysis	750 mg	500 mg q48h
CAPD	750 mg	500 mg q48h
Complicated UTI / Acute Pyelonephritis		
$CL_{CR} \geq 20$ mL/min	No dosage adjustment required	
CL_{CR} from 10 to 19 mL/min	250 mg	250 mg q48h
Uncomplicated UTI	No dosage adjustment required	

CL_{CR}=creatinine clearances
CAPD=chronic ambulatory peritoneal dialysis

slowly over a period of not less than 60 or 90 minutes, depending on the dosage. (See **PRECAUTIONS**.)
Single-use vials require dilution prior to administration. (See **PREPARATION FOR ADMINISTRATION.**)
The usual dose of LEVAQUIN Tablets/Injection is 250 mg or 500 mg administered orally or by slow infusion over 60 minutes every 24 hours or 750 mg administered by slow infusion over 90 minutes every 24 hours, as indicated by infection and described in the following dosing chart. These recommendations apply to patients with normal renal function (i.e., creatinine clearance > 80 mL/min). For patients with altered renal function see the **Patients with Impaired Renal Function** subsection. Oral doses should be administered at least two hours before or two hours after antacids containing magnesium, aluminum, as well as sucralfate, metal cations such as iron, and mul-

tivitamin preparations with zinc or Videx®, (Didanosine), chewable/buffered tablets or the pediatric powder for oral solution.
Patients with Normal Renal Function
[See first table above]
Patients with Impaired Renal Function
[See second table above]
When only the serum creatinine is known, the following formula may be used to estimate creatinine clearance.

Men: Creatinine clearance (mL/min) =

$$\frac{\text{Weight (kg)} \times (140 - \text{age})}{72 \times \text{serum creatinine (mg/dL)}}$$

Women: $0.85 \times$ the value calculated for men.

The serum creatinine should represent a steady state of renal function.

Desired Dosage Strength	From Appropriate Vial, Withdraw Volume	Volume of Diluent	Infusion Time
250 mg	10 mL (20 mL Vial)	40 mL	60 min
500 mg	20 mL (20 mL Vial)	80 mL	60 min
750 mg	30 mL (30 mL Vial)	120 mL	90 min

Preparation of Levofloxacin Injection for Administration

LEVAQUIN Injection in Single-Use Vials: LEVAQUIN Injection is supplied in single-use vials containing a concentrated levofloxacin solution with the equivalent of 500 mg (20 mL vial) and 750 mg (30 mL vial) of levofloxacin in Water for Injection, USP. The 20 mL and 30 mL vials each contain 25 mg of levofloxacin/mL. **THESE LEVAQUIN INJECTION SINGLE-USE VIALS MUST BE FURTHER DILUTED WITH AN APPROPRIATE SOLUTION PRIOR TO INTRAVENOUS ADMINISTRATION. (See COMPATIBLE INTRAVENOUS SOLUTIONS.)** The concentration of the resulting diluted solution should be 5 mg/mL prior to administration.

This intravenous drug product should be inspected visually for particulate matter prior to administration. Samples containing visible parties should be discarded.

Since no preservative or bacteriostatic agent is present in this product, aseptic technique must be used in preparation of the final intravenous solution. **Since the vials are for single-use only, any unused portion remaining in the vial should be discarded. When used to prepare two 250 mg doses from the 20 mL vial containing 500 mg of levofloxacin, the full content of the vial should be withdrawn at once using a single-entry procedure, and a second dose should be prepared and stored for subsequent use. (See Stability of LEVAQUIN Injection Following Dilution.)**

Since only limited data are available on the compatibility of levofloxacin intravenous injection with other intravenous substances, **additives or other medications should not be added to LEVAQUIN Injection in single-use vials or infused simultaneously through the same intravenous line.** If the same intravenous line is used for sequential infusion of several different drugs, the line should be flushed before and after infusion of LEVAQUIN Injection with an infusion solution compatible with LEVAQUIN Injection and with any other drug(s) administered via this common line.

Prepare the desired dosage of levofloxacin according to the following chart:

[See table above]

For example, to prepare a 500-mg dose using the 20 mL vial (25 mg/mL), withdraw 20 mL and dilute with a compatible intravenous solution to a total volume of 100 mL.

Compatible Intravenous Solutions: Any of the following intravenous solutions may be used to prepare a 5 mg/mL levofloxacin solution with the approximate pH values:

Intravenous Fluids	Final pH of LEVAQUIN Solution
0.9% Sodium Chloride Injection, USP	4.71
5% Dextrose Injection, USP	4.58
5% Dextrose/0.9% NaCl Injection	4.62
5% Dextrose in Lactated Ringers	4.92
Plasma-Lyte® 56/5% Dextrose Injection	5.03
5% Dextrose, 0.45% Sodium Chloride, and 0.15% Potassium Chloride Injection	4.61
Sodium Lactate Injection (M/6)	5.54

LEVAQUIN Injection Premix in Single-Use Flexible Containers: LEVAQUIN Injection is also supplied in flexible containers containing a premixed, ready-to-use levofloxacin solution in D_5W for single-use. The fill volume is either 50 or 100 mL for the 100 mL flexible container or 150 mL for the 150 mL container. **NO FURTHER DILUTION OF THESE PREPARATIONS ARE NECESSARY** Consequently each 50 mL, 100 mL, and 150 mL premix flexible container already contains a dilute solution with the equivalent of 250 mg, 500 mg, and 750 mg of levofloxacin, respectively (5 mg/mL) in 5% Dextrose (D_5W).

This parenteral drug product should be inspected visually for particulate matter prior to administration. Samples containing visible parties should be discarded.

Since the premix flexible containers are for single-use only, any unused portion should be discarded.

Since only limited data are available on the compatibility of levofloxacin intravenous injection with other intravenous substances, **additives or other medications should not be added to LEVAQUIN Injection in flexible containers or infused simultaneously through the same intravenous line.** If the same intravenous line is used for sequential infusion of several different drugs, the line should be flushed before and after infusion of LEVAQUIN Injection with an infusion solution compatible with LEVAQUIN Injection and with any other drug(s) administered via this common line.

Instructions for the Use of LEVAQUIN Injection Premix in Flexible Containers

To open:

1. Tear outer wrap at the notch and remove solution container.

2. Check the container for minute leaks by squeezing the inner bag firmly. If leaks are found, or if the seal is not intact, discard the solution, as the sterility may be compromised.

3. Do not use if the solution is cloudy or a precipitate is present.

4. Use sterile equipment.

5. **WARNING: Do not use flexible containers in series connections.** Such use could result in air embolism due to residual air being drawn from the primary container before administration of the fluid from the secondary container is complete.

Preparation for administration:

1. Close flow control clamp of administration set.

2. Remove cover from port at bottom of container.

3. Insert piercing pin of administration set into port with a twisting motion until the pin is firmly seated. **NOTE: See full directions on administration set carton.**

4. Suspend container from hanger.

5. Squeeze and release drip chamber to establish proper fluid level in chamber during infusion of LEVAQUIN Injection in Premix Flexible Containers.

6. Open flow control clamp to expel air from set. Close clamp.

7. Regulate rate of administration with flow control clamp.

Stability of LEVAQUIN Injection as Supplied

When stored under recommended conditions, LEVAQUIN Injection, as supplied in 20 mL and 30 mL vials, or 100 mL and 150 mL flexible containers, is stable through the expiration date printed on the label.

Stability of LEVAQUIN Injection Following Dilution

LEVAQUIN Injection, when diluted in a compatible intravenous fluid to a concentration of 5 mg/mL, is stable for 72 hours when stored at or below 25°C (77°F) and for 14 days when stored under refrigeration at 5°C (41°F) in plastic intravenous containers. Solutions that are diluted in a compatible intravenous solution and frozen in glass bottles or plastic intravenous containers are stable for 6 months when stored at -20°C (-4°F). **THAW FROZEN SOLUTIONS AT ROOM TEMPERATURE 25°C (77°F) OR IN A REFRIGERATOR 8°C (46°F). DO NOT FORCE THAW BY MICROWAVE IRRADIATION OR WATER BATH IMMERSION. DO NOT REFREEZE AFTER INITIAL THAWING.**

HOW SUPPLIED

LEVAQUIN Tablets

LEVAQUIN (levofloxacin tablets) Tablets are supplied as 250, 500, and 750 mg modified rectangular, film-coated tablets.

LEVAQUIN Tablets are packaged in bottles and in unit-dose blister strips in the following configurations:

250 mg tablets: color: terra cotta pink
debossing: "LEVAQUIN" on side 1 and "250" on side 2
bottles of 50 (NDC 0045-1520-50)
unit-dose/100 tablets (NDC 0045-1520-10)
500 mg tablets: color: peach
debossing: "LEVAQUIN" on side 1 and "500" on side 2
bottles of 50 (NDC 0045-1525-50)
unit-dose/100 tablets (NDC 0045-1525-10)
750 mg tablets: color: white
debossing: "LEVAQUIN" on side 1 and "750" on side 2
bottles of 50 (NDC 0045-1530-50)
unit-dose/100 tablets (NDC 0045-1530-10)

LEVAQUIN Tablets should be stored at 15° to 30°C (59° to 86°F) in well-closed containers.

LEVAQUIN Tablets are manufactured for OMP DIVISION, ORTHO-McNEIL PHARMACEUTICAL, INC. by Janssen Ortho LLC, Gurabo, Puerto Rico 00778.

LEVAQUIN Injection

Single-Use Vials: LEVAQUIN (levofloxacin injection) Injection is supplied in single-use vials. Each vial contains a concentrated solution with the equivalent of 500 mg of levofloxacin in 20 mL vials and 750 mg of levofloxacin in 30 mL vials.

25 mg/mL, 20 mL vials (NDC 0045-0069-51)
25 mg/mL, 30 mL vials (NDC 0045-0065-55)

LEVAQUIN Injection in Single-Use Vials should be stored at controlled room temperature and protected from light.

LEVAQUIN Injection in Single-Use Vials is manufactured for OMP DIVISION, ORTHO-McNEIL PHARMACEUTICAL, INC. by OMJ Pharmaceuticals, Inc., San German, Puerto Rico, 00683.

Premix in Flexible Containers: LEVAQUIN (levofloxacin injection) Injection is supplied as a single-use, premixed solution in flexible containers. Each bag contains a dilute solution with the equivalent of 250, 500, or 750 mg of levofloxacin, respectively, in 5% Dextrose (D_5W).

5 mg/mL (250 mg), 50 mL flexible container (NDC 0045-0067-01)
5 mg/mL (500 mg), 100 mL flexible container (NDC 0045-0068-01)
5 mg/mL (750 mg), 150 mL flexible container (NDC 0045-0066-01)

LEVAQUIN Injection Premix in Flexible Containers should be stored at or below 25°C (77°F); however, brief exposure up to 40°C (104°F) does not adversely affect the product. Avoid excessive heat and protect from freezing and light.

LEVAQUIN Injection Premix in Flexible Containers is manufactured for OMP DIVISION, ORTHO-McNEIL PHARMACEUTICAL, INC. by ABBOTT Laboratories, North Chicago, IL 60064.

CLINICAL STUDIES

Community-Acquired Bacterial Pneumonia

Adult inpatients and outpatients with a diagnosis of community-acquired bacterial pneumonia were evaluated in two pivotal clinical studies. In the first study, 590 patients were enrolled in a prospective, multi-center, un-blinded randomized trial comparing levofloxa-cin 500 mg once daily orally or intravenously for 7 to 14 days to ceftriaxone 1 to 2 grams in-travenously once or in equally divided doses twice daily followed by cefuroxime axetil 500 mg orally twice daily for a total of 7 to 14 days. Patients assigned to treatment with the control regimen were allowed to receive eryth-romycin (or doxycyine if intolerant of erythro-mycin) if an infection due to atypical patho-gens was suspected or proven. Clinical and mi-crobiologic evaluations were performed during treatment, 5 to 7 days posttherapy, and 3 to 4 weeks posttherapy. Clinical success (cure plus improvement) with levofloxacin at 5 to 7 days posttherapy, the primary efficacy variable in this study, was superior (95%) to the control group (83%) [95% CI of -19,-6]. In the second study, 264 patients were enrolled in a prospec-tive, multi-center, non-comparative trial of 500 mg levofloxacin administered orally or in-travenously once daily for 7 to 14 days. Clini-cal success for clinically evaluable patients was 93%. For both studies, the clinical success rate in patients with atypical pneumonia due to *Chlamydia pneumoniae*, *Mycoplasma pneu-moniae*, and *Legionella pneumophila* were 96%, 96%, and 70%, respectively. Microbio-logic eradication rates across both studies were as follows:

Pathogen	No. Pathogens	Microbiologic Eradication Rate (%)
H. influenzae	55	98
S. pneumoniae	83	95
S. aureus	17	88
M. catarrhalis	18	94
H. parainfluenzae	19	95
K. pneumoniae	10	100.0

Additional studies were initiated to evaluate the utility of LEVAQUIN in community-acquired pneumonia due to *S. pneumoniae*, with particular interest in penicillin-resistant strains (MIC value for penicillin ≥ 2 µg/mL). In addition to the studies previously dis-cussed, inpatients and outpatients with mild to severe community-acquired pneumonia were evaluated in six additional clinical stud-ies; one double-blind study, two open label ran-domized studies, and three open label non-comparative studies. The total number of clin-ically evaluable patients with *S. pneumoniae* across all 8 studies was 250 for levofloxacin and 41 for comparators. The clinical success rate (cured or improved) among the 250 levo-floxacin-treated patients with *S. pneumoniae* was 245/250 (98%). The clinical success rate among the 41 comparator-treated patients with *S. pneumoniae* was 39/41 (95%).

Across these 8 studies, 18 levofloxacin-treated and 4 non-quinolone comparator-treated pa-tients with community-acquired pneumonia

due to penicillin-resistant *S. pneumoniae* (MIC value for penicillin ≥ 2 µg/mL) were identified. Of the 18 levofloxacin-treated pa-tients, 15 were evaluable following the com-pletion of therapy. Fifteen out of the 15 evalu-able levofloxacin-treated patients with com-munity-acquired pneumonia due to penicillin-resistant *S. pneumoniae* achieved clinical success (cure or improvement). Of these 15 pa-tients, 6 were bacteremic and 5 were classified as having severe disease. Of the 4 comparator-treated patients with community-acquired pneumonia due to penicillin-resistant *S. pneu-moniae*, 3 were evaluable for clinical efficacy. Three out of the 3 evaluable comparator-treated patients achieved clinical success. All three of the comparator-treated patients were bacteremic and had disease classified as severe.

Complicated Skin And Skin Structure Infec-tions

Three hundred ninety-nine patients were en-rolled in an open-label, randomized, compari-tive study for complicated skin and skin struc-ture infections. The patients were randomized to receive either levofloxacin 750mg QD (IV followed by oral), or an approved comparator for a median of 10 ± 4.7 days. As is expected in complicated skin and skin structure infec-tions, surgical procedures were performed in the levofloxacin and comparator groups. Sur-gery (incision and drainage or debridement) was performed on 45% of the levofloxacin treated patients and 44% of the comparator treated patients, either shortly before or dur-ing antibiotic treatment and formed an inte-gral part of therapy for this indication.

Among those who could be evaluated clinically 2-5 days after completion of study drug, over-all success rates (improved or cured) were 116/138 (84.1%) for patients treated with levo-floxacin and 106/132 (80.3%) for patients treated with the comparator.

Success rates varied with the type of diagnosis ranging from 68% in patients with infected ul-cers to 90% in patients with infected wounds and abscesses. These rates were equivalent to those seen with comparator drugs.

ANIMAL PHARMACOLOGY

Levofloxacin and other quinolones have been shown to cause arthropathy in immature ani-mals of most species tested. (See **WARN-INGS**.) In immature dogs (4–5 months old), oral doses of 10 mg/kg/day for 7 days and in-travenous doses of 4 mg/kg/day for 14 days of levofloxacin resulted in arthropathic lesions. Administration at oral doses of 300 mg/kg/day for 7 days and intravenous doses of 60 mg/kg/day for 4 weeks produced arthropathy in juve-nile rats.

When tested in a mouse ear swelling bioassay, levofloxacin exhibited phototoxicity similar in magnitude to ofloxacin, but less phototoxicity than other quinolones.

While crystalluria has been observed in some intravenous rat studies, urinary crystals are not formed in the bladder, being present only after micturition and are not associated with nephrotoxicity.

In mice, the CNS stimulatory effect of quinolones is enhanced by concomitant administration of non-steroidal anti-inflammatory drugs. In dogs, levofloxacin administered at 6 mg/kg or higher by rapid intravenous injection produced hypotensive effects. These effects were considered to be related to histamine release. In vitro and in vivo studies in animals indicate that levofloxacin is neither an enzyme inducer or inhibitor in the human therapeutic plasma concentration range; therefore, no drug metabolizing enzyme-related interactions with other drugs or agents are anticipated.

REFERENCES

1. National Committee for Clinical Laboratory Standards. Methods for Dilution Antimicrobial Susceptibility Tests for Bacteria That Grow Aerobically Fourth Edition. Approved Standard NCCLS Document M7-A4, Vol. 17, No. 2, NCS, Wayne, PA, January, 1997.
2. National Committee for Clinical Laboratory Standards. Performance Standards for Antimicrobial Disk Susceptibility Tests Sixth Edition. Approved Standard NCCLS Document M2-A6, Vol. 17, No. 1, NCCLS, Wayne, PA, January, 1997.

Patient Information About:
LEVAQUIN®
(levofloxacin tablets)
250 mg Tablets, 500 mg Tablets, and 750 mg Tablets

This leaflet contains important information about LEVAQUIN® (levofloxacin), and should be read completely before you begin treatment. This leaflet does not take the place of discussions with your doctor or health care professional about your medical condition or your treatment. This leaflet does not list all benefits and risks of LEVAQUIN®. The medicine described here can be prescribed only by a licensed health care professional. If you have any questions about LEVAQUIN® talk to your health care professional. Only your health care professional can determine if LEVAQUIN® is right for you.

What is LEVAQUIN?
LEVAQUIN® is a quinolone antibiotic used to treat lung, sinus, skin, and urinary tract infections caused by certain germs called bacteria. LEVAQUIN® kills many of the types of bacteria that can infect the lungs, sinuses, skin, and urinary tract and has been shown in a large number of clinical trials to be safe and effective for the treatment of bacterial infections.

Sometimes viruses rather than bacteria may infect the lungs and sinuses (for example the common cold). LEVAQUIN®, like other antibiotics, does not kill viruses.

You should contact your health care professional if you think that your condition is not improving while taking LEVAQUIN®. LEVAQUIN® Tablets are terra cotta pink for the 250 mg tablet, peach colored for the 500 mg tablet, or white for the 750 mg tablet.

How and when should I take LEVAQUIN?
LEVAQUIN® should be taken once a day for 3, 7, 10, or 14 days depending on your prescription. It should be swallowed and may be taken with or without food. Try to take the tablet at the same time each day and drink fluids liberally.

You may begin to feel better quickly; however, in order to make sure that all bacteria are killed, you should complete the full course of medication. Do not take more than the prescribed dose of LEVAQUIN® even if you missed a dose by mistake. You should not take a double dose.

Who should not take LEVAQUIN®?
You should not take LEVAQUIN® if you have ever had a severe allergic reaction to any of the group of antibiotics known as "quinolones" such as ciprofloxacin. Serious and occasionally fatal allergic reactions have been reported in patients receiving therapy with quinolones, including LEVAQUIN®.

If you are pregnant or are planning to become pregnant while taking LEVAQUIN®, talk to your health care professional before taking this medication. LEVAQUIN® is not recommended for use during pregnancy or nursing, as the effects on the unborn child or nursing infant are unknown.

LEVAQUIN® is not recommended for children.

What are possible side effects of LEVAQUIN®?
LEVAQUIN® is generally well tolerated. The most common side effects caused by LEVAQUIN®, which are usually mild, include nausea, diarrhea, itching, abdominal pain, dizziness, flatulence, rash and vaginitis in women.

You should be careful about driving or operating machinery until you are sure LEVAQUIN® is not causing dizziness.

Allergic reactions have been reported in patients receiving quinolones including LEVAQUIN®, even after just one dose. If you develop hives, skin rash or other symptoms of an allergic reaction, you should stop taking this medication and call your health care professional.

Ruptures of shoulder, hand, or Achilles tendons have been reported in patients receiving quinolones, including LEVAQUIN®. If you develop pain, swelling, or rupture of a tendon you should stop taking LEVAQUIN® and contact your health care professional.

Some quinolone antibiotics have been associated with the development of phototoxicity ("sunburns" and "blistering sunburns") following exposure to sunlight or other sources of ultraviolet light such as artificial ultraviolet light used in tanning salons. LEVAQUIN® has been infrequently associated with phototoxicity. You should avoid excessive exposure to sunlight or artificial ultraviolet light while you are taking LEVAQUIN®.

If you have diabetes and you develop a hypoglycemic reaction while on LEVAQUIN, you should stop taking LEVAQUIN® and call your health care professional.

Convulsions have been reported in patients receiving quinolone antibiotics including LEVAQUIN®. If you have experienced convulsions in the past, be sure to let your physician know that you have a history of convulsions.

Quinolones, including LEVAQUIN®, may also cause central nervous system stimulation which may lead to tremors, restlessness, anxiety, lightheadedness, confusion, hallucinations, paranoia, depression, nightmares, insomnia, and rarely, suicidal thoughts or acts.

If you notice any side effects not mentioned in this leaflet or you have concerns about the side effects you are experiencing, please inform your health care professional.

For more complete information regarding levofloxacin, please refer to the full prescribing information, which may be obtained from your health care professional, pharmacist, or the Physicians Desk Reference (PDR).

What about other medicines I am taking?

Taking warfarin (Coumadin®) and LEVAQUIN® together can further predispose you to the development of bleeding problems. If you take warfarin, be sure to tell your health care professional.

Many antacids and multivitamins may interfere with the absorption of LEVAQUIN® and may prevent it from working properly. You should take LEVAQUIN® either 2 hours before or 2 hours after taking these products.

It is important to let your health care professional know all of the medicines you are using.

Other information

Take your dose of LEVAQUIN® once a day.

Complete the course of medication even if you are feeling better.

Keep this medication out of the reach of children.

This information does not take the place of discussions with your doctor or health care professional about your medical condition or your treatment.

ORTHO-McNEIL

OMP DIVISION

ORTHO-McNEIL PHARMACEUTICAL, INC.

Raritan, New Jersey, USA 08869

U.S. Patent No. 4,382,892 and U.S. Patent No. 5,053,407

7518201

© OMP 2000   Revised November 2000

633-10-816-2

MINOCIN®   ℞
[*mĭ-nō-sĭn*]
Sterile
Minocycline Hydrochloride
Intravenous
100 mg/Vial

DESCRIPTION

MINOCIN minocycline hydrochloride, a semi-synthetic derivative of tetracycline, is named [4S -(4α,4aα,5aα,12aα)]-4,7-bis (dimethylamino)-1, 4, 4a, 5, 5a, 6, 11, 12a-octahydro-3, 10, 12,12a-tetrahydroxy-1, 11-dioxo-2-naphtha-cenecarboxamide monohydrochloride.

Each vial, dried by cryodesiccation, contains sterile minocycline HCl equivalent to 100 mg minocycline. When reconstituted with 5 mL of Sterile Water for Injection USP, the pH ranges from 2.0 to 2.8.

ACTIONS

Microbiology

The tetracyclines are primarily bacteriostatic and are thought to exert their antimicrobial effect by the inhibition of protein synthesis. Minocycline HCl is a tetracycline with antibacterial activity comparable to other tetracyclines with activity against a wide range of gram-negative and gram-positive organisms.

Tube dilution testing: Microorganisms may be considered susceptible (likely to respond to minocycline therapy) if the minimum inhibitory concentration (MIC) is not more than 4 mcg/mL. Microorganisms may be considered intermediate (harboring partial resistance) if the MIC is 4 to 12.5 mcg/mL and resistant (not likely to respond to minocycline therapy) if the MIC is greater than 12.5 mcg/mL.

Susceptibility plate testing: If the Kirby-Bauer method of susceptibility testing (using a 30 mcg tetracycline disc) gives a zone of 18 mm or greater, the bacterial strain is considered to be susceptible to any tetracycline. Minocycline shows moderate *in vitro* activity against certain strains of staphylococci which have been found resistant to other tetracyclines. For such strains, minocycline susceptibility powder may be used for additional susceptibility testing.

Human Pharmacology

Following a single dose of 200 mg administered intravenously to 10 healthy male volunteers, serum levels ranged from 2.52 to 6.63 mcg/mL (average 4.18), after 12 hours they ranged from 0.82 to 2.64 mcg/mL (average 1.38). In a group of five healthy male volunteers, serum levels of 1.4 to 1.8 mcg/mL were maintained at 12 and 24 hours with doses of 100 mg every 12 hours for three days. When given 200 mg once daily for three days, the serum levels had fallen to approximately 1 mcg/mL at 24 hours. The serum half-life following I.V. doses of 100 mg every 12 hours or 200 mg once daily did not differ significantly and ranged from 15 to 23 hours. The serum half-life following a single 200 mg oral dose in 12 essentially normal volunteers ranged from 11 to 17 hours, in 7 patients with hepatic dysfunction ranged from 11 to 16 hours, and in 5 patients with renal dysfunction from 18 to 69 hours.

Intravenously administered minocycline appears similar to oral doses in excretion. The urinary and fecal recovery of oral minocycline when administered to 12 normal volunteers is one-half to one-third that of other tetracyclines.

INDICATIONS

MINOCIN is indicated in infections caused by the following microorganisms:

Rickettsiae: (Rocky Mountain spotted fever, typhus fever and the typhus group, Q fever, rickettsialpox, tick fevers).

Mycoplasma pneumoniae (PPLO, Eaton agent).

Agents of psittacosis and ornithosis.

Agents of lymphogranuloma venereum and granuloma inguinale.

The spirochetal agent of relapsing fever (*Borrelia recurrentis*).

The following gram-negative microorganisms:

Haemophilus ducreyi (chancroid),

Yersinia pestis and *Francisella tularensis,* formerly *Pasteurella pestis* and *Pasteurella tularensis,*

Bartonella bacilliformis,

Bacteroides species,

Vibrio comma and *Vibrio fetus,*

Brucella species (in conjunction with streptomycin).

Because many strains of the following groups of microorganisms have been shown to be resistant to tetracyclines, culture and susceptibility testing are recommended.

MINOCIN is indicated for treatment of infections caused by the following gram-negative microorganisms when bacteriologic testing indicates appropriate susceptibility to the drug:

Escherichia coli,

Enterobacter aerogenes (formerly *Aerobacter aerogenes*),

Shigella species,

Mima species and *Herellea* species,

Haemophilus influenzae (respiratory infections),

Klebsiella species (respiratory and urinary infections).

MINOCIN is indicated for treatment of infections caused by the following gram-positive microorganisms when bacteriologic testing indicates appropriate susceptibility to the drug:

Streptococcus species:

Up to 44% of strains of *Streptococcus pyogenes* and 74% of *Streptococcus faecalis* have been found to be resistant to tetracycline drugs. Therefore, tetracyclines should not be used for streptococcal disease unless the organism has been demonstrated to be sensitive.

For upper respiratory infections due to Group A beta-hemolytic streptococci, penicillin is the usual drug of choice, including prophylaxis of rheumatic fever.

Streptococcus pneumoniae,
Staphylococcus aureus, skin and soft tissue infections.

Tetracyclines are not the drugs of choice in the treatment of any type of staphylococcal infection.

When penicillin is contraindicated, tetracyclines are alternative drugs in the treatment of infections due to:

Neisseria gonorrhoeae, and *Neisseria meningitidis,*
Treponema pallidum and *Treponema pertenue* (syphilis and yaws),
Listeria monocytogenes,
Clostridium species,
Bacillus anthracis,
Fusobacterium fusiforme (Vincent's infection),
Actinomyces species.

In acute intestinal amebiasis, the tetracyclines may be a useful adjunct to amebicides.

MINOCIN minocycline HCl is indicated in the treatment of trachoma, although the infectious agent is not always eliminated, as judged by immunofluorescence.

Inclusion conjunctivitis may be treated with oral tetracyclines or with a combination of oral and topical agents.

CONTRAINDICATIONS

This drug is contraindicated in persons who have shown hypersensitivity to any of the tetracyclines.

WARNINGS

In the presence of renal dysfunction, particularly in pregnancy, intravenous tetracycline therapy in daily doses exceeding 2 g has been associated with deaths through liver failure.

When the need for intensive treatment outweighs its potential dangers (mostly during pregnancy or in individuals with known or suspected renal or liver impairment), it is advisable to perform renal and liver function tests before and during therapy. Also, tetracycline serum concentrations should be followed. If renal impairment exists, even usual oral or parenteral doses may lead to excessive systemic accumulation of the drug and possible liver toxicity. Under such conditions, lower than usual total doses are indicated, and if therapy is prolonged, serum level determinations of the drug may be advisable. This hazard is of particular importance in the parenteral administration of tetracyclines to pregnant or postpartum patients with pyelonephritis. When used under these circumstances, the blood level should not exceed 15 mcg/mL and liver function tests should be made at frequent intervals. Other potentially hepatotoxic drugs should not be prescribed concomitantly.

THE USE OF TETRACYCLINES DURING TOOTH DEVELOPMENT (LAST HALF OF PREGNANCY, INFANCY, AND CHILDHOOD TO THE AGE OF 8 YEARS) MAY CAUSE PERMANENT DISCOLORATION OF THE TEETH (YELLOW-GRAY-BROWN). This adverse reaction is more common during long-term use of the drugs but has been observed following repeated short-term courses. Enamel hypoplasia has also been reported. TETRACYCLINES, THEREFORE, SHOULD NOT BE USED IN THIS AGE GROUP UNLESS OTHER DRUGS ARE NOT LIKELY TO BE EFFECTIVE OR ARE CONTRAINDICATED.

Photosensitivity manifested by an exaggerated sunburn reaction has been observed in some individuals taking tetracyclines. Patients apt to be exposed to direct sunlight or ultraviolet light should be advised that this reaction can occur with tetracycline drugs, and treatment should be discontinued at the first evidence of skin erythema. Studies to date indicate that photosensitivity is rarely reported with MINOCIN minocycline HCl.

The anti-anabolic action of the tetracyclines may cause an increase in BUN. While this is not a problem in those with normal renal function, in patients with significantly impaired function, higher serum levels of tetracycline may lead to azotemia, hyperphosphatemia, and acidosis.

CNS side effects including light-headedness, dizziness or vertigo have been reported. Patients who experience these symptoms should be cautioned about driving vehicles or using hazardous machinery while on minocycline therapy. These symptoms may disappear during therapy and usually disappear rapidly when the drug is discontinued.

Usage in Pregnancy
(See above **WARNINGS** about use during tooth development.)

Results of animal studies indicate that tetracyclines cross the placenta, are found in fetal tissues and can have toxic effects on the developing fetus (often related to retardation of skeletal development). Evidence of embryotoxicity has also been noted in animals treated early in pregnancy.

The safety of MINOCIN for use during pregnancy has not been established.

Usage in Newborns, Infants, and Children
(See above **WARNINGS** about use during tooth development.)

All tetracyclines form a stable calcium complex in any bone-forming tissue. A decrease in the fibula growth rate has been observed in prematures given oral tetracycline in doses of 25 mg/kg every 6 hours. This reaction was shown to be reversible when the drug was discontinued.

Tetracyclines are present in the milk of lactating women who are taking a drug in this class.

PRECAUTIONS

General

Pseudotumor cerebri (benign intracranial hypertension) in adults has been associated with the use of tetracyclines. The usual clinical manifestations are headache and blurred vision. Bulging fontanels have been associated with the use of tetracyclines in infants. While both of these conditions and related symptoms usually resolve soon after discontinuation of the tetracycline, the possibility for permanent sequelae exists.

As with other antibiotic preparations, use of this drug may result in overgrowth of nonsusceptible organisms, including fungi. If superinfection occurs, the antibiotic should be discontinued and appropriate therapy should be instituted.

In venereal diseases when coexistent syphilis is suspected, darkfield examination should be done before treatment is started and the blood serology repeated monthly for at least 4 months.

In long-term therapy, periodic laboratory evaluation of organ systems, including hematopoietic, renal, and hepatic studies should be performed.

All infections due to Group A beta-hemolytic streptococci should be treated for at least ten days.

Drug Interactions

Because tetracyclines have been shown to depress plasma prothrombin activity, patients who are on anticoagulant therapy may require downward adjustment of their anticoagulant dosage.

Since bacteriostatic drugs may interfere with the bactericidal action of penicillin, it is advisable to avoid giving tetracycline in conjunction with penicillin.

Concurrent use of tetracyclines with oral contraceptives may render oral contraceptives less effective.

ADVERSE REACTIONS

Gastrointestinal: Anorexia, nausea, vomiting, diarrhea, glossitis, dysphagia, enterocolitis, pancreatitis, inflammatory lesions (with monilial overgrowth) in the anogenital region, and increases in liver enzymes. Rarely, hepatitis and liver failure have been reported.

These reactions have been caused by both the oral and parenteral administration of tetracyclines.

Skin: Maculopapular and erythematous rashes. Exfoliative dermatitis has been reported but is uncommon. Fixed drug eruptions, including balanitis, have been rarely reported. Erythema multiforme and rarely Stevens-Johnson syndrome have been reported. Photosensitivity is discussed above. (See **WARNINGS**.)

Pigmentation of the skin and mucous membranes has been reported.

Tooth discoloration has been reported, rarely, in adults.

Renal Toxicity: Rise in BUN has been reported and is apparently dose related. (See **WARNINGS**.) Reversible acute renal failure has been rarely reported.

Hypersensitivity Reactions: Urticaria, angioneurotic edema, polyarthralgia, anaphylaxis, anaphylactoid purpura, pericarditis, exacerbation of systemic lupus erythematosus, and rarely, pulmonary infiltrates with eosinophilia have been reported. A transient lupus-like syndrome has also been reported.

Blood: Hemolytic anemia, thrombocytopenia, neutropenia, and eosinophilia have been reported.

CNS: (See **WARNINGS**.) Pseudotumor cerebri (benign intracranial hypertension) in adults and bulging fontanels in infants. (See **PRECAUTIONS—General**.) Headache has also been reported.

Other: When given over prolonged periods, tetracyclines have been reported to produce brown-black microscopic discoloration of the thyroid glands. Very rare cases of abnormal thyroid function have been reported.

Decreased hearing has been rarely reported in patients on MINOCIN.

DOSAGE AND ADMINISTRATION

Note: Rapid administration is to be avoided. Parenteral therapy is indicated only when oral therapy is not adequate or tolerated. Oral therapy should be instituted as soon as possible. If intravenous therapy is given over prolonged periods of time, thrombophlebitis may result.

ADULTS: Usual adult dose: 200 mg followed by 100 mg every 12 hours and should not exceed 400 mg in 24 hours. The cryodesiccated powder should be reconstituted with 5 mL Sterile Water for Injection USP and immediately further diluted to 500 mL to 1,000 mL with Sodium Chloride Injection USP, Dextrose Injection USP, Dextrose and Sodium Chloride Injection USP, Ringer's Injection USP, or Lactated Ringer's Injection USP, but not other solutions containing calcium because a precipitate may form. When further diluted in 500 mL to 1,000 mL compatible solutions (except Lactated Ringers), the pH usually ranges from 2.5 to 4.0. The pH of MINOCIN IV 100 mg in Lactated Ringers 500 mL to 1,000 mL usually ranges from 4.5 to 6.0.

Final dilutions (500 mL to 1,000 mL) should be administered immediately but product and diluents are compatible at room temperature for 24 hours without a significant loss of potency. Any unused portions must be discarded after that period.

For children above eight years of age: Usual pediatric dose: 4 mg/kg followed by 2 mg/kg every 12 hours.

In patients with renal impairment: (See **WARNINGS**.)

Total dosage should be decreased by reduction of recommended individual doses and/or by extending time intervals between doses.

Parenteral drug products should be inspected visually for particulate matter and discoloration prior to administration, whenever solution and container permit.

HOW SUPPLIED

MINOCIN® minocycline HCl Intravenous is supplied as 100 mg vials of sterile cryodesiccated powder.

Product No. NDC 0205-5305-94
Store at Controlled Room Temperature 15–30°C (59–86°F).
Manufactured by:
LEDERLE PARENTERALS, INC.
Carolina, Puerto Rico 00987
50422-95   Revised January 1995

MINOCIN®   ℞
Minocycline Hydrochloride
Pellet-Filled Capsules

DESCRIPTION

MINOCIN minocycline hydrochloride, a semi-synthetic derivative of tetracycline, is [4S-(4α,4aα,5aα,12aα)] -4,7-bis(dimethylamino)-1,4,4a,5,5a,6,11,12a-octahydro-3,10,12,12a-tetrahydroxy-1,11-dioxo-2-naphthacenecarboxamide monohydrochloride.

MINOCIN minocycline hydrochloride pellet-filled capsules for oral administration contain pellets of minocycline HCl equivalent to 50 mg or 100 mg of minocycline in microcrystalline cellulose.

The capsule shells contain the following inactive ingredients: Blue 1, Gelatin, Titanium Dioxide and Yellow 10. The 50 mg capsule shells also contain Black and Yellow Iron Oxides.

CLINICAL PHARMACOLOGY

MINOCIN minocycline hydrochloride pellet-filled capsules are rapidly absorbed from the gastrointestinal tract following oral administration. Following a single dose of two 100 mg pellet-filled capsules of MINOCIN minocycline HCl administered to 18 normal fasting adult volunteers, maximum serum concentrations were attained in 1 to 4 hours (average 2.1 hours) and ranged from 2.1 to 5.1 mcg/mL (average 3.5 mcg/mL). The serum half-life in the normal volunteers ranged from 11.1 to 22.1 hours (average 15.5 hours).

When MINOCIN minocycline hydrochloride pellet-filled capsules were given concomitantly with a meal which included dairy products, the extent of absorption of MINOCIN minocycline hydrochloride pellet-filled capsules was not noticeably influenced. The peak plasma concentrations were slightly decreased (11.2%) and delayed by one hour when administered with food, compared to dosing under fasting conditions.

In previous studies with other minocycline dosage forms, the minocycline serum half-life ranged from 11 to 16 hours in 7 patients with hepatic dysfunction, and from 18 to 69 hours in 5 patients with renal dysfunction. The urinary and fecal recovery of minocycline when administered to 12 normal volunteers is one-half to one-third that of other tetracyclines.

Microbiology

The tetracyclines are primarily bacteriostatic and are thought to exert their antimicrobial effect by the inhibition of protein synthesis. The tetracyclines, including minocycline, have similar antimicrobial spectra of activity against a wide range of gram-positive and gram-negative organisms. Cross-resistance of these organisms to tetracyclines is common. While *in vitro* studies have demonstrated the susceptibility of most strains of the following microorganisms, clinical efficacy for infections other than those included in the **INDICATIONS AND USAGE** section has not been documented.

GRAM-NEGATIVE BACTERIA:
Bartonella bacilliformis
Brucella species
Calymmatobacterium granulomatis
Campylobacter fetus
Francisella tularensis
Haemophilus ducreyi
Haemophilus influenzae
Listeria monocytogenes
Neisseria gonorrhoeae
Vibrio cholerae
Yersinia pestis

Because many strains of the following groups of gram-negative microorganisms have been shown to be resistant to tetracyclines, culture and susceptibility tests are especially recommended:
Acinetobacter species
Bacteroides species
Enterobacter aerogenes
Escherichia coli
Klebsiella species
Shigella species

GRAM-POSITIVE BACTERIA:
Because many strains of the following groups of gram-positive microorganisms have been shown to be resistant to tetracyclines, culture and susceptibility testing are especially recommended. Up to 44 percent of *Streptococcus pyogenes* strains have been found to be resistant to tetracycline drugs. Therefore, tetracyclines should not be used for streptococcal disease unless the organism has been demonstrated to be susceptible.
Enterococcus group [*Enterococcus faecalis* (formerly *Streptococcus faecalis*) and *Enterococcus faecium* (formerly *Streptococcus faecium*)]
Streptococcus pneumoniae
Streptococcus pyogenes
Viridans group streptococci

OTHER MICROORGANISMS:
Actinomyces species
Bacillus anthracis
Balantidium coli
Borrelia recurrentis
Chlamydia psittaci
Chlamydia trachomatis
Clostridium species
Entamoeba species
Fusobacterium fusiforme
Mycoplasma pneumoniae
Propionibacterium acnes
Rickettsiae
Treponema pallidum
Treponema pertenue
Ureaplasma urealyticum

Susceptibility Tests

Diffusion Techniques

The use of antibiotic disk susceptibility test methods which measure zone diameter gives an accurate estimation of susceptibility of microorganisms to MINOCIN. One such standard procedure[1] has been recommended for use with disks for testing antimicrobials. Either the 30 mcg tetracycline-class disk or the 30 mcg minocycline disk should be used for the determination of the susceptibility of microorganisms to minocycline.

With this type of procedure a report of "susceptible" from the laboratory indicates that the infecting organism is likely to respond to therapy. A report of "intermediate susceptibility" suggests that the organism would be susceptible if a high dosage is used or if the infection is confined to tissues and fluids (e.g., urine) in which high antibiotic levels are attained. A report of "resistant" indicates that the infecting organism is not likely to respond to therapy. With either the tetracycline-class disk or the minocycline disk, zone sizes of 19 mm or greater indicate susceptibility, zone sizes of 14 mm or less indicate resistance, and zone sizes of 15 to 18 mm indicate intermediate susceptibility.

Standardized procedures require the use of laboratory control organisms. The 30 mcg tetracycline disk should give zone diameters between 19 and 28 mm for *Staphylococcus aureus* ATCC 25923 and between 18 and 25 mm for *Escherichia coli* ATCC 25922. The 30 mcg minocycline disk should give zone diameters between 25 and 30 mm for *S. aureus* ATCC 25923 and between 19 and 25 mm for *E. coli* ATCC 25922.

Dilution Techniques

When using the NCCLS agar dilution or broth dilution (including microdilution) method[2] or equivalent, a bacterial isolate may be considered susceptible if the MIC (minimal inhibitory concentration) of minocycline is 4 mcg/mL or less. Organisms are considered resistant if the MIC is 16 mcg/mL or greater. Organisms with an MIC value of less than 16 mcg/mL but greater than 4 mcg/mL are expected to be susceptible if a high dosage is used or if the infection is confined to tissues and fluids (e.g., urine) in which high antibiotic levels are attained.

As with standard diffusion methods, dilution procedures require the use of laboratory control organisms. Standard tetracycline or minocycline powder should give MIC values of 0.25 mcg/mL to 1.0 mcg/mL for *S. aureus* ATCC 25923, and 1.0 mcg/mL to 4.0 mcg/mL for *E. coli* ATCC 25922.

INDICATIONS AND USAGE

MINOCIN minocycline hydrochloride pellet-filled capsules are indicated in the treatment of the following infections due to susceptible strains of the designated microorganisms:

Rocky Mountain spotted fever, typhus fever and the typhus group, Q fever, rickettsialpox and tick fevers caused by *Rickettsiae.*

Respiratory tract infections caused by *Mycoplasma pneumoniae.*

Lymphogranuloma venereum caused by *Chlamydia trachomatis.*

Psittacosis (Ornithosis) due to *Chlamydia psittaci.*

Trachoma caused by *Chlamydia trachomatis,* although the infectious agent is not always eliminated, as judged by immunofluorescence.

Inclusion conjunctivitis caused by *Chlamydia trachomatis.*

Nongonococcal urethritis in adults caused by *Ureaplasma urealyticum* or *Chlamydia trachomatis.*

Relapsing fever due to *Borrelia recurrentis.*

Chancroid caused by *Haemophilus ducreyi.*

Plague due to *Yersinia pestis.*

Tularemia due to *Francisella tularensis.*

Cholera caused by *Vibrio cholerae.*

Campylobacter fetus infections caused by *Campylobacter fetus.*

Brucellosis due to *Brucella* species (in conjunction with streptomycin).

Bartonellosis due to *Bartonella bacilliformis.*

Granuloma inguinale caused by *Calymmatobacterium granulomatis.*

Minocycline is indicated for treatment of infections caused by the following gram-negative microorganisms, when bacteriologic testing indicates appropriate susceptibility to the drug:

Escherichia coli.

Enterobacter aerogenes.

Shigella species.

Acinetobacter species.

Respiratory tract infections caused by *Haemophilus influenzae.*

Respiratory tract and urinary tract infections caused by *Klebsiella* species.

MINOCIN minocycline hydrochloride pellet-filled capsules are indicated for the treatment of infections caused by the following gram-positive microorganisms when bacteriologic testing indicates appropriate susceptibility to the drug:

Upper respiratory tract infections caused by *Streptococcus pneumoniae.*

Skin and skin structure infections caused by *Staphylococcus aureus.* (Note: Minocycline is not the drug of choice in the treatment of any type of staphylococcal infection.)

Uncomplicated urethritis in men due to *Neisseria gonorrhoeae* and for the treatment of other gonococcal infections when penicillin is contraindicated.

When penicillin is contraindicated, minocycline is an alternative drug in the treatment for the following infections:

Infections in women caused by *Neisseria gonorrhoeae.*

Syphilis caused by *Treponema pallidum.*

Yaws caused by *Treponema pertenue.*

Listeriosis due to *Listeria monocytogenes.*

Anthrax due to *Bacillus anthracis.*

Vincent's infection caused by *Fusobacterium fusiforme.*

Actinomycosis caused by *Actinomyces israelii.*

Infections caused by *Clostridium* species.

In *acute intestinal amebiasis,* minocycline may be a useful adjunct to amebicides.

In severe *acne,* minocycline may be useful adjunctive therapy.

Oral minocycline is indicated in the treatment of asymptomatic carriers of *Neisseria meningitidis* to eliminate meningococci from the nasopharynx. In order to preserve the usefulness of minocycline in the treatment of asymptomatic meningococcal carrier, diagnostic laboratory procedures, including serotyping and susceptibility testing, should be performed to establish the carrier state and the correct treatment. It is recommended that the prophylactic use of minocycline be reserved for situations in which the risk of meningococcal meningitis is high.

Oral minocycline is not indicated for the treatment of meningococcal infection.

Although no controlled clinical efficacy studies have been conducted, limited clinical data show that oral minocycline hydrochloride has been used successfully in the treatment of infections caused by *Mycobacterium marinum.*

CONTRAINDICATIONS

This drug is contraindicated in persons who have shown hypersensitivity to any of the tetracyclines.

WARNINGS

MINOCIN PELLET-FILLED CAPSULES, LIKE OTHER TETRACYCLINE-CLASS ANTIBIOTICS, CAN CAUSE FETAL HARM WHEN ADMINISTERED TO A PREGNANT WOMAN. IF ANY TETRACYCLINE IS USED DURING PREGNANCY OR IF THE PATIENT BECOMES PREGNANT WHILE TAKING THESE DRUGS, THE PATIENT SHOULD BE APPRISED OF THE POTENTIAL HAZARD TO THE FETUS. THE USE OF DRUGS OF THE TETRACYCLINE CLASS DURING TOOTH DEVELOPMENT (LAST HALF OF PREGNANCY, INFANCY, AND CHILDHOOD TO THE AGE OF 8 YEARS) MAY CAUSE PERMANENT DISCOLORATION OF THE TEETH (YELLOW-GRAY-BROWN).

This adverse reaction is more common during long-term use of the drug but has been observed following repeated short-term courses. Enamel hypoplasia has also been reported. TETRACYCLINE DRUGS, THEREFORE, SHOULD NOT BE USED DURING TOOTH DEVELOPMENT UNLESS OTHER DRUGS ARE NOT LIKELY TO BE EFFECTIVE OR ARE CONTRAINDICATED.

All tetracyclines form a stable calcium complex in any bone-forming tissue. A decrease in fibula growth rate has been observed in premature human infants given oral tetracycline in doses of 25 mg/kg every six hours. This reaction was shown to be reversible when the drug was discontinued.

Results of animal studies indicate that tetracyclines cross the placenta, are found in fetal tissues, and can have toxic effects on the developing fetus (often related to retardation of skeletal development). Evidence of embryotoxicity has been noted in animals treated early in pregnancy.

The anti-anabolic action of the tetracyclines may cause an increase in BUN. While this is not a problem in those with normal renal function, in patients with significantly impaired function, higher serum levels of tetracycline may lead to azotemia, hyperphosphatemia, and acidosis. If renal impairment exists, even usual oral or parenteral doses may lead to excessive systemic accumulations of the drug and possible liver toxicity. Under such conditions, lower than usual total doses are indicated, and if therapy is prolonged, serum level determinations of the drug may be advisable. Photosensitivity manifested by an exaggerated sunburn reaction has been observed in some individuals taking tetracyclines. This has been reported rarely with minocycline.

Central nervous system side effects including lightheadedness, dizziness, or vertigo have been reported with minocycline therapy. Patients who experience these symptoms should be cautioned about driving vehicles or using hazardous machinery while on minocycline therapy. These symptoms may disappear during therapy and usually disappear rapidly when the drug is discontinued.

PRECAUTIONS
General
As with other antibiotic preparations, use of this drug may result in overgrowth of nonsusceptible organisms, including fungi. If superinfection occurs, the antibiotic should be discontinued and appropriate therapy instituted.

Pseudotumor cerebri (benign intracranial hypertension) in adults has been associated with the use of tetracyclines. The usual clinical manifestations are headache and blurred vision. Bulging fontanels have been associated with the use of tetracyclines in infants. While both of these conditions and related symptoms usually resolve after discontinuation of the tetracycline, the possibility for permanent sequelae exists.

Incision and drainage or other surgical procedures should be performed in conjunction with antibiotic therapy when indicated.

Information For Patients
Photosensitivity manifested by an exaggerated sunburn reaction has been observed in some individuals taking tetracyclines. Patients apt to be exposed to direct sunlight or ultraviolet light should be advised that this reaction can occur with tetracycline drugs, and treatment should be discontinued at the first evidence of skin erythema. This reaction has been reported rarely with use of minocycline. Patients who experience central nervous system symptoms (see **WARNINGS**) should be

cautioned about driving vehicles or using hazardous machinery while on minocycline therapy.

Concurrent use of tetracycline may render oral contraceptives less effective (see **Drug Interactions**).

Laboratory Tests

In venereal disease when coexistent syphilis is suspected, a dark-field examination should be done before treatment is started and the blood serology repeated monthly for at least four months.

In long-term therapy, periodic laboratory evaluations of organ systems, including hematopoietic, renal, and hepatic studies, should be performed.

Drug Interactions

Because tetracyclines have been shown to depress plasma prothrombin activity, patients who are on anticoagulant therapy may require downward adjustment of their anticoagulant dosage.

Since bacteriostatic drugs may interfere with the bactericidal action of penicillin, it is advisable to avoid giving tetracycline-class drugs in conjunction with penicillin.

Absorption of tetracyclines is impaired by antacids containing aluminum, calcium or magnesium, and iron-containing preparations.

The concurrent use of tetracycline and methoxyflurane has been reported to result in fatal renal toxicity.

Concurrent use of tetracyclines with oral contraceptives may render oral contraceptives less effective.

Drug/Laboratory Test Interactions

False elevations of urinary catecholamine levels may occur due to interference with the fluorescence test.

Carcinogenesis, Mutagenesis, Impairment of Fertility

Dietary administration of minocycline in long term tumorigenicity studies in rats resulted in evidence of thyroid tumor production. Minocycline has also been found to produce thyroid hyperplasia in rats and dogs. In addition, there has been evidence of oncogenic activity in rats in studies with a related antibiotic, oxytetracycline (i.e., adrenal and pituitary tumors). Likewise, although mutagenicity studies of minocycline have not been conducted, positive results in *in vitro* mammalian cell assays (i.e., mouse lymphoma and Chinese hamster lung cells) have been reported for related antibiotics (tetracycline hydrochloride and oxytetracycline). Segment I (fertility and general reproduction) studies have provided evidence that minocycline impairs fertility in male rats.

Teratogenic Effects: Pregnancy: *Pregnancy Category D:* (See **WARNINGS**.) *Nonteratogenic Effects:* (See **WARNINGS**.)

Labor and Delivery

The effect of tetracyclines on labor and delivery is unknown.

Nursing Mothers

Tetracyclines are excreted in human milk. Because of the potential for serious adverse reactions in nursing infants from the tetracyclines, a decision should be made whether to discontinue nursing or discontinue the drug, taking into account the importance of the drug to the mother (see **WARNINGS**).

Pediatric Use

See **WARNINGS**.

ADVERSE REACTIONS

Due to oral minocycline's virtually complete absorption, side effects to the lower bowel, particularly diarrhea, have been infrequent. The following adverse reactions have been observed in patients receiving tetracyclines.

Gastrointestinal: Anorexia, nausea, vomiting, diarrhea, glossitis, dysphagia, enterocolitis, pancreatitis, inflammatory lesions (with monilial overgrowth) in the anogenital region, and increases in liver enzymes. Rarely, hepatitis and liver failure have been reported. Rare instances of esophagitis and esophageal ulcerations have been reported in patients taking the tetracycline-class antibiotics in capsule and tablet form. Most of these patients took the medication immediately before going to bed (see **DOSAGE AND ADMINISTRATION**).

Skin: Maculopapular and erythematous rashes. Exfoliative dermatitis has been reported but is uncommon. Fixed drug eruptions have been rarely reported. Lesions occurring on the glans penis have caused balanitis. Erythema multiforme and rarely Stevens-Johnson syndrome have been reported. Photosensitivity is discussed above (see **WARNINGS**). Pigmentation of the skin and mucous membranes has been reported.

Renal toxicity: Elevations in BUN have been reported and are apparently dose related (see **WARNINGS**). Reversible acute renal failure has been rarely reported.

Hypersensitivity reactions: Urticaria, angioneurotic edema, polyarthralgia, anaphylaxis, anaphylactoid purpura, pericarditis, exacerbation of systemic lupus erythematosus and rarely pulmonary infiltrates with eosinophilia have been reported. A transient lupus-like syndrome has also been reported.

Blood: Hemolytic anemia, thrombocytopenia, neutropenia, and eosinophilia have been reported.

Central nervous system: Bulging fontanels in infants and benign intracranial hypertension (Pseudotumor cerebri) in adults (see **PRECAUTIONS—General**) have been reported. Headache has also been reported.

Other: When given over prolonged periods, tetracyclines have been reported to produce brown-black microscopic discoloration of the thyroid glands. Very rare cases of abnormal thyroid function have been reported.

Decreased hearing has been rarely reported in patients on MINOCIN®.

Tooth discoloration in children less than 8 years of age (see **WARNINGS**) and also, rarely, in adults has been reported.

OVERDOSAGE

Minocycline is not removed in significant quantities by hemodialysis or peritoneal dialysis. In one study, four patients received 200 mg oral doses 3 hours prior to hemodialysis, following flow rates of 100 to 200 mL/min there was no consistent difference between venous and arterial minocycline concentrations and no detectable minocycline was found in the dialysate. In another study, four patients were administered IP minocycline over 72 to 96 hours and achieved blood concentrations of 1.5 to 2 mcg/mL, over the following 12 hours drug free dialysate was used. No detectable minocycline was found to transfer from the blood to the dialysate.

In case of overdosage, discontinue medication, treat symptomatically, and institute supportive measures.

DOSAGE AND ADMINISTRATION

THE USUAL DOSAGE AND FREQUENCY OF ADMINISTRATION OF MINOCYCLINE DIFFERS FROM THAT OF THE OTHER TETRACYCLINES. EXCEEDING THE RECOMMENDED DOSAGE MAY RESULT IN AN INCREASED INCIDENCE OF SIDE EFFECTS.

MINOCIN minocycline hydrochloride pellet-filled capsules may be taken with or without food (see **CLINICAL PHARMACOLOGY**).

Adults

The usual dosage of MINOCIN minocycline hydrochloride pellet-filled capsules is 200 mg initially followed by 100 mg every 12 hours. Alternatively, if more frequent doses are preferred, two or four 50 mg pellet-filled capsules may be given initially followed by one 50 mg capsule four times daily.

For children above 8 years of age

The usual dosage of MINOCIN minocycline hydrochloride pellet-filled capsules is 4 mg/kg initially followed by 2 mg/kg every 12 hours.

Uncomplicated gonococcal infections other than urethritis and anorectal infections in men: 200 mg initially, followed by 100 mg every 12 hours for a minimum of four days, with post-therapy cultures within 2 to 3 days.

In the treatment of uncomplicated gonococcal urethritis in men, 100 mg every 12 hours for five days is recommended.

For the treatment of syphilis, the usual dosage of MINOCIN minocycline hydrochloride pellet-filled capsules should be administered over a period of 10 to 15 days. Close follow-up, including laboratory tests, is recommended.

In the treatment of meningococcal carrier state, the recommended dosage is 100 mg every 12 hours for five days.

Mycobacterium marinum infections: Although optimal doses have not been established, 100 mg every 12 hours for 6 to 8 weeks have been used successfully in a limited number of cases.

Uncomplicated nongonococcal urethral infection in adults caused by *Chlamydia trachomatis* or *Ureaplasma urealyticum:* 100 mg orally, every 12 hours for at least seven days.

Ingestion of adequate amounts of fluids along with capsule and tablet forms of drugs in the tetracycline-class is recommended to reduce the risk of esophageal irritation and ulceration.

In patients with renal impairment (see **WARNINGS**), the total dosage should be decreased by either reducing the recommended individual doses and/or by extending the time intervals between doses.

HOW SUPPLIED

MINOCIN® minocycline hydrochloride pellet-filled capsules are supplied as capsules containing minocycline hydrochloride equivalent to 100 mg and 50 mg minocycline.

100 mg, two-piece, hard-shell capsule with an opaque light green cap and a transparent green body, printed in white ink with Lederle over M46 on one half and Lederle over 100 mg on the other half. Each capsule contains pellets of minocycline HCl equivalent to 100 mg of minocycline, supplied as follows:
NDC 0005-5344-18—Bottle of 50

50 mg, two-piece, hard-shell capsule with an opaque yellow cap and a transparent green body, printed in black ink with Lederle over M45 on one half and Lederle over 50 mg on the other half. Each capsule contains pellets of minocycline HCl equivalent to 50 mg of minocycline, supplied as follows:
NDC 0005-5343-23—Bottle of 100
NDC 0005-5343-27—Bottle of 250

Store at Controlled Room Temperature 20°–25°C (68°–77°F).

Protect from light, moisture and excessive heat.

ANIMAL PHARMACOLOGY AND TOXICOLOGY

MINOCIN minocycline HCl has been observed to cause a dark discoloration of the thyroid in experimental animals (rats, minipigs, dogs, and monkeys). In the rat, chronic treatment with MINOCIN has resulted in goiter accompanied by elevated radioactive iodine uptake and evidence of thyroid tumor production. MINOCIN has also been found to produce thyroid hyperplasia in rats and dogs.

REFERENCES

1. National Committee for Clinical Laboratory Standards, Approved Standard: *Performance Standards for Antimicrobial Disk Susceptibility Tests,* 3rd Edition, Vol. 4(16):M2-A3, Villanova, PA, December 1984.

2. National Committee for Clinical Laboratory Standards, Approved Standard: *Methods for Dilution Antimicrobial Susceptibility Tests for Bacteria that Grow Aerobically,* 2nd Edition, Vol. 5(22):M7-A, Villanova, PA, December 1985.

©1992
Manufactured by:
LEDERLE PHARMACEUTICAL DIVISION

American Cyanamid Company
Pearl River, NY 10965
CI 4957-2   Revised August 18, 1998

MINOCIN®   ℞
[*mĭ′nō-sĭn*]
Minocycline Hydrochloride
Oral Suspension

DESCRIPTION

MINOCIN minocycline hydrochloride, a semisynthetic derivative of tetracycline, is named
[4*S*-(4α, 4aα, 5aα, 12aα)]-4,7-bis(dimethylamino)-1,4,4a,5,5a,6,11,12a-octahydro- 3,10,
12, 12a-tetrahydroxy-1, 11-dioxo-2-naphtha-
cenecarboxamide monohydrochloride.
Its structural formula is:

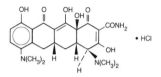

$C_{23}H_{27}N_3O_7\cdot HCl$ M.W. 493.94

MINOCIN Oral Suspension contains minocycline HCl equivalent to 50 mg of minocycline
per 5 mL (10 mg/mL) and the following inactive ingredients: Alcohol, Butylparaben, Calcium Hydroxide, Cellulose, Decaglyceryl Tet-
raoleate, Edetate Calcium Disodium, Glycol,
Guar Gum, Polysorbate 80, Propylparaben,
Propylene Glycol, Sodium Saccharin, Sodium
Sulfite (see **WARNINGS**) and Sorbitol.

ACTIONS
Microbiology
The tetracyclines are primarily bacteriostatic
and are thought to exert their antimicrobial
effect by the inhibition of protein synthesis.
Minocycline HCl is a tetracycline with antibacterial activity comparable to other tetracyclines with activity against a wide range of
gram-negative and gram-positive organisms.
Tube dilution testing: Microorganisms may
be considered susceptible (likely to respond to
minocycline therapy) if the minimum inhibitory concentration (MIC) is not more than
4 mcg/mL. Microorganisms may be considered
intermediate (harboring partial resistance) if
the MIC is 4 to 12.5 mcg/mL and resistant (not
likely to respond to minocycline therapy) if the
MIC is greater than 12.5 mcg/mL.
Susceptibility plate testing: If the Kirby-
Bauer method of susceptibility testing (using a
30 mcg tetracycline disc) gives a zone of 18
mm or greater, the bacterial strain is considered to be susceptible to any tetracycline. Minocycline shows moderate *in vitro* activity
against certain strains of staphylococci which
have been found resistant to other tetracyclines. For such strains minocycline susceptibility powder may be used for additional susceptibility testing.
Human Pharmacology
Following a single dose of two 100 mg minocycline HCl capsules administered to ten normal

adult volunteers, serum levels ranged from
0.74 to 4.45 mcg/mL in one hour (average
2.24), after 12 hours, they ranged from 0.34 to
2.36 mcg/mL (average 1.25). The serum half-
life following a single 200 mg dose in 12 essentially normal volunteers ranged from 11 to 17
hours. In seven patients with hepatic dysfunction it ranged from 11 to 16 hours, and in 5
patients with renal dysfunction from 18 to 69
hours. The urinary and fecal recovery of minocycline when administered to 12 normal volunteers is one half to one third that of other
tetracyclines.

INDICATIONS

MINOCIN is indicated in infections caused by
the following microorganisms:
> Rickettsiae: (Rocky Mountain spotted fe-
> ver, typhus fever and the typhus group, Q
> fever, rickettsialpox, tick fevers).
> *Mycoplasma pneumoniae* (PPLO, Eaton
> agent).
> Agents of psittacosis and ornithosis.
> Agents of lymphogranuloma venereum and
> granuloma inguinale.
> The spirochetal agent of relapsing fever
> (*Borrelia recurrentis*).

The following gram-negative microorganisms:
> *Haemophilus ducreyi* (chancroid),
> *Yersinia pestis* and *Francisella tularensis*
> (formerly *Pasteurella pestis* and *Pasteurella
> tularensis*),
> *Bartonella bacilliformis,*
> *Bacteroides* species,
> *Vibrio comma* and *Vibrio fetus,*
> *Brucella species* (in conjunction with strep-
> tomycin).

Because many strains of the following groups
of microorganisms have been shown to be resistant to tetracyclines, culture and susceptibility testing are recommended.
MINOCIN is indicated for treatment of infections caused by the following gram-negative
microorganisms when bacteriologic testing indicates appropriate susceptibility to the drug:
> *Escherichia coli,*
> *Enterobacter aerogenes* (formerly *Aerobacter
> aerogenes*),
> *Shigella species,*
> *Acinetobacter calcoaceticus* (formerly Herel-
> lea, Mima),
> *Haemophilus influenzae* (respiratory infec-
> tions),
> *Klebsiella species* (respiratory and urinary
> infections).

MINOCIN is indicated for treatment of infections caused by the following gram-positive
microorganisms when bacteriologic testing indicates appropriate susceptibility to the drug:
> *Streptococcus* species;

Up to 44% of strains of *Streptococcus pyogenes*
and 74% of *Streptococcus faecalis* have been
found to be resistant to tetracycline drugs.
Therefore, tetracyclines should not be used for
streptococcal disease unless the organism has
been demonstrated to be sensitive.

For upper respiratory infections due to Group A beta-hemolytic streptococci, penicillin is the usual drug of choice, including prophylaxis of rheumatic fever.

> *Streptococcus pneumoniae* (formerly Diplococcus pneumoniae),
> *Staphylococcus aureus*, skin and soft tissue infections.

Tetracyclines are not the drugs of choice in the treatment of any type of staphylococcal infection.

MINOCIN is indicated for the treatment of uncomplicated gonococcal urethritis in men due to *Neisseria gonorrhoeae*.

When penicillin is contraindicated, tetracyclines are alternative drugs in the treatment of infections due to:

> *Neisseria gonorrhoeae* (in women),
> *Treponema pallidum* and *Treponema pertenue* (syphilis and yaws),
> *Listeria monocytogenes*,
> *Clostridium* species,
> *Bacillus anthracis*,
> *Fusobacterium fusiforme* (Vincent's infection),
> *Actinomyces* species.

In acute intestinal amebiasis, the tetracyclines may be a useful adjunct to amebicides. In severe acne, the tetracyclines may be useful adjunctive therapy.

MINOCIN minocycline HCl is indicated in the treatment of trachoma, although the infectious agent is not always eliminated, as judged by immunofluorescence.

MINOCIN is indicated for the treatment of uncomplicated urethral, endocervical or rectal infections in adults caused by *Chlamydia trachomatis* or *Ureaplasma urealyticum*.[1]

Inclusion conjunctivitis may be treated with oral tetracyclines or with a combination of oral and topical agents.

MINOCIN is indicated in the treatment of asymptomatic carriers of *Neisseria meningitidis* to eliminate meningococci from the nasopharynx.

In order to preserve the usefulness of MINOCIN in the treatment of asymptomatic meningococcal carriers, diagnostic laboratory procedures, including serotyping and susceptibility testing, should be performed to establish the carrier state and the correct treatment. It is recommended that the drug be reserved for situations in which the risk of meningococcal meningitis is high.

MINOCIN by oral administration is not indicated for the treatment of meningococcal infection.

Although no controlled clinical efficacy studies have been conducted, limited clinical data show that oral MINOCIN has been used successfully in the treatment of infections caused by Mycobacterium marinum.

CONTRAINDICATIONS

This drug is contraindicated in persons who have shown hypersensitivity to any of the tetracyclines.

WARNINGS

THE USE OF DRUGS OF THE TETRACYCLINE CLASS DURING TOOTH DEVELOPMENT (LAST HALF OF PREGNANCY, INFANCY, AND CHILDHOOD TO THE AGE OF 8 YEARS) MAY CAUSE PERMANENT DISCOLORATION OF THE TEETH (YELLOW-GRAY-BROWN). This adverse reaction is more common during long-term use of the drugs but has been observed following repeated short-term courses. Enamel hypoplasia has also been reported. TETRACYCLINE DRUGS, THEREFORE, SHOULD NOT BE USED IN THIS AGE GROUP UNLESS OTHER DRUGS ARE NOT LIKELY TO BE EFFECTIVE OR ARE CONTRAINDICATED.

If renal impairment exists, even usual oral or parenteral doses may lead to excessive systemic accumulations of the drug and possible liver toxicity. Under such conditions, lower than usual total doses are indicated, and if therapy is prolonged, serum level determinations of the drug may be advisable.

Photosensitivity manifested by an exaggerated sunburn reaction has been observed in some individuals taking tetracyclines. Patients apt to be exposed to direct sunlight or ultraviolet light should be advised that this reaction can occur with tetracycline drugs, and treatment should be discontinued at the first evidence of skin erythema. Studies to date indicate that photosensitivity is rarely reported with MINOCIN minocycline HCl.

The anti-anabolic action of the tetracyclines may cause an increase in BUN. While this is not a problem in those with normal renal function, in patients with significantly impaired function, higher serum levels of tetracycline may lead to azotemia, hyperphosphatemia, and acidosis.

CNS side effects including light-headedness, dizziness, or vertigo have been reported. Patients who experience these symptoms should be cautioned about driving vehicles or using hazardous machinery while on minocycline therapy. These symptoms may disappear during therapy and usually disappear rapidly when the drug is discontinued.

MINOCIN Oral Suspension contains sodium sulfite, a sulfite that may cause allergic-type reactions including anaphylactic symptoms and life-threatening or less severe asthmatic episodes in certain susceptible people. The overall prevalence of sulfite sensitivity in the general population is unknown and probably low. Sulfite sensitivity is seen more frequently in asthmatic than in nonasthmatic people.

Usage in Pregnancy (See above **WARNINGS** about use during tooth development.)

Results of animal studies indicate that tetracyclines cross the placenta, are found in fetal tissues and can have toxic effects on the developing fetus (often related to retardation of skeletal development). Evidence of embryotoxicity has also been noted in animals treated early in pregnancy.

The safety of MINOCIN for use during pregnancy has not been established.

Usage in Newborns, Infants, and Children (See above **WARNINGS** about use during tooth development.)

All tetracyclines form a stable calcium complex in any bone forming tissue. A decrease in the fibula growth rate has been observed in prematures given oral tetracycline in doses of 25 mg/kg every six hours. This reaction was shown to be reversible when the drug was discontinued.

Tetracyclines are present in the milk of lactating women who are taking a drug in this class.

PRECAUTIONS
General

Pseudotumor cerebri (benign intracranial hypertension) in adults has been associated with the use of tetracyclines. The usual clinical manifestations are headache and blurred vision. Bulging fontanels have been associated with the use of tetracyclines in infants. While both of these conditions and related symptoms usually resolve soon after discontinuation of the tetracycline, the possibility for permanent sequelae exists.

As with other antibiotic preparations, use of this drug may result in overgrowth of nonsusceptible organisms, including fungi. If superinfection occurs, the antibiotic should be discontinued and appropriate therapy should be instituted.

In venereal diseases when coexistent syphilis is suspected, darkfield examination should be done before treatment is started and the blood serology repeated monthly for at least 4 months.

In long-term therapy, periodic laboratory evaluation of organ systems, including hematopoietic, renal and hepatic studies should be performed.

All infections due to Group A beta-hemolytic streptococci should be treated for at least ten days.

Drug Interactions

Because tetracyclines have been shown to depress plasma prothrombin activity, patients who are on anticoagulant therapy may require downward adjustment of their anticoagulant dosage.

Since bacteriostatic drugs may interfere with the bactericidal action of penicillin, it is advisable to avoid giving tetracycline in conjunction with penicillin.

Concurrent use of tetracyclines with oral contraceptives may render oral contraceptives less effective.

ADVERSE REACTIONS

Gastrointestinal: Anorexia, nausea, vomiting, diarrhea, glossitis, dysphagia, enterocolitis, pancreatitis, inflammatory lesions (with monilial overgrowth) in the anogenital region and increases in liver enzymes. Rarely, hepatitis and liver failure have been reported.

These reactions have been caused by both the oral and parenteral administration of tetracyclines.

Skin: Maculopapular and erythematous rashes. Exfoliative dermatitis has been reported but is uncommon. Fixed drug eruptions, including balanitis, have been rarely reported. Erythema multiforme and rarely Stevens-Johnson syndrome have been reported. Photosensitivity is discussed above. (See **WARNINGS**.)

Pigmentation of the skin and mucous membranes has been reported.

Tooth discoloration has been reported rarely in adults.

Renal toxicity: Rise in BUN has been reported and is apparently dose related. (See **WARNINGS**.) Reversible acute renal failure has been rarely reported.

Hypersensitivity reactions: Urticaria, angioneurotic edema, polyarthralgia, anaphylaxis, anaphylactoid purpura, pericarditis, exacerbation of systemic lupus erythematosus and rarely pulmonary infiltrates with eosinophilia have been reported. A transient lupus-like syndrome has also been reported.

Blood: Hemolytic anemia, thrombocytopenia, neutropenia and eosinophilia have been reported.

CNS: (See **WARNINGS**.) Pseudotumor cerebri (benign intracranial hypertension) in adults and bulging fontanels in infants. (See **PRECAUTIONS—General**.) Headache has also been reported.

Other: When given over prolonged periods, tetracyclines have been reported to produce brown-black microscopic discoloration of the thyroid glands. Very rare cases of abnormal thyroid function have been reported.

Decreased hearing has been rarely reported in patients on MINOCIN.

DOSAGE AND ADMINISTRATION

Therapy should be continued for at least 24 to 48 hours after symptoms and fever have subsided.

Concomitant therapy: Antacids containing aluminum, calcium, or magnesium impair absorption and should not be given to patients taking oral tetracycline.

Studies to date have indicated that the absorption of MINOCIN is not notably influenced by foods and dairy products.

In patients with renal impairment: (See **WARNINGS**.) Total dosage should be decreased by reduction of recommended individual doses and/or extending time intervals between doses.

In the treatment of streptococcal infections, a therapeutic dose of tetracycline should be administered for at least ten days.

ADULTS: The usual dosage of MINOCIN is 200 mg initially followed by 100 mg every 12 hours.

For children above eight years of age: The usual dosage of MINOCIN minocycline HCl is 4 mg/kg initially followed by 2 mg/kg every 12 hours.

For treatment of syphilis, the usual dosage of MINOCIN should be administered over a period of 10 to 15 days. Close follow up, including laboratory tests, is recommended.

Gonorrhea patients sensitive to penicillin may be treated with MINOCIN, administered as 200 mg initially followed by 100 mg every twelve hours for a minimum of four days, with post-therapy cultures within 2 to 3 days.

In the treatment of meningococcal carrier state, recommended dosage is 100 mg every 12 hours for five days.

Mycobacterium marinum infections: Although optimal doses have not been established, 100 mg twice a day for 6 to 8 weeks have been used successfully in a limited number of cases.

Uncomplicated urethral, endocervical, or rectal infection in adults caused by *Chlamydia trachomatis* or *Ureaplasma urealyticum:* 100 mg, by mouth, 2 times a day for at least seven days.[1]

In the treatment of uncomplicated gonococcal urethritis in men, 100 mg twice a day orally for five days is recommended.

HOW SUPPLIED

MINOCIN® minocycline hydrochloride Oral Suspension contains minocycline hydrochloride equivalent to 50 mg minocycline per teaspoonful (5 mL). Preserved with propylparaben 0.10% and butylparaben 0.06% with Alcohol USP 5% v/v, Custard-flavored.

NDC 0005-5313-56　　　Bottle 2 fl. oz. (60 mL)

Store at controlled room temperature, between 20°C and 25°C (68°F and 77°F).

DO NOT FREEZE.

Animal Pharmacology and Toxicology

MINOCIN has been found to produce high blood concentrations following oral dosage to various animal species and to be extensively distributed to all tissues examined in ^{14}C-labeled drug studies in dogs. MINOCIN has been found experimentally to produce discoloration of the thyroid glands. This finding has been observed in rats and dogs. Changes in thyroid function have also been found in these animal species. However, no change in thyroid function has been observed in humans.

Reference: 1. CDC Sexually Transmitted Diseases Treatment Guidelines 1982.

Manufactured by:

LEDERLE PHARMACEUTICAL DIVISION

American Cyanamid Company

Pearl River, NY 10965

CI 6016-1　Issued February 23, 1999

Buffered
PFIZERPEN®   ℞
(penicillin G potassium)
for Injection

DESCRIPTION

Buffered Pfizerpen® (penicillin G potassium) for Injection is a sterile, pyrogen-free powder for reconstitution. Buffered Pfizerpen for Injection is an antibacterial agent for intramuscular, continuous intravenous drip, intrapleural or other local infusion, and intrathecal administration.

Each million units contains approximately 6.8 milligrams of sodium (0.3 mEq) and 65.6 milligrams of potassium (1.68 mEq).

Chemically, Pfizerpen is monopotassium 3,3-dimethyl-7-oxo-6-(2-phenylacetamido)-4-thia-1-azabicyclo (3.2.0) heptane-2-carboxylate. It has a molecular weight of 372.48 and the following chemical structure:

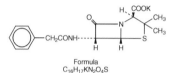

Formula
$C_{16}H_{17}KN_2O_4S$

Penicillin G potassium is a colorless or white crystal, or a white crystalline powder which is odorless, or practically so, and moderately hygroscopic. Penicillin G potassium is very soluble in water. The pH of the reconstituted product is between 6.0–8.5.

CLINICAL PHARMACOLOGY

Aqueous penicillin G is rapidly absorbed following both intramuscular and subcutaneous injection. Initial blood levels following parenteral administration are high but transient. Penicillins bind to serum proteins, mainly albumin. Therapeutic levels of the penicillins are easily achieved under normal circumstances in extracellular fluid and most other body tissues. Penicillins are distributed in varying degrees into pleural, pericardial, peritoneal, ascitic, synovial, and interstitial fluids. Penicillins are excreted in breast milk. Penetration into the cerebrospinal fluid, eyes, and prostate is poor. Penicillins are rapidly excreted in the urine by glomerular filtration and active tubular secretion, primarily as unchanged drug. Approximately 60 percent of the total dose of 300,000 units is excreted in the urine within this 5-hour period. For this reason, high and frequent doses are required to maintain the elevated serum levels desirable in treating certain severe infections in individuals with normal kidney function. In neonates and young infants, and in individuals with impaired kidney function, excretion is considerably delayed.

Microbiology

Penicillin G exerts a bactericidal action against penicillin-susceptible microorganisms during the stage of active multiplication. It acts through the inhibition of biosynthesis of cell wall mucopeptide rendering the cell wall osmotically unstable. It is not active against the penicillinase-producing bacteria, which include many strains of staphylococci. While *in vitro* studies have demonstrated that susceptibility of most strains of the following organisms, clinical efficacy for infections other than those included in the INDICATIONS AND USAGE section has not been documented. Penicillin G exerts high *in vitro* activity against staphylococci (except penicillinase-producing strains), streptococci (groups A, C, G, H, L, and M), and pneumococci. Other organisms susceptible to penicillin G are *N. gonorrhoeae, Corynebacterium diphtheriae, Bacillus anthracis,* Clostridia, *Actinomyces bovis, Streptobacillus moniliformis, Listeria monocytogenes* and Leptospira. *Treponema pallidum* is extremely sensitive to the bactericidal action of penicillin G. Some species of gram-negative bacilli are sensitive to moderate to high concentrations of the drug obtained with intravenous administration. These include most strains of *Escherichia coli;* all strains of *Proteus mirabilis,* Salmonella and Shigella; and some strains of *Aerobacter aerogenes* and *Alcaligenes faecalis.*

Penicillin acts synergistically with gentamicin or tobramycin against many strains of enterococci.

Susceptibility Testing: Penicillin G Susceptibility Powder or 10 units Penicillin G Susceptibility Discs may be used to determine microbial susceptibility to penicillin G using one of the following standard methods recommended by the National Committee for Laboratory Standards:

M2-A3, "Performance Standards for Antimicrobial Disk Susceptibility Tests"

M7-A, "Methods for Dilution Antimicrobial Susceptibility Tests for Bacteria that Grow Aerobically"

M11-A, "Reference Agar Dilution Procedure for Antimicrobial Susceptibility Testing of Anaerobic Bacteria"

M17-P, "Alternative Methods for Antimicrobial Susceptibility Testing of Anaerobic Bacteria"

Tests should be interpreted by the following criteria:

[See first table at bottom of next page]
[See second table at bottom of next page]

Interpretations of susceptible, intermediate, and resistant correlate zone size diameters with MIC values. A laboratory report of "susceptible" indicates that the suspected causative microorganism most likely will respond to therapy with penicillin G. A laboratory report of "resistant" indicates that the infecting microorganism most likely will not respond to therapy. A laboratory report of "moderately susceptible" indicates that the microorganism is most likely susceptible if a high dosage of penicillin G is used, or if the infection is such that high levels of penicillin G may be attained, as in urine. A report of "intermediate" using the disk diffusion method may be considered an equivocal result, and dilution tests may be indicated.

Control organisms are recommended for susceptibility testing. Each time the test is performed the following organisms should be included. The range for zones of inhibition is shown below:

Control Organism	Zone of Inhibition Range
Staphylococcus aureus (ATCC 25923)	27–35

INDICATIONS AND USAGE

Aqueous penicillin G (parenteral) is indicated in the therapy of severe infections caused by penicillin G-susceptible microorganisms when rapid and high penicillin levels are required in the conditions listed below. Therapy should be guided by bacteriological studies (including susceptibility tests) and by clinical response.

The following infections will usually respond to adequate dosage of penicillin G (parenteral):

Streptococcal infections.

NOTE: Streptococci in groups A, C, H, G, L, and M are very sensitive to penicillin G. Some group D organisms are sensitive to the high serum levels obtained with aqueous penicillin G.

Aqueous penicillin G (parenteral) is the penicillin dosage form of choice for bacteremia, empyema, severe pneumonia, pericarditis, endocarditis, meningitis, and other severe infections caused by sensitive strains of the gram-positive species listed above.

Pneumococcal infections.

Staphylococcal infections—penicillin G sensitive.

Other infections:

Anthrax.

Actinomycosis.

Clostridial infections (including tetanus).

Diphtheria (to prevent carrier state).

Erysipeloid *(Erysipelothrix insidiosa)* endocarditis.

Fusospirochetal infections—severe infections of the oropharynx (Vincent's), lower respiratory tract and genital area due to *Fusobacterium fusiformisans* spirochetes.

Gram-negative bacillary infections (bacteremias)–*(E. coli, A. aerogenes, A. faecalis,* Salmonella, Shigella and *P. mirabilis).*

Listeria infections *(Listeria monocytogenes).*

Meningitis and endocarditis.

Pasteurella infections *(Pasteurella multocida).*

Bacteremia and meningitis.

Rat-bite fever *(Spirillum minus* or *Streptobacillus moniliformis).*

Gonorrheal endocarditis and arthritis *(N. gonorrhoeae).*

Syphilis *(T. pallidum)* including congenital syphilis.

Meningococcic meningitis.

Although no controlled clinical efficacy studies have been conducted, aqueous crystalline penicillin G for injection and penicillin G procaine suspension have been suggested by the American Heart Association and the American Dental Association for use as part of a combined parenteral-oral regimen for prophylaxis against bacterial endocarditis in patients with congenital heart disease or rheumatic, or other acquired valvular heart disease when they undergo dental procedures and surgical procedures of the upper respiratory tract.[1] Since it may happen that *alpha* hemolytic streptococci relatively resistant to penicillin may be found when patients are receiving continuous oral penicillin for secondary prevention of rheumatic fever, prophylactic agents other than penicillin may be chosen for these patients and prescribed in addition to their continuous rheumatic fever prophylactic regimen.

NOTE: When selecting antibiotics for the prevention of bacterial endocarditis, the physi-

Zone Diameter, nearest whole mm			
	Susceptible	Moderately Susceptible	Resistant
Staphylococci	≥29	—	≤28
N. gonorrhoeae	≥20	—	≤19
Enterococci	—	≥15	≤14
Non-enterococcal streptococci and *L. monocytogenes*	≥28	20–27	≤19

Approximate MIC Correlates		
	Susceptible	Resistant
Staphylococci	≤0.1 µg/mL	β-lactamase
N. gonorrhoeae	≤0.1 µg/mL	β-lactamase
Enterococci	—	≥16 µg/mL
Non-enterococcal streptococci and *L. monocytogenes*	≤0.12 µg/mL	≥ 4 µg/mL

cian or dentist should read the full joint statement of the American Heart Association and the American Dental Association.[1]

CONTRAINDICATIONS

A history of a previous hypersensitivity reaction to any penicillin is a contraindication.

WARNINGS

Serious and occasionally fatal hypersensitivity (anaphylactoid) reactions have been reported in patients on penicillin therapy. These reactions are more likely to occur in individuals with a history of penicillin hypersensitivity and/or a history of sensitivity to multiple allergens. There have been reports of individuals with a history of penicillin hypersensitivity who have experienced severe reactions when treated with cephalosporins. Before initiating therapy with any penicillin, careful inquiry should be made concerning previous hypersensitivity reactions to penicillin, cephalosporins, or other allergens. If an allergic reaction occurs, the drug should be discontinued and the appropriate therapy instituted. Serious anaphylactoid reactions require immediate emergency treatment with epinephrine. Oxygen, intravenous steroids, and airway management including intubation, should also be administered as indicated.

PRECAUTIONS

General: Penicillin should be used with caution in individuals with histories of significant allergies and/or asthma.

Intramuscular Therapy: Care should be taken to avoid intravenous or accidental intraarterial administration, or injection into or near major peripheral nerves or blood vessels, since such injections may produce neurovascular damage. Particular care should be taken with IV administration because of the possibility of thrombophlebitis.

In streptococcal infections, therapy must be sufficient to eliminate the organism (10 days minimum), otherwise the sequelae of streptococcal disease may occur. Cultures should be taken following the completion of treatment to determine whether streptococci have been eradicated.

The use of antibiotics may result in overgrowth of nonsusceptible organisms. Constant observation of the patient is essential. If new infections due to bacteria or fungi appear during therapy, the drug should be discontinued and appropriate measures taken. Whenever allergic reactions occur, penicillin should be withdrawn unless, in the opinion of the physician, the condition being treated is life threatening and amenable only to penicillin therapy. Aqueous penicillin G by the intravenous route in high doses (above 10 million units) should be administered slowly because of the adverse effects of electrolyte imbalance from either the potassium or sodium content of the penicillin. Penicillin G potassium contains 1.7 mEq potassium and 0.3 mEq sodium per million units. The patient's renal, cardiac, and vascular status should be evaluated and if impairment of function is suspected or known to exist a reduction in the total dosage should be considered. Frequent evaluation of electrolyte balance, renal and hematopoietic function is recommended during therapy when high doses of intravenous aqueous penicillin G are used.

Laboratory Tests: In prolonged therapy with penicillin, periodic evaluation of the renal, hepatic, and hematopoietic systems is recommended for organ system dysfunction. This is particularly important in prematures, neonates and other infants, and when high doses are used.

Positive Coomb's tests have been reported after large intravenous doses.

Monitor serum potassium and implement corrective measures when necessary.

When treating gonococcal infections in which primary and secondary syphilis are suspected, proper diagnostic procedures, including dark field examinations, should be done before receiving penicillin and monthly serological tests made for at least four months. All cases of penicillin treated syphilis should receive clinical and serological examinations every six months for two to three years.

In suspected staphylococcal infections, proper laboratory studies, including susceptibility tests, should be performed.

In streptococcal infections, cultures should be taken following completion of treatment to determine whether streptococci have been eradicated. Therapy must be sufficient to eliminate the organism (a minimum of 10 days), otherwise the sequelae of streptococcal disease (e.g., endocarditis, rheumatic fever) may occur.

Drug Interactions: Concurrent administration of bacteriostatic antibiotics (e.g., erythromycin, tetracycline) may diminish the bactericidal effects of penicillins by slowing the rate of bacterial growth. Bactericidal agents work most effectively against the immature cell wall of rapidly proliferating microorganisms. This has been demonstrated *in vitro;* however, the clinical significance of this interaction is not well documented. There are few clinical situations in which the concurrent use of "static" and "cidal" antibiotics are indicated. However, in selected circumstances in which such therapy is appropriate, using adequate doses of antibacterial agents and beginning penicillin therapy first, should minimize the potential for interaction.

Penicillin blood levels may be prolonged by concurrent administration of probenecid which blocks the renal tubular secretion of penicillins.

Displacement of penicillin from plasma protein binding sites will elevate the level of free penicillin in the serum.

Carcinogenesis, Mutagenesis, Impairment of Fertility: No information on long-term studies are available on the carcinogenesis, mutagenesis, or the impairment of fertility with the use of penicillins.

Pregnancy Category B–*Teratogenic Effects:* Reproduction studies performed in the mouse, rat, and rabbit have revealed no evidence of impaired fertility or harm to the fetus due to penicillin G. Human experience with the penicillins during pregnancy has not shown any positive evidence of adverse effects on the fetus. There are, however, no adequate and well controlled studies in pregnant women showing conclusively that harmful effects of these drugs on the fetus can be excluded. Because animal reproduction studies are not always predictive of human response, this drug should be used during pregnancy only if clearly needed.

Nursing Mothers: Penicillins are excreted in human milk. Caution should be exercised when penicillin G is administered to a nursing woman.

Pediatric Use: Penicillins are excreted largely unchanged by the kidney. Because of incompletely developed renal function in infants, the rate of elimination will be slow. Use caution in administering to newborns and evaluate organ system function frequently.

ADVERSE REACTIONS

Penicillin is a substance of low toxicity but does have a significant index of sensitization. The following hypersensitivity reactions have been reported: skin rashes ranging from maculopapular eruptions to exfoliative dermatitis; urticaria; and reactions resembling serum sickness, including chills, fever, edema, arthralgia and prostration. Severe and occasionally fatal anaphylaxis has occurred (see WARNINGS).

Hemolytic anemia, leucopenia, thrombocytopenia, nephropathy, and neuropathy are rarely observed adverse reactions and are usually associated with high intravenous dosage. Patients given continuous intravenous therapy with penicillin G potassium in high dosage (10 million to 100 million units daily) may suffer severe or even fatal potassium poisoning, particularly if renal insufficiency is present. Hyperreflexia, convulsions, and coma may be indicative of this syndrome.

Cardiac arrhythmias and cardiac arrest may also occur. (High dosage of penicillin G sodium may result in congestive heart failure due to high sodium intake.)

The Jarisch-Herxheimer reaction has been reported in patients treated for syphilis.

OVERDOSAGE

Neurological adverse reactions, including convulsions, may occur with the attainment of high CSF levels of beta-lactams. In case of overdosage, discontinue medication, treat symptomatically, and institute supportive measures as required.

Penicillin G potassium is hemodialyzable.

DOSAGE AND ADMINISTRATION

Severe infections due to Susceptible Strains of Streptococci, Pneumococci, and Staphylococ-

ci—bacteremia, pneumonia, endocarditis, pericarditis, empyema, meningitis, and other severe infections—a minimum of 5 million units daily.

Syphilis—Aqueous penicillin G may be used in the treatment of acquired and congenital syphilis, but because of the necessity of frequent dosage, hospitalization is recommended. Dosage and duration of therapy will be determined by age of patient and stage of disease.

Gonorrheal endocarditis—a minimum of 5 million units daily.

Meningococcic meningitis—1–2 million units intramuscularly every 2 hours, or continuous IV drip of 20–30 million units/day.

Actinomycosis—1–6 million units/day for cervicofacial cases; 10–20 million units/day for thoracic and abdominal disease.

Clostridial infections—20 million units/day; penicillin is adjunctive therapy to antitoxin.

Fusospirochetal infections—severe infections of oropharynx, lower respiratory tract, and genital area–5–10 million units/day.

Rat-bite fever (Spirillum minus or Streptobacillus moniliformis)—12–15 million units/day for 3–4 weeks.

Listeria infections (Listeria monocytogenes)
Neonates—500,000 to 1 million units/day.
Adults with meningitis—15–20 million units/ day for 2 weeks.
Adults with endocarditis—15–20 million units/day for 4 weeks.

Pasteurella infections (Pasteurella multocida)
Bacteremia and meningitis—4–6 million units/day for 2 weeks.

Erysipeloid (Erysipelothrix insidiosa)
Endocarditis—2–20 million units/day for 4–6 weeks.

Gram-negative bacillary infections (E. coli, Enterobacter aerogenes, A. faecalis, Salmonella, Shigella and Proteus mirabilis)
Bacteremia—20–80 million units/day.

Diphtheria (carrier state)—300,000–400,000 units of penicillin/day in divided doses for 10–12 days.

Anthrax—A minimum of 5 million units of penicillin/day in divided doses until cure is effected.

For prophylaxis against bacterial endocarditis[1] in patients with congenital heart disease or rheumatic or other acquired valvular heart disease, when undergoing dental procedures or surgical procedures of the upper respiratory tract, use a combined parenteral-oral regimen. One million units of aqueous crystalline penicillin G (30,000 units/kg in children) intramuscularly, mixed with 600,000 units procaine penicillin G (600,000 units for children) should be given one-half to one hour before the procedure. Oral penicillin V (phenoxymethyl penicillin), 500 mg for adults or 250 mg for children less than 60 lb, should be given every 6 hours for 8 doses. Doses for children should not exceed recommendations for adults for a single dose or for a 24 hour period.

Approx. Desired Concentration (units/mL)	Approx. Volume (mL) 1,000,000 units	Solvent for Vial of 5,000,000 units	Infusion Only 20,000,000 units
50,000	20.0	—	—
100,000	10.0	—	—
250,000	4.0	18.2	75.0
500,000	1.8	8.2	33.0
750,000	—	4.8	—
1,000,000	—	3.2	11.5

Reconstitution
The following table shows the amount of solvent required for solution of various concentrations:
[See table above]
When the required volume of solvent is greater than the capacity of the vial, the penicillin can be dissolved by first injecting only a portion of the solvent into the vial, then withdrawing the resultant solution and combining it with the remainder of the solvent in a larger sterile container.
Buffered Pfizerpen (penicillin G potassium) for Injection is highly water soluble. It may be dissolved in small amounts of Water for Injection, or Sterile Isotonic Sodium Chloride Solution for Parenteral Use. All solutions should be stored in a refrigerator. When refrigerated, penicillin solutions may be stored for seven days without significant loss of potency.
Buffered Pfizerpen for Injection may be given intramuscularly or by continuous intravenous drip for dosages of 500,000, 1,000,000, or 5,000,000 units. It is also suitable for intrapleural, intraarticular, and other local instillations.
THE 20,000,000 UNIT DOSAGE MAY BE ADMINISTERED BY INTRAVENOUS INFUSION ONLY.
(1) Intramusclar Injection: Keep total volume of injection small. The intramuscular route is the preferred route of administration. Solutions containing up to 100,000 units of penicillin per mL of diluent may be used with a minimum of discomfort. Greater concentration of penicillin G per mL is physically possible and may be employed where therapy demands. When large dosages are required, it may be advisable to administer aqueous solutions of penicillin by means of continuous intravenous drip.
(2) Continuous Intravenous Drip: Determine the volume of fluid and rate of its administration required by the patient in a 24 hour period in the usual manner for fluid therapy, and add the appropriate daily dosage of penicillin to this fluid. For example, if an adult patient requires 2 liters of fluid in 24 hours and a daily dosage of 10 million units of penicillin,

add 5 million units to 1 liter and adjust the rate of flow so the liter will be infused in 12 hours.
(3) Intrapleural or Other Local Infusion: If fluid is aspirated, give infusion in a volume equal to ¼ or ½ the amount of fluid aspirated, otherwise, prepare as for intramuscular injection.
(4) Intrathecal Use: The intrathecal use of penicillin in meningitis must be highly individualized. It should be employed only with full consideration of the possible irritating effects of penicillin when used by this route. The preferred route of therapy in bacterial meningitides is intravenous, supplemented by intramuscular injection.
Parenteral drug products should be inspected visually for particulate matter and discoloration prior to administration, whenever solution and container permit.
Sterile solution may be left in refrigerator for one week without significant loss of potency.

HOW SUPPLIED
Buffered Pfizerpen® (penicillin G potassium) for Injection is available in vials containing respectively 1,000,000 units × 10's (NDC 0049-0510-83), 1,000,000 units × 100's (NDC 0049-0510-95), 5,000,000 units × 10's (NDC 0049-0520-83), 5,000,000 units × 100's (NDC 0049-0520-95), 20,000,000 units × 1's (NDC 0049-0530-28), and a bulk pharmacy package of 20,000,000 units × 10's (NDC 0049-0530-83) of dry powder for reconstitution; buffered with sodium citrate and citric acid to an optimum pH.
Each million units contains approximately 6.8 milligrams of sodium (0.3 mEq) and 65.6 milligrams of potassium (1.68 mEq).
Store the dry powder below 86°F (30°C).

Reference
1. American Heart Association, 1977. Prevention of bacterial endocarditis. Circulation. **56**:139A–143A.
                              ©1997 PFIZER INC
Roerig
Division of Pfizer Inc, NY, NY 10017
70-4209-44-6   Revised April 1998

RIFADIN® ℞
[*rif' uh-din*]
(rifampin capsules USP)
and
RIFADIN® IV
(rifampin for injection USP)

Prescribing Information as of August 2000

DESCRIPTION

RIFADIN (rifampin capsules USP) for oral administration contain 150 mg or 300 mg of rifampin per capsule. The 150 mg and 300 mg capsules also contain, as inactive ingredients: corn starch, D&C Red No. 28, FD&C Blue No. 1, FD&C Red No. 40, gelatin, magnesium stearate, and titanium dioxide.

RIFADIN IV (rifampin for injection USP) contains rifampin 600 mg, sodium formaldehyde sulfoxylate 10 mg, and sodium hydroxide to adjust pH.

Rifampin is a semisynthetic antibiotic derivative of rifamycin SV. Rifampin is a red-brown crystalline powder very slightly soluble in water at neutral pH, freely soluble in chloroform, soluble in ethyl acetate and in methanol. Its molecular weight is 822.95 and its chemical formula is $C_{43}H_{58}N_4O_{12}$. The chemical name for rifampin is either:

3-[[(4-Methyl-1-piperazinyl)imino] methyl]rifamycin

or

5,6,9,17,19,21-hexahydroxy-23-methoxy-2,4, 12, 16, 20, 22–heptamethyl-8-[N-(4-methyl-1-piperazinyl)formimidoyl]-2,7 -(epoxypentadeca[1,11,13]trienimino)naphtho[2,1-*b*]furan-1,11(2H)-dione 21-acetate.

Its structural formula is:

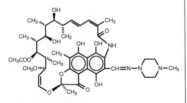

CLINICAL PHARMACOLOGY
Oral Administration

Rifampin is readily absorbed from the gastrointestinal tract. Peak serum concentrations in healthy adults and pediatric populations vary widely from individual to individual. Following a single 600 mg oral dose of rifampin in healthy adults, the peak serum concentration averages 7 μg/mL but may vary from 4 to 32 μg/mL. Absorption of rifampin is reduced by about 30% when the drug is ingested with food.

Rifampin is widely distributed throughout the body. It is present in effective concentrations in many organs and body fluids, including cerebrospinal fluid. Rifampin is about 80% protein bound. Most of the unbound fraction is not ionized and, therefore, diffuses freely into tissues.

In healthy adults, the mean biological half-life of rifampin in serum averages 3.35 ± 0.66 hours after a 600 mg oral dose, with increases up to 5.08 ± 2.45 hours reported after a 900 mg dose. With repeated administration, the half-life decreases and reaches average values of approximately 2 to 3 hours. The half-life does not differ in patients with renal failure at doses not exceeding 600 mg daily, and consequently, no dosage adjustment is required. Following a single 900 mg oral dose of rifampin in patients with varying degrees of renal insufficiency, the mean half-life increased from 3.6 hours in healthy adults to 5.0, 7.3, and 11.0 hours in patients with glomerular filtration rates of 30 to 50 mL/min, less than 30 mL/min, and in anuric patients, respectively. Refer to the WARNINGS section for information regarding patients with hepatic insufficiency.

Rifampin is rapidly eliminated in the bile, and an enterohepatic circulation ensues. During this process, rifampin undergoes progressive deacetylation so that nearly all the drug in the bile is in this form in about 6 hours. This metabolite is microbiologically active. Intestinal reabsorption is reduced by deacetylation, and elimination is facilitated. Up to 30% of a dose is excreted in the urine, with about half of this being unchanged drug.

Intravenous Administration

After intravenous administration of a 300 or 600 mg dose of rifampin infused over 30 minutes to healthy male volunteers (n=12), mean peak plasma concentrations were 9.0 ± 3.0 and 17.5 ± 5.0 μg/mL, respectively. Total body clearance after the 300 and 600 mg IV doses were 0.19 ± 0.06 and 0.14 ± 0.03 L/hr/kg, respectively. Volumes of distribution at steady state were 0.66 ± 0.14 and 0.64 ± 0.11 L/kg for the 300 and 600 mg IV doses, respectively. After intravenous administration of 300 or 600 mg doses, rifampin plasma concentrations in these volunteers remained detectable for 8 and 12 hours, respectively (see Table).

[See table below]

Plasma Concentrations (mean ± standard deviation, μg/mL)						
Rifampin Dosage IV	30 min	1 hr	2 hr	4 hr	8 hr	12 hr
300 mg	8.9±2.9	4.9±1.3	4.0±1.3	2.5±1.0	1.1±0.6	<0.4
600 mg	17.4±5.1	11.7±2.8	9.4±2.3	6.4±1.7	3.5±1.4	1.2±0.6

Plasma concentrations after the 600 mg dose, which were disproportionately higher (up to 30% greater than expected) than those found after the 300 mg dose, indicated that the elimination of larger doses was not as rapid.

After repeated once-a-day infusions (3 hr duration) of 600 mg in patients (n=5) for 7 days, concentrations of IV rifampin decreased from 5.81 ± 3.38 µg/mL 8 hours after the infusion on day 1 to 2.6 ± 1.88 µg/mL 8 hours after the infusion on day 7.

Rifampin is widely distributed throughout the body. It is present in effective concentrations in many organs and body fluids, including cerebrospinal fluid. Rifampin is about 80% protein bound. Most of the unbound fraction is not ionized and therefore diffuses freely into tissues.

Rifampin is rapidly eliminated in the bile and undergoes progressive enterohepatic circulation and deacetylation to the primary metabolite, 25-desacetyl-rifampin. This metabolite is microbiologically active. Less than 30% of the dose is excreted in the urine as rifampin or metabolites. Serum concentrations do not differ in patients with renal failure at a studied dose of 300 mg and consequently, no dosage adjustment is required.

Pediatrics

Oral Administration. In one study, pediatric patients 6 to 58 months old were given rifampin suspended in simple syrup or as dry powder mixed with applesauce at a dose of 10 mg/kg body weight. Peak serum concentrations of 10.7 ± 3.7 and 11.5 ± 5.1 µg/mL were obtained 1 hour after preprandial ingestion of the drug suspension and the applesauce mixture, respectively. After the administration of either preparation, the $t_{1/2}$ of rifampin averaged 2.9 hours. It should be noted that in other studies in pediatric populations, at doses of 10 mg/kg body weight, mean peak serum concentrations of 3.5 µg/mL to 15 µg/mL have been reported.

Intravenous Administration. In pediatric patients 0.25 to 12.8 years old (n=12), the mean peak serum concentration of rifampin at the end of a 30 minute infusion of approximately 300 mg/m² was 25.9 ± 1.3 µg/mL; individual peak concentrations 1 to 4 days after initiation of therapy ranged from 11.7 to 41.5 µg/mL; individual peak concentrations 5 to 14 days after initiation of therapy were 13.6 to 37.4 µg/mL. The individual serum half-life of rifampin changed from 1.04 to 3.81 hours early in therapy to 1.17 to 3.19 hours 5 to 14 days after therapy was initiated.

Microbiology

Rifampin inhibits DNA-dependent RNA polymerase activity in susceptible cells. Specifically, it interacts with bacterial RNA polymerase but does not inhibit the mammalian enzyme. Rifampin at therapeutic levels has demonstrated bactericidal activity against both intracellular and extracellular *Mycobacterium tuberculosis* organisms.

Organisms resistant to rifampin are likely to be resistant to other rifamycins.

Rifampin has bactericidal activity against slow and intermittently growing *M tuberculosis* organisms. It also has significant activity against *Neisseria meningitidis* isolates (see INDICATIONS AND USAGE).

In the treatment of both tuberculosis and the meningococcal carrier state (see INDICATIONS AND USAGE), the small number of resistant cells present within large populations of susceptible cells can rapidly become predominant. In addition, resistance to rifampin has been determined to occur as single-step mutations of the DNA-dependent RNA polymerase. Since resistance can emerge rapidly, appropriate susceptibility tests should be performed in the event of persistent positive cultures.

Rifampin has been shown to be active against most strains of the following microorganisms, both in vitro and in clinical infections as described in the INDICATIONS AND USAGE section.

Aerobic Gram-Negative Microorganisms:
Neisseria meningitidis

"Other" Microorganisms:
Mycobacterium tuberculosis

The following in vitro data are available, but their clinical significance is unknown.

Rifampin exhibits in vitro activity against most strains of the following microorganisms; however, the safety and effectiveness of rifampin in treating clinical infections due to these microorganisms have not been established in adequate and well-controlled trials.

Aerobic Gram-Positive Microorganisms:
Staphylococcus aureus (including Methicillin-Resistant *S. aureus*/MRSA)
Staphylococcus epidermidis

Aerobic Gram-Negative Microorganisms:
Haemophilus influenzae

"Other" Microorganisms:
Mycobacterium leprae

β-lactamase production should have no effect on rifampin activity.

Susceptibility Tests

Prior to initiation of therapy, appropriate specimens should be collected for identification of the infecting organism and in vitro susceptibility tests.

In vitro testing for *Mycobacterium tuberculosis* isolates:

Two standardized in vitro susceptibility methods are available for testing rifampin against *M tuberculosis* organisms. The agar proportion method (CDC or NCCLS[1] M24-P) utilizes Middlebrook 7H10 medium impregnated with rifampin at a final concentration of 1.0 µg/mL to determine drug resistance. After three weeks of incubation MIC_{99} values are calculated by comparing the quantity of organisms growing in the medium containing drug to the control cultures. Mycobacterial growth in the presence of drug, of at least 1% of the growth in the control culture, indicates resistance.

The radiometric broth method employs the BACTEC 460 machine to compare the growth index from untreated control cultures to cultures grown in the presence of 2.0 µg/mL of rifampin. Strict adherence to the manufacturer's instructions for sample processing and data interpretation is required for this assay. Susceptibility test results obtained by the two different methods can only be compared if the appropriate rifampin concentration is used for each test method as indicated above. Both procedures require the use of *M tuberculosis* H37Rv ATCC 27294 as a control organism.

The clinical relevance of in vitro susceptibility test results for mycobacterial species other than *M tuberculosis* using either the radiometric or the proportion method has not been determined.

In vitro testing for *Neisseria meningitidis* isolates:

Dilution Techniques: Quantitative methods that are used to determine minimum inhibitory concentrations provide reproducible estimates of the susceptibility of bacteria to antimicrobial compounds. One such standardized procedure uses a standardized dilution method[2,4] (broth, agar, or microdilution) or equivalent with rifampin powder. The MIC values obtained should be interpreted according to the following criteria for *Neisseria meningitidis:*

MIC (µg/mL)	Interpretation
≤1	(S) Susceptible
2	(I) Intermediate
≥4	(R) Resistant

A report of "susceptible" indicates that the pathogen is likely to be inhibited by usually achievable concentrations of the antimicrobial compound in the blood. A report of "intermediate" indicates that the result should be considered equivocal, and if the microorganism is not fully susceptible to alternative, clinically feasible drugs, the test should be repeated. This category implies possible clinical applicability in body sites where the drug is physiologically concentrated or in situations where the maximum acceptable dose of drug can be used. This category also provides a buffer zone that prevents small uncontrolled technical factors from causing major discrepancies in interpretation. A report of "resistant" indicates that usually achievable concentrations of the antimicrobial compound in the blood are unlikely to be inhibitory and that other therapy should be selected.

Measurement of MIC or minimum bactericidal concentrations (MBC) and achieved antimicrobial compound concentrations may be appropriate to guide therapy in some infections. (See CLINICAL PHARMACOLOGY section for further information on drug concentrations

achieved in infected body sites and other pharmacokinetic properties of this antimicrobial drug product.)

Standardized susceptibility test procedures require the use of laboratory control microorganisms. The use of these microorganisms does not imply clinical efficacy (see INDICATIONS AND USAGE); they are used to control the technical aspects of the laboratory procedures. Standard rifampin powder should give the following MIC values:

Microorganism		MIC (µg/mL)
Staphylococcus aureus	ATCC 29213	0.008–0.06
Enterococcus faecalis	ATCC 29212	1–4
Escherichia coli	ATCC 25922	8–32
Pseudomonas aeruginosa	ATCC 27853	32–64
Haemophilus influenzae	ATCC 49247	0.25–1

Diffusion Techniques: Quantitative methods that require measurement of zone diameters provide reproducible estimates of the susceptibility of bacteria to antimicrobial compounds. One such standardized procedure[3,4] that has been recommended for use with disks to test the susceptibility of microorganisms to rifampin uses the 5 µg rifampin disk. Interpretation involves correlation of the diameter obtained in the disk test with the MIC for rifampin.

Reports from the laboratory providing results of the standard single-disk susceptibility test with a 5 µg rifampin disk should be interpreted according to the following criteria for *Neisseria meningitidis:*

Zone Diameter (mm)	Interpretation
≥20	(S) Susceptible
17–19	(I) Intermediate
≤16	(R) Resistant

Interpretation should be as stated above for results using dilution techniques.

As with standard dilution techniques, diffusion methods require the use of laboratory control microorganisms. The use of these microorganisms does not imply clinical efficacy (see INDICATIONS AND USAGE); they are used to control the technical aspects of the laboratory procedures. The 5 µg rifampin disk should provide the following zone diameters in these quality control strains:

Microorganism		Zone Diameter (mm)
S. aureus	ATCC 25923	26–34
E. coli	ATCC 25922	8–10
H. influenzae	ATCC 49247	22–30

INDICATIONS AND USAGE

In the treatment of both tuberculosis and the meningococcal carrier state, the small number of resistant cells present within large populations of susceptible cells can rapidly become the predominant type. Bacteriologic cultures should be obtained before the start of therapy to confirm the susceptibility of the organism to rifampin and they should be repeated throughout therapy to monitor the response to treatment. Since resistance can emerge rapidly, susceptibility tests should be performed in the event of persistent positive cultures during the course of treatment. If test results show resistance to rifampin and the patient is not responding to therapy, the drug regimen should be modified.

Tuberculosis

Rifampin is indicated in the treatment of all forms of tuberculosis.

A three-drug regimen consisting of rifampin, isoniazid, and pyrazinamide (eg, RIFATER®) is recommended in the initial phase of short-course therapy which is usually continued for 2 months. The Advisory Council for the Elimination of Tuberculosis, the American Thoracic Society, and Centers for Disease Control and Prevention recommend that either streptomycin or ethambutol be added as a fourth drug in a regimen containing isoniazid (INH), rifampin, and pyrazinamide for initial treatment of tuberculosis unless the likelihood of INH resistance is very low. The need for a fourth drug should be reassessed when the results of susceptibility testing are known. If community rates of INH resistance are currently less than 4%, an initial treatment regimen with less than four drugs may be considered.

Following the initial phase, treatment should be continued with rifampin and isoniazid (eg, RIFAMATE®) for at least 4 months. Treatment should be continued for longer if the patient is still sputum or culture positive, if resistant organisms are present, or if the patient is HIV positive.

RIFADIN IV is indicated for the initial treatment and retreatment of tuberculosis when the drug cannot be taken by mouth.

Meningococcal Carriers

Rifampin is indicated for the treatment of asymptomatic carriers of *Neisseria meningitidis* to eliminate meningococci from the nasopharynx. **Rifampin is not indicated for the treatment of meningococcal infection because of the possibility of the rapid emergence of resistant organisms.** (See WARNINGS.)

Rifampin should not be used indiscriminately, and therefore, diagnostic laboratory procedures, including serotyping and susceptibility testing, should be performed for establishment of the carrier state and the correct treatment. So that the usefulness of rifampin in the treatment of asymptomatic meningococcal carriers is preserved, the drug should be used only when the risk of meningococcal disease is high.

CONTRAINDICATIONS

Rifampin is contraindicated in patients with a history of hypersensitivity to any of the rifamycins. (See WARNINGS.)

WARNINGS

Rifampin has been shown to produce liver dysfunction. Fatalities associated with jaundice have occurred in patients with liver disease and in patients taking rifampin with other hepatotoxic agents. Patients with impaired liver function should be given rifampin only in cases of necessity and then with caution and under strict medical supervision. In these patients, careful monitoring of liver function, especially SGPT/ALT and SGOT/AST should be carried out prior to therapy and then every 2 to 4 weeks during therapy. If signs of hepatocellular damage occur, rifampin should be withdrawn.

In some cases, hyperbilirubinemia resulting from competition between rifampin and bilirubin for excretory pathways of the liver at the cell level can occur in the early days of treatment. An isolated report showing a moderate rise in bilirubin and/or transaminase level is not in itself an indication for interrupting treatment; rather, the decision should be made after repeating the tests, noting trends in the levels, and considering them in conjunction with the patient's clinical condition.

Rifampin has enzyme-inducing properties, including induction of delta amino levulinic acid synthetase. Isolated reports have associated porphyria exacerbation with rifampin administration.

The possibility of rapid emergence of resistant meningococci restricts the use of RIFADIN to short-term treatment of the asymptomatic carrier state. **RIFADIN is not to be used for the treatment of meningococcal disease.**

PRECAUTIONS

General

For the treatment of tuberculosis, rifampin is usually administered on a daily basis. Doses of rifampin greater than 600 mg given once or twice weekly have resulted in a higher incidence of adverse reactions, including the "flu syndrome" (fever, chills and malaise), hematopoietic reactions (leukopenia, thrombocytopenia, or acute hemolytic anemia), cutaneous, gastrointestinal, and hepatic reactions, shortness of breath, shock, anaphylaxis, and renal failure. Recent studies indicate that regimens using twice-weekly doses of rifampin 600 mg plus isoniazid 15 mg/kg are much better tolerated.

Intermittent therapy may be used if the patient cannot (or will not) self-administer drugs on a daily basis. Patients on intermittent therapy should be closely monitored for compliance and cautioned against intentional or accidental interruption of prescribed therapy, because of the increased risk of serious adverse reactions.

Rifampin has enzyme induction properties that can enhance the metabolism of endogenous substrates including adrenal hormones, thyroid hormones, and vitamin D. Rifampin and isoniazid have been reported to alter vitamin D metabolism. In some cases, reduced levels of circulating 25-hydroxy vitamin D and 1,25-dihydroxy vitamin D have been accompanied by reduced serum calcium and phosphate, and elevated parathyroid hormone.

RIFADIN IV

For intravenous infusion only. Must not be administered by intramuscular or subcutaneous route. Avoid extravasation during injection: local irritation and inflammation due to extravascular infiltration of the infusion have been observed. If these occur, the infusion should be discontinued and restarted at another site.

Information for Patients

The patient should be told that rifampin may produce a reddish coloration of the urine, sweat, sputum, and tears, and the patient should be forewarned of this. Soft contact lenses may be permanently stained.

The patients should be advised that the reliability of oral or other systemic hormonal contraceptives may be affected; consideration should be given to using alternative contraceptive measures.

Patients should be instructed to take rifampin either 1 hour before or 2 hours after a meal with a full glass of water.

Patients should be instructed to notify their physicians promptly if they experience any of the following: fever, loss of appetite, malaise, nausea and vomiting, darkened urine, yellowish discoloration of the skin and eyes, and pain or swelling of the joints.

Compliance with the full course of therapy must be emphasized, and the importance of not missing any doses must be stressed.

Laboratory Tests

Adults treated for tuberculosis with rifampin should have baseline measurements of hepatic enzymes, bilirubin, serum creatinine, a complete blood count, and a platelet count (or estimate). Baseline tests are unnecessary in pediatric patients unless a complicating condition is known or clinically suspected.

Patients should be seen at least monthly during therapy and should be specifically questioned concerning symptoms associated with adverse reactions. All patients with abnormalities should have follow-up, including laboratory testing, if necessary. Routine laboratory monitoring for toxicity in people with normal baseline measurements is generally not necessary.

Drug Interactions

ENZYME INDUCTION: Rifampin is known to induce certain cytochrome P-450 enzymes. Administration of rifampin with drugs that undergo biotransformation through these meta-bolic pathways may accelerate elimination of coadministered drugs. To maintain optimum therapeutic blood levels, dosages of drugs metabolized by these enzymes may require adjustment when starting or stopping concomitantly administered rifampin.

Rifampin has been reported to accelerate the metabolism of the following drugs: anticonvulsants (eg, phenytoin), antiarrhythmics (eg, disopyramide, mexiletine, quinidine, tocainide), oral anticoagulants, antifungals (eg, fluconazole, itraconazole, ketoconazole), barbiturates, beta-blockers, calcium channel blockers (eg, diltiazem, nifedipine, verapamil), chloramphenicol, clarithromycin, corticosteroids, cyclosporine, cardiac glycoside preparations, clofibrate, oral or other systemic hormone contraceptives, dapsone, diazepam, doxycycline, fluoroquinolones (eg ciprofloxacin), haloperidol, oral hypoglycemic agents (sulfonylureas), levothyroxine, methadone, narcotic analgesics, nortriptyline, progestins, quinine, tacrolimus, theophylline tricyclic antidepressants (eg, amitriptyline, nortriptyline), and zidovudine. It may be necessary to adjust the dosages of these drugs if they are given concurrently with rifampin.

Patients using oral or other systemic hormonal contraceptives should be advised to change to nonhormonal methods of birth control during rifampin therapy.

Rifampin has been observed to increase the requirements for anticoagulant drugs of the coumarin type. In patients receiving anticoagulants and rifampin concurrently, it is recommended that the prothrombin time be performed daily or as frequently as necessary to establish and maintain the required dose of anticoagulant.

Diabetes may become more difficult to control.

OTHER INTERACTIONS: When the two drugs were taken concomitantly, decreased concentrations of atovaquone and increased concentrations of rifampin were observed.

Concurrent use of ketoconazole and rifampin has resulted in decreased serum concentrations of both drugs. Concurrent use of rifampin and enalapril has resulted in decreased concentrations of enalaprilat, the active metabolite of enalapril. Dosage adjustments should be made if indicated by the patient's clinical condition.

Concomitant antacid administration may reduce the absorption of rifampin. Daily doses of rifampin should be given at least 1 hour before the ingestion of antacids.

Probenecid and cotrimoxazole have been reported to increase the blood level of rifampin. When rifampin is given concomitantly with either halothane or isoniazid, the potential for hepatotoxicity is increased. The concomitant use of rifampin and halothane should be avoided. Patients receiving both rifampin and isoniazid should be monitored close for hepatotoxicity.

Plasma concentrations of sulfapyridine may be reduced following the concomitant administration of sulfasalazine and rifampin. This finding may be the result of alteration in the colonic bacteria responsible for the reduction of sulfasalazine to sulfapyridine and mesalamine.

Drug/Laboratory Interactions

Cross-reactivity and false-positive urine screening tests for opiates have been reported in patients receiving rifampin when using the KIMS (Kinetic Interaction of Microparticles in Solution) method (eg, Abuscreen OnLine opiates assay; Roche Diagnostic Systems). Confirmatory tests, such as gas chromatography/mass spectrometry, will distinguish rifampin from opiates.

Therapeutic levels of rifampin have been shown to inhibit standard microbiological assays for serum folate and vitamin B_{12}. Thus, alternate assay methods should be considered. Transient abnormalities in liver function tests (eg, elevation in serum bilirubin, alkaline phosphatase, and serum transaminases) and reduced biliary excretion of contrast media used for visualization of the gallbladder have also been observed. Therefore, these tests should be performed before the morning dose of rifampin.

Carcinogenesis, Mutagenesis, Impairment of Fertility

There are no known human data on long-term potential for carinogenicity, mutagenicity, or impairment of fertility. A few cases of accelerated growth of lung carcinoma have been reported in man, but a causal relationship with the drug has not been established. An increase in the incidence of hepatomas in female mice (of a strain known to be particularly susceptible to the spontaneous development of hepatomas) was observed when rifampin was administered in doses 2 to 10 times the average daily human dose for 60 weeks, followed by an observation period of 46 weeks. No evidence of carcinogenicity was found in male mice of the same strain, mice of a different strain, or rats under similar experimental conditions.

Rifampin has been reported to possess immunosuppressive potential in rabbits, mice, rats, guinea pigs, human lymphocytes in vitro, and humans. Antitumor activity in vitro has also been shown with rifampin.

There was no evidence of mutagenicity in bacteria, *Drosophila melanogaster*, or mice. An increase in chromotid breaks was noted when whole blood cell cultures were treated with rifampin. Increased frequency of chromosomal aberrations was observed in vitro in lymphocytes obtained from patients treated with combinations of rifampin, isoniazid, and pyrazinamide and combinations of streptomycin, rifampin, isoniazid, and pyrazinamide.

Pregnancy—Teratogenic Effects

Category C. Rifampin has been shown to be teratogenic in rodents given oral doses of rifampin 15 to 25 times the human dose. Although rifampin has been reported to cross the placental barrier and appear in cord blood, the effect of RIFADIN, alone or in combination with other antituberculosis drugs, on the human fetus is not known. Neonates of rifampin-treated mothers should be carefully observed for any evidence of adverse effects. Isolated cases of fetal malformations have been reported; however, there are no adequate and well-controlled studies in pregnant women. Rifampin should be used during pregnancy only if the potential benefit justifies the potential risk to the fetus. Rifampin in oral doses of 150 to 250 mg/kg produced teratogenic effects in mice and rats. Malformations were primarily cleft palate in the mouse and spina bifida in the rat. The incidence of these anomalies was dose-dependent. When rifampin was given to pregnant rabbits in doses up to 20 times the usual daily human dose, imperfect osteogenesis and embryotoxicity were reported.

Pregnancy—Non-Teratogenic Effects

When administered during the last few weeks of pregnancy, rifampin can cause post-natal hemorrhages in the mother and infant for which treatment with vitamin K may be indicated.

Nursing Mothers

Because of the potential for tumorigenicity shown for rifampin in animal studies, a decision should be made whether to discontinue nursing or discontinue the drug, taking into account the importance of the drug to the mother.

Pediatric Use

See CLINICAL PHARMACOLOGY—Pediatrics; see also DOSAGE AND ADMINISTRATION.

ADVERSE REACTIONS

Gastrointestinal

Heartburn, epigastric distress, anorexia, nausea, vomiting, jaundice, flatulence, cramps, and diarrhea have been noted in some patients. Although *Clostridium difficile* has been shown in vitro to be sensitive to rifampin, pseudomembranous colitis has been reported with the use of rifampin (and other broad spectrum antibiotics). Therefore, it is important to consider this diagnosis in patients who develop diarrhea in association with antibiotic use. Rarely, hepatitis or a shock-like syndrome with hepatic involvement and abnormal liver function tests has been reported.

Hematologic

Thrombocytopenia has occurred primarily with high dose intermittent therapy, but has also been noted after resumption of interrupted treatment. It rarely occurs during well supervised daily therapy. This effect is reversible if the drug is discontinued as soon as purpura occurs. Cerebral hemorrhage and fatalities have been reported when rifampin administration has been continued or resumed after the appearance of purpura.

Rare reports of disseminated intravascular coagulation have been observed.

Transient leukopenia, hemolytic anemia, and decreased hemoglobin have been observed.

Central Nervous System

Headache, fever, drowsiness, fatigue, ataxia, dizziness, inability to concentrate, mental confusion, behavioral changes, pain in extremities, and generalized numbness have been observed.

Psychoses has been rarely reported.

Ocular

Visual disturbances have been observed.

Endocrine

Menstrual disturbances have been observed. Rare reports of adrenal insufficiency in patients with compromised adrenal function have been observed.

Renal

Elevations in BUN and serum uric acid have been reported. Rarely, hemolysis, hemoglobinuria, hematuria, interstitial nephritis, acute tubular necrosis, renal insufficiency, and acute renal failure have been noted. These are generally considered to be hypersensitivity reactions. They usually occur during intermittent therapy or when treatment is resumed following intentional or accidental interruption of a daily dosage regimen, and are reversible when rifampin is discontinued and appropriate therapy instituted.

Dermatologic

Cutaneous reactions are mild and self-limiting and do not appear to be hypersensitivity reactions. Typically, they consist of flushing and itching with or without a rash. More serious cutaneous reactions which may be due to hypersensitivity occur but are uncommon.

Hypersensitivity Reactions

Occasionally, pruritus, urticaria, rash, pemphigoid reaction, erythema multiforme including Stevens-Johnson Syndrome, toxic epidermal necrolysis, vasculitis, eosinophilia, sore mouth, sore tongue, and conjunctivitis have been observed.

Anaphylaxis has been reported rarely.

Miscellaneous

Rare reports of myopathy and muscular weakness have also been observed.

Edema of the face and extremities has been reported. Other reactions reported to have occurred with intermittent dosage regimens include "flu syndrome" (such as episodes of fever, chills, headache, dizziness, and bone pain), shortness of breath, wheezing, decrease in blood pressure and shock. The "flu syndrome" may also appear if rifampin is taken irregularly by the patient or if daily administration is resumed after a drug free interval.

OVERDOSAGE

Signs and Symptoms

Nausea, vomiting, abdominal pain, pruritus, headache, and increasing lethargy will probably occur within a short time after ingestion; unconsciousness may occur when there is severe hepatic disease. Transient increases in liver enzymes and/or bilirubin may occur.

Brownish-red or orange discoloration of the skin, urine, sweat, saliva, tears, and feces will occur, and its intensity is proportional to the amount ingested.

Facial or periorbital edema has also been reported in pediatric patients. Hypotension, sinus tachycardia, ventricular arrhythmias, seizures and cardiac arrest were reported in some fatal cases.

Acute Toxicity

The LD_{50} of rifampin is approximately 885 mg/kg in the mouse, 1720 mg/kg in the rat, and 2120 mg/kg in the rabbit.

The minimum acute lethal or toxic dose is not well established. However, nonfatal acute overdoses in adults have been reported with doses ranging from 9 to 12 gm rifampin. Fatal acute overdoses in adults have been reported with doses ranging from 14 to 60 gm. Alcohol or a history of alcohol abuse was involved in some of the fatal and nonfatal reports. Nonfatal overdoses in pediatric patients ages 1 to 4 years old of 100 mg/kg for one to two doses has been reported.

Treatment

Intensive support measures should be instituted and individual symptoms treated as they arise. Since nausea and vomiting are likely to be present, gastric lavage is probably preferable to induction of emesis. Following evacuation of the gastric contents, the instillation of activated charcoal slurry into the stomach may help absorb any remaining drug from the gastrointestinal tract. Antiemetic medication may be required to control severe nausea and vomiting. Active diuresis (with measured intake and output) will help promote excretion of the drug. Hemodialysis may be of value in some patients.

DOSAGE AND ADMINISTRATION

Rifampin can be administered by the oral route or by IV infusion (see INDICATIONS AND USAGE). IV doses are the same as those for oral.

See CLINICAL PHARMACOLOGY for dosing information in patients with renal failure.

Tuberculosis

Adults: 10 mg/kg, in a single daily administration, not to exceed 600 mg/day, oral or IV

Pediatric Patients: 10–20 mg/kg, not to exceed 600 mg/day, oral or IV

It is recommended that oral rifampin be administered once daily, either 1 hour before or 2 hours after a meal with a full glass of water.

Rifampin is indicated in the treatment of all forms of tuberculosis. A three-drug regimen consisting of rifampin, isoniazid, and pyrazinamide (eg, RIFATER®) is recommended in the initial phase of short-course therapy which is usually continued for 2 months. The Advisory Council for the Elimination of Tuberculosis, the American Thoracic Society, and the Centers for Disease Control and Prevention recommend that either streptomycin or ethambutol be added as a fourth drug in a regimen containing isoniazid (INH), rifampin and pyrazinamide for initial treatment of tuberculosis unless the likelihood of INH resistance is very low. The need for a fourth drug should be reassessed when the results of susceptibility testing are known. If community rates of INH resistance are currently less than 4%, an initial treatment regimen with less than four drugs may be considered.

Following the initial phase, treatment should be continued with rifampin and isoniazid (eg, RIFAMATE®) for at least 4 months. Treatment should be continued for longer if the patient is still sputum or culture positive, if resistant organisms are present, or if the patient is HIV positive.

Preparation of Solution for IV Infusion: Reconstitute the lyophilized powder by transferring 10 mL of sterile water for injection to a vial containing 600 mg of rifampin for injection. Swirl vial gently to completely dissolve the antibiotic. The reconstituted solution contains 60 mg rifampin per mL and is stable at room temperature for 24 hours. Prior to administration, withdraw from the reconstituted solution a volume equivalent to the amount of rifampin calculated to be administered and add to 500 mL of infusion medium. Mix well and infuse at a rate allowing for complete infusion within 3 hours. Alternatively, the amount of rifampin calculated to be administered may be added to 100 mL of infusion medium and infused in 30 minutes.

Dilutions in dextrose 5% for injection (D5W) are stable at room temperature for up to 4 hours and should be prepared and used within this time. Precipitation of rifampin from the infusion solution may occur beyond this time. Dilutions in normal saline are stable at room temperature for up to 24 hours and should be prepared and used within this time. Other infusion solutions are not recommended.

Incompatibilities: Physical incompatibility (precipitate) was observed with undiluted (5 mg/mL) and diluted (1 mg/mL in normal saline) diltiazem hydrochloride and rifampin (6 mg/mL in normal saline) during simulated Y-site administration.

Meningococcal Carriers

Adults: For adults, it is recommended that 600 mg rifampin be administered twice daily for two days.

Pediatric Patients: Pediatric patients 1 month of age or older: 10 mg/kg (not to exceed 600 mg per dose) every 12 hours for two days.

Pediatric patients under 1 month of age: 5 mg/kg every 12 hours for two days.

Preparation of Extemporaneous Oral Suspension

For pediatric and adult patients in whom capsule swallowing is difficult or where lower doses are needed, a liquid suspension may be prepared as follows:

RIFADIN 1% w/v suspension (10 mg/mL) can be compounded using one of four syrups—Simple Syrup (Syrup NF), Simple Syrup (Humco

Laboratories), Syrpalta® Syrup (Emerson Laboratories), or Raspberry Syrup (Humco Laboratories).

1. Empty the contents of four RIFADIN 300 mg capsules or eight RIFADIN 150 mg capsules onto a piece of weighing paper.
2. If necessary, gently crush the capsule contents with a spatula to produce a fine powder.
3. Transfer the rifampin powder blend to a 4-ounce amber glass or plastic (high density polyethylene [HDPE], polypropylene, or polycarbonate) prescription bottle.
4. Rinse the paper and spatula with 20 mL of one of the above-mentioned syrups, and add the rinse to the bottle. Shake vigorously.
5. Add 100 mL of syrup to the bottle and shake vigorously.

This compounding procedure results in a 1% w/v suspension containing 10 mg rifampin/mL. Stability studies indicate that the suspension is stable when stored at room temperature (25 ± 3°C) or in a refrigerator (2–8°C) for four weeks. This extemporaneously prepared suspension must be shaken well prior to administration.

HOW SUPPLIED

150 mg maroon and scarlet capsules imprinted "RIFADIN 150."

Bottles of 30 (NDC 0068-0510-30)

300 mg maroon and scarlet capsules imprinted "RIFADIN 300."

Bottles of 30 (NDC 0068-0508-30)
Bottles of 60 (NDC 0068-0508-60)
Bottles of 100 (NDC 0068-0508-61)

Storage: Keep tightly closed. Store in a dry place. Avoid excessive heat.

RIFADIN IV (rifampin for injection USP) is available in glass vials containing 600 mg rifampin (NDC 0068-0597-01).

Storage: Avoid excessive heat (temperatures above 40°C or 104°F). Protect from light.

References:

1. National Committee for Clinical Laboratory Standards, Antimycobacterial Susceptibility Testing. Proposed Standard NCCLS Document M24-P, Vol. 10, No. 10, NNCLS, Villanova, PA, 1990.

2. National Committee for Clinical Laboratory Standards. Methods for Dilution Antimicrobial Susceptibility Tests for Bacteria that Grow Aerobically—Third Edition. Approved Standard NCCLS Document M7-A3, Vol. 13, No. 25, NCCLS, Villanova, PA, December 1993.

3. National Committee for Clinical Laboratory Standards. Performance Standards for Antimicrobial Disk Susceptibility Tests—Fifth Edition. Approved Standard NCCLS Document M2-A5, Vol. 13, No. 24, NCCLS, Villanova, PA, December 1993.

4. National Committee for Clinical Laboratory Standards. Performance Standards for Antimicrobial Susceptibility Testing; Fifth In-

formational Supplement, NCCLS Document M100-S5, Vol. 14, No. 16, NCCLS, Villanova, PA, December 1994.

Rx Only

Prescribing Information as of August 2000

Merrell Pharmaceuticals Inc.

Subsidiary of Aventis Pharmaceuticals Inc.

Kansas City, MO 64137 USA

www.aventispharma-us.com

Rifadin IV (rifampin for injection USP) is
manufactured by:

GRUPPO LEPETIT S.p.A.

20020 Lainate, Italy

Made in Italy   50059044

STREPTOMYCIN SULFATE Injection, USP   ℞
1 g/2.5 mL Ampules
For Intramuscular Use Only

> **WARNING**
> THE RISK OF SEVERE NEUROTOXIC REACTIONS IS SHARPLY INCREASED IN PATIENTS WITH IMPAIRED RENAL FUNCTION OR PRE-RENAL AZOTEMIA. THESE INCLUDE DISTURBANCES OF VESTIBULAR AND COCHLEAR FUNCTION. OPTIC NERVE DYSFUNCTION, PERIPHERAL NEURITIS, ARACHNOIDITIS, AND ENCEPHALOPATHY MAY ALSO OCCUR. THE INCIDENCE OF CLINICALLY DETECTABLE, IRREVERSIBLE VESTIBULAR DAMAGE IS PARTICULARLY HIGH IN PATIENTS TREATED WITH STREPTOMYCIN.
> RENAL FUNCTION SHOULD BE MONITORED CAREFULLY; PATIENTS WITH RENAL IMPAIRMENT AND/OR NITROGEN RETENTION SHOULD RECEIVE REDUCED DOSAGES. THE PEAK SERUM CONCENTRATION IN INDIVIDUALS WITH KIDNEY DAMAGE SHOULD NOT EXCEED 20 TO 25 MCG/ML.
> THE CONCURRENT OR SEQUENTIAL USE OF OTHER NEUROTOXIC AND/OR NEPHROTOXIC DRUGS WITH STREPTOMYCIN SULFATE, INCLUDING NEOMYCIN, KANAMYCIN, GENTAMICIN, CEPHALORIDINE, PAROMOMYCIN, VIOMYCIN, POLYMYXIN B, COLISTIN, TOBRAMYCIN AND CYCLOSPORINE SHOULD BE AVOIDED.
> THE NEUROTOXICITY OF STREPTOMYCIN CAN RESULT IN RESPIRATORY PARALYSIS FROM NEUROMUSCULAR BLOCKAGE, ESPECIALLY WHEN THE DRUG IS GIVEN SOON AFTER THE USE OF ANESTHESIA OR OF MUSCLE RELAXANTS.
> THE ADMINISTRATION OF STREPTOMYCIN IN PARENTERAL FORM SHOULD BE RESERVED FOR PATIENTS WHERE ADEQUATE LABORATORY AND AUDIOMETRIC TESTING FACILITIES ARE AVAILABLE DURING THERAPY.

DESCRIPTION

Streptomycin is a water-soluble aminoglycoside derived from *Streptomyces griseus*. It is marketed as the sulfate salt of streptomycin. The chemical name of streptomycin sulfate is D-Streptamine, *O*-2-deoxy-2-(methylamino)-α-L-glucopyranosyl-(1→2)-*O*-5-deoxy-3-*C*-formyl-α-L-lyxofuranosyl-(1⁻4)-*N*,*N* ′-bis(aminoiminomethyl)-, sulfate (2:3) (salt). The empirical formula for Streptomycin Sulfate is $(C_{21}H_{39}N_7O_{12})_2.3H_2SO_4$ and the molecular weight is 1457.38. It has the following structure:

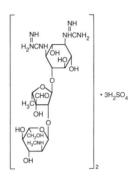

Streptomycin Sulfate Injection, 1 g/2.5 mL (400 mg/mL), is supplied as a sterile, nonpyrogenic solution for intramuscular use.
Each mL contains: Streptomycin sulfate equivalent to 400 mg of streptomycin, sodium citrate dihydrate 12 mg, phenol 0.25% w/v as preservative, sodium metabisulfite 2 mg in Water for Injection. pH range 5.0 to 8.0.

CLINICAL PHARMACOLOGY

Following intramuscular injection of 1 g of streptomycin, as the sulfate, a peak serum level of 25 to 50 mcg/mL is reached within 1 hour, diminishing slowly to about 50 percent after 5 to 6 hours.
Appreciable concentrations are found in all organ tissues except the brain. Significant amounts have been found in pleural fluid and tuberculous cavities. Streptomycin passes through the placenta with serum levels in the cord blood similar to maternal levels. Small amounts are excreted in milk, saliva, and sweat.
Streptomycin is excreted by glomerular filtration. In patients with normal kidney function, between 29% and 89% of a single 600 mg dose is excreted in the urine within 24 hours. Any reduction of glomerular function results in decreased excretion of the drug and concurrent rise in serum and tissue levels.
Microbiology
Streptomycin sulfate is a bactericidal antibiotic. It acts by interfering with normal protein synthesis.
Streptomycin has been shown to be active against most strains of the following organisms both *in vitro* and in clinical infection. (See INDICATIONS AND USAGE.):
Brucella (brucellosis),
Calymmatobacterium granulomatis (donovanosis, granuloma inguinale),
Escherichia coli, Proteus spp., Aerobacter aerogenes, Klebsiella pneumoniae, and *Enterococcus faecalis* in urinary tract infections,

Francisella tularensis,
Haemophilus ducreyi (chancroid),
Haemophilus influenzae (in respiratory, endocardial, and meningeal infections—concomitantly with another antibacterial agent),
Klebsiella pneumoniae pneumonia (concomitantly with another antibacterial agent),
Mycobacterium tuberculosis,
Pasteurella pestis
Streptococcus viridans, *Enterococcus faecalis* (in endocardial infections—concomitantly with penicillin).

SUSCEPTIBILITY TESTS: Diffusion Techniques

Quantitative methods that require measurement of zone diameters give the most precise estimate of the susceptibility of bacteria to antimicrobial agents. One such standard procedure[1] which has been recommended for use with disks to test susceptibility of organisms to streptomycin uses the 10 mcg streptomycin disk. Interpretation involves the correlation of the diameter obtained in the disk test with the minimum inhibitory concentration (MIC) for streptomycin.

Reports from the laboratory giving results of the standard single disk susceptibility test with a 10 mcg streptomycin disk should be interpreted according to the following criteria:

Zone Diameter (mm)	Interpretation
≥15	(S) Susceptible
11–12	(I) Intermediate
≤10	(R) Resistant

A report of "Susceptible" indicates that the pathogen is likely to respond to monotherapy with streptomycin. A report of "Intermediate" indicates that the result be considered equivocal, and, if the organism is not fully susceptible to alternative clinically feasible drugs, the test should be repeated. This category provides a buffer zone which prevents small uncontrolled technical factors from causing major discrepancies in interpretations. A report of "Resistant" indicates that achievable drug concentrations are unlikely to be inhibitory and other therapy should be selected.

Standardized procedures require the use of laboratory control organisms. The 10 mcg streptomycin disk should give the following zone diameter:

Organism	Zone diameter (mm)
E. coli ATCC 25922	12–20
S. aureus ATCC 25923	14–22

Methods Section:

Two standardized *in vitro* susceptibility methods are available for testing streptomycin against *Mycobacterium tuberculosis* organisms. The agar proportion method (CDC or NCCLS M24–P) utilizes middlebrook 7H10 medium impregnated with streptomycin at two final concentrations, 2.0 and 10.0 mcg/mL. MIC_{90} values are calculated by comparing the quantity of organisms growing in the medium containing drug to the control cultures. Mycobacterial growth in the presence of drug ≥ 1% of the control indicates resistance.

The radiometric broth method employs the BACTEC 460 machine to compare the growth index from untreated control cultures to cultures grown in the presence of 6.0 mcg/mL of streptomycin. Strict adherence to the manufacturer's instructions for sample processing and data interpretation is required for this assay.

Susceptibility test results obtained by these two different methods cannot be compared unless equivalent drug concentrations are evaluated.

The clinical relevance of *in vitro* susceptibility test results for mycobacterial species other than *M. tuberculosis* using either the BACTEC or the proportion method has not been determined.

INDICATIONS AND USAGE

Streptomycin is indicated for the treatment of individuals with moderate to severe infections caused by susceptible strains of microorganisms in the specific conditions listed below:

1. Mycobacterium tuberculosis: The Advisory Council for the Elimination of Tuberculosis, the American Thoracic Society, and the Center for Disease Control recommend that either streptomycin or ethambutol be added as a fourth drug in a regimen containing isoniazid (INH), rifampin and pyrazinamide for initial treatment of tuberculosis unless the likelihood of INH or rifampin resistance is very low. The need for a fourth drug should be reassessed when the results of susceptibility testing are known. In the past when the national rate of primary drug resistance to isoniazid was known to be less than 4% and was either stable or declining, therapy with two and three drug regimens was considered adequate. If community rates of INH resistance are currently less than 4%, an initial treatment regimen with less than four drugs may be considered.

Streptomycin is also indicated for therapy of tuberculosis when one or more of the above drugs is contraindicated because of toxicity or intolerance. The management of tuberculosis has become more complex as a consequence of increasing rates of drug resistance and concomitant HIV infection. Additional consultation from experts in the treatment of tuberculosis may be desirable in those settings.

2. Non-tuberculosis infections: The use of streptomycin should be limited to the treatment of infections caused by bacteria which have been shown to be susceptible to the antibacterial effects of streptomycin and which are not amenable to therapy with less potentially toxic agents.

a. *Pasteurella pestis* (plague),
b. *Francisella tularensis* (tularemia),
c. *Brucella,*

d. *Calymmatobacterium granulomatis* (donovanosis, granuloma inguinale),

e. *H. ducreyi* (chancroid),

f. *H. influenzae* (in respiratory, endocardial, and meningeal infections—concomitantly with another antibacterial agent),

g. *K. pneumoniae* pneumonia (concomitantly with another antibacterial agent),

h. *E. coli, Proteus, A. aerogenes, K. pneumoniae,* and *Enterococcus faecalis* in urinary tract infections,

i. *Streptococcus* viridans, *Enterococcus faecalis* (in endocardial infections—concomitantly with penicillin),

j. Gram-negative bacillary bacteremia (concomitantly with another antibacterial agent).

CONTRAINDICATIONS

A history of clinically significant hypersensitivity to streptomycin is a contraindication to its use. Clinically significant hypersensitivity to other aminoglycosides may contraindicate the use of streptomycin because of the known cross-sensitivity of patients to drugs in this class.

WARNINGS

Ototoxicity: Both vestibular and auditory dysfunction can follow the administration of streptomycin. The degree of impairment is directly proportional to the dose and duration of streptomycin administration, to the age of the patient, to the level of renal function and to the amount of underlying existing auditory dysfunction. The ototoxic effects of the aminoglycosides, including streptomycin, are potentiated by the co-administration of ethacrynic acid, mannitol, furosemide and possibly other diuretics.

The vestibulotoxic potential of streptomycin exceeds that of its capacity for cochlear toxicity. Vestibular damage is heralded by headache, nausea, vomiting and disequilibrium. Early cochlear injury is demonstrated by the loss of high frequency hearing. Appropriate monitoring and early discontinuation of the drug may permit recovery prior to irreversible damage to the sensorineural cells.

Sulfites: Streptomycin contains sodium metabisulfite, a sulfite that may cause allergic type reactions including anaphylactic symptoms and life-threatening or less severe asthmatic episodes in certain susceptible people. The overall prevalence of sulfite sensitivity in the general population is unknown and probably low. Sulfite sensitivity is seen more frequently in asthmatic than in non-asthmatic people.

Pregnancy: Streptomycin can cause fetal harm when administered to a pregnant woman. Because streptomycin readily crosses the placental barrier, caution in use of the drug is important to prevent ototoxicity in the fetus. If this drug is used during pregnancy, or if the patient becomes pregnant while taking this drug, the patient should be apprised of the potential hazard to the fetus.

PRECAUTIONS

General: Baseline and periodic caloric stimulation tests and audiometric tests are advisable with extended streptomycin therapy. Tinnitus, roaring noises, or a sense of fullness in the ears indicates need for audiometric examination or termination of streptomycin therapy or both.

Care should be taken by individuals handling streptomycin for injection to avoid skin sensitivity reactions. As with all intramuscular preparations, Streptomycin Sulfate Injection should be injected well within the body of a relatively large muscle and care should be taken to minimize the possibility of damage to peripheral nerves. (See DOSAGE AND ADMINISTRATION.)

Extreme caution must be exercised in selecting a dosage regimen in the presence of preexisting renal insuffiency. In severely uremic patients a single dose may produce high blood levels for several days and the cumulative effect may produce ototoxic sequelae. When streptomycin must be given for prolonged periods of time alkalinization of the urine may minimize or prevent renal irritation.

A syndrome of apparent central nervous system depression, characterized by stupor and flaccidity, occasionally coma and deep respiratory depression, has been reported in very young infants in whom streptomycin dosage had exceeded the recommended limits. Thus, infants should not receive streptomycin in excess of the recommended dosage.

In the treatment of venereal infections such as granuloma inguinale, and chancroid, if concomitant syphilis is suspected, suitable laboratory procedures such as a dark field examination should be performed before the start of treatment, and monthly serologic tests should be done for at least four months.

As with other antibiotics, use of this drug may result in overgrowth of nonsusceptible organisms, including fungi. If superinfection occurs, appropriate therapy should be instituted.

Drug Interactions: The ototoxic effects of the aminoglycosides, including streptomycin, are potentiated by the co-administration of ethacrynic acid, furosemide, mannitol and possibly other diuretics.

Pregnancy: Category D: See WARNINGS section.

Nursing Mothers: Because of the potential for serious adverse reactions in nursing infants from streptomycin, a decision should be made whether to discontinue nursing or to discontinue the drug, taking into account the importance of the drug to the mother.

Pediatric Use: (See DOSAGE AND ADMINISTRATION.)

ADVERSE REACTIONS

The following reactions are common: vestibular ototoxicity (nausea, vomiting, and vertigo); paresthesia of face; rash; fever; urticaria; angioneurotic edema; and eosinophilia.

The following reactions are less frequent: cochlear ototoxicity (deafness); exfoliative dermatitis; anaphylaxis; azotemia; leucopenia; thrombocytopenia, pancytopenia; hemolytic anemia; muscular weakness; and amblyopia.

Vestibular dysfunction resulting from the parenteral administration of streptomycin is cumulatively related to the total daily dose. When 1.8 to 2 g/day are given, symptoms are likely to develop in the large percentage of patients—especially in the elderly or patients with impaired renal function—within four weeks. Therefore, it is recommended that caloric and audiometric tests be done prior to, during, and following intensive therapy with streptomycin in order to facilitate detection of any vestibular dysfunction and/or impairment of hearing which may occur.

Vestibular symptoms generally appear early and usually are reversible with early detection and cessation of streptomycin administration. Two to three months after stopping the drug, gross vestibular symptoms usually disappear, except for the relative inability to walk in total darkness or on very rough terrain.

Although streptomycin is the least nephrotoxic of the aminoglycosides, nephrotoxicity does occur rarely.

Clinical judgment as to termination of therapy must be exercised when side effects occur.

DOSAGE AND ADMINISTRATION

Intramuscular Route Only

Adults: The preferred site is the upper outer quadrant of the buttock, (*i.e.*, gluteus maximus), or the mid-lateral thigh.

Children: It is recommended that intramuscular injections be given preferably in the mid-lateral muscles of the thigh. In infants and small children the periphery of the upper outer quadrant of the gluteal region should be used only when necessary, such as in burn patients, in order to minimize the possibility of damage to the sciatic nerve.

The deltoid area should be used only if well developed such as in certain adults and older children, and then only with caution to avoid radial nerve injury. Intramuscular injections should not be made into the lower and mid-third of the upper arm. As with all intramuscular injections, aspiration is necessary to help avoid inadvertent injection into a blood vessel.

Injection sites should be alternated. As higher doses or more prolonged therapy with streptomycin may be indicated for more severe or fulminating infections (endocarditis, meningitis, etc.), the physician should always take adequate measures to be immediately aware of any toxic signs or symptoms occurring in the patient as a result of streptomycin therapy.

1. TUBERCULOSIS: The standard regimen for the treatment of drug susceptible tuberculosis has been two months of INH, rifampin and pyrazinamide followed by four months of INH and rifampin (patients with concomitant infection with tuberculosis and HIV may require treatment for a longer period). When streptomycin is added to this regimen because of suspected or proven drug resistance (see **INDICATIONS AND USAGE** section), the recommended dosing for streptomycin is as follows:

	Daily	Twice Weekly	Thrice Weekly
Children	20–40 mg/kg Max 1 g	25–30 mg/kg Max 1.5 g	25–30 mg/kg Max 1.5 g
Adults	15 mg/kg Max 1 g	25–30 mg/kg Max 1.5 g	25–30 mg/kg Max 1.5 g

Streptomycin is usually administered daily as a single intramuscular injection. A total dose of not more than 120 g over the course of therapy should be given unless there are no other therapeutic options. In patients older than 60 years of age the drug should be used at a reduced dosage due to the risk of increased toxicity. (See **BOXED WARNING**).

Therapy with streptomycin may be terminated when toxic symptoms have appeared, when impending toxicity is feared, when organisms become resistant, or when full treatment effect has been obtained. The total period of drug treatment of tuberculosis is a minimum of 1 year; however, indications for terminating therapy with streptomycin may occur at any time as noted above.

2. TULAREMIA: One to 2 g daily in divided doses for 7 to 14 days until the patient is afebrile for 5 to 7 days.

3. PLAGUE: Two grams of streptomycin daily in two divided doses should be administered intramuscularly. A minimum of 10 days of therapy is recommended.

4. BACTERIAL ENDOCARDITIS:

    a. *Streptococcal endocarditis:* In penicillin-sensitive alpha and non-hemolytic streptococcal endocarditis (penicillin MIC≤0.1 mcg/mL), streptomycin may be used for 2-week treatment concomitantly with penicillin. The streptomycin regimen is 1 g b.i.d. for the first week, and 500 mg b.i.d. for the second week. If the patient is over 60 years of age, the dosage should be 500 mg b.i.d. for the entire 2-week period.

    b. *Enterococcal endocarditis:* Streptomycin in doses of 1 g b.i.d. for 2 weeks and 500 mg b.i.d. for an additional 4 weeks is given in combination with penicillin. Ototoxicity may require termination of the streptomycin prior to completion of the 6-week course of treatment.

5. CONCOMITANT USE WITH OTHER AGENTS: For concomitant use with other agents to which the infecting organism is also sensitive: Streptomycin is considered a second-line agent for the treatment of gram-negative bacillary bacteremia, meningitis, and pneumonia; brucellosis; granuloma inguinale; chancroid; and urinary tract infection.

For adults: 1 to 2 grams in divided doses every six to twelve hours for moderate to severe infections. Doses should generally not exceed 2 grams per day.

For children: 20 to 40 mg/kg/day (8 to 20 mg/lb/day) in divided doses every 6 to 12 hours. (Particular care should be taken to avoid excessive dosage in children.)

Parenteral drug products should be inspected visually for particulate matter and discoloration prior to administration, whenever solution and container permit.

HOW SUPPLIED

Streptomycin Sulfate Injection, USP is supplied in packages of 10 ampules (NDC 0049-0620-33). Each ampule contains streptomycin sulfate equivalent to 1 g of streptomycin in 2.5 mL.

Store under refrigeration at 36° to 46°F (2° to 8°C).

REFERENCES

[1] National Committee for Clinical Laboratory Standards. Performance Standards for Antimicrobial Disk Susceptibility Tests—Fourth Edition. Approved Standard NCCLS Document M2-A4. Vol. 10, No. 7. NCCLS, Villanova, PA 1990.

70-4895-00-0   Issued April 1993

VIBRAMYCIN® Hyclate   ℞
[*vī "bra-mī 'sin*]
doxycycline hyclate for injection
INTRAVENOUS
For Intravenous Use Only

DESCRIPTION

Vibramycin (doxycycline hyclate for injection) Intravenous is a broad–spectrum antibiotic synthetically derived from oxytetracycline, and is available as Vibramycin Hyclate (doxycycline hydrochloride hemiethanolate hemihydrate). The chemical designation of this light-yellow crystalline powder is alpha-6-deoxy-5-oxytetracycline. Doxycycline has a high degree of lipoid solubility and a low affinity for calcium binding. It is highly stable in normal human serum.

ACTIONS

Doxycycline is primarily bacteriostatic and thought to exert its antimicrobial effect by the inhibition of protein synthesis. Doxycycline is active against a wide range of gram-positive and gram-negative organisms.

The drugs in the tetracycline class have closely similar antimicrobial spectra and cross resistance among them is common. Microorganisms may be considered susceptible to doxycycline (likely to respond to doxycycline therapy) if the minimum inhibitory concentration (M.I.C.) is not more than 4.0 mcg/mL. Microorganisms may be considered intermediate (harboring partial resistance) if the M.I.C. is 4.0 to 12.5 mcg/mL and resistant (not likely to respond to therapy) if the M.I.C. is greater than 12.5 mcg/mL.

Susceptibility plate testing: If the Kirby-Bauer method of disc susceptibility testing is used, a 30 mcg doxycycline disc should give a zone of at least 16 mm when tested against a doxycycline-susceptible bacterial strain. A tetracycline disc may be used to determine microbial susceptibility. If the Kirby-Bauer method of disc susceptibility testing is used, a 30 mcg tetracycline disc should give a zone of at least 19 mm when tested against a tetracycline-susceptible bacterial strain.

Tetracyclines are readily absorbed and are bound to plasma proteins in varying degree. They are concentrated by the liver in the bile, and excreted in the urine and feces at high concentrations and in a biologically active form.

Following a single 100 mg dose administered in a concentration of 0.4 mg/mL in a one-hour infusion, normal adult volunteers average a peak of 2.5 mcg/mL, while 200 mg of a concentration of 0.4 mg/mL administered over two hours averaged a peak of 3.6 mcg/mL.

Excretion of doxycycline by the kidney is about 40 percent/72 hours in individuals with normal function (creatinine clearance about 75 mL/min.). This percentage excretion may fall as low as 1-5 percent/72 hours in individuals with severe renal insufficiency (creatinine

clearance below 10 mL/min.). Studies have shown no significant difference in serum half-life of doxycycline (range 18-22 hours) in individuals with normal and severely impaired renal function.

Hemodialysis does not alter this serum half-life of doxycycline.

INDICATIONS

Doxycycline is indicated in infections caused by the following microorganisms:
> Rickettsiae (Rocky Mountain spotted fever, typhus fever, and the typhus group, Q fever, rickettsialpox and tick fevers).
> *Mycoplasma pneumoniae* (PPLO, Eaton Agent).
> Agents of psittacosis and ornithosis.
> Agents of lymphogranuloma venereum and granuloma inguinale.
> The spirochetal agent of relapsing fever (*Borrelia recurrentis*).

The following gram-negative microorganisms:
> *Haemophilus ducreyi* (chancroid),
> *Pasteurella pestis* and *Pasteurella tularensis,*
> *Bartonella bacilliformis,*
> *Bacteroides* species,
> *Vibrio comma* and *Vibrio fetus,*
> *Brucella* species (in conjunction with streptomycin).

Because many strains of the following groups of microorganisms have been shown to be resistant to tetracyclines, culture and susceptibility testing are recommended.

Doxycycline is indicated for treatment of infections caused by the following gram-negative microorganisms when bacteriologic testing indicates appropriate susceptibility to the drug:
> *Escherichia coli,*
> *Enterobacter aerogenes* (formerly *Aerobacter aerogenes),*
> *Shigella* species,
> *Mima* species and *Herellea* species,
> *Haemophilus influenzae* (respiratory infections),
> *Klebsiella* species (respiratory and urinary infections).

Doxycycline is indicated for treatment of infections caused by the following gram-positive microorganisms when bacteriologic testing indicates appropriate susceptibility to the drug:
Streptococcus species:
> Up to 44 percent of strains of *Streptococcus pyogenes* and 74 percent of *Streptococcus faecalis* have been found to be resistant to tetracycline drugs. Therefore, tetracyclines should not be used for streptococcal disease unless the organism has been demonstrated to be sensitive. For upper respiratory infections due to group A beta-hemolytic streptococci, penicillin is the usual drug of choice, including prophylaxis of rheumatic fever.
> *Diplococcus pneumoniae,*
> *Staphylococcus aureus*, respiratory, skin and soft tissue infections. Tetracyclines are not the drugs of choice in the treatment of any type of staphylococcal infections.

When penicillin is contraindicated, doxycycline is an alternative drug in the treatment of infections due to:

Neisseria gonorrhoeae and *N. meningitidis,*
Treponema pallidum and *Treponema pertenue* (syphilis and yaws),
Listeria monocytogenes,
Clostridium species,
Bacillus anthracis,
Fusobacterium fusiforme (Vincent's infection),
Actinomyces species.

In acute intestinal amebiasis, doxycycline may be a useful adjunct to amebicides.

Doxycycline is indicated in the treatment of trachoma, although the infectious agent is not always eliminated, as judged by immunofluorescence.

CONTRAINDICATIONS

This drug is contraindicated in persons who have shown hypersensitivity to any of the tetracyclines.

WARNINGS

THE USE OF DRUGS OF THE TETRACYCLINE CLASS DURING TOOTH DEVELOPMENT (LAST HALF OF PREGNANCY, INFANCY AND CHILDHOOD TO THE AGE OF 8 YEARS) MAY CAUSE PERMANENT DISCOLORATION OF THE TEETH (YELLOW-GRAY-BROWN). This adverse reaction is more common during long-term use of the drugs but has been observed following repeated short-term courses. Enamel hypoplasia has also been reported. *TETRACYCLINE DRUGS, THEREFORE, SHOULD NOT BE USED IN THIS AGE GROUP UNLESS OTHER DRUGS ARE NOT LIKELY TO BE EFFECTIVE OR ARE CONTRAINDICATED.*

Photosensitivity manifested by an exaggerated sunburn reaction has been observed in some individuals taking tetracyclines. Patients apt to be exposed to direct sunlight or ultraviolet light should be advised that this reaction can occur with tetracycline drugs, and treatment should be discontinued at the first evidence of skin erythema.

The antianabolic action of the tetracyclines may cause an increase in BUN. Studies to date indicate that this does not occur with the use of doxycycline in patients with impaired renal function.

Usage in Pregnancy

(See above WARNINGS about use during tooth development.)

Vibramycin Intravenous has not been studied in pregnant patients. It should not be used in pregnant women unless, in the judgment of the physician, it is essential for the welfare of the patient.

Results of animal studies indicate that tetracyclines cross the placenta, are found in fetal tissues and can have toxic effects on the developing fetus (often related to retardation of skeletal development). Evidence of embryotoxicity has also been noted in animals treated early in pregnancy.

Usage in Children

The use of Vibramycin Intravenous in children under 8 years is not recommended because safe conditions for its use have not been established.

(See above WARNINGS about use during tooth development.)

As with other tetracyclines, doxycycline forms a stable calcium complex in any bone-forming tissue. A decrease in the fibula growth rate has been observed in prematures given oral tetracycline in doses of 25 mg/kg every 6 hours. This reaction was shown to be reversible when the drug was discontinued.

Tetracyclines are present in the milk of lactating women who are taking a drug in this class.

PRECAUTIONS

As with other antibiotic preparations, use of this drug may result in overgrowth of nonsusceptible organisms, including fungi. If superinfection occurs, the antibiotic should be discontinued and appropriate therapy instituted. In venereal diseases when coexistent syphilis is suspected, a dark field examination should be done before treatment is started and the blood serology repeated monthly for at least 4 months.

Because tetracyclines have been shown to depress plasma prothrombin activity, patients who are on anticoagulant therapy may require downward adjustment of their anticoagulant dosage.

In long-term therapy, periodic laboratory evaluation of organ systems, including hematopoietic, renal, and hepatic studies should be performed.

All infections due to group A beta-hemolytic streptococci should be treated for at least 10 days.

Since bacteriostatic drugs may interfere with the bactericidal action of penicillin, it is advisable to avoid giving tetracycline in conjunction with penicillin.

ADVERSE REACTIONS

Gastrointestinal: anorexia, nausea, vomiting, diarrhea, glossitis, dysphagia, enterocolitis, and inflammatory lesions (with monilial overgrowth) in the anogenital region. Hepatotoxicity has been reported rarely. These reactions have been caused by both the oral and parenteral administration of tetracyclines.

Skin: maculopapular and erythematous rashes. Exfoliative dermatitis has been reported but is uncommon. Photosensitivity is discussed above. (See WARNINGS.)

Renal toxicity: Rise in BUN has been reported and is apparently dose related. (See WARNINGS.)

Hypersensitivity reactions: urticaria, angioneurotic edema, anaphylaxis, anaphylactoid purpura, pericarditis and exacerbation of systemic lupus erythematosus.

Bulging fontanels in infants and benign intracranial hypertension in adults have been reported in individuals receiving full therapeutic dosages. These conditions disappeared rapidly when the drug was discontinued.

Blood: Hemolytic anemia, thrombocytopenia, neutropenia and eosinophilia have been reported.

When given over prolonged periods, tetracyclines have been reported to produce brown-black microscopic discoloration of thyroid glands. No abnormalities of thyroid function studies are known to occur.

DOSAGE AND ADMINISTRATION

Note: Rapid administration is to be avoided. Parenteral therapy is indicated only when oral therapy is not indicated. Oral therapy should be instituted as soon as possible. If intravenous therapy is given over prolonged periods of time, thrombophlebitis may result.

THE USUAL DOSAGE AND FREQUENCY OF ADMINISTRATION OF VIBRAMYCIN I.V. (100-200 MG/DAY) DIFFERS FROM THAT OF THE OTHER TETRACYCLINES (1-2 G/DAY). EXCEEDING THE RECOMMENDED DOSAGE MAY RESULT IN AN INCREASED INCIDENCE OF SIDE EFFECTS. Studies to date have indicated that Vibramycin at the usual recommended doses does not lead to excessive accumulation of the antibiotic in patients with renal impairment.

Adults: The usual dosage of Vibramycin I.V. is 200 mg on the first day of treatment administered in one or two doses. Subsequent daily dosage is 100 to 200 mg depending upon the severity of infection, with 200 mg administered in one or two infusions.

In the treatment of primary and secondary syphilis, the recommended dosage is 300 mg daily for at least 10 days.

For children above eight years of age: The recommended dosage schedule for children weighing 100 pounds or less is 2 mg/lb of body weight on the first day of treatment, administered in one or two infusions. Subsequent daily dosage is 1 to 2 mg/lb of body weight given as one or two infusions, depending on the severity of the infection. For children over 100 pounds the usual adult dose should be used. (See WARNINGS Section for Usage in Children.)

General: The duration of infusion may vary with the dose (100 to 200 mg per day), but is usually one to four hours. A recommended minimum infusion time for 100 mg of a 0.5 mg/mL solution is one hour. Therapy should be continued for at least 24-48 hours after symptoms and fever have subsided. The therapeutic antibacterial serum activity will usually persist for 24 hours following recommended dosage.

Intravenous solutions should not be injected intramuscularly or subcutaneously. Caution should be taken to avoid the inadvertent introduction of the intravenous solution into the adjacent soft tissue.

PREPARATION OF SOLUTION

To prepare a solution containing 10 mg/mL, the contents of the vial should be reconstituted with 10 mL (for the 100 mg/vial container) or 20 mL (for the 200 mg/vial container) of Sterile Water for Injection or any of the ten intravenous infusion solutions listed below. Each 100 mg of Vibramycin (i.e., withdraw entire solution from the 100 mg vial) is further diluted with 100 mL to 1000 mL of the intravenous solutions listed below. Each 200 mg of Vibramycin (i.e., withdraw entire solution from the 200 mg vial) is further diluted with 200 mL to 2000 mL of the following intravenous solutions:

1. Sodium Chloride Injection, USP
2. 5% Dextrose Injection, USP
3. Ringer's Injection, USP
4. Invert Sugar, 10% in Water
5. Lactated Ringer's Injection, USP
6. Dextrose 5% in Lactated Ringer's
7. Normosol-M® in D5-W (Abbott)
8. Normosol-R® in D5-W (Abbott)
9. Plasma-Lyte® 56 in 5% Dextrose (Travenol)
10. Plasma-Lyte® 148 in 5% Dextrose (Travenol)

This will result in desired concentrations of 0.1 to 1.0 mg/mL. Concentrations lower than 0.1 mg/mL or higher than 1.0 mg/mL are not recommended.

Stability

Vibramycin IV is stable for 48 hours in solution when diluted with Sodium Chloride Injection, USP, or 5% Dextrose Injection, USP, to concentrations between 1.0 mg/mL and 0.1 mg/ mL and stored at 25°C. Vibramycin IV in these solutions is stable under fluorescent light for 48 hours, but must be protected from direct sunlight during storage and infusion. Reconstituted solutions (1.0 to 0.1 mg/mL) may be stored up to 72 hours prior to start of infusion if refrigerated and protected from sunlight and artificial light. Infusion must then be completed within 12 hours. Solutions must be used within these time periods or discarded.

Vibramycin IV, when diluted with Ringer's Injection, USP, or Invert Sugar, 10% in Water, or Normosol-M® in D5-W (Abbott), or Normosol-R®in D5-W (Abbott), or Plasma-Lyte® 56 in 5% Dextrose (Travenol), or Plasma-Lyte® 148 in 5% Dextrose (Travenol) to a concentration between 1.0 mg/mL and 0.1 mg/mL, must be completely infused within 12 hours after reconstitution to ensure adequate stability. During infusion, the solution must be protected from direct sunlight. Reconstituted solutions (1.0 to 0.1 mg/mL) may be stored up to 72 hours prior to start of infusion if refrigerated and protected from sunlight and artifical light. Infusion must then be completed within 12 hours. Solutions must be used within these time periods or discarded.

When diluted with Lactated Ringer's Injection, USP, or Dextrose 5% in Lactated Ringer's, infusion of the solution (ca. 1.0 mg/mL) or lower concentrations (not less than 0.1 mg/mL) must be completed within six hours after reconstitution to ensure adequate stability. During infusion, the solution must be protected from direct sunlight. Solutions must be used within this time period or discarded.

Solutions of Vibramycin (doxycycline hyclate for injection) at a concentration of 10 mg/mL in Sterile Water for Injection, when frozen immediately after reconstitution are stable for 8 weeks when stored at −20°C. If the product is warmed, care should be taken to avoid heating it after the thawing is complete. Once thawed the solution should not be refrozen.

HOW SUPPLIED

Vibramycin (doxycycline hyclate for injection) Intravenous is available as a sterile powder in a vial containing doxycycline hyclate equivalent to 100 mg of doxycycline with 480 mg of ascorbic acid, packages of 5 (NDC 0049-0960-77), and in individually packaged vials containing doxycycline hyclate equivalent to 200 mg of doxycycline with 960 mg of ascorbic acid (0049–0980–81).

65-1940-00-2

LITERATURE AVAILABLE

Yes.

Revised March 1991

VIBRAMYCIN® Calcium ℞
[vī-brə 'mīs-ᵊn]
doxycycline calcium
oral suspension
SYRUP

VIBRAMYCIN® Hyclate
[vī-brə 'mīs-ᵊn]
doxycycline hyclate
CAPSULES

VIBRAMYCIN® Monohydrate
[vī-brə 'mīs-ᵊn]
doxycycline monohydrate
for ORAL SUSPENSION

VIBRA–TABS®
[vī-brə 'mīs-ᵊn]
doxycycline hyclate
FILM COATED TABLETS

DESCRIPTION

Vibramycin is a broad-spectrum antibiotic synthetically derived from oxytetracycline, and is available as Vibramycin Monohydrate (doxycycline monohydrate); Vibramycin Hyclate and Vibra-Tabs (doxycycline hydrochloride hemiethanolate hemihydrate); and Vibramycin Calcium (doxycycline calcium) for oral administration.
The structural formula of doxycycline monohydrate is

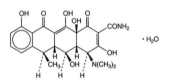

with a molecular formula of $C_{22}H_{24}N_2O_8 \cdot H_2O$ and a molecular weight of 462.46. The chemical designation for doxycycline is 4-(Dimethylamino)-1, 4, 4a, 5, 5a, 6, 11, 12a-octahydro-3, 5, 10, 12, 12a-pentahydroxy-6-methyl-1, 11-dioxo-2-naphthacenecarboxamide monohydrate. The molecular formula for doxycycline hydrochloride hemiethanolate hemihydrate is $(C_{22}H_{24}N_2O_8 \cdot HCl)_2 \cdot C_2H_6O \cdot H_2O$ and the molecular weight is 1025.89. Doxycycline is a light-yellow crystalline powder. Doxycycline hyclate is soluble in water, while doxycycline monohydrate is very slightly soluble in water.
Doxycycline has a high degree of lipoid solubility and a low affinity for calcium binding. It is highly stable in normal human serum. Doxycycline will not degrade into an epianhydro form.
Inert ingredients in the syrup formulation are: apple flavor; butylparaben; calcium chloride; carmine; glycerin; hydrochloric acid; magnesium aluminum silicate; povidone; propylene glycol; propylparaben; raspberry flavor; simethicone emulsion; sodium hydroxide; sodium metabisulfite; sorbitol solution; water.

Inert ingredients in the capsule formulations are: hard gelatin capsules (which may contain Blue 1 and other inert ingredients); magnesium stearate; microcrystalline cellulose; sodium lauryl sulfate.
Inert ingredients for the oral suspension formulation are: carboxymethylcellulose sodium; Blue 1; methylparaben; microcrystalline cellulose; propylparaben; raspberry flavor; Red 28; simethicone emulsion; sucrose.
Inert ingredients for the tablet formulation are: ethylcellulose; hydroxypropyl methylcellulose; magnesium stearate; microcrystalline cellulose; propylene glycol; sodium lauryl sulfate; talc; titanium dioxide; Yellow 6 Lake.

CLINICAL PHARMACOLOGY

Tetracyclines are readily absorbed and are bound to plasma proteins in varying degree. They are concentrated by the liver in the bile, and excreted in the urine and feces at high concentrations and in a biologically active form. Doxycycline is virtually completely absorbed after oral administration.
Following a 200 mg dose, normal adult volunteers averaged peak serum levels of 2.6 mcg/mL of doxycycline at 2 hours decreasing to 1.45 mcg/mL at 24 hours. Excretion of doxycycline by the kidney is about 40%/72 hours in individuals with normal function (creatinine clearance about 75 mL/min.). This percentage excretion may fall as low as 1–5%/72 hours in individuals with severe renal insufficiency (creatinine clearance below 10 mL/min.). Studies have shown no significant difference in serum half-life of doxycycline (range 18–22 hours) in individuals with normal and severely impaired renal function. Hemodialysis does not alter serum half-life.
Results of animal studies indicate that tetracyclines cross the placenta and are found in fetal tissues.

Microbiology
The tetracyclines are primarily bacteriostatic and are thought to exert their antimicrobial effect by the inhibition of protein synthesis. The tetracyclines, including doxycycline, have a similar antimicrobial spectrum of activity against a wide range of gram-positive and gram-negative organisms. Cross-resistance of these organisms to tetracyclines is common.

Gram-Negative Bacteria
Neisseria gonorrhoeae
Calymmatobacterium granulomatis
Haemophilus ducreyi
Haemophilus influenzae
Yersinia pestis (formerly *Pasteurella pestis*)
Francisella tularensis (formerly *Pasteurella tularensis*)
Vibro cholera (formerly *Vibrio comma*)
Bartonella bacilliformis
Brucella species
Because many strains of the following groups of gram-negative microorganisms have been shown to be resistant to tetracyclines, culture and susceptibility testing are recommended:

Escherichia coli
Klebsiella species
Enterobacter aerogenes
Shigella species
Acinetobacter species (formerly *Mima* species and *Herellea* species)
Bacteroides species

Gram-Positive Bacteria

Because many strains of the following groups of gram-positive microorganisms have been shown to be resistant to tetracycline, culture and susceptibility testing are recommended. Up to 44 percent of strains of *Streptococcus pyogenes* and 74 percent of *Streptococcus faecalis* have been found to be resistant to tetracycline drugs. Therefore, tetracycline should not be used for streptococcal disease unless the organism has been demonstrated to be susceptible.

Streptococcus pyogenes
Streptococcus pneumoniae
Enterococcus group *(Streptococcus faecalis* and *Streptococcus faecium)*
Alpha-hemolytic streptococci (viridans group)

Other Microorganisms

Rickettsiae
Chlamydia psittaci
Chlamydia trachomatis
Mycoplasma pneumoniae
Ureaplasma urealyticum
Borrelia recurrentis
Treponema pallidum
Treponema pertenue
Clostridium species
Fusobacterium fusiforme
Actinomyces species
Bacillus anthracis
Propionbacterium acnes
Entamoeba species
Balantidium coli
Plasmodium falciparum

Doxycycline has been found to be active against the asexual erythrocytic forms of *Plasmodium falciparum* but not against the gametocytes of *P. falciparum*. The precise mechanism of action of the drug is not known.

Susceptibility tests: Diffusion techniques: Quantitative methods that require measurement of zone diameters give the most precise estimate of the susceptibility of bacteria to antimicrobial agents. One such standard procedure[1] which has been recommended for use with disks to test susceptibility of organisms to doxycycline uses the 30-mcg tetracycline-class disk or the 30-mcg doxycycline disk. Interpretation involves the correlation of the diameter obtained in the disk test with the minimum inhibitory concentration (MIC) for tetracycline or doxycycline, respectively.

Reports from the laboratory giving results of the standard single-disk susceptibility test with a 30-mcg tetracycline-class disk or the 30-mcg doxycycline disk should be interpreted according to the following criteria:

Zone Diameter (mm)		Interpretation
tetracycline	doxycycline	
≥19	≥16	Susceptible
15–18	13–15	Intermediate
≤14	≤12	Resistant

A report of "Susceptible" indicates that the pathogen is likely to be inhibited by generally achievable blood levels. A report of "Intermediate" suggests that the organism would be susceptible if a high dosage is used or if the infection is confined to tissues and fluids in which high antimicrobial levels are attained. A report of "Resistant" indicates that achievable concentrations are unlikely to be inhibitory, and other therapy should be selected.

Standardized procedures require the use of laboratory control organisms. The 30-mcg tetracycline-class disk or the 30-mcg doxycycline disk should give the following zone diameters:

Organism	Zone Diameter (mm)	
	tetracycline	doxycycline
E. coli ATCC 25922	18–25	18–24
S. aureus ATCC 25923	19–28	23–29

Dilution techniques: Use a standardized dilution method[2] (broth, agar, microdilution) or equivalent with tetracycline powder. The MIC values obtained should be interpreted according to the following criteria:

MIC (mcg/mL)	Interpretation
≤4	Susceptible
8	Intermediate
≥16	Resistant

As with standard diffusion techniques, dilution methods require the use of laboratory control organisms. Standard tetracycline powder should provide the following MIC values:

Organism	MIC (mcg/mL)
E. coli ATCC 25922	1.0–4.0
S. aureus ATCC 29213	0.25–1.0
E. faecalis ATCC 29212	8–32
P. aeruginosa ATCC 27853	8–32

INDICATIONS AND USAGE

Treatment:

Doxycycline is indicated for the treatment of the following infections:

Rocky mountain spotted fever, typhus fever and the typhus group, Q fever, rickettsialpox, and tick fevers caused by Rickettsiae.

Respiratory tract infections caused by *Mycoplasma pneumoniae*.

Lymphogranuloma venereum caused by *Chlamydia trachomatis*.

Psittacosis (ornithosis) caused by *Chlamydia psittaci*.

Trachoma caused by *Chlamydia trachomatis*, although the infectious agent is not always eliminated as judged by immunofluorescence. Inclusion conjunctivitis caused by *Chlamydia trachomatis*.

Uncomplicated urethral, endocervical or rectal infections in adults caused by *Chlamydia trachomatis.*

Nongonococcal urethritis caused by *Ureaplasma urealyticum.*

Relapsing fever due to *Borrelia recurrentis.*

Doxycycline is also indicated for the treatment of infections caused by the following gram-negative microorganisms:

Chancroid caused by *Haemophilus ducreyi.*

Plague due to *Yersinia pestis* (formerly *Pasteurella pestis*).

Tularemia due to *Francisella tulerensis* (formerly *Pasteurella tulerensis*).

Cholera caused by *Vibrio cholerae* (formerly *Vibrio comma*).

Campylobacter fetus infections caused by *Campylobacter fetus* (formerly *Vibrio fetus*).

Brucellosis due to *Brucella* species (in conjunction with streptomycin).

Bartonellosis due to *Bartonella bacilliformis.*

Granuloma inguinale caused by *Calymmatobacterium granulomatis.*

Because many strains of the following groups of microorganisms have been shown to be resistant to doxycycline, culture and susceptibility testing are recommended.

Doxycycline is indicated for treatment of infections caused by the following gram-negative microorganisms, when bacteriologic testing indicates appropriate susceptibility to the drug:

Escherichia coli.

Enterobacter aerogenes (formerly *Aerobacter aerogenes*).

Shigella species.

Acinetobacter species (formerly *Mima* species and *Herellea* species).

Respiratory tract infections caused by *Haemophilus influenzae.*

Respiratory tract and urinary tract infections caused by *Klebsiella* species.

Doxycycline is indicated for treatment of infections caused by the following gram-positive microorganisms when bacteriologic testing indicates appropriate susceptibility to the drug:

Upper respiratory infections caused by *Streptococcus pneumoniae* (formerly *Diplococcus pneumoniae*).

When penicillin is contraindicated, doxycycline is an alternative drug in the treatment of the following infections:

Uncomplicated gonorrhea caused by *Neisseria gonorrhoeae.*

Syphilis caused by *Treponema pallidum.*

Yaws caused by *Treponema pertenue.*

Listeriosis due to *Listeria monocytogenes.*

Anthrax due to *Bacillus anthracis.*

Vincent's infection caused by *Fusobacterium fusiforme.*

Actinomycosis caused by *Actinomyces israelii.*

Infections caused by *Clostridium* species.

In acute intestinal amebiasis, doxycycline may be a useful adjunct to amebicides.

In severe acne, doxycycline may be useful adjunctive therapy.

Prophylaxis:

Doxycycline is indicated for the prophylaxis of malaria due to *Plasmodium falciparum* in short-term travelers (<4 months) to areas with chloroquine and/or pyrimethamine-sulfadoxine resistant strains. See DOSAGE AND ADMINISTRATION section and Information for Patients subsection of the PRECAUTIONS section.

CONTRAINDICATIONS

This drug is contraindicated in persons who have shown hypersensitivity to any of the tetracyclines.

WARNINGS

THE USE OF DRUGS OF THE TETRACYCLINE CLASS DURING TOOTH DEVELOPMENT (LAST HALF OF PREGNANCY, INFANCY AND CHILDHOOD TO THE AGE OF 8 YEARS) MAY CAUSE PERMANENT DISCOLORATION OF THE TEETH (YELLOW-GRAY-BROWN). This adverse reaction is more common during long-term use of the drugs, but has been observed following repeated short-term courses. Enamel hypoplasia has also been reported. TETRACYCLINE DRUGS, THEREFORE, SHOULD NOT BE USED IN THIS AGE GROUP UNLESS OTHER DRUGS ARE NOT LIKELY TO BE EFFECTIVE OR ARE CONTRAINDICATED.

All tetracyclines form a stable calcium complex in any bone-forming tissue. A decrease in fibula growth rate has been observed in prematures given oral tetracycline in doses of 25 mg/kg every 6 hours. This reaction was shown to be reversible when the drug was discontinued.

Results of animal studies indicate that tetracyclines cross the placenta, are found in fetal tissues, and can have toxic effects on the developing fetus (often related to retardation of skeletal development). Evidence of embryotoxicity has also been noted in animals treated early in pregnancy. If any tetracycline is used during pregnancy or if the patient becomes pregnant while taking this drug, the patient should be apprised of the potential hazard to the fetus.

The antianabolic action of the tetracyclines may cause an increase in BUN. Studies to date indicate that this does not occur with the use of doxycycline in patients with impaired renal function.

Photosensitivity manifested by an exaggerated sunburn reaction has been observed in some individuals taking tetracyclines. Patients apt to be exposed to direct sunlight or ultraviolet light should be advised that this reaction can occur with tetracycline drugs, and treatment should be discontinued at the first evidence of skin erythema.

Vibramycin Syrup contains sodium metabisulfite, a sulfite that may cause allergic-type reactions including anaphylactic symptoms and life-threatening or less severe asthmatic episodes in certain susceptible people. The overall prevalence of sulfite sensitivity in the general population is unknown and probably low. Sulfite sensitivity is seen more frequently in asthmatic than in non-asthmatic people.

PRECAUTIONS

General

As with other antibiotic preparations, use of this drug may result in overgrowth of nonsusceptible organisms, including fungi. If superinfection occurs, the antibiotic should be discontinued and appropriate therapy instituted. Bulging fontanels in infants and benign intracranial hypertension in adults have been reported in individuals receiving tetracyclines. These conditions disappeared when the drug was discontinued.

Incision and drainage or other surgical procedures should be performed in conjunction with antibiotic therapy, when indicated.

Doxycycline offers substantial but not complete suppression of the asexual blood stages of *Plasmodium* strains.

Doxycycline does not suppress *P. falciparum's* sexual blood stage gametocytes. Subjects completing this prophylactic regimen may still transmit the infection to mosquitoes outside endemic areas.

Information for Patients

Patients taking doxycycline for malaria prophylaxis should be advised:

—that no present-day antimalarial agent, including doxycycline, guarantees protection against malaria.

—to avoid being bitten by mosquitoes by using personal protective measures that help avoid contact with mosquitoes, especially from dusk to dawn (e.g., staying in well-screened areas, using mosquito nets, covering the body with clothing, and using an effective insect repellent.)

—that doxycycline prophylaxis:

—should begin 1–2 days before travel to the malarious area,

—should be continued daily while in the malarious area and after leaving the malarious area,

—should be continued for 4 further weeks to avoid development of malaria after returning from an endemic area,

—should not exceed 4 months.

All patients taking doxycycline should be advised:

—to avoid excessive sunlight or artificial ultraviolet light while receiving doxycycline and to discontinue therapy if phototoxicity (e.g., skin eruption, etc.) occurs. Sunscreen or sunblock should be considered. (See WARNINGS.)

—to drink fluids liberally along with doxycycline to reduce the risk of esophageal irritation and ulceration. (See ADVERSE REACTIONS.)

—that the absorption of tetracyclines is reduced when taken with foods, especially those which contain calcium. However, the absorp-

tion of doxycycline is not markedly influenced by simultaneous ingestion of food or milk. (See DRUG INTERACTIONS.)

—that the absorption of tetracyclines is reduced when taking bismuth subsalicylate. (See DRUG INTERACTIONS.)

—that the use of doxycycline might increase the incidence of vaginal candidiasis.

Laboratory Tests

In venereal disease, when co-existent syphilis is suspected, dark field examinations should be done before treatment is started and the blood serology repeated monthly for at least 4 months.

In long-term therapy, periodic laboratory evaluation of organ systems, including hematopoietic, renal, and hepatic studies, should be performed.

Drug Interactions

Because tetracyclines have been shown to depress plasma prothrombin activity, patients who are on anticoagulant therapy may require downward adjustment of their anticoagulant dosage.

Since bacteriostatic drugs may interfere with the bactericidal action of penicillin, it is advisable to avoid giving tetracyclines in conjunction with penicillin.

Absorption of tetracyclines is impaired by antacids containing aluminum, calcium, or magnesium, and iron-containing preparations.

Absorption of tetracyclines is impaired by bismuth subsalicylate.

Barbiturates, carbamazepine, and phenytoin decrease the half-life of doxycycline.

The concurrent use of tetracycline and Penthrane (methoxyflurane) has been reported to result in fatal renal toxicity.

Concurrent use of tetracycline may render oral contraceptives less effective.

Drug/Laboratory Test Interactions

False elevations of urinary catecholamine levels may occur due to interference with the fluorescence test.

Carcinogenesis, Mutagenesis, Impairment of Fertility

Long-term studies in animals to evaluate carcinogenic potential of doxycycline have not been conducted. However, there has been evidence of oncogenic activity in rats in studies with the related antibiotics, oxytetracycline (adrenal and pituitary tumors), and minocycline (thyroid tumors).

Likewise, although mutagenicity studies of doxycycline have not been conducted, positive results in *in vitro* mammalian cell assays have been reported for related antibiotics (tetracycline, oxytetracycline).

Doxycycline administered orally at dosage levels as high as 250 mg/kg/day had no apparent effect on the fertility of female rats. Effect on male fertility has not been studied.

Pregnancy Category

Teratogenic effects: Category "D" — (See WARNINGS).

Nonteratogenic effects: (See WARNINGS).

Labor and Delivery

The effect of tetracyclines on labor and delivery is unknown.

Nursing Mothers

Tetracyclines are excreted in human milk. Because of the potential for serious adverse reactions in nursing infants from doxycycline, a decision should be made whether to discontinue nursing or to discontinue the drug, taking into account the importance of the drug to the mother. (See WARNINGS.)

Pediatric Use

See WARNINGS and DOSAGE AND ADMINISTRATION.

ADVERSE REACTIONS

Due to oral doxycycline's virtually complete absorption, side effects of the lower bowel, particularly diarrhea, have been infrequent. The following adverse reactions have been observed in patients receiving tetracyclines:

Gastrointestinal: anorexia, nausea, vomiting, diarrhea, glossitis, dysphagia, enterocolitis, and inflammatory lesions (with monilial overgrowth) in the anogenital region. Hepatotoxicity has been reported rarely. These reactions have been caused by both the oral and parenteral administration of tetracyclines. Rare instances of esophagitis and esophageal ulcerations have been reported in patients receiving capsule and tablet forms of the drugs in the tetracycline class. Most of these patients took medications immediately before going to bed. (See DOSAGE AND ADMINISTRATION.)

Skin: maculopapular and erythematous rashes. Exfoliative dermatitis has been reported but is uncommon. Photosensitivity is discussed above. (See WARNINGS.)

Renal toxicity: Rise in BUN has been reported and is apparently dose related. (See WARNINGS.)

Hypersensitivity reactions: urticaria, angioneurotic edema, anaphylaxis, anaphylactoid purpura, serum sickness, pericarditis, and exacerbation of systemic lupus erythematosus.

Blood: Hemolytic anemia, thrombocytopenia, neutropenia, and eosinophilia have been reported.

Other: bulging fontanels in infants and intracranial hypertension in adults. (See PRECAUTIONS—General.)

When given over prolonged periods, tetracyclines have been reported to produce brownblack microscopic discoloration of the thyroid gland. No abnormalities of thyroid function studies are known to occur.

OVERDOSAGE

In case of overdosage, discontinue medication, treat symptomatically and institute supportive measures. Dialysis does not alter serum half-life and thus would not be of benefit in treating cases of overdosage.

DOSAGE AND ADMINISTRATION

THE USUAL DOSAGE AND FREQUENCY OF ADMINISTRATION OF DOXYCYCLINE DIFFERS FROM THAT OF THE OTHER TETRACYCLINES. EXCEEDING THE RECOMMENDED DOSAGE MAY RESULT IN AN INCREASED INCIDENCE OF SIDE EFFECTS. Adults: The usual dose of oral doxycycline is 200 mg on the first day of treatment (administered 100 mg every 12 hours) followed by a maintenance dose of 100 mg/day. The maintenance dose may be administered as a single dose or as 50 mg every 12 hours.

In the management of more severe infections (particularly chronic infections of the urinary tract), 100 mg every 12 hours is recommended.

For children above eight years of age: The recommended dosage schedule for children weighing 100 pounds or less is 2 mg/lb of body weight divided into two doses on the first day of treatment, followed by 1 mg/lb of body weight given as a single daily dose or divided into two doses, on subsequent days. For more severe infections up to 2 mg/lb of body weight may be used. For children over 100 lb the usual adult dose should be used.

The therapeutic antibacterial serum activity will usually persist for 24 hours following recommended dosage.

When used in streptococcal infections, therapy should be continued for 10 days.

Administration of adequate amounts of fluid along with capsule and tablet forms of drugs in the tetracycline class is recommended to wash down the drugs and reduce the risk of esophageal irritation and ulceration. (See ADVERSE REACTIONS.)

If gastric irritation occurs, it is recommended that doxycycline be given with food or milk. The absorption of doxycycline is not markedly influenced by simultaneous ingestion of food or milk.

Studies to date have indicated that administration of doxycycline at the usual recommended doses does not lead to excessive accumulation of the antibiotic in patients with renal impairment.

Uncomplicated gonococcal infections in adults (except anorectal infections in men): 100 mg, by mouth, twice a day for 7 days. As an alternate single visit dose, administer 300 mg stat followed in one hour by a second 300 mg dose. The dose may be administered with food, including milk or carbonated beverage, as required.

Uncomplicated urethral, endocervical, or rectal infection in adults caused by *Chlamydia trachomatis:* 100 mg by mouth twice a day for 7 days.

Nongonococcal urethritis (NGU) caused by *C. trachomatis* or *U. urealyticum:* 100 mg by mouth twice a day for 7 days.

Syphilis—early: Patients who are allergic to penicillin should be treated with doxycycline 100 mg by mouth twice a day for 2 weeks.

Syphilis of more than one year's duration: Patients who are allergic to penicillin should be treated with doxycycline 100 mg by mouth twice a day for 4 weeks.

Acute epididymo-orchitis caused by *N. gonor-rhoeae:* 100 mg, by mouth, twice a day for at least 10 days.

Acute epididymo-orchitis caused by *C. tracho-matis:* 100 mg, by mouth, twice a day for at least 10 days.

For prophylaxis of malaria: For adults, the recommended dose is 100 mg daily. For children over 8 years of age, the recommended dose is 2 mg/kg given once daily up to the adult dose. Prophylaxis should begin 1–2 days before travel to the malarious area. Prophylaxis should be continued daily during travel in the malarious area and for 4 weeks after the traveler leaves the malarious area.

HOW SUPPLIED

Vibramycin Hyclate (doxycycline hyclate) is available in capsules containing doxycycline hyclate equivalent to:

50 mg doxycycline
bottles of 50 (NDC 0069-0940-50),
unit-dose pack of 100 (10 × 10's) (NDC 0069-0940-41).
The capsules are white and light blue and are imprinted with "VIBRA" on one half and "PFIZER 094" on the other half.

100 mg doxycycline
bottles of 50 (NDC 0069-0950-50) and 500 (NDC 0069-0950-73),
unit-dose pack of 100 (10 × 10's) (NDC 0069-0950-41).
The capsules are light blue and are imprinted with "VIBRA" on one half and "PFIZER 095" on the other half.

Vibra-Tabs (doxycycline hyclate) is available in salmon colored film-coated tablets containing doxycycline hyclate equivalent to:

100 mg doxycycline
bottles of 50 (NDC 0069-0990-50) and 500 (NDC 0069-0990-73),
The tablets are imprinted on one side with "VIBRA-TABS" and "PFIZER 099" on the other side.

Vibramycin Calcium Syrup (doxycycline calcium oral suspension) is available as a raspberry-apple flavored oral suspension. Each teaspoonful (5 mL) contains doxycycline calcium equivalent to 50 mg of doxycycline: bottles of 1 oz (30 mL) (NDC 0069-0971-51), and 1 pint (473 mL) (NDC 0069-0971-93).

Vibramycin Monohydrate (doxycycline mono-hydrate) for Oral Suspension is available as a raspberry-flavored, dry powder for oral suspension. When reconstituted, each teaspoonful (5 mL) contains doxycycline monohydrate equivalent to 25 mg of doxycycline: 2 oz (60 mL) bottles (NDC 0069-0970-65).

All products are to be stored below 86°F (30°C) and dispensed in tight, light-resistant containers (USP). The unit dose packs should also be stored in a dry place.

ANIMAL PHARMACOLOGY AND ANIMAL TOXICOLOGY

Hyperpigmentation of the thyroid has been produced by members of the tetracycline class in the following species: in rats by oxytetracycline, doxycycline, tetracycline PO_4, and methacycline; in minipigs by doxycycline, minocycline, tetracycline PO_4, and methacycline; in dogs by doxycycline and minocycline; in monkeys by minocycline.

Minocycline, tetracycline PO_4, methacycline, doxycycline, tetracycline base, oxytetracycline HCl, and tetracycline HCl were goitrogenic in rats fed a low iodine diet. This goitrogenic effect was accompanied by high radioactive iodine uptake. Administration of minocycline also produced a large goiter with high radioiodine uptake in rats fed a relatively high iodine diet.

Treatment of various animal species with this class of drugs has also resulted in the induction of thyroid hyperplasia in the following: in rats and dogs (minocycline); in chickens (chlortetracycline); and in rats and mice (oxytetracycline). Adrenal gland hyperplasia has been observed in goats and rats treated with oxytetracycline.

REFERENCES

1. National Committee for Clinical Laboratory Standards, *Performance Standards for Antimicrobial Disk Susceptibility Tests,* Fourth Edition. Approved Standard NCCLS Document M2-A4, Vol. 10, No. 7 NCCLS, Villanova, PA, April 1990.
2. National Committee for Clinical Laboratory Standards, *Methods for Dilution Antimicrobial Susceptibility Tests for Bacteria that Grow Aerobically,* Second Edition. Approved Standard NCCLS Document M7-A2, Vol. 10, No. 8 NCCLS, Villanova, PA, April 1990.

69-1680-00-5   Revised April 1993

Section 5

Vaccine Information

Anthrax Vaccine

Overview

Anthrax vaccines induce active immunity against *Bacillus anthracis*. Three vaccines have been developed: U.S. and U.K. vaccines (avirulent) and Russian vaccine (live attenuated spore formulation). This monograph discusses the U.S. vaccine (Anthrax Vaccine Adsorbed).

The dosing recommendation for anthrax prophylaxis in persons at risk of exposure is three doses of the U.S. vaccine separated by 2-week intervals, followed by additional doses at 6, 12, and 18 months; yearly booster doses should be given. For use after exposure to anthrax aerosol, the vaccine is used in conjunction with antibiotic therapy (eg, ciprofloxacin); one vaccine dose should be given as soon as possible, with repeat doses at 2 and 4 weeks. Local reactions (eg, erythema, tenderness, pruritus) have been reported frequently; systemic reactions (eg, fever) are uncommon.

Only limited efficacy data are available for any anthrax vaccine. The US vaccine is indicated as prophylaxis in individuals at risk of anthrax exposure (eg, industrial exposures). Anthrax vaccine is also indicated for postexposure prophylaxis in combination with antibiotics. It is not presently known if the vaccine will provide effective protection in the event of an inhalational-based, bioterrorist attack. However, pivotal studies in non-human primates demonstrate approximately 95% protection against *Bacillus anthracis* infection following exposure to more than 100 times the median lethal dose of the pathogen.

Dosing Information

Dosage Forms

Anthrax Vaccine Adsorbed is manufactured in the U.S. by BioPort Corporation. Formerly known as MDPH-PA and MDPH-AVA, it carries the trade name BioThrax™. It can be requested through the CDC in the event of a biowarfare emergency. Information regarding the vaccine and its use in military personnel can be obtained from the United States Department of Defense (Anthrax Vaccine Immunization Program; AVIP) at (877)438-8222, or from the AVIP web site: http://www.anthrax.osd.mil (CDC, 2000).

Storage and Stability

Anthrax vaccines are temperature-sensitive (Frank, 1999). Vials of Anthrax Vaccine Adsorbed (BioPort) should be stored at 2 to 8 degrees Centigrade (35 to 46 degrees Fahrenheit). Vials should not be used after the expiration date on the package (Prod Info Anthrax Vaccine Adsorbed, 1999; Frank, 1999).

Adult Dosage

PREEXPOSURE PROPHYLAXIS:
Anthrax Vaccine Adsorbed
(BioPort) is administered subcutaneously. The recommended dose
for primary immunization is 0.5
mL SC at 0, 2, and 4 weeks, followed by additional 0.5-mL injections at 6, 12, and 18 months.
Thereafter, yearly booster doses
(0.5 mL) are indicated to maintain
immunity (Friedlander et al, 1999;
Prod Info Anthrax Vaccine
Adsorbed, 1999; Ibrahim et al,
1999; Anon, 1998). The administration technique provided by the
manufacturer should be followed;
in particular, vials should be shak-
en thoroughly before use and different subcutaneous sites should be
used for each injection (Prod Info
Anthrax Vaccine Adsorbed, 1999).

POSTEXPOSURE PROPHYLAX-
IS: For postexposure prophylaxis,
including inhalational exposure
following a bioterrorist attack, the
vaccine is indicated in conjunction
with chemoprophylaxis. One dose
(0.5 mL) of the vaccine should be
given as soon as possible postexposure, with repeat doses 2 and 4
weeks later (total of 3 doses)
(CDC, 1999).

One of the following antibiotics
should also be administered:

- Oral ciprofloxacin 500 mil-
  ligrams (mg) twice daily
- Levofloxacin 500 mg once daily
- Ofloxacin 400 mg twice daily

If fluoroquinolones are unavailable,
doxycycline 100 mg twice daily
should be given (CDC, 1999).
Therapy should continue until
exposure to *B. anthracis* has been
excluded. If exposure is confirmed,
therapy should be continued for 4
weeks and until three doses of vaccine have been administered, or for
8 weeks if vaccine is unavailable
(CDC, 1999).

Pediatric Dosage

Anthrax vaccines have not been
studied in children. However, the
Working Group on Civilian
Biodefense suggests that the U.S.
vaccine is likely to be safe and
effective in pediatric patients
(Inglesby et al, 1999).

Onset and Duration

Initial response is seen in 3 weeks
(Anon, 1998). For the U.S. vaccine, protective antibody responses
have been reported approximately
7 days after the second dose (during full immunization schedule)
(Anon, 1998). However, a clear
minimum therapeutic antibody
level (ie, anti-protective antigen
(PA) level) has not been established in animals or humans
(Ibrahim et al, 1999; Nass, 1999).

Geometric mean titers of anti-protective antigen antibody (APAA)
increased significantly as the dosing
interval between the first and second
dose of the anthrax vaccine increased
from 2 to 4 weeks. In 2 retrospective

analyses of banked sera taken from vaccinated at-risk employees (group 1, n=89 and group 2, n=51, respectively) of the U.S. Army Research Institute of Infectious Diseases (USAMRIID), APAA titers increased 3-to-4 fold with increasing dosing intervals (from 2 weeks, to 3 and 4 weeks, respectively) in groups 1 and 2 (p=0.0005, and p=0.029 to 0.013, respectively), (Pittman et al, 2001). Anti-PA, anti-LF, and anti-EF levels have been determined by ELISA (Ibrahim et al, 1999).

Response lasts 6 to 12 months (booster periods) (Ibrahim et al, 1999). Following a full immunization schedule, protective antibody titers are reportedly achieved with each annual booster dose, and remain stable for approximately 6 months (Ibrahim et al, 1999).

Contraindications

- Prior hypersensitivity or other severe reaction to any anthrax vaccine
- Contraindicated in persons who have recovered after a prior clinical exposure to anthrax

Precautions

Use Cautiously In:
- Immunocompromised patients (potential for blunted antibody response)
- Patients undergoing corticosteroids/other immunosuppressant therapy (potential for blunted antibody response). In patients receiving short courses of steroids, the manufacturer of the U.S. vaccine recommends deferment of vaccination until therapy is completed; in those receiving long-term therapy, an extra vaccine dose is suggested a month or more after discontinuation
- Infection/febrile illness (potential confusion of vaccine adverse effects with those of the illness)
- Patients with allergies, asthma, or history of hypersensitivity to other medications (enhanced risk of allergic phenomena/anaphylaxis)
- Pregnancy or breastfeeding period (animal/human data unavailable)
- The U.S. vaccine has not been studied in subjects under 18 years of age or over 65 years of age. However, the Working Group on Civilian Biodefense suggests that it is likely to be safe and effective in children (Inglesby et al, 1999).

Teratogenicity
U.S. Food and Drug Administration Pregnancy Category C (Prod Info Anthrax Vaccine Adsorbed, 1999). The propensity of this vaccine to cause teratogenic or other adverse fetal effects has not been investigated in animal studies. There are no published reports of its use in pregnant women.

Adverse Reactions

Central Nervous System
Headache, malaise, and lassitude are infrequent systemic adverse effects (less than 0.5% of patients)

associated with the U.S. vaccine, and are transient (Friedlander et al, 1999; Prod Info Anthrax Vaccine Adsorbed, 1999).

Gastrointestinal

Transient nausea and heartburn have occurred rarely after injection of the U.S. vaccine (less than 0.5% of patients); these symptoms are transient (Friedlander et al, 1999; Prod Info Anthrax Vaccine Adsorbed, 1999).

Skin

Cutaneous adverse effects of the U.S. vaccine have included erythema, tenderness, pruritus, forearm edema, and subcutaneous nodules. Most reactions are transient. Antihistamines may be useful.

In safety studies with the U.S. vaccine (including follow-up of vaccinated military personnel), mild local cutaneous reactions (1 to 5 cm in diameter) consisting of erythema, local tenderness, and induration, have occurred in up to 30% of subjects. These reactions generally developed within 24 hours of the second injection and began to subside within 48 hours; they have tended to increase in severity until the fifth injection, and were milder thereafter. Moderate local inflammatory reactions (5 to 12 cm) with or without pruritus have been seen in 1 to 5% of recipients/doses (after the second injection) (Friedlander et al, 1999; Prod Info Anthrax Vaccine Adsorbed, 1999; Anon, 1998).

Severe reactions (12 cm or greater), characterized by extensive forearm edema plus local inflammatory reactions, have occurred in less than 1% of patients/doses (Friedlander et al, 1999; Prod Info Anthrax Vaccine Adsorbed, 1999). In one safety study (CDC) involving approximately 7,000 subjects (16,000 injections of U.S. vaccine), mild and moderate local reactions were seen after 3 to 20% and 1 to 3% of doses, respectively; the incidence of severe reactions (12 cm or greater) was less than 1%. This study evaluated four lots of the vaccine (Friedlander et al, 1999).

The pattern of onset and increased severity of reactions with repeat injections suggests an allergic reaction to the vaccine or components. Antihistamines have been useful for local reactions (Ibrahim et al, 1999).

Subcutaneous nodules at the injection site have been reported occasionally, and have persisted in some subjects (Friedlander et al, 1999; Prod Info Anthrax Vaccine Adsorbed, 1999).

Musculoskeletal

Infrequently, muscle or joint aches have accompanied injection of the U.S. vaccine (less than 0.5% of patients). These symptoms are transient (Friedlander et al, 1999; Prod Info Anthrax Vaccine Adsorbed, 1999).

Other

Unconfirmed reports linking Gulf War-related illness to the anthrax vaccine have focused upon the adjuvant component squalene as a potential causative agent. Antisqualene antibodies were detected in hundreds of military personnel presenting with post-Gulf War illness. Squalene-containing adjuvants have been effective in boosting the immunity produced by the vaccine in animal studies. However, military officials have denied use of unlicensed adjuvants (Nass, 1999).

Fevers with or without chills are rare systemic effects of the U.S. vaccine (less than 0.5% in larger studies), and are transient (Friedlander et al, 1999; Prod Info Anthrax Vaccine Adsorbed, 1999). The manufacturer recommends discontinuation of the immunization protocol if fever is observed.

Hypersensitivity reactions are possible. A 34-year-old man developed a delayed hypersensitivity-type reaction within 24 hours of receiving the third in a series of injections of anthrax vaccine. The patient presented with dyspnea, diaphoresis, pallor, and urticarial wheals on his face, arms, and torso. He recovered within 2 hours of receiving treatment with hydrocortisone and diphenhydramine (Swanson-Biearman & Krenzelok, 2001). By history, the patient described feeling diaphoretic and weak approximately 24 hours after the second anthrax vaccination but did not report it.

Monitoring Parameters

Therapeutic

1. Anti-PA levels in selected patients
2. Culture *(B. anthracis)*. C/S indicated particularly in exposed patients

Toxic

1. Temperature; first-dose blood pressure and signs of anaphylaxis in patients with allergies or prior allergic responses to medications (may be impractical during mass postexposure prophylaxis)
2. Other signs/symptoms of toxicity (eg, local reactions, flu-like symptoms)

Place in Therapy

In general, the U.S. anthrax vaccine is indicated for primary immunization in individuals at risk of exposure to anthrax spores (eg, high-risk industries). This was expanded to include all U.S. Armed Forces in a 1998 mandate from the Secretary of Defense, although the decision was met with criticism. Some military personnel have refused the vaccine (Morris, 1999). Although the threat of a biowarfare attack is real, mass vaccination of civilians is not recommended, related in part to limited U.S. vaccine supplies (and modest production capacity); even if sufficient vaccine were available, specialists would not recommend population wide immunization at present due to cost, logistics, and the unlikely occurrence of a bioterrorist attack in any given community (Inglesby et al, 1999; CDC, 1999). However, the vaccine is indicated for postexposure vaccination in conjunction with chemoprophylaxis following a proven biologic event (CDC, 1999). No clinical data exist for children, but the vaccine will most likely be safe for administration (Inglesby et al, 1999).

Whether the U.S. vaccine will actually prove effective in the event of a bioterrorist attack is of major concern. No studies have evaluated the field efficacy of the current BioPort vaccine (Anthrax Vaccine Adsorbed). As mutant *Bacillus anthracis* strains can be developed, potentially unaffected by chemoprophylaxis or the current vaccine, this concern is of even greater significance. Newer and higher-efficacy vaccines with a simpler dose regimen are urgently needed.

Pharmacology

Anthrax Vaccine Adsorbed induces active immunity against *Bacillus anthracis* (Prod Info, 1999; Turnbull, 1991). Development of an anthrax vaccine for human use is based on the two exotoxin complexes (binary toxins) released by *Bacillus anthracis,* lethal toxin and edema toxin.

Edema toxin consists of edema factor (EF), a calmodulin-dependent adenylate cyclase, and protective antigen (PA), an 82 kilodalton (kD) protein binding moiety which enables entry of EF into host cells; edema toxin is responsible for the edema and neutrophil-function impairment associated with cutaneous anthrax infection (Dixon et al, 1999; Ibrahim et al, 1999; Nass, 1999; Farrar, 1994).

Lethal toxin is composed of lethal factor (LF), a zinc metalloprotease, plus PA to permit cell entry; stimulation of tumor necrosis factor-alpha (TNF-alpha) and interleukin-1-beta by lethal toxin appear at least partly responsible for shock and sudden death in anthrax (Dixon et al, 1999; Ibrahim et al, 1999).

Both toxin complexes are encoded by plasmid pXO1, and the presence of PA is a requirement for their virulence (Ibrahim et al, 1999; Nass, 1999). The virulence of *B. anthracis* is also dependent upon its outer capsule, encoded by plasmid pXO2, which protects the vegetative bacilli against phagocytosis and antibacterial proteins (Dixon et al, 1999; Ibrahim et al, 1999).

Although serologically active, the EF and LF components are nonimmunizing when administered alone (Ibrahim et al, 1999). However, protection is observed when either toxin is combined with PA, and even PA alone is immunizing. Most human vaccines have emphasized high PA contents (Demicheli et al, 1998; Ibrahim et al, 1999).

The U.S. vaccine, Anthrax Vaccine Adsorbed (BioPort) is a culture filtrate from the toxigenic, nonencapsulated strain of *Bacillus anthracis* V770-NP1-R (from a case of bovine anthrax in 1951). This strain appears to produce PA in the relative absence of LF and EF. The PA in the vaccine is produced anaerobically, which creates higher yields than under aerobic conditions. The PA is then adsorbed onto preformed aluminum hydroxide gel. It was licensed in 1970.

The PA content can only be measured indirectly (ie, antibody titers in animals/humans). Based on antibody-titer determinations, the PA content appears significantly higher, and LF and EF contents are significantly lower, compared to the UK vaccine. The U.S. vaccine is avirulent, incapable of causing disease. A disadvantage is the multiple injections required over an 18-month period for immunity. Other deficiencies include the undefined nature of the vaccine's components, the need for numerous booster doses, a relatively high incidence of adverse effects, variable efficacy against virulent *B. anthracis* strains in animal studies, and variable potency between vaccine lots (Nass, 1999; Ibrahim et al, 1999; Demicheli et al, 1998).

Newer vaccines of potentially greater efficacy and safety are under development. Some strategies include use of new adjuvants, recombinant PA vaccines, mutant PA vaccines, and a DNA vaccine encoding PA (Gu et al, 1999; Ivins et al, 1995; Barnard & Friedlander, 1999; Ibrahim et al, 1999). An oral vaccine (lactobacillus vector) is under evaluation (Zegers et al, 1999). Although some of these vaccines have been tested in animals, none is considered ready for routine clinical use.

Animal challenge studies have been used extensively to evaluate the efficacy of anthrax vaccines. In guinea pigs and mice, results have been highly variable, related in part to differing study designs, challenge strains, vaccine batches, and doses. Better responses have been observed in rabbits and nonhuman primates. It is known that different animal species vary in their sensitivity/resistance to anthrax; how closely animal responses parallel those in humans is not known, and clear extrapolation to humans is not possible.

Following parenteral anthrax-spore challenge of guinea pigs vaccinated with the U.S. vaccine, survival rates have ranged from 0 to 100%; rates were generally higher in animals receiving Vollum strains (characteristically vaccine-sensitive) compared to the Ames, New Hampshire, and penicillin-resistant strains (characteristically vaccine resistant, although this is a relative term). In mice, protection was inadequate against all anthrax strains (Turnbull, 1991; Nass, 1999).

In guinea-pig aerosol spore challenge studies (the most likely route of a biological warfare attack), survival rates of 23 to 71% and 0 to 100% (usual, 50%) have been observed with the U.S. and U.K. vaccines, respectively (Nass, 1999; Friedlander et al, 1999). In rabbits immunized with the U.S. vaccine, survival rates of over 95% have been reported following aerosol anthrax challenge in some studies (Friedlander et al, 1999). Collective data from other studies indicated aerosol-challenge survival in 52 of 55 nonhuman primates administered two doses of U.S. vaccine (Friedlander et al, 1999; Inglesby et al, 1999); many of these studies used the Ames strain. When used for postexposure prophylaxis (monkeys), one study reported that poor survival rates were seen when the U.S. vaccine was given on days 1 and 15 following aerosol challenge (Friedlander et al, 1993).

References

- Anon: Anthrax vaccine. *Med Lett Drugs Ther* 1998; 40(1026):52-53.
- Anon: Anthrax vaccine trial of 1,500 patients could begin in summer 2000. *FDC Reports: The Pink Sheet*. February 28, 2000; 62(9):24-25.
- Anon: Recommendations of the Advisory Committee on Immunization Practices (ACIP): Use of anthrax vaccine in the United States. *MMWR* 2000; 49(RR15):1-20.
- Baillie LWJ, Fowler K & Turnbull PCB: Human immune responses to the UK human anthrax vaccine. *J Appl Microbiol* 1999; 87:306-308.
- Barnard JP & Friedlander AM: Vaccination against anthrax with attenuated recombinant strains of *Bacillus anthracis* that produce protective antigen. *Infect Immun* 1999; 67(2):562-567.
- CDC: Bioterrorism alleging use of anthrax and interim guidelines for management - United States, 1998. *MMWR* 1999; 48:69-73.
- CDC: Surveillance for adverse effects associated with anthrax vaccination - U.S. Department of Defense, 1998-2000. *MMWR* 2000; 49(16):341-345.
- Demicheli V, Rivetti D, Deeks JJ et al: The effectiveness and safety of vaccines against human anthrax: a systematic review. *Vaccine* 1998; 16(9/10):880-884.
- Dixon TC, Meselson M, Gullemin J et al: Anthrax. *N Engl J Med* 1999; 341(11):815-826.
- Farrar WE: Anthrax: virulence and vaccines. *Ann Intern Med* 1994; 121(5):379-380.
- Frank KJ: Monitoring temperature-sensitive vaccines and immunologic drugs, including anthrax vaccine. *Am J Health-*

Syst Pharm 1999; 56:2052-2055.

- Freedman ML & Thorpe MEC: Anthrax: a case report and a short review of anthrax in Australia. *Med J Aust* 1969; 1(4):154-157.

- Friedlander AM, Pittman PR & Parker GW: Anthrax vaccine: evidence for safety and efficacy against inhalational anthrax. *JAMA* 1999; 282(22):2104-2106.

- Friedlander AM, Welkos SL, Pitt MLM et al: Postexposure prophylaxis against experimental inhalation anthrax. *J Infect Dis* 1993; 167:1239-1242.

- Gordon SM: The threat of bioterrorism: a reason to learn more about anthrax and small-pox. *Cleveland Clin J Med* 1999; 66(10):592-600.

- Gu M-L, Leppla SH & Klinman DM: Protection against anthrax toxin by vaccination with a DNA plasmid encoding anthrax protective antigen. *Vaccine* 1999; 17:340-344.

- Hambleton P, Carman JA & Melling J: Anthrax: the disease in relation to vaccines. *Vaccine* 1984; 2:125-132.

- Ibrahim KH, Brown G, Wright DH et al: *Bacillus anthracis:* medical issues of biological warfare. *Pharmacotherapy* 1999; 19(6):690-701.

- Inglesby TV, Henderson DA, Bartlett JG et al: Anthrax as a biological weapon: medical and public health management. *JAMA* 1999; 281:1735-1745.

- Ivins B, Fellows P, Pitt L et al: Experimental anthrax vaccines: efficacy of adjuvants combined with protective antigen against an aerosol *Bacillus anthracis* spore challenge in guinea pigs. *Vaccine* 1995; 13(18):1779-1784.

- Morris K: U.S. military face punishment for refusing anthrax vaccine. *Lancet* 1999; 353(9147):130.

- Nass M: Anthrax vaccine: model of a response to the biologic warfare threat. *Infect Dis Clin N Am* 1999; 13(1):187-208.

- Parfitt M (ed): *Martindale: The Complete Drug Reference.* London: Pharmaceutical Press (electronic version). Micromedex, Inc., Englewood, CO (edition expired 5/2000).

- Pittman PR, Mangiafico JA, Rossi CA et al: Anthrax vaccine: increasing intervals between the first two doses enhances anti-body response in humans. *Vaccine* 2001; 19:213-216.

- Product Information: Anthrax vaccine adsorbed. BioPort Corporation, Lansing, MI, (PI revised 8/1999) reviewed 4/2000.

- Russell PK: Vaccines in civilian defense against bioterrorism. *Emerg Infect Dis* 1999; 5(4):531-533.

- Swanson-Biearman B & Krenzelok EP: Delayed life-threatening reaction to anthrax vaccine. *Clin Toxicol* 2001; 39(1):81-84.

- Turnbull PCB: Anthrax vac-cines: past, present and future. *Vaccine* 1991; 9(8):533-539.

- Zegers ND, Kluter E, van der Stap H et al: Expression of the protective antigen of *Bacillus anthracis* by *Lactobacillus casei:* towards the development of an oral vaccine against anthrax. *J Appl Microbiol* 1999; 87:309-314.

- Zoon KC: Vaccines, pharmaceutical products, and bioterrorism: challenges for the U.S. Food and Drug Administration. *Emerg Infect Dis* 1999.

Smallpox Vaccine

Overview

Smallpox vaccine (vaccinia virus) is a highly effective immunizing agent against smallpox. A controlled percutaneous dose of approximately 2.5 x 10(5) PFU is given by multiple-puncture technique for routine nonemergency vaccination as well as routine nonemergency revaccination. Adverse reactions reported with smallpox vaccine include vaccinia necrosum, painful facial rash, erythema, herpes simplex infection at the site of vaccination, and allergic reactions.

There is no evidence of smallpox transmission anywhere in the world. At this time smallpox vaccine is indicated only for civilians who are laboratory workers occupationally exposed to smallpox or other closely related orthopox viruses. In the event of an intentional release of smallpox virus (bioterrorism), postrelease vaccination is recommended for the following groups (CDC, 2001):

- Persons who were exposed to the initial release of the virus
- Persons who had face-to-face, household, or close-proximity contact (<6.5 feet or 2 meters) (84) with a confirmed or suspected smallpox patient at any time from the onset of the patient's fever until all scabs have separated
- Personnel involved in the direct medical or public health evaluation, care, or transportation of confirmed or suspected smallpox patients
- Laboratory personnel involved in the collection or processing of clinical specimens from confirmed or suspected smallpox patients
- Other persons who have an increased likelihood of contact with infectious materials from a smallpox patient (e.g., personnel responsible for medical waste disposal, linen disposal or disinfection, and room disinfection in a facility where smallpox patients are present).

Although smallpox vaccination has been suggested for the treatment and prevention of recurrent herpes simplex infection, warts, or other diseases, smallpox vaccine should never be used therapeutically for any of these indications.

Dosing Information

Availability

The production of Dryvax®, manufactured by Wyeth-Ayerst, was discontinued in 1981. However, the Centers for Disease Control and Prevention maintain a supply to protect laboratory workers occupationally exposed to smallpox virus and other closely related orthopox viruses. Postrelease (bioterrorism) vaccination within a few days after exposure may prevent the disease in previously vaccinated patients and prevent death in those not previously vaccinated (CDC, 2001; Anon, 1999). Requests for the vaccine, including the reason for the request, should be referred to:

Center for Disease Control and Prevention
Drug Service
Mailstop D09
1600 Clifton Road
Atlanta, GA 30333
Telephone: (404) 639-3670
Fax: (404) 639-3717

Dosing Information

Storage and Stability
Smallpox vaccine (Dryvax®, Wyeth) is stored at room temperature during transport and is stable for 10 days at this temperature (Prod Info Dryvax®), 1995).

Disposal Procedures
The vaccine vial, the stopper, the diluent cartridge, the needle used for administration, and any cotton or gauze that came in contact with the vaccine should be burned, boiled, or autoclaved before disposal (Prod Info Dryvax®), 1995).

Important Note
Recently vaccinated individuals should prevent contact of the site by unvaccinated individuals; a porous bandage may be used to loosely cover the site and should be changed daily. Vaccinia virus can be cultured from the site of vaccination for up to 21 days after vaccination, and contact transmission of vaccinia has been reported (CDC, 2001).

The CDC can assist physicians in the diagnosis and management of patients with suspected complications of vaccinia vaccination. VIG (Vaccinia immune globulin) is available when indicated (day (404) 639-3670; evenings and weekends (404) 639-3311). Complications should be reported to the Vaccine Adverse Event Reporting System (800-822-7967) or the state or local health department.

Adult Dosage
SMALLPOX PROPHYLAXIS:
Using a bifurcated needle (provided with Dryvax®) pick up a drop of vaccine and deposit it on a clean, dry site of skin. With the same needle (using multiple puncture technique) vaccinate through the drop of vaccine, using 15 rapid punctures. After completion of vaccination, blot off any vaccine remaining on the skin. The vaccination site should be checked 6 to 8 days after vaccination for a response. Each percutaneous dose contains approximately $2.5 \times 10^{(5)}$

PFU of low pathogenicity vaccinia virus (CDC, 2001).

REVACCINATION: Revaccination is recommended for laboratory workers directly involved with smallpox or related orthopox viruses. Revaccination should be administered at least every 10 years. Fifteen needle punctures are recommended for revaccination (CDC, 2001).

POSTRELEASE (BIOTERRORISM) VACCINATION: The recommended dose is the same as that used for smallpox prophylaxis (CDC, 2001).

Pediatric Dosage
SMALLPOX PROPHYLAXIS: Smallpox vaccination is no longer indicated for infants and children for routine nonemergency indications (CDC, 2001).

POSTRELEASE (BIOTERRORISM) VACCINATION: The recommended dose is the same as that used for smallpox prophylaxis (CDC, 2001).

Duration
With a single dose, substantial (but waning) immunity can persist for 10 years or longer (CDC, 2001). With multiple doses, immunity can continue for 30 years (El-Ad et al, 1990). Neutralizing antibodies against smallpox in 140 patients lasted 30 years (geometric mean titer 10.5, 95% confidence interval 6.8 to 16.4), after the patients had been vaccinated in infancy and

again at 8 and 18 years. Routine revaccination beyond the primary injection and two revaccinations is not needed. However, persons at high risk are recommended to receive revaccination regardless of vaccination status.

Contraindications

Contraindications for routine non-emergency vaccination include:
- Infants and children
- Individuals with eczema, other skin conditions, wounds, or burns, or whose household contacts have such conditions
- Persons receiving therapy with radiation, high-dose corticosteroids, or immunosuppressive drugs, or whose household contacts are receiving such therapy
- Individuals with leukemia, lymphomas of any type, and other malignant neoplasms affecting the bone-marrow or lymphatic systems, or whose household contacts have such conditions
- Persons with congenital or acquired deficiencies of the immune system, including individuals infected with the human immunodeficiency virus, or whose household contacts have such conditions
- Pregnancy
- Allergies to the smallpox vaccine components

Contraindications during a smallpox emergency include:
- For individuals exposed to

smallpox virus, there are NO contraindications for vaccination
- For individuals with no exposure to smallpox virus, contraindications for nonemergency use apply.

Precautions

Autoinoculation
Inadvertent autoinoculation to other sites and contact spread of vaccinia from recently vaccinated patients has been reported; any contact with the vaccination site should be avoided.

Teratogenicity
U.S. Food and Drug Administration Pregnancy Category C (Prod Info Dryvax®, 1995). Animal reproduction studies have not been conducted. Smallpox vaccine should NOT be given to a pregnant woman.

Adverse Reactions

Central Nervous System
Although extremely rare, postvaccinial encephalitis is the most serious complication associated with the vaccinia virus vaccine. The majority of cases have occurred in children less than 1 year of age or individuals receiving the primary vaccination. Of affected vaccinees, 25% suffer permanent neurologic sequelae and 15 to 25% die (CDC, 2001).

Ocular
Accidental autoinoculation to the eye may result in vaccinial keratitis

and blindness (CDC, 2001; Prod Info Dryvax®, 1995).

Skin
Eczema vaccinatum occurs in individuals with a history of eczema or other chronic skin conditions and involves a localized or systemic dissemination of vaccinia virus after vaccination. Although generally mild and self-limiting, severe and even fatal cases have been reported in vaccine recipients as well as contacts of vaccine recipients with eczema (CDC, 2001).

Generalized vaccinia, characterized by a self-limiting, vesicular rash, has been reported after smallpox vaccination (CDC, 2001).

Vaccinia necrosum (progressive vaccinia) has occurred almost exclusively in individuals with cellular immunodeficiency; it is a severe, potentially fatal illness characterized by progressive necrosis at the site of vaccination (CDC, 2001).

A 2.5-year-old male developed a painful facial rash with marked erythema and edema following contact with his mother and a sibling who had received a smallpox vaccination 2 weeks earlier. The patient recovered without adverse sequelae (Birrer & Laude, 1981).

Other
The most frequent complication of vaccinia vaccination is the inadvertent inoculation of virus transferred from the vaccination site to another anatomical site; the most common

sites include the face, nose, eyelid, mouth, genitalia, and rectum (CDC, 2001).

Recurrent herpes simplex infection has been noted to occur at the site of smallpox vaccination. This occurrence was reported (Mintz, 1982) in a 27-year-old male who had received repeated (7) smallpox vaccinations to treat a recurrent genital herpes simplex virus infection. Recurrences of herpes simplex infection at the smallpox vaccination site increased from 4 to 6 times per year to a monthly basis. Despite therapy with smallpox vaccination, genital lesions continued unabated. Genital recurrences and deltoid recurrences continued at monthly intervals, however, rarely occurred simultaneously.

For information on hypersensitivity reactions, see Micromedex Drug Consult reference, "Immunizations-Induced Hypersensitivity Reactions."

Drug Interactions

Azathioprine

1. *Summary:* Azathioprine is cleaved in vivo to mercaptopurine. While alterations in specific immune response in transplant patients are difficult to directly relate to the immunosuppression caused by azathioprine, this population has subnormal responses to vaccines (Prod Info Imuran®, 1998). Vaccination with a live vaccine in a patient immunocompromised by a chemotherapeutic agent has resulted in severe and fatal infections (MMWR, 1989; Rosenblaum et al, 1966). One patient experienced disseminated vaccinia infection after receiving a smallpox vaccine while on concomitant methotrexate therapy (Allison, 1968). Live virus and bacterial vaccines should not be administered to a patient receiving an immunosuppressive chemotherapeutic agent. At least three months should elapse between the discontinuation of chemotherapy and vaccination with a live vaccine (MMWR, 1989).

2. *Adverse Effect:* An increased risk of infection by the live vaccine

3. *Clinical Management:* Patients receiving azathioprine should be vaccinated with a live vaccine only when the risk outweighs the benefit.

4. *Severity:* Major

5. *Onset:* Delayed

6. *Documentation:* Fair

7. *Probable Mechanism:* Decreased immune response allows live vaccine to produce infection

Chemotherapeutic Agents

1. *Summary:* Vaccination with a live vaccine in a patient immunocompromised by a chemotherapeutic agent has resulted in severe and fatal infections (MMWR, 1989; Rosenbaum et al, 1966). One

patient experienced disseminated vaccinia infection after receiving a smallpox vaccine while on concomitant methotrexate therapy (Allison, 1968). Live virus and bacterial vaccines should not be administered to a patient receiving an immunosuppressive chemotherapeutic agent. At least three months should elapse between the discontinuation of chemotherapy and vaccination with a live vaccine (MMWR, 1989).

2. *Adverse Effect:* An increased risk of infection by the live vaccine

3. *Clinical Management:* Patients receiving immunosuppressive chemotherapy should not be vaccinated with a live vaccine. In patients with leukemia in remission, allow at least three months between the end of chemotherapy and vaccination with a live vaccine.

4. *Severity:* Major

5. *Onset:* Delayed

6. *Documentation:* Fair

7. *Probable Mechanism:* Decreased immune response allows live vaccine to produce infection

Corticosteroids

1. *Summary:* As a general rule, live-attenuated viral or bacterial vaccines should not be administered to patients who are immunosuppressed as a result of large amounts of corticosteroids (more than 10 mg of prednisone or equivalent for more than two weeks). However, an inadequate

response to inactivated vaccines may also occur with immunosuppression due to large doses of steroids. Low- to moderate-dose short-term systemic corticosteroid therapy (less than 14 days), topical steroid therapy, long-term alternative-day treatment with low to moderate doses of short-acting systemic steroids, and intra-articular, bursal, or tendon injections of corticosteroids should not be considered contraindications to vaccine administration (CDC, 1989). Likewise, doses of steroids given as replacement therapy, such as in Addison's disease, are not considered immunosuppressive (Grabenstein, 1990). The exact interval between discontinuing immunosuppressives and regaining the ability to respond to individual vaccines is not known. Estimates vary from three months to one year (Anon, 1991).

2. *Adverse Effect:* An inadequate immunological response to the vaccine

3. *Clinical Management:* If possible, delay the administration of vaccines, especially live viral or bacterial types, in persons immunosuppressed with large doses of corticosteroids. However, the clinical judgment of the responsible physician should prevail.

4. *Severity:* Moderate

5. *Onset:* Delayed

6. *Documentation:* Fair

7. *Probable Mechanism:* Suppression of the immune system

Cyclosporine

1. *Summary:* Cyclosporine abolishes T-lymphocyte involvement in both cellular and humoral immunity, including interleukin-2 production. Because most vaccines and toxoids require helper T-lymphocyte involvement to achieve an immunologic response, a decreased immune response may occur when immunization is performed during cyclosporine therapy (Grabenstein, 1990). In general, the use of live attenuated vaccines should be avoided in patients receiving cyclosporine (Prod Info Sandimmune®, 1996). The exact interval between discontinuing immunosuppressives and regaining the ability to respond to individual vaccines is not known. Estimates vary from three months to one year (Anon, 1991).

2. *Adverse Effect:* An inadequate immunological response to the vaccine

3. *Clinical Management:* When possible, immunization should occur two to four weeks before initiating therapy with cyclosporine.

4. *Severity:* Moderate

5. *Onset:* Delayed

6. *Documentation:* Fair

7. *Probable Mechanism:* Suppression of the immune system

Cytomegalovirus Immune Globulin

1. *Summary:* Live-virus vaccines may not replicate successfully, and antibody response could be reduced when the vaccine is administered after cytomegalovirus immune globulin because of the presence of antibodies in the immune globulin. Live-virus vaccines should ideally be administered at least three months after therapy with cytomegalovirus immune globulin is discontinued. If the administration of an immune globulin preparation becomes necessary because of exposure to disease, live-virus vaccines can be given simultaneously with the immune globulin at a site remote from that chosen for the immune globulin. Vaccine virus replication and stimulation of immunity will occur one to two weeks after vaccination. Therefore, if the interval between administration of the vaccine and immune globulin is less than 14 days, or if they were administered simultaneously, vaccination should be repeated at least three months after the immune globulin preparation was given, unless serologic testing indicates that adequate antibodies were formed (CDC, 1989; Prod Info CytoGam®, 1995).

2. *Adverse Effect:* Interference with the immune response to the live vaccine

3. *Clinical Management:* The administration of live viral vac-

cines should be deferred, if possible, until three months after the discontinuation of cytomegalovirus immune globulin. If the live-virus vaccine was administered less than 14 days before or at the same time as the immune globulin, vaccination may need to be repeated at least three months after the discontinuation of the immune globulin, unless serologic testing indicates that adequate antibodies were produced.

4. *Severity:* Moderate
5. *Onset:* Delayed
6. *Documentation:* Fair
7. *Probable Mechanism:* Presence of antibodies in the immune globulin

Etanercept

1. *Summary:* Although no data are available regarding the effects of vaccination in patients receiving etanercept therapy, vaccination with live vaccines is not recommended. The possibility exists for etanercept to affect host defenses against infections since the cellular immune response may be altered (Prod Info Enbrel®, 1999).
2. *Adverse Effect:* secondary transmission of infection by the live vaccine
3. *Clinical Management:* The administration of live vaccines is not recommended in patients receiving etanercept.
4. *Severity:* Moderate
5. *Onset:* Delayed

6. *Documentation:* Poor
7. *Probable Mechanism:* Altered cellular immune response

Hepatitis B Immune Globulin

1. *Summary:* Live-virus vaccines may not replicate successfully, and antibody response could be reduced when the vaccine is administered after hepatitis B immune globulin because of the presence of antibodies in the immune globulin. Even though administration of hepatitis B immune globulin did not interfere with measles vaccination, live-virus vaccines should ideally be administered at least three months after therapy with hepatitis B immune globulin is discontinued. If the administration of an immune globulin preparation becomes necessary because of exposure to disease, live-virus vaccines can be given simultaneously with the immune globulin at a site remote from that chosen for the immune globulin. Vaccine virus replication and stimulation of immunity will occur one to two weeks after vaccination. Therefore, if the interval between administration of the vaccine and immune globulin is less than 14 days, or if they were administered simultaneously, vaccination should be repeated at least three months after the immune globulin preparation was given, unless serologic testing indicates that adequate antibodies were formed.

However, ACIP recommendations indicate that neonates who receive hepatitis B immune globulin and hepatitis virus vaccine shortly after birth can receive the MMR vaccine, live, according to the usual immunization schedule (ACIP, 1985; CDC, 1989; Prod Info HyperHep®, 1995; Prod Info Nabi-HB®, 1999).

2. *Adverse Effect:* Interference with the immune response to the live vaccine

3. *Clinical Management:* The administration of live viral vaccines should be deferred, if possible, until three months after the discontinuation of hepatitis B immune globulin. If the live-virus vaccine was administered less than 14 days before or at the same time as the immune globulin, vaccination may need to be repeated at least three months after the discontinuation of the immune globulin, unless serologic testing indicates that adequate antibodies were produced.

4. *Severity:* Moderate

5. *Onset:* Delayed

6. *Documentation:* Fair

7. *Probable Mechanism:* Presence of antibodies in the immune globulin

Immune Globulin

1. *Summary:* Live-virus vaccines may not replicate successfully, and antibody response could be reduced when the vaccine is administered after immune globulin because of the presence of antibodies in the immune globulin. Live-virus vaccines should ideally be administered three months after therapy with intramuscular immune globulin and six months after therapy with intravenous immune globulin. If the administration of an immune globulin preparation becomes necessary because of exposure to disease, live-virus vaccines can be given simultaneously with the immune globulin at a site remote from that chosen for the immune globulin. Vaccine virus replication and stimulation of immunity will occur one to two weeks after vaccination. Therefore, if the interval between administration of the vaccine and immune globulin is less than 14 days, or if they were administered simultaneously, vaccination should be repeated at least three months after the immune globulin preparation was given, unless serologic testing indicates that adequate antibodies were formed (CDC, 1989; Prod Info Gamimune® N, 1995; Prod Info Gammar®, 1990).

2. *Adverse Effect:* Interference with the immune response to the live vaccine

3. *Clinical Management:* The administration of live viral vaccines should be deferred, if possible, until three to six months after the discontinuation of immune globulin, depending on the route of administration of the

immune globulin. If the live-virus vaccine was administered less than 14 days before or at the same time as the immune globulin, vaccination may need to be repeated at least three months after the immune globulin, unless serologic testing indicates that adequate antibodies were produced.

4. *Severity:* Moderate
5. *Onset:* Delayed
6. *Documentation:* Fair
7. *Probable Mechanism:* Presence of antibodies in the immune globulin

Infliximab

1. *Summary:* Although no data are available on the response to vaccination or on the secondary transmission of infection by live vaccines in patients receiving infliximab therapy, it is recommended that live vaccines not be given concurrently (Prod Info Remicade™, 1999).
2. *Adverse Effect:* An increased risk of infection by the live vaccine
3. *Clinical Management:* Vaccination with a live vaccine while receiving infliximab therapy is not recommended.
4. *Severity:* Moderate
5. *Onset:* Delayed
6. *Documentation:* Poor
7. *Probable Mechanism:* Decreased immune response allows live vaccine to produce infection

Leflunomide

1. *Summary:* Although there is no efficacy or safety data available regarding vaccination during leflunomide therapy, the manufacturer of leflunomide recommends that vaccination with a live vaccine not be performed during leflunomide treatment. The long half-life of leflunomide should be taken into consideration following the discontinuation of the drug when administration with a live vaccine is considered. A rapid drug elimination procedure is available to accelerate the elimination of leflunomide (Prod Info Arava™, 1998).
2. *Adverse Effect:* Interference with the immune response to the live vaccine
3. *Clinical Management:* Vaccination with live vaccines is not recommended during therapy with leflunomide. In cases where vaccination is unavoidable, consider interrupting leflunomide therapy and performing the leflunomide elimination procedure prior to vaccination.
4. *Severity:* Moderate
5. *Onset:* Delayed
6. *Documentation:* Poor
7. *Probable Mechanism:* Immunosuppression caused by leflunomide

Rabies Immune Globulin

1. *Summary:* Live-virus vaccines may not replicate successfully, and antibody response could be reduced when the vaccine is

administered after rabies immune globulin because of the presence of antibodies in the immune globulin. Live-virus vaccines should ideally be administered at least three months after therapy with rabies immune globulin is discontinued. If the administration of an immune globulin preparation becomes necessary because of exposure to disease, live-virus vaccines can be given simultaneously with the immune globulin at a site remote from that chosen for the immune globulin. Vaccine virus replication and stimulation of immunity will occur one to two weeks after vaccination. Therefore, if the interval between administration of the vaccine and immune globulin is less than 14 days, or if they were administered simultaneously, vaccination should be repeated at least three months after the immune globulin preparation was given, unless serologic testing indicates that adequate antibodies were formed (CDC, 1989; Prod Info Hyperab®, 1995).

2. *Adverse Effect:* Interference with the immune response to the live vaccine

3. *Clinical Management:* The administration of live viral vaccines should be deferred, if possible, until three months after the discontinuation of rabies immune globulin. If the live-virus vaccine was administered less than 14 days before or at the same time as the immune globulin, vaccination may need to be repeated at least three months after the discontinuation of the immune globulin, unless serologic testing indicates that adequate antibodies were produced.

4. *Severity:* Moderate

5. *Onset:* Delayed

6. *Documentation:* Fair

7. *Probable Mechanism:* Presence of antibodies in the immune globulin

Respiratory Syncytial Virus Immune Globulin

1. *Summary:* Live-virus vaccines may not replicate successfully, and antibody response could be reduced when the vaccine is administered after respiratory syncytial virus immune globulin because of the presence of antibodies in the immune globulin. Live-virus vaccines should ideally be administered at ten months after therapy with respiratory syncytial virus immune globulin. If the administration of an immune globulin preparation becomes necessary because of exposure to disease, live-virus vaccines can be given simultaneously with the immune globulin at a site remote from that chosen for the immune globulin. Vaccine virus replication and stimulation of immunity will occur one to two weeks after vaccination. Therefore, if the interval between administration of the vaccine and immune globulin is less than 14

days, or if they were administered simultaneously, vaccination should be repeated at least three months after the immune globulin preparation was given, unless serologic testing indicates that adequate antibodies were formed (CDC, 1989; Prod Info RespiGam™, 1996).

2. *Adverse Effect:* Interference with the immune response to the live vaccine

3. *Clinical Management:* The administration of live viral vaccines should be deferred, if possible, until ten months after the discontinuation of respiratory syncytial virus immune globulin. If the live-virus vaccine was administered less than 14 days before or at the same time as the immune globulin, vaccination may need to be repeated at least three months after the administration of the immune globulin, unless serologic testing indicates that adequate antibodies were produced.

4. *Severity:* Moderate

5. *Onset:* Delayed

6. *Documentation:* Fair

7. *Probable Mechanism:* Presence of antibodies in the immune globulin

Rho(D) Immune Globulin

1. *Summary:* Live-virus vaccines may not replicate successfully, and antibody response could be reduced when the vaccine is administered after Rho(D) immune globulin because of the presence of antibodies in the immune globulin. Live-virus vaccines should ideally be administered at least three months after therapy with Rho(D) immune globulin. If the administration of an immune globulin preparation becomes necessary because of exposure or potential exposure to disease, live-virus vaccines can be given simultaneously with the immune globulin at a site remote from that chosen for the immune globulin. Such is the case with rubella vaccine and Rho(D) immune globulin, which should both be administered postpartum in a Rho(D) negative mother who is not vaccinated against rubella virus. Vaccine virus replication and stimulation of immunity will occur one to two weeks after vaccination. Therefore, if the interval between administration of the vaccine and immune globulin is less than 14 days, or if they were administered simultaneously, vaccination should be repeated at least three months after the immune globulin preparation was given, unless serologic testing indicates that adequate antibodies were formed (CDC, 1989; Prod Info RhoGAM™, 1995).

2. *Adverse Effect:* Interference with the immune response to the live vaccine

3. *Clinical Management:* The administration of live viral vaccines should be deferred, if possible, until three months after the

administration of Rho(D) immune globulin. If the live-virus vaccine was administered less than 14 days before or at the same time as the immune globulin, vaccination may need to be repeated at least three months after the immune globulin, unless serologic testing indicates that adequate antibodies were produced.

4. *Severity:* Moderate
5. *Onset:* Delayed
6. *Documentation:* Fair
7. *Probable Mechanism:* Presence of antibodies in the immune globulin

Sirolimus

1. *Summary:* Sirolimus is an immunosuppressant which may affect the response to vaccinations, resulting in vaccination being less effective. The use of live vaccines should be avoided in patients receiving sirolimus therapy (Prod Info Rapamune®, 1999).
2. *Adverse Effect:* Decreased vaccination efficacy
3. *Clinical Management:* The use of live vaccines should be avoided in patients receiving sirolimus.
4. *Severity:* Major
5. *Onset:* Delayed
6. *Documentation:* Fair
7. *Probable Mechanism:* Decreased immune response due to immunosuppression

Tacrolimus

1. *Summary:* The manufacturer recommends that vaccination with live vaccines be avoided while tacrolimus is being administered (Prod Info Prograf®, 1994). Live vaccines administered to patients with tacrolimus-induced immune system depression could produce potentially life-threatening infections in these patients. The manufacturer also indicates that vaccination of patients receiving an immunosuppressant such as tacrolimus may result in an impaired immunologic response to that vaccine.
2. *Adverse Effect:* Risk of infection in immunocompromised hosts; reduced effectiveness of vaccine
3. *Clinical Management:* Avoid administering live vaccines in patients receiving this immunosuppressant. Also, administration of a vaccine in patients receiving tacrolimus is likely to result in an impaired immunologic response to the vaccine.
4. *Severity:* Major
5. *Onset:* Delayed
6. *Documentation:* Fair
7. *Probable Mechanism:* Interference with the immune response to the live vaccine

Tetanus Immune Globulin

1. *Summary:* Live-virus vaccines may not replicate successfully, and antibody response could be reduced when the vaccine is administered after tetanus immune globulin because of the presence of antibodies in the immune globulin. Live-virus

vaccines should ideally be administered at least three months after therapy with tetanus immune globulin. If the administration of an immune globulin preparation becomes necessary because of exposure to disease, live-virus vaccines can be given simultaneously with the immune globulin at a site remote from that chosen for the immune globulin. Vaccine virus replication and stimulation of immunity will occur one to two weeks after vaccination. Therefore, if the interval between administration of the vaccine and immune globulin is less than 14 days, or if they were administered simultaneously, vaccination should be repeated at least three months after the immune globulin preparation was given, unless serologic testing indicates that adequate antibodies were formed (CDC, 1989; Prod Info Hyper-Tet®, 1995).

2. *Adverse Effect:* Interference with the immune response to the live vaccine

3. *Clinical Management:* The administration of live viral vaccines should be deferred, if possible, until three months after the administration of tetanus immune globulin. If the live-virus vaccine was administered less than 14 days before or at the same time as the immune globulin, vaccination may need to be repeated at

least three months after the immune globulin, unless serologic testing indicates that adequate antibodies were produced.

4. *Severity:* Moderate
5. *Onset:* Delayed
6. *Documentation:* Fair
7. *Probable Mechanism:* Presence of antibodies in the immune globulin

Tuberculin

1. *Summary:* Because live-virus vaccines can suppress the reactivity to tuberculin testing, tuberculin tests should be done preceding vaccination or on the same day as vaccination with a live-virus vaccine. If this is not possible, administer the tuberculin test four to six weeks prior to live-virus vaccination (MMWR, 1989).

2. *Adverse Effect:* Suppressed reactivity to the tuberculin test

3. *Clinical Management:* Tuberculin testing should be performed preceding or on the same day as immunization with a live-virus vaccine. If this is not possible, allow four to six weeks to elapse between tuberculin testing and the administration of live-virus vaccines.

4. *Severity:* Minor
5. *Onset:* Delayed
6. *Documentation:* Poor
7. *Probable Mechanism:* Unknown

Varicella-Zoster Immune Globulin

1. *Summary:* Live-virus vaccines may not replicate successfully,

and antibody response could be reduced when the vaccine is administered after varicella-zoster immune globulin because of the presence of antibodies in the immune globulin. Live-virus vaccines should ideally be administered at least three months after therapy with vari-cella-zoster immune globulin. If the administration of an immune globulin preparation becomes necessary because of exposure to disease, live-virus vaccines can be given simultaneously with the immune globulin at a site remote from that chosen for the immune globulin. Vaccine virus replication and stimulation of immunity will occur one to two weeks after vaccination. Therefore, if the interval between administration of the vaccine and immune globulin is less than 14 days, or if they were administered simultaneously, vaccination should be repeated at least three months after the immune globulin preparation was given, unless serologic test-ing indicates that adequate anti-bodies were formed (CDC, 1989; Prod Info Varicella Zoster Immune Globulin®, 1996).

2. *Adverse Effect:* Interference with the immune response to the live vaccine

3. *Clinical Management:* The administration of live viral vac-cines should be deferred, if possi-ble, until three months after the administration of varicella-zoster immune globulin. If the live-virus vaccine was administered less than 14 days before or at the same time as the immune globulin, vac-cination may need to be repeated at least three months after the immune globulin, unless serologic testing indicates that adequate antibodies were produced.

4. *Severity:* Moderate
5. *Onset:* Delayed
6. *Documentation:* Fair
7. *Probable Mechanism:* Presence of antibodies in the immune globulin

Monitoring Parameters

Therapeutic

The vaccination site should be evaluated 6 to 8 days after vaccina-tion. Primary vaccination is suc-cessful if a typical Jennerian vesi-cle is present. The vesicle may be accompanied by fever, regional lymphadenopathy, and malaise per-sisting for a few days. If the vesi-cle is not present the vaccination should be repeated with a different lot. Additionally, the vaccination procedure should be re-evaluated. If the vaccination is successful, the vesicle will crust over and the crust will come off approximately 21 days after vaccination (Prod Info Dryvax®, 1995).

Following revaccination, a "major reaction" is considered a successful revaccination. A "major reaction" is a vesicle or pustular lesion on an area of induration surrounding a central lesion which may be a crust or an ulcer. The patient may experience fever, regional lymphadenopathy, and malaise persisting for a few days. The course of reaction may be accelerated or the same as the course of the reaction in primary vaccination. Any other reaction is considered "equivocal." In this case the revaccination procedures should be checked and revaccination repeated with another lot of vaccine (Prod Info Dryvax®, 1995).

Toxic

The only available product to treat the complications of vaccinia vaccination is vaccinia immune globulin (VIG) (CDC, 1991). It is effective for vaccination and some cases of progressive vaccinia, and may be helpful in ocular vaccinia resulting from inadvertent implementation. VIG is also recommended for severe generalized vaccinia if the patient has a toxic condition or a serious underlying disease. VIG is of no benefit in the treatment of post-vaccinial encephalitis.

The recommended dose of VIG is 0.6 mL/kg (CDC, 1991). VIG must be administered intramuscularly and as soon as possible after the onset of symptoms. Since the dose may be large, it may be given in divided doses over 24 to 36 hours. Doses may be repeated, usually at intervals of 2 to 3 days, until recovery begins. The CDC is the only source of VIG for civilians.

Place In Therapy

The Centers for Disease Control recommend that smallpox vaccination be administered prophylatically ONLY to laboratory workers who directly handle a culture or animals contaminated or infected with vaccinia, recombinant vaccinia viruses, or other orthopox viruses that infect humans (monkeypox or cowpox). These individuals should be revaccinated at least every 10 years (CDC, 2001). In addition, the CDC's Advisory Committee on Immunization Practices (ACIP) has recommended the use of vaccinia vaccine in certain at-risk individuals in the event of intentional release of the virus as an act of bioterrorism. (CDC, 2001).

The Centers for Disease Control state that there is no additional therapeutic use for vaccinia vaccine. There is no evidence that it has any value in the treatment or prevention of recurrent herpes simplex, warts, or any disease other than those caused by human orthopox viruses (CDC, 2001).

Mechanism of Action

Smallpox vaccine contains live vaccinia virus; introduction of the vaccine into the superficial layers of the skin results in the development of antibodies to all viral antigens as well as increased vaccinia-specific cell-mediated immunity.

Neutralizing antibodies appear approximately 10 days after the primary vaccination and 7 days after revaccination (CDC, 2001).

References

- ACIP: Recommendations for protection against viral hepatitis. *MMWR* 1985; 34:313-335.
- Allison J: Methotrexate and smallpox vaccination. *Lancet* 1968; 2:1250.
- Allison J: Methotrexate and small pox vaccination (letter). *Lancet* 1968; 2:1250.
- Amstey M: Therapy for genital herpes virus infection. *Drug Ther Bull* 1974.
- Anon: American Academy of Pediatrics Committee on Infectious Diseases. Report of the Committee on Infectious Diseases. 22nd ed. American Academy of Pediatrics, Elk Grove Village, IL, 1991.
- Anon: California State Dept of Health Services: Another tragic case from misuse of smallpox vaccine. *California Morbidity Weekly Report* 1978; (6 April).
- Anon: Drugs and vaccines against biological weapons. *Med Lett Drugs Ther* 1999; 41(1046):15-16.
- Bedson S & Bland J: On the supposed relationship between the viruses of herpes febralis and vaccinia. *Br J Exp Path* 1928; 174.
- Birrer RB & Laude TA: Vaccinia reaction in a sibling. *NY State J Med* 1981; 5:774.
- CDC: Adverse reactions to smallpox vaccination - 1978. *MMWR* 1979; 28:265-267.
- CDC: General recommendations on immunization. *MMWR* 1989; 38:205-214, 219-227.
- CDC: Vaccinia (smallpox) vaccine. Recommendations of the Advisory Committee for Immunization Practices (ACIP). *MMWR* 2001; 50(No. RR-10):1-25.
- el-Ad B, Roth Y, Winder A et al: The persistence of neutralizing antibodies after revaccination against smallpox. *J Infect Dis* 1990; 161:446-448.
- Funk EA & Strausbaugh LJ: Vaccinia necrosum after smallpox vaccination for Herpes Labialis. *South Med J* 1981; 74:383-384.
- Godlee F: Smallpox virus to be destroyed. *Br Med J* 1991; 302:373.
- Grabenstein JD & Baker JR: Comment: cyclosporine and vaccination (letter). *Drug Intell Clin Pharm* 1985; 19:679-680.
- Grabenstein JD: Drug interactions involving immunologic agents. Part 1. Vaccine-vaccine, vaccine-immunoglobulin, and vaccine-drug interactions. *DICP* 1990; 24:67-81.
- Kern A & Schiff B: Smallpox vaccinations in the management of recurrent herpes simplex: a controlled evaluation. *J Invest Derm* 1959; 33:99.
- Maddocks AC: Indomethacin and vaccination. *Lancet* 1973; 2:215.

- Miller LG & Loomis JH: Advice of manufacturers about effects of temperature on biologicals. *Am J Hosp Pharm* 1985; 42:843-848.

- Mintz L: Recurrent herpes simplex infection at a smallpox vaccination site. *JAMA* 1982; 247:2704-2705.

- MMWR: General recommendations on immunization. *MMWR* 1989; 38:205-214, 219-227.

- Neff J & Lane J: Vaccinia necrosum following smallpox vaccination for chronic herpetic ulcers. *JAMA* 1970; 213:123.

- Product Information: Arava™, leflunomide. Hoechst Marion Roussel, Inc., Kansas City, MO, 1998.

- Product Information: CytoGam®, cytomegalovirus immune globulin intravenous (human). MedImmune, Inc., Gaithersburg, MD, 1995.

- Product Information: Dryvax®, smallpox vaccine. Wyeth Laboratories, Inc, Marietta, PA, 1995.

- Product Information: Enbrel®, etanercept. Immunex Corporation, Seattle, WA, 1999.

- Product Information: Gamimune® N, immune globulin intravenous (human). Bayer Corporation Biological Products, West Haven, CT, 1995.

- Product Information: Gammar®, immune globulin (human). Armour Pharmaceutical Company, Kankakee, IL, 1990.

- Product Information: Habi-HB®, hepatitis B immune globulin (human). Nabi, Boca Raton, FL, 1999.

- Product Information: Hyperab®, rabies immune globulin (human). Bayer Corporation Biological Products, West Haven, CT, 1995.

- Product Information: HyperHep®, hepatitis B immune globulin (human). Bayer Corporation Biological Products, West Haven, CT, 1995.

- Product Information: Hyper-Tet®, tetanus immune globulin (human). Bayer Corporation Biological Products, West Haven, CT, 1995.

- Product Information: Imuran®, azathioprine. Glaxo Wellcome Inc., Research Triangle Park, NC, 1998.

- Product Information: Prograf®, tacrolimus. Fujisawa USA, Inc., Deerfield, IL, 1994.

- Product Information: Rapamune®, sirolimus. Wyeth Laboratories, Philadelphia, PA, 1999.

- Product Information: Remicade™, infliximab. Centocor, Inc., Malvern, PA, 1999.

- Product Information: RespiGam™, respiratory syncytial virus immune globulin intravenous (human). Medimmune, Inc., Gaithersburg, MD, 1996.

- Product Information: RhoGAM™, Rho(D) immune globulin (human). Ortho Diagnostic Systems Inc., Raritan, NJ, 1995.

- Product Information: Sandimmune®, cyclosporine. Novartis Pharmaceuticals Corporation, East Hanover, NJ, 1996.
- Product Information: Varicella Zoster Immune Globulin®, varicella-zoster immune globulin (human). American Red Cross, Blood Services, Dedham, MA, 1996.
- Rosenbaum EH, Cohen RA & Glatstein HR: Vaccination of a patient receiving immunosuppressive therapy for lymphosarcoma. *JAMA* 1966; 198:737-740.
- Yettra M: Remission of chronic lymphocytic leukemia after smallpox vaccination. *Arch Intern Med* 1979; 139:603.

Section 6

Medical
Safety

Precautionary Measures During Bioterror Attack

This section summarizes the precautionary measures recommended when caring for patients incapacitated by a biological warfare agent. Standard infection-control precautions are as follows.

Standard Precautions

- Avoid direct contact with all body fluids (including blood), secretions, excretions, non-intact skin (including rashes), and mucous membranes.
- Wear gloves when contact with the above.
- Wash hands.
- Use a mask/eye protection/face shield while performing procedures that can cause a splash or spray.
- Use a gown to protect skin and clothing during procedures.

Recommendations for specific agents are listed below. The information was drawn from the Texas Department of Health Bioterrorism web page, http://www.tdh.state. tx.us/bioterrorism/, as of October 24, 2001.

Aflatoxins

Follow standard precautions.

Anthrax

Standard precautions should be practiced. Airborne precautions are not indicated as respiratory anthrax is not transmitted person-to-person. In the absence of large amounts of organic material, wash surfaces with a sporicidal agent such as 0.5% sodium hypochlorite (1 part household bleach added to 9 parts water). Hydrogen peroxide, peracetic acid, and other agents are effective disinfectants. Persons exposed to the aerosol should shower thoroughly with soap and water. Bed linens, clothing, and other exposed articles should be washed according to hospital policy.

Botulism

Standard precautions should be practiced, but isolation is not required. The toxin is not dermally active and secondary aerosols from patients are not a hazard. The toxin is destroyed by boiling for 5 to 10 minutes. Surfaces may be decontaminated with 0.5% sodium hypochlorite solution (1 part household bleach added to 9 parts water) and/or soap and water.

Brucellosis

Standard precautions should be exercised by health care workers. Person-to-person transmission has been noted but is insignificant. Decontamination can be accomplished with a 0.5% sodium hypochlorite solution (1 part household bleach added to 9 parts water). Proper treatment of water, through boiling, chlorination, or iodination would also be important in areas intentionally subjected to Brucella aerosols.

Crimean-Congo Hemorrhagic Fever
Follow standard precautions.

Ebola and Marburg Filoviruses
Follow standard precautions.

E. Coli O157:H7
Follow standard precautions.

Glanders
Follow standard precautions.

Hantavirus Pulmonary Syndrome
Follow standard precautions. Use of full face-piece air-purifying respirators with P100 particulate filters is also recommended.

Junin (Argentine Hemorrhagic Fever)
Follow standard precautions.

Lassa Fever
Follow standard precautions.

Paralytic Shellfish Toxins
Follow standard precautions.

Plague
Although buboes may be aspirated for diagnostic purposes, incision and drainage may pose a hazard to medical personnel. Droplet precautions in addition to standard precautions should be strictly enforced for at least 72 hours after the initia-

tion of effective therapy. Surface decontamination may be accomplished by using 0.5% sodium hypochlorite solution (1 part household bleach added to nine parts water).

Q Fever
Standard precautions should be practiced. Decontaminate surfaces with soap and water or with a 0.5% hypochlorite solution (1 part household bleach added to 9 parts water).

Ricin (Toxalbumins)
Standard precautions should be taken. Decontaminate exposed skin by washing with soap and water and/or 0.1% sodium hypochlorite (1 part household bleach added to 49 parts water).

Rocky Mountain Spotted Fever
Follow standard precautions.

Shigella
Follow standard precautions.

Smallpox
Patients should be considered infectious until scabs separate, which usually takes about three weeks from the time of infection. Isolation with droplet and airborne precautions should be exercised for patients and all contacts for a minimum of 16 to 17 days following exposure. Isolation in the home or other non-hospital facilities should be considered where possible, since the risk for transmission is high and few hospitals will have enough negative pressure rooms for proper

isolation. Immediate vaccination, if available, should be given to all medical personnel. Outside of the hospital setting, patients and household contacts should wear a N95 or better mask. Care-givers should wear disposable gowns and gloves, as well. Bed linens, clothing, and other exposed articles must be sterilized or incinerated.

Staphylococcus

Standard precautions should be taken. Decontaminate surfaces with 0.5% sodium hypochlorite (1 part household bleach added to 9 parts water) with 10 to 15 minutes contact time, and/or soap and water.

Tetrodotoxin

Follow standard precautions.

Trichothecene Mycotoxins

Standard precautions should be taken. A chemical protective mask and clothing are required to avoid exposure. Exposed skin should be washed with soap and water. Bed linens, clothing, other exposed articles, and wash waste can be decontaminated through the use of a hypochlorite solution under alkaline conditions, such as 1% sodium hypochlorite and 0.1M NaOH with one hour contact time.

Tularemia

No evidence exists of person-to-person transmission. Standard precautions should be practiced; strict isolation is not required. Organisms are rendered harmless by mild heat (55°C for 10 minutes) and/or standard disinfectants such as 0.5% sodium hypochlorite solution (1 part household bleach added to 9 parts water).

Typhus

Follow standard precautions.

Venezuelan Equine Encephalitis

Standard blood precautions and barrier-nursing techniques must be employed. Patients should be isolated. The virus is destroyed by heat (80°C for 30 minutes) and regular disinfectants.

Interim Recommendations for the Selection and Use of Protective Clothing and Respirators Against Biological Agents

The approach to any potentially hazardous atmosphere, including biological hazards, must be made with a plan that includes an assessment of hazard and exposure potential, respiratory protection needs, entry conditions, exit routes, and decontamination strategies. Any plan involving a biological hazard should be based on relevant infectious disease or biological safety recommendations by the Centers for Disease Control and Prevention (CDC) and other expert bodies including emergency first responders, law enforcement, and public health officials. The need for decontamination and for treatment of all first responders with antibiotics or other medications should be decided in consultation with local public health authorities.

This INTERIM STATEMENT is based on current understanding of the potential threats and existing recommendations issued for biological aerosols. CDC makes this judgment because:

1. Biological weapons may expose people to bacteria, viruses, or toxins as fine airborne particles. Biological agents are infectious through one or more of the following mechanisms of exposure, depending upon the particular type of agent: inhalation, with infection through respiratory mucosa or lung tissues; ingestion; contact with the mucous membranes of the eyes, or nasal tissues; or penetration of the skin through open cuts (even very small cuts and abrasions of which employees might be unaware). Organic airborne particles share the same physical characteristics in air or on surfaces as inorganic particles from hazardous dusts. This has been demonstrated in military research on biological weapons and in civilian research to control the spread of infection in hospitals.

2. Because biological weapons are particles, they will not penetrate the materials of properly assembled and fitted respirators or protective clothing.

3. Existing recommendations for protecting workers from biological hazards require the use of half-mask or full facepiece air-purifying respirators with particulate filter efficiencies ranging from N95 (for hazards such as pulmonary tuberculosis) to P100 (for hazards such as hantavirus) as a minimum level of protection.

4. Some devices used for intentional biological terrorism may have the capacity to disseminate large quantities of biological materials in aerosols.

5. Emergency first responders typically use self-contained breathing apparatus (SCBA) respirators with a full facepiece operated in the most protective, positive pressure (pressure demand) mode during emergency responses. This type of SCBA provides the highest level of protection against airborne hazards when properly fitted to the user's face and properly used. National Institute for Occupational Safety and Health (NIOSH) respirator policies state that, under those conditions, SCBA reduces the user's exposure to the hazard by a factor of at least 10,000. This reduction is true whether the hazard is from airborne particles, a chemical vapor, or a gas. SCBA respirators are used when hazards and airborne concentrations are either unknown or expected to be high. Respirators providing lower levels of protection are generally allowed once conditions are understood and exposures are determined to be at lower levels.

Interim Recommendations

When using respiratory protection, the type of respirator is selected on the basis of the hazard and its airborne concentration. For a biological agent, the air concentration of infectious particles will depend upon the method used to release the agent. Current data suggest that the self-contained breathing apparatus (SCBA) which first responders currently use for entry into potentially hazardous atmospheres will provide responders with respiratory protection against biological exposures associated with a suspected act of biological terrorism.

Protective clothing, including gloves and booties, also may be required for the response to a suspected act of biological terrorism. Protective clothing may be needed to prevent skin exposures and/or contamination of other clothing. The type of protective clothing needed will depend upon the type of agent, concentration, and route of exposure.

The interim recommendations for personal protective equipment, including respiratory protection and protective clothing, are based upon the anticipated level of exposure risk associated with different response situations, as follows:

1. Responders should use a NIOSH-approved, pressure-demand SCBA in conjunction with a Level A protective suit in responding to a suspected biological incident where any of the following information is unknown or the event is uncontrolled:

- the type(s) of airborne agent(s);
- the dissemination method;

- if dissemination via an aerosol-generating device is still occurring or it has stopped but there is no information on the duration of dissemination, or what the exposure concentration might be.

2. Responders may use a Level B protective suit with an exposed or enclosed NIOSH- approved pressure-demand SCBA if the situation can be defined in which:

- the suspected biological aerosol is no longer being generated;
- other conditions may present a splash hazard.

3. Responders may use a full face-piece respirator with a P100 filter or powered air-purifying respirator (PAPR) with high efficiency particulate air (HEPA) filters when it can be determined that:

- an aerosol-generating device was not used to create high airborne concentration,
- dissemination was by a letter or package that can be easily bagged.

These types of respirators reduce the user's exposure by a factor of 50 if the user has been properly fit tested.

Care should be taken when bagging letters and packages to minimize creating a puff of air that could spread pathogens. It is best to avoid large bags and to work very slowly and carefully when placing objects in bags. Disposable hooded coveralls, gloves, and foot coverings also should be used. NIOSH recommends against wearing standard firefighter turnout gear into potentially contaminated areas when responding to reports involving biological agents.

Decontamination of protective equipment and clothing is an important precaution to make sure that any particles that might have settled on the outside of protective equipment are removed before taking off gear. Decontamination sequences currently used for hazardous material emergencies should be used as appropriate for the level of protection employed. Equipment can be decontaminated using soap and water, and 0.5% hypochlorite solution (one part household bleach to 10 parts water) can be used as appropriate or if gear had any visible contamination. Note that bleach may damage some types of firefighter turnout gear (one reason why it should not be used for biological agent response actions). After taking off gear, response workers should shower using copious quantities of soap and water.

From the Centers for Disease Control, Public Health Emergency Preparedness and Response. Available at URL:
http://www.bt.cdc.gov/Documents App/Anthrax/Protective/10242001 Protect.asp.

As Accessed 2001 Oct. 25.

Directory of Protective Clothing Suppliers

Containment Systems

ILC Dover, Inc.
P.O. Box 266
Frederica, DE 19946
Phone: 800-631-9567
Web site: www.ilcdover.com
Products: Protective Clothing,
   Containment Systems

Eye Protection

Magid Glove & Safety
2060 North Kolmar Ave.
Chicago, IL 60639
Phone: 800-444-8030
Web site: www.magidglove.com
Products: Eye Protection,
   Face/Head Protection,
   Hand Protection, Protective
   Clothing, Respiratory Protection,
   Protective Footwear

North Safety Products
2000 Plainfield Pike
Cranston, RI 02921
Phone: 800-430-4110
Web site: www.northsafety.com
Products: Eye Protection,
   Face/Head Protection,
   Hand Protection, Protective
   Clothing, Respiratory Protection,
   Protective Footwear

Norcross Safety Products
1136 Second Street
Rock Island, IL 61202
Phone: 800-777-9021
Web site: www.servusproducts.com
Products: Eye Protection,
   Face/Head Protection,
   Hand Protection, Protective
   Footwear

Face/Head Protection

Kimberly-Clark, Inc.
Health Care Division
1400 Holcomb Bridge Road
Building 200
Roswell, GA 30076
Phone: 800-324-3577
Web site: www.kchealthcare.com
Products: Hand Protection,
   Protective Clothing, Face/Head
   Protection

Magid Glove & Safety
2060 North Kolmar Ave.
Chicago, IL 60639
Phone: 800-444-8030
Web site: www.magidglove.com
Products: Eye Protection,
   Face/Head Protection,
   Hand Protection, Protective
   Clothing, Respiratory Protection,
   Protective Footwear

Norcross Safety Products
1136 Second Street
Rock Island, IL 61202
Phone: 800-777-9021
Web site: www.servusproducts.com
Products: Eye Protection,
    Face/Head Protection, Hand
    Protection, Protective Clothing,
    Respiratory Protection,
    Protective Footwear

North Safety Products
2000 Plainfield Pike
Cranston, RI 02921
Phone: 800-430-4110
Web site: www.northsafety.com
Products: Eye Protection,
    Face/Head Protection,
    Hand Protection, Protective
    Clothing, Respiratory Protection,
    Protective Footwear

Hand Protection

Ansell Occupational Healthcare
1300 Walnut Street
Box 6000
Coshocton, OH 43812
Phone: 800-800-0444
Web site: www.ansellpro.com
E-mail: info@ansell.com
Products: Hand Protection,
    Protective Clothing

Best Manufacturing
P.O. Box 8
579 Edison Street
Menlo, GA 30731
Phone: 800-241-0323
Web site: www.bestglove.com
E-mail: sales@bestglove.com
Products: Hand Protection

Boss Manufacturing Company
221 W. First Street
Kewanee, IL 61443
Phone: 800-447-4581
Web site: www.bossgloves.com
Products: Hand Protection

Comasec Safety, Inc.
P.O. Box 1219
8 Niblick Road
Enfield, CT 06083-1219
Phone: 800-333-0219
Web site: www.comasecsafety.com
Products: Hand Protection

Guardian Manufacturing Company
302 Conwell Avenue
Willard, OH 44890
Phone: 800-243-7379
Web site: www.guardian-mfg.com
E-mail: susanl@willard-oh.com
Products: Hand Protection

Kappler, Inc.
P.O. Box 218
Guntersville,AL 35976
Phone: 800-633-2410
Web site: www.kappler.com
E-mail: info@kappler.com.
Products: Protective Clothing,
    Protective Footwear, Hand
    Protection

Kimberly-Clark, Inc.
Health Care Division
1400 Holcomb Bridge Road
Building 200
Roswell, GA 30076
Phone: 800-324-3577
Web site: www.kchealthcare.com
Products: Hand Protection,
    Protective Clothing, Face/Head
    Protection

Magid Glove & Safety
2060 North Kolmar Ave.
Chicago, IL 60639
Phone: 800-444-8030
Web site: www.magidglove.com
Products: Eye Protection, Face/Head
Protection, Hand Protection,
Protective Clothing, Respiratory
Protection, Protective Footwear

Marigold Industrial
Division of SSL Americas, Inc
3585 Engineering Dr., Ste. 200
Norcross, GA 30092
Phone: 888-733-0987
Web site:
www.marigoldindustrial.com
Products: Hand Protection

MAPA Professional
Perfect Fit Glove Co., Inc.
Industrial Glove Division
85 Innsbruck Drive
Buffalo, NY 14227
Phone: 800-245-6837
Web site: www.mapaglove.com
E-mail: sales@mapaglove.com
Products: Hand Protection

Memphis Glove Company
P.O. Box 171814
Memphis, TN 38187
Phone: 800-955-6887
Web site: www.memphisglove.com
Products: Hand Protection

Montgomery Safety Products
1117 Marion Avenue, SW
Canton, OH 44707
Phone: 800-562-0600
Web site:
www.montgomerysafety.com
Products: Hand Protection

Norcross Safety Products
1136 Second Street
Rock Island, IL 61202
Phone: 800-777-9021
Web site: www.servusproducts.com
Products: Eye Protection,
Face/Head Protection,
Hand Protection, Protective
Clothing, Respiratory Protection,
Protective Footwear

North Safety Products
2000 Plainfield Pike
Cranston, RI 02921
Phone: 800-430-4110
Web site: www.northsafety.com
Products: Eye Protection,
Face/Head Protection,
Hand Protection, Protective
Clothing, Respiratory Protection,
Protective Footwear

Protective Clothing

Ansell Occupational Healthcare
1300 Walnut Street
Box 6000
Coshocton, OH 43812
Phone: 800-800-0444
Web site: www.ansellpro.com
E-mail: info@ansell.com
Products: Hand Protection,
Protective Clothing

Chemfab Corporation
701 Daniel Webster Highway
P.O. Box 1137
Merrimack, NH 03054 USA
Phone: 800-451-6101
Web site: www.chemfab.com
Products: Protective Clothing

DuPont
P.O. Box 80705
Wilmington, DE 19880
Phone: 877-797-5907
  (*USA DuPont Tyvek®*
  Customer Information Center)
888-577-6960
  (*Dupont Customer Service*)
Web site:
  www.tyvekprotectiveapprl.com
E-mail: afscdt@usa.dupont.com
Products: Protective Clothing

ILC Dover, Inc.
P.O. Box 266
Frederica, DE 19946
Phone: 800-631-9567
Web site: www.ilcdover.com
Products: Protective Clothing,
  Containment Systems

Kappler, Inc.
P.O. Box 218
Guntersville, AL 35976
Phone: 800-633-2410
Web site: www.kappler.com
E-mail: info@kappler.com
Products: Protective Clothing,
  Protective Footwear,
  Hand Protection

Kimberly-Clark, Inc.
Health Care Division
1400 Holcomb Bridge Road
Building 200
Roswell, GA 30076
Phone: 800-324-3577
Web site: www.kchealthcare.com
Products: Hand Protection,
  Protective Clothing, Face/Head
  Protection

LaCrosse-Rainfair
3600 South Memorial Drive
Racine, WI 53403
Phone: 800-557-7246
Web site:
  www.lacrosserainfair.com
Products: Protective Clothing,
  Protective Footwear

Magid Glove & Safety
2060 North Kolmar Ave.
Chicago, IL 60639
Phone: 800-444-8030
Web site: www.magidglove.com
Products: Eye Protection,
  Face/Head Protection, Hand
  Protection, Protective Clothing,
  Respiratory Protection,
  Protective Footwear

Mar-Mac Manufacturing, Inc.
P.O. Box 278
McBee, SC 29101
Phone: 843-335-8211
Web site: www.marmac.com
Products: Protective Clothing

Nat-Wear
5 High Street
Miora, New York 12957
Phone: 800-833-7270
Web site: www.natwear.com
Products: Protective Clothing

Neese Industries, Inc.
P.O. Box 1059
Gonzales, LA 70707
Phone: 800-535-8042
Web site: www.neeseind.com
Products: Protective Clothing

Norcross Safety Products
1136 Second Street
Rock Island, IL 61202
Phone: 800-777-9021
Web site: www.servusproducts.com
Products: Eye Protection,
Face/Head Protection, Hand
Protection, Protective Clothing,
Respiratory Protection,
Protective Footwear

North Safety Products
2000 Plainfield Pike
Cranston, RI 02921
Phone: 800-430-4110
Web site: www.northsafety.com
Products: Eye Protection,
Face/Head Protection, Hand
Protection, Protective Clothing,
Respiratory Protection,
Protective Footwear

River City
P.O. Box 171814
Memphis,TN 38187
Phone: 800-888-0347
Web site: www.protectivewear.com
Products: Protective Clothing

Standard Safety Equipment Company
1407 Ridgeview Drive
McHenry, IL 60050
Phone: 815-363-8565
Web site: www.standardsafety.com
Products: Protective Clothing

Trelleborg-Viking, Inc.
170 West Road, Suite 1
Portsmouth, NH 03801
Phone: 800-344-4458
Web site:
www.trelleborg.com/protective/
Products: Protective Clothing

Wells Lamont Industrial
8145 River Dr.
Morton Grove, IL 60053
Phone: 800-247-3295
Web site:
www.wellslamontindustry.com
Products: Protective Clothing

Workrite
500 East Third Street
P.O. Box 1192
Oxnard, CA 93032
Phone: 800-521-1888
Fax: www.workrite.com.
Products: Protective Clothing

Protective Footwear

Kappler, Inc.
P.O. Box 218
Guntersville,AL 35976
Phone: 800-633-2410
Web site: www.kappler.com
E-mail: info@kappler.com.
Products: Protective Clothing,
Protective Footwear, Hand
Protection

LaCrosse-Rainfair
3600 South Memorial Drive
Racine, WI 53403
Phone: 800-557-7246
Web site:
www.lacrosserainfair.com
Products: Protective Clothing,
Protective Footwear

Magid Glove & Safety
2060 North Kolmar Ave.
Chicago, IL 60639
Phone: 800-444-8030
Web site: www.magidglove.com
Products: Eye Protection,
    Face/Head Protection, Hand
    Protection, Protective Clothing,
    Respiratory Protection,
    Protective Footwear

Norcross Safety Products
1136 Second Street
Rock Island, IL 61202
Phone: 800-777-9021
Web site: www.servusproducts.com
Products: Eye Protection,
    Face/Head Protection, Hand
    Protection, Protective Clothing,
    Respiratory Protection,
    Protective Footwear

North Safety Products
2000 Plainfield Pike
Cranston, RI 02921
Phone: 800-430-4110
Web site: www.northsafety.com
Products: Eye Protection,
    Face/Head Protection, Hand
    Protection, Protective Clothing,
    Respiratory Protection,
    Protective Footwear

Onguard Industries
4501 Pulaski Highway
Belcamp, MD 21017
Phone: 800-365-2282
Products: Protective Footwear

Tingley
P.O. Box 100
South Plainfield, NJ 07080
Phone: 800-631-5498
Products: Protective Footwear

Repiratory Protection

Magid Glove & Safety
2060 North Kolmar Ave.
Chicago, IL 60639
Phone: 800-444-8030
Web site: www.magidglove.com
Products: Eye Protection,
    Face/Head Protection, Hand
    Protection, Protective Clothing,
    Respiratory Protection,
    Protective Footwear

Norcross Safety Products
1136 Second Street
Rock Island, IL 61202
Phone: 800-777-9021
Web site: www.servusproducts.com
Products: Eye Protection,
    Face/Head Protection, Hand
    Protection, Protective Clothing,
    Respiratory Protection,
    Protective Footwear

North Safety Products
2000 Plainfield Pike
Cranston, RI 02921
Phone: 800-430-4110
Web site: www.northsafety.com
Products: Eye Protection,
    Face/Head Protection, Hand
    Protection, Protective Clothing,
    Respiratory Protection,
    Protective Footwear

Section 7

Government Guidelines and Advisories

Interim Guidelines for Investigation of and Response to *Bacillus Anthracis* Exposures

Environmental Sampling

Environmental testing to detect *B. anthracis* on surfaces or in the air can be used to investigate known or suspected exposure events. The highest priority of an investigation is to evaluate the risk for exposure to aerosolized *B. anthracis* spores. Persons collecting and testing samples should 1) obtain adequate samples, 2) avoid cross-contamination during processing, and 3) ensure proficient laboratory testing and interpretation of test results. A positive laboratory test for *B. anthracis* from a sample of an environmental surface may be caused by cross-contamination from an exposure vehicle (eg, contact with an envelope containing *B. anthracis*), background occurrence of *B. anthracis* spores in the environment, or previously aerosolized *B. anthracis* that has settled onto environmental surfaces. Laboratory test results of environmental surface samples should not be the only criterion for starting, continuing, or stopping antimicrobial prophylaxis for inhalational disease.

Environmental sampling can be directed, prospective, or random. In directed sampling, air and/or surface samples are obtained as part of an investigation of a specific threat, a known exposure, or of persons with bioterrorism-related anthrax. Directed environmental sampling may play a critical role in characterizing potential exposures and guiding public health action (Box 1).

Prospective environmental sampling is defined as ongoing sampling and testing of air or surfaces for *B. anthracis* spores. The value of prospective sampling is not known. Current technologies for monitoring air for *B. anthracis* and other agents are not validated and their performance has not been assessed during bioterrorism events. Prospective environmental sampling of surfaces may have a role in detecting *B. anthracis* contamination, especially at facilities or events determined to be at high risk for bioterrorism (Box 1).

The testing of random environmental samples (ie, sampling air or surfaces of facilities that are not directly associated with confirmed anthrax disease or a known *B. anthracis* exposure) is of uncertain utility in detecting past exposures. Random positive tests for *B.*

anthracis spores may represent cross-contamination from an exposure vehicle (eg, letter) that poses negligible risks for inhalational anthrax. These positive test results may prompt more extensive evaluation to direct cleanup, if needed.

Nasal Swab Cultures

Nasal swab cultures should not be used to diagnose cases of anthrax or to evaluate whether a person had been exposed. Nasal swab cultures may be useful in the investigation of known or suspected airborne *B. anthracis* (Box 1). Because the sensitivity of nasal swab cultures decreases over time, cultures should be obtained within 7 days of the exposure. The presence of *B. anthracis* from a nasal swab culture cannot be determined by gram stain or colony characteristics alone and requires confirmatory testing by qualified laboratories.

Antimicrobial Prophylaxis

Antimicrobial prophylaxis is used to prevent cases of inhalational anthrax (Box 1). Public health authorities often start prophylaxis before the extent of exposure is known. Subsequent epidemiologic and laboratory test data may indicate that some persons started on prophylaxis were not exposed. These persons should stop antimicrobial prophylaxis. Persons who were exposed should complete 60 days of therapy.

No shorter course of antimicrobial prophylaxis exists. The choice of an antimicrobial agent should be based on antimicrobial susceptibility, the drug's effectiveness, adverse events, and cost. *B. anthracis* isolates from patients with bioterrorism-related anthrax have been susceptible to ciprofloxacin, doxycycline, and other agents; the use of doxycycline may be preferable to prevent development of ciprofloxacin resistance in more common bacteria (1). Respiratory transmission of *B. anthracis* from person-to-person does not occur; no antimicrobial prophylaxis is indicated.

Closing Facilities

The decision to close a facility is made to prevent cases of inhalational anthrax (Box 1). The facility should remain closed until the risk for inhalational disease is eliminated.

Reference

1. CDC. Update: investigation of bioterrorism-related anthrax and interim guidelines for exposure management and antimicrobial therapy. October 2001. *MMWR*. 2001;50:909--919.

BOX 1. Interim guidelines for investigation of and response to B. anthracis exposures

Environmental Sampling

Directed sampling of environmental surfaces may be indicated:

- To identify a site or source of *Bacillus anthracis* exposure that has resulted in a case(s) of anthrax
- To trace the route of an exposure vehicle (eg, a powder-containing letter)
- To obtain the *B. anthracis* strain when isolates from patients are not available
- To guide cleanup activities in a contaminated area or building
- To assess biosafety procedures in laboratories processing *B. anthracis* specimens

Prospective sampling of environmental surfaces may be indicated:

- To identify receipt of a contaminated exposure vehicle in high risk facilities (eg, mailrooms of targeted persons or groups)
- To detect aerosolized *B. anthracis* in high risk areas or events

Laboratory testing of environmental surface samples should not be the only means to determine the need for antimicrobial prophylaxis.

Nasal Swab Cultures

Collection of nasal swabs for culture of *B. anthracis* may be useful:

- To help define an area of exposure to aerosolized *B. anthracis*
- To help ascertain where a person with inhalational anthrax was exposed if the time and place of exposure are not already known

Collection of nasal swabs for culture of *B. anthracis* is not indicated:

- To diagnose anthrax
- To determine a person's risk of exposure and the need for antimicrobial prophylaxis
- To determine when antimicrobial prophylaxis should be stopped
- To supplement random environmental sampling

Antimicrobial Prophylaxis

Antimicrobial prophylaxis may be initiated pending additional information when:

- A person is exposed to an air space where a suspicious material may have been aerosolized (eg, near a suspicious powder-containing letter during opening)
- A person has shared the air space likely to be the source of an inhalational anthrax case

Antimicrobial prophylaxis should be continued for 60 days for:
- Persons exposed to an air space known to be contaminated with aerosolized *B. anthracis*
- Persons exposed to an air space known to be the source of an inhalational anthrax case
- Persons along the transit path of an envelope or other vehicle containing *B. anthracis* that may have been aerosolized (eg, a postal sorting facility in which an envelope containing *B. anthracis* was processed)
- Unvaccinated laboratory workers exposed to confirmed *B. anthracis* cultures

Antimicrobial prophylaxis is not indicated:
- For prevention of cutaneous anthrax
- For autopsy personnel examining bodies infected with anthrax when appropriate isolation precautions and procedures are followed
- For hospital personnel caring for patients with anthrax
- For persons who routinely open or handle mail in the absence of a suspicious letter or credible threat

A positive test for B. anthracis from a randomly collected specimen does not require implementation of antimicrobial prophylaxis or the closing of a facility.

Closing a Facility

Closing a facility or a part of a facility may be indicated:
- After an inhalational anthrax case is detected and a probable site of exposure in the facility is identified
- When there is a known aerosolization of *B. anthracis* in the facility
- When evidence strongly suggests an aerosolization of *B. anthracis* in the facility
- As determined by law enforcement authorities in a criminal investigation

Closing a facility is not indicated:
- Based only on the identification of *B. anthracis* from samples of environmental surfaces
- Based only on the identification of a cutaneous anthrax case

Source: MMWR 50(44); November 9, 2001

Considerations for Distinguishing Influenza-Like Illness from Inhalational Anthrax

CDC has issued guidelines on the evaluation of persons with a history of exposure to *Bacillus anthracis* spores or who have an occupational or environmental risk for anthrax exposure (1). This notice describes the clinical evaluation of persons who are not known to be at increased risk for anthrax but who have symptoms of influenza-like illness (ILI). Clinicians evaluating persons with ILI should consider a combination of epidemiologic, clinical, and, if indicated, laboratory and radiographic test results to evaluate the likelihood that inhalational anthrax is the basis for ILI symptoms.

ILI is a nonspecific respiratory illness characterized by fever, fatigue, cough, and other symptoms. The majority of ILI cases is not caused by influenza but by other viruses (eg, rhinoviruses and respiratory syncytial virus [RSV]), adenoviruses, and parainfluenza viruses). Less common causes of ILI include bacteria such as *Legionella spp., Chlamydia pneumoniae, Mycoplasma pneumoniae,* and *Streptococcus pneumoniae.* Influenza, RSV, and certain bacterial infections are particularly important causes of ILI because these infections can lead to serious complications requiring hospitalization (2,3,4). Yearly, adults and children can average one to three and three to six ILI, respectively (5).

Epidemiologic Considerations

To date, 10 confirmed cases of inhalational anthrax have been identified (1). The epidemiologic profile of these 10 cases caused by bioterrorism can guide the assessment of persons with ILI. All but one case have occurred among postal workers, persons exposed to letters or areas known to be contaminated by anthrax spores, and media employees. The 10 confirmed cases have been identified in a limited number of communities. Inhalational anthrax is not spread from person-to-person. In comparison, millions of ILI cases associated with other respiratory pathogens occur each year and in all communities. Respiratory infections associated with bacteria can occur throughout the year; pneumococcal disease peaks during the winter, and mycoplasma and legionellosis are more common during the summer and fall (4). Cases of ILI resulting from influenza and RSV infection generally peak during the winter; rhinoviruses and parainfluenza virus infections usually peak during the fall and spring; and adenoviruses circulate throughout the year. All of these viruses are highly communicable and spread easily from person to person.

Clinical Considerations

Although many different illnesses might present with ILI symptoms, the presence of certain signs and symptoms might help to distinguish other causes of ILI from inhalational anthrax. Nasal congestion and rhinorrhea are features of most ILI cases not associated with anthrax (Table 1) (6,7). In comparison, rhinorrhea was reported in one of the 10 persons who had inhalational anthrax diagnosed since September 2001. All 10 persons with inhalational anthrax had abnormal chest radiographs on initial presentation; seven had mediastinal widening, seven had infiltrates, and eight had pleural effusion. Findings might be more readily discernable on posteroanterior with lateral views, compared with anteroposterior views (ie, portable radiograph alone) (1). Most cases of ILI are not associated with radiographic findings of pneumonia, which occurs most often among the very young, elderly, or those with chronic lung disease (2,3). Influenza associated pneumonia

occurs in approximately 1% to 5% of community-dwelling adults with influenza and can occur in >20% of influenza-infected elderly (2). Influenza-associated pneumonia might be caused by the primary virus infection or, more commonly, by bacterial infection occurring coincident with or following influenza illness (2).

Testing

No rapid screening test is available to diagnose inhalational anthrax in the early stages. Blood cultures grew *B. anthracis* in all seven patients with inhalational anthrax who had not received previous antimicrobial therapy. However, blood cultures should not be obtained routinely on all patients with ILI symptoms who have no probable exposure to anthrax but should be obtained for persons in situations in which bacteremia is suspected.

Rapid tests for influenza and RSV are available, and, if used, should be conducted within the first 3 to 4 days of a person's illness when viral shedding is most likely. RSV antigen detection tests have a peak sensitivity of 75% to 95% in infants but do not have enough sensitivity to warrant their routine use among adults (8).

Among the influenza tests available for point-of-care testing, the reported sensitivities and specificities range from 45% to 90% and 60% to 95%, respectively (9). Two tests (Quidel Quickvue Influenza test and ZymeTx Zstatflu test®) can be performed in any physician's office, and three are classified as moderately complex tests (Biostar FLU OIA; Becton-Dickinson Directigen Flu A+B; and Becton-Dickinson Directigen Flu A™).

The clinical usefulness of rapid influenza tests for the diagnosis of influenza in individual patients is limited because the sensitivity of the influenza rapid tests is relatively low (45% to 90%), and a large proportion of persons with influenza might be missed with these tests. Therefore, the rapid influenza tests should not be done on every person presenting with ILI. However, rapid influenza testing used with viral culture can help indicate whether influenza viruses are circulating among specific populations, (eg, nursing home residents or patients attending a clinic). This type of epidemiologic information on specific populations can aid in diagnosing ILI.

Vaccination against influenza is the best means to prevent influenza and its severe complications. The influenza vaccine is targeted towards persons aged >65 years and to persons aged 6 months to 64 years who have a high risk medical condition because these groups are at increased risk for influenza-related complications. The vaccine also is targeted towards health-care workers to prevent transmission of influenza to high-risk persons. In addition, vaccination is recommended for household members of high-risk persons and for healthy persons aged 50 to 64 years. The vaccine can prevent 70% to 90% of influenza infections in healthy adults. However, the vaccine does not prevent ILI caused by infectious agents other than influenza, and many persons vaccinated against influenza will still get ILI. Therefore, receipt of vaccine will not definitely exclude influenza from the differential diagnosis of ILI or increase the probability of inhalational anthrax as a cause, especially among persons who have no probable exposure to anthrax. Frequent hand washing can reduce the number of respiratory illnesses (10) and pneumococcal polysaccharide vaccine can reduce the risk for serious pneumococcal disease.

Additional information about anthrax is available at:

http://www.hhs.gov/hottopics/healing/biological.html
http://www.bt.cdc.gov/DocumentsApp/FactsAbout/FactsAbout.asp

Additional information about influenza, RSV and other viral respiratory infections, and pneumococcal disease is available at:

TABLE 1. Symptoms and signs of inhalational anthrax, laboratory-confirmed influenza, and influenza-like illness (ILI) from other causes

Symptom/Sign	Inhalational anthrax (n=10)	Laboratory-confirmed influenza	ILI from other causes
Elevated temperature	70%	68%-77%	40%-73%
Fever or chills	100%	83%-90%	75%-89%
Fatigue/malaise	100%	75%-94%	62%-94%
Cough (minimal or nonproductive)	90%	84%-93%	72%-80%
Shortness of breath	80%	6%	6%
Chest discomfort or pleuritic chest pain	60%	35%	23%
Headache	50%	84%-91%	74%-89%
Myalgias	50%	67%-94%	73%-94%
Sore throat	20%	64%-84%	64%-84%
Rhinorrhea	10%	79%	68%
Nausea or vomiting	80%	12%	12%
Abdominal pain	30%	22%	22%

http://www.cdc.gov/ncidod/diseases/flu/fluvirus.htm
http://www.cdc.gov/nip/flu/default.htm
http://www.cdc.gov/ncidod/dvrd/revb/index.htm
http://www.cdc.gov/ncidod/dbmd/diseaseinfo/streppneum_t.htm
http://www.cdc.gov/nip/diseases/Pneumo/vac-chart.htm

References

1. CDC. Update: investigation of bioterrorism-related anthrax and interim guidelines for clinical evaluation of persons with possible anthrax. *MMWR.* 2001;50:941-948.

2. Nicholson KG. Human influenza. In: Nicholson KG, Webster RG, Hay AJ, eds. *Textbook of influenza.* Malden, Massachusetts: Blackwell Science 1998:219-264.

3. Hall CB. Medical progress: respiratory syncytial virus and parainfluenza virus. *N Engl J Med.* 2001;344:1917-1928.

4. Bartlett JG, Dowell SF, Mandell LA, File TM Jr, Musher DM, Fine MJ. Practice guidelines for the management of community-acquired pneumonia in adults. *Clin Infect Dis.* 2000;31:347-382.

5. Monto AS. Viral respiratory infections in the community: epidemiology, agents, and interventions. *Am J Med.* 1995;99:6B24S-6B27S.

6. Carrat F, Tachet A, Rouzioux C, Housset B, Valleron AJ. Evaluation of clinical case definitions of influenza: detailed investigation of patients during the 1995—1996 epidemic in France. *Clin Infect Dis.* 1999;28:283-290.

7. Monto AS, Gravenstein S, Elliott M, Colopy M, Schweinle J. Clinical signs and symptoms predicting influenza infection. *Arch Intern Med.* 2000;160:3243-3247.

8. Kellogg JA. Culture vs. direct antigen assays for detection of microbial pathogens from lower respiratory tract specimens suspected of containing the respiratory syncytial virus. *Arch Pathol Lab Med.* 1991;115:451-458.

9. Munoz FM, Galasso GJ, Gwaltney JM, et al. Current research on influenza and other respiratory viruses: II International Symposium. *Antiviral Res.* 2000;46:91-124.

10. Ryan MAK, Christian RS, Wohlrabe J. Handwashing and respiratory illness among young adults in military training. *Am J Prevent Med.* 2001;21:79-83.

Source: MMWR 50(44); November 9, 2001

Updated Recommendations for Antimicrobial Prophylaxis Among Asymptomatic Pregnant Women After Exposure to *Bacillus Anthracis*

The antimicrobial of choice for initial prophylactic therapy among asymptomatic pregnant women exposed to *Bacillus anthracis* is ciprofloxacin, 500 mg twice a day for 60 days. In instances in which the specific *B. anthracis* strain has been shown to be penicillin-sensitive, prophylactic therapy with amoxicillin, 500 mg three times a day for 60 days, may be considered. Isolates of *B. anthracis* implicated in the current bioterrorist attacks are susceptible to penicillin in laboratory tests, but may contain penicillinase activity (2). Pencillins are not recommended for treatment of anthrax, where such penicillinase activity may decrease their effectiveness. However, penicillins are likely to be effective for preventing anthrax, a setting where relatively few organisms are present. Doxycycline should be used with caution in asymptomatic pregnant women and only when contraindications are indicated to the use of other appropriate antimicrobial drugs.

Pregnant women are likely to be among the increasing number of persons receiving antimicrobial prophylaxis for exposure to *B. anthracis*. Clinicians, public health officials, and women who are candidates for treatment should weigh the possible risks and benefits to the mother and fetus when choosing an antimicrobial for postexposure anthrax prophylaxis. Women who become pregnant while taking antimicrobial prophylaxis should continue the medication and consult a health-care provider or public health official to discuss these issues.

No formal clinical studies of ciprofloxacin have been performed during pregnancy. Based on limited human information, ciprofloxacin use during pregnancy is unlikely to be associated with a high risk for structural malformations in fetal development. Data on ciprofloxacin use during pregnancy from the Teratogen Information System indicate that therapeutic doses during pregnancy are unlikely to pose a substantial teratogenic risk, but data are insufficient to determine that there is no risk (1). Doxycycline is a tetracycline antimicrobial. Potential dangers of tetracyclines to fetal development include risk for dental staining of the primary teeth and concern about possible depressed bone growth and defective dental enamel. Rarely, hepatic necrosis has been reported in pregnant women using tetracyclines. Penicillins generally are considered safe for use during pregnancy and are not associated with an increased risk for fetal malformation. Pregnant women should be advised that congenital malformations occur in approximately 2% to 3% of births, even in the absence of known teratogenic exposure.

Additional information about the treatment of anthrax infection is available at: <http://www.cdc.gov/mmwr/preview/mmwrhtml/mm5042a1.htm>.

Reference

1. Friedman JM, Polifka JE. Teratogenic effects of drugs: a resource for clinicians *(TERIS)*. Baltimore, Maryland: Johns Hopkins University Press; 2000:149-195.

2. CDC. Update: investigation of bioterrorism-related anthrax and interim guidelines for exposure management and antimicrobial therapy, October 2001. *MMWR*. 2001;50:909-919.

Source: MMWR 50(43); November 2, 2001

Update: Interim Recommendations for Antimicrobial Prophylaxis for Children and Breastfeeding Mothers and Treatment of Children with Anthrax

Ciprofloxacin or doxycycline is recommended for antimicrobial prophylaxis and treatment of adults and children with *Bacillus anthracis* infection associated with the recent bioterrorist attacks in the United States. Amoxicillin is an option for antimicrobial prophylaxis for children and pregnant women and to complete treatment of cutaneous disease when *B. anthracis* is susceptible to penicillin, as is the case in the recent attacks (1,2,3). Use of ciprofloxacin or doxycycline might be associated with adverse effects in children (4,5), and liquid formulations of these drugs are not widely available. This notice provides further information about prophylaxis and treatment of children and breastfeeding mothers, including the use of amoxicillin.

Ciprofloxacin, doxycycline, and penicillin G procaine have been effective as antimicrobial prophylaxis for inhalational *B. anthracis* infection in nonhuman primates and are approved for this use in humans by the Food and Drug Administration (FDA) (5,6). Amoxicillin has not been studied in animal models and is not approved by FDA for the prophylaxis or treatment of anthrax. Other data indicate that *B. anthracis* strains produce a cephalosporinase and suggest that the strains contain an inducible beta-lactamase that might decrease the effectiveness of penicillins, especially when a large number of organisms is present (2). In addition, penicillin achieves low intracellular concentrations that might be detrimental to its ability to kill germinating spores in macrophages.

Because of these concerns, penicillins (including amoxicillin) are not recommended for initial treatment of anthrax, but are likely to be effective for antimicrobial prophylaxis following exposure to *B. anthracis*, a setting where relatively few organisms are expected to be present. Therefore, amoxicillin* may be used for the 60-day antimicrobial prophylaxis in infants and children when the isolate involved in the exposure is determined to be susceptible to penicillin. Isolates of *B. anthracis* implicated in the recent bioterrorist attacks are susceptible to ciprofloxacin, doxycycline, and penicillin (2).

Initial treatment of infants and children with inhalational or systemic (including gastrointestinal or oropharyngeal) anthrax should consist of intravenous ciprofloxacin† or doxycyline§, plus one or two additional antimicrobial¶ agents. If meningitis is suspected, ciprofloxacin might be more effective than doxycycline because of better central nervous system penetration (2). Experience with fluoroquinolones other than ciprofloxacin in children is limited.

Ciprofloxacin or doxycycline should be the initial treatment of localized cutaneous anthrax in infants and children. Intravenous therapy with multiple antimicrobial agents is recommended for cutaneous anthrax with systemic involvement, extensive edema, or lesions on the head or neck (2). Whether infants and young children are at increased risk for systemic dissemination of cutaneous infection is not known; a 7-month-old patient infected during the recent bioterrorism attacks developed systemic illness after onset of cutaneous anthrax (7). For young children (eg, aged <2 years), initial therapy of cutaneous anthrax should be intravenous, and combination therapy with additional antimicrobials should be considered.

After clinical improvement following intravenous treatment for inhalational or cutaneous anthrax, oral therapy with one or two antimicrobial agents (including either ciprofloxacin or doxycycline) may be used to complete the first 14 to 21 days of treatment for inhalational anthrax or the first 7 to 10 days for uncomplicated cutaneous anthrax. The optimal oral treatment regimen is unknown; some adults with inhalational anthrax as a result of the recent bioterrorist attacks are receiving ciprofloxacin and rifampin. For both inhalational and cutaneous anthrax in the setting of this bioterrorist attack, antimicrobial therapy should be continued for 60 days because of the likelihood of exposure to aerosolized *B. anthracis* and the need to protect against persistent spores that might germinate in the respiratory tract. Because of potential adverse effects of prolonged use of ciprofloxacin or doxycycline in children, amoxicillin is an option for completion of the remaining 60 days of therapy for persons infected in these bioterrorist attacks.

Because of its known safety for infants, amoxicillin is an option for antimicrobial prophylaxis in breast-feeding mothers when *B. anthracis* is known to be penicillin-susceptible and no contraindication to maternal amoxicillin use is indicated. The American Academy of Pediatrics also considers ciprofloxacin and tetracyclines (which include doxycycline) to be usually compatible with breastfeeding because the amount of either drug absorbed by infants is small, but little is known about the safety of long-term use (8). Mothers concerned about the use of ciprofloxacin or doxycycline for antimicrobial prophylaxis should consider expressing and then discarding breast milk so that breast-feeding can be resumed when antimicrobial prophylaxis is completed. Decisions about antimicrobial choice and continuation of breastfeeding should be made by the mother and her and the infant's health-care providers. Consideration should be given to antimicrobial efficacy, safety for the infant, and the benefits of breastfeeding.

Health-care providers prescribing antimicrobial drugs for the prophylaxis or treatment of anthrax should be aware of their adverse effects and consult with an infectious disease specialist as needed. Additional information about recognition, prophylaxis, and treatment of anthrax infection is available at <http://www.bt.cdc.gov>.

References

1. CDC. Update: investigation of anthrax associated with intentional exposure and interim public health guidelines, October 2001. *MMWR.* 2001;50:889-893.

2. CDC. Update: investigation of bioterrorism-related anthrax and interim guidelines for exposure management and antimicrobial therapy, October 2001. *MMWR.* 2001;50:909-919.

3. CDC. Updated recommendations for antimicrobial prophylaxis among asymptomatic pregnant women after exposure to *Bacillus anthracis. MMWR.* 2001;50:960.

4. Bayer Corporation. Ciprofloxacin®. In: *Physicians' Desk Reference.* Montvale, New Jersey: Medical Economics Company, 2000:678-683.

5. Food and Drug Administration. Prescription drug products; Doxycycline and Penicillin G Procaine administration for inhalational anthrax (post-exposure). *Federal Register.* 2001;66:55679.

6. Friedlander AM, Welkos SL, Pitt MLM, et al. Postexposure prophylaxis against experimental inhalation anthrax. *J Infect Dis.* 1993;167:1239-1243.

7. Roche KJ, Chang MW, Lazarus H. Cutaneous anthrax infection: images in clinical medicine. *N Engl J Med.* 2001. Available at <http://www.nejm.org>. Accessed November 6, 2001.

8. American Academy of Pediatrics Committee on Drugs. The transfer of drugs and other chemicals into human milk. *Pediatrics.* 2001;108:776-789.

Source: MMWR 50(45); November 16, 2001

* The recommended dose of amoxicillin is 80 mg/kg/day orally divided every 8 hours (maximum 500 mg/dose).

† The recommended dose of ciprofloxacin is 10 mg/kg/dose every 12 hours intravenously (maximum 400 mg/dose) or 15 mg/kg/dose every 12 hours orally (maximum 500 mg/dose).

§ The recommended dose of doxycycline is 2.2 mg/kg/dose every 12 hours intravenously or orally (maximum 100 mg/dose).

¶ Options for additional drugs, based on in vitro sensitivity testing of isolates in the recent attacks, include rifampin, vancomycin, penicillin, ampicillin, chloramphenicol, imipenem, clindamycin, and clarithromycin (2).

Children and Anthrax:
A Fact Sheet for Clinicians

Anthrax is an acute infectious disease caused by the bacterium *Bacillus anthracis*. Children, like adults, may be affected by three clinical forms: cutaneous, inhalational, or gastrointestinal. The symptoms and signs of anthrax infection in children older than 2 months of age are similar to those in adults. The clinical presentation of anthrax in young infants is not well defined. When children become ill and present for treatment, making a diagnosis may be more difficult than in adults because young children have difficulty reporting what has happened to them or telling a doctor exactly how they feel. Because respiratory illnesses are much more common in children than adults, the examining clinician should have an understanding of disease manifestations in children.

The following are clinical descriptions (based on experience with adults) of the three forms of anthrax (*MMWR* 2001;50(41):889-893).

- **Inhalational.** Inhalational anthrax begins with a brief prodrome resembling an influenza-like viral respiratory illness followed by development of dyspnea, systemic symptoms, and shock, with radiographic evidence of mediastinal widening and pleural effusion. Inhalational anthrax is the most lethal form of anthrax. The incubation period of inhalational anthrax among humans typically ranges from 1 to 7 days but may be up to 60 days. Host factors, dose of exposure, and chemoprophylaxis may affect the duration of the incubation period. Patients frequently develop meningitis. Case-fatality estimates for inhalational anthrax are extremely high; the risk for death is high even if patients are provided with supportive care, including appropriate antimicrobial treatment.

- **Cutaneous.** Cutaneous anthrax is characterized by a skin lesion evolving from a papule, through a vesicular stage, to a depressed black eschar. The incubation period ranges from 1 to 12 days. The lesion is usually painless, but patients also may have fever, malaise, headache, and regional lymphadenopathy. The case fatality rate for cutaneous anthrax is 20% without, and <1% with, antimicrobial treatment.

- **Gastrointestinal.**

    Gastrointestinal anthrax is characterized by severe abdominal pain followed by fever and signs of septicemia. This form of anthrax usually results from eating raw or undercooked meat containing *B. anthracis*, and the incubation period is usually 1 to 7 days. An oropharyngeal and an abdominal form of the disease have been described. Involvement of the pharynx is usually characterized by lesions at the base of the tongue, dysphagia, fever, and regional lymphadenopathy. Lower bowel inflammation typically causes nausea, loss of appetite, and fever followed by abdominal pain, hematemesis, and bloody diarrhea. The case-fatality rate is estimated to be between 25% and 60%. The effect of early antibiotic treatment on the case-fatality rate has not been established.

Neither CDC nor the American Academy of Pediatrics (AAP) recommend dispensing antibiotics for parents to have on hand in case of a possible exposure to *Bacillus anthracis*. CDC and its partner organizations will dispense antibiotics through the National Pharmaceutical Stockpile (NPS) program if exposure occurs. The NPS was designed to ensure the availability of lifesaving pharmaceuticals; antimicrobials; chemical interventions; and medical, surgical, and patient-support supplies, as well as equipment for prompt delivery to disaster sites. Disasters include a possible biological or chemical terrorist event anywhere in the United States. For more detailed information about the NPS, see CDC's Web site at www.bt.cdc.gov.

Vaccination

At this time, anthrax vaccine is not recommended for people younger than 18 years of age. Military personnel and civilians at high risk for repeated exposure (eg, laboratory workers handling powders containing *Bacillus anthracis* may benefit from the vaccine.

Prophylaxis

Post-exposure prophylaxis is indicated to prevent inhalational anthrax after a confirmed or suspected aerosol exposure to *Bacillus anthracis*. Consultation with public health authorities is strongly encouraged to identify people who should receive prophylaxis. When no information is available about the antimicrobial susceptibility of the implicated strain of *Bacillus anthracis*, CDC recommends initial therapy with either ciprofloxacin or doxycycline for children, as follows:

Ciprofloxacin:

- 10-15 mg/kg/dose po Q12 hours (not to exceed 1 gram per day) for 60 days.

Doxycycline:
- 8 years or older and weighing more than 45 kg: 100 mg po BID for 60 days.
- 8 years or older and weighing 45 kg or less: 2.2 mg/kg/dose po BID for 60 days.
- 8 years or younger: 2.2 mg/kg/dose po BID for 60 days

Reference: CDC. Update: Investigation of anthrax associated with intentional exposure and interim public health guidelines, October, 2001. *MMWR* 2001;50 (41):889-893.

The National Pharmaceutical Stockpile (NSP) contains oral and liquid types of both drugs for use by children who are too small to tolerate pills. Both tetracyclines and fluoroquinolones can cause adverse health effects in children. These risks must be weighed carefully against the risk of developing a life-threatening disease due to *Bacillus anthracis*. As soon as the penicillin susceptibility of the organism has been confirmed, prophylactic therapy for children should be changed to oral amoxicillin 80 mg/kg of body mass per day divided every 8 hours (not to exceed 500 mg three times daily). The NSP also includes amoxicillin suspension for children. *Bacillus anthracis* is not susceptible to cephalosporins or to trimethoprim/sulfamethoxazole, and these agents should not be used for prophylaxis.

Drug Recommendations For Pediatric Anthrax Cases

Some antibiotics and other treatments that have proven effective against anthrax in adults have not been studied as extensively in children. Therefore, CDC provides the following recommendations for treating anthrax in children:

For inhalational anthrax:

Initial Therapy (intravenous)	Duration
Ciprofloxacin* 10-15 mg/kg/dose every 12 hours **OR** Doxycycline:¶ ■ 8 years and >45 kg: 100 mg every 12 hours ■ 8 years and 45 kg or less: 2.2 mg/kg/dose every 12 hours ■ 8 years or younger: 2.2 mg/kg/dose every 12 hours **AND** One or two additional antimicrobials§	IV treatment initially. Switch to oral antimicrobial therapy when clinically appropriate: Ciprofloxacin 10-15mg/kg/dose po every 12 hours **OR** Doxycycline:¶ ■ 8 years and >45 kg: 100 mg po BID ■ 8 years and 45 kg or less: 2.2 mg/kg/dose po BID ■ 8 years or younger: 2.2 mg/kg/dose po BID Continue for 60 days (IV and po combined)

Antimicrobial therapy should be continued for 60 days because of the potential persistence of spores after an aerosol exposure. Initial therapy may be altered on the basis of the clinical course of the patient; one or two antimicrobial agents (eg, ciprofloxacin or doxycycline) may be adequate as the patient improves.

* If intravenous ciprofloxacin is not available, oral ciprofloxacin may be acceptable because it is rapidly and well absorbed from the gastrointestinal tract with no substantial loss by first-pass metabolism. Maximum serum concentrations are attained 1 to 2 hours after oral dosing but may not be achieved if vomiting or ileus is present. In children, ciprofloxacin dosage should not exceed 1 g/day.

¶ The AAP recommends treatment of young children with tetracyclines for serious infections (eg, Rocky Mountain spotted fever). If meningitis is suspected, doxycycline may be less optimal because of poor central nervous system penetration.

§ Other agents with *in vitro* activity include rifampin, vancomycin, penicillin, ampicillin, chloramphenicol, imipenem, clindamycin, and clarithromycin. Because of concerns of constitutive and inducible beta-lactamases in *Bacillus anthracis* isolates involved in the current bioterrorist attack, penicillin and ampicillin should not be used alone. Consultation with an infectious disease specialist is advised.

For cutaneous anthrax:

CDC recommends the following treatment:

Initial Therapy (oral)	Duration
Ciprofloxacin: 10-15 mg/kg/dose every 12 hours (not to exceed 1 g/day) **OR**	60 days
Doxycycline: ■ >8 years and >45 kg: 100 mg every 12 hours ■ >8 years and 45 kg or less: 2.2 mg/kg/dose every 12 hours ■ 8 years or younger: 2.2 mg/kg/dose every 12 hours	60 days

Cutaneous anthrax with signs of systemic involvement, extensive edema, or lesions on the head or neck requires intravenous therapy, and a multidrug approach is recommended. Ciprofloxacin or doxycycline should be considered first-line therapy. Amoxicillin 80 mg/kg/day divided every 8 hours is an option for completion of therapy after clinical improvement, if the organism is susceptible. Previous guidelines have suggested treating cutaneous anthrax for 7 to 10 days, but 60 days is recommended in the setting of this attack, given the likelihood of exposure to aerosolized *Bacillus anthracis.*

For gastrointestinal and oropharyngeal anthrax:

Use regimens recommended for inhalational anthrax.

Children are more likely than adults to suffer side affects from some antibiotics used to prevent or treat the disease. If a child does develop side effects, testing should be done to determine whether the bacteria to which the child was exposed are susceptible to other drugs with fewer side effects, such as amoxicillin.

For additional information

The American Academy of Pediatrics offers more extensive information about children and anthrax at its Web site, http://www.aap.org/advocacy/releases/smlpoxanthrax.htm. For information related to preparedness and bioterrorism, see CDC's Web site at http://www.bt.cdc.gov.

Sources: MMWR 50(41); October 19, 2001; *MMWR* 50(42); October 26, 2001; American Academy of Pediatrics fact sheet at: http://www.aap.org/advocacy/releases/smlpoxanthrax.htm.

Statement by The Department of Health and Human Services Regarding Additional Options for Preventive Treatment for Those Exposed to Inhalational Anthrax

Many of those who were exposed to inhalational anthrax in the recent mail attacks are presently concluding their 60-day course of preventive antibiotic treatment. Some of these persons, especially those who may have been exposed to very high levels of anthrax spores, may wish to take additional precautions. The Department of Health and Human Services (HHS) is providing two additional options beyond the 60-day antibiotic course, for those who may wish to pursue them: an extended course of antibiotics, and investigational post-exposure treatment with anthrax vaccine.

HHS will make anthrax vaccine available to those who were exposed to inhalational anthrax, who have concluded their antibiotic treatment and who wish to receive the vaccine as an investigational product. The vaccine is being made available in this investigational mode, under an investigational new drug application (IND) at the option of the individual, in recognition of the limited nature of the data now available concerning inhalation anthrax treatment and the factors underlying development of the disease, as well as uncertainty concerning the extent of exposure to spores that some persons may have received in the recent anthrax incidents. The decision to use this vaccine is at the discretion of the individual, in consultation with his or her physician.

Background

Existing data, based especially on animal models, indicate that inhalational anthrax is unlikely to occur after 60 days following exposure. This is the basis of the recommendation for 60 days treatment with an effective antibiotic. So far, no known cases have developed in individuals who were recently exposed to inhalation anthrax and who were prescribed the 60-day antibiotic course. HHS health agencies continue to recommend that those who were prescribed the 60-day antibiotic course and who conclude this course of treatment, or who stopped taking the medicine prior to 60 days, should remain watchful of their health and be in close communication with a physician who is aware of their exposure status. A number of individuals have already concluded the 60-day course, or have stopped taking the antibiotics prior to the 60-day conclusion, and no cases have been reported among them.

At the same time, other animal data indicate that live spores may continue to reside in the lungs beyond the 60-day period, even though these animals did not develop disease. Traces of live spores have been detected in the lungs up to 100 days following exposure. This raises the theoretical possibility that the spores remaining in the lung area might still, after 60 days, result in anthrax.

If such a late infection were to occur, HHS scientists believe that the infection could be successfully treated, as were cases of inhalation anthrax that were identified early during the anthrax mail attacks. At the same time, HHS recognizes that some individuals may wish to take extra precautions, especially those whose exposure may have been especially high.

Options

There are three options for individuals exposed to inhalational anthrax:

Current Recommendation: 60 days of antibiotic treatment, accompanied by careful monitoring for illness.

Additional Option 1: 40 additional days of antibiotic treatment -- This course would be intended to provide protection against the theoretical possibility that spores might cause infection up to 100 days after exposure. It should be accompanied by monitoring for illness or adverse reactions.

Additional Option 2: 40 additional days of antibiotic treatment, plus anthrax vaccine as an investigational treatment -- In addition to the 40 days of additional protection, this option would involve three doses of anthrax vaccine over a four-week period, to provide immunity to infection over a longer period of time. This is not currently an FDA-approved use of the vaccine, however the vaccine may provide additional protection by inducing an immune response to the anthrax organism. As an investigational new drug, the vaccine would need to be administered with the full informed consent of the individual as to possible risks. Individuals would also be asked to take part in a follow-up study measuring the effect of the vaccine when administered after exposure.

All those who are concluding a 60-day course of antibiotic treatment should monitor their health and be in close contact with their physician. Those who may wish to continue taking antibiotics for an additional 40 days should consult their physician about this course. Those who may wish to take part in the investigational post-exposure use of the anthrax vaccine should consult their physician or a physician at the site where vaccine is being administered.

Source: HHS News Release, 12/18/2001

Smallpox Vaccine for Bioterrorism Preparedness: Excerpt from the Recommendations of the Advisory Committee on Immunization Practices (ACIP), 2001

Although use of biological agents is an increasing threat, use of conventional weapons (eg, explosives) is still considered more likely in terrorism scenarios (1). Moreover, use of smallpox virus as a biological weapon might be less likely than other biological agents because of its restricted availability; however, its use would have substantial public health consequences. Therefore, in support of current public health bioterrorism preparedness efforts, ACIP has developed the following recommendations if this unlikely event occurs.

Surveillance

A suspected case of smallpox is a public health emergency. Smallpox surveillance in the United States includes detecting a suspected case or cases, making a definitive diagnosis with rapid laboratory confirmation at CDC, and preventing further smallpox transmission. A suspected smallpox case should be reported immediately by telephone to state or local health officials and advice obtained regarding isolation and laboratory specimen collection. State or local health officials should notify CDC immediately at (404) 639-2184, (404) 639-0385, or (770) 488-7100 if a suspected case of smallpox is reported. Because of the problems encountered previously in Europe with health-care-associated smallpox transmission from imported cases present in a hospital setting (2,3), health officials should be diligent regarding use of adequate isolation facilities and precautions (see Infection Control Measures). Currently, specific therapies with proven treatment effectiveness for clinical smallpox are unavailable. Medical care of more seriously ill smallpox patients would include supportive measures only. If the patient's condition allows, medical and public health authorities should consider isolation and observation outside a hospital setting to prevent health-care-associated smallpox transmission and overtaxing of medical resources. Clinical consultation and a preliminary laboratory diagnosis can be completed within 8-24 hours. Surveillance activities, including notification procedures and laboratory confirmation of cases, might change if smallpox is confirmed.

Prerelease Vaccination

The risk for smallpox occurring as a result of a deliberate release by terrorists is considered low, and the population at risk for such an exposure cannot be determined. Therefore, preexposure vaccination is not recommended for any group other than laboratory or medical personnel working with nonhighly attenuated Orthopoxviruses.

Recommendations regarding preexposure vaccination should be on the basis of a calculable risk assessment that considers the risk for disease and the benefits and risks regarding vaccination. Because the current risk for exposure is considered low, benefits of vaccination do not outweigh the risk regarding vaccine complications. If the potential or an intentional release of smallpox virus increases later, preexposure vaccination might become indicated for selected groups (eg, medical and public health personnel or laboratorians) who would have an identified higher risk for exposure because of work-related contact with smallpox patients or infectious materials.

Postrelease Vaccination

If an intentional release of smallpox (variola) virus does occur, vaccinia vaccine will be recommended for certain groups. Groups for whom vaccination would be indicated include

- persons who were exposed to the initial release of the virus;
- persons who had face-to-face, household, or close-proximity contact (<6.5 feet or 2 meters) (4) with a confirmed or suspected smallpox patient at any time from the onset of the patient's fever until all scabs have separated;
- personnel involved in the direct medical or public health evaluation, care, or transportation of confirmed or suspected smallpox patients;
- laboratory personnel involved in the collection or processing of clinical specimens from confirmed or suspected smallpox patients; and
- other persons who have an increased likelihood of contact with infectious materials from a smallpox patient (eg, personnel responsible for medical waste disposal, linen disposal or disinfection, and room disinfection in a facility where smallpox patients are present).

Using recently vaccinated personnel (ie, <3 years) for patient care activities would be the best practice. However, because recommendations for routine smallpox vaccination in the United States were rescinded in 1971 and smallpox vaccination is currently recommended only for specific groups (see Routine Nonemergency Vaccine Use), having recently vaccinated personnel available in the early stages of a smallpox emergency would be unlikely. Smallpox vaccine can prevent or decrease the severity of clinical disease, even when administered 3-4 days after exposure to the smallpox virus (5,6,7). Preferably, healthy persons with no contraindications to vaccination, who can be vaccinated immediately before patient contact or very soon after patient contact (ie, <3 days), should be selected for patient care activities or activities involving potentially infectious materials. Persons who have received a previous vaccination (ie, childhood vaccination or vaccination >3 years before) against smallpox might demonstrate a more accelerated immune response after revaccination than those receiving a primary vaccination (8). If possible, these persons should be revaccinated and assigned to patient care activities in the early stages of a smallpox outbreak until additional personnel can be successfully vaccinated.

Personnel involved with direct smallpox patient care activities should observe strict contact and airborne precautions (9) (ie, gowns, gloves, eye shields, and correctly fitted N-95 masks) for additional protection until postvaccination immunity has been demonstrated (ie, 6-8 days after

vaccination). Shoe covers should be used in addition to standard contact isolation protective clothing to prevent transportation of the virus outside the isolation area. After postvaccination immunity has occurred, contact precautions with shoe covers should still be observed to prevent the spread of infectious agents (see Infection Control Measures). If possible, the number of personnel selected for direct contact with confirmed or suspected smallpox patients or infectious materials should be limited to reduce the number of vaccinations and to prevent unnecessary vaccination complications.

Children who have had a definite risk regarding exposure to smallpox (ie, face-to-face, household, or close-proximity contact with a smallpox patient) should be vaccinated regardless of age (10,11). Pregnant women who have had a definite exposure to smallpox virus (ie, face-to-face, household, or close-proximity contact with a smallpox patient) and are, therefore, at high risk for contracting the disease, should also be vaccinated (11). Smallpox infection among pregnant women has been reported to result in a more severe infection than among nonpregnant women (8). Therefore, the risks to the mother and fetus from experiencing clinical smallpox substantially outweigh any potential risks regarding vaccination. In addition, vaccinia virus has not been documented to be teratogenic, and the incidence of fetal vaccinia is low (11,12,13,14). When the level of exposure risk is undetermined, the decision to vaccinate should be made after assessment by the clinician and patient of the potential risks versus the benefits of smallpox vaccination.

In a postrelease setting, vaccination might be initiated also for other groups whose unhindered function is deemed essential to the support of response activities (eg, selected law enforcement, emergency response, or military personnel) and who are not otherwise engaged in patient care activities but who have a reasonable probability of contact with smallpox patients or infectious materials. If vaccination of these groups is initiated by public health authorities, only personnel with no contraindications to vaccination should be vaccinated before initiating activities that could lead to contact with suspected smallpox patients or infectious materials. Steps should be taken (eg, reassignment of duties) to prevent contact of any unvaccinated personnel with infectious smallpox patients or materials.

Because of increased transmission rates that have been described in previous outbreaks of smallpox involving aerosol transmission in hospital settings (2,3,15), potential vaccination of nondirect hospital contacts should be evaluated by

public health officials. Because hospitalized patients might have other contraindications to vaccination (eg, immunosuppression), vaccination of these nondirect hospital contacts should occur after prudent evaluation of the hospital setting with determination of the exposure potential through the less-common aerosol transmission route.

Contraindications to Vaccination During a Smallpox Emergency

No absolute contraindications exist regarding vaccination of a person with a high-risk exposure to smallpox. Persons at greatest risk for experiencing serious vaccination complications are also at greatest risk for death from smallpox (10,11). If a relative contraindication to vaccination exists, the risk for experiencing serious vaccination complications must be weighed against the risk for experiencing a potentially fatal smallpox infection. When the level of exposure risk is undetermined, the decision to vaccinate should be made after prudent assessment by the clinician and the patient of the potential risks versus the benefits of smallpox vaccination.

Infection Control Measures

Isolation of confirmed or suspected smallpox patients will be necessary to limit the potential exposure of nonvaccinated and, therefore, non-immune persons. Although droplet spread is the major mode of person-to-person smallpox transmission, airborne transmission through fine-particle aerosol can occur. Therefore, airborne precautions using correct ventilation (eg, negative air-pressure rooms with high-efficiency particulate air filtration) should be initiated for hospitalized confirmed or suspected smallpox patients, unless the entire facility has been restricted to smallpox patients and recently vaccinated persons (16,17). Although personnel who have been vaccinated recently and who have a demonstrated immune response should be fully protected against infection with variola virus, they should continue to observe standard and contact precautions (ie, using protective clothing and shoe covers) when in contact with smallpox patients or contaminated materials to prevent inadvertent spread of variola virus to susceptible persons and potential self-contact with other infectious agents. Personnel should remove and correctly dispose of all protective clothing before contact with nonvaccinated persons. Reuseable bedding and clothing can be autoclaved or laundered in hot water with bleach to inactivate the virus (5,6). Laundry handlers should be vaccinated before handling contaminated materials.

Nonhospital isolation of confirmed or suspected smallpox patients should be of a sufficient degree to prevent the spread of disease to nonimmune persons during the time the patient is considered potentially infectious (ie, from the onset of symptoms until all scabs have separated). Private residences or other nonhospital facilities that are used to isolate confirmed or suspected smallpox patients should have nonshared ventilation, heating, and air-conditioning systems. Access to those facilities should be limited to recently vaccinated persons with a demonstrated immune response. If suspected smallpox patients are placed in the same isolation facility, they should be vaccinated to guard against accidental exposure caused by misclassification as someone with smallpox.

In addition to isolation of infectious smallpox patients, careful surveillance of contacts during their potential incubation period is required. Transmission of smallpox virus rarely occurs before the appearance of the rash that develops 2-4 days after the prodromal fever (3). If a vaccinated or unvaccinated contact experiences a fever >101° F (38° C) during the 17-day period after his or her last exposure to a smallpox patient, the contact should be isolated immediately to prevent contact with nonvaccinated or nonimmune persons until smallpox can be ruled out by clinical or laboratory examination.

VIG for Prophylaxis and Treatment of Adverse Reactions During a Smallpox Emergency

If vaccination of persons with contraindications is required because of exposure to smallpox virus after an intentional release as a bioterrorism agent, current stores of VIG are insufficient to allow its prophylactic use with vaccination. Because of the limited stores of VIG, its use in such a scenario should be reserved for severe, life-threatening complications (eg, progressive vaccinia, eczema vaccinatum, or severe, toxic generalized vaccinia). If additional VIG becomes available in sufficient quantities to allow its prophylactic use, VIG should be administered intramuscularly as a dose of 0.3 mg/kg along with vaccinia vaccine to persons with contraindications who require vaccination.

References

1. Federal Bureau of Investigation, Counterterrorism Threat Assessment and Warning Unit, National Security Division. Terrorism in the United States, 1998. Washington, DC: US Department of Justice, FBI, 1998. Available at: <http://www.fbi.gov/publications/terror/terror98.pdf>. Accessed May 2, 2001.

2. Mack TM. Smallpox in Europe, 1950-1971. *J Infect Dis* 1972;125:161-9.

3. Gelfand HM, Posch J. Recent outbreak of smallpox in Meschede, West Germany. *Am J Epidemiol* 1971;93:234-7.

4. CDC. Prevention of plague: recommendations of the Advisory Committee on Immunization Practices (ACIP). *MMWR* 1996;45(RR-14):1-15.

5. Dixon CW. *Smallpox*. London, England: Churchill, 1962.

6. Henderson DA, Inglesby TV, Bartlett JG, et al. for the Working Group on Civilian Biodefense. Smallpox as a biological weapon: medical and public health management. *JAMA* 1999;281:2127-37.

7. Dixon CW. Smallpox in Tripolitania, 1946: an epidemiological and clinical study of 500 cases, including trials of penicillin treatment. *J Hyg* 1948;46:351-77.

8. Fenner F, Henderson DA, Arita I, Jezek Z, Ladnyi ID. *Smallpox and its eradication.* Geneva, Switzerland: World Health Organization, 1988.

9. Garner JS, the Hospital Infection Control Practices Advisory Committee. Guideline for isolation precautions in hospitals. *Infect Control Hosp Epidemiol* 1996;17:53-80.

10. Public Health Service. Recommendations of the Public Health Service Advisory

Committee on Immunization Practices: Smallpox vaccine. Washington, DC: Public Health Service, 1972.

11. Goldstein JA, Neff JM, Lane JM, Koplan JP. Smallpox vaccination reactions, prophylaxis, and therapy of complications. *Pediatrics* 1975;55:342-7.

12. Greenberg M, Yankauer A, Krugman S, Osborn JJ, Ward RS, Dancis J. Effect of smallpox vaccination during pregnancy on the incidence of congenital malformations. *Pediatrics* 1949;3:456.

13. Green DM, Reid SM, Rhaney K. Generalized vaccinia in the human fetus. *Lancet* 1966;I:1296.

14. Harley JD, Gillespie AM. Case of complicated congenital vaccinia. *Pediatrics* 1972;50: 150-2.

15. Wehrle PF, Posch J, Richter KH, Henderson DA. Airborne outbreak of smallpox in a German hospital and its cance with respect to ot recent outbreaks in Eur *Bull World Health Orga* 1970;43:669-79.

16. Garner JS, Simmons BF Guideline for isolation tions in hospitals. *Infect* 1983;4(suppl):245-325.

17. Advisory Committee on Infection Control (APIC Hospital Infections Prog Bioterrorism Working C Bioterrorism readiness template for healthcare ties. Atlanta, GA: US Department of Health a Human Services, CDC, Available at <http://www.cdc.gov/nc hip/Bio/13apr99APIC-CDCBioterrorism.pdf>. Accessed May 2, 2001.

Source: MMWR 50(RR-10)
June 22, 2001